# Exam 70-647: *PRO: Windows Server® 2008, Enterprise Administrator*

| Objective | Chapter | Lesson |
|---|---|---|
| **Planning Network and Application Services (23 percent)** | | |
| Plan for name resolution and IP addressing. | 1 | 1, 2 |
| Design for network access. | 5 | 1, 2 |
| Plan for application delivery. | 7 | 2 |
| Plan for Terminal Services. | 7 | 1 |
| **Designing Core Identity and Access Management Components (25 percent)** | | |
| Design Active Directory forests and domains. | 2 | 1 |
| Design the Active Directory physical topology. | 2 | 2 |
| Design the Active Directory administrative model. | 4 | 1 |
| Design the enterprise-level group policy strategy. | 4 | 2 |
| **Designing Support Identity and Access Management Components (29 percent)** | | |
| Plan for domain or forest migration, upgrade, and restructuring. | 3 | 1 |
| Design the branch office deployment. | 6 | 1, 2 |
| Design and implement public key infrastructure. | 9 | 1, 2, 3 |
| Plan for interoperability. | 3 | 2 |
| **Designing for Business Continuity and Data Availability (23 percent)** | | |
| Plan for business continuity. | 10 | 3 |
| Design for software updates and compliance management. | 11 | 1, 2 |
| Design the operating system virtualization strategy. | 8 | 1, 2 |
| Design for data management and data access. | 2, 4, 10 | Chapter 2, Lesson 1<br>Chapter 4, Lesson 1<br>Chapter 10, Lessons 1, 2 |

**Note:** Exam objectives are subject to change at any time without prior notice and at Microsoft's sole discretion. Please visit the Microsoft Learning Certification Web site (*www.microsoft.com/learning/mcp/*) for the most current listing of exam objectives.

# MCITP Self-Paced Training Kit (Exam 70-647): Windows® Server Enterprise Administration

*Orin Thomas, John Policelli, Ian McLean, J.C. Mackin,*
*Paul Mancuso, and David R. Miller, with GrandMasters*

PUBLISHED BY
Microsoft Press
A Division of Microsoft Corporation
One Microsoft Way
Redmond, Washington 98052-6399

Library of Congress Control Number: 2008927270

Printed and bound in the United States of America.

2 3 4 5 6 7 8 9   QWT   3 2 1 0 9 8

Distributed in Canada by H.B. Fenn and Company Ltd.

A CIP catalogue record for this book is available from the British Library.

Microsoft Press books are available through booksellers and distributors worldwide. For further information about international editions, contact your local Microsoft Corporation office or contact Microsoft Press International directly at fax (425) 936-7329. Visit our Web site at www.microsoft.com/mspress. Send comments to tkinput@microsoft.com.

Microsoft, Microsoft Press, Access, Active Directory, ActiveX, BitLocker, ESP, Excel, Forefront, Hyper-V, InfoPath, Internet Explorer, OneCare, Outlook, PowerPoint, ReadyBoost, SharePoint, SQL Server, Visual Studio, Windows, Windows NT, Windows PowerShell, Windows Server, and Windows Vista are either registered trademarks or trademarks of Microsoft Corporation in the United States and/or other countries. Other product and company names mentioned herein may be the trademarks of their respective owners.

The example companies, organizations, products, domain names, e-mail addresses, logos, people, places, and events depicted herein are fictitious. No association with any real company, organization, product, domain name, e-mail address, logo, person, place, or event is intended or should be inferred.

This book expresses the author's views and opinions. The information contained in this book is provided without any express, statutory, or implied warranties. Neither the authors, Microsoft Corporation, nor its resellers, or distributors will be held liable for any damages caused or alleged to be caused either directly or indirectly by this book.

**Acquisitions Editor:** Ken Jones
**Developmental Editor:** Laura Sackerman
**Project Editor:** Victoria Thulman
**Editorial Production:** nSight, Inc.
**Technical Reviewer:** Roazanne Murphy Whalen
**Cover:** Tom Draper Design

Body Part No. X14-37562

*This book is dedicated to my beautiful fiancée, Maria. Thank you for your*
*love and support and especially for your patience through another*
*long project that tied up our evenings and weekends.*

*–John Policelli*

*Somewhat unusually I wrote my part of this book and, more or less at the same time,*
*underwent a quadruple cardiac bypass operation. This book is dedicated to*
*the skilled team of doctors and nurses that got me smoothly through the*
*procedure and back to work (if not quite fully fit) in record time. I*
*would also like to acknowledge the helpfulness and considerable*
*ability of my co-author Orin Thomas, who stepped in*
*and completed tasks for me in a most professional*
*fashion when I was unable to do so.*

*–Ian McLean*

*I dedicate my contribution to this book to*
*my wife Yaneth and my son Anthony.*

*–Paul Mancuso*

*For Ross and Veronica. You mean the world to me.*
*All my love,*

*–David R. Miller*

# About the Authors

## Orin Thomas

**Orin Thomas** (MCSE, MVP) is an author and systems administrator who has worked with Microsoft Windows Server operating systems for more than a decade. He is the coauthor of numerous self-paced training kits for Microsoft Press, including *MCSA/MCSE Self-Paced Training Kit (Exam 70-290): Managing and Maintaining a Microsoft Windows Server 2003 Environment*, second edition, and a contributing editor for *Windows IT Pro* magazine.

## John Policelli

**John Policelli** (Microsoft MVP for Directory Services, MCTS, MCSA, ITSM, iNet+, Network+, and A+) is a solutions-focused IT consultant with more than a decade of combined success in architecture, security, strategic planning, and disaster recovery planning. He has designed and implemented dozens of complex directory service, e-Messaging, Web, networking, and security enterprise solutions. John has spent the past nine years focused on identity and access management and provided thought leadership for some of the largest installations of Active Directory Domain Services in Canada. He has been involved as an author, technical reviewer, and subject matter expert for more than 50 training, exam-writing, press, and white paper projects related to Windows Server 2008 identity and access management, networking, and collaboration.

## Ian McLean

**Ian McLean** (MCSE, MCITP, MCT) has more than 40 years' experience in industry, commerce, and education. He started his career as an electronics engineer before going into distance learning and then education as a university professor. He currently provides technical support for a government organization and runs his own consultancy company. Ian has written 22 books in addition to many papers and technical articles. Books he has previously coauthored include *MCITP Self-Paced Training Kit (Exam 70-444): Optimizing and Maintaining a Database Administration Solution Using Microsoft SQL Server 2005* and *MCITP Self-Paced Training Kit (Exam 70-646): Windows Server Administration: Windows Server 2008 Administrator*. When not writing, Ian annoys everyone by playing guitar very badly. However, he is forced to play instrumentals because his singing is even worse.

## J.C. Mackin

**J.C. Mackin** (MCITP, MCTS, MCSE, MCDST, MCT) is a writer, editor, consultant, and trainer who has been working with Microsoft networks for more than a decade. Books he has previously authored or coauthored include *MCSA/MCSE Self-Paced Training Kit (Exam 70-291): Implementing, Managing, and Maintaining a Microsoft Windows Server 2003 Network Infrastructure, MCITP Self-Paced Training Kit (Exam 70-443): Designing a Database Server Infrastructure Using Microsoft SQL Server 2005*, and *MCITP Self-Paced Training Kit (Exam 70-622): Supporting and Troubleshooting Applications on a Windows Vista Client for Enterprise Support Technicians*. He also holds a master's degree in Telecommunications and Network Management.

When not working with computers, J.C. can be found with a panoramic camera photographing medieval villages in Italy or France.

## Paul Mancuso

**Paul Mancuso** (MCITP, MCSE: Security and Messaging, MCT, CCSI, CCNP, VCP, CCISP) has been in the IT field lecturing, writing, training, and consulting for more than 20 years. As co-owner of National IT Training and Certification Institute (NITTCI), Paul has extensive experience in authoring training materials as well as four books. Books he has recently coauthored include *MCITP 70-622 Exam Cram: Supporting and Troubleshooting Applications on a Windows Vista Client for Enterprise Support Technicians* for Que Publishing; and *Designing a Messaging Infrastructure Using Exchange Server 2007* for Microsoft Press. He has recently taken up golf and enjoys hacking up luscious green golf courses in his spare time.

# David R. Miller

**David R. Miller** (SME; MCT; MCITPro; MCSE Windows NT 4.0, Windows 2000, and Windows 2003: Security; CISSP; LPT; ECSA; CEH; CWNA; CCNA; CNE; Security+; A+; N+) is an information technology and network engineering consultant; instructor; author; and technical editor of books, curricula, certification exams, and computer-based training videos. He regularly performs as a Microsoft Subject Matter Expert (SME) on product lines including Windows Vista, Windows Server 2008, and Microsoft Exchange Server 2007. He is the principal author of the information systems security book titled *Security Administrator Street Smarts* for Sybex and Wiley Publishing and is scheduled to write the second edition of this book in summer 2008. David is writing *MCITP 70-622 PRO: Supporting and Troubleshooting Applications on a Windows Vista Client for Enterprise Support Technicians* and *MCITP 70-632 PRO: Supporting and Troubleshooting Applications on a Windows Vista Client for Consumer Support Technicians* for Que Publishing, due to be released in the first half of 2008. In addition to this book, he is an author on another Microsoft Certified IT Professional book for Microsoft Press, entitled *MCITP 70-237 PRO: Designing Messaging Solutions with Exchange Server 2007*. The two Microsoft Press books are due to be published in the first half of 2008.

# Contents at a Glance

1   Planning Name Resolution and Internet Protocol Addressing . . . . . . . . . 1

2   Designing Active Directory Domain Services . . . . . . . . . . . . . . . . . . . . . . . 79

3   Planning Migrations, Trusts, and Interoperability. . . . . . . . . . . . . . . . . . 141

4   Designing Active Directory Administration
    and Group Policy Strategy . . . . . . . . . . . . . . . . . . . . . . . . . . . . . . . . . . . . . . 169

5   Designing a Network Access Strategy . . . . . . . . . . . . . . . . . . . . . . . . . . . 227

6   Design a Branch Office Deployment. . . . . . . . . . . . . . . . . . . . . . . . . . . . . 287

7   Planning Terminal Services and Application Deployment. . . . . . . . . . . 333

8   Server and Application Virtualization. . . . . . . . . . . . . . . . . . . . . . . . . . . . 361

9   Planning and Designing a Public Key Infrastructure . . . . . . . . . . . . . . . 391

10  Designing Solutions for Data Sharing, Data Security,
    and Business Continuity . . . . . . . . . . . . . . . . . . . . . . . . . . . . . . . . . . . . . . . 429

11  Designing Software Update Infrastructure
    and Managing Compliance . . . . . . . . . . . . . . . . . . . . . . . . . . . . . . . . . . . . . 475

    Answers . . . . . . . . . . . . . . . . . . . . . . . . . . . . . . . . . . . . . . . . . . . . . . . . . . . . . . 513

    Glossary . . . . . . . . . . . . . . . . . . . . . . . . . . . . . . . . . . . . . . . . . . . . . . . . . . . . . . 545

    Index . . . . . . . . . . . . . . . . . . . . . . . . . . . . . . . . . . . . . . . . . . . . . . . . . . . . . . . . . 549

# Table of Contents

Introduction. . . . . . . . . . . . . . . . . . . . . . . . . . . . . . . . . . . . . . . . . . . . . . . . . . . xxv
    Lab Setup Instructions. . . . . . . . . . . . . . . . . . . . . . . . . . . . . . . . . . . . . . . . . . xxv
        Hardware Requirements . . . . . . . . . . . . . . . . . . . . . . . . . . . . . . . . . . . . xxvi
        Preparing the Computer Running Windows Server 2008 Enterprise. . . . . . . xxvi
        Preparing the Computer Running Windows Vista . . . . . . . . . . . . . . . . . . . xxvi
    Using the CD. . . . . . . . . . . . . . . . . . . . . . . . . . . . . . . . . . . . . . . . . . . . . . . xxvii
        How to Install the Practice Tests. . . . . . . . . . . . . . . . . . . . . . . . . . . . . . xxviii
        How to Use the Practice Tests . . . . . . . . . . . . . . . . . . . . . . . . . . . . . . . xxviii
        How to Uninstall the Practice Tests . . . . . . . . . . . . . . . . . . . . . . . . . . . . xxix
    Microsoft Certified Professional Program . . . . . . . . . . . . . . . . . . . . . . . . . . . xxix
    Technical Support. . . . . . . . . . . . . . . . . . . . . . . . . . . . . . . . . . . . . . . . . . . . . xxx

**1    Planning Name Resolution and Internet Protocol Addressing. . . . . . . . . 1**
    Before You Begin . . . . . . . . . . . . . . . . . . . . . . . . . . . . . . . . . . . . . . . . . . . . . . .2
    Lesson 1: Planning Name Resolution. . . . . . . . . . . . . . . . . . . . . . . . . . . . . . . . .3
        Planning Windows Server 2008 DNS . . . . . . . . . . . . . . . . . . . . . . . . . . . .4
        Using New DNS Features and Enhancements . . . . . . . . . . . . . . . . . . . . . .15
        Planning a DNS Infrastructure . . . . . . . . . . . . . . . . . . . . . . . . . . . . . . . .22
        Configuring DNS . . . . . . . . . . . . . . . . . . . . . . . . . . . . . . . . . . . . . . . . .30
        Lesson Summary. . . . . . . . . . . . . . . . . . . . . . . . . . . . . . . . . . . . . . . . . .34
        Lesson Review . . . . . . . . . . . . . . . . . . . . . . . . . . . . . . . . . . . . . . . . . . .34
    Lesson 2: Planning Internet Protocol Addressing. . . . . . . . . . . . . . . . . . . . . . .36
        Analyzing the IPv6 Address Structure . . . . . . . . . . . . . . . . . . . . . . . . . . .37

**What do you think of this book? We want to hear from you!**

Microsoft is interested in hearing your feedback so we can continually improve our books and learning resources for you. To participate in a brief online survey, please visit:

**www.microsoft.com/learning/booksurvey/**

Investigating the Advantages of IPv6 . . . . . . . . . . . . . . . . . . . . . . . . . . . . . . . 45

Implementing IPv4-to-IPv6 Compatibility . . . . . . . . . . . . . . . . . . . . . . . . . . . . 48

Planning an IPv4-to-IPv6 Transition Strategy. . . . . . . . . . . . . . . . . . . . . . . . . 51

Using IPv6 Tools . . . . . . . . . . . . . . . . . . . . . . . . . . . . . . . . . . . . . . . . . . . . . . . 54

Configuring Clients Through DHCPv6. . . . . . . . . . . . . . . . . . . . . . . . . . . . . . . 60

Planning an IPv6 Network. . . . . . . . . . . . . . . . . . . . . . . . . . . . . . . . . . . . . . . . 62

Configuring IPv6 Connectivity . . . . . . . . . . . . . . . . . . . . . . . . . . . . . . . . . . . . 66

Lesson Summary. . . . . . . . . . . . . . . . . . . . . . . . . . . . . . . . . . . . . . . . . . . . . . . 73

Lesson Review . . . . . . . . . . . . . . . . . . . . . . . . . . . . . . . . . . . . . . . . . . . . . . . . 74

Chapter Review. . . . . . . . . . . . . . . . . . . . . . . . . . . . . . . . . . . . . . . . . . . . . . . . . . . 76

Chapter Summary. . . . . . . . . . . . . . . . . . . . . . . . . . . . . . . . . . . . . . . . . . . . . . . . . 76

Case Scenarios. . . . . . . . . . . . . . . . . . . . . . . . . . . . . . . . . . . . . . . . . . . . . . . . . . . 76

Case Scenario 1:  Configuring DNS . . . . . . . . . . . . . . . . . . . . . . . . . . . . . . . . 76

Case Scenario 2:  Implementing IPv6 Connectivity . . . . . . . . . . . . . . . . . . . . 77

Suggested Practices . . . . . . . . . . . . . . . . . . . . . . . . . . . . . . . . . . . . . . . . . . . . . . . 77

Configure DNS . . . . . . . . . . . . . . . . . . . . . . . . . . . . . . . . . . . . . . . . . . . . . . . 77

Configure IPv6 Connectivity . . . . . . . . . . . . . . . . . . . . . . . . . . . . . . . . . . . . . 78

Take a Practice Test. . . . . . . . . . . . . . . . . . . . . . . . . . . . . . . . . . . . . . . . . . . . . . . 78

**2      Designing Active Directory Domain Services. . . . . . . . . . . . . . . . . . . . . . . 79**

Before You Begin . . . . . . . . . . . . . . . . . . . . . . . . . . . . . . . . . . . . . . . . . . . . . . . . . 80

Lesson 1:  Designing AD DS Forests and Domains . . . . . . . . . . . . . . . . . . . . . . . . 81

Designing the Forest Structure. . . . . . . . . . . . . . . . . . . . . . . . . . . . . . . . . . . . 81

Designing the Domain Structure . . . . . . . . . . . . . . . . . . . . . . . . . . . . . . . . . . 90

Designing Functional Levels . . . . . . . . . . . . . . . . . . . . . . . . . . . . . . . . . . . . . 97

Designing the Schema. . . . . . . . . . . . . . . . . . . . . . . . . . . . . . . . . . . . . . . . . 101

Designing Trusts to Optimize Intra-Forest Authentication. . . . . . . . . . . . . . 103

Designing AD DS Forests and Domains . . . . . . . . . . . . . . . . . . . . . . . . . . . 106

Lesson Summary. . . . . . . . . . . . . . . . . . . . . . . . . . . . . . . . . . . . . . . . . . . . . 110

Lesson Review . . . . . . . . . . . . . . . . . . . . . . . . . . . . . . . . . . . . . . . . . . . . . . . 110

Lesson 2:  Designing the AD DS Physical Topology. . . . . . . . . . . . . . . . . . . . . . . 112

Designing the Site Structure . . . . . . . . . . . . . . . . . . . . . . . . . . . . . . . . . . . . 114

Designing Replication . . . . . . . . . . . . . . . . . . . . . . . . . . . . . . . . . . . . . . . . . 117

Designing the Placement of Domain Controllers . . . . . . . . . . . . . . . . . . . . . 122

Designing Printer Location Policies. . . . . . . . . . . . . . . . . . . . . . . . . . . . . . . 127

Designing the Active Directory Domain Services Physical Topology. . . . . . . 130

Lesson Summary. . . . . . . . . . . . . . . . . . . . . . . . . . . . . . . . . . . . . . . . . . . . 135

Lesson Review . . . . . . . . . . . . . . . . . . . . . . . . . . . . . . . . . . . . . . . . . . . . . 135

Chapter Review. . . . . . . . . . . . . . . . . . . . . . . . . . . . . . . . . . . . . . . . . . . . . . . . . 137

Chapter Summary . . . . . . . . . . . . . . . . . . . . . . . . . . . . . . . . . . . . . . . . . . . . . . 137

Case Scenarios . . . . . . . . . . . . . . . . . . . . . . . . . . . . . . . . . . . . . . . . . . . . . . . . 137

Case Scenario 1: Designing the AD DS Forest . . . . . . . . . . . . . . . . . . . . . 138

Case Scenario 2: Designing AD DS Sites . . . . . . . . . . . . . . . . . . . . . . . . . . 138

Case Scenario 3: Designing the Placement of Domain Controllers. . . . . . . 138

Suggested Practices. . . . . . . . . . . . . . . . . . . . . . . . . . . . . . . . . . . . . . . . . . . . . 139

Implement Forests, Domains, and the Physical Topology . . . . . . . . . . . . . 139

Watch a Webcast . . . . . . . . . . . . . . . . . . . . . . . . . . . . . . . . . . . . . . . . . . . 140

Read a White Paper . . . . . . . . . . . . . . . . . . . . . . . . . . . . . . . . . . . . . . . . . 140

Take a Practice Test . . . . . . . . . . . . . . . . . . . . . . . . . . . . . . . . . . . . . . . . . . . . . 140

**3     Planning Migrations, Trusts, and Interoperability. . . . . . . . . . . . . . . . . . 141**

Before You Begin . . . . . . . . . . . . . . . . . . . . . . . . . . . . . . . . . . . . . . . . . . . . . . . 141

Lesson 1: Planning for Migration, Upgrade, and Restructuring. . . . . . . . . . . . . 143

Migration Paths . . . . . . . . . . . . . . . . . . . . . . . . . . . . . . . . . . . . . . . . . . . . 143

Upgrading an Existing Domain to Windows Server 2008 . . . . . . . . . . . . . . 145

Cross-Forest Authentication. . . . . . . . . . . . . . . . . . . . . . . . . . . . . . . . . . . . 146

Planning Forest Migration to Windows Server 2008 . . . . . . . . . . . . . . . . . . 148

Lesson Summary. . . . . . . . . . . . . . . . . . . . . . . . . . . . . . . . . . . . . . . . . . . . 149

Lesson Review . . . . . . . . . . . . . . . . . . . . . . . . . . . . . . . . . . . . . . . . . . . . . 150

Lesson 2: Planning for Interoperability . . . . . . . . . . . . . . . . . . . . . . . . . . . . . . 152

Planning AD FS. . . . . . . . . . . . . . . . . . . . . . . . . . . . . . . . . . . . . . . . . . . . . 152

Microsoft Identity Lifecycle Manager 2007 Feature Pack 1. . . . . . . . . . . . . 154

Planning for UNIX Interoperability . . . . . . . . . . . . . . . . . . . . . . . . . . . . . . 155

Planning for Interoperability . . . . . . . . . . . . . . . . . . . . . . . . . . . . . . . . . . . 161

Lesson Summary. . . . . . . . . . . . . . . . . . . . . . . . . . . . . . . . . . . . . . . . . . . . 162

Lesson Review . . . . . . . . . . . . . . . . . . . . . . . . . . . . . . . . . . . . . . . . . . . . . 163

Chapter Review . . . . . . . . . . . . . . . . . . . . . . . . . . . . . . . . . . . . . . . . . . . . . . . . . . . 165

Chapter Summary . . . . . . . . . . . . . . . . . . . . . . . . . . . . . . . . . . . . . . . . . . . . . . . . . . 165

Case Scenario . . . . . . . . . . . . . . . . . . . . . . . . . . . . . . . . . . . . . . . . . . . . . . . . . . . . . 165

    Case Scenario: Phasing Out a UNIX-Based Computer at Tailspin Toys . . . . . 166

Suggested Practices . . . . . . . . . . . . . . . . . . . . . . . . . . . . . . . . . . . . . . . . . . . . . . . . 166

    Plan for Domain or Forest Migration, Upgrade, and Restructuring . . . . . . . 166

    Plan for Interoperability . . . . . . . . . . . . . . . . . . . . . . . . . . . . . . . . . . . . . . . . . . 167

Take a Practice Test . . . . . . . . . . . . . . . . . . . . . . . . . . . . . . . . . . . . . . . . . . . . . . . . 167

**4    Designing Active Directory Administration
and Group Policy Strategy. . . . . . . . . . . . . . . . . . . . . . . . . . . . . . . . . . 169**

Before You Begin . . . . . . . . . . . . . . . . . . . . . . . . . . . . . . . . . . . . . . . . . . . . . . . . . . 169

Lesson 1: Designing the Active Directory Administrative Model . . . . . . . . . . . . . 171

    Delegating Active Directory Administration . . . . . . . . . . . . . . . . . . . . . . . . . . 172

    Using Group Strategy to Delegate Management Tasks . . . . . . . . . . . . . . . . 178

    Planning to Audit AD DS and Group Policy Compliance . . . . . . . . . . . . . . . 191

    Planning Organizational Structure . . . . . . . . . . . . . . . . . . . . . . . . . . . . . . . . . 193

    Creating a Forest Trust . . . . . . . . . . . . . . . . . . . . . . . . . . . . . . . . . . . . . . . . . . . 195

    Lesson Summary . . . . . . . . . . . . . . . . . . . . . . . . . . . . . . . . . . . . . . . . . . . . . . . . 197

    Lesson Review . . . . . . . . . . . . . . . . . . . . . . . . . . . . . . . . . . . . . . . . . . . . . . . . . . 198

Lesson 2: Designing Enterprise-Level Group Policy Strategy . . . . . . . . . . . . . . . . 200

    Planning a Group Policy Hierarchy . . . . . . . . . . . . . . . . . . . . . . . . . . . . . . . . . 201

    Controlling Device Installation . . . . . . . . . . . . . . . . . . . . . . . . . . . . . . . . . . . . 206

    Planning Authentication and Authorization . . . . . . . . . . . . . . . . . . . . . . . . . 213

    Implementing Fine-Grained Password Policies . . . . . . . . . . . . . . . . . . . . . . . 219

    Lesson Summary . . . . . . . . . . . . . . . . . . . . . . . . . . . . . . . . . . . . . . . . . . . . . . . . 222

    Lesson Review . . . . . . . . . . . . . . . . . . . . . . . . . . . . . . . . . . . . . . . . . . . . . . . . . . 222

Chapter Review . . . . . . . . . . . . . . . . . . . . . . . . . . . . . . . . . . . . . . . . . . . . . . . . . . . 224

Chapter Summary . . . . . . . . . . . . . . . . . . . . . . . . . . . . . . . . . . . . . . . . . . . . . . . . . . 224

Case Scenarios . . . . . . . . . . . . . . . . . . . . . . . . . . . . . . . . . . . . . . . . . . . . . . . . . . . . 224

    Case Scenario 1: Designing a Delegation Strategy . . . . . . . . . . . . . . . . . . . . 224

    Case Scenario 2: Planning Authentication and Authorization . . . . . . . . . . . 225

Suggested Practices . . . . . . . . . . . . . . . . . . . . . . . . . . . . . . . . . . . . . . . . . . . . . . . . 225

Designing the Active Directory Administrative Model. . . . . . . . . . . . . . . . . 226

Designing Enterprise-Level Group Policy Strategy . . . . . . . . . . . . . . . . . . . . 226

Take a Practice Test . . . . . . . . . . . . . . . . . . . . . . . . . . . . . . . . . . . . . . . . . . . . . . . 226

**5    Designing a Network Access Strategy** . . . . . . . . . . . . . . . . . . . . . . . . . . . .**227**

Before You Begin . . . . . . . . . . . . . . . . . . . . . . . . . . . . . . . . . . . . . . . . . . . . . . . . . . . 228

Lesson 1: Perimeter Networks and Remote Access Strategies . . . . . . . . . . . . . . . 230

Designing the Perimeter Network. . . . . . . . . . . . . . . . . . . . . . . . . . . . . . . . . 231

Deploying Strategic Services in the Perimeter Network . . . . . . . . . . . . . . 236

Designing a Remote Access Strategy . . . . . . . . . . . . . . . . . . . . . . . . . . . . . . 238

Designing a RADIUS Solution for Remote Access. . . . . . . . . . . . . . . . . . . . 245

Designing a RADIUS Solution for a Mid-Size Enterprise . . . . . . . . . . . . . . 250

Lesson Summary. . . . . . . . . . . . . . . . . . . . . . . . . . . . . . . . . . . . . . . . . . . . . . . . 252

Lesson Review . . . . . . . . . . . . . . . . . . . . . . . . . . . . . . . . . . . . . . . . . . . . . . . . . . 253

Lesson 2: Network Access Policy and Server and Domain Isolation . . . . . . . . . . . 255

Network Access Protection Overview. . . . . . . . . . . . . . . . . . . . . . . . . . . . . . 255

Considerations for NAP Enforcement. . . . . . . . . . . . . . . . . . . . . . . . . . . . . . 262

Planning NAP IPsec Enforcement . . . . . . . . . . . . . . . . . . . . . . . . . . . . . . . . . 262

Planning NAP VPN Enforcement. . . . . . . . . . . . . . . . . . . . . . . . . . . . . . . . . . 269

Planning NAP 802.1x Enforcement . . . . . . . . . . . . . . . . . . . . . . . . . . . . . . . 271

Planning NAP DHCP Enforcement . . . . . . . . . . . . . . . . . . . . . . . . . . . . . . . . 275

Domain and Server Isolation . . . . . . . . . . . . . . . . . . . . . . . . . . . . . . . . . . . . . 277

Lesson Summary. . . . . . . . . . . . . . . . . . . . . . . . . . . . . . . . . . . . . . . . . . . . . . . . 279

Lesson Review . . . . . . . . . . . . . . . . . . . . . . . . . . . . . . . . . . . . . . . . . . . . . . . . . . 280

Chapter Review. . . . . . . . . . . . . . . . . . . . . . . . . . . . . . . . . . . . . . . . . . . . . . . . . . . . . 281

Chapter Summary . . . . . . . . . . . . . . . . . . . . . . . . . . . . . . . . . . . . . . . . . . . . . . . . . . 281

Case Scenario . . . . . . . . . . . . . . . . . . . . . . . . . . . . . . . . . . . . . . . . . . . . . . . . . . . . . . 282

Case Scenario: Designing a NAP Solution for a Large Enterprise. . . . . . . . . 282

Suggested Practices. . . . . . . . . . . . . . . . . . . . . . . . . . . . . . . . . . . . . . . . . . . . . . . . . . 283

Implement VPNs, RADIUS Solution, and NAP Enforcement . . . . . . . . . . . . . 283

Watch a Webcast . . . . . . . . . . . . . . . . . . . . . . . . . . . . . . . . . . . . . . . . . . . . . . . 284

Read a White Paper . . . . . . . . . . . . . . . . . . . . . . . . . . . . . . . . . . . . . . . . . . . . . 284

Take a Practice Test . . . . . . . . . . . . . . . . . . . . . . . . . . . . . . . . . . . . . . . . . . . . . . . . . 285

**6    Design a Branch Office Deployment** . . . . . . . . . . . . . . . . . . . . . . . . . **287**

Before You Begin . . . . . . . . . . . . . . . . . . . . . . . . . . . . . . . . . . . . . . . . . . . . . . 287

Lesson 1: Branch Office Deployment . . . . . . . . . . . . . . . . . . . . . . . . . . . . . . 290

Branch Office Services . . . . . . . . . . . . . . . . . . . . . . . . . . . . . . . . . . . . . . 290

Branch Office Communications Considerations . . . . . . . . . . . . . . . . . . 304

Lesson Summary . . . . . . . . . . . . . . . . . . . . . . . . . . . . . . . . . . . . . . . . . . . 306

Lesson Review . . . . . . . . . . . . . . . . . . . . . . . . . . . . . . . . . . . . . . . . . . . . . 306

Lesson 2: Branch Office Server Security . . . . . . . . . . . . . . . . . . . . . . . . . . . 308

Overview of Security for the Branch Office . . . . . . . . . . . . . . . . . . . . . 309

Securing Windows Server 2008 in the Branch Office . . . . . . . . . . . . . . 310

Security Overview for the Information System in the Branch Office . . . . . . . 311

Securing Windows Server 2008 in the Branch Office . . . . . . . . . . . . . . 312

Lesson Summary . . . . . . . . . . . . . . . . . . . . . . . . . . . . . . . . . . . . . . . . . . . 325

Lesson Review . . . . . . . . . . . . . . . . . . . . . . . . . . . . . . . . . . . . . . . . . . . . . 326

Chapter Review . . . . . . . . . . . . . . . . . . . . . . . . . . . . . . . . . . . . . . . . . . . . . . . 328

Chapter Summary . . . . . . . . . . . . . . . . . . . . . . . . . . . . . . . . . . . . . . . . . . . . . 328

Case Scenarios . . . . . . . . . . . . . . . . . . . . . . . . . . . . . . . . . . . . . . . . . . . . . . . . 329

Case Scenario 1: Contoso Trucking . . . . . . . . . . . . . . . . . . . . . . . . . . . . 329

Case Scenario 2: Contoso Trucking, Part 2 . . . . . . . . . . . . . . . . . . . . . . 329

Case Scenario 3: Contoso Trucking, Part 3 . . . . . . . . . . . . . . . . . . . . . . 330

Suggested Practices . . . . . . . . . . . . . . . . . . . . . . . . . . . . . . . . . . . . . . . . . . . . 330

Branch Office Deployment . . . . . . . . . . . . . . . . . . . . . . . . . . . . . . . . . . 330

Read a White Paper . . . . . . . . . . . . . . . . . . . . . . . . . . . . . . . . . . . . . . . . 331

Take a Practice Test . . . . . . . . . . . . . . . . . . . . . . . . . . . . . . . . . . . . . . . . . . . . 331

**7    Planning Terminal Services and Application Deployment** . . . . . . . . . . **333**

Before You Begin . . . . . . . . . . . . . . . . . . . . . . . . . . . . . . . . . . . . . . . . . . . . . . 333

Lesson 1: Planning a Terminal Services Deployment . . . . . . . . . . . . . . . . . . 334

Planning a Terminal Services Deployment . . . . . . . . . . . . . . . . . . . . . . 334

Terminal Services Licensing . . . . . . . . . . . . . . . . . . . . . . . . . . . . . . . . . . 335

Deploying Applications Using Terminal Services Web Access . . . . . . . . . . . . 340

Planning the Deployment of Applications by Using RemoteApp . . . . . . . . . 341

Planning the Deployment of Terminal Server Farms . . . . . . . . . . . . . . . 342

Planning the Deployment of Terminal Services Gateway Servers . . . . . . . . . 343

Planning Terminal Services . . . . . . . . . . . . . . . . . . . . . . . . . . . . . . . . . . . 344

Lesson Summary. . . . . . . . . . . . . . . . . . . . . . . . . . . . . . . . . . . . . . . . . . . 346

Lesson Review . . . . . . . . . . . . . . . . . . . . . . . . . . . . . . . . . . . . . . . . . . . . 346

Lesson 2: Planning Application Deployment . . . . . . . . . . . . . . . . . . . . . . . . . . . 348

Planning the Deployment of Applications by Using Group Policy. . . . . . . . . 348

Planning Application Deployment with System Center Essentials . . . . . . . . 350

Planning the Deployment of Applications by Using SCCM 2007. . . . . . . . . . 351

Planning Application Deployment . . . . . . . . . . . . . . . . . . . . . . . . . . . . . . 354

Lesson Summary. . . . . . . . . . . . . . . . . . . . . . . . . . . . . . . . . . . . . . . . . . . 355

Lesson Review . . . . . . . . . . . . . . . . . . . . . . . . . . . . . . . . . . . . . . . . . . . . 356

Chapter Review. . . . . . . . . . . . . . . . . . . . . . . . . . . . . . . . . . . . . . . . . . . . . . . . 358

Chapter Summary . . . . . . . . . . . . . . . . . . . . . . . . . . . . . . . . . . . . . . . . . . . . . . 358

Case Scenario . . . . . . . . . . . . . . . . . . . . . . . . . . . . . . . . . . . . . . . . . . . . . . . . . 358

Case Scenario: Planning a Terminal Services Strategy
for Winqtip Toys . . . . . . . . . . . . . . . . . . . . . . . . . . . . . . . . . . . . . . . . . . . 359

Suggested Practices. . . . . . . . . . . . . . . . . . . . . . . . . . . . . . . . . . . . . . . . . . . . . 359

Provision Applications . . . . . . . . . . . . . . . . . . . . . . . . . . . . . . . . . . . . . . . 359

Take a Practice Test . . . . . . . . . . . . . . . . . . . . . . . . . . . . . . . . . . . . . . . . . . . . . 360

**8    Server and Application Virtualization. . . . . . . . . . . . . . . . . . . . . . . . . 361**

Before You Begin . . . . . . . . . . . . . . . . . . . . . . . . . . . . . . . . . . . . . . . . . . . . . . . 361

Lesson 1: Planning Operating System Virtualization. . . . . . . . . . . . . . . . . . . . . . 362

Virtual Server 2005 R2. . . . . . . . . . . . . . . . . . . . . . . . . . . . . . . . . . . . . . . 364

Hyper-V . . . . . . . . . . . . . . . . . . . . . . . . . . . . . . . . . . . . . . . . . . . . . . . . . . 365

Managing Virtualized Servers . . . . . . . . . . . . . . . . . . . . . . . . . . . . . . . . . 366

Candidates for Virtualization . . . . . . . . . . . . . . . . . . . . . . . . . . . . . . . . . . 370

Planning for Server Consolidation. . . . . . . . . . . . . . . . . . . . . . . . . . . . . . . 371

Designing Virtual Server Deployment . . . . . . . . . . . . . . . . . . . . . . . . . . . . 375

Lesson Summary. . . . . . . . . . . . . . . . . . . . . . . . . . . . . . . . . . . . . . . . . . . 376

Lesson Review . . . . . . . . . . . . . . . . . . . . . . . . . . . . . . . . . . . . . . . . . . . . 377

Lesson 2: Planning Application Virtualization . . . . . . . . . . . . . . . . . . . . . . . . . . . 379

Microsoft SoftGrid Application Virtualization . . . . . . . . . . . . . . . . . . . . . . 379

Planning Application Virtualization . . . . . . . . . . . . . . . . . . . . . . . . . . . . . . . . 383

Lesson Summary . . . . . . . . . . . . . . . . . . . . . . . . . . . . . . . . . . . . . . . . . . . . . . . 385

Lesson Review . . . . . . . . . . . . . . . . . . . . . . . . . . . . . . . . . . . . . . . . . . . . . . . . 385

Chapter Review . . . . . . . . . . . . . . . . . . . . . . . . . . . . . . . . . . . . . . . . . . . . . . . . . . . 388

Chapter Summary . . . . . . . . . . . . . . . . . . . . . . . . . . . . . . . . . . . . . . . . . . . . . . . . . . 388

Case Scenario . . . . . . . . . . . . . . . . . . . . . . . . . . . . . . . . . . . . . . . . . . . . . . . . . . . . 388

Case Scenario: Tailspin Toys Server Consolidation . . . . . . . . . . . . . . . . . . . . 388

Suggested Practices . . . . . . . . . . . . . . . . . . . . . . . . . . . . . . . . . . . . . . . . . . . . . . . 389

Windows Server Virtualization . . . . . . . . . . . . . . . . . . . . . . . . . . . . . . . . . . . 389

Plan Application Virtualization . . . . . . . . . . . . . . . . . . . . . . . . . . . . . . . . . . . 389

Take a Practice Test . . . . . . . . . . . . . . . . . . . . . . . . . . . . . . . . . . . . . . . . . . . . . . . . 390

**9    Planning and Designing a Public Key Infrastructure . . . . . . . . . . . . . . 391**

Before You Begin . . . . . . . . . . . . . . . . . . . . . . . . . . . . . . . . . . . . . . . . . . . . . . . . . 391

Lesson 1: Identifying PKI Requirements . . . . . . . . . . . . . . . . . . . . . . . . . . . . . . . . 393

Reviewing PKI Concepts . . . . . . . . . . . . . . . . . . . . . . . . . . . . . . . . . . . . . . . . . 393

Identifying PKI-Enabled Applications . . . . . . . . . . . . . . . . . . . . . . . . . . . . . . 394

Identifying Certificate Requirements . . . . . . . . . . . . . . . . . . . . . . . . . . . . . . . 395

Reviewing the Company Security Policy . . . . . . . . . . . . . . . . . . . . . . . . . . . . 398

Assessing Business Requirements . . . . . . . . . . . . . . . . . . . . . . . . . . . . . . . . . 399

Assessing External Requirements . . . . . . . . . . . . . . . . . . . . . . . . . . . . . . . . . 400

Assessing Active Directory Requirements . . . . . . . . . . . . . . . . . . . . . . . . . . . 400

Assessing Certificate Template Requirements . . . . . . . . . . . . . . . . . . . . . . . 401

Lesson Summary . . . . . . . . . . . . . . . . . . . . . . . . . . . . . . . . . . . . . . . . . . . . . . . 401

Lesson Review . . . . . . . . . . . . . . . . . . . . . . . . . . . . . . . . . . . . . . . . . . . . . . . . 402

Lesson 2: Designing the CA Hierarchy . . . . . . . . . . . . . . . . . . . . . . . . . . . . . . . . . 403

Planning the CA Infrastructure . . . . . . . . . . . . . . . . . . . . . . . . . . . . . . . . . . . 403

Lesson Summary . . . . . . . . . . . . . . . . . . . . . . . . . . . . . . . . . . . . . . . . . . . . . . . 412

Lesson Review . . . . . . . . . . . . . . . . . . . . . . . . . . . . . . . . . . . . . . . . . . . . . . . . 412

Lesson 3: Creating a Certificate Management Plan . . . . . . . . . . . . . . . . . . . . . . . 414

Selecting a Certificate Enrollment Method . . . . . . . . . . . . . . . . . . . . . . . . . . 414

Creating a CA Renewal Strategy . . . . . . . . . . . . . . . . . . . . . . . . . . . . . . . . . . 418

Defining a Revocation Policy . . . . . . . . . . . . . . . . . . . . . . . . . . . . . . . . . . . . . 419

Planning a PKI Management Strategy . . . . . . . . . . . . . . . . . . . . . . . . . . . . . 423

Lesson Summary. . . . . . . . . . . . . . . . . . . . . . . . . . . . . . . . . . . . . . . . . . . . . 424

Lesson Review . . . . . . . . . . . . . . . . . . . . . . . . . . . . . . . . . . . . . . . . . . . . . . 425

Chapter Review. . . . . . . . . . . . . . . . . . . . . . . . . . . . . . . . . . . . . . . . . . . . . . . . . 426

Chapter Summary . . . . . . . . . . . . . . . . . . . . . . . . . . . . . . . . . . . . . . . . . . . . . . 426

Case Scenario . . . . . . . . . . . . . . . . . . . . . . . . . . . . . . . . . . . . . . . . . . . . . . . . . . 426

Case Scenario: Planning a PKI . . . . . . . . . . . . . . . . . . . . . . . . . . . . . . . . . 426

Suggested Practices. . . . . . . . . . . . . . . . . . . . . . . . . . . . . . . . . . . . . . . . . . . . . 427

Watch a Webcast . . . . . . . . . . . . . . . . . . . . . . . . . . . . . . . . . . . . . . . . . . . . 427

Read a White Paper . . . . . . . . . . . . . . . . . . . . . . . . . . . . . . . . . . . . . . . . . . 427

Take a Practice Test . . . . . . . . . . . . . . . . . . . . . . . . . . . . . . . . . . . . . . . . . . . . . 428

**10    Designing Solutions for Data Sharing, Data Security, and Business Continuity** . . . . . . . . . . . . . . . . . . . . . . . . . . . . . . . . .**429**

Before You Begin . . . . . . . . . . . . . . . . . . . . . . . . . . . . . . . . . . . . . . . . . . . . . . . 429

Lesson 1: Planning for Data Sharing and Collaboration. . . . . . . . . . . . . . . . . 431

Planning a DFS Deployment. . . . . . . . . . . . . . . . . . . . . . . . . . . . . . . . . . . 431

DFS Namespaces Advanced Settings and Features . . . . . . . . . . . . . . . . . . 434

DFS Replication Advanced Settings and Features. . . . . . . . . . . . . . . . . . . . 436

Overview of the DFS Design Process. . . . . . . . . . . . . . . . . . . . . . . . . . . . . 438

Planning a SharePoint Infrastructure. . . . . . . . . . . . . . . . . . . . . . . . . . . . . 439

Designing a Data Sharing Solution . . . . . . . . . . . . . . . . . . . . . . . . . . . . . . 445

Lesson Summary. . . . . . . . . . . . . . . . . . . . . . . . . . . . . . . . . . . . . . . . . . . . 446

Lesson Review . . . . . . . . . . . . . . . . . . . . . . . . . . . . . . . . . . . . . . . . . . . . . . 447

Lesson 2: Choosing Data Security Solutions . . . . . . . . . . . . . . . . . . . . . . . . . . 448

Protecting Volume Data with BitLocker . . . . . . . . . . . . . . . . . . . . . . . . . . 448

Choosing a BitLocker Authentication Mode . . . . . . . . . . . . . . . . . . . . . . . 449

BitLocker Security Design Considerations . . . . . . . . . . . . . . . . . . . . . . . . . 450

Planning for EFS . . . . . . . . . . . . . . . . . . . . . . . . . . . . . . . . . . . . . . . . . . . . 451

Using AD RMS. . . . . . . . . . . . . . . . . . . . . . . . . . . . . . . . . . . . . . . . . . . . . . 453

Designing Data Storage Security. . . . . . . . . . . . . . . . . . . . . . . . . . . . . . . . 456

Lesson Summary. . . . . . . . . . . . . . . . . . . . . . . . . . . . . . . . . . . . . . . . . . . . 457

Lesson Review . . . . . . . . . . . . . . . . . . . . . . . . . . . . . . . . . . . . . . . . . . . . . . 458

Lesson 3:  Planning for System Recoverability and Availability . . . . . . . . . . . . . . . . 459

Planning AD DS Maintenance and Recovery Procedures. . . . . . . . . . . . . . . 459

Seizing Operations Master Roles . . . . . . . . . . . . . . . . . . . . . . . . . . . . . . . . . . . 463

Using Network Load Balancing to Support High-Usage Servers . . . . . . . . . 464

Using Failover Clusters to Maintain High Availability . . . . . . . . . . . . . . . . . . 467

Lesson Summary. . . . . . . . . . . . . . . . . . . . . . . . . . . . . . . . . . . . . . . . . . . . . . . . . . 470

Lesson Review . . . . . . . . . . . . . . . . . . . . . . . . . . . . . . . . . . . . . . . . . . . . . . . . . . . 471

Chapter Review . . . . . . . . . . . . . . . . . . . . . . . . . . . . . . . . . . . . . . . . . . . . . . . . . . . . . . . 472

Chapter Summary . . . . . . . . . . . . . . . . . . . . . . . . . . . . . . . . . . . . . . . . . . . . . . . . . . . . . 472

Case Scenario . . . . . . . . . . . . . . . . . . . . . . . . . . . . . . . . . . . . . . . . . . . . . . . . . . . . . . . . 473

Case Scenario:  Designing Solutions for Sharing,
Security, and Availability . . . . . . . . . . . . . . . . . . . . . . . . . . . . . . . . . . . . . . . . . 473

Suggested Practices . . . . . . . . . . . . . . . . . . . . . . . . . . . . . . . . . . . . . . . . . . . . . . . . . . . 474

Watch a Webcast . . . . . . . . . . . . . . . . . . . . . . . . . . . . . . . . . . . . . . . . . . . . . . . . 474

Read a White Paper . . . . . . . . . . . . . . . . . . . . . . . . . . . . . . . . . . . . . . . . . . . . . . 474

Take a Practice Test. . . . . . . . . . . . . . . . . . . . . . . . . . . . . . . . . . . . . . . . . . . . . . . . . . . . 474

**11    Designing Software Update Infrastructure
and Managing Compliance . . . . . . . . . . . . . . . . . . . . . . . . . . . . . . . . . 475**

Before You Begin . . . . . . . . . . . . . . . . . . . . . . . . . . . . . . . . . . . . . . . . . . . . . . . . . . . . . 475

Lesson 1:  Designing a Software Update Infrastructure . . . . . . . . . . . . . . . . . . . . . . . 477

Microsoft Update as a Software Update Solution . . . . . . . . . . . . . . . . . . . . . 477

Windows Server Update Services as a Software Update Solution . . . . . . . . . 478

System Center Essentials 2007 . . . . . . . . . . . . . . . . . . . . . . . . . . . . . . . . . . . . . 485

System Center Configuration Manager 2007. . . . . . . . . . . . . . . . . . . . . . . . . . 487

Windows Server 2008 Software Update Infrastructure. . . . . . . . . . . . . . . . . . 488

Lesson Summary. . . . . . . . . . . . . . . . . . . . . . . . . . . . . . . . . . . . . . . . . . . . . . . . . . 493

Lesson Review . . . . . . . . . . . . . . . . . . . . . . . . . . . . . . . . . . . . . . . . . . . . . . . . . . . 494

Lesson 2:  Managing Software Update Compliance . . . . . . . . . . . . . . . . . . . . . . . . . . 496

Microsoft Baseline Security Analyzer. . . . . . . . . . . . . . . . . . . . . . . . . . . . . . . . 496

SCCM 2007 Compliance and Reporting . . . . . . . . . . . . . . . . . . . . . . . . . . . . . 500

Planning and Deploying Security Baselines . . . . . . . . . . . . . . . . . . . . . . . . . . 501

Role-Based Security and SCE Reporting . . . . . . . . . . . . . . . . . . . . . . . . . . . . . 505

Lesson Summary. . . . . . . . . . . . . . . . . . . . . . . . . . . . . . . . . . . . . . . . . . . . . . . . . . 506

Lesson Review . . . . . . . . . . . . . . . . . . . . . . . . . . . . . . . . . . . . . . . . . . . . . . . 507

Chapter Review. . . . . . . . . . . . . . . . . . . . . . . . . . . . . . . . . . . . . . . . . . . . . . . 509

Chapter Summary . . . . . . . . . . . . . . . . . . . . . . . . . . . . . . . . . . . . . . . . . . . . . 509

Case Scenarios . . . . . . . . . . . . . . . . . . . . . . . . . . . . . . . . . . . . . . . . . . . . . . . . 509

Case Scenario 1: Deploying WSUS 3.0 SP1 at Fabrikam, Inc. . . . . . . . . . . . . 509

Case Scenario 2: Security Policies at Coho Vineyard and Coho Winery . . . . 510

Suggested Practices. . . . . . . . . . . . . . . . . . . . . . . . . . . . . . . . . . . . . . . . . . . . 511

Designing for Software Updates and Compliance Management . . . . . . . . . 511

Take a Practice Test . . . . . . . . . . . . . . . . . . . . . . . . . . . . . . . . . . . . . . . . . . . . 511

**Answers.** . . . . . . . . . . . . . . . . . . . . . . . . . . . . . . . . . . . . . . . . . . . . . . . . . . . . . . . **513**

**Glossary.** . . . . . . . . . . . . . . . . . . . . . . . . . . . . . . . . . . . . . . . . . . . . . . . . . . . . . . . **545**

**Index** . . . . . . . . . . . . . . . . . . . . . . . . . . . . . . . . . . . . . . . . . . . . . . . . . . . . . . . . . . **549**

**What do you think of this book? We want to hear from you!**

Microsoft is interested in hearing your feedback so we can continually improve our books and learning resources for you. To participate in a brief online survey, please visit:

**www.microsoft.com/learning/booksurvey**

# Acknowledgements

The authors would like to express their sincere gratitude to the following people who helped put this title together: Ken Jones, Rozanne Murphy Whalen, Chris Norton, Kerin Forsyth, Joe Gustaitis, Laura Sackerman, Chris Howd, Ron Thomas, Lisa Kreissler, Richard Kobylka, Chris McCain, and Victoria Thulman. Books like these only come together through a prolonged team effort and the authors would like to deeply thank you for working so hard to make all of us look so good!

# Introduction

This training kit is designed for enterprise administrators who have several years' experience managing the overall IT environment and architecture of medium to large organizations. As an enterprise administrator, you likely are responsible for translating business goals into technology decisions and designs and for developing mid-range and long-term strategies. You are responsible for making key decisions and recommendations about network infrastructure, directory services, identity management, security policies, business continuity, IT administrative structure, best practices, standards, and Service Level Agreements (SLAs). Your job role involves 20 percent operations, 60 percent engineering, and 20 percent support tasks.

By using this training kit, you will learn how to do the following:

- Plan network and application services
- Design core identity and access management components
- Design support identity and access management components
- Design for business continuity and data availability

---

**MORE INFO**   **Find additional content online**

As new or updated material that complements this book becomes available, it will be posted on the Microsoft Press Online Windows Server and Client Web site. Based on the final build of Windows Server 2008, the type of material you might find includes updates to book content, articles, links to companion content, errata, sample chapters, and more. This Web site will be available soon at *http://www.microsoft.com/learning/books/online/serverclient* and will be updated periodically.

---

## Lab Setup Instructions

The exercises in this training kit require a minimum of two computers or virtual machines:

- One server running Windows Server 2008 Enterprise configured as a domain controller
- One computer running Windows Vista (Enterprise, Business, or Ultimate)

You can obtain an evaluation version of Windows Server 2008 Enterprise from the Microsoft download center at *http://www.microsoft.com/Downloads/Search.aspx*.

All computers must be physically connected to the same network. It is recommended that you use an isolated network that is not part of your production network to do the practice exercises in this book. To minimize the time and expense of configuring physical computers, using virtual machines is recommended. To run computers as virtual machines within Windows, you can use Virtual PC 2007, Virtual Server 2005 R2, or third-party virtual machine software. To download Virtual PC 2007, visit *http://www.microsoft.com/windows/downloads/virtualpc/default.mspx*. To download an evaluation version of Virtual Server 2005 R2, visit *http://www.microsoft.com/technet/virtualserver/evaluation/default.mspx*.

# Hardware Requirements

You can complete almost all practice exercises in this book using virtual machines rather than real server hardware. The minimum and recommended hardware requirements for Windows Server 2008 are listed in the following table:

**Windows Server 2008 Minimum Hardware Requirements**

| Hardware Component | Minimum Requirements | Recommended |
|---|---|---|
| Processor | 1GHz (x86), 1.4GHz (x64) | 2GHz or faster |
| RAM | 512 MB | 2 GB |
| Disk Space | 15 GB | 40 GB |

If you intend to implement several virtual machines on the same computer (recommended), a higher specification will enhance your user experience. In particular, a computer with 4 GB of RAM and 60 GB of free disk space can host all the virtual machines specified for all the practice exercises in this book.

# Preparing the Computer Running Windows Server 2008 Enterprise

Detailed instructions for preparing for Windows Server 2008 installation and installing and configuring the Windows Server 2008 Enterprise domain controller are given in Chapter 1, "Planning Name Resolution and Internet Protocol Addressing." The required server roles are added in the practice exercises in subsequent chapters.

# Preparing the Computer Running Windows Vista

Perform the following steps to prepare your computer running Windows Vista for the exercises in this training kit.

## Check Operating System Version Requirements

In System Control Panel (found in the System And Maintenance category), verify that the operating system version is Windows Vista Enterprise, Windows Vista Business, or Windows Vista Ultimate. If necessary, choose the option to upgrade to one of these versions.

### Name the Computer

In System Control Panel, specify the computer name as **Melbourne**.

### Configure Networking

To configure networking carry out the following tasks:

1. In Control Panel, click Set Up File Sharing.
2. In Network And Sharing Center, verify that the network is configured as a Private network and that File Sharing is enabled.
3. In Network And Sharing Center, click Manage Network Connections.
4. In Network Connections, open the properties of the Local Area Connection. Specify a static IPv4 address that is on the same subnet as the domain controller.

   For example, the setup instructions for the domain controller specify an IPv4 address 10.0.0.11. If you use this address, you can configure the client computer with an IP address of 10.0.0.21. The subnet mask is 225.225.225.0, and the Domain Name System (DNS) address is the IPv4 address of the domain controller. You do not require a default gateway. You can choose other network addresses if you want to, provided that the client and server are on the same subnet.

# Using the CD

The companion CD included with this training kit contains the following:

- **Practice tests**  You can reinforce your understanding of how to configure Windows Vista by using electronic practice tests you customize to meet your needs from the pool of Lesson Review questions in this book, or you can practice for the 70-647 certification exam by using tests created from a pool of 200 realistic exam questions to ensure that you are prepared.
- **An eBook**  An electronic version (eBook) of this book is included for when you do not want to carry the printed book with you. The eBook is in Portable Document Format (PDF), and you can view it by using Adobe Acrobat or Adobe Reader.
- **Sample chapters**  Sample chapters from other Microsoft Press titles on Windows Server 2008 are also included. These chapters are in PDF format.

> **Digital Content for Digital Book Readers:** If you bought a digital-only edition of this book, you can enjoy select content from the print edition's companion CD.
> Visit **http://go.microsoft.com/fwlink/?/LinkId=116279** to get your downloadable content. This content is always up-to-date and available to all readers.

# How to Install the Practice Tests

To install the practice test software from the companion CD to your hard disk, do the following:

1. Insert the companion CD into your CD drive and accept the license agreement. A CD menu appears.

   **NOTE  If the CD menu does not appear**

   If the CD menu or the license agreement does not appear, AutoRun might be disabled on your computer. Refer to the Readme.txt file on the CD-ROM for alternative installation instructions.

2. Click Practice Tests and follow the instructions on the screen.

# How to Use the Practice Tests

To start the practice test software, follow these steps:

1. Click Start, click All Programs, and then select Microsoft Press Training Kit Exam Prep.

   A window appears that shows all the Microsoft Press training kit exam prep suites installed on your computer.

2. Double-click the lesson review or practice test you want to use.

   **NOTE  Lesson reviews vs. practice tests**

   Select the (70-647) Windows Server 2008, Enterprise Administration lesson review to use the questions from the "Lesson Review" sections of this book. Select the (70-647) Windows Server 2008, Enterprise Administration practice test to use a pool of 200 questions similar to those that appear on the 70-647 certification exam.

## Lesson Review Options

When you start a lesson review, the Custom Mode dialog box appears so that you can configure your test. You can click OK to accept the defaults, or you can customize the number of questions you want, how the practice test software works, which exam objectives you want the questions to relate to, and whether you want your lesson review to be timed. If you are retaking a test, you can select whether you want to see all the questions again or only the questions you missed or did not answer.

After you click OK, your lesson review starts.

- To take the test, answer the questions and use the Next and Previous buttons to move from question to question.

- After you answer an individual question, if you want to see which answers are correct—along with an explanation of each answer—click Explanation.

- If you prefer to wait until the end of the test to see how you did, answer all the questions, and then click Score Test. You will see a summary of the exam objectives you chose and the percentage of questions you got right overall and per objective. You can print a copy of your test, review your answers, or retake the test.

### Practice Test Options

When you start a practice test, you choose whether to take the test in Certification Mode, Study Mode, or Custom Mode.

- **Certification Mode** Closely resembles the experience of taking a certification exam. The test has a set number of questions. It is timed, and you cannot pause and restart the timer.
- **Study Mode** Creates an untimed test during which you can review the correct answers and the explanations after you answer each question.
- **Custom Mode** Gives you full control over the test options so that you can customize them as you like.

In all modes, the user interface when you are taking the test is basically the same but with different options enabled or disabled, depending on the mode. The main options are discussed in the previous section, "Lesson Review Options."

When you review your answer to an individual practice test question, a "References" section is provided that lists where in the training kit you can find the information that relates to that question and provides links to other sources of information. After you click Test Results to score your entire practice test, you can click the Learning Plan tab to see a list of references for every objective.

## How to Uninstall the Practice Tests

To uninstall the practice test software for a training kit, use the Programs And Features option in Windows Control Panel.

# Microsoft Certified Professional Program

The Microsoft certifications provide the best method to prove your command of current Microsoft products and technologies. The exams and corresponding certifications are developed to validate your mastery of critical competencies as you design and develop, or implement and support, solutions with Microsoft products and technologies. Computer professionals who become Microsoft-certified are recognized as experts and are sought after industry-wide. Certification brings a variety of benefits to the individual and to employers and organizations.

---

**MORE INFO**  **All the Microsoft certifications**

For a full list of Microsoft certifications, go to *http://www.microsoft.com/learning/mcp/default.asp*.

---

# Technical Support

Every effort has been made to ensure the accuracy of this book and the contents of the companion CD. If you have comments, questions, or ideas regarding this book or the companion CD, please send them to Microsoft Press by using either of the following methods:

- E-mail: tkinput@microsoft.com
- Postal mail at:

  Microsoft Press
  Attn: *MCITP Self-Paced Training Kit (Exam 70-647): Windows Server Enterprise Administration*, Editor
  One Microsoft Way
  Redmond, WA 98052-6399

For additional support information regarding this book and the CD-ROM (including answers to commonly asked questions about installation and use), visit the Microsoft Press Technical Support Web site at *http://www.microsoft.com/learning/support/books/*. To connect directly to the Microsoft Knowledge Base and enter a query, visit *http://support.microsoft.com/search/*. For support information regarding Microsoft software, connect to *http://support.microsoft.com*.

Chapter 1

# Planning Name Resolution and Internet Protocol Addressing

As an enterprise administrator, you will be responsible for the overall IT environment and architecture within your organization. Enterprise administrators translate business goals into technology decisions; design mid-range to long-term strategies; and make key decisions and recommendations about, for example, network infrastructure, directory services, security policies, business continuity, administrative structure, best practices, standards, and service-level agreements (SLAs).

The enterprise administrator is responsible for infrastructure design and global configuration changes. If you intend to extend your career and become an enterprise administrator, or if you already carry out enterprise administrator tasks and want to acquire a certification that matches your experience, you will already be an experienced network and server administrator with typically two or more years' experience administering corporate networks. The 70-647 examination is not designed for beginners, nor is this training kit.

As an experienced administrator, you will almost certainly be familiar with name resolution and IPv4 addressing. You will probably have come across IPv6 addresses but might not be familiar with them. This chapter does not attempt to cover old ground but, rather, looks at the new features and approaches implemented in Windows Server 2008.

---

**IMPORTANT** Examination Objectives

The objectives related to name resolution and IP addressing in the 70-647 examination are similar to those in the 70-646 Windows Server 2008 Server Administration examination. If you have previously prepared for 70-646, you will find that this chapter discusses topics that you have already studied. In this case, please treat this material as review.

---

## Exam objectives in this chapter:
- Plan for name resolution and IP addressing.

## Lessons in this chapter:
- Lesson 1: Planning Name Resolution . . . . . . . . . . . . . . . . . . . . . . . . . . . . . . . . . . . . . . . .3
- Lesson 2: Planning Internet Protocol Addressing . . . . . . . . . . . . . . . . . . . . . . . . . . . . . 36

# Before You Begin

To complete the lessons in this chapter, you must have done the following:

- Installed Windows Server 2008 Enterprise on a server configured as a domain controller in the *contoso.internal* domain. Active Directory–integrated Domain Name System (DNS) is installed by default on the first domain controller in a domain. The computer name is Glasgow. Configure a static IPv4 address of 10.0.0.11 with a subnet mask 255.255.255.0. The IPv4 address of the DNS server is 10.0.0.11. Other than IPv4 configuration and the computer name, accept all the default installation settings. You can obtain an evaluation version of the Windows Server 2008 Enterprise software from the Microsoft Download Center at *http://www.microsoft.com/downloads/search.aspx*.

- Installed Windows Vista Business, Enterprise, or Windows Vista Ultimate on a client computer joined to the *contoso.internal* domain. The computer name is Melbourne. Initially, this computer should have a static IPv4 address of 10.0.0.21 with a subnet mask 255.255.255.0. The IPv4 address of the DNS server is 10.0.0.11. You can obtain evaluation software that enables you to implement Windows Vista Enterprise 30-Day evaluation virtual hard disk (VHD) at *http://www.microsoft.com/downloads/details.aspx?FamilyID =c2c27337-d4d1-4b9b-926d-86493c7da1aa&DisplayLang=en*.

- Created a user account with the username Kim_Akers and password P@ssw0rd. Add this account to the Domain Admins, Enterprise Admins, and Schema Admins groups.

- It's recommended that you use an isolated network that is not part of your production network to do the practice exercises in this book. Internet access is not required for the exercises, and you do not need to configure a default gateway. To minimize the time and expense of configuring physical computers, it's recommended that you use virtual machines. To run computers as virtual machines within Windows, you can use Virtual PC 2007, Virtual Server 2005 R2, or third-party virtual machine software. To download Virtual PC 2007, visit *http://www.microsoft.com/windows/downloads/virtualpc/default.mspx*. To download Virtual Server 2005 R2, visit *http://www.microsoft.com/technet/virtualserver /evaluation/default.mspx*.

# Lesson 1:  Planning Name Resolution

As an experienced administrator, you will have worked with DNS and with Microsoft dynamic DNS. You should also be familiar with Network Basic Input Output System (NetBIOS) names, the NetBIOS Extended User Interface (NetBEUI), and the Windows Internet Name Service (WINS). It is not, therefore, the purpose of this lesson to explain the basic operation of these features but rather to look at Windows Server 2008 enhancements, particularly to DNS, and to discuss the planning of a name resolution infrastructure across an enterprise network.

Possibly one of the first planning decisions you need to make is whether to use WINS to resolve NetBIOS names. When Microsoft introduced dynamic DNS, this was seen as a replacement to WINS, but WINS is still in use in many networks and is supported in Windows Server 2008. Microsoft, however, describes WINS as approaching obsolescence and introduces the GlobalNames DNS zone to provide single-label name resolution for large enterprise networks that do not deploy WINS. If you do not use WINS, you can consider disabling NetBIOS over TCP/IP (NetBT) on your network.

When planning a DNS infrastructure, you must decide when to use Active Directory–integrated, standard primary, secondary, stub, reverse lookup, and GlobalNames DNS zones. You need to plan DNS forwarding and when to use conditional forwarding, which is especially relevant to the enterprise environment in which you can have multiple Active Directory Domain Services (AD DS) forests in the same intranetwork. Enterprise networks are also likely to include or need to integrate with non-Microsoft DNS servers, and you need to know how Microsoft DNS interoperates with, for example, Berkley Internet Daemon (BIND) servers. Windows Server 2008 (and Windows Vista) supports IPv6 by default, and you need to understand and use the IPv6 records in DNS. Setting up a reverse lookup IPv6 DNS zone can be described best as a potentially confusing procedure and is one of the exercises in the practice session later in this chapter.

---

**After this lesson, you will be able to:**

- Consider Windows Server 2008 DNS features when planning your name resolution infrastructure.
- Identify Windows Server 2008 enhancements to DNS and use these in your planning process.
- Configure static IPv6 DNS records.
- Configure an IPv6 reverse lookup zone.
- Administer DNS using the Microsoft Management Console (MMC) snap-in and command-line tools.

**Estimated lesson time:  45 minutes**

> **Real World**
>
> *John Policelli*
>
> I recall performing an assessment of a client's Active Directory Domain Services environment, which underscored to me the importance of properly designing name resolution.
>
> Our client had engaged us to assist in identifying the root cause of authentication issues, Group Policy processing issues, and Microsoft Outlook to Exchange Server communication issues. Knowing that each of these is heavily dependent on name resolution, I was almost certain that the culprit of our client's issues was name resolution before even starting the assessment. Through performing the assessment, I was able to validate that the issues were indeed related to name resolution. Through further analysis, I was able to identify a number of name resolution design flaws that were causing these issues. In reality, our client did not have any issue with authentication, Group Policy processing, or Outlook to Exchange Server communication. Rather, these were all symptoms of the name resolution issues that were caused by the insufficient name resolution design.
>
> Designing name resolution and IP address assignment are perhaps the most crucial tasks an enterprise administrator will perform. The Windows operating system, Active Directory Domain Services, and virtually all technologies discussed in this training kit rely heavily on both name resolution and IP address assignment. Without properly designed name resolution and IP address assignment solutions, an organization's network is severely hampered.

## Planning Windows Server 2008 DNS

DNS resolves IP host names to IP addresses and can also resolve IP addresses to host names in reverse lookup DNS zones. Name resolution is important for IPv4 because IPv4 addresses are difficult to remember, and users mostly use host names or fully qualified domain names (FQDNs), for example, in Internet addresses such as *http://www.litware.com*. Remembering IPv6 addresses is almost impossible, and name resolution is even more important on the IPv6 region of the World Wide Web. This section covers the enhancements to DNS introduced in Windows Server 2008 and how DNS deals with IPv6 addresses.

The Windows Server 2008 DNS server role retains the features introduced by Microsoft Windows Server 2003 DNS, including dynamic configuration and incremental zone transfer, and introduces several new features and significant enhancements.

Windows Server 2008 DNS in a Windows-based network supports Active Directory Domain Services (AD DS). If you install the AD DS role on a server or run the *dcpromo* command, and a DNS server that meets AD DS requirements cannot be located, you can automatically install and configure a DNS server and, by default, create an Active Directory–integrated DNS zone. Typically, this happens when you are installing the first domain controller (DC) in a forest.

A partition is a data container in AD DS that holds data for replication. You can store DNS zone data in either the domain or application directory partitions of AD DS, and then you can specify which partition should store the zone. This choice defines the set of DCs to which that zone's data is replicated. Microsoft recommends that you use the Windows Server 2008 DNS Server service for this purpose, although other types of DNS servers can support AD DS deployment. Partitions help ensure that only updates to DNS zones are replicated to other DNS servers. Incremental zone transfer is discussed later in this lesson.

---

**NOTE   File-backed DNS servers**

A file-backed DNS server is a DNS server that is not integrated with AD DS. You can install file-backed DNS servers on any standalone computer on your network. Typically, file-backed DNS servers are used in peripheral zones where the use of member servers (and especially DCs) could be seen as a security risk. File-backed servers typically contain standard primary or secondary zones, although they can also contain stub zones or exist as caching-only servers that do not hold any DNS zones but instead cache name resolution records.

---

> ## Windows Server 2008 DNS Compliance
>
> The DNS Server role in Windows Server 2008 complies with all Request for Comments (RFCs) that define and standardize the DNS protocol. It uses standard DNS data file and resource record formats and can work successfully with most other DNS server implementations, such as DNS implementations that use the BIND software. Windows Server 2008 DNS is fully compliant with the dynamic update protocol defined in RFC 2136.

## Configuring Windows Server 2008 DNS

Close integration with other Windows services, including AD DS, WINS (if enabled), and Dynamic Host Configuration Protocol (DHCP and DHCPv6) ensures that Windows Server 2008 dynamic DNS requires little or no manual configuration. Computers that run the DNS Client service register their host names and IPv4 and IPv6 addresses (although not link-local IPv6 addresses) dynamically. You can configure the DNS Server and DNS Client services to perform secure dynamic updates. This ensures that only authenticated users with the appropriate rights can update resource records on the DNS server. Figure 1-1 shows a zone being configured to allow only secure dynamic updates. More information about IPv6 addresses, including link-local addresses, is given in Lesson 2, "Planning Internet Protocol Addressing."

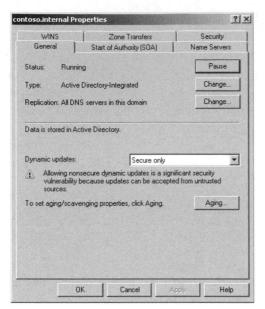

**Figure 1-1** Allowing only secure dynamic updates

---

**MORE INFO** Dynamic update protocol

For more information about the dynamic update protocol, see *http://www.ietf.org/rfc/rfc2136.txt* and *http://www.ietf.org/rfc/rfc3007*.

---

**NOTE** Secure dynamic updates

Secure dynamic updates are available only for zones that are integrated with AD DS.

---

## Using Stub Zones

A *stub zone*, supported in Windows Server 2008 DNS, is a zone copy that contains only the resource records necessary to identify the authoritative DNS servers for that zone. Stub zones ensure that DNS servers hosting parent zones can determine authoritative DNS servers for child zones, thus helping maintain efficient DNS name resolution. Figure 1-2 shows a stub zone specified in the New Zone Wizard.

You can use stub zones when name servers in the target zone are in transition, such as if part or all of the company network is undergoing IP address transition, and resolution of names is problematic. For example Contoso, Ltd., recently acquired the sales organization Litware, Inc. Contoso has a Windows Server 2008 domain. Litware has a Microsoft Windows 2000 Server mixed-mode domain and, for historical reasons, uses standalone Microsoft Windows NT 4.0 DNS servers and BIND servers for name resolution. Contoso has decided that the Litware name will no longer be used and the Litware organization will instead be the Contoso sales division with a *sales.contoso.com* subdomain. You are currently planning to configure the new *sales.contoso.com* subdomain with a new name resolution and IP addressing structure to comply with Contoso company policy.

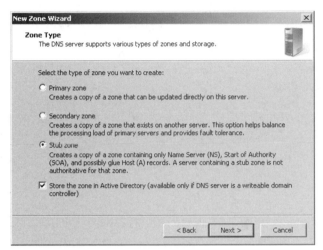

**Figure 1-2**   Creating a stub zone

In this case, your plan would include a stub zone in the Contoso Active Directory *contoso.com* domain that contains resource records that identify the authoritative DNS servers for the *sales.contoso.com* subdomain. As the *sales.contoso.com* domain is implemented and the names and IP addresses of its DNS servers change, the stub zone in the *contoso.com* domain can be easily updated.

Stub zones are typically used to hold the records for DNS servers in delegated zones. In this case, a name server (NS) record in the parent zone lists the name server that is authoritative for the delegated zone. For example, the name server for the *contoso.com* zone can delegate authority for the *sales.contoso.com* zone to a DNS server in that delegated zone. You can use stub zones to keep delegated zone information current, improve name resolution, and simplify DNS administration.

---

**NOTE**   Delegation and glue records in Windows Server 2008

The DNS Server role in Windows Server 2008 automatically adds delegation and glue records when you delegate a subdomain. Delegated name servers are listed by name rather than by IP address. Thus, a resolving name server needs to find out the IP address of the server to which it has been referred and must issue another DNS request to do so. This can introduce a circular dependency in which a name server accesses an NS record that refers to itself. To prevent this from happening, the name server providing the delegation can provide the IP address of the next name server. This record is called a glue record.

---

## DNS Forwarding

DNS servers to which other DNS servers forward requests are known as *forwarders*. If a DNS server does not have an entry in its database for the remote host specified in a client request, it can return the address of a DNS server more likely to have that information to the client, or it can query the other DNS server itself. This process takes place recursively until either the client computer receives the IP address or the DNS server establishes that the queried name cannot be resolved.

The Windows 2008 DNS Server service uses *conditional forwarders* to extend the standard forwarder configuration. A conditional forwarder is a DNS server that forwards DNS queries according to the DNS domain name in the query. For example, you can configure a DNS server to forward all the queries that it receives for names ending with *adatum.com* to the IP address of one or more specified DNS servers that are authoritative for the *adatum.com* domain. This feature is particularly useful on enterprise extranets, where several organizations and domains access the same private internetwork.

---

**Exam Tip**   In Windows Server 2008, conditional forwarding entries can be stored in AD DS and configured to replicate to all DNS servers in the forest, all DNS servers in the domain, or all DCs in the domain.

---

Figure 1-3 shows the dialog box used to create a conditional forwarder. You cannot actually configure this on your test network because you have only one DNS server.

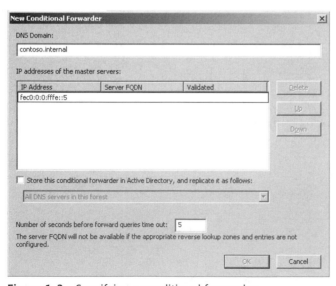

**Figure 1-3**   Specifying a conditional forwarder

## Zone Replication

Windows Server 2008 DNS zones are replicated between DNS servers for failover and to improve DNS name resolution efficiency. Zone transfers implement zone replication and synchronization. If you add a new DNS server to the network and configure it as a secondary DNS server for an existing zone, it performs a full zone transfer to obtain a read-only copy of resource records for the zone. Any further changes to the authoritative zone are replicated to the secondary zone. Windows Server 2003 introduced incremental zone transfer that replicates only changes to the authoritative zone, and Windows Server 2008 supports this functionality. Prior to Windows Server 2003, a full zone transfer was required to replicate any changes in the authoritative DNS zone to the secondary DNS server. Incremental transfer enables a secondary server to pull only those zone changes that it needs to synchronize its copy of the zone with its source zone, which can be either a primary or secondary copy of the zone that is maintained by another DNS server.

You can allow zone transfers to any DNS server, to specified DNS servers only, and to DNS servers listed on the Name Servers tab (any server that has registered an NS record). Figure 1-4 shows a DNS zone configured to allow zone transfers only to DNS servers listed on the Name Servers tab.

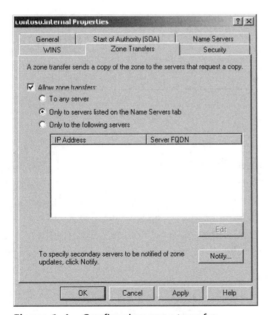

**Figure 1-4**   Configuring zone transfer

## DNS Records

As a network professional, you should be familiar with standard DNS record types such as IPv4 host (A), Start of Authority (SOA), Pointer (PTR), canonical name (CNAME), name server (NS), Mail Exchanger (MX), service location (SRV), and so on. You might use other DNS record types, such as Andrew File System Database (AFSDB) and Asynchronous Transfer Mode (ATM) address if you are configuring compatibility with non-Windows DNS systems. Figure 1-5 shows some of the record types available in Windows Server 2008 DNS. If you need to create an IPv6 record for a client that cannot register itself with Active Directory, you need to create an AAAA record manually.

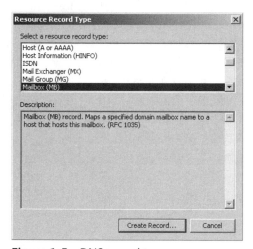

**Figure 1-5**   DNS record types

## Administering DNS

You can use the DNS Manager MMC snap-in GUI to manage and configure the DNS Server service. Windows Server 2008 also provides configuration wizards for performing common server administration tasks. Figure 1-6 shows the DNS Manager tool as well as IPv4 and IPv6 host records dynamically registered in DNS. Note that if you access this tool at this point in the lesson, IPv6 records will not be displayed because you have not yet configured IPv6 addresses. You do this in the practice session later in this lesson and in Lesson 2 of this chapter.

Windows Server 2008 provides command-line tools that help you better manage and support DNS servers and clients on your network. You can use the *dnscmd* tool to configure and administer both IPv4 and IPv6 records and to create reverse lookup zones. Figure 1-7 lists the command-line switches you can use with this tool. Typically, you need to run the command console (or command prompt) as an administrator to use the *dnscmd* tool.

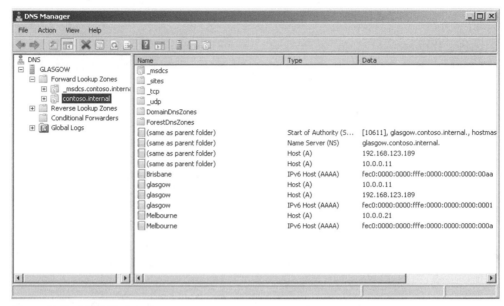

**Figure 1-6**  DNS Manager

```
Command Prompt                                                            _ □ ×

C:\Users\kim_akers>dnscmd /help

Usage: DnsCmd <ServerName> <Command> [<Command Parameters>]

<ServerName>:
  IP address or host name  -- remote or local DNS server
                           -- DNS server on local machine
<Command>:
  /Info                    -- Get server information
  /Config                  -- Reset server or zone configuration
  /EnumZones               -- Enumerate zones
  /Statistics              -- Query/clear server statistics data
  /ClearCache              -- Clear DNS server cache
  /WriteBackFiles          -- Write back all zone or root-hint datafile(s)
  /StartScavenging         -- Initiates server scavenging
  /IpValidate              -- Validate remote DNS servers
  /ResetListenAddresses    -- Set server IP address(es) to serve DNS requests
  /ResetForwarders         -- Set DNS servers to forward recursive queries to
  /ZoneInfo                -- View zone information
  /ZoneAdd                 -- Create a new zone on the DNS server
  /ZoneDelete              -- Delete a zone from DNS server or DS
  /ZonePause               -- Pause a zone
  /ZoneResume              -- Resume a zone
  /ZoneReload              -- Reload zone from its database (file or DS)
  /ZoneWriteBack           -- Write back zone to file
  /ZoneRefresh             -- Force refresh of secondary zone from master
  /ZoneUpdateFromDs        -- Update a DS integrated zone by data from DS
  /ZonePrint               -- Display all records in the zone
  /ZoneResetType           -- Change zone type
  /ZoneResetSecondaries    -- Reset secondary\notify information for a zone
  /ZoneResetScavengeServers -- Reset scavenging servers for a zone
  /ZoneResetMasters        -- Reset secondary zone's master servers
  /ZoneExport              -- Export a zone to file
  /ZoneChangeDirectoryPartition -- Move a zone to another directory partition
  /EnumRecords             -- Enumerate records at a name
  /RecordAdd               -- Create a record in zone or RootHints
  /RecordDelete            -- Delete a record from zone, RootHints or cache
  /NodeDelete              -- Delete all records at a name
  /AgeAllRecords           -- Force aging on node(s) in zone
  /EnumDirectoryPartitions -- Enumerate directory partitions
  /DirectoryPartitionInfo  -- Get info on a directory partition
  /CreateDirectoryPartition -- Create a directory partition
  /DeleteDirectoryPartition -- Delete a directory partition
  /EnlistDirectoryPartition -- Add DNS server to partition replication scope
  /UnenlistDirectoryPartition -- Remove DNS server from replication scope
  /CreateBuiltinDirectoryPartitions -- Create built-in partitions
  /ExportSettings          -- Output settings to DnsSettings.txt in the DNS se
```

**Figure 1-7**  The *dnscmd* tool

You can use the *ipconfig* command to view interface adapter configurations. You can also release IPv4 and IPv6 configurations by using *ipconfig /release* and *ipconfig /release6*, respectively. Similarly, you can renew configurations with *ipconfig /renew* and *ipconfig /renew6*. Although an ordinary user can use *ipconfig* and *ipconfig /all* to view IP configuration, you usually need to run the command console (or command prompt) as an administrator to use the other switches provided with the *ipconfig* tool.

If a client sends a request to a DNS server and the remote host name cannot be resolved, the DNS cache on the client stores the information that resolution failed. This is known as negative caching and is designed to prevent clients from continually accessing DNS servers and attempting to resolve unresolvable host names. However, the disadvantage of negative caching is that if the remote host name cannot be resolved because of a server problem, and that problem is subsequently repaired, the client cannot obtain resolution for that host name until the information stating that it is not resolvable is cleared from the cache. In this situation, you can use *ipconfig /flushdns* on the client to clear the cache immediately. Typically, the cache is refreshed every 15 minutes, so this problem will fix itself even if you are not present to issue the command.

A new client on a network takes some time to register with dynamic DNS. You can speed up this process by using the *ipconfig /registerdns* command. You can display DNS information by using the *ipconfig /displaydns* command. The *ipconfig* commands that display information can be run without elevated privileges, but the commands that configure interfaces, release configuration, flush the cache, or register the client require you to run the command console as an administrator. Figure 1-8 shows the command-line switches available with the *ipconfig* command.

---

### Quick Check

1.  Which command-line interface command can you use to create reverse lookup zones?
2.  Which command-line interface commands release and renew nonstatic IPv6 configurations?

### Quick Check Answers

1.  *dnscmd*
2.  *ipconfig /release6* and *ipconfig /renew6*

---

If a client cannot obtain remote host name resolution from a DNS server, and you have used the *ping* command to ensure that you have network connectivity between the server and the host, you can use *nslookup* to check whether the server is providing a DNS service. If, for example, you enter the *nslookup glasgow* command from the Melbourne client computer on your test network, this tests connectivity to the *glasgow.contoso.internal* server.

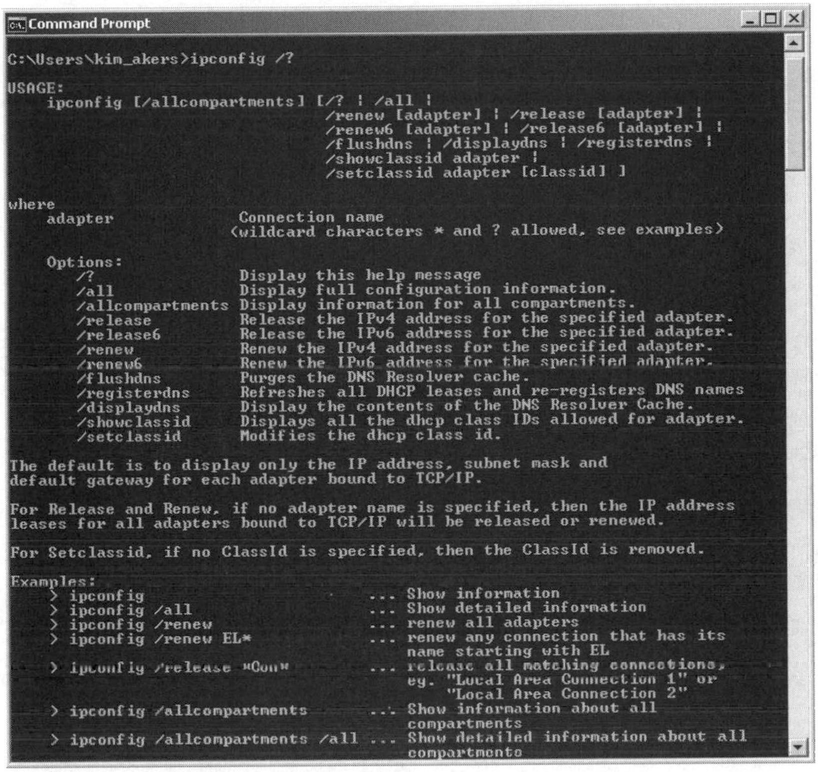

**Figure 1-8**  The *ipconfig* tool

You can issue the *nslookup contoso.internal* command from the same client computer. This returns the IPv4 addresses of DNS servers in the *contoso.internal* domain.

If you enter *nslookup* on Melbourne and then enter *ls –d contoso.internal* at the nslookup> prompt, this lists all the DNS records in the *contoso.internal* domain, as shown in Figure 1-9.

---

**NOTE**  *Nslookup ls -d <domain>*

This command does not work unless you have enabled zone transfer (shown in Figure 1-4), even if you run it on the server that hosts the domain. If you cannot get this to work, try selecting To Any Server on the Zone Transfers tab, but be aware that doing so compromises your security.

---

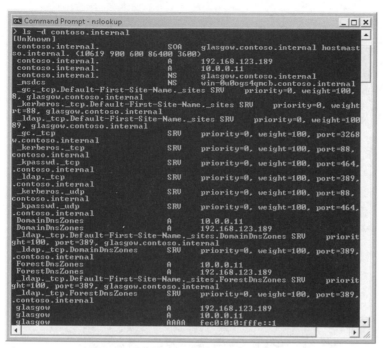

**Figure 1-9** DNS records in the *contoso.internal* domain

A list of *nslookup* commands is shown in Figure 1-10.

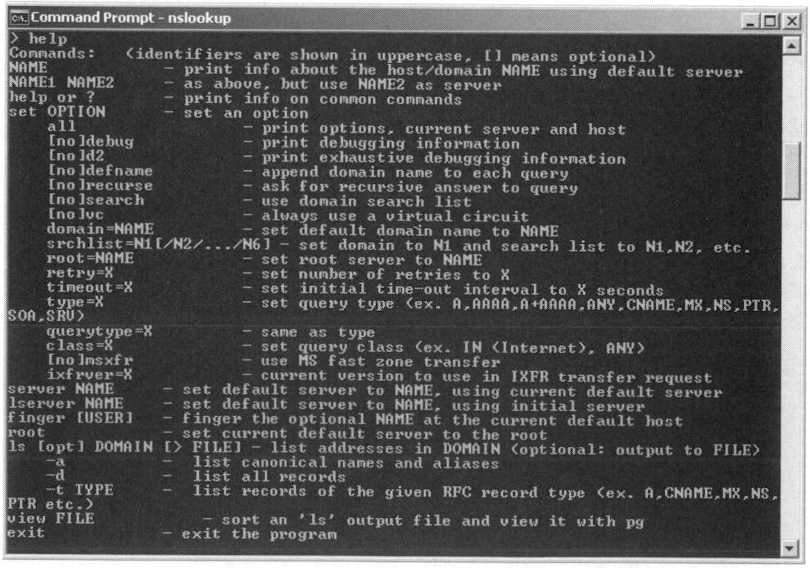

**Figure 1-10** *Nslookup* commands

The *netsh interface ipv6 show dnsservers* command displays IPv6 DNS configurations and indicates which DNS server addresses are statically configured.

## Using New DNS Features and Enhancements

The DNS Server role in Windows Server 2008 provides the following new or enhanced features:

- **Support for read-only domain controllers**  The Windows Server 2008 DNS Server role provides primary read-only zones on read-only domain controllers (RODCs). A DNS zone on an RODC is authoritative but is not dynamically updated whenever a new network entity (client, server, network printer, or network projector) is added to the domain. If a network entity is added on the same site as an RODC, the RODC can pull its corresponding DNS records from a writable DC, provided the writable DC is configured to allow this. This enables name resolution to be performed locally on a site rather than over a wide area network (WAN).

**MORE INFO**  RODCs

For more information about RODCs, go to *http://technet2.microsoft.com/windowsserver2008 /en/library/ea8d253e-0646-490c-93d3-b78c5e1d9db71033.mspx?mfr=true* and follow the links.

- **Background zone loading**  Loading DNS zone data is a background operation in Windows Server 2008. If you need to restart a DNS server that hosts one or more large DNS zones that are stored in AD DS, the server is able to respond to client queries more quickly because it does not need to wait until all zone data is loaded.
- **GlobalNames**  The GlobalNames DNS zone provides single-label name resolution for large enterprise networks that do not deploy WINS. This zone is used when it is impractical to use DNS name suffixes to provide single-label name resolution.
- **IPv6 support**  The Windows Server 2008 DNS Server role fully supports IPv6 addresses. It implements AAAA and IPv6 records and supports IPv6 reverse lookup zones.

### Supporting RODCs

An RODC provides a shadow copy of a DC and cannot be directly configured. This makes it less vulnerable to attack. Microsoft advises using RODCs in locations where you cannot guarantee the physical security of a DC. You can delegate RODC configuration to nonadministrative accounts and do not need to have domain or enterprise administrators working at branch offices.

Windows Server 2008 supports primary read-only authoritative zones (sometimes called branch office zones). When a Windows Server 2008 server is configured as an RODC, it replicates a read-only copy of all Active Directory partitions that DNS uses, including the domain partition, ForestDNSZones, and DomainDNSZones. A user with the appropriate permissions can view the contents of a primary read-only zone but cannot change its contents. The contents of a read-only zone in an RODC change only when the DNS zone on the master DC changes and the master DC is configured to allow the RODC to pull these changes.

## Background Zone Loading

In a large organization with large Windows Server 2003 (or earlier) zones that store DNS data in AD DS, restarting a DNS server can take considerable time. The DNS server needs to retrieve zone data from AD DS and is unavailable to service client requests while this is happening.

Windows Server 2008 DNS addresses this situation through background zone loading. A Windows Server 2008 DNS server loads zone data from AD DS in the background and can respond almost immediately to client requests when it restarts, instead of waiting until its zones are fully loaded. Also, because zone data is stored in AD DS rather than in a file, that data can be accessed asynchronously and immediately when a query is received. File-based zone data can be accessed only through a sequential file read and takes longer to access than data in AD DS.

When the DNS server starts, it identifies all zones to be loaded, loads root hints from files or AD DS storage, loads any file-backed zones, and starts to respond to queries and remote procedure calls (RPCs) while using background processes (additional processor threads) to load zones that are stored in AD DS.

If a DNS client requests data for a host in a zone that has already been loaded, the DNS server responds as required. If the request is for information that has not yet been loaded into memory, the DNS server reads the required data from AD DS so that the request can be met.

When you are planning your name resolution infrastructure, plan to have more than one DNS server servicing name resolution requests. Usually, all DCs (writable and RODC) in an Active Directory domain host Active Directory–integrated DNS zones. Both Active Directory–integrated and standard primary zones can use secondary zones for load sharing and failover. Secondary DNS servers are good candidates for virtualization and can be hosted on virtual machines. If a primary server is rebooting, DNS requests are normally answered by other Active Directory–integrated DNS servers or by secondary servers. The effect of background loading in this situation is that a rebooted DNS server comes online more quickly to share the load of satisfying client requests.

> ### Quick Check
> - Which DNS record enables a host name to be resolved to an IPv6 address?
> ### Quick Check Answer
> - AAAA

## Using the GlobalNames DNS Zone for Legacy Support

WINS uses NetBT, which Microsoft describes as approaching obsolescence. Nevertheless, it provides static, global records with single-label names and is still widely used. Windows Server 2008 DNS introduces the GlobalNames zone to hold single-label names and provide legacy support for networks that previously used WINS for NetBIOS name resolution. Typically, the replication scope of this zone is the entire forest, which ensures that the zone can provide single-label names that are unique in the forest. The GlobalNames zone also supports single-label name resolution throughout an organization that contains multiple forests—provided that you use service location (SRV) resource records to publish the GlobalNames zone location. This enables organizations to disable WINS and NetBT, which will probably not be supported in future Windows Server releases. You need to keep this in mind when planning changes in your name resolution structure and deciding whether to retain WINS. Disabling NetBT reduces the attack surface of your servers and makes them less vulnerable to malicious users.

The GlobalNames zone provides single-label name resolution for a limited set of host names, usually centrally managed corporate servers and Web sites, and is not used for peer-to-peer name resolution. Client workstation name resolution and dynamic updates are not supported. Instead, the GlobalNames zone holds CNAME resource records to map a single-label name to an FQDN. In networks that are currently using WINS, the GlobalNames zone usually contains resource records for centrally managed names that are already statically configured on the WINS server.

Microsoft recommends that you integrate the GlobalNames zone with AD DS and that you configure each authoritative DNS server with a local copy of the GlobalNames zone. This provides maximum performance and scalability. AD DS integration of the GlobalNames zone is required to support deployment of the GlobalNames zone across multiple forests.

---

**NOTE  Enabling a DNS server to support GlobalNames zones**

The /config switch in the dnscmd command-line tool enables a DNS server to support GlobalNames zones.

---

**Exam Tip**    Unlike WINS, GlobalNames zone functionality does not permit host name entries to be registered dynamically. All host name entries in the GlobalNames zone must be created manually.

---

## Planning WINS Replication for Legacy Support

As an enterprise administrator, you need to support earlier networks, for example, Windows NT 4.0 domains. Although WINS is nearly obsolescent, you need to know how to support it and include it in your planning and design process. Questions about WINS are likely to appear in the 70-647 examination. The major planning and design decisions you need to make when planning WINS services will be about which WINS replication topology to use. You might not have looked at WINS for some time and, therefore, this section includes some basic information for the purpose of review.

WINS database replication occurs whenever the WINS database changes on any WINS server, for example, when a NetBIOS name is released. WINS replication enables a WINS server to resolve NetBIOS names of hosts registered with other WINS servers. To replicate database entries, each WINS server must be configured as either a pull or a push partner with at least one other WINS server.

A push partner sends a message to its pull partners, notifying them when its WINS database has changed. When a WINS server's pull partners respond to the message with a replication request, the WINS server pushes a copy of its new database entries to its pull partners. A pull partner is a WINS server that requests new database entries from its push partners by requesting entries with a higher version number than the entries it received during the last replication.

Push replication occurs when a specified number of updates to the WINS database have occurred and works best when you have fast links between your WINS servers that can support a high bandwidth. You can configure pull replication to occur at specific intervals, and you can control the replication traffic by adjusting the bandwidth. Pull replication is used between sites connected by slow WAN links. To replicate database entries in both directions, configure each server to be both a push and a pull partner. Every WINS server must be both a push partner and a pull partner (but not necessarily with each other) for the replication to complete.

---

**Exam Tip**   Push replication occurs when a specified number of updated WINS database entries is reached. Pull replication can be configured to occur at specific intervals.

---

How you plan your WINS replication topology primarily depends on the network topology and disaster recovery requirements in your organization. The following WINS replication topologies are available:

- **Centralized WINS topology**   This topology uses a single centralized high availability WINS server or WINS server cluster. Centralized WINS topology simplifies deployment and maintenance. No server-to-server replication overhead exists, and all clients are configured with the same WINS server address. Fault tolerance can be achieved by using clustering. If, however, the shared cluster database is corrupted, it needs to be restored from backup. No WINS replication occurs in this topology. Centralized WINS topology does not provide WINS database fault tolerance.

- **Full mesh WINS topology**   This topology is a distributed WINS design with multiple WINS servers or clusters deployed across the enterprise. You need to plan WINS replication to ensure synchronization of the WINS database between all WINS servers. All WINS servers replicate with all other WINS servers. You can configure replication manually or by using the WINS autodiscovery (automatic partner configuration) feature. In a full mesh WINS topology, some clients can be configured to use one WINS server as their primary, and the remaining clients can use another WINS server, which enables you to implement load balancing. Full mesh WINS topology is typically used when the network topology consists of multiple data centers and remote offices. Each WINS server replicates with every other WINS server in this topology, which causes a significant amount of network traffic. This topology can introduce security risks and requires more management and support than other technologies. The full mesh WINS topology is illustrated in Figure 1-11.

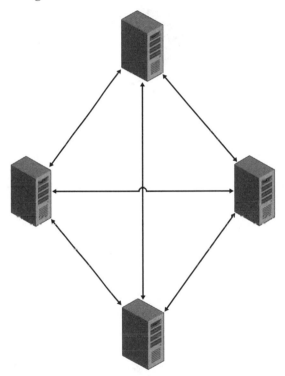

**Figure 1-11**   Full mesh WINS topology

■ **Ring WINS topology**   This topology is a distributed WINS design in which each WINS server replicates with a specific neighboring partner, forming a circle. This topology needs to be created manually because relationships between each server pair must be determined and configured by a WINS administrator. A ring WINS topology is easier to maintain than a full mesh WINS topology, and you can provision for load balancing by distributing your clients across WINS servers. However, troubleshooting is more difficult in a ring WINS topology, and the *convergence time*, which is the time it takes for a database change to replicate to all WINS servers, is longer because updates are passed sequentially from server to server. The ring mesh WINS topology is illustrated in Figure 1-12.

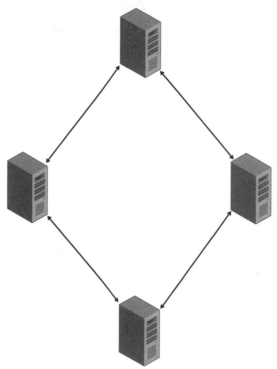

**Figure 1-12**    Ring WINS topology

- **Hub and spoke WINS topology**    This is a distributed WINS design in which a central WINS server is designated as the hub, and additional WINS servers replicate only with the hub in the site where they are located. A hub and spoke WINS topology provides efficient convergence, simple management, and convenient provisioning for load balancing. It is typically used when the network topology consists of a central data center and multiple remote offices or branch offices. The central data center usually provides name resolution for the majority of the computers on the network, and the branch offices provide name resolution for local computers. The hub and spoke WINS topology is illustrated in Figure 1-13.

When you have planned your WINS replication topology, you can determine the number of WINS servers required. This depends on the number of clients that need WINS name resolution services, on the available bandwidth for client name queries and registrations, and on server-to-server replication between sites. As a guideline, there should be one WINS server for every 10,000 clients, with a minimum of two WINS servers to provide redundancy in sites that require highly available WINS services.

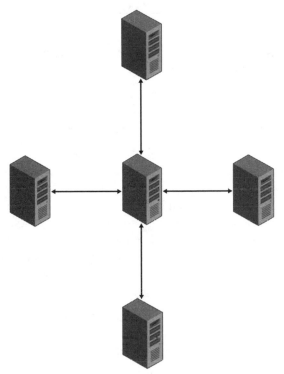

**Figure 1-13**   Hub and spoke WINS topology

## Supporting IPv6 Addresses

Windows Server 2008 DNS supports IPv6 addresses as fully as it supports IPv4 addresses. IPv6 addresses register dynamically, and you can create an AAAA host record for any computer on the network whose operating system does not support dynamic registration. You can also create IPv6 reverse lookup zones. You configure an AAAA record and create an IPv6 reverse lookup zone in the practice session later in this lesson.

---

**MORE INFO**   **IPv6 reverse lookup zones**

For more information about IPv6 reverse lookup zones and additional information about a wide range of IPv6 topics, see *http://www.microsoft.com/technet/network/ipv6/ipv6faq.mspx*.

---

The *dnscmd* command-line tool accepts addresses in both IPv4 and IPv6 format. Windows Server 2008 DNS servers can send recursive queries to IPv6-only servers, and a DNS server forwarder list can contain both IPv4 and IPv6 addresses. DHCP clients can register IPv6 addresses in addition to (or instead of) IPv4 addresses. Windows Server 2008 DNS servers support the *ip6.arpa* domain namespace for reverse lookups.

> **Quick Check**
> - What feature does Windows Server 2008 DNS introduce that will help organizations phase out WINS and NetBT?
>
> **Quick Check Answer**
> - The GlobalNames zone

# Planning a DNS Infrastructure

As a network professional, you will almost certainly know that in a dynamic DNS system, most hosts and servers register their host (A) records automatically, and you can configure DHCP to create DNS records when it allocates configurations. In comparison with former static DNS, in which records needed to be added manually (unless DNS was integrated with WINS), dynamic DNS requires very little manual configuration. Although you have probably created IPv4 reverse lookup zones, and will create an IPv6 lookup zone in the practice exercise at the end of this lesson, you might not have experience planning a DNS infrastructure.

As you advance in your chosen profession, you will discover that planning takes up much of your time, and the examination guide mentions planning tasks carried out and decisions made by enterprise administrators; therefore, you need to consider the process of planning a DNS infrastructure.

## Planning a DNS Namespace

Planning and defining a DNS namespace is typically a task for the enterprise administrator. You need to know the options available so that you can plan and implement enterprise-level decisions more efficiently.

If you use a DNS namespace for internal purposes only, the name does not need to conform to the standard defined in RFC 1123, "Requirements for Internet Hosts - Application and Support"; RFC 2181, "Clarifications to the DNS Specification"; and the character set specified in RFC2044, "UTF-8, a Transformation Format of Unicode and ISO 10646." The *contoso.internal* namespace you configured in your test network is an example of this type of namespace.

However, when you specify a corporate namespace to be used on the Internet, it needs to be registered with the appropriate authority and conform to the relevant RFC standards. Examples of corporate namespaces are *treyresearch.net* and *tailspintoys.com*. Most organizations have both a private and a public network. You can implement the DNS infrastructure by using one of the following schemes:

- Use separate namespaces for your external and internal namespaces, such as *tailspintoys.com* and *tailspintoys.private*. This improves security by isolating the two namespaces from each other and preventing internal resources from being exposed directly to the

Internet. Zone transfers do not need to be performed between the two namespaces, and the existing DNS namespace remains unchanged.

■ Use a corporate namespace for both the internal and external (Internet) portions of your network. This configuration is straightforward to implement and provides access to both internal and external resources. However, you need to ensure that the appropriate records are being stored on the internal and external DNS servers and that the security of your internal network is protected.

---

**NOTE   Internal users require access to external resources**

Using a single corporate namespace presents a challenge when internal users require name resolution for publicly accessible resources, because the external DNS zone is not configured to resolve internal resources. This challenge can be overcome by duplicating the external zone on internal DNS servers for clients to resolve resources. You can also configure split DNS, which is described later in this lesson.

---

**Exam Tip**   Using the same namespace internally and externally requires duplicating the external zone on internal DNS servers for clients to resolve external resources.

---

■ Use delegated namespaces to identify your organization's internal network. For example, Trey Research could have the public namespace *treyresearch.net* and the private namespace *intranet.treyresearch.net*. This fits neatly with Active Directory structure and is easily implemented if you use Active Directory–integrated DNS. You need to ensure that internal clients can resolve external namespace addresses but that external clients cannot resolve internal namespace addresses. All internal domain data is isolated in the domain tree and requires its own DNS server infrastructure. An internal DNS server will forward requests for an external namespace address to an external DNS server. The disadvantage of namespace delegation is that FQDNs can become quite long. The maximum length of an FQDN is 255 bytes. FQDNs for DCs are limited to 155 bytes.

Active Directory–integrated DNS provides several advantages. Not least of these benefits is that DNS zone information is automatically replicated with other AD DS information through distributed file system replication (DFSR). You can implement RODCs that hold authoritative read-only DNS zones and provide secure local name resolution in branch offices where the physical security of servers cannot be guaranteed. You can implement secondary DNS zones on Windows DNS or BIND servers that need not be part of the Active Directory structure. For example, DNS servers on peripheral zones are frequently standalone servers.

How you implement Active Directory on your network plays a critical role in determining how domains should be created and nested within each other. Your zone structure typically mirrors your Active Directory domain structure, although this is not compulsory. You can easily create delegated zones. For example, you could use *engineering.tailspintoys.com* rather than *tailspintoys.com/engineering*.

You can partition your DNS namespace by geographical location, by department, or by both. For example, if Tailspin Toys has several locations but only a single human resources department located at the central office, you could use the namespace *hr.tailspintoys.com*. If Contoso, Ltd., has a main office in Denver and manufacturing facilities in Boston and Dallas, you could configure namespaces *denver.contoso.com*, *boston.contoso.com*, and *dallas.contoso.com*. You can combine both systems: *manufacturing.dallas.contoso.com*. If you are concerned that the design implements too many hierarchical levels, you can choose instead to use Active Directory organizational units (OUs) such as *dallas.contoso.com/manufacturing*.

## Using Split DNS

In a split DNS infrastructure, you create two zones on two separate name servers for the same domain. The zones have the same name, for example, *contoso.com*. Internal network clients use one of the zones, and external network clients use the other. You require at least two name servers because a single name server cannot host two zones with the same name.

The zone used by external clients resolves host names to public IP addresses. For example, the zone database on the external zone for *contoso.com* could contain the DNS records shown in Table 1-1.

**Table 1-1  DNS Records for the External *contoso.com* Zone**

| Host Name | Record Type | Resolves To |
|---|---|---|
| www | A | 206.46.41.10 |
| ftp | A | 206.46.41.12 |
| mail | A | 206.46.41.14 |
| - | MX | mail.corp.net |

The zone used by internal clients resolves host names to private IP addresses and provides aliases for the external hostnames. The zone database on the internal zone for *contoso.com* could contain the DNS records shown in Table 1-2.

**Table 1-2  DNS Records for the Internal *contoso.com* Zone**

| Host Name | Record Type | Resolves To |
|---|---|---|
| www | CNAME | webserver.corp.net |
| ftp | CNAME | ftpserver.corp.net |
| mail | CNAME | exchange.corp.net |
| exchange | A | 10.0.0.25 |
| webserver | A | 10.0.0.27 |
| ftpserver | A | 10.0.0.29 |

When external network clients resolve the name *www.contoso.com*, they obtain the external IP address of the Web server, 206.46.41.10, which is what is required. External network clients should not receive the private IP address of the internal network server.

When internal network clients access *www.contoso.com*, they connect to the server Web server, using the internal, private IP address, 10.0.0.27. The CNAME record for www resolves to the Host (A) record of *webserver.contoso.com*, and requests are forwarded to 10.0.0.27. You also need to configure Internet Security and Acceleration (ISA) Server on your network to support split DNS, but ISA Server configuration is beyond the scope of this book.

---

**MORE INFO** Split-brain and split-split DNS

For more information about split DNS, split-brain DNS, and split-split DNS, see *http:// www.microsoft.com/serviceproviders/resources/techresarticlesdnssplit.mspx*.

---

## Planning DNS Forwarding

A DNS forwarder accepts forwarded recursive lookups from another DNS server and then resolves the request for that DNS server. For example, a local DNS server can forward DNS queries to a central DNS server that is authoritative for an internal DNS zone. If the forwarding server does not receive a valid resolution from the server to which it forwards the request, it attempts to resolve the request itself unless it is a subordinate server. Subordinate servers do not try to resolve a resolution request if they do not receive a valid response to a forwarded DNS request. In general, subordinate servers are used in conjunction with secure Internet connections.

Windows Server 2003 introduced conditional forwarding, described earlier in this lesson, and this can be used in Windows Server 2008. You should plan to use conditional forwarders if, for example, you want requests made for internal name resolution to be forwarded to a master DNS server that stores internal DNS zones and name resolution requests for Internet domains to be sent to the Internet where they can be satisfied through recursion. You can also use conditional forwarding on an extranet where resolution requests that specify domains in the extranet can be sent to DNS servers authoritative for the DNS zones corresponding to the domains, and requests for the resolution of names external to the extranet can be sent to the Internet for recursive resolution.

---

**Exam Tip**   Forwarding DNS requests requires the DNS server to be capable of making recursive queries. Examination answers that suggest that you should configure forwarding and disable recursion can be discarded as possible correct answers.

---

A typical DNS forwarding scenario could specify a DNS server that is permitted to forward queries to DNS servers outside the corporate firewall. This implementation enables the firewall to be configured to allow DNS traffic only from this specific DNS server and to allow only valid replies back to the DNS server to enter the protected network. By using this approach, all other DNS traffic—both inbound and outbound—can be dropped at the firewall. This improves the overall security of the network and the DNS service.

## Planning the Zone Type

Active Directory networks typically use Active Directory–integrated zones for internal name resolution. In this case, DNS zone information is held on writable DCs in the domain (usually all the writable DCs). This gives the advantages of DFSR, failover if one DC goes down, and increased availability through a multimaster arrangement. Standard primary zones installed on Windows standalone servers can be used where a writable DNS server is required but access to the Active Directory database is seen as a security risk, for example, in peripheral zones. RODCs can be used when you want the advantages of Active Directory–integrated DNS but cannot guarantee the physical security of your servers, such as in branch offices.

Both Active Directory–integrated and standard primary zones can provide zone information to standard secondary DNS zones. In Windows Server 2008 networks, secondary DNS zones can be implemented on member servers, standalone servers, and RODCs. Installing a secondary DNS server at a remote location can significantly improve the speed of name resolution at that location. Secondary zone servers increase redundancy by providing name resolution even if the primary zone server is unresponsive and reduce the load on primary servers by distributing name resolution requests among more DNS servers. A secondary zone server does not need to be part of the Active Directory domain (except in the case of RODCs), and you can install secondary zones on non-Windows servers. You can also configure secondary zone servers on virtual machines.

As a network professional, you have probably configured the aging and scavenging settings for DNS records, configured dynamic updates, specified zone replication scopes, and configured zone transfers. However, it is one thing to know how to configure these settings. It is quite another to plan your zones and decide what the optimum settings are for your name resolution structure. This is a job for the enterprise administrator.

---

### Quick Check

- Which type of record in a stub zone can prevent circular dependency by ensuring that the name server providing the delegation can provide the IP address of the next name server?

### Quick Check Answer

- A glue record

If a large number of stale resource records remain in zones, they take up server disk space and cause unnecessarily long zone transfers. DNS servers that load zones containing stale resource records risk using outdated information to answer client queries, potentially causing name resolution problems. DNS servers and zones can be configured to scavenge stale resource records within a period of time. In environments in which resource records can become stale, you need to ensure that you enable the scavenging of these records.

The design of aging and scavenging settings is dependent on your name resolution traffic and on how often your network changes. A network that is reasonably stable with few stations being added or removed can probably be configured with long aging settings and less frequent scavenging cycles than can a more dynamic environment. Frequent scavenging and short aging periods can increase your network traffic.

DNS zones can also be configured to allow or disallow dynamic updates, although it is unusual for dynamic updates to be disallowed in modern networks. Active Directory–integrated zones can also be configured to allow secure dynamic updates only. Secure dynamic updates, discussed earlier in this lesson, are strongly recommended because they ensure that only authorized changes are made to DNS data.

---

**Exam Tip**    Only Active Directory–integrated zones support secure dynamic updates.

---

When you plan the replication scope of Active Directory–integrated zones, you need to decide whether the zone should be replicated to all DNS servers in the forest, all DNS servers in the domain (the default), or all DCs in the domain. If you need to broaden the replication scope, you can configure the zone to replicate to all DNS servers in the forest. Replicating to all DCs in the domain is recommended only if you have Windows 2000 Server DCs in your environment.

You can configure the primary name server, the refresh interval, and the minimum default Time-to-Live (TTL) values for zone resource records in the zone's Start of Authority (SOA) record. The TTL controls the minimum amount of time clients, including other DNS servers, cache resource records for the zone. If your environment is dynamic with frequent IP addresses changes, plan to configure the minimum TTL to a low value such as one day.

When planning DNS zones, you need to specify whether zone transfers are permitted and, if so, to which servers. You can configure zone transfers to any server, to the name servers listed on the Name Servers tab or the zone, or to a specific list of name servers.

## Planning Root Hints

When you install a Windows Server 2008 DNS server that has access to the Internet, the server is automatically configured with a list of root servers. If a DNS server receives a query for a DNS zone for which it is not authoritative, the server will send a query to one of the root servers that initiates a series of queries until the name is resolved. You can use root hints to prepare servers that are authoritative for non-root zones so that they can discover authoritative servers that manage domains at a higher level or in other subtrees of the DNS domain namespace.

Root hints are essential for servers that are authoritative at lower levels of the namespace when locating and finding other servers. By default, the DNS Server service implements root hints by using a file named *cache.dns* that normally contains the NS and A resource records for the Internet root servers. If, however, you are using the DNS Server service on a private network, you should plan to edit or replace this file with similar records that point to your own internal root DNS servers.

## Planning to Integrate AD DS with an Existing DNS Infrastructure

Many enterprise-level organizations already use one or more BIND servers. BIND provides name resolution for UNIX systems or Internet name resolution for internal users. In this case, Windows Active Directory–integrated DNS needs to interoperate with the BIND DNS infrastructure.

Two options are available within the Windows Server 2008 DNS infrastructure:

- You can use the existing DNS infrastructure to host the DNS zone for AD DS. Potentially, this can reduce hardware requirements and administrative effort. However, this option can also mean that the DNS infrastructure is supported by a different team than that which supports AD DS. As an enterprise administrator, one of your tasks is to rationalize your support organization, and you, or your line manager, might find this option unacceptable.

- You can deploy Windows Server 2008 DNS and use forwarders to integrate both DNS infrastructures. This can give you more flexibility for DNS infrastructure design, DNS namespace design, and DNS administration model. Windows-based DNS is required for Active Directory–integrated zones, and you can use forwarders to provide interoperability between Windows Server 2008 DNS infrastructure and the existing DNS infrastructure. Windows Server 2008 DNS servers can forward any DNS queries for records hosted on the existing DNS infrastructure to the existing DNS servers.

Figure 1-14 depicts the forwarding of DNS queries between a Windows Server 2008 DNS infrastructure and a BIND DNS infrastructure.

For example, Contoso, Ltd., has an existing BIND-based DNS infrastructure with a DNS domain name of *contoso.com*. Contoso plans to deploy a new Windows Server 2008 DNS infrastructure for AD DS with a DNS domain name of *sales.contoso.com*. A conditional forwarding entry for *contoso.com* has been created on the Windows Server 2008 DNS server in the *sales.contoso.com* domain. A conditional forwarding entry for *sales.contoso.com* has been created on a BIND-based DNS server in the *contoso.com* domain.

When a client in the *sales.contoso.com* domain needs to access a UNIX Web server in the *contoso.com* domain, it first queries its primary DNS server in the *sales.contoso.com* domain. This server is not authoritative for the *contoso.com* zone, but it does have a conditional forwarding entry for the *contoso.com* zone. Through the conditional forwarding entry on its DNS server in the *sales.contoso.com* domain, it contacts the BIND-based DNS server in the *contoso.com* domain to retrieve the name resolution for *web.contoso.com*.

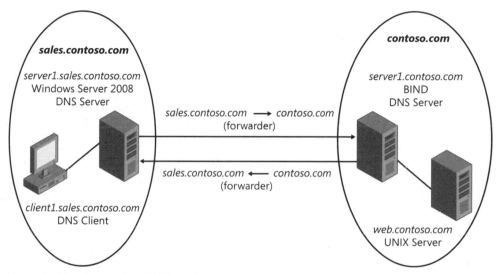

**Figure 1-14**  Forwarding DNS queries

## Planning the GlobalNames Zone

To plan your GlobalNames Zone design, you need to understand the deployment scenarios in which a GlobalNames zone can be configured. You can deploy a GlobalNames zone in a single-forest environment or a multiple-forest environment. A single-forest deployment of a GlobalNames zone allows single-label name resolution through DNS, using a single Active Directory–integrated GlobalNames zone. A multiple-forest deployment of a GlobalNames zone allows single-label name resolution through DNS, using an Active Directory–integrated GlobalNames zone for each forest within the multiple-forest environment.

You can adapt a single-forest GlobalNames zone deployment to meet an assortment of single-label name resolution requirements in the following ways:

- **All domains and client computers in a forest**  Microsoft recommends this scenario for organizations that have a single forest and a small number of domains. Single-label name resolution is provided to all domain-joined client computers in the forest. In this scenario, you need to ensure that all authoritative DNS servers in the forest are Windows Server 2008 domain controllers. You then need to create an AD DS integrated GlobalNames zone on one DNS server in the forest and replicate this to all domain controllers in the forest that are DNS servers. You then add CNAME records for single-label names pointing to the FQDNs of the resource servers.

- **A multiple-forest GlobalNames zone**   This deployment scenario is recommended for companies that have multiple domains and multiple forests. You can customize a multiple-forest DNS server to meet diverse single-label name resolution requirements for all domains and client computers in all forests by ensuring that all authoritative DNS servers in the forest are Windows Server 2008 domain controller DNS servers. You also need to ensure that GlobalNames zone functionality has been enabled on each DNS server in the forest. You create an AD DS integrated GlobalNames zone on one DNS server in a forest and replicate the GlobalNames zone to all domain controllers in the forest that are DNS servers. You then add CNAME records for single-label names pointing to the FQDN of the resource servers. In each of the other forests, you add SRV resource records pointing to each remote domain controller DNS server that hosts a local copy of the Global-Names zone to the forest-wide _msdcs zone.

- **A selected set of DNS servers host the GlobalNames zone**   Microsoft recommends this deployment scenario for companies that have multiple domains and multiple forests but want to limit the GlobalNames zone to a selected set of DNS servers. This deployment scenario provides single-label name resolution to all client computers in the forests.

- **Selected domains across multiple forests**   Microsoft recommends this deployment when you want to deploy a GlobalNames zone in a multiple-forest environment in a set of selected domains as a pilot program.

## PRACTICE Configuring DNS

In this practice, you configure a static IPv6 configuration on the Glasgow DC. You then configure a static AAAA record and an IPv6 reverse lookup zone. Finally, you create a PTR record in the reverse lookup zone for the Glasgow computer.

---

**IMPORTANT   70-647 Lab configuration**

As a deliberate policy, the TK 70-647 test network configuration in this training kit is as similar as possible to the test network configuration in TK 70-646. The exercises in this chapter are very similar to the practice exercises in Chapter 2 in TK 70-646, which configured this network. If you used TK 70-646 to study for that examination, you should not need to configure IPv6 on your Glasgow computer or create an AAAA record, nor should you need to configure IPv6 on your client computer as described in Lesson 2 of this chapter. However, if you created an IPv6 reverse lookup zone, it's recommended that you delete this and create it again because this is a procedure you should practice. If you did not do any of the practice exercises in TK 70-646, you need to do all the exercises in this practice.

---

▶ **Exercise 1   Configure IPv6 on the Glasgow Computer**

In this exercise, you configure IPv6 on the Glasgow computer (the DC). You need to do this because you create a reverse lookup IPv6 zone and a PTR record for the Glasgow computer in subsequent exercises. The exercise asks you to log on interactively to the DC. If you want to make this more realistic, you can log on to the Melbourne client instead and connect to the DC through Remote Desktop. If you recently used TK 70-646 to study for that examination, your Glasgow computer might already be configured with these settings.

1. Log on at the Glasgow DC with the Kim_Akers account.
2. Start Network And Sharing Center from Control Panel. Under Tasks, click Manage Network Connections.
3. Right-click the network connection to your private network and choose Properties.
4. If a Universal Access Control (UAC) dialog box appears, click Continue to close it.
5. Select Internet Protocol Version 6 (TCP/IPv6) and click Properties.
6. Configure the static site-local IPv6 address **fec0:0:0:fffe::1**.
7. Configure the preferred DNS server address **fec0:0:0:fffe::1**. The Properties dialog box should look similar to Figure 1-15.

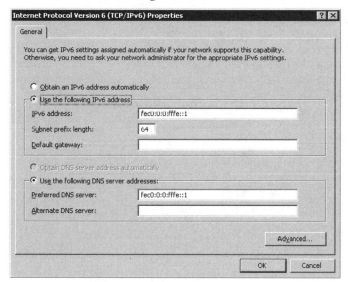

**Figure 1-15**    IPv6 configuration on the domain controller

8. Click OK. Close the Local Area Connections Properties dialog box.
9. Close the Network Connections window.
10. Close Network And Sharing Center.

---

**NOTE    Virtual machines**

If you are using a virtual machine to implement your server and client on the same computer, it is a good idea to close your virtual machine and restart your computer after configuring interfaces.

---

▶ **Exercise 2    Configure an AAAA Record**

The standalone server Brisbane has an operating system that cannot register in Windows Server 2008 DNS. Therefore, you need to create a manual AAAA record for this server. Its IPv6 address is fec0:0:0:fffe::aa. Note that you can create an AAAA record for this server even though it does not currently exist on your network.

1. If necessary, log on to the Glasgow DC with the Kim_Akers account.
2. In Administrative Tools, open DNS Manager.
3. If a UAC dialog box appears, click Continue.
4. In DNS Manager, expand Forward Lookup Zones. Right-click *contoso.internal* and choose New Host (A or AAAA).
5. Enter the server name and IPv6 address as shown in Figure 1-16. Ensure that the Create Associated Pointer (PTR) Record check box is not selected.

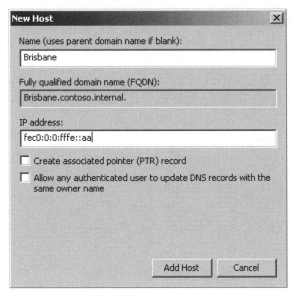

**Figure 1-16**   Specifying a DNS host record

6. Click Add Host. Click OK to clear the DNS message box.
7. Click Done. Ensure that the new record exists in DNS Manager.
8. Close DNS Manager.

▶ **Exercise 3    Configure a Reverse Lookup IPv6 Zone**

In this exercise, you will create an IPv6 reverse lookup zone for all site-local IPv6 addresses—that is, addresses starting with fec0. You will then create a PTR record in the zone. Note that in IPv6, reverse lookup zone addresses are entered as reverse-order 4-bit nibbles, so fec0 becomes 0.c.e.f.

1.  If necessary, log on to the DC with the Kim_Akers account.

2.  Click Start. Right-click Command Prompt and choose Run As Administrator.

3.  If a UAC dialog box appears, click Continue.

4.  Enter **dnscmd glasgow /ZoneAdd 0.c.e.f.ip6.arpa /DsPrimary**. Figure 1-17 shows that the zone was created successfully. Close the command console.

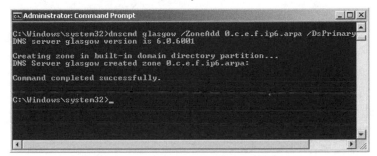

**Figure 1-17**   Creating an IPv6 reverse lookup zone

5.  Open DNS Manager in Administrative Tools. If a UAC dialog box appears, click Continue.

6.  Expand Forward Lookup Zones. Select *contoso.internal*.

7.  Right-click the AAAA record for Glasgow, and then choose Properties.

8.  Select the Update Associated Pointer (PTR) Record check box, as shown in Figure 1-18. Click OK.

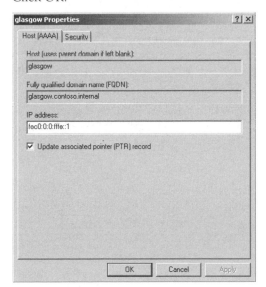

**Figure 1-18**   Creating a PTR record

9.  Expand Reverse Lookup Zones and select 0.c.e.f.ip6.arpa. Ensure that the PTR record for Glasgow exists, as shown in Figure 1-19.

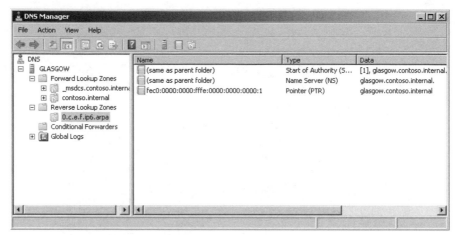

**Figure 1-19** The PTR record for Glasgow

10. Log off from the domain controller.

## Lesson Summary

■ The DNS Server role in Windows Server 2008 complies with all current standards and can work successfully with most other DNS server implementations.

■ Windows Server 2008 DNS is dynamic and typically requires very little static configuration. You can use the DNS Manager GUI or command-line interface tools such as *dnscmd*, *nslookup*, *ipconfig*, and *netsh* to configure and manage DNS.

■ New Windows Server 2008 DNS functions include background zone loading, support for RODCs, and the GlobalNames DNS zone. Windows Server 2008 DNS fully supports IPv6 forward lookup and reverse lookup zones.

■ WINS resolves NetBIOS names to IP addresses. Windows Server 2008 supports WINS to provide support for previous networks. The GlobalNames DNS zone provides single-label name resolution for large enterprise networks that do not deploy WINS.

## Lesson Review

Use the following questions to test your knowledge of the information in Lesson 1, "Planning Name Resolution." The questions are also available on the companion CD if you prefer to review them in electronic form.

**NOTE** Answers

Answers to these questions and explanations of why each answer choice is correct or incorrect are located in the "Answers" section at the end of the book.

1. Which WINS topology uses a distributed WINS design with multiple WINS servers or clusters deployed across the enterprise, with each server or cluster replicating with every other server or cluster?

    A. Centralized WINS topology

    B. Full mesh WINS topology

    C. Ring WINS topology

    D. Hub and spoke WINS topology

2. Which DNS record enables you to specify refresh interval and TTL settings?

    A. SOA

    B. NS

    C. SRV

    D. CNAME

3. Which command enables a DNS server to support GlobalNames zones?

    A. *dnscmd /createdirectorypartition*

    B. *dnscmd /enlistdirectorypartition*

    C. *dnscmd /config*

    D. *dnscmd /createbuiltindirectorypartitions*

4. You want to list all the DNS records in the *adatum.internal* domain. You connect to the *Edinburgh.adatum.internal* DNS server by using Remote Desktop and open the command console. You type **nslookup**. At the nslookup> prompt, you type **ls −d adatum.internal**. An error message tells you that zone data cannot be loaded to that computer. You know all the DNS records in the domain exist on Edinburgh. Why were they not displayed?

    A. You have not configured the *adatum.internal* forward lookup zone to allow zone transfers.

    B. You need to run the command console as an administrator to use *nslookup*.

    C. You should have typed **nslookup ls −d adatum.internal** directly from the command prompt. You cannot use the *ls* function from the nslookup> prompt.

    D. You need to log on to the DNS server interactively to use *nslookup*. You cannot use it over a Remote Desktop connection.

5. A user tries to access the company internal Web site from a client computer but cannot do so because of a network problem. You fix the network problem, but the user still cannot reach the Web site, although she can reach other Web sites. Users on other client computers have no problem reaching the internal Web site. How can you quickly resolve the situation?

    A. Create a static host record for your local Web server in DNS.

    B. Run *ipconfig /flushdns* on the primary DNS server.

    C. Run *ipconfig /registerdns* on the user's computer.

    D. Run *ipconfig /flushdns* on the user's computer.

# Lesson 2: Planning Internet Protocol Addressing

As an experienced network professional, you are familiar with IPv4 addresses. You know that the private IP address ranges are 10.0.0.0/8, 172.16.0.0/12, and 192.168.0.0/16 and that the automatic IP addressing (APIPA) range is 169.254.0.0/16. You are aware that Network Address Translation (NAT) typically enables you to use relatively few public IP addresses to enable Internet access to many internal clients with private IP addresses. You are able to identify Class A, B, and C networks, but you are also aware that most modern network design uses classless interdomain routing (CIDR). You know that Class D addresses (224.0.0.0/4) are used for multicasting.

You know that DHCP can allocate IPv4 addresses, subnet masks, default gateways, DNS and WINS servers, and many other settings and that APIPA can automatically configure IPv4 addresses for use in an isolated private network. You are aware that three DHCP infrastructure models exist: the centralized DHCP infrastructure model, the decentralized DHCP infrastructure model, and the combined DHCP infrastructure model. You know that DHCP works with DNS so that Host and (if appropriate) PTR records are added to DNS zones when DHCP allocates IP addresses.

You might be less familiar with the IPv6 infrastructure, the advantages of IPv6, the types of IPv6 addresses, the operation of DHCPv6 and how to set up a DHCPv6 scope, and how to install the Windows Server 2008 DHCP server role. As IPv6 usage increases, you need to be aware of IPv4-to-IPv6 transition strategies and Ipv4 and IPv6 interoperability, particularly the use of Teredo addresses. This lesson looks at IPv6, DHCPv6, transition strategy, and interoperability. Note that the objectives of the 70-646 and 70-647 examinations are very similar for this topic. If you studied IPv6 for the 70-646 examination, please treat this lesson as review.

---

**After this lesson, you will be able to:**
- Identify the various types of IPv6 addresses and explain their uses.
- Describe the advantages of IPv6 and how these are achieved.
- Identify IPv6 addresses that can be routed on the IPv4 Internet.
- Recommend an appropriate IPv4-to-IPv6 transition strategy.
- Implement IPv4 and IPv6 interoperability.
- Use IPv6 tools.
- Configure DHCPv6 scopes.

**Estimated lesson time: 55 minutes**

---

---

**Real World**

*Ian McLean*

Sometimes I wonder whether NAT and CIDR did us any good in the long run.

They solved a problem. IPv4 address space exhaustion was suddenly no longer an issue. (It will be again.) We were granted breathing space to transition to IPv6. There was and still is a huge amount of money invested in the IPv4 intranet, and there would have been severe problems had we suddenly found that no addresses were left. Many of us sighed with relief.

However, the other problems haven't gone away. Backbone routers still host huge route tables; quality of service remains problematic when traffic is encrypted. End-to-end security is not ensured.

Had we seen NAT and CIDR for the temporary fixes they are and implemented a controlled but steady IPv6 transition, things would all have been well. Alas, it is only now, years after the crisis loomed, that operating systems such as Windows Server 2008 and Windows Vista that support IPv6 by default are being released. The acronym WYKIWYL (what you know is what you like) reigned supreme. We were happy with IPv4. Why worry about that nasty IPv6 thing? Some even grew to love NAT, seeing it as a security enhancement. (That's an argument I won't go into.)

IPv6 is coming, and we can't afford to ignore it. We need it too much. Sometimes I'm reminded of the argument that the airplane would never catch on. It frightened the horses.

---

## Analyzing the IPv6 Address Structure

IPv4 and IPv6 addresses can be readily distinguished. An IPv4 address uses 32 bits, resulting in an address space of just over 4 billion. An IPv6 address uses 128 bits, resulting in an address space of $2^{128}$, or 340,282,366,920,938,463,463,374,607,431,768,211,456—a number too large to comprehend. This represents $6.5 \times 2^{23}$ or 54,525,952 addresses for every square meter of the earth's surface. In practice, the IPv6 address space allows for multiple levels of subnetting and address allocation between the Internet backbone and individual subnets within an organization. The vastly increased address space available enables users to allocate not one but several unique IPv6 addresses to a network entity, with each address being used for a different purpose.

IPv6 provides addresses that are equivalent to IPv4 address types and others that are unique to IPv6. A node can have several IPv6 addresses, each of which has its own unique purpose. This section describes the IPv6 address syntax and the various classes of IPv6 address.

## IPv6 Address Syntax

The IPv6 128-bit address is divided at 16-bit boundaries, and each 16-bit block is converted to a 4-digit hexadecimal number. Colons are used as separators. This representation is called *colon-hexadecimal*.

Global unicast IPv6 addresses are equivalent to IPv4 public unicast addresses. To illustrate IPv6 address syntax, consider the following IPv6 global unicast address:

21cd:0053:0000:0000:03ad:003f:af37:8d62

IPv6 representation can be simplified by removing the leading zeros within each 16-bit block. However, each block must have at least a single digit. With leading zero suppression, the address representation becomes:

21cd:53:0:0:3ad:3f:af37:8d62

A contiguous sequence of 16-bit blocks set to 0 in the colon-hexadecimal format can be compressed to ::. Thus, the previous example address could be written:

21cd:53::3ad:3f:af37:8d62

Some types of addresses contain long sequences of zeros and thus provide good examples of when to use this notation. For example, the multicast address ff05:0:0:0:0:0:0:2 can be compressed to ff05::2.

## IPv6 Address Prefixes

The prefix is the part of the address that indicates either the bits that have fixed values or the network identifier bits. IPv6 prefixes are expressed in the same way as CIDR IPv4 notation, or *slash notation*. For example, 21cd:53::/64 is the subnet on which the address 21cd:53::23ad:3f:af37:8d62 is located. In this case, the first 64 bits of the address are the network prefix. An IPv6 subnet prefix (or subnet ID) is assigned to a single link. Multiple subnet IDs can be assigned to the same link. This technique is called *multinetting*.

---

**NOTE    IPv6 does not use dotted decimal notation in subnet masks**

Only prefix-length notation is supported in IPv6. IPv4 dotted decimal subnet mask representation (such as 255.255.255.0) has no direct equivalent.

---

## IPv6 Address Types

The three types of IPv6 address are unicast, multicast, and anycast.

- **Unicast**   Identifies a single interface within the scope of the unicast address type. Packets addressed to a unicast address are delivered to a single interface. RFC 2373 allows multiple interfaces to use the same address, provided that these interfaces appear as a single interface to the IPv6 implementation on the host. This accommodates load-balancing systems.

- **Multicast**   Identifies multiple interfaces. Packets addressed to a multicast address are delivered to all interfaces that are identified by the address.

- **Anycast**   Identifies multiple interfaces. Packets addressed to an anycast address are delivered to the nearest interface identified by the address. The nearest interface is the closest in terms of routing distance, or number of hops. An anycast address is used for one-to-one-of-many communication, with delivery to a single interface.

---

**MORE INFO   IPv6 addressing architecture**

For more information about IPv6 address structure and architecture, see RFC 2373 at *http://www.ietf.org/rfc/rfc2373.txt*.

---

**NOTE   Interfaces and nodes**

IPv6 addresses identify interfaces rather than nodes. A node is identified by any unicast address that is assigned to one of its interfaces.

---

## IPv6 Unicast Addresses

IPv6 supports the following types of unicast address:

- Global
- Link-local
- Site-local
- Special
- Network Service Access Point (NSAP) and Internetwork Packet Exchange (IPX) mapped addresses

## Global Unicast Addresses

Global unicast addresses are the IPv6 equivalent of IPv4 public addresses and are globally routable and reachable on the Internet. These addresses can be aggregated to produce an efficient routing infrastructure and are, therefore, sometimes known as aggregatable global unicast addresses. An aggregatable global unicast address is unique across the entire Internet. (The region over which an IP address is unique is called the *scope* of the address.)

The Format Prefix (FP) of a global unicast address is held in the three most significant bits, which are always 001. The next 13 bits are allocated by the Internet Assigned Numbers Authority (IANA) and are known as the top-level aggregator (TLA). IANA allocates TLAs to local Internet registries that, in turn, allocate individual TLAs to large ISPs. The next 8 bits of the address are reserved for future expansion.

The next 24 bits of the address contain the next-level aggregator (NLA). This identifies a specific customer site. The NLA enables an ISP to create multiple levels of addressing hierarchy within a network. The next 16 bits contain the site-level aggregator, which is used to organize addressing and routing for downstream ISPs and to identify sites or subnets within a site.

The next 64 bits identify the interface within a subnet. This is the 64-bit Extended Unique Identifier (EUI-64) address as defined by the Institute of Electrical and Electronics Engineers (IEEE). EUI-64 addresses are either assigned directly to network adapter cards or derived from the 48-bit Media Access Control (MAC) address of a network adapter as defined by the IEEE 802 standard. Put simply, the interface identity is provided by the network adapter hardware.

---

### Privacy Extensions for Stateless Address Autoconfiguration in IPv6

Concerns have been expressed that deriving an interface identity (ID) directly from computer hardware could enable the itinerary of a laptop and, hence, that of its owner to be tracked. This raises privacy issues, and future systems might allocate interface IDs differently.

RFC 3041 and RFC 4941 address this problem. For more information, see *http://www.ietf.org/rfc/rfc3041.txt* and *http://www.ietf.org/rfc/rfc4191.txt*.

---

To summarize, the FP, TLA, reserved bits, and NLA identify the public topology; the site-level aggregator identifies the site topology; and the ID identifies the interface. Figure 1-20 illustrates the structure of an aggregatable global unicast address.

**Figure 1-20**    Global unicast address structure

---

**MORE INFO**    Global unicast address format

For more information about aggregatable global unicast addresses, see RFC 2374 at *http://www.ietf.org/rfc/rfc2374.txt*.

**Exam Tip**  You need to know that an aggregatable global unicast address is the IPv6 equivalent of an IPv4 public unicast address. You should be able to identify a global unicast address from the value of its three most significant bits. Knowing the various components of the address helps you understand how IPv6 addressing works, but the 70-647 examination is unlikely to test this knowledge in the depth of detail provided by the RFCs.

**Link-Local Addresses**  Link-local IPv6 addresses are equivalent to IPv4 addresses that are autoconfigured through APIPA and use the 169.254.0.0/16 prefix. You can identify a link-local address by an FP of 1111 1110 10, which is followed by 54 zeros. (Link-local addresses always begin with fe8.) Nodes use link-local addresses when communicating with neighboring nodes on the same link. The scope of a link-local address is the local link. A link-local address is required for Neighbor Discovery (ND) and is always automatically configured, even if no other unicast address is allocated.

**Site-Local Addresses**  Site-local IPv6 addresses are equivalent to the IPv4 private address space (10.0.0.0/8, 172.16.0.0/12, and 192.168.0.0/16). Private intranets that do not have a direct, routed connection to the Internet can use site-local addresses without conflicting with aggregatable global unicast addresses. The scope of a site-local address is the site (or organization internetwork).

Site-local addresses can be allocated by using stateful address configuration such as from a DHCPv6 scope. A host uses stateful address configuration when it receives router advertisement messages that do not include address prefixes. A host will also use a stateful address configuration protocol when no routers are present on the local link.

Site-local addresses can also be configured through stateless address configuration. This is based on router advertisement messages that include stateless address prefixes and require that hosts do not use a stateful address configuration protocol.

Alternatively, address configuration can use a combination of stateless and stateful configuration. This occurs when router advertisement messages include stateless address prefixes but require that hosts use a stateful address configuration protocol.

---

**MORE INFO**  IPv6 address autoconfiguration

For more information about how IPv6 addresses are configured, see *http://www.microsoft.com/technet/technetmag/issues/2007/08/CableGuy/*. Although the article is titled "IPv6 Autoconfiguration in Windows Vista," it also covers Windows Server 2008 autoconfiguration and describes the differences between autoconfiguration on a client and on a server operating system.

---

Site-local addresses begin with fec0 followed by 32 zeros and then by a 16-bit subnet identifier that you can use to create subnets within your organization. The *64-bit Interface ID* field identifies a specific interface on a subnet.

Figure 1-21 shows link-local and site-local addresses (for DNS servers) configured on interfaces on the Windows Server 2008 DC Glasgow. No global addresses exist in the configuration because DCs are never exposed directly to the Internet. The IPv6 addresses on your test computer will probably be different. Note that in this figure, the Glasgow DC has a virtual interface to the virtual machine that hosts the Melbourne client.

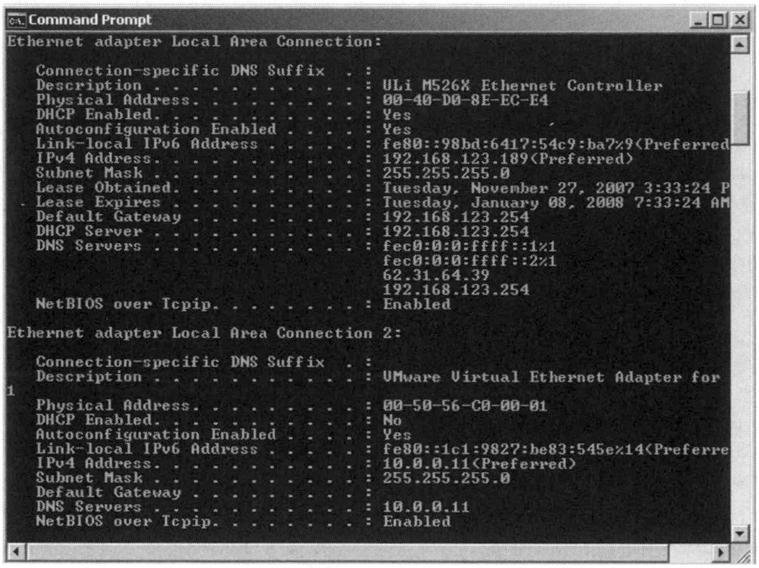

**Figure 1-21**    IPv6 addresses on computer interfaces

## Link-Local and Site-Local Addresses

You can implement IPv6 connectivity between hosts on an isolated subnet by using link-local addresses. However, you cannot assign link-local addresses to router interfaces (default gateways), and you cannot route from one subnet to another if only link-local addresses are used. DNS servers cannot use only link-local addresses. If you use link-local addresses, you need to specify their interface IDs—that is the number after the % symbol at the end of the address, as shown previously in Figure 1-21. Link-local addresses are not dynamically registered in Windows Server 2008 DNS.

For these reasons, site-local addresses are typically used on the subnets of a private network to implement IPv6 connectivity over the network. If every device on the network has its own global address (a stated aim of IPv6 implementation), global addresses can route between internal subnets, to peripheral zones, and to the Internet.

**Special Addresses**    Two special IPv6 addresses exist—the unspecified address and the loop-back address. The unspecified address 0:0:0:0:0:0:0:0 (or ::) indicates the absence of an address and is equivalent to the IPv4 unspecified address 0.0.0.0. It is typically used as a source address for packets attempting to verify whether a tentative address is unique. It is never assigned to an interface or used as a destination address. The loopback address 0:0:0:0:0:0:0:1 (or ::1) identifies a loopback interface and is equivalent to the IPv4 loopback address 127.0.0.1.

**NSAP and IPX Addresses**    NSAP addresses are identifying labels for network endpoints used in Open Systems Interconnection (OSI) networking. They are used to specify a piece of equipment connected to an Asynchronous Transfer Mode (ATM) network. IPX is no longer widely used because modern Novell Netware networks support TCP/IP. IPv6 addresses with an FP of 0000001 map to NSAP addresses. IPv6 addresses with an FP of 0000010 map to IPX addresses.

---

**Exam Tip**    The 70-647 examination is unlikely to include questions about NSAP or IPX mapping.

---

## IPv6 Multicast Addresses

IPv6 multicast addresses enable an IPv6 packet to be sent to a number of hosts, all of which have the same multicast address. They have an FP of 11111111. (They always start with ff.) Subsequent fields specify flags, scope, and group ID, as shown in Figure 1-22.

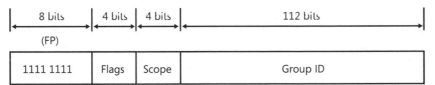

**Figure 1-22**    Multicast address structure

The *flags* field holds the flag settings. Currently, the only flag defined is the *Transient (T)* flag that uses the low-order field bit. If this flag is set to 0, the multicast address is well known—in other words, it is permanently assigned and has been allocated by IANA. If the flag is set to 1, the multicast address is transient.

---

### Quick Check
- Which type of address is fec0:0:0:eadf::1ff?

**Quick Check Answer**
- Unicast site-local

---

The *scope* field indicates the scope of the IPv6 internetwork for which the multicast traffic is intended. Routers use the multicast scope together with information provided by multicast routing protocols to determine whether multicast traffic can be forwarded. For example, traffic with the multicast address ff02::2 has a link-local scope and is never forwarded beyond the local link. Table 1-3 lists the assigned *scope* field values.

**Table 1-3   *Scope* Field Values**

| Value | Scope |
| --- | --- |
| 0 | Reserved |
| 1 | Node-local scope |
| 2 | Link-local scope |
| 5 | Site-local scope |
| 8 | Organization-local scope |
| e | Global scope |
| f | Reserved |

The group ID represents the multicast group and is unique within the scope. Permanently assigned group IDs are independent of the scope. Transient group IDs are relevant only to a specific scope. Multicast addresses from ff01:: through ff0f:: are reserved, well-known addresses.

In theory, $2^{112}$ group IDs are available. In practice, because of the way that IPv6 multicast addresses are mapped to Ethernet multicast MAC addresses, RFC 2373, "IP Version 6 Addressing Architecture," recommends assigning the group ID from the low-order 32 bits of the IPv6 multicast address and setting the remaining original group ID bits to zero. In this way, each group ID maps to a unique Ethernet multicast MAC address.

---

**MORE INFO   Assigning group IDs**

For more information about assigning group IDs, see *http://www.ietf.org/rfc/rfc2373.txt*.

---

**The Solicited-Node Multicast Address**   The solicited-node multicast address facilitates the querying of network nodes during address resolution. IPv6 uses the ND message to resolve a link-local IPv6 address to a node MAC address. Rather than use the local-link scope all-nodes multicast address (which would be processed by all nodes on the local link) as the neighbor solicitation message destination, IPv6 uses the solicited-node multicast address. This address comprises the prefix ff02::1:ff00:0/104 and the last 24 bits of the IPv6 address that is being resolved.

For example, if a node has the link-local address fe80::6b:28c:16d2:c97, the corresponding solicited-node address is ff02::1:ffd2:c97.

The result of using the solicited-node multicast address is that address resolution uses a mechanism that is not processed by all network nodes. Because of the relationship between the MAC address, the Interface ID, and the solicited-node address, the solicited-node address acts as a pseudo-unicast address for efficient address resolution.

### IPv6 Anycast Addresses

An anycast address is assigned to multiple interfaces. Packets sent to an anycast address are forwarded by the routing infrastructure to the nearest of these interfaces. The routing infrastructure must be aware of the interfaces that are assigned anycast addresses and their distance in terms of routing metrics. Currently, anycast addresses are used only as destination addresses and are assigned only to routers. Anycast addresses are assigned from the unicast address space, and the scope of an anycast address is the scope of the unicast address type from which the anycast address is assigned.

**The Subnet-Router Anycast Address**    The subnet-router anycast address is created from the subnet prefix for a given interface. In a subnet-router anycast address, the bits in the subnet prefix retain their current values, and the remaining bits are set to zero.

All router interfaces attached to a subnet are assigned the subnet-router anycast address for that subnet. The subnet-router anycast address is used for communication with one of multiple routers that are attached to a remote subnet.

---

### Quick Check
- A node has the link-local address fe80::aa:cdfe:aaa4:cab7. What is its corresponding solicited-node address?

### Quick Check Answer
- ff02::1:ffa4:cab7 (the prefix ff02::1:ff00:0/104 and the last 24 bits of the link-local address, which are a4:cab7)

---

# Investigating the Advantages of IPv6

IPv6 was designed to overcome the limitations of IPv4. This section lists the advantages that IPv6 has over its predecessor.

### Increased Address Space

In retrospect, the 32-bit structure that IPv4 uses was not sufficient for an addressing structure. IPv6 offers 128 bits. This gives enough addresses for every device that requires one to have a unique public IPv6 address. In addition, the 64-bit host portion (interface ID) of an IPv6 address can be automatically generated from the network adapter hardware.

## Automatic Address Configuration

Typically, IPv4 is configured either manually or by using DHCP. Automatic configuration (autoconfiguration) through APIPA is available for isolated subnets that are not routed to other networks. IPv6 deals with the need for simpler and more automatic address configuration by supporting both stateful and stateless address configuration. Stateful configuration uses DHCPv6. If stateless address configuration is used, hosts on a link automatically configure themselves with IPv6 addresses for the link and (optionally) with addresses that are derived from prefixes advertised by local routers. You can also configure a stateless DHCPv6 configuration that does not assign addresses to hosts but can assign settings to (for example) DNS servers whose domain names are not included in the router advertisements.

## Network-Level Security

Private communication over the Internet requires encryption to protect data from being viewed or modified in transit. Internet Protocol Security (IPsec) provides this facility, but its use is optional in IPv4. IPv6 makes IPsec mandatory. This provides a standards-based solution for network security needs and improves interoperability among different IPv6 implementations.

## Real-Time Data Delivery

Quality of service (QoS) exists in IPv4, and bandwidth can be guaranteed for real-time traffic (such as video and audio transmissions) over a network. However, IPv4 real-time traffic support relies on the *Type of Service (ToS)* field and the identification of the payload, typically using a User Datagram Protocol (UDP) or Transmission Control Protocol (TCP) port.

The *IPv4 ToS* field has limited functionality, and payload identification using a TCP port and a UDP port is not possible when an IPv4 packet payload is encrypted. Payload identification is included in the *Flow Label* field of the IPv6 header, so payload encryption does not affect QoS operation.

---

### Quick Check

1. How many bits are in an IPv4 address?
2. How many bits are in an IPv6 address?

**Quick Check Answers**

1. 32
2. 128

---

## Routing Table Size

The IPv6 global addresses used on the Internet are designed to create an efficient, hierarchical, and summarizable routing infrastructure based on the common occurrence of multiple levels of ISPs. On the Internet, backbone routers have greatly reduced routing tables that use route aggregation and correspond to the routing infrastructure of top-level aggregators.

---

### Route Aggregation

Route aggregation provides for routing of traffic for networks with smaller prefixes to networks with larger prefixes. In other words, it permits a number of contiguous address blocks to be combined and summarized as a larger address block. Route aggregation reduces the number of advertised routes on large networks. When an ISP breaks its network into smaller subnets to provide service to smaller providers, it needs to advertise the route only to its main supernet for traffic to be sent to smaller providers.

Route aggregation is used when a large ISP has a contiguous range of IP addresses to manage. IP addresses (IPv4 or IPv6) that are capable of summarization are termed *aggregatable addresses*.

---

## Header Size and Extension Headers

IPv4 and IPv6 headers are not compatible, and a host or router must use both IPv4 and IPv6 implementations to recognize and process both header formats. Therefore, the IPv6 header was designed to be as small as was practical. Nonessential and optional fields are moved to extension headers placed after the IPv6 header. As a result, the IPv6 header is only twice as large as the IPv4 header, and the size of IPv6 extension headers is constrained only by the size of the IPv6 packet.

## Removal of Broadcast Traffic

IPv4 relies on Address Resolution Protocol (ARP) broadcasts to resolve IP addresses to the MAC addresses of network interface cards (NICs). Broadcasts increase network traffic and are inefficient because every host processes them.

The ND protocol for IPv6 uses a series of Internet Control Message Protocol for IPv6 (ICMPv6) messages that manage the interaction of nodes on the same link (neighboring nodes). ND replaces ARP broadcasts, ICMPv4 router discovery, and ICMPv4 Redirect messages with efficient multicast and unicast ND messages.

# Implementing IPv4-to-IPv6 Compatibility

In addition to the various types of addresses described earlier in this lesson, IPv6 provides the following types of compatibility addresses to aid migration from IPv4 to IPv6 and to implement transition technologies.

## IPv4-Compatible Address

The IPv4-compatible address 0:0:0:0:0:0:w.x.y.z (or ::w.x.y.z) is used by dual stack nodes that are communicating with IPv6 over an IPv4 infrastructure. The last four octets (w.x.y.z) represent the dotted decimal representation of an IPv4 address. Dual stack nodes are nodes with both IPv4 and IPv6 protocols. When the IPv4-compatible address is used as an IPv6 destination, the IPv6 traffic is automatically encapsulated with an IPv4 header and sent to the destination using the IPv4 infrastructure.

## IPv4-Mapped Address

The IPv4-mapped address 0:0:0:0:0:ffff:w.x.y.z (or ::ffff:w.x.y.z) is used to represent an IPv4-only node to an IPv6 node and, hence, to map IPv4 devices that are not compatible with IPv6 into the IPv6 address space. The IPv4-mapped address is never used as the source or destination address of an IPv6 packet.

## Teredo Address

A Teredo address consists of a 32-bit Teredo prefix. In Windows Server 2008 (and Windows Vista), this is 2001::/32. The prefix is followed by the IPv4 (32-bit) public address of the Teredo server that assisted in the configuration of the address. The next 16 bits are reserved for Teredo flags. Currently, only the highest ordered flag bit is defined. This is the *cone* flag and is set when the NAT device connected to the Internet is a cone NAT. A cone NAT stores the mapping between an internal address and port number and the public address and port number.

---

**NOTE**    **Windows XP and Windows Server 2003**

In Windows XP and Windows Server 2003, the Teredo prefix was originally 3ffe:831f::/32. Computers running Windows XP and Windows Server 2003 use the 2001::/32 Teredo prefix when updated with Microsoft Security Bulletin MS06-064.

---

The next 16 bits store an obscured version of the external UDP port that corresponds to all Teredo traffic for the Teredo client interface. When a Teredo client sends its initial packet to a Teredo server, NAT maps the source UDP port of the packet to a different, external UDP port. All Teredo traffic for the host interface uses the same external, mapped UDP port. The value representing this external port is masked or obscured by XORing it with 0xffff. Obscuring the external port prevents NATs from translating it within the payload of packets that are being forwarded.

The final 32 bits store an obscured version of the external IPv4 address that corresponds to all Teredo traffic for the Teredo client interface. The external address is obscured by XORing the external address with 0xffffffff. As with the UDP port, this prevents NAT devices from translating the external IPv4 address within the payload of packets that are being forwarded. For example, the obscured version of the public IPv4 address 131.107.0.1 in colon-hexadecimal format is 7c94:fffe. (131.107.0.1 equals 0x836b0001 in hexadecimal, and 0x836b0001 XOR 0xffffffff equals 0x7c94fffe.) Obscuring the external address prevents NAT devices from translating it within the payload of the packets that are being forwarded. You can perform this operation using the Windows Calculator program in Scientific View.

As a further example, Northwind Traders currently implements the following IPv4 private networks at its headquarters and branch offices:

- Headquarters: 10.0.100.0 /24
- Branch1: 10.0.0.0 /24
- Branch2: 10.0.10.0 /24
- Branch3: 10.0.20.0 /24

The company wants to establish IPv6 communication between Teredo clients and other Teredo clients and between Teredo clients and IPv6-only hosts. The presence of Teredo servers on the IPv4 Internet enables this communication to take place. A Teredo server is an IPv6/IPv4 node connected to both the IPv4 Internet and the IPv6 Internet that supports a Teredo tunneling interface. The Teredo addresses of the Northwind Traders networks depend on a number of factors such as the port and type of NAT server used, but they could, for example, be the following:

- Headquarters: 2001::ce49:7601:e866:efff:f5ff:9bfe through 2001::0a0a:64fe:e866:efff:f5ff:9b01
- Branch 1: 2001:: ce49:7601:e866:efff:f5ff:fffe through 2001::0a0a:0afe:e866:efff: f5ff:ff01
- Branch 2: 2001:: ce49:7601:e866:efff:f5ff:f5fe through 2001::0a0a:14fe:e866:efff:f5ff:f501
- Branch 3: 2001:: ce49:7601:e866:efff:f5ff:ebfe through 2001::0a0a:1efe:e866:efff:f5ff:ebfe

Note that, for example, 10.0.100.1 is the equivalent of 0a00:6401, and 0a00:6401 XORed with ffff:ffff is f5ff:9bfe.

---

**Exam Tip**  The 70-647 examination objectives specifically mention Teredo addresses, which are supported by Microsoft. However, the examination is unlikely to ask you to generate a Teredo address. You might, however, be asked to identify such an address and work out its included IPv4 address. Fortunately, you have access to a scientific calculator during the examination.

---

---

### Cone NATs

Cone NATs can be full cone, restricted cone, or port restricted cone. In a full cone NAT, all requests from the same internal IP address and port are mapped to the same external IP address and port, and any external host can send a packet to the internal host by sending a packet to the mapped external address.

In a restricted cone NAT, all requests from the same internal IP address and port are mapped to the same external IP address and port, but an external host can send a packet to the internal host if the internal host had previously sent a packet to the external host.

In a port restricted cone NAT, the restriction includes port numbers. An external host with a specified IP address and source port can send a packet to an internal host only if the internal host had previously sent a packet to that IP address and port.

---

## ISATAP Addresses

IPv6 can use an Intra-site Automatic Tunnel Addressing Protocol (ISATAP) address to communicate between two nodes over an IPv4 intranet. An ISATAP address starts with a 64-bit unicast link-local, site-local, global, or 6to4 global prefix. The next 32 bits are the ISATAP identifier 0:5efe. The final 32 bits hold the IPv4 address in either dotted decimal or hexadecimal notation. An ISATAP address can incorporate either a public or a private IPv4 address.

For example, the ISATAP address fe80::5efe:w.x.y.z address has a link-local prefix; the fec0::1111:0:5efe:w.x.y.z address has a site-local prefix; the 3ffe:1a05:510:1111:0:5efe:w.x.y.z address has a global prefix; and the 2002:9d36:1:2:0:5efe:w.x.y.z address has a 6to4 global prefix. In all cases, w.x.y.z represents an IPv4 address.

By default, Windows Server 2008 automatically configures the ISATAP address fe80::5efe:w.x.y.z for each IPv4 address that is assigned to a node. This link-local ISATAP address enables two hosts to communicate over an IPv4 network by using each other's ISATAP address.

You can implement IPv6-to-IPv4 configuration by using the *netsh interface ipv6 6to4*, *netsh interface ipv6 isatap*, and *netsh interface ipv6 add v6v4tunnel* IPv6 commands. For example, to create an IPv6-in-IPv4 tunnel between the local address 10.0.0.11 and the remote address 192.168.123.116 on an interface named *Remote*, you would type **netsh interface ipv6 add v6v4tunnel "Remote" 10.0.0.11 192.168.123.116**.

You can also configure the appropriate compatibility addresses manually by using the *netsh interface ipv6 set address* command or the Internet Protocol Version 6 (TCP/IPv6) GUI as described in the next section of this lesson.

**NOTE  6to4cfg**

Windows Server 2008 does not support the 6to4cfg tool.

# Planning an IPv4-to-IPv6 Transition Strategy

No specific time frame is mandated for IPv4-to-IPv6 transition. As an enterprise administrator, one of your decisions is whether to be an early adopter and take advantage of IPv6 enhancements such as addressing and stronger security or wait and take advantage of the experience of others. Both are valid strategies.

However, you do need to find out whether your upstream ISPs support IPv6 and whether the networking hardware in your organization (or the several organizations in your enterprise) also supports the protocol. The most straightforward transition method, dual stack, requires that both IPv4 and IPv6 be supported. By the same token, do not delay the decision to transition to IPv6 for too long. If you wait until the IPv4 address space is fully depleted, dual stack will no longer be available, and you (and the users you support) will find the transition process much more challenging.

Currently, the underlying assumption in transition planning is that an existing IPv4 infrastructure is available and that your most immediate requirement is to transport IPv6 packets over existing IPv4 networks so that isolated IPv6 network islands do not occur. As more networks make the transition, the requirement will change to transporting IPv4 packets over IPv6 infrastructures to support earlier IPv4 applications and avoid isolated IPv4 islands.

Several transition strategies and technologies exist because no single strategy fits all. RFC 4213, "Basic Transition Mechanisms for Hosts and Routers," describes the key elements of these transition technologies, such as dual stack and configured tunneling. The RFC also defines a number of node types based upon their protocol support, including previous systems that support only IPv4, future systems that will support only IPv6, and the dual node that implements both IPv6 and IPv4.

**MORE INFO  IPv4-to-IPv6 transition**

For more information about basic transition mechanisms, see *http://www.ietf.org/rfc/rfc4213.txt* and download the white paper, "IPv6 Transition Technologies," from *http://technet.microsoft.com/en-us /library/bb726951.aspx*.

## Dual Stack Transition

Dual stack (also known as a dual IP layer) is arguably the most straightforward approach to transition. It assumes that hosts and routers provide support for both protocols and can send and receive both IPv4 and IPv6 packets. Thus, a dual stack node can interoperate with an IPv4 device by using IPv4 packets and interoperate with an IPv6 device by using IPv6 packets. It can also operate in one of the following three modes:

- Only the IPv4 stack enabled
- Only the IPv6 stack enabled
- Both IPv4 and IPv6 stacks enabled

Because a dual stack node supports both protocols, you can configure it with both IPv4 32-bit addresses and IPv6 128-bit addresses. It can use, for example, DHCP to acquire its IPv4 addresses and stateless autoconfiguration or DHCPv6 to acquire its IPv6 addresses. Current IPv6 implementations are typically dual stack. An IPv6-only product would have very few communication partners.

## Configured Tunneling Transition

If a configured tunneling transition strategy is employed, the existing IPv4 routing infrastructure remains functional but also carries IPv6 traffic while the IPv6 routing infrastructure is under development. A tunnel is a bidirectional, point-to-point link between two network endpoints. Data passes through a tunnel using encapsulation, in which the IPv6 packet is carried inside an IPv4 packet. The encapsulating IPv4 header is created at the tunnel entry point and removed at the tunnel exit point. The tunnel endpoint addresses are determined from configuration information that is stored at the encapsulating endpoint.

Configured tunnels are also called *explicit tunnels.* You can configure them as router-to-router, host-to-router, host-to-host, or router-to-host, but they are most likely to be used in a router-to-router configuration. The configured tunnel can be managed by a *tunnel broker.* A tunnel broker is a dedicated server that manages tunnel requests coming from end users, as described in RFC 3053, "IPv6 Tunnel Broker."

---

**MORE INFO**  Tunnel broker

For more information about tunnel brokers, see *http://www.ietf.org/rfc/rfc3053.txt.*

---

## Automatic Tunneling

RFC 2893, "Transition Mechanisms for IPv6 Hosts and Routers" (replaced by RFC 4213), describes automatic tunneling. This enables IPv4/IPv6 nodes to communicate over an IPv4 routing infrastructure without using preconfigured tunnels. The nodes that perform automatic tunneling are assigned a special type of address called an IPv4-compatible address, which carries the 32-bit IPv4 address within a 128-bit IPv6 address format. The IPv4address can be automatically extracted from the IPv6 address.

MORE INFO  **Automatic tunneling**

For more information about automatic tunneling, see *http://www.ietf.org/rfc/rfc2893.txt*. Be aware, however, that the status of this document is obsolete, and RFC 4213 is the current standard.

## 6to4

RFC 3056, "Connection of IPv6 Domains via IPv4 Clouds," describes the 6to4 tunneling scheme. 6to4 tunneling enables IPv6 sites to communicate with each other via an IPv4 network without using explicit tunnels and to communicate with native IPv6 domains by relay routers. This strategy treats the IPv4 Internet as a single data link.

MORE INFO  **6to4 tunneling**

For more information about 6to4 tunneling, see *http://www.ietf.org/rfc/rfc3056.txt*.

## Teredo

RFC 4380, "Teredo: Tunneling IPv6 over UDP through Network Address Translations (NATs)," describes Teredo, which is an enhancement to the *6to4* method and is supported by Windows Server 2008. Teredo enables nodes that are located behind an IPv4 NAT device to obtain IPv6 connectivity by using UDP to tunnel packets. Teredo requires the use of server and relay elements to assist with path connectivity. Teredo address structure was discussed earlier in this lesson.

MORE INFO  **Teredo**

For more information about Teredo, see *http://www.ietf.org/rfc/rfc4380.txt* and *http://www.microsoft.com/technet/network/ipv6/teredo.mspx*.

## Intra-Site Automatic Tunneling Addressing Protocol

RFC 4214, "Intra-Site Automatic Tunnel Addressing Protocol (ISATAP)," defines ISATAP, which connects IPv6 hosts and routers over an IPv4 network, using a process that views the IPv4 network as a link layer for IPv6, and other nodes on the network as potential IPv6 hosts or routers. This creates a host-to-host, host-to-router, or router-to-host automatic tunnel.

MORE INFO  **ISATAP**

For more information about ISATAP, see *http://www.ietf.org/rfc/rfc4214.txt* and download the "Manageable Transition to IPv6 Using ISATAP" white paper from *http://www.microsoft.com/downloads/details.aspx?FamilyId=B8F50E07-17BF-4B5C-A1F9-5A09E2AF698B&displaylang=en*.

# Using IPv6 Tools

Windows Server 2008 provides tools with which you can configure IPv6 interfaces and check IPv6 connectivity and routing. Tools also exist that implement and check IPv4 to IPv6 compatibility.

In Windows Server 2008, the standard command-line tools such as *ping*, *ipconfig*, *pathping*, *tracert*, *netstat*, and *route* have full IPv6 functionality. For example, Figure 1-23 shows the *ping* command used to check connectivity with a link-local IPv6 address on a test network. The IPv6 addresses on your test network will be different. Note that if you were pinging from one host to another, you would also need to include the interface ID, for example, *ping fe80::fd64:b38b:cac6:cdd4%15*. Interface IDs are discussed later in this lesson.

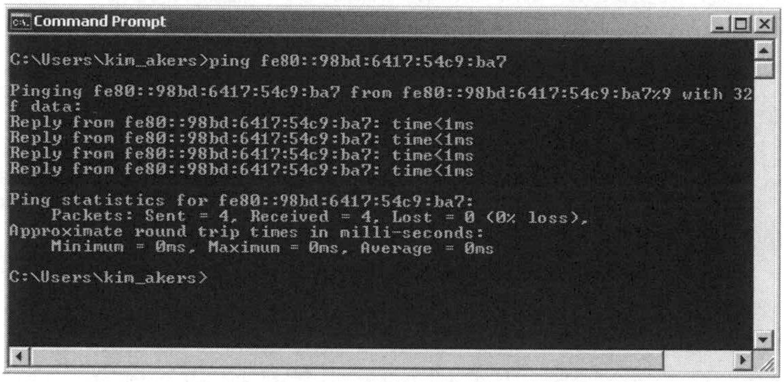

**Figure 1-23** Pinging an IPv6 address

---

**NOTE** *Ping6*

The *ping6* command-line tool is not supported in Windows Server 2008.

---

Tools specific to IPv6 are provided in the *netsh* (network shell) command structure. For example, the *netsh interface ipv6 show neighbors* command shows the IPv6 interfaces of all hosts on the local subnet. You use this command in the practice session later in this lesson, after you have configured IPv6 connectivity on a subnet.

## Verifying IPv6 Configuration and Connectivity

If you are troubleshooting connectivity problems or merely want to check your configuration, arguably the most useful tool—and certainly one of the most used—is *ipconfig*. The *ipconfig /all* tool displays both IPv4 and IPv6 configuration. The output from this tool was shown in Figure 1-21 earlier in this lesson.

If you want to display the configuration of only the IPv6 interfaces on the local computer, you can use the *netsh interface ipv6 show address* command. Figure 1-24 shows the output of this command run on the Glasgow computer. Note the % character followed by a number after each IPv6 address. This is the interface ID, which identifies the interface that is configured with the IPv6 address.

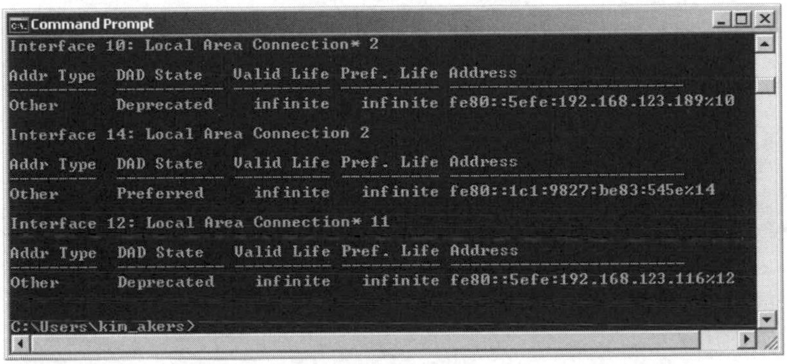

**Figure 1-24**   Displaying IPv6 addresses and interface IDs

If you are administering an enterprise network with a number of sites, you also need to know site IDs. You can obtain a site ID by using the *netsh interface ipv6 show address level=verbose* command. Part of the output from this command is shown in Figure 1-25.

**Figure 1-25**   Displaying IPv6 addresses and site IDs

## Configuring IPv6 Interfaces

Typically, most IPv6 addresses are configured through autoconfiguration or DHCPv6. However, if you need to configure an IPv6 address manually, you can use the *netsh interface ipv6 set address* command, as in this example: *netsh interface ipv6 set address "local area connection 2" fec0:0:0:fffe::2* where "local area connection 2" is the name of the network connection that you wish to configure. You need to run the command console (also known as the command prompt) as an administrator to use this command. In Windows Server 2008 (and in Windows Vista), you can also manually configure IPv6 addresses from the properties of the TCP/IPv6 GUI. Figure 1-26 shows this configuration.

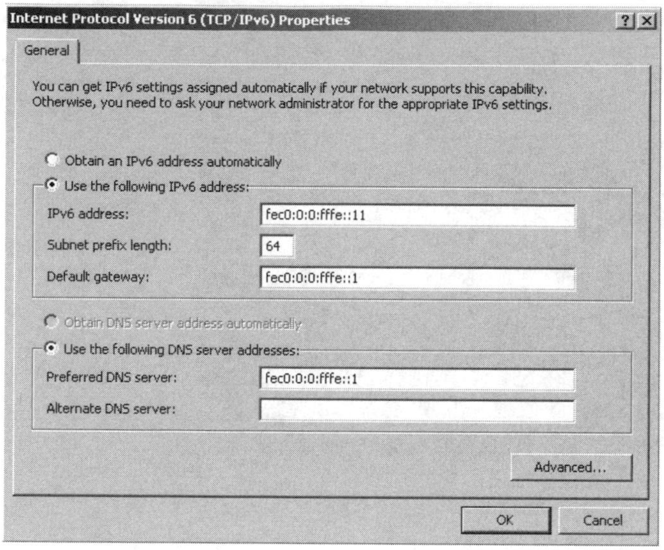

**Figure 1-26**    Configuring an IPv6 address through a GUI

The advantage of using the TCP/IPv6 GUI is that you can specify the IPv6 addresses of one or more DNS servers in addition to specifying the interface address. If, however, you choose to use command-line interface commands, the command to add the IPv6 addresses of DNS servers is *netsh interface ipv6 add dnsserver*, as in this example: *netsh interface ipv6 add dnsserver "local area connection 2" fec0:0:0:fffe::1*. To change the properties of IPv6 interfaces (but not their configuration), use the *netsh interface ipv6 set interface* command, as in this example: *netsh interface ipv6 set interface "local area connection 2" forwarding=enabled*. You need to run the command console (command prompt) as an administrator to use the *netsh interface ipv6 add* and *netsh interface ipv6 set* commands.

---

## Quick Check

- Which *netsh* command lists site IDs?

**Quick Check Answer**

- *netsh interface ipv6 show address level=verbose*

---

## Verifying IPv6 Connectivity

To verify connectivity on a local network, your first step should be to flush the neighbor cache, which stores recently resolved link-layer addresses and might give a false result if you are checking changes that involve address resolution. You can check the contents of the neighbor cache by using the *netsh interface ipv6 show neighbors* command. The *netsh interface ipv6 delete neighbors* command flushes the cache. You need to run the command console as an administrator to use the *netsh* tool.

You can test connectivity to a local host on your subnet and to your default gateway by using the *ping* command. You can add the interface ID to the IPv6 interface address to ensure that the address is configured on the correct interface. Figure 1-27 shows a *ping* command using an IPv6 address and an interface ID.

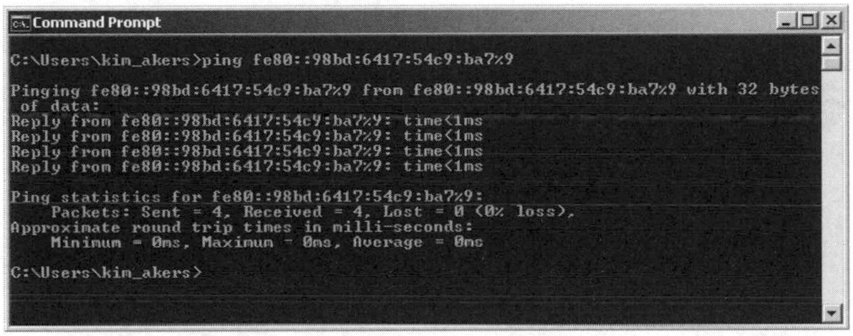

**Figure 1-27**   Pinging an IPv6 address with an interface ID

To check connectivity to a host on a remote network, your first task should be to check and clear the destination cache, which stores next-hop IPv6 addresses for destinations. You can display the current contents of the destination cache by using the *netsh interface ipv6 show destinationcache* command. To flush the destination cache, use the *netsh interface ipv6 delete destinationcache* command. You need to run the command console as an administrator to use this command.

Your next step is to check connectivity to the default router interface on your local subnet. This is your default gateway. You can identify the IPv6 address of your default router interface by using the *ipconfig*, *netsh interface ipv6 show routes*, or *route print* commands. You can also specify the zone ID, which is the interface ID for the default gateway on the interface on which you want the ICMPv6 Echo Request messages to be sent. When you have ensured that you can reach the default gateway on your local subnet, ping the remote host by its IPv6 address. Note that you cannot ping a remote host (or a router interface) by its link-local IPv6 address because link-local addresses are not routable.

If you can connect to the default gateway but cannot reach the remote destination address, trace the route to the remote destination by using the *tracert –d* command followed by the destination IPv6 address. The *–d* command-line switch prevents the *tracert* tool from performing a DNS reverse query on router interfaces in the routing path. This speeds up the display of the routing path. If you want more information about the routers in the path and, particularly if you want to verify router reliability, use the *pathping -d* command, again followed by the destination IPv6 address.

> ## Quick Check
> - Which *netsh* command could you use to identify the IPv6 address of your default router interface?
> ### Quick Check Answer
> - *netsh interface ipv6 show route*

## Troubleshooting Connectivity

As an experienced administrator, you know that if you cannot connect to a remote host, you (or more probably a more junior member of your team) first want to check the various hardware connections (wired and wireless) in your organization and ensure that all network devices are running. If these basic checks do not find the problem, the IPsec configuration might not be properly configured, or firewall problems (such as incorrectly configured packet filters) might exist.

You can use the IP Security Policies Management Microsoft Management Console (MMC) snap-in to check and configure IPsec policies and the Windows Firewall With Advanced Security snap-in to check and configure IPv6-based packet filters. Figures 1-28 and 1-29 show these tools.

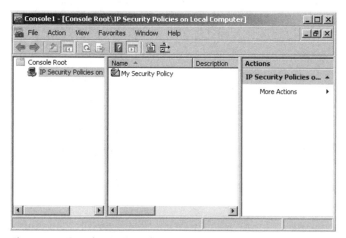

**Figure 1-28**   The IP Security Policies Management snap-in

---

**NOTE   IPSec6**

The IPSec6 tool is not implemented in Windows Server 2008.

---

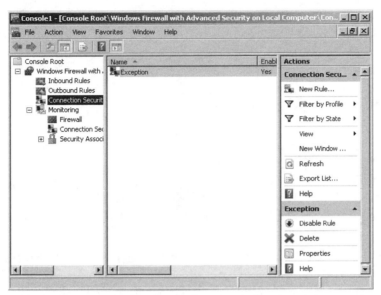

**Figure 1-29**    The Windows Firewall With Advanced Security snap-in

You might be unable to reach a local or remote destination because of incorrect or missing routes in the local IPv6 routing table. You can use the *route print*, *netstat –r*, or *netsh interface ipv6 show route* commands to view the local IPv6 routing table and verify that you have a route corresponding to your local subnet and to your default gateway. Note that the *netstat –r* command displays both IPv4 and IPv6 routing tables.

If you have multiple default routes with the same metric, you might need to modify your IPv6 router configurations so that the default route with the lowest metric uses the interface that connects to the network with the largest number of subnets. You can use the *netsh interface ipv6 set route* command to modify an existing route. To add a route to the IPv6 routing table, use the *netsh interface ipv6 add route* command. The *netsh interface ipv6 delete route* command removes an existing route. You need to run the command console as an administrator to use these commands.

If you can access a local or remote host by IPv4 address but not by host name, you might have a DNS problem. Tools to configure, check, and debug DNS include *dnscmd*, *ipconfig*, *netsh interface ipv6 show dnsservers*, *netsh interface ipv6 add dnsserver*, *nslookup*, and the TCP/IPv6 GUI. This chapter has discussed these tools in earlier sections of both lessons.

### Verifying IPv6-Based TCP Connections

If the Telnet client tool is installed, you can verify that a TCP connection can be established to a TCP port by entering the *telnet* command followed by the destination IPv6 address and the TCP port number, as in this example: *telnet fec0:0:0:fffe::1 80*. If Telnet successfully creates a

TCP connection, the telnet> prompt appears, and you can type Telnet commands. If the tool cannot create a connection, it will return an error message.

---

**MORE INFO    Installing the Telnet client**

For more information about Telnet, including how to install the Telnet client, search Windows Server 2008 Help for "Telnet: frequently asked questions."

---

# Configuring Clients Through DHCPv6

You can choose stateless or stateful configuration when configuring hosts by using DHCPv6. Stateless configuration does not generate a host address—which is instead autoconfigured— but it can, for example, specify the address of a DNS server. Stateful configuration specifies host addresses.

Whether you choose stateful or stateless configuration, you can assign the IPv6 addresses of DNS servers through the DNS Recursive Name Server DHCPv6 option (option 0023). If you choose stateful configuration, the IPv6 addresses of DNS servers can be configured as a scope option, so different scopes could have different DNS servers. Scope options override server options for that scope. This is the preferred method of configuring DNS server IPv6 addresses, which are not configured through router discovery.

With DHCPv6, an IPv6 host can receive subnet prefixes and other configuration parameters. A common use of DHCPv6 for Windows-based IPv6 hosts is to configure the IPv6 addresses of DNS servers automatically.

Currently, when you configure an IPv6 scope, you specify the 64-bit prefix. By default, DHCPv6 can allocate host addresses from the entire 64-bit range for that prefix. This allows for IPv6 host addresses that are configured through adapter hardware. You can specify exclusion ranges, so if you wanted to allocate only host addresses in the range fec0::0:0:0:1 through fec0::0:0:0:fffe, you would exclude addresses fec0::0:0:1:1 through fec0::ffff:ffff:ffff:fffe.

Several DHCPv6 options exist. Arguably, the most useful option specifies the DNS server. Other options are concerned with compatibility with other systems that support IPv6, such as the UNIX Network Information Service (NIS).

DHCPv6 is similar to DHCP in many respects. For example, scope options override server options, and DHCPv6 requests and acknowledgements can pass through BootP-enabled routers and layer-3 switches (almost all modern routers and switches act as DHCP relay agents) so that a DHCPv6 server can configure clients on a remote subnet.

---

**Exam Tip**    If you want to configure a Windows Server 2008 server as a DHCP relay agent, you need to install the Routing and Remote Access Services (RRAS) role service.

---

As with DHCP, you can implement the 80:20 rule so that a DHCPv6 server is configured with a scope for its own subnet that contains 80 percent of the available addresses for that subnet and a second scope for a remote subnet that contains 20 percent of the available addresses for that subnet. A similarly configured DHCPv6 server on the remote subnet provides failover. If either server fails, the hosts on both subnets still receive their configurations.

For example, the Tailspin Toys Melbourne office network has two private virtual local area networks (VLANs) that have been allocated the following site-local networks:

- VLAN1: fec0:0:0:aaaa::1 through fec0:0:0:aaaa::fffe
- VLAN2: fec0:0:0:aaab::1 through fec0:0:0:aaab::fffe

Exceptions are defined so that IPv6 addresses on the VLANS can be statically allocated to servers. In this case, you could implement the 80:20 rule by configuring the following DHCPv6 scopes on the DHCP server on VLAN1:

- fec0:0:0:aaaa::1 through fec0:0:0:aaaa::cccb
- fec0:0:0:aaab::cccc through fec0:0:0:aaab::fffe

You would then configure the following DHCPv6 scopes in the DHCP server on VLAN2:

- fec0:0:0:aaab::1 through fec0:0:0:aaab::cccb
- fec0:0:0:aaaa::cccc through fec0:0:0:aaaa::fffe

DHCP servers, and especially DHCP servers that host 20-percent scopes, are excellent candidates for virtualization because they experience only limited I/O activity. Additionally, you can deploy this role on a Server Core installation of Windows Server 2008. This technique is particularly applicable to more complex networks.

---

**NOTE**   Virtual DNS servers

Like DHCP servers, DNS servers—particularly secondary DNS servers—are good candidates for virtualization.

---

For example, Trey Research is a single-site organization but has five buildings within its site, connected by fiber-optic links to a layer-3 switch configured to allocate a VLAN to each building. VLAN1, allocated to the main office, supports the majority of the company's computers. VLAN3 supports most of the remainder. VLAN2, VLAN4, and VLAN5 each support only a few computers.

In this case, you can configure the DHCP server on VLAN1 to host 80 percent of the VLAN1 address range. You can configure a virtual DHCP server on the same VLAN to host 20 percent of the VLAN2 through VLAN5 address ranges. On VLAN3, you can configure a DHCP server to host the 80-percent ranges for VLAN2 through VLAN5 and a virtual server to host the 20-percent range for VLAN1. If either server fails, hosts on all the VLANs can continue to receive their configurations through DHCP.

---

**NOTE** The 80:20 rule

The 80:20 rule is typically implemented within an Active Directory site because a WAN link (with routers over which you have no control) might not pass DHCP traffic. In general, if you implement DHCP failover by using the 80:20 rule, you need at least two DHCP servers per site.

---

Installing the DHCP server role and configuring a DHCPv6 scope are practical procedures and are, therefore, covered in detail in the practice session later in this lesson.

# Planning an IPv6 Network

Configuring IPv6 and implementing IPv6 are relatively straightforward. Planning an IPv6 network is rather more complex. Every scenario has unique features, but in general, you might want to deploy IPv6 in conjunction with an existing IPv4 network. You might have applications that require IPv6, although your network is principally IPv4. You might want to design a new network or restructure a current one so it is primarily IPv6. You could be designing a network for a large multinational company with multiple sites and thousands of users or for a small organization with a head office and a single branch office.

Whatever the scenario, you will need to maintain interoperability with former functions and with IPv4. Even in a new IPv6 network, it is (currently) unlikely that you can ignore IPv4 completely.

## Analyzing Hardware Requirements

An early step in the design process is to identify and analyze the required network infrastructure components. Hardware components could include the following:

- Routers
- Layer-3 switches
- Printers
- Faxes
- Firewalls
- Intrusion-detection equipment
- Hardware load balancers
- Load-balancing server clusters
- Virtual private network (VPN) entry and exit points
- Servers and services
- Network interconnect hardware
- Intelligent NICs

This list is not exhaustive, and you might need to consider other hardware devices, depending upon the scenario. Which of these hardware devices store, display, or allow the input of IP addresses? Can all the necessary hardware be upgraded to work with IPv6? If not, what are the workarounds? If you need to replace hardware, is there a budget and a time frame for hardware refresh?

## Analyzing Software and Application Requirements

From the software and applications viewpoint, network management is the area most likely to be affected by the version of IP used, although some line-of-business (LOB) applications could also be affected. You might need to consider the IPv6 operation and compatibility of the following components:

- Network infrastructure management, such as WINS
- Network management systems, such as systems based on Simple Network Management Protocol (SNMP)
- Performance management systems
- High-level network management applications (typically third-party applications)
- Configuration management, such as DHVP and DHCPv6
- Security policy management and enforcement
- LOB applications
- Transition tools

Consideration of transition tools implies the requirement—except in a new IPv6 network—of determining the transition strategy you want to deploy. Transition strategies were discussed earlier in this lesson and depend largely on the planned scenario and whether both IPv4 and IPv6 stacks are available. If some previous components do not support IPv6, you need to consider how to support them while transitioning is in progress and whether you will continue to support them in a dual stack network when transitioning is complete. You need to ensure interoperability between IPv4 and IPv6 components.

Possibly your first step in configuration management is to decide whether to use stateful or stateless configuration. With IPv6, it is possible to have every component on your network configured with its own global unicast address. Security is implemented by firewalls, virus filters, spam filters, IP filtering, and all the standard security methods. IPsec provides end-to-end encryption. You can configure peripheral zones in IPv6 networks as you can in IPv4 networks. DHCPv6 in stateless mode can configure options—for example, DNS servers—that are not configured through router discovery. In either case, you need to ensure that your ISP is IPv6-compliant and obtain a range of IPv6 addresses.

---

### Integrating DHCP with Network Access Protection

You can further increase security on your network by integrating DHCP and DHCPv6 with Network Access Protection (NAP). NAP provides policy enforcement components that help ensure that computers connecting to or communicating on a network comply with administrator-defined requirements for system health and limiting the access of computers that do not meet these requirements to a restricted network. The restricted network contains the resources needed to update computers so that they meet the health requirements. When you integrate DHCP with NAP, a computer must be compliant to obtain an unlimited access IP address configuration from a DHCP server. Network access for noncompliant computers is limited through an IP address configuration that allows access only to a restricted network. DHCP enforcement ensures that clients conform to health policy requirements every time a DHCP client attempts to lease or renew an IP address configuration. DHCP enforcement also actively monitors the health status of the NAP client and renews the IP address configuration for access only to the restricted network if the client becomes noncompliant.

When planning DHCP integration with NAP, you must decide whether DHCP NAP enforcement will be enabled on all DHCP scopes, selected DHCP scopes, or no DHCP scopes at all. In addition, you must configure which NAP profile to use for DHCP NAP enforcement. Last, you must determine how a DHCP server will behave when the Network Policy Server (NPS) is unreachable. A DHCP server can be configured to allow full access, allow restricted access, or drop client packets when the NPS server is unreachable.

To learn more about NAP, see *http://technet.microsoft.com/en-us/network/bb545879.aspx*.

---

You might decide that exposing the global unicast addresses of all your network components to the Internet represents a security risk. This is a matter of debate in the networking community and outside the scope of this book. If you do make that decision, you can choose to implement site-local IPv6 addresses on your internal subnets, assuming your NAT servers support IPv6. You can choose stateful configuration by DHCPv6. Assuming that your routers or layer-3 switches can pass DHCP traffic, you can follow the 80:20 rule across your subnets or VLANs to ensure that configuration still occurs if a DHCP server is down.

When you have made the basic decisions about network infrastructure and transitioning strategy, and have discovered whether you current network (or proposed new network) is capable of supporting IPv6, you then need to address other requirements and considerations. For example, unless you are implementing a new IPv6 network, you need to ensure that IPv4 infrastructure is not disrupted during the transition. With this requirement in mind, it might not be feasible to deploy IPv6 on all parts of your network immediately.

Alternatively, if your only requirement is to deploy a set of specified IPv6 applications (such as peer-to-peer communication), your IPv6 deployment might be limited to the minimum required to operate this set of applications.

## Documenting Requirements

Your next step is to determine and document exactly what is required. For example, you might need to address the following questions:

- Is external connectivity (to the Internet, for example) required?
- Does the organization have one site or several sites? If the latter, what are the geographical locations of the sites, and how is information currently passed securely between them?
- What is the current IPv4 structure of the internetwork?
- What IPv6 address assignment plan is available from the provider?
- What IPv6 services does the provider offer?
- How should prefix allocation be delegated in the enterprise?
- Are site-external and site-internal IPv6 routing protocols required? If so, which ones?
- Does the enterprise currently use an external data center? (For example, are servers located at the provider?)
- Is IPv6 available using the same access links as IPv4?
- Which applications need to support IPv6 and can they be upgraded to do so? Will these applications need to support both IPv4 and IPv6?
- Do the enterprise platforms support both IPv4 and IPv6? Is IPv6 installed by default on server and client platforms?
- Is NAT v4–v6 available, and do the applications have any issues with using it?
- Do the applications need globally routable IP addresses?
- Will multicast and anycast addresses be used?

You also need to analyze and document the working patterns and support structure within the organization. You need to obtain the following information:

- Who takes ownership of the network? For example, is network support in-house or outsourced?
- Does a detailed asset management database exist?
- Does the organization support home workers? If so, how?
- Is IPv6 network mobility used or required for IPv6?
- What is the enterprise's policy for geographical numbering?
- Do separate sites in the enterprise have different providers?

- What is the current IPv4 QoS policy (assuming you are not designing a new IPv6-only network)? Will this change when IPv6 is implemented?
- What proposals are in place for training technical staff in the use of IPv6?

Documenting and analyzing this information will take some time. However, without this documentation, you will not know the precise requirements for IPv6 implementation, and the project will take much longer and result in a less satisfactory outcome. When you have gathered the information, you can plan the tasks you and your team need to perform and the requirements for each. You will have a better idea of the time and cost of the project and whether it should be implemented in stages.

Your next step is to draw up and implement a project plan. Project planning is beyond the scope of this book. However, you would be wise to heed a word of warning: Do not ignore what might seem to be peripheral or nontime-critical activities. Training your technical staff is a good example. Every part of the final plan is important, and unless every aspect is implemented, the result will be less than optimal. In the worst case, the project can fail completely because of an unconsidered component.

---

**MORE INFO**    **IPv6 network scenarios**

For more information about IPv6 planning and specific scenario examples, see RFC 4057, "IPv6 Enterprise Network Scenarios," at *http://www.ietf.org/rfc/rfc4057*.

---

## PRACTICE Configuring IPv6 Connectivity

In this practice, you will configure a site-local IPv6 address on your client computer interface that connects to your private subnet (the IPv4 10.0.0.0/24 subnet). You will test IPv6 connectivity between your client and domain controller. You will then install the DHCP Server role on your domain controller and configure a DHCPv6 scope.

---

**NOTE**    **Logging on to the domain controller**

You perform the server configurations in this practice session by logging interactively on to the domain controller with an administrative-level account. However, in a production network, this would be bad practice. If you want to make the exercises more realistic, you can log on to your client computer and connect to your server through Remote Desktop or run Administrative Tools on a client and specify the server within the tool.

---

▶ Exercise 1    Configure IPv6

In this exercise, you will configure IPv6 site-local addresses on your client computer and test connectivity. You need to have configured the IPv6 settings on your domain controller in Lesson 1 before you start this exercise.

1. Log on to your client computer on the *contoso.internal* domain by using the Kim_Akers account.

2. From Control Panel, double-click Network And Sharing Center. If you are not using Classic View, first click Network And Internet, and then click Network And Sharing Center. Click Manage Network Connections.

3. Right-click the interface that connects to your private network and choose Properties.

4. If a UAC dialog box appears, click Continue.

5. Select Internet Protocol Version 6 (TCP/IPv6) and click Properties.

6. Configure a static site-local IPv6 address, fec0:0:0:fffe::a.

7. Configure a DNS server address, fec0:0:0:fffe::1. The Properties dialog box should look similar to Figure 1-30.

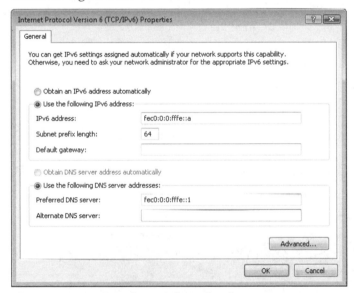

**Figure 1-30**   IPv6 configuration on the client

8. Click OK. Close the Local Area Connections Properties dialog box.

9. Close the Network And Connections dialog box.

10. Close Network And Sharing Center.

**NOTE   Virtual machines**

If you are using a virtual machine to implement your server and client on the same computer, it is a good idea to close your virtual machine and restart your computer after configuring interfaces.

11. Open the command console on the client computer. Enter **ping fec0:0:0:fffe::1**. You should get the response from the domain controller shown in Figure 1-31.

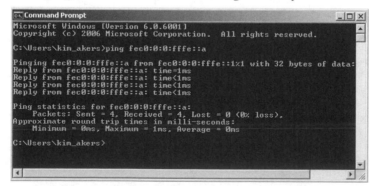

**Figure 1-31**    Pinging the DC from the client

---

**NOTE    Firewall configuration**

If the firewall on either your Glasgow domain controller or your Melbourne client blocks ICMP traffic, you need to reconfigure this setting (or settings) before this command will work.

---

12. Enter **ping glasgow**. Note that the DC host name resolves to the IPv6 address.

13. Log off from the client computer.

14. Log on to your DC, using the Kim_Akers account.

15. Open the command console on your domain controller.

16. Enter **ping fec0:0:0:fffe::a**. You should get the response shown in Figure 1-32.

```
Command Prompt                                              _ □ x
Microsoft Windows [Version 6.0.6001]
Copyright (c) 2006 Microsoft Corporation.  All rights reserved.

C:\Users\kim_akers>ping fec0:0:0:fffe::a

Pinging fec0:0:0:fffe::a from fec0:0:0:fffe::1%1 with 32 bytes of data:
Reply from fec0:0:0:fffe::a: time=1ms
Reply from fec0:0:0:fffe::a: time<1ms
Reply from fec0:0:0:fffe::a: time<1ms
Reply from fec0:0:0:fffe::a: time<1ms

Ping statistics for fec0:0:0:fffe::a:
    Packets: Sent = 4, Received = 4, Lost = 0 (0% loss),
Approximate round trip times in milli-seconds:
    Minimum = 0ms, Maximum = 1ms, Average = 0ms

C:\Users\kim_akers>
```

**Figure 1-32**    Pinging the client from the DC

17. Enter **netsh interface ipv6 show neighbors**. Figure 1-33 shows the fec0:0:0:fffe::a interface as a neighbor on the same subnet as the domain controller.

**Figure 1-33**  Showing the DC neighbors

▶ **Exercise 2    Install the DHCP Server Role**

In this exercise, you will install the DHCP Server role and specify that DHCPv6 can provide stateful IPv6 configuration.

1.  If necessary, log on to the DC with the Kim_Akers account.

2.  If the Initial Configuration Tasks window opens when you log on, click Add Roles. Otherwise, open Server Manager from Administrative Tools, right-click Roles in the console tree, and choose Add Roles

3.  The Add Roles Wizard starts. If the Before You Begin page appears, click Next.

4.  Select the DHCP Server check box as shown in Figure 1-34 and click Next. On the Introduction To DHCP Server page, click Next.

5.  On the Select Network Connection Bindings page, ensure that only the 10.0.0.11 IPv4 interface check box is selected for DHCP. Click Next.

6.  On the Specify IPv4 DNS Server Settings page, verify that the domain is *contoso.internal* and the Preferred DNS Server IPv4 Address is 10.0.0.11. Click Next.

7.  On the Specify IPv4 WINS Settings page, verify that WINS Is Not Required For Applications On This Network is selected. Click Next.

8.  On the Add Or Edit DHCP Scopes page, you can define only IPv4 scopes, so the scope list should be empty. Click Next.

9.  On the Configure DHCPv6 Stateless Mode page, select Disable DHCPv6 Stateless Mode For This Server. This enables you to use the DHCP Management Console to configure DHCPv6 after the DHCP Server role has been installed. Figure 1-35 shows this setting. Click Next.

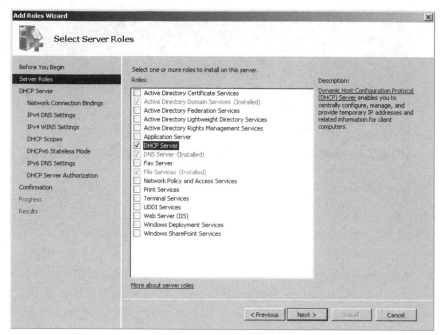

**Figure 1-34**    Selecting to install the DHCP Server role

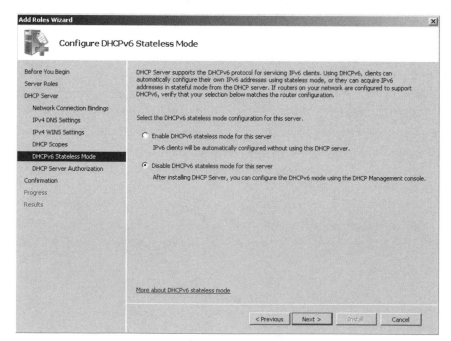

**Figure 1-35**    Disabling DHCPv6 stateless mode

10. On the Authorize DHCP Server page, ensure that Use Current Credentials is selected.

11. On the Confirm Installation Selections page, check your settings.

12. Click Install. Click Close when installation completes.

13. Restart the domain controller.

    Note that a reboot is always a good idea after you have installed a server role, even if you are not prompted to do so, especially if you are using virtual machines.

▶ **Exercise 3    Set Up a DHCPv6 Scope**

In this exercise, you will configure a DHCPv6 scope. You need to have configured the IPv6 settings on your client and DC computers and installed the DHCP Server role on your DC before you carry out this exercise.

1. If necessary, log on to the DC with the Kim_Akers account.

2. In Administrative Tools, choose DHCP.

3. If a UAC dialog box appears, click Continue to close it.

4. Expand *glasgow.contoso.internal*. Expand IPv6. Ensure that a green arrow appears beside the IPv6 icon. This confirms that the DHCPv6 Server is authorized.

5. Right-click IPv6 and choose New Scope. The New Scope Wizard opens. Click Next.

6. Give the scope a name (such as Private Network Scope) and type a brief description. Click Next.

7. Set Prefix to fec0::fffe. You are configuring only one IPv6 scope on this subnet and do not need to set Preference. Your screen should look similar to Figure 1-36. Click Next.

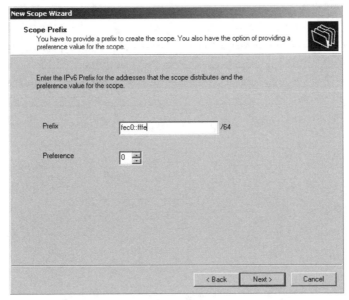

**Figure 1-36**    Setting a DHCPv6 prefix

8. You want to exclude IPv6 addresses fec0:0:0:fffe::1 through fec0:0:0:fffe::ff from the scope. Specify a Start Address of 0:0:0:1 and an End Address of 0:0:0:ff on the Add Exclusions page and click Add, as shown in Figure 1-37.

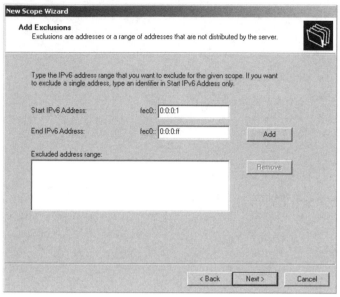

**Figure 1-37**   Configuring scope exclusions

9. Click Next. You can set the scope lease on the Scope Lease page. For the purposes of this practice, the lease periods are acceptable. Click Next. Check the scope summary, ensure that Yes is selected under Activate Scope Now, and then click Finish.

10. In the DHCP console, expand the scope, right-click Scope Options, choose Configure Options, and examine the available options. Select Option 0023 DNS Recursive Server IPv6 Address List. Specify fec0:0:0:fffe::1 as the DNS Server IPv6 address, as shown in Figure 1-38.

11. Click Add, and then click OK. Close the DHCP console.

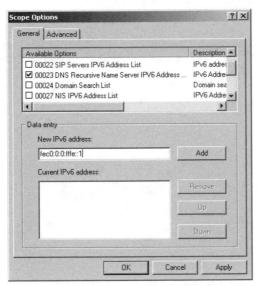

**Figure 1-38**  Specifying a DNS server for DHCPv6 configuration

## Lesson Summary

- IPv6 supports unicast, multicast, and anycast addresses. Unicast addresses can be global, site-local, link-local, or special. IPX and NSAP mapped addresses are also supported.

- IPv6 is fully supported in Windows Server 2008 and addresses problems such as lack of address space that are associated with IPv4.

- IPv6 is designed to be backward-compatible, and IPv4-compatible addresses can be specified. Transitioning strategies include dual stack, configured tunneling, automatic tunneling, 6to4, Teredo, and ISATAP.

- IPv6 addresses can be configured through stateful (DHCPv6) and stateless (autoconfiguration) methods. DHCPv6 can also be used statelessly to configure (for example) DNS servers when hosts are autoconfigured.

- Tools to configure and troubleshoot IPv6 include *ping*, *ipconfig*, *tracert*, *pathping*, and *netsh*. You can also configure IPv6 by using the TCP/IPv6 Properties GUI.

## Lesson Review

Use the following questions to test your knowledge of the information in Lesson 2, "Planning Internet Protocol Addressing." The questions are also available on the companion CD if you prefer to review them in electronic form.

---

**NOTE   Answers**

Answers to these questions and explanations of why each answer choice is correct or incorrect are located in the "Answers" section at the end of the book.

---

1. Which type of IPv6 address is the equivalent of a public unicast IPv4 address?

    A. Site-local

    B. Global

    C. Link-local

    D. Special

2. A node has a link-local IPv6 address of fe80::6b:28c:16a7:d43a. What is its corresponding solicited-node address?

    A. ff02::1:ffa7:d43a

    B. ff02::1:ff00:0:16a7:d43a

    C. fec0::1:ff a7:d43a

    D. fec0::1:ff00:0:16a7:d43a

3. Which protocol uses ICMPv6 messages to manage the interaction of neighboring nodes?

    A. ARP

    B. EUI-64

    C. DHCPv6

    D. ND

4. Which IPv6-to-IPv4 transition strategy uses preconfigured tunnels and encapsulates an IPv6 packet within an IPv4 packet?

    A. Configured tunneling

    B. Dual stack

    C. ISATAP

    D. Teredo

5. Which command enables you to configure an IPv6 address manually on a specified interface?

    A. *netsh interface ipv6 show address*

    B. *netsh interface ipv6 add address*

    C. *netsh interface ipv6 set interface*

    D. *netsh interface ipv6 set address*

6. Trey Research is an innovative research organization that prides itself on being at the forefront of technology. The company currently has 82 client computers all running Windows Vista Ultimate. All its servers—including its DCs—have recently been upgraded to Windows Server 2008 Enterprise. Trey's site consists of two buildings linked by a fiber-optic cable. Each building has its own VLAN, and Trey's peripheral zone is on a separate VLAN. All Trey's clients receive their IPv4 configurations through DHCP, and the 80:20 rule is used to implement failover if a DHCP server fails. All servers and router interfaces are configured manually, as are the company's network printers and network projectors. Trey has a Class C public IPv4 allocation and sees no need to implement NAT. It uses a network management system based on SNMP. It uses a number of high-level graphics applications in addition to business software and the Microsoft Office 2007 suite. The company wants to introduce IPv6 configuration and access the Internet. It has verified that its provider and all its network hardware fully support IPv6. Which of the following are likely to form part of Trey's IPv6 implementation plan? (Choose all that apply.)

    A. Trey is likely to adopt a dual stack transition strategy.

    B. Trey is likely to adopt a configured tunneling transition strategy.

    C. Trey is likely to configure its internal network hosts with site-local unicast addresses.

    D. Trey is likely to configure its internal network hosts with global unicast addresses.

    E. Trey needs to ensure that its servers and clients support IPv6.

    F. Trey needs to ensure that its network projectors and network printers support IPv6.

    G. Trey needs to ensure that its network management system is compatible with IPv6.

    H. Trey needs to ensure that its graphic applications are compatible with IPv6.

# Chapter Review

To further practice and reinforce the skills you learned in this chapter, you can perform the following tasks:

- Review the chapter summary.
- Complete the case scenarios. These scenarios set up real-world situations involving the topics in this chapter and ask you to create a solution.
- Complete the suggested practices.
- Take a practice test.

## Chapter Summary

- IPv6 is fully supported in Windows Server 2008 and is installed by default. It supports unicast, multicast, and anycast addresses. It is backward-compatible with IPv4 and offers a selection of transitioning strategies.
- IPv6 addresses can be configured through stateful and stateless configuration. Both GUI and command-line interface tools are available to configure IPv6 and check network connectivity.
- Windows Server 2008 DNS fully supports IPv6 in addition to offering several new and enhanced features. It conforms to all current standards. GUI and command-line interface tools are available to configure DNS and check DNS functionality.

## Case Scenarios

In the following case scenarios, you will apply what you have learned about planning name resolution and IP addressing. You can find answers to these questions in the "Answers" section at the end of this book.

## Case Scenario 1:  Configuring DNS

You administer the Windows Server 2008 AD DS network at Blue Yonder Airlines. When the company upgraded to Windows Server 2008, it also introduced Active Directory–integrated DNS, although two BIND servers are still used as secondary DNS servers. Answer the following questions:

1. Blue Yonder has set up wireless hotspots for the convenience of its customers. However, management is concerned that attackers might attempt to register their computers in the company's DNS. How can you ensure against this?

2. Your boss is aware of the need to replicate DNS zones to the two standalone BIND servers. She is concerned that an attacker might attempt to replicate DNS zone information to an unauthorized server, thus exposing the names and IP addresses of company computers. How do you reassure her?

3. For additional security, Blue Yonder uses RODCs at its branch locations. Management is concerned that DNS zone information on these computers is kept up to date. What information can you provide?

4. Blue Yonder wants to use an application that needs to resolve IPv6 addresses to host names. How do you implement this functionality?

## Case Scenario 2: Implementing IPv6 Connectivity

You are a senior network administrator at Wingtip Toys. Your corporate network consists of two subnets with contiguous private IPv4 networks configured as Virtual Local Area Networks (VLANs) connected to a layer-3 switch. Wingtip Toys accesses its ISP and the Internet through a dual-homed server running ISA Server that provides NAT and firewall services and connects through a peripheral zone to a hardware firewall and, hence, to its ISP. The company wants to implement IPv6 connectivity. All of the network hardware supports IPv6, as does the ISP. Answer the following questions:

1. What options are available for the type of unicast address used on the subnets?

2. Given that the Wingtip Toys network can support both IPv4 and IPv6, what is the most straightforward transition strategy?

3. You decide to use stateful configuration to allocate IPv6 configuration on the two subnets. How should you configure your DHCPv6 servers to provide failover protection?

# Suggested Practices

To help you successfully master the exam objective presented in this chapter, complete the following tasks.

## Configure DNS

Do both practices in this section.

- **Practice 1**  Use the command-line interface tools. It would take an entire book to do justice to the *nslookup*, *dnscmd*, *ipconfig*, and *netsh* tools. The only way to become familiar with these tools is to use them.

- **Practice 2**  Configure IPv6 reverse lookup zones. This procedure was described earlier in the lesson. Specifying IPv6 reverse lookup zones in DNS can be an error-prone procedure because of the way the prefixes are specified. You will become comfortable with this notation only through practice.

## Configure IPv6 Connectivity

Do Practice 1 and Practice 2. Practice 3 is optional.

- **Practice 1**   Investigate *netsh* commands. The *netsh* command structure provides you with many powerful commands. In particular, use the help function in the command console to investigate the *netsh interface ipv6 set*, *netsh interface ipv6 add*, and *netsh interface ipv6 show* commands. Investigate the *netsh dhcp* commands also.

- **Practice 2**   Find out more about DHCPv6 scope and server options. Use the DHCP administrative tool to list the DHCP scope and server options. Access Windows Server 2008 Help and the Internet to find out more about these options. In the process, you should learn something about NIS networks. Although the 70-647 examination objectives do not cover NIS, you should, as a network professional, know what it is.

- **Practice 3**   Test DHCPv6 address allocation. If you have access to additional computers with suitable client operating systems, connect them to your network and configure them to obtain IPv6 configuration automatically. Ensure that the DHCPv6 scope you have configured provides configuration for these computers. Ensure that the host IPv6 addresses configured fall outside the fec0:0:0:fffe::1 through fec0:0:0:fffe::ff range, which includes the IPv6 addresses for the Glasgow and Melbourne computers.

## Take a Practice Test

The practice tests on this book's companion CD offer many options. For example, you can test yourself on just one exam objective, or you can test yourself on all the 70-647 certification exam content. You can set up the test so that it closely simulates the experience of taking a certification exam, or you can set it up in study mode so that you can look at the correct answers and explanations after you answer each question.

---

**MORE INFO**   **Practice tests**

For details about all the practice test options available, see the "How to Use the Practice Tests" section in this book's introduction.

---

# Chapter 2
# Designing Active Directory Domain Services

Active Directory Domain Services (AD DS) is arguably one of the most important server roles in Windows Server 2008. AD DS provides the basis for authentication and authorization for virtually all other server roles in Windows Server 2008 and is the foundation for the Microsoft Identity and Access solutions. Additionally, a number of enterprise products, such as Microsoft Exchange Server and Microsoft Windows SharePoint Services, require AD DS.

As an enterprise administrator, you are likely accountable for the architecture of AD DS in your organization. Even though virtually all large organizations already have deployed AD DS, you will inevitably need to design it because of the constantly changing business and technical requirements. Designing AD DS for large organizations is a complex task. As an enterprise administrator, you must be able to gather the relevant business and technical requirements and design AD DS to meet these requirements.

This chapter will empower you to design AD DS forests and domains as well as the AD DS physical topology.

## Exam objectives in this chapter:
- Design Active Directory forests and domains.
- Design Active Directory physical topology.
- Design for data management and data access.

## Lessons in this chapter:

- Lesson 1: Designing AD DS Forests and Domains . . . . . . . . . . . . . . . . . . . . . . . . . . . . . .81
- Lesson 2: Designing the AD DS Physical Topology . . . . . . . . . . . . . . . . . . . . . . . . . . . 112

# Before You Begin

No special setup is required for this chapter.

---

### Real World

*John Policelli*

When Active Directory directory service was first released as part of the Microsoft Windows 2000 Server operating system, many organizations quickly made a decision to migrate from Microsoft Windows NT 4.0 to Active Directory. The buzz on the street was that Active Directory was a more robust directory service than the security accounts manager (SAM) database used in Windows NT 4.0, it provided significant scalability, and it promised to reduce administrative overhead. Unfortunately, many organizations failed to realize the full benefits of Active Directory because they did not spend enough time gathering requirements, and their design was inadequate.

When moving from Windows NT 4.0 to Active Directory, most organizations failed to reassess business and technical requirements and, as a result, were left with an Active Directory structure that was almost identical to the Windows NT 4.0 structure they were trying to move away from. Many of these same organizations have since realized that insufficient planning and lack of business requirements gathering has left them with a bloated Active Directory structure. A number of these organizations have multiple-year plans to consolidate the number of forests and domains so that they can fully realize the benefits of Active Directory Domain Services (AD DS).

Designing AD DS requires a thorough understanding of business and technical requirements. Investing the time to gather these requirements properly at the outset and then designing AD DS based on these requirements can save you a significant amount of time and pain in the future.

---

# Lesson 1: Designing AD DS Forests and Domains

When designing AD DS in Windows Server 2008, you need to start with forests and domains. Forests and domains act as the security, administration, and replication boundary for AD DS and are required before you can design the physical topology.

The first part of your design will be the forest structure. To design the forest structure, you need to start by gathering a number of requirements. When you have gathered the relevant forest requirements, you can determine the number of forests you require and finally design the forest model. After you have completed the forest design, you need to design the domain structure. Designing the domain structure also starts with gathering a set of business and technical requirements that will enable you to determine the domain model and the number of domains you require. Because most organizations already have AD DS, you will also need to decide whether to upgrade existing domains or deploy new ones. Last, you will need to design the forest root domain and domain trees. When you have designed the forest and domain structure, you need to design forest and domain functional levels, design the schema, and design trusts to optimize intra-forest authentication.

This lesson will provide you with the knowledge to gather relevant business and technical requirements and then create a forest and domain design in Windows Server 2008 based on these requirements.

---

**After this lesson, you will be able to:**
- Gather forest and domain design requirements.
- Determine the number of forests and domains required.
- Design the forest model.
- Design the domain model.
- Decide whether to upgrade existing domains or deploy new ones.
- Design the forest root domain.
- Design forest and domain functional levels.
- Design the AD DS schema.
- Design trusts to optimize intra-forest authentication.

**Estimated lesson time: 45 minutes**

---

## Designing the Forest Structure

Every AD DS design starts with designing the forest structure. Without a design for the forest structure, you will not be able to design the subsequent logical and physical components within AD DS. Designing the forest structure consists of identifying the role of AD DS in your organization; gathering business, technical, security, and network requirements; gathering autonomy and isolation requirements; determining the number of forests required; and designing the forest model.

---

**MORE INFO    What's new in AD DS in Windows Server 2008?**

For more information about the changes in AD DS functionality from Microsoft Windows Server 2003 with SP1 to Windows Server 2008, go to *http://technet2.microsoft.com/windowsserver2008 /en/library/40046b6c-2d64-46a6-94d5-cd483cffd0911033.mspx*.

---

## Identifying the Role of AD DS

Before you can design the forest structure, you need to understand the role AD DS will have in your organization. It can be used in a variety of ways. For example, it can be used as a network operating system (NOS), as an enterprise directory, or as an Internet directory. Also, an organization can have requirements to use AD DS for more than one purpose, for instance, as a NOS directory and an enterprise directory. How AD DS will be used in your organization will have an effect on the forest structure.

When AD DS will be used strictly as a NOS directory, a single forest is usually sufficient. However, as you will see, there are exceptions to this general rule when diverse organizational structure or operational or legal requirements exist within an organization.

When AD DS will be used as an enterprise directory, you must consider a number of factors before you will be able to design the forest structure, and you must understand the requirements to store information within the enterprise directory. First, identify whether the enterprise directory will store confidential employee information such as payroll information. If so, determine whether access to this information needs to be restricted, because authenticated users have read access to virtually all attributes in AD DS. If the enterprise directory will store confidential employee information, and access to this information should be restricted, it is more effective to deploy a separate forest for the enterprise directory or deploy an Active Directory Lightweight Directory Services (AD LDS) instance, both of which will affect the design of the forest structure. Although it is technically possible to modify permissions on attributes, doing so when attributes are shared by a NOS directory and an enterprise directory can be a very complex undertaking.

After you have an understanding of the requirements to store confidential information, determine whether the enterprise directory will require custom attributes and classes. Enterprise directories usually store more information, such as organizational information and payroll information, than a NOS directory. Because this information varies for each organization, most enterprise directories introduce a requirement to modify the default AD DS schema, and you must identify any requirements for custom attributes and classes and assess the impact of these modifications on the schema when designing the forest structure. As previously mentioned, new attributes are visible to authenticated users. If the enterprise directory requires custom attributes, and access to these attributes must be restricted, a separate AD DS forest or an AD LDS instance is better suited as the enterprise directory. By using either a separate AD DS forest or a separate AD LDS instance, the enterprise directory will have a dedicated schema that will not conflict with the schema for the NOS directory.

Last, when AD DS will be used as an Internet directory, there are a number of additional factors to consider as part of the design of the forest structure. Internet directories are typically used to store customer or partner identity information, which is accessed through publicly accessible servers and applications. Most organizations are legally required to restrict access to customer information. Additionally, most organizations want to separate customer and partner identities from employee identities for organizational structure and operational and security requirements. If AD DS will be used as an Internet directory, a separate AD DS forest or an AD LDS instance is required to meet organizational structure and operational, legal, and security requirements.

## Gathering Business, Technical, Security, and Network Requirements

After you have a thorough understanding of the role AD DS will have in your organization, you must gather the business, technical, and security requirements. These requirements for the forest structure typically fall into one or more of the following categories:

- Organizational structural requirements
- Operational requirements
- Legal requirements
- Limited connectivity requirements

A proper understanding of the organizational structure is essential in designing the forest structure. For example, there might be a requirement for a particular business unit to operate independently from the rest of the organization so that the business unit can be divested in the future with minimal effort. Also, a particular business unit might have a requirement to install a number of directory-enabled applications that require changes to the AD DS schema. In both cases, the business unit's unique requirements might have a negative impact on the rest of the organization if the business unit belongs to the same forest as the rest of the organization. To gather organizational structure requirements, start by identifying the various groups within the organization that will take advantage of AD DS. Next, determine whether any of these groups requires the ability to operate separately from the rest of the organization. If you do find organizational structure requirements that are unique to a specific group, you must determine whether these requirements will adversely affect the rest of the organization. In most cases, this impact can be mitigated only by deploying a separate forest for each business unit that has diverse requirements from the rest of the organization.

After you have identified the organizational structure requirements, gather the operational requirements that will influence the forest structure design. Organizations such as the military and hosting companies that use AD DS are commonly bound by unique operational requirements. To identify operational requirements, start by inventorying the operational teams in the organization along with the operational requirements for each team. By completing this inventory of requirements, you will be able to select the appropriate forest design model.

You must have an understanding of the legal requirements to which an organization must adhere to design the forest structure, too. Some organizations, such as financial institutions and government organizations, have legal requirements to function in a specific way such as restricting access to certain information as specified in a business contract. Failure to meet these requirements can result in loss of the contract and possible legal action. When gathering legal requirements as part of your forest structure design, start by identifying the legal obligations the organization must comply with. Next, determine whether these legal obligations can be met by using a single AD DS forest. If not, a separate forest will be required as part of the forest structure design.

Finally, identifying any limited connectivity requirements is also essential in the design of the forest structure. Some organizations have limited connectivity requirements, such as groups that are located on restricted or isolated networks. Start by identifying all groups within the organization that have such limitations. For each group with limited connectivity requirements, gather the details of which networks these groups are permitted to connect to or are restricted from accessing.

---

### Real World

*John Policelli*

One of the most important, and overdue, changes Windows Server 2008 addresses is the new fine-grained password policies feature. Since the introduction of Active Directory in Windows 2000 Server, password policies and account lockout policies could be applied only at the domain level, which meant that all users in the domain would have to adhere to the same password policy and account lockout policy.

I cannot begin to count the number of times I have been involved in a project in which there were business, technical, or both requirements to create a unique password policy. In the past, the abovementioned limitation meant we were unable to meet these unique password policy requirements. A number of third-party products that provide custom password policy functionality exist, but very few projects were willing to cover this additional cost. With enough convincing, project teams were usually able to sway the security team to provide exemptions to the existing password policy, which often resulted in service accounts being configured to have a password that never expires.

---

With the new fine-grained password policies feature in Windows Server 2008, we can finally create multiple password policies and account lockout policies for users in the same domain. Moreover, the fact that the fine-grained password policies feature in Windows Server 2008 maps password policies to users, groups, or both means that we have virtually unlimited flexibility when it comes to password policy and account lockout policy requirements.

## Gathering Autonomy and Isolation Requirements

In addition to the forest design requirements, you must identify the autonomy and isolation requirements to design the forest structure effectively.

Autonomy involves independent control of a resource. With autonomy, the control is not exclusive. When you achieve autonomy, administrators have the authority to manage resources independently; however, administrators with greater authority exist who also have control over those resources and can take control away if necessary. The forest structure can be designed to achieve the following types of autonomy:

- **Service autonomy**  Service autonomy involves control over all or part of service management. Service autonomy might be required for a group within an organization that wants to be able to control the service level of AD DS by adding and removing domain controllers as needed.

- **Data autonomy**  Data autonomy involves control over all or part of the data stored in the directory or on member computers (member computers implies they are joined to the directory). Data autonomy does not prevent service administrators in the forest from accessing the data.

Isolation consists of independent, exclusive control of a resource. When you achieve isolation, administrators have the authority to manage a resource independently, and no other administrators can take control of the resource away. The forest structure can be designed to achieve the following types of isolation:

- **Service isolation**  Service isolation prevents administrators other than those specifically designated to control service management from controlling or interfering with service management. Operational or legal requirements typically create a need for service isolation.

- **Data isolation**  Data isolation prevents administrators other than those specifically designated to control or view data from controlling or viewing a subset of data in the directory or on member computers. Because data stored in AD DS and on computers joined to AD DS cannot be isolated from service administrators, the only way for a group within an organization to achieve complete data isolation is to create a separate forest for that data.

**MORE INFO**    Autonomy vs. isolation

For more information about autonomy vs. isolation, go to *http://technet2.microsoft.com /windowsserver2008/en/library/022fd4ef-c9c3-403b-8561-7bd21190bff01033.mspx.*

## Determining the Number of Forests Required

After you have collected the forest design requirements, the next step is to determine the number of forests required. Start by reviewing the role of AD DS in your organization. If you are designing a forest for a NOS directory, a single forest can be used. If you are designing a forest as an enterprise directory, determine whether the existing NOS directory can be extended to act as an enterprise directory also. As previously mentioned, if the schema and data confidentiality of the enterprise directory will differ from those in the NOS directory, a separate forest is required for the enterprise directory. Alternatively, if the schema and data confidentiality requirements between the NOS directory and the enterprise directory are consistent, a single forest will suffice. Finally, if you are designing the forest as an Internet directory, you will need to deploy a dedicated forest to ensure the separation of employee and client data.

After you have reviewed the role of AD DS in your organization, review the autonomy and isolation requirements to determine the number of forests required. Remember that with autonomy, control is not exclusive. As such, if you have identified data autonomy and service autonomy requirements, use a single forest. Conversely, if you have identified data isolation and service isolation requirements, deploy a separate forest because isolation consists of independent control.

When determining the number of forests required, it is also imperative to incorporate the cost and administrative differences between a single forest model and a multiple forest model into your design decision. A single forest requires the least amount of hardware and administrative effort, which makes this model the most cost effective. Multiple forests require additional hardware and administrative effort. When determining the number of forests required, you must weigh the costs of additional forests against the requirements to deploy these additional forests.

**MORE INFO**    Determining the number of forests required

For more information about determining the number of forests required, go to *http:// technet2.microsoft.com/windowsserver2008/en/library/a2936b2a-1d3e-4549-a2f5 -8de82851e2671033.mspx.*

## Designing the Forest Model

When you have collected the forest design requirements, select the appropriate forest model to meet them by first understanding the different forest models that exist. You can select from three forest models when designing the forest structure:

- **Organizational forest model**  In the organizational forest model, user accounts and resources exist in the same forest and are managed separately. The organizational forest model is used to provide service autonomy, service isolation, or data isolation. Figure 2-1 illustrates the organizational forest model.

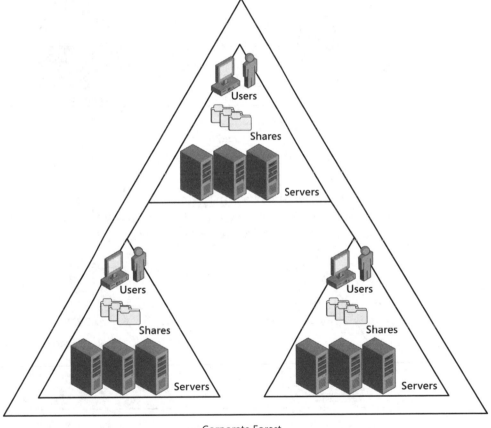

Corporate Forest

**Figure 2-1**  Organizational forest model

Use the organizational forest model when you need to provide exclusive or inclusive control of the AD DS infrastructure or when you need to prevent administrators from controlling or viewing a subset of data in the directory or on member computers joined to the directory.

- **Resource forest model**    In the resource forest model, a separate forest is used to manage resources. Resource forests do not contain user accounts other than those required for services. Forest trusts are established so that users from other forests can access the resources contained in the resource forest. Resource forests, illustrated in Figure 2-2, provide service isolation.

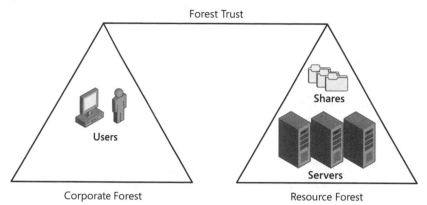

**Figure 2-2**    Resource forest model

Use the resource forest model when you need to provide exclusive control of the AD DS infrastructure.

- **Restricted access forest model**    In the restricted access forest model, illustrated in Figure 2-3, a separate forest is created to contain user accounts and data that must be isolated from the rest of the organization. Restricted access forests provide data isolation.

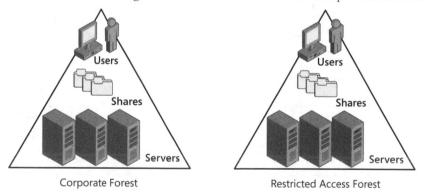

**Figure 2-3**    Restricted access forest model

Use the restricted access forest model when you need to prevent administrators from controlling or viewing a subset of data in the directory or on member computers.

---

**MORE INFO**  Forest design models

For more information about forest design models, go to *http://technet2.microsoft.com /windowsserver2008/en/library/066d1fe4-cd49-4efb-9e24-3ab0612620fc1033.mspx*.

---

Now that you have an understanding of the three forest models that exist, you are ready to map the forest design requirements to the appropriate design model. Some organizations might have a single forest requirement that maps directly to a forest design model, which makes the selection of a forest design model straightforward. However, there will be cases in which an organization has multiple design requirements, which will make mapping these requirements to a forest design model more complex. You can use the information in Table 2-1 to map forest design requirements to the appropriate forest design model.

**Table 2-1   Mapping Forest Design Requirements to Forest Design Models**

| Limited Connectivity | Data Isolation | Data Autonomy | Service Isolation | Service Autonomy | Scenario |
|---|---|---|---|---|---|
| No | No | Yes | No | No | Join an existing forest for data autonomy. |
| No | No | N/A | No | Yes | Use an organizational forest or domain for service autonomy. |
| No | No | N/A | Yes | N/A | Use an organizational or resource forest for service isolation. |
| N/A | Yes | N/A | N/A | N/A | Use an organizational or restricted access forest for data isolation. |
| Yes | No | N/A | No | No | Use an organizational forest or reconfigure the firewall for limited connectivity. |
| Yes | No | N/A | No | Yes | Use an organizational forest or domain and reconfigure the firewall for service autonomy with limited connectivity. |
| Yes | No | N/A | Yes | N/A | Use a resource forest and reconfigure the firewall for service isolation with limited connectivity. |

---

**MORE INFO**   **Mapping design requirements to forest design models**

For more information about mapping design requirements to design models, go to *http:// technet2.microsoft.com/windowsserver2008/en/library/c7b00aad-8e05-4e28-90fb-52923b2bc38f1033.mspx.*

---

# Designing the Domain Structure

After you have designed the forest structure, you are ready to design the domain structure for each forest. Every AD DS forest must contain at least one domain. Designing the domain structure consists of gathering domain design requirements, designing the domain model, determining the number of domains required, determining whether to upgrade existing domains or deploy new domains, designing the forest root domain, and designing domain trees.

## Gathering Domain Design Requirements

Because AD DS domains are mostly used to partition a large forest into smaller components for administration and replication purposes, you must gather the security, administration, and replication requirements before you can design the domain structure. It is these requirements that will aid you in determining how best to partition the AD DS data through domains.

Gathering security requirements is essential when designing the domain structure. Certain security policies, such as the domain-wide password policy, can be applied only at the domain level. When gathering security requirements, you must assess the domain-wide security requirements for the various groups in the organization. Because these security settings are domain-wide, you need to determine whether the different groups in the organization can use the same security settings. In reality, it is difficult in large organizations to have several groups agree on a common security policy. If there are groups in your organization that represent a subset of the users and that have unique security requirements, you use fine-grained password policies. Alternatively, if the group represents a large portion of your organization, it is more efficient to deploy a dedicated domain to satisfy the group's unique security requirements. The administrative effort required to maintain the security groups used for fine-grained password policies increases substantially when the number of users the fine-grained password policy applies to is large. Generally, any group that has unique security requirements that can be applied only at the domain level requires a dedicated domain.

After you have gathered the relevant security requirements, gather the administration requirements for the domain structure. Gathering these administrative requirements will enable you to understand better how the domains will be managed and effectively aid you in designing the domain structure. Start by identifying the team or teams that will be responsible for AD DS service management in your organization. If you determine that a single team will require administrative access to AD DS, you can deploy a single domain to meet the administrative requirements. However, if multiple teams require administrative access to AD DS, you then need to determine whether a single domain will meet those requirements. To do so, establish the level of administrative access that is required by each team and whether the required access must be exclusive. If the access does not need to be exclusive, deploy a single AD DS domain to meet the administrative requirements because all teams will have the same level of access. Alternatively, if the level of access needs to be exclusive to one or more teams, deploy a dedicated domain for each team.

Because the domain partition is a writable copy of all attributes on every object in the domain, you need to ensure that you account for the replication requirements when designing the domain structure so that you can partition the AD DS forest into smaller portions that will replicate more efficiently on your network. Start by identifying each location that will contain AD DS users. Then determine the number of users in each location and the business unit each user belongs to. Next, gather the relevant network configuration information for each location. When designing a domain structure, it is important to understand how each location is connected to the remainder of the network. Collect the available bandwidth, network usage, and connection information for each location in your organization. If all the locations are interconnected through high-speed network links that have ample bandwidth, the additional network bandwidth consumed by AD DS replication will not be a concern, and a single domain will suffice. However, if there are one or more locations that have limited network bandwidth or saturated network connections, then partitioning that location through a dedicated domain will ensure that AD DS replication operates more efficiently.

## Designing the Domain Model

Now that you have gathered the relevant domain structure design requirements, you can design the domain model for AD DS. To select the appropriate domain design model, you must first understand the different models that exist. You can select from two when designing the domain structure:

- **Single domain model**   The single domain model, illustrated in Figure 2-4, consists of a forest with a single domain. Any domain controller can authenticate any user in the forest, and all domain controllers can be global catalog servers. In this model, all directory data is replicated to all locations that host domain controllers. The single domain model is the simplest because it is easier to administer and less expensive to maintain. However, it creates the most replication traffic, especially when domain controllers are decentralized. It is sufficient when security requirements, administrative requirements, and replication requirements are consistent across the organization.

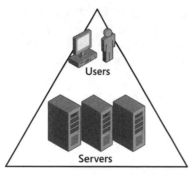

*woodgrovebank.com*

**Figure 2-4**    Single domain model

Use the single domain model when fast network connections exist between domain controllers, bandwidth consumption is not a concern, the administration of AD DS is centralized, and security requirements are consistent across the organization.

■ **Regional domain model**    The regional domain model consists of a forest root domain and one or more regional domains, which represent the geographic locations within an organization. The regions used to define each domain in this model typically represent fixed elements, such as countries. Wide area network (WAN) connectivity is a key factor when planning to use a regional domain model, which is more complex to design and requires a thorough analysis of the WAN connectivity and number of users in each region. However, because all object data within a domain is replicated to all domain controllers in that domain, regional domains can reduce network traffic over the WAN link. This model is better suited when diverse security requirements, administrative requirements, or replication requirements exist across the organization. Figure 2-5 illustrates the regional domain model.

Use the regional domain model when not all domain controllers are connected to the rest of the network through fast connections, network traffic needs to be minimized, the administration of AD DS is decentralized, and security requirements are diverse across the organization.

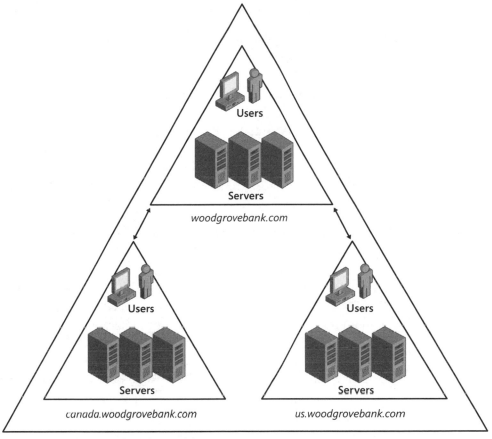

**Figure 2-5**   Regional domain model

---

**MORE INFO**   Domain models

For more information about domain models, go to *http://technet2.microsoft.com/windowsserver2008
/en/library/a9cea3ca-3f39-4f78-81f3-71f9a23cc49e1033.mspx.*

---

## Determining the Number of Domains Required

After you have selected a domain model, determine the number of domains required, which
will vary depending on the domain model you choose. Additionally, the maximum number of
users that a domain can contain will vary depending on the slowest link that must accommodate replication between domain controllers and the amount of network bandwidth you can
allocate to AD DS replication. For example, if all the domain controllers are connected by network links that have a speed of 1,500 kilobits per second (Kbps), and you are able to allocate
five percent of bandwidth to AD DS replication, the domain can contain approximately

100,000 users and maintain efficient replication. However, if you have a domain controller connected with a 64-Kbps link, and you are able to allocate five percent of bandwidth to AD DS replication, the domain can contain approximately only 50,000 users while maintaining efficient replication. If you are unable to accommodate all users in a single domain, use the regional domain model so you can divide your organization into regions in a way that makes sense for your organization and your existing network.

---

**MORE INFO    Determining the number of domains required**

For more information about determining the number of domains required, go to *http:// technet2.microsoft.com/windowsserver2008/en/library/bf0230ae-4f1a-4200-892f -b621278657ec1033.mspx.*

---

## Determining Whether to Upgrade Existing Domains or Deploy New Ones

As part of your domain structure design, determine whether to upgrade existing domains or deploy new domains. AD DS in Windows Server 2008 can be installed as a new domain or by upgrading an existing domain, which is known as an in-place upgrade. If you choose to install a new domain as opposed to using the in-place upgrade path, you must migrate users from the existing domain to the new domain. User account migrations between domains can be a costly and time-consuming task and potentially affect end users.

---

**MORE INFO    Determining whether to upgrade existing domains or deploy new ones**

For more information about determining whether to upgrade existing domain or deploy new domains, go to *http://technet2.microsoft.com/windowsserver2008/en/library /6499cf42-558a-48ce-a16c-edfcbad43d491033.mspx.*

---

You must consider a number of factors when determining whether to upgrade existing domains or deploy new ones. First, you need to determine whether the existing domain model still meets the requirements of your organization. In large organizations, requirements tend to change over time, which is why you need to determine your satisfaction level with the existing domain model. If no major changes are desired of the domain model as part of the upgrade to Windows Server 2008, and the existing domain structure meets the business and technical requirements, the in-place upgrade will provide the easiest migration path. Conversely, if the existing domain structure does not meet the business and migration goals of the organization, the deployment of a new domain is required. By deploying a new domain, you can design and deploy the domain according to the current domain structure requirements and then migrate objects from the old domain into the new domain structure.

Next, determine how much downtime can be incurred when moving to Windows Server 2008 and how much downtime is acceptable in your organization. Review any Service Level Agreements (SLAs) that exist for AD DS in your organization to identify the acceptable downtime and maintenance windows. The in-place upgrade performs an upgrade of the operating system on each domain controller. Although this can be phased, the in-place upgrade does result in downtime. Alternatively, the deployment of a new domain does not require you to take the existing domain or any domain controllers offline, so downtime is minimal. If downtime is a concern, deploy a new domain instead of upgrading an existing domain.

The next key criterion to consider is time constraints. You need to know how much time you have been allocated to upgrade to Windows Server 2008. If the upgrade to Windows Server 2008 needs to occur sooner rather than later, the in-place upgrade is the right path to take. The in-place upgrade takes roughly 60–90 minutes per domain controller. The deployment of new domains and migrating objects to them is time intensive and should be avoided if time constraints exist.

Last, consider budget. Determine the budget you have been allocated to upgrade to Windows Server 2008. If budget is limited, use the in-place upgrade because the costs are typically lower than those with a new domain deployment. Because the existing domain controllers are upgraded, in-place upgrades do not require additional hardware or software. Also, in-place upgrades require less resource time to perform. If budget is not a concern, and you have other factors that will make the deployment of a new domain more beneficial, use the new domain deployment strategy.

## Designing the Forest Root Domain

If you decide to deploy new AD DS domains, you must first design the forest root domain—the first domain you deploy in an AD DS forest. After you deploy the forest root domain, it remains the forest root domain for the life of the AD DS deployment. It is not possible to change the forest root domain, so designing it involves determining whether you need to deploy a dedicated one.

A dedicated forest root domain is an AD DS domain created exclusively to function as the forest root domain. A dedicated forest root domain does not contain any end user accounts and allows the separation of forest-level service administrators from domain-level service administrators. Additionally, a dedicated forest root domain is not usually affected by organizational changes that can result in the restructuring or renaming of domains. However, the use of a dedicated forest root domain introduces additional management overhead.

---

**MORE INFO** Selecting the forest root domain

For more information about selecting the forest root domain, go to *http://technet2.microsoft.com /windowsserver2008/en/library/3e6a25db-b784-4b16-bfe8-d96585de9c201033.mspx*.

---

If you will not use a dedicated forest root domain, you must select a regional domain to function as the forest root domain. That regional domain will be the first domain in the forest to be deployed. Using a regional domain as a forest root domain does not generate the additional management overhead that a dedicated forest root domain does, as Figure 2-6 illustrates.

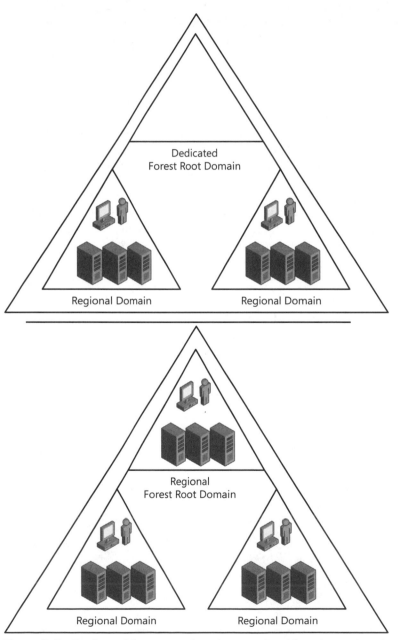

**Figure 2-6**   Dedicated forest root domain vs. regional forest root domain

---

**MORE INFO**   Deploying a Windows Server 2008 forest root domain

For more information about deploying a Windows Server 2008 forest root domain, go to *http://technet2.microsoft.com/windowsserver2008/en/library/92406e8d-dc1c-4740-a00a-2c4032896dd11033.mspx*.

---

Use a dedicated forest root domain to separate the responsibility of forest management and domain management.

## Designing Domain Trees

When the forest root domain is in place, additional domains can be added to the forest in the same domain tree as the forest root domain or in additional domain trees. All domains in the same domain tree will share a contiguous namespace whereas domains that are added through a new domain tree will have a different namespace.

Using the same domain tree or a new domain tree does not provide any difference in functionality. In both cases, each domain within an AD DS forest will share a transitive trust with all other domains, and each domain will share the schema directory partition, configuration directory partition, and global catalog directory partition. The principles for deciding whether to use existing domain trees or additional domain trees are the same as those in planning a Domain Name System (DNS) namespace for AD DS. A domain tree is warranted when one group in the organization has a requirement for a DNS namespace that is not contiguous with the existing DNS namespace AD DS uses. Consider the example of an AD DS forest that has an existing domain with the DNS name of *tailspintoys.com*. If the business unit called Wingtip Toys needs to have its own DNS domain name for AD DS, you would deploy a second domain tree that has a DNS domain name of *wingtiptoys.com*.

# Designing Functional Levels

When you have designed the forest structure and the domain structure, you are ready to design the functional levels, which provide a way to enable domain-wide features or forest-wide AD DS features. Different levels of domain functionality and forest functionality are available, depending on your network environment. Designing functional levels includes designing domain functional levels and then designing forest functional levels.

---

**MORE INFO**   Understanding AD DS functional levels

For more information about AD DS functional levels, go to *http://technet2.microsoft.com/windowsserver2008/en/library/dbf0cdec-d72f-4ba3-bc7a-46410e02abb01033.mspx*.

---

## Designing Domain Functional Levels

Designing functional levels starts with designing domain functional levels. Domain functional levels enable features that affect the entire domain and are dependent on the version of Windows that is installed on the domain controllers in the domain. Therefore, start by identifying the version of Windows that is installed on each domain controller in each domain in the forest. If you have domain controllers in a domain that have Windows 2000 Server installed on them, the highest domain functional level you can set for that domain is Windows 2000 Native. If you have domain controllers in a domain that have Windows Server 2003 installed on them, the highest domain functional level you can set for that domain is Windows Server 2003. If all domain controllers in the domain have Windows Server 2008 installed on them, you can set the domain functional level to Windows Server 2008.

---

**TIP    Determining the operating system installed on existing domain controllers**

In large environments, it is not practical to log on to each domain controller to determine the version of operating system. The *Systeminfo* command in Windows Server 2008 enables you to retrieve operating system information remotely from multiple computers. For more information about the *Systeminfo* command in Windows Server 2008, go to *http://technet2.microsoft.com /windowsserver2008/en/library/39954968-3c2e-4d3e-9d89-c9c43347461e1033.mspx*.

---

Table 2-2 lists the domain functional levels and their corresponding supported domain controllers.

**Table 2-2    Domain Functional Levels and Supported Domain Controllers**

| Domain Functional Level | Domain Controllers Supported |
| --- | --- |
| Windows 2000 Native | Windows 2000 Server<br>Windows Server 2003<br>Windows Server 2008 |
| Windows Server 2003 | Windows Server 2003<br>Windows Server 2008 |
| Windows Server 2008 | Windows Server 2008 |

When designing domain functional levels, determine which advanced AD DS features you need to enable in each domain. If you find that the domain functional level you require cannot be achieved because of domain controllers with earlier versions of Windows, you will have to upgrade those domain controllers or decommission them from the domain. Table 2-3 lists the domain-wide features that are enabled for the Windows Server 2008 domain functional levels.

**Table 2-3  Domain-Wide Features for Domain Functional Levels**

| Domain Functional Level | Enabled Features |
| --- | --- |
| Windows 2000 Native | All default Active Directory features and the following features:<br>■ Universal groups for both distribution groups and security groups<br>■ Group nesting<br>■ Group conversion, which makes conversion possible between security groups and distribution groups<br>■ Security identifier (SID) history |
| Windows Server 2003 | All default Active Directory features, all features from the Windows 2000 Native domain functional level, plus the following features:<br>■ The availability of the domain management tool, *Netdom.exe*, to prepare for a domain controller rename.<br>■ Update of the logon time stamp<br>■ The ability to set the *userPassword* attribute as the effective password on the *inetOrgPerson* object and user objects<br>■ The ability to redirect Users and Computers containers<br>■ Authorization Manager, to store its authorization policies in AD DS<br>■ Constrained delegation<br>■ Support for selective authentication |
| Windows Server 2008 | All default Active Directory features, all features from the Windows Server 2003 domain functional level, plus the following features:<br>■ Distributed File System Replication support for SYSVOL<br>■ Advanced Encryption Services (AES 128 and 256) support for the Kerberos authentication protocol<br>■ Last Interactive Logon Information<br>■ Fine-grained password policies |

**CAUTION  Raising the domain functional level**

When the domain functional level is raised, domain controllers running earlier operating systems cannot be introduced into the domain.

## Designing Forest Functional Levels

After you have designed the domain functional levels, you are ready to design the forest functional levels. Forest functional levels enable features that affect the entire forest and are dependent on the domain functional levels of the domains in the forest. To design forest functional levels, start by identifying the domain functional level for each domain in the forest. If domains in the forest have a domain functional level of Windows 2000 Native, the highest forest functional level that can be set is Windows 2000. If domains in the forest have a domain functional level of Windows Server 2003, the highest forest functional level that can be set is Windows Server 2003. If all domains in the forest have a domain functional level of Windows Server 2008, the forest functional level can be set to Windows Server 2008. Table 2-4 lists the forest functional levels and their corresponding supported domain functional levels.

**Table 2-4    Forest-Wide Features for Forest Functional Levels**

| Forest Functional Level | Domain Functional Levels Supported |
|---|---|
| Windows 2000 | Windows 2000 Native<br>Windows Server 2003<br>Windows Server 2008 |
| Windows Server 2003 | Windows Server 2003<br>Windows Server 2008 |
| Windows Server 2008 | Windows Server 2008 |

When designing forest functional levels, determine which advanced AD DS features you need to enable across the forest. If you find that the forest functional level you require cannot be achieved because of domains with earlier, lower-level domain functional levels, you will have to upgrade the domain functional level for these domains. Table 2-5 lists the forest-wide features that are enabled for the Windows Server 2008 forest functional levels.

**Table 2-5    Forest Functional Levels Features**

| Forest Functional Level | Domain Functional Levels Supported |
|---|---|
| Windows 2000 | All default Active Directory features. |
| Windows Server 2003 | All default Active Directory features, plus the following features:<br>■ Support for forest trusts.<br>■ Support for renaming domains.<br>■ Support for linked-value replication, which enables domain controllers to replicate individual property values for objects instead of the complete object to reduce network bandwidth usage.<br>■ The ability to deploy a read-only domain controller (RODC) that runs Windows Server 2008.<br>■ Improved Knowledge Consistency Checker (KCC) algorithms and scalability.<br>■ The ability to create instances of the dynamic auxiliary class called *dynamicObject* in a domain directory partition.<br>■ The ability to convert an *inetOrgPerson* object instance into a *User* object instance and the reverse.<br>■ The ability to create instances of the new group types, called application basic groups and Lightweight Directory Access Protocol (LDAP) query groups, to support role-based authorization.<br>■ Deactivation and redefinition of attributes and classes in the schema. |

Table 2-5    Forest Functional Levels Features

| Forest Functional Level | Domain Functional Levels Supported |
|---|---|
| Windows Server 2008 | This functional level provides all the features available at the Windows Server 2003 forest functional level but no additional features. |

**CAUTION    Raising the forest functional level**

When the forest functional level is raised, domain controllers running earlier operating systems cannot be introduced into the forest.

# Designing the Schema

After you have designed the forest structure, domain structure, and functional levels, you are ready to design the AD DS schema. Because there is a single schema for the entire forest and schema changes are global, designing the schema requires careful planning and testing and consists of designing a schema modification process, upgrading the schema to support Windows Server 2008, and designing schema attributes and classes.

## Designing a Schema Modification Process

Because schema modifications are global changes that cannot be reversed, designing a schema modification process is imperative when designing the schema. A properly designed schema modification process will aid in mitigating the impact of a problematic schema modification.

To start, scrutinize the requirement for a schema modification. If it is required for an enterprise-wide application such as Exchange Server, then it is usually warranted. However, if it is required for an application that will be used by only a small population of the organization, determine whether you want to deploy a global change to satisfy the needs of those users. As previously mentioned, schema modifications are global, so schema modifications that are required for a non-enterprise-wide product will still require a global change that is not reversible. Additionally, schema modifications that are required for a subset of users in the organization are typically required on a short-term basis, so you must analyze the duration of the requirement. Although schema attributes can be deactivated at a later time, attributes still consume space in the schema partition, which is replicated to all domain controllers in the forest. Whenever possible, aim to limit schema changes to requirements that are enterprise-wide and long-term.

When you have decided to proceed with a proposed schema modification, you are ready to test it, an absolutely critical process that should never be ignored in view of the permanent nature of the change. When testing a schema modification, ensure that the test environment has a schema that is consistent with production. After you have deployed the schema change in your test environment, perform a level of regression testing against AD DS to determine that the schema change was not problematic. When performing regression testing, verify that AD DS is still able to replicate the schema partition to all domain controllers in the test environment. Next, modify the object type or object class that was changed as part of the schema modification. For example, if you created a new attribute and added it to the *User* class, you must modify it on a user object as part of your regression testing. Next, verify that you are still able to modify attributes that existed prior to the schema modification.

When you have thoroughly tested the schema modification in a test environment, you are ready to modify the schema in the production AD DS forest. Even though you tested the schema modification in a test environment, it is still imperative to perform a staged schema modification when deploying the change into production to further mitigate risk. When deploying the schema modification in production, use the following staged process:

- Disable outbound replication on the server that holds the schema master operations master role.
- Implement the schema modification on the server that holds the schema master operations master role.
- Perform a thorough set of regression tests on the server that holds the schema master operations master role.
- Enable outbound replication on the server that holds the schema master operations master role.
- Verify that the schema modification successfully replicated to all domain controllers in the forest.
- Perform a thorough set of regression tests on all domain controllers in the forest.

By following this staged schema modification process, you can minimize the impact of a problematic schema change to the server that holds the schema master operations master role. You do this by disabling outbound replication on this server before implementing the schema change and performing a thorough set of regression tests after implementing the schema change. If the schema change is problematic, you will need to decommission this server because the problematic schema change on the server cannot be reversed. Decommissioning the schema master operations master role holder after a problematic schema change consists of taking this server off the network, seizing the schema master operations master role on another domain controller, and then forcibly deleting the problematic domain controller from AD DS.

## Upgrading the Schema to Support Windows Server 2008

AD DS in Windows Server 2008 introduces a number of changes to the schema. If you are installing a new Windows Server 2008–based AD DS forest, you do not need to prepare the forest for Windows Server 2008. However, if you are installing Windows Server 2008 domain controllers into an existing Windows 2000 Server or Windows Server 2003 forest, you need to perform a number of tasks to prepare it for Windows Server 2008.

Before you can add the first Windows Server 2008 domain controller to an existing Windows 2000 Server or Windows Server 2003 forest, you must prepare the existing forest, introducing a number of schema changes and forest-wide changes by running the *adprep /forestprep* command on the server that holds the schema master operations master role.

After you have prepared the forest for Windows Server 2008, prepare each domain in which you will install Windows Server 20008 domain controllers. Doing so introduces a number of domain-wide changes and consists of running the *adprep /domainprep /gpprep* command on the server in each domain that holds the infrastructure operations master role.

Finally, if you are installing RODCs into an existing Windows Server 2003 forest, you must also prepare the forest for them by modifying the permissions in each domain. You do this by running the *adprep /rodcprep* command on any computer in the forest.

---

**MORE INFO**  **Windows Server 2008 schema changes**

For more information about schema changes in Windows Server 2008, go to *http://technet2.microsoft.com/windowsserver2008/en/library /7120ec57-ad86-4369-af22-773ed9b097fc1033.mspx.*

---

# Designing Trusts to Optimize Intra-Forest Authentication

The final component in forest and domain design consists of designing trusts to optimize intra-forest authentication. In a complex forest with multiple domain trees, intra-forest authentication can take a substantial amount of time because the authentication request must traverse the trust path. Figure 2-7 shows the default trust path in a complex forest.

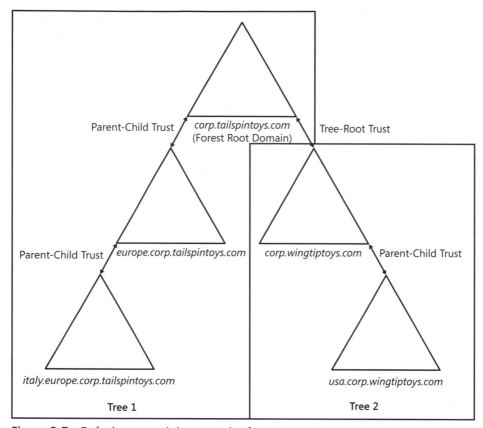

**Figure 2-7**   Default trust path in a complex forest

In this example, when a user in the *usa.corp.wingtiptoys.com* domain needs to access a resource in the *italy.europe.corp.tailspintoys.com* domain, the authentication request must traverse through the following path:

1. *corp.wingtiptoys.com* domain
2. *corp.tailspintoys.com* domain
3. *europe.tailspintoys.com* domain
4. *italy.europe.tailspintoys.com* domain

This amount of time can be reduced significantly through using a shortcut trust. Figure 2-8 shows a shortcut trust in the same forest.

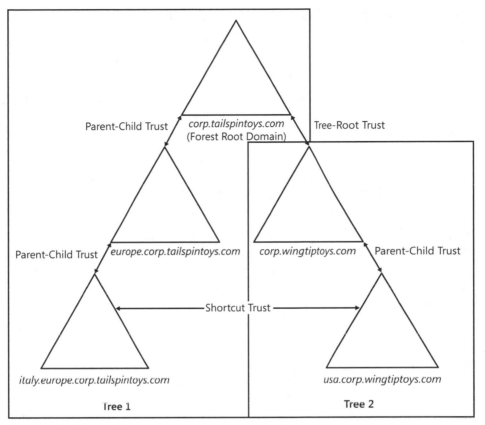

**Figure 2-8**   Shortcut trust

A shortcut trust between the *usa.corp.wingtiptoys.com* domain and the *italy.europe.corp.tailspintoys* *.com* optimizes intra-forest authentication because the authentication request does not have to traverse the default trust path but rather is sent directly between these two domains.

When designing trusts to optimize intra-forest authentication, start by identifying each domain in the forest that has frequent cross-domain resource access requirements. For these domains, deploy a shortcut trust. When deploying the shortcut trust, you can use a one-way trust or a two-way trust. To determine the direction of the trust, you need to understand the resource access requirements in your organization. If bidirectional resource access is required, use a two-way shortcut trust. If unidirectional resource access is required, use a one-way shortcut trust.

---

**MORE INFO   Understanding when to create a shortcut trust**

For more information about when to create a shortcut trust, go to *http://go.microsoft.com/fwlink /?LinkId=107061*.

---

PRACTICE **Designing AD DS Forests and Domains**

You are the enterprise administrator at Contoso, Ltd. Contoso is a large corporation with offices located throughout the United Kingdom. As an enterprise administrator, it is your role to design AD DS for Contoso and its subsidiaries.

Contoso's head office is located in Glasgow, Scotland, and contains 15,000 employees. It has remote offices in England, Wales, and Northern Ireland, each containing approximately 5,000 employees. Each of the remote offices is connected to the head office through the corporate WAN.

All the Windows-based workstations and servers for Contoso and its subsidiaries will use AD DS for authentication and authorization. Contoso has a number of publicly accessible applications that require customer accounts to reside in AD DS for authentication and authorization.

For legal and security reasons, Contoso must separate employee information from customer information. The company has an IT department, located in its head office, that will be responsible for AD DS forest service management and local IT departments situated in each location, which are responsible for the AD DS service management and data management in their respective location.

To comply with Contoso's IT security policies, forest-level service management and domain-level service management must be performed by different teams. Each of Contoso's locations has its own password policy requirements. The amount of bandwidth AD DS replication uses must be minimized. The domain controllers for the NOS directory will be decentralized, but the domain controllers for the Internet directory will be centralized. Contoso plans to implement fine-grained password policies in the future. It also wants to use AES 128 and 256 for the Kerberos authentication protocol for its publicly accessible applications. All AD DS domain controllers will have Windows Server 2008 installed.

Contoso recently acquired a subsidiary named Fabrikam, Inc., whose office is located in Seattle, Washington, and contains 5,000 employees. Fabrikam has diverse requirements for the internal DNS name used for resources in AD DS. Active Directory service management and data management for Fabrikam will be performed by Contoso's IT departments. Fabrikam's employees will frequently access resources located on servers in the Wales remote office. Contoso wants to ensure that the authentication process for Fabrikam users accessing resources in the Wales Contoso remote office is fast.

▶ **Exercise 1   Design the Forest Structure**

In this exercise, you will review the business and technical requirements to design the forest structure for Contoso and its subsidiaries.

1.  What are the relevant forest design requirements for Contoso and its subsidiaries?
    The relevant forest design requirements for Contoso and its subsidiaries are:

- ❑ AD DS will act as the NOS directory and as an Internet directory for Contoso and its subsidiaries.
- ❑ Service management requirements suggest the need for service autonomy. Multiple teams will be managing the AD DS infrastructure, but control for any one team does not need to be exclusive.
- ❑ Data management requirements suggest the need for data autonomy. Multiple teams will be managing the AD DS data, but control for any one team does not need to be exclusive.
- ❑ Data management requirements also suggest the need for data isolation in the case of customer information. Employee information must be separated from customer information.

2. Based on your analysis of the requirements, how many forests are required for Contoso and its subsidiaries?

   Two AD DS forests are required to meet the business and technical requirements. The first forest will be used as the NOS directory for Contoso and its Fabrikam subsidiary. Both companies can reside in the same forest because they have consistent data autonomy and services autonomy requirements; the AD DS data and service will be managed by the same IT departments.

   A second forest is required to serve as Contoso's Internet directory. The Internet directory requires a dedicated forest because of the data isolation requirement; Contoso must separate employee information from customer information.

3. Which forest model(s) will be used in the design?

   The first forest, which will be used as the NOS directory, will use the organizational forest model because user accounts will be stored in this forest and managed separately. There are no limited connectivity or service isolation requirements to suggest the need for a resource forest model.

   The second forest, which will be used as the Internet directory, will use the restricted access forest model because there are data isolation requirements.

### ▶ Exercise 2   Design the Domain Structure

In this exercise, you will review the business and technical requirements to design the domain structure for Contoso and its subsidiaries.

1. What are the relevant domain design requirements for Contoso and its subsidiaries?

   The relevant domain design requirements for Contoso and its subsidiaries are:
   - ❑ The security requirements state that each Contoso location has its own password policy requirements.
   - ❑ The security requirements state that forest-level service management and domain-level service management must be performed by different teams.

- ❏ The business requirements state that the DNS name used for the Fabrikam subsidiary must be different than the DNS name used for the rest of the organization.
- ❏ The technical requirements state that the amount of bandwidth used by AD DS replication must be minimized.
- ❏ The technical requirements state that the domain controllers for the NOS directory forest will be decentralized, but the domain controllers for the Internet directory forest will be centralized.

2. Which domain model will be used for each forest?

   The forest used as the NOS directory will use the regional domain model because users are distributed throughout various remote locations. Additionally, by using the regional domain model for this forest, the amount of bandwidth AD DS replication uses will be minimized in accordance with the technical requirement to do so.

   The forest used as the Internet directory will use the single domain model because all domain controllers will be centralized.

3. What will the forest root domain design be for the NOS directory forest?

   The forest root design for the NOS directory forest will consist of a dedicated forest root domain, which is necessary to meet the security requirement to have forest-level and domain-level service management performed by different teams.

4. Based on your analysis of the requirements, how many domains are required for each forest?

   The forest used as the NOS directory will require six domains. The first domain in this forest will be the dedicated forest root domain. Four additional domains are required for the remote Contoso locations in Scotland, England, Wales, and Northern Ireland because of the security requirement to create separate password policies for each location. Additionally, the Fabrikam subsidiary requires its own domain in this forest because of the business requirement to use a different DNS name for Fabrikam's resources.

   The forest used as the Internet directory will have a single domain to store customer information, and there are no technical or business requirements that suggest the need for multiple domains.

5. How many domain trees will be required for each forest?

   The forest used as the NOS directory will require two domain trees because there are diverse DNS namespace requirements between Contoso and its Fabrikam subsidiary. A separate domain tree is required for the Fabrikam subsidiary to meet its unique DNS namespace requirements.

▶ **Exercise 3   Design the Functional Levels**

In this exercise, you will review the business and technical requirements to design the functional levels for Contoso and its subsidiaries.

1. What are the relevant functional level design requirements for Contoso and its subsidiaries?

   The relevant functional level design requirements for Contoso and its subsidiaries are that:

   ❑ Contoso plans to implement fine-grained password policies in the future.

   ❑ Contoso wants to use AES 128 and 256 for the Kerberos authentication protocol for its publicly accessible applications.

   ❑ All AD DS domain controllers will have Windows Server 2008 installed.

2. What will the domain functional level design be for each forest?

   The domain functional level design for the NOS directory forest will consist of a domain functional level of Windows Server 2008 for each domain so that Contoso can use fine-grained password policies in the future. This functional level is recommended for this forest also because all the domain controllers will have Windows Server 2008 installed.

   The domain functional level design for the Internet directory forest will consist of a domain functional level of Windows Server 2008 so that Contoso can use Advanced AES 128 and 256 for the Kerberos authentication protocol for its publicly accessible applications. This functional level is also recommended for this forest because all the domain controllers will have Windows Server 2008 installed.

3. What will the forest functional level design be for each forest?

   Both forests will have a forest functional level of Windows Server 2008. Although this forest functional level does not provide any additional features over the Windows Server 2003 functional level, it is recommended because all the domains will have a domain functional level of Windows Server 2008.

▶ **Exercise 4    Design Shortcut Trusts**

In this exercise, you will review the business and technical requirements to design the functional levels for Contoso and its subsidiaries.

1. What are the relevant shortcut trust design requirements for Contoso and its subsidiaries?

   The relevant shortcut trust design requirements for Contoso and its subsidiaries are that:

   ❑ Fabrikam's employees will frequently access resources located on servers in the Wales remote office.

   ❑ Authentication should be optimized for Fabrikam's employees accessing resources in the Wales remote office.

2. What will the shortcut trust design be?

   The shortcut trust design will consist of a shortcut trust between the Wales Contoso domain and the Fabrikam domain. This is required to optimize authentication between Fabrikam users and resources in the Wales Contoso domain.

# Lesson Summary

- Gathering forest design requirements consists of identifying the role of AD DS in your organization, gathering business, technical, security, network, autonomy, and isolation requirements.

- You can choose the organizational forest model, resource forest model, or the restricted access forest model when designing forests.

- You can choose either the single domain model or the regional domain model when designing the domains within a forest.

- A dedicated forest root domain enables the separation of forest-level service administrators from domain-level service administrators.

- Domain functional levels enable features that affect the entire domain, and forest functional levels enable features that affect the entire forest.

- Before you can add the first Windows Server 2008 domain controller to an existing Windows 2000 or Windows Server 2003 forest, you must prepare the existing forest by using the *adprep* command. If you are installing RODCs into an existing Windows 2000 Server or Windows Server 2003 forest, you must also prepare the forest for RODCs.

- You can use shortcut trusts to optimize intra-forest authentication.

# Lesson Review

You can use the following questions to test your knowledge of the information in Lesson 1, "Designing AD DS Forests and Domains." The questions are also available on the companion CD if you prefer to review them in electronic form.

---

**NOTE** Answers

Answers to these questions and explanations of why each answer choice is correct or incorrect are located in the "Answers" section at the end of the book.

---

1. How can you achieve data autonomy when designing the forest structure?
   A. Create a new forest, using the resource forest model.
   B. Join an existing forest.
   C. Create a new forest, using the organizational forest model.
   D. Create a new forest, using the restricted access forest model.

2. How can you achieve service autonomy when designing the forest structure?
   A. Create a new forest, using the restricted access forest model.
   B. Create a new forest, using the resource forest model.
   C. Create a new forest, using the organizational forest model.
   D. Join an existing forest.

3. You are examining an existing AD DS environment to determine whether to upgrade the existing domains or deploy new domains. What factors must you consider? (Choose all that apply.)

   A. Existing domain model

   B. The amount of downtime that can be incurred

   C. Time constraints

   D. Budget

4. You are in the process of deploying an attribute into your production AD DS forest. The new attribute will be added to the user class. You have successfully tested the schema extension in your lab environment. What should you do prior to installing the schema extension into production to minimize the impact of a problematic schema change?

   A. Disable outbound replication on the server that holds the schema master operations master role.

   B. Disable inbound replication on the server that holds the schema master operations master role.

   C. Deactivate the user class.

   D. Restart the computer that holds the schema master operations master role into Directory Services Restore Mode.

5. You have an existing AD DS forest that has a domain functional level of Windows Server 2003 and a forest functional level of Windows 2000. You have deployed a number of writable Windows Server 2008 domain controllers into this forest. The forest now has a mixture of Windows Server 2003 and Windows Server 2008 domain controllers. You need to deploy an RODC into this forest. What should you do?

   A. Raise the forest functional level to Windows Server 2008.

   B. Raise the forest functional level to Windows Server 2003.

   C. Run the *adprep /forestprep* command.

   D. Run the *adprep /domainprep /gpprep* command.

# Lesson 2:  Designing the AD DS Physical Topology

Now that you have designed the forest and domain structure in Lesson 1, you are ready to complete the AD DS design by designing the physical topology, which is required so AD DS can replicate the directory data to domain controllers in the various locations on your network. Also, it is the physical topology that defines how clients are directed to the appropriate domain controller for authentication and that enables clients to search for printers based on location information.

The design of the physical topology starts with designing the site structure, which represents the physical structure of your network and that AD DS uses to build the most efficient replication topology. Designing the site structure consists of selecting a site model based on the relevant site design requirements. After you have designed the site structure, you must design replication to control how the directory data is replicated between the various domain controllers on your network. Designing replication involves designing the replication topology as well as site links, site link properties, and site link bridging. Next, you must design the placement of domain controllers, specifically, forest root domain controllers, regional domain controllers, read-only domain controllers, global catalog servers, and operations master role holders. Last, you must design printer location policies so that users can search for printers based on location information stored in AD DS.

This lesson will provide you with the knowledge to gather relevant business and technical requirements and then design the AD DS physical topology in Windows Server 2008.

> **After this lesson, you will be able to:**
> - Gather site design requirements.
> - Design the site model.
> - Select a replication topology.
> - Design site links and site link properties.
> - Design site link bridging.
> - Design the placement of forest root domain controllers, regional domain controllers, RODCs, global catalog servers, and operations master role holders.
> - Design a location schema for printer location policies.
>
> **Estimated lesson time:  35 minutes**

## Real World

*John Policelli*

I recently spearheaded a site and replication redesign initiative, which emphasized the importance of reevaluating networking information and location data on an ongoing basis as part of an AD DS physical topology design.

When our client, a large financial institution with a global presence, first deployed Active Directory seven years ago, a requirement forced it to disable the Intersite Topology Generator (ISTG) on all sites. Effectively, all intersite replication connections had to be created manually. As you would expect, the network topology and location data had changed drastically from the time when the original replication design was created. However, because the client did not experience any issues with replication, it never reevaluated these requirements or its AD DS physical topology design.

We were faced with a major initiative to replace 25 percent of our client's former domain controllers with new domain controllers that would be located in a new data center. To make this even more complex, this was being driven by a time-sensitive data center consolidation project, which would result in a significant change to the physical topology design.

I made a conscious decision to reevaluate our client's network topology, location data, and requirements as part of the site and replication redesign initiative I was leading. As a result, I was able to validate that ISTG could be re-enabled. Given the benefits of ISTG in a large environment, we decided to re-enable the ISTG on all sites as part of our AD DS site and replication redesign. We saved a significant amount of time introducing the new domain controllers and decommissioning the earlier domain controllers during the data center consolidation project. Furthermore, the decision to re-enable the ISTG on all sites improved the client's disaster recovery readiness. All this was exactly what I expected, knowing the benefits of ISTG. However, what surprised me the most was the fact that the forest convergence time, or the time it takes for a change to the AD DS database to reach all domain controllers in the forest, was reduced by almost 40 percent as a result of re-enabling the ISTG on all sites. Effectively, changes to the database were being replicated faster and more efficiently.

As you will see in this lesson, one of the most important tasks when designing the AD DS physical topology is collecting network information and location data. However, as was true in the site and replication redesign initiative that I led, this is not only required during the initial design phase but rather is something you need to do on an ongoing basis to ensure that your physical topology meets the constantly changing needs of your organization.

# Designing the Site Structure

Designing the AD DS physical topology begins with designing the site structure, which is the foundation for the physical topology AD DS uses. Designing the site structure consists of gathering site design requirements, designing the site model, and designing site settings.

---

**MORE INFO**    **Designing the site topology for Windows Server 2008 AD DS**

For more information about designing the site topology for Windows Server 2008 AD DS, go to *http://go.microsoft.com/fwlink/?LinkId=89026.*

---

## Gathering Site Design Requirements

To begin the site structure design, you need to gather the existing network information. Because sites in AD DS represent the physical structure of your network, AD DS uses network topology information to build the most efficient replication topology. Domain controllers are placed into sites according to where the domain data is needed, and sites are used for replication, authentication, and service location.

Start by creating a location map that represents the physical network infrastructure of your organization. Most large organizations have a network group you will need to consult with to obtain the necessary information. On the location map, identify the geographic locations that contain groups of computers and users. For each location, gather the relevant network information, including the type of communication link, the link speed, and the available bandwidth between locations. Figure 2-9 shows a sample location map.

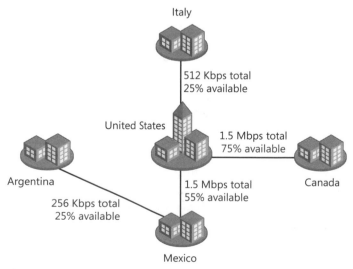

**Figure 2-9**    Sample location map

When you have collected the relevant network information, collect location data as part of your site design. Location data is required to determine the placement of domain controllers. Begin by gathering the IP subnets in each location; the AD DS authentication process uses IP subnets to direct clients to the closest domain controller. If you do not know the subnet mask and network address within each location, consult your networking group. Next, for each location, detail the number of users for each domain, the number of workstations, and the number of servers. Table 2-6 is a sample table you can use to document the relevant network information and location data for each region.

**Table 2-6   Sample Network Information and Location Data Gathering Table**

| Name of Region | Total Bandwidth | Available Bandwidth | Network Segments | Number of Users | Domains |
|---|---|---|---|---|---|
|  |  |  |  |  |  |
|  |  |  |  |  |  |
|  |  |  |  |  |  |

The location map you create and the location data you collect are required to identify the site model that best matches the physical topology of your network and to design the site structure. By collecting this information, you will be able to determine which physical locations need a dedicated site object as well as the physical locations that can be combined into a single site object. Additionally, you'll use this information to design the placement of domain controllers and global catalog servers.

**MORE INFO   Collecting network information**

For more information about collecting network information, go to *http://technet2.microsoft.com/ windowsserver2008/en/library/7aa1f2f8-3cd1-4a74-8991-1a063fda5ad11033.mspx.*

## Designing the Site Model

When you have obtained or created a location map and collected the location data, you are ready to design the site model AD DS replication will use. The two available site models are:

- **Single site model**   The single site model consists of a single site object. In this model, all domains in the forest belong to the same site object, and all IP subnets are associated with this site object. In the single site model, all authentication requests are directed to domain controllers in the same site. Additionally, all replication occurs through intrasite replication.

   The goal of the single site model is to reduce AD DS replication latency by ensuring that all domain controllers in the site are updated as quickly as possible. Through intrasite replication, replication occurs more or less immediately after a change has been made, replication traffic is not compressed, the replication process is initiated by a notification from the sending domain controller, replication traffic is sent to several replication partners during each replication cycle, and replication traffic within a single site requires virtually no customization. Use the single site model when all domain controllers are interconnected through fast network connections and there is ample available bandwidth.

- **Multiple sites model**  The multiple sites model consists of domain controllers distributed between two or more site objects. IP subnets are associated with sites based on network information and location data. As a result, authentication requests are directed to domain controllers in the site closest to the authenticating client. Replication between domain controllers in the same site occurs through intrasite replication, but replication between domain controllers in different sites occurs through intersite replication.

  The goal of the multiple sites model is to reduce the amount of bandwidth used for AD DS replication. Through intersite replication, replication is initiated according to a schedule, replication traffic is compressed, the replication schedule determines when domain controllers will replicate, replication can use either IP or Simple Mail Transfer Protocol (SMTP) transport, and replication traffic is sent through bridgehead servers rather than to multiple replication partners. However, the multiple sites model requires more configuration than the single site model. Use the multiple sites model when the physical network topology on your network includes locations that are not connected through fast connections, and bandwidth consumption is a concern.

---

**NOTE**   How does automatic site coverage work?

There can be cases in which sites do not contain domain controllers for each domain in the forest. The clients in these sites still need to locate a domain controller for their domain for authentication. Through automatic site coverage, Windows Server 2008 registers DNS service location (SRV) resource records to ensure that clients can locate a domain controller in the nearest available site. These resource records map to the sites that contain no domain controller for the domain of which they are a member. Automatic site coverage uses an algorithm that factors in the cost associated with the site links of a site that does not contain a domain controller. As a result, the appropriate domain controller registers its SRV resource records for that site.

---

Now that you have an understanding of the available site models, you must determine which model best meets the requirements of your AD DS physical topology. To map the appropriate site model to the site design requirements you gathered earlier, you need to examine each location independently. Start by reviewing the number of users in the location. Assess whether this number warrants the costs and administrative effort of a domain controller.

Next, review the business continuity requirements for each location. If the location needs to continue to operate if the WAN link is down, then deploying a dedicated site object for that location is a necessity. Users in a location that is not represented by a dedicated site object and does not have a local domain controller must cross the WAN when authenticating to AD DS.

You must also identify and incorporate site-aware applications when designing the site model. Site-aware application, such as Exchange Server and DFS, publish service information in the Sites container in AD DS so that clients can locate the services provided by these applications more efficiently. Then, determine where the servers hosting these site-aware applications will be physically located. You will need to create a dedicated site object for each location that will include servers hosting site-aware applications.

A site object should be created for each location that has 100 or more users so that users in such locations can continue to authenticate even if the WAN link is unavailable. A site object is also required for each location that will contain one or more domain controllers and for each location that will have site-aware applications installed locally. Last, if a site is not required for a location, ensure that you add the subnet of the location to a site for which the location has the maximum WAN speed and available bandwidth.

# Designing Replication

After you have designed the site structure, design replication so that data is synchronized between the domain controllers in the forest and domains. Designing replication includes designing the replication topology, designing site links, designing site link properties, and designing site link bridging.

## Designing the Replication Topology

The first step to designing replication is designing the replication topology, which defines the logical connections that AD DS replication uses to replicate among domain controllers. To minimize the network bandwidth required for replication, identify where bandwidth is highest and lowest on the network and model the replication topology after the physical topology of the network. There are three AD DS replication topologies:

- **Hub and spoke**  In the hub and spoke replication topology, one site is designated as the hub, and other sites, called spokes, connect to the hub. In this topology, AD DS replicates from the hub servers to the spoke servers and vice versa, but replication does not occur directly between two spoke servers. When you choose this topology, you must decide which site will act as the hub. If you want to set up multiple hubs, use a hybrid topology. Figure 2-10 shows an example of the hub and spoke replication topology.

  Use the hub and spoke replication topology for WANs that consist of faster network connections between major computing hubs and slower links connecting branch offices.

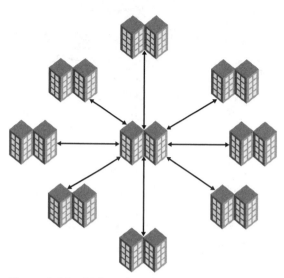

**Figure 2-10**    Hub and spoke replication topology

■ **Full mesh**    In a full mesh replication topology, every site connects to every other site. An AD DS change on a domain controller in one site replicates directly to all other domain controllers in all other sites. Figure 2-11 shows an example of the full mesh replication topology.

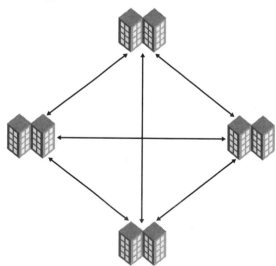

**Figure 2-11**    Full mesh replication topology

Because each site connects to every other site, the propagation of change orders for replicating AD DS can impose a heavy burden on the network. To reduce unnecessary traffic, use a different topology or delete connections you do not actually need.

■ **Hybrid**  The hybrid replication topology is a combination of a hub and spoke and a full mesh. One example of a hybrid topology is a redundant hub and spoke topology. In this configuration, a hub site might contain two domain controllers that are connected by a high-speed link. Each of these two hub servers might connect with four branch domain controllers in a hub and spoke arrangement. Figure 2-12 shows an example of the hybrid replication topology.

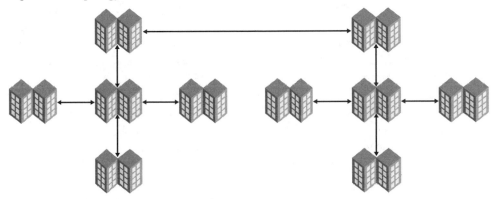

**Figure 2-12**  Hybrid Replication Topology

Use the hybrid replication topology to provide redundancy for a hub and spoke topology. By using the hybrid replication topology instead of only the hub and spoke replication topology, the single point of failure (the hub) is eliminated.

## Designing Site Links

After you have designed the site model and the replication topology, design site links. Site links connect the sites to form the desired replication topology. Without site links, intersite replication cannot occur, which means domain controllers in different sites will not be able to replicate with one another.

To design site links, identify the sites you need to connect and create a site link for each connection. For example, if you identify the need to connect a site named Seattle and a site named Redmond, create a site link called Seattle-Redmond and associate the Seattle and Redmond sites with this site link. Next, ensure that the sites are not members of any other site links. When sites are created, they are usually added to the Default-First-Site-Link by default. When you associate the site with another site link, remember to change the original site link membership of the site. Ensuring site link membership accuracy is important because the KCC will make routing decisions based on the membership of both site links, which might result in incorrect routing.

---

**MORE INFO**   Creating a site link design

For more information about creating a site link design, go to *http://technet2.microsoft.com/ windowsserver2008/en/library/d35bcae0-fe46-4f6f-8cf2-df09e58965461033.mspx.*

---

When designing site links, you need to design the transport the site link uses. The Inter-Site Transports container provides the means for mapping site links to that transport. When you create a site link object, you create it in either the IP container, which associates the site link with the remote procedure call (RPC) over IP transport, or the SMTP container, which associates the site link with the SMTP transport. When you create a site link object in the respective Inter-Site Transports container, AD DS uses RPC over IP to transfer both intersite and intrasite replication between domain controllers. To keep data secure while in transit, RPC over IP replication uses both the Kerberos authentication protocol and data encryption. When a direct IP connection is not available, you can configure replication between sites to use SMTP. However, SMTP replication functionality is limited and requires an enterprise certification authority (CA). SMTP can replicate only the configuration, schema, and application directory partitions and does not support the replication of domain directory partitions. Use RPC over IP for site links if at all possible. Use SMTP when a direct IP connection is not available. Avoid using SMTP if possible; use it only as an interim solution because SMTP replication will not be supported in future versions of AD DS, and SMTP replication has many limitations, as previously mentioned.

## Designing Site Link Properties

After you have designed site links, design site link properties by determining the cost, the schedule, and the replication interval.

Designing site link properties starts with determining the cost for each site link. Determining the cost associated with that replication path is required because the KCC uses cost to determine the least expensive route for replication between two sites that replicate the same directory partition. To start, refer back to the network map and location data you collected earlier. For each network connection in each location, determine the available bandwidth. Assign the lowest cost to the highest available bandwidth. For example, assign a cost of 283 when the available bandwidth is 4,096 Kbps and assign a cost of 1,042 when the available bandwidth is 9.6 Kbps.

---

**MORE INFO**   Determining the cost

For more information about determining the cost, go to *http://technet2.microsoft.com /WindowsServer2008/en/library/56650a8d-8f76-4f6c-a30d-669b14a18a2f1033.mspx.*

---

When you have determined the cost of each site link, determine the schedule so you can control site link availability. To design the site link schedule, create two overlapping schedules between site links that contain domain controllers that directly replicate with each other. Use the default (100 percent available) schedule on those links unless you want to block replication traffic during peak hours. By blocking replication, you give priority to other traffic, but you also increase replication latency.

---

**MORE INFO**  **Determining the schedule**

For more information about determining the schedule, go to *http://technet2.microsoft.com /windowsserver2008/en/library/afeaea89-8ca0-43ed-bd44-4c822d6535081033.mspx.*

---

After you have determined the schedule, determine the interval to indicate how frequently you want replication to occur during the times when the schedule allows replication. Consider the example of a schedule that allows replication between the hours of midnight and 7:00 A.M. with the replication interval set to 60 minutes. In this example, replication can occur up to seven times. When determining the schedule, remember that a small interval decreases latency but increases the amount of WAN traffic. Conversely, a large interval increases latency but decreases WAN traffic. If you need to keep domain partitions up to date, you can minimize latency by setting a shorter interval, such as 15 minutes. If you need to decrease WAN traffic, increase latency by setting a larger interval, such as 360 minutes.

---

**MORE INFO**  **Determining the interval**

For more information about determining the interval, go to *http://technet2.microsoft.com /windowsserver2008/en/library/988f01e8-ba59-4b34-8b71-60e0fa0746741033.mspx.*

---

## Designing Site Link Bridging

The final component in designing replication is designing site link bridging. A site link bridge connects two or more site links and enables transitivity between site links. Each site link in a bridge must have a site in common with another site link in the bridge. Site link transitivity enables the KCC to re-route replication when necessary. When site links are bridged, the cost of replication from a domain controller at one end of the bridge to a domain controller at the other end is the sum of the costs on each of the intervening site links. Site link transitivity is enabled by default and should remain enabled unless the IP network contains segments that are not fully routed or if you need to control the replication flow of the changes made in AD DS.

If your IP network is composed of IP segments that are not fully routed, you can disable the Bridge All Site Links option for the IP transport. In this case, all IP site links are considered nontransitive, and you can create and configure site link bridge objects to model the actual routing behavior of your network. A site link bridge has the effect of providing routing for a disjointed network. When you add site links to a site link bridge, all site links within the bridge can route transitively. Each site link in a manual site link bridge must have at least one site in common with another site link in the bridge. Otherwise, the bridge cannot compute the cost from sites in one link to the sites in other links of the bridge. If bridgehead servers that are capable of the transport used by the site link bridge are not available in two linked sites, a route is not available.

---

**MORE INFO**    **Creating a site link bridge design**

For more information about creating a site link bridge design, go to *http://technet2.microsoft.com* */windowsserver2008/en/library/455a4a18-5c97-4559-ac5a-b0109abd647b1033.mspx.*

---

## Designing the Placement of Domain Controllers

After you have designed the site structure and replication, design the placement of domain controllers, including forest root domain controllers, regional domain controllers, RODCs, global catalog servers, and operations master role holders.

---

### Real World

*John Policelli*

I have spent a great deal of my career both identifying and mitigating AD DS security risks. Through my many AD DS security assessments, I saw a common theme that was independent of the size of the AD DS deployment, the type of organization, or the administrative model used. For business and technical reasons, a significant number of organizations have had to deploy domain controllers in locations where physical security cannot be guaranteed. In these cases, the entire AD DS forest was at risk. Prior to Windows Server 2008, organizations have had very few options to mitigate this risk adequately.

RODCs in Windows Server 2008 now provide organizations with an adequate means to mitigate the security risk associated with placing domain controllers in locations where physical security cannot be guaranteed. The introduction of the RODC is one of the most important new features relating to the AD DS physical topology in Windows Server 2008. Prior to Windows Server 2008, if users in a branch office could not authenticate over the WAN, a writable domain controller was required in the branch office. This has always presented a significant risk because physical security in branch offices is usually nonexistent. As with most software, if an attacker gains physical access to a domain controller, he or she can compromise the domain controller. Additionally, if an attacker gains access to a writable domain controller, the security of the entire forest is in jeopardy.

As an enterprise administrator, it is inevitable that you will design the placement of new domain controllers. However, you should also use the guidelines in this section to reevaluate the existing physical topology design in your organization.

---

## Designing the Placement of Forest Root Domain Controllers

When designing the placement of domain controllers, you must start with the forest root domain controllers. They are the first domain controllers you deploy because the forest root domain is the first domain you add to the forest. The primary role of forest root domain controllers is to create trust paths for clients that need to access resources in domains other than their own. Regardless of whether you choose to deploy a dedicated forest root domain or to use a regional domain as the forest root domain, the placement of forest root domain controllers is imperative for end-user authentication.

Start by placing forest root domain controllers in hub locations and at data center locations. Next, examine the intra-organizational authentication requirements for your organization. If users in a remote location need to access resources from other domains, they need to contact the forest root domain controllers. Because you began by placing the forest root domain controllers in the hub and data center locations, these users will have to cross the WAN for this intra-organizational authentication. At this point, you need to determine whether the reliability of the WAN link between the remote location and the hub and data center locations is sufficient. If reliability is sufficient, and the WAN links are fast, you do not need to deploy additional forest root domain controllers. However, if reliability issues exist, you can either deploy a forest root domain controller in the remote location or use a shortcut trust. By deploying a forest root domain controller in the remote location, users will not have to cross the WAN for intra-organizational authentication, and the authentication time will be optimized. However, deploying forest root domain controllers in remote locations will introduce additional hardware, software, and administrative costs. Additionally, deploying forest root domain controllers in remote locations can introduce unwanted security risks. As an alternative, you can use a shortcut trust to optimize the intra-organizational authentication.

Designing shortcut trusts was discussed in the "Designing Trusts to Optimize Intra-Forest Authentication" section in Lesson 1 of this chapter.

## Designing the Placement of Regional Domain Controllers

Now that you have designed the placement of forest root domain controllers, you need to design the placement of regional domain controllers, which is applicable only if you are using the regional domain model. The single domain model does not require regional domain controllers. To minimize hardware and software costs, plan to deploy as few regional domain controllers as possible. Because every AD DS site needs to have a domain controller, the placement of regional domain controllers is heavily dependent on the site design and replication topology.

Start by placing regional domain controllers in every location that has an associated site object. If there are locations that contain users from multiple domains, place a regional domain controller for each domain in that location. During the authentication process, users will try to authenticate against a domain controller in the domain they belong to in their local site. Finally, examine the organization's business continuity requirements. If they state that users should not cross the WAN in the event of a domain controller failure, place multiple domain controllers for each domain that users in the location belong to.

## Designing the Placement of RODCs

The placement of RODCs is also imperative when designing the placement of domain controllers. An RODC makes it possible for organizations to deploy a domain controller easily in scenarios in which physical security cannot be guaranteed. An RODC helps with the lack of physical security that is a common concern for domain controllers in the branch offices. An RODC must replicate domain data from a domain controller running Windows Server 2008. Consequently, replication is among the most important considerations for determining where to place RODCs. Start by identifying the locations where physical security cannot be guaranteed, such as branch offices. Review network information and location data you previously collected for these locations. The locations that are not connected to the rest of the network through fast links or have bandwidth limitations will benefit from a local domain controller. Because the physical security cannot be guaranteed in these locations, deploy an RODC as opposed to a writable domain controller. Next, for each location that will have an RODC, you need to ensure that a writable domain controller running Windows Server 2008 is in an adjacent site. Each RODC requires a writable domain controller running Windows Server 2008 for the same domain from which the RODC can directly replicate. Typically, this requires that a writable domain controller running Windows Server 2008 be placed in the nearest site in the topology, defined as the site that has the lowest-cost site link for the site that includes the RODC.

## Designing the Placement of Global Catalog Servers

Next, design the placement of global catalog servers. The design of global catalog server placement is applicable only if the domain model you have selected is a single domain model. Because every domain controller stores the only domain directory partition in the forest, configuring each domain controller as a global catalog server does not require any additional disk space usage, CPU usage, or replication traffic. In a multiple domain model, the design of global catalog server placement must incorporate the application requirements, number of users, available bandwidth, and universal group membership caching for each site.

Start by reviewing network information and location data you previously collected to identify locations that are connected to the rest of the network through fast networks and have ample bandwidth available. These locations do not require a local global catalog server because users can access a global catalog server over the WAN link. Next, determine whether any applications need a local global catalog server. Certain applications, such as Exchange Server, Message Queuing, and applications using DCOM need a global catalog infrastructure to provide low query latency. Deploy a global catalog server in each location containing applications that need a local global catalog server. Next, review the location data to determine the number of users in each location. When the number of users exceeds 100, communication to global catalog servers is substantial, so deploy a global catalog server in each such location. Last, consider universal group membership caching to eliminate the need for a local global catalog server. For locations that include fewer than 100 users and that do not include a large number of roaming users or applications that require a global catalog server, you can deploy domain controllers that are running Windows Server 2008 and enable universal group membership caching.

---

**MORE INFO**  How universal group caching works

For more information about how universal group caching works, go to *http://go.microsoft.com /fwlink/?LinkId=107063*.

---

## Designing the Placement of Operations Master Role Holders

To complete the placement of domain controllers design, you need to design the placement of operations master role holders. The most important operations master for day-to-day operations is the primary domain controller (PDC) emulator. The PDC emulator receives priority updates for user password changes. Therefore, the PDC emulator should be placed in a central location where the maximum number of clients can connect to the server. The placement of the other operations masters is not as crucial as the PDC emulator; however, you must still properly design the placement of these role holders.

The schema master, domain naming master, and relative identifier (RID) master should be located in a site where another domain controller is a direct replication partner. This will provide adequate disaster recovery. If one of these servers fails, you might have to seize the operations master role on another domain controller. Ideally, you would like to seize the role on another domain controller that is fully replicated with the original operations master. This is more likely to be the case if the two domain controllers are in the same site and are configured as directory replication partners. The RID master must be accessible to all domain controllers through an RPC connection. When a domain controller requires more RIDs, it will use an RPC connection to request them from the RID master.

The placement of the infrastructure master role is dependent on the number of domains in the forest and the forest model and whether all domain controllers are global catalog servers. As a general rule, the infrastructure master should be located on a nonglobal catalog server that has a direct connection object to some global catalog in the forest, preferably in the same site. The role of the infrastructure master is to update user display name references between domains. Because the global catalog server holds a partial replica of every object in the forest, the infrastructure master, if placed on a global catalog server, will never update anything because it does not contain any references to objects that it does not hold. There are two exceptions to this general rule:

- **Single domain forest**   In a forest that contains a single AD DS domain, there are no phantoms, so the infrastructure master has no work to do. The infrastructure master can be placed on any domain controller in the domain, regardless of whether that domain controller hosts the global catalog.
- **Multiple domain forest where every domain controller in a domain holds the global catalog**   If every domain controller in a domain that is part of a multiple domain forest also hosts the global catalog, there are no phantoms or work for the infrastructure master to do. The infrastructure master can be put on any domain controller in that domain.

---

## The Infrastructure Master Role and Global Catalog Servers

Recommendations regarding the placement of the infrastructure master role have been confusing and contradictory since the introduction of Active Directory in Windows 2000 Server. Most of the confusion stems from ambiguous wording. In some documentation, you will read that the infrastructure master can never be placed on a server that hosts the global catalog. In other documentation, you will read that the infrastructure master role can be placed on a global catalog server provided that all domain controllers in the domain are global catalog servers. To an extent, both camps are not entirely accurate.

The infrastructure master role is a domain-level operations master role. Its role is to compare objects of the local domain against objects in other domains in the same forest. The global catalog server holds a partial copy of every object in the forest. If the server holding the infrastructure master role is also a global catalog server, it will never see any differences. As a result, the infrastructure master will not make any changes in its local domain. Alternatively, if every domain controller in the domain is also a global catalog server, there is nothing for the infrastructure master to do, given that the global catalog already knows about the objects in the other domains.

In a single domain AD DS forest model, there is no need for the infrastructure master to pull updates from other domains. In that case, the infrastructure master can reside on a global catalog server.

In a multiple domain forest that has all domain controllers configured as global catalog servers, there is no need for the infrastructure master to pull updates from other domains because, as a global catalog server, it knows about all objects already. Therefore, the infrastructure master role can reside on a global catalog server.

# Designing Printer Location Policies

After you have designed the placement of domain controllers, the final design for the physical topology involves designing printer location policies. Printers can be published in AD DS so that clients can locate printers based on their name, location, and other criteria. Designing printer location policies consists of creating a location schema, associating locations with subnets in AD DS, and enabling physical location tracking.

Designing printer location policies starts with creating a location schema, which enables users across the organization to search for location. Location information for large organizations can change frequently, so you must ensure that the design for the location schema is flexible enough to describe all locations printers can be placed and facilitates future changes in your organization. Because end users use location names, it is important to select simple and recognizable names as part of the location schema. Use the following guidelines when selecting names for the location schema:

- Use the name/name/name/name/... form for location names. (The slash (/) must be the dividing character.)
- Use any characters except for the slash (/).
- Avoid using special characters in the name.
- Keep names to a maximum of 32 characters to ensure visibility of the whole name in the user interface.
- Remember that the number of levels to a name is limited to 256.
- Remember that the maximum length of an entire location name is 260 characters.

Now that you have an understanding of the role of the location schema and the guidelines to follow when creating the location schema, you are ready to create a location schema. To start, examine the network map and location data you collected earlier for your organization to determine the top-level geographic locations. Use static locations for the top-level geographic locations in your location schema, such as continents or countries. Next, use static locations for the second level geographic locations, such as countries, states, or provinces. Next, for the third level geographic locations, use fairly static locations, such as cities or buildings. Last, identify as many more levels as are required according to the geographical boundaries of your organization. For levels four and beyond, use locations, divisions, and departments, all of which can change more frequently than the previous levels.

To understand fully how to create the location schema, consider the following example, shown in Table 2-7, of an organization that has a worldwide presence. The organization operates in a number of countries throughout North America, South America, and Europe. The organization has multiple offices in some countries and multiple offices in some states throughout the United States. In some offices, the organization occupies multiple floors.

**Table 2-7  Sample Network Information and Location Data-Gathering Table**

| Top Level | Second Level | Third Level | Fourth Level | Fifth Level | Sixth Level |
|-----------|--------------|-------------|--------------|-------------|-------------|
| North America | United States | Washington | Redmond | Building 40 | Floor 1 |
| North America | United States | Washington | Redmond | Building 40 | Floor 2 |
| North America | United States | New York | New York | Finance | |
| North America | United States | New York | New York | Marketing | |
| North America | Canada | Ontario | Ottawa | | |
| North America | Canada | Ontario | Toronto | Bloor Street | |
| North America | Canada | Ontario | Toronto | Bay Street | |
| South America | Argentina | Mendoza | Mendoza | | |
| South America | Chile | Santiago | Santiago | | |
| Europe | Italy | Lazio | Rome | Development | |
| Europe | Italy | Lazio | Rome | HR | |
| Europe | Spain | Madrid | Madrid | | |

- Continent names are used for the top-level locations.
- Country names are used for the second-level locations.
- State and province names are used for the third-level locations.
- City names are used for the fourth-level locations.
- Department names are used for the fifth-level locations when more than one department exists in a location.
- Building names are also used for the fifth-level locations when more than one building exists in a given city.
- Floor names are used for the sixth-level locations when more than one floor exists in a building.

This location schema provides the organization with the flexibility to add locations to the schema in the future. Additionally, users can perform searches based on broad location details such as continent, country, state/province, or city, and they can perform searches based on granular location details, such as department or floor. Also, the tree varies in depth depending on the location. For example, the full name of Floor 1 in Redmond is North America/United States/Washington/Redmond/Building 40/Floor 1 whereas the full name of the HR building in Rome is Europe/Italy/Lazio/Rome/HR.

Now that you have created the location schema, you must associate locations with subnets in AD DS. By setting location information about subnets, AD DS automatically associates a printer to a location based on the subnet on which the printer is located. Figure 2-13 shows the location information for a subnet in AD DS.

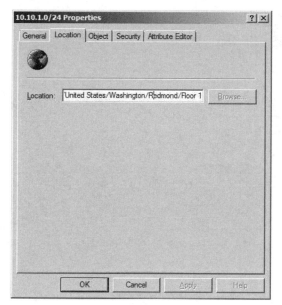

**Figure 2-13**   Subnet location information

Ensure that you define a location on all subnets in AD DS so that users can search printers based on the location information.

The last step in designing printer location policies consists of enabling physical location tracking. Physical location tracking is a feature that was introduced in Windows 2000 Server; it enables users to browse for printers based on the location schema. Because physical location tracking is not enabled by default, you must enable it through Group Policy. Then, a Browse button appears beside the Location field in the Find Printers dialog box. When designing printer location policies, you must decide the Group Policy level in which physical location tracking will be enabled. Because printers are usually installed at the computer level as opposed to the user level, physical location tracking is a Group Policy setting that is definable under the Computer Configuration settings, as shown in Figure 2-14.

Designing an enterprise Group Policy strategy is discussed in Chapter 4, "Designing Active Directory Administration and Group Policy Strategy."

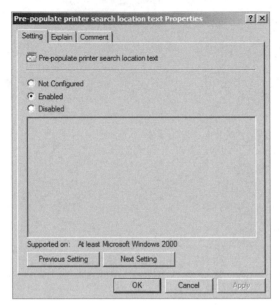

**Figure 2-14**   Subnet location information

PRACTICE **Designing the Active Directory Domain Services Physical Topology**

You are an enterprise administrator at Blue Yonder Airlines. Blue Yonder Airlines is a large multinational corporation with office locations located in five countries. It is currently running Windows Server 2003 but is beginning to implement Windows Server 2008. As an enterprise administrator, it is your role to design the AD DS infrastructure for Blue Yonder Airlines.

The company has expanded significantly since it implemented Windows Server 2003, to different countries located in different regions of the world, and has acquired several subsidiaries. As a result, the organization has decided to evaluate the current AD DS design to determine whether that infrastructure should be modified as part of the migration project.

Blue Yonder Airlines has a single AD DS forest that has a dedicated forest root domain named *blueyonderairlines.com*. The forest functional level in the *blueyonderairlines.com* forest is set to Windows Server 2003 and contains users from the five countries Blue Yonder Airlines operates in. This includes 25,000 users from the United States; 10,000 users from Canada; 5,000 users from Mexico; 3,000 users from Italy; and 100 users from Argentina. Users in the U.S. belong to the *us.blueyonderairlines.com* regional domain. Likewise, users in Canada belong to the *canada.blueyonderairlines.com* regional domain, but those in Mexico and Argentina both belong to the *mexico.blueyonderairlines.com* regional domain.

The Canada location has a direct connection to the United States location through a 1.5-Mbps network link. The average available bandwidth on this network link is 75 percent. The Mexico location also has a direct connection to the United States location through a 1.5-Mbps network link. The average available bandwidth on this network link is 55 percent. The Italy location has a direct connection to the United States location through a 512-Kbps network link. The average available bandwidth on this network link is 25 percent during business hours and 5 percent between 2:00 A.M. and 6:00 A.M. AD DS replication should not occur after business hours. Blue Yonder Airlines has a retail outlet in Argentina where physical security is a concern. The Argentina location is connected to the Mexico location through a 256-Kbps network connection, which has an average available bandwidth of 25 percent. Blue Yonder Airlines does not want users in Argentina to authenticate over the WAN; however, it does want to ensure that users in each region are able to log on even if a network outage occurs.

▶ **Exercise 1   Design the Site Structure**

In this exercise, you will review the business and technical requirements to design the site structure for Blue Yonder Airlines.

1. Based on your analysis of the network location, draw a location map for Blue Yonder Airlines.

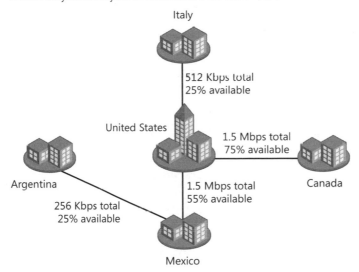

**Figure 2-15**   Location map for Blue Yonder Airlines

2. Use the following table to record the relevant location information for Blue Yonder Airlines.

| Name of Region | Total Bandwidth | Available Bandwidth | Network Segment | # of Users | Domains |
|---|---|---|---|---|---|
|  |  |  |  |  |  |
|  |  |  |  |  |  |
|  |  |  |  |  |  |
|  |  |  |  |  |  |

| Name of Region | Total Bandwidth | Available Bandwidth | Network Segment | # of Users | Domains |
|---|---|---|---|---|---|
| U.S. | 1.5 Mbps | 75% | 10.10.1.0/24 | 0 25,000 | *blueyonderairlines.com* *us.blueyonderairlines.com* |
| Canada | 1.5 Mbps | 75% | 10.10.2.0/24 | 10,000 | *canada.blueyonderairlines.com* |
| Mexico | 1.5 Mbps | 55% | 10.10.3.0/24 | 5,000 | *mexico.blueyonderairlines.com* |
| Italy | 512 kbps | 25% – day 5% – night | 10.10.4.0/24 | 3,000 | *italy.blueyonderairlines.com* |
| Argentina | 256 kbps | 25% | 10.10.5.0/24 | 100 | *mexico.blueyonderairlines.com* |

3. Which site model will be used for Blue Yonder Airlines?

The multiple sites model will be used because Blue Yonder Airlines wants to ensure that users in each region are able to log on even if a network outage occurs. Additionally, each region has its own domain, so the multiple sites model will ensure that domain data is replicated only to domain controllers for a given domain instead of across the WAN.

▶ **Exercise 2  Design Replication**

In this exercise, you will review the business and technical requirements to design replication for Blue Yonder Airlines.

1. What are the relevant replication design requirements for Blue Yonder Airlines?

The relevant replication design requirements for Blue Yonder Airlines are:

❑ Domain data for the *blueyonderairlines.com* domain is required in the U.S. location.

❑ Domain data for the *us.blueyonderairlines.com* domain is required in the U.S. location.

❑ Domain data for the *canada.blueyonderairlines.com* domain is required in the Canada location.

❑ Domain data for the *italy.blueyonderairlines.com* domain is required in the Italy location.

❑ Domain data for the *mexico.blueyonderairlines.com* domain is required in the Mexico and Argentina locations.

❑ The Canada location has a direct connection to the U.S. location through a 1.5-Mbps network link that has an average available bandwidth of 75 percent.

❑ The Mexico location has a direct connection to the U.S. location through a 1.5-Mbps network link that has an average available bandwidth of 55 percent.

❑ The Italy location has a direct connection to the U.S. location through a 512-Kbps network link that has an average available bandwidth of 25 percent during business hours and 5 percent between 2:00 AM and 6:00 AM.

❑ AD DS replication should not occur between the Italy location and the U.S. location after business hours.

❑   The Argentina location is connected to the Mexico location through a 256-Kbps network connection that has an average available bandwidth of 25 percent.

❑   Blue Yonder Airlines wants to ensure that users in each region are able to log on even if a network outage occurs.

2.  Which replication topology will be used for the replication design?

The hub and spoke replication topology will be used for the replication design. It's best suited for this design because the locations that will have a writable domain controller all have a direct connection to the U.S. location, which is the hub.

3.  Which site links are required to facilitate the replication design?

The following site links are required for the replication design:

U.S.–Canada

U.S.–Mexico

U.S.–Italy

Argentina–Mexico

4.  What will the cost of each site link be?

There are no requirements to have diverse costs on the site links. Therefore, the cost on each site link can remain at the default of 100.

5.  What will the replication schedule design be for each site link?

The replication schedule design for each site link will be as follows:

The U.S.–Canada site link will have a default replication schedule.

The U.S.–Mexico site link will have a default replication schedule.

The U.S.–Italy site will have a custom replication schedule, preventing AD DS replication between the hours of 2:00 A.M. and 6:00 A.M.

The Argentina–Mexico site link will have a default replication schedule.

6.  What will the replication interval design be for each site link?

The replication interval design for each site link will be as follows:

❑   The U.S.–Canada site link will have the default replication interval of 180.

❑   The U.S.–Mexico site link will have the default replication interval of 180.

❑   The U.S.–Italy site link will have the default replication interval of 180.

❑   The Argentina–Mexico site link will have a replication interval of 360.

▶ **Exercise 3   Design the Placement of Domain Controllers**

In this exercise, you will review the business and technical requirements to design placement of domain controllers for Blue Yonder Airlines.

1.  Where will the forest root domain controllers be placed as part of the design?

The forest root domain controllers will be placed in the U.S. location. This is the only location that has users for the forest root domain. Additionally, because all domains belong to the same tree, forest root domain controllers do not need to be placed in any of the remote locations to speed up authentication.

2. Where will the regional domain controllers be placed as part of the design?

The placement of regional domain controllers for the remote offices will be as follows:

- ❑ The domain controllers for the *us.blueyonderairlines.com* domain will be placed in the U.S. location.
- ❑ The domain controllers for the *canada.blueyonderairlines.com* domain will be placed in the Canada location.
- ❑ The domain controllers for the *mexico.blueyonderairlines.com* domain will be placed in the Mexico location.
- ❑ No writable domain controllers will be placed in the Argentina location because of the lack of physical security in this location.

3. Where will global catalog servers be placed as part of the design?

Global catalog servers are required in each location except the Argentina location because of the lack of physical security there. The remaining locations (U.S., Canada, Italy, and Mexico) all require local global catalog servers because of the requirement to ensure that users do not cross the WAN for authentication.

4. Where will RODCs be placed as part of the design?

An RODC will be placed in the Argentina location because of the lack of physical security in this location.

5. Where will the operations master role holders be placed as part of the design?

The placement of operations master role holders will be as follows:

- ❑ Because the schema master and the domain naming master role are forest-level roles, and the forest root domain is in the U.S. site, these roles will reside on a server in the U.S. site.
- ❑ Because the infrastructure master role, RID master role, and PDC emulator role are domain-level roles, and the *blueyonderairlines.com* domain is in the U.S. site, these roles will reside on a server in the U.S. site.
- ❑ Because the infrastructure master role, RID master role, and PDC emulator role are domain-level roles, and the *us.blueyonderairlines.com* domain is in the U.S. site, these roles will reside on a server in the U.S. site.
- ❑ Because the infrastructure master role, RID master role, and PDC emulator role are domain-level roles, and the *canada.blueyonderairlines.com* domain is in the Canada site, these roles will reside on a server in the Canada site.
- ❑ Because the infrastructure master role, RID master role, and PDC emulator role are domain-level roles, and the *italy.blueyonderairlines.com* domain is in the Italy site, these roles will reside on a server in the Italy site.

## Lesson Summary

- Gathering site design requirements consists of creating a location map and gathering location data.
- You can implement sites using the single site model to reduce AD DS replication latency or the multiple sites model to reduce the amount of bandwidth used for AD DS replication.
- Configure intersite replication topology using the hub and spoke, full mesh, or hybrid replication topology.
- Place forest root domain controllers in hub locations and at data center locations. Place regional domain controllers in every location that has an associated site object. Place RODCs in locations that require a local domain controller but lack physical security.
- At least one global catalog server should be placed in each location that has an associated site object unless universal group caching is enabled on the site object.
- Place the PDC emulator in a central location where the maximum number of clients can connect to the server.
- The schema master, domain naming master, and the relative identifier (RID) master should be located in a site where another domain controller is a direct replication partner.
- In a forest that contains a single AD DS domain, the infrastructure master can be placed on any domain controller in the domain. If every domain controller in a domain that is part of a multiple domain forest also hosts the global catalog, you can place the infrastructure master on any domain controller in that domain.

## Lesson Review

You can use the following questions to test your knowledge of the information in Lesson 2, "Designing the AD DS Physical Topology." The questions are also available on the companion CD if you prefer to review them in electronic form.

**NOTE  Answers**

Answers to these questions and explanations of why each answer choice is correct or incorrect are located in the "Answers" section at the end of the book.

1. Which of the following uses intrasite replication only?
   - A. Single site model
   - B. Multiple sites model
   - C. Hub and spoke replication topology
   - D. Full mesh replication topology

2. Which replication topology would you use if your network consists of faster network connections between major computing hubs and slower links connecting branch offices?

   A. Single site model

   B. Ring replication topology

   C. Hub and spoke replication topology

   D. Full mesh replication topology

3. You have a single AD DS forest with a single domain that is using the hub and spoke replication topology. Where should you place the server that holds the PDC emulator operations master role?

   A. In the location represented by the hub site

   B. In one of the locations represented by a spoke site

   C. In every location represented by a spoke site

   D. On the server that holds the global catalog server role in a location represented by a spoke site

4. You have an AD DS forest that consists of multiple domains. Each domain has a number of global catalog servers, but not all domain controllers are global catalog servers. Where should you place the infrastructure master role?

   A. On a server that is not a global catalog server

   B. On a server that is also a global catalog server

   C. On every global catalog server forest

   D. On a single server in the forest root domain

# Chapter Review

To further practice and reinforce the skills you learned in this chapter, you can perform the following tasks:

- Review the chapter summary.
- Complete the case scenarios. These scenarios set up real-world situations involving the topics of this chapter and ask you to create a solution.
- Complete the suggested practices.
- Take a practice test.

# Chapter Summary

- Gathering forest design requirements consists of identifying the role of AD DS in your organization and gathering business, technical, security, network, autonomy, and isolation requirements.
- The three forest models are the organizational forest model, the resource forest model, and the restricted access forest model.
- Domain design requires you to consider an organization's security, administrative, and replication requirements. You can implement two domain models: the single domain model and the regional domain model.
- Gathering site design requirements consists of creating a location map and gathering location data. You can implement two site models: the single site model and the multiple sites model.
- The three replication topologies are the hub and spoke replication topology, the hybrid replication topology, and the full mesh replication topology.
- Place the PDC emulator in a central location where the maximum number of clients can connect to the server.
- The schema master, domain naming master, and the relative identifier (RID) master should be located in a site where another domain controller is a direct replication partner.

# Case Scenarios

In the following case scenarios, you will apply what you've learned about designing AD DS forests and domains and their topologies. You can find answers to these questions in the "Answers" section at the end of this book.

# Case Scenario 1:  Designing the AD DS Forest

You work as an enterprise administrator at Tailspin Toys, which has an existing AD DS forest supported by the Tailspin Toys IT department. Tailspin Toys recently purchased Wingtip Toys.

Wingtip Toys does not use AD DS. It has been mandated, however, to move to a centralized model for authentication and authorization and thus will begin using AD DS. Wingtip Toys has its own IT department that will support AD DS.

You have been asked to design a forest for Wingtip Toys. The administrators from Tailspin Toys should be permitted only to manage the AD DS forest for Tailspin Toys. The administrators from Wingtip Toys should be permitted only to manage the AD DS forest for Wingtip Toys.

1.  Will joining the Wingtip Toys computers to the existing Tailspin Toys forest meet the requirements?
2.  Will creating a new organizational forest for Wingtip Toys meet the requirements?

# Case Scenario 2:  Designing AD DS Sites

You are an enterprise administrator at Woodgrove Bank, which has a single AD DS forest with a dedicated forest root domain named *woodgrovebank.com*.

The *woodgrovebank.com* forest contains users from the five countries Woodgrove Bank operates in. The Canada location has a direct connection to the United States location through a 1.5-Mbps network link with an average available bandwidth of 75 percent. The Mexico location has a direct connection to the United States location through a 1.5-Mbps network link with an average available bandwidth of 55 percent. The Italy location has a direct connection to the United States location through a 512-Kbps network link with an average available bandwidth of 25 percent. The Argentina location is connected to the Mexico location through a 256-Kbps network connection with an average available bandwidth of 25 percent. Woodgrove Bank does not want users in Argentina to authenticate over the WAN.

You need to determine which AD DS site replication topology to use for Woodgrove Bank.

1.  Will using a hub and spoke AD DS replication topology meet the requirements?
2.  Will using a hybrid AD DS replication topology meet the requirements?

# Case Scenario 3:  Designing the Placement of Domain Controllers

You are an enterprise administrator at Woodgrove Bank, which has a single AD DS forest with a dedicated forest root domain named *woodgrovebank.com*.

The *woodgrovebank.com* forest contains users from the five countries Woodgrove Bank operates in. This includes 25,000 users from the United States; 10,000 users from Canada; 5,000 users from Mexico; 3,000 users from Italy; and 100 users from Argentina. Users in the U.S. location belong to the *us.woodgrovebank.com* regional domain. Users in the Canada location belong to the *canada.woodgrovebank.com* regional domain. Users in the Mexico and Argentina locations belong to the *mexico.woodgrovebank.com* regional domain.

Woodgrove Bank has a retail outlet in Argentina where physical security is a concern. The Argentina location is connected to the Mexico location through a network connection. Woodgrove Bank does not want users in Argentina to authenticate over the WAN.

You need to determine how users in the Argentina location will authenticate without compromising physical security.

1. Will placing a global catalog server in the Argentina location meet the requirements?
2. Will placing an RODC in the Argentina location meet the requirements?

# Suggested Practices

To help you successfully master the exam objectives presented in this chapter, complete the following tasks.

## Implement Forests, Domains, and the Physical Topology

- **Practice 1**   Implement an AD DS forest with a child domain by performing the following procedure. Using either virtual or physical machines, install the Active Directory Domain Services Server role on two installations of Windows Server 2008. On the first server, install a new AD DS forest and domain. On the second server, install a new AD DS domain, following the same namespace as the first domain.
- **Practice 2**   Implement an AD DS site and replication design by performing the following procedure. Using either virtual or physical machines, create a multiple domain AD DS forest. Create one site object for each domain controller in the forest. Create site links between each site object, using the full mesh topology. Configure the cost, schedule, and frequency on each site link.
- **Practice 3**   Implement a domain controller placement design by performing the following procedure. Using either virtual or physical machines, create a multiple domain AD DS forest. Transfer the schema master role. Transfer the domain naming master role. Transfer the RID master role in each domain in the forest. Transfer the infrastructure master role in each domain in the forest. Transfer the PDC emulator role in each domain in the forest.

## Watch a Webcast

- **Practice 1**    Watch the "Technical Overview of Active Directory Domain Services in Windows Server 2008" webcast. You can find this by searching *http://msevents .microsoft.com* for event ID # 1032343629 or by visiting *http://msevents.microsoft.com/CUI /WebCastEventDetails.aspx?EventID=1032343629&EventCategory=5&culture=en -US&CountryCode=US.*

- **Practice 2**    Watch the "TechNet Webcast: Active Directory Inside Out (Part 2 of 11)— Active Directory Physical Concepts—Level 200" webcast. You can find this by searching *http://msevents.microsoft.com* for event ID # 1032316700 or by visiting *http:// msevents.microsoft.com/cui/WebCastEventDetails.aspx?culture=en-US&EventID =1032259125&CountryCode=US.*

- **Practice 3**    Watch the "Active Directory Inside Out (Part 3 of 11)—Active Directory Replication and the Operations Masters Role—Level 200" webcast. You can find this by searching *http://msevents.microsoft.com* for event ID # 1032259125 or by visiting *http:// msevents.microsoft.com/cui/WebCastEventDetails.aspx?culture=en-US&EventID =1032259125&CountryCode=US.*

    NOTE: This is a WS03 webcast—there are no relevant WS08 webcasts at present.

## Read a White Paper

- **Practice 1**    Read the "Scenarios for Installing AD DS" white paper from Microsoft at *http://technet2.microsoft.com/windowsserver2008/en/library/c1f9eb95-563e-40ba-b74a -9113152a59271033.mspx?mfr=true.*

- **Practice 2**    Read the "Steps for Installing AD DS" white paper from Microsoft at *http:// technet2.microsoft.com/windowsserver2008/en/library/c1f9eb95-563e-40ba -b74a9113152a59271033.mspx?mfr=true.*

# Take a Practice Test

The practice tests on this book's companion CD offer many options. For example, you can test yourself on just one exam objective, or you can test yourself on all the 70-647 certification exam content. You can set up the test so that it closely simulates the experience of taking a certification exam, or you can set it up in study mode so that you can look at the correct answers and explanations after you answer each question.

---

**MORE INFO    Practice tests**

For details about all the practice test options available, see the "How to Use the Practice Tests" section in this book's introduction.

---

# Chapter 3

# Planning Migrations, Trusts, and Interoperability

This chapter focuses on how to get Windows Server 2008 working with other technologies and other operating systems. In the first lesson, you will learn which factors you need to consider when planning an organization's move from an existing Active Directory directory service environment to one based on Windows Server 2008 Active Directory Domain Services (AD DS). You will also learn what steps to consider when planning a trust relationship between one AD DS environment and another. The second lesson in this chapter focuses on the topic of interoperability, which includes ensuring that users of Windows-based and UNIX-based computers are able to work seamlessly together. This lesson also includes information about technologies by which you can migrate services and applications that traditionally run on UNIX-based computers only, so that they can be hosted off computers on which the Windows Server 2008 operating system is installed.

## Exam objectives in this chapter:
- Plan for domain or forest migration, upgrade, and restructuring.
- Plan for interoperability.

## Lessons in this chapter:
- Lesson 1: Planning for Migration, Upgrade, and Restructuring . . . . . . . . . . . . . . . . 143
- Lesson 2: Planning for Interoperability . . . . . . . . . . . . . . . . . . . . . . . . . . . . . . . . . . . 152

# Before You Begin

To complete the lessons in this chapter, you must have installed a Windows Server 2008 Enterprise domain controller named Glasgow as described in Chapter 1, "Planning Name Resolution and Internet Protocol Addressing." No additional configuration is required for this chapter.

## Real World

*Orin Thomas*

My formal IT career (when I was paid with money rather than with coffee, cakes, and the occasional doughnut) started in college. In the 1990s, Australian universities were notoriously diverse IT environments. The faculty had a great deal of freedom in selecting the operating system of their desktop computers, and many of them exercised this right. It was up to the IT staff to make the desktop computers work with each department's existing IT infrastructure or to modify the infrastructure to meet the needs of the faculty. The crew I worked with had to get Windows-based, pre-OS X Macintosh–based, and UNIX-based computers—and some stuff you've probably never heard of—all using the same set of shared departmental printers and file servers. Some of our solutions to these challenges were straightforward. Some were so ad hoc that they would stop working when someone looked at a printer the wrong way. More than a decade later, enabling disparate operating systems to interoperate and use the same set of resources is a much simpler process. The ability to "play well with others" has become a feature. The easier it is to integrate an operating system into a diverse environment, the less likely it is that the IT department will object to allowing that operating system into the environment. If this philosophy had been more prevalent in the 1990s, it would have saved the crew that I worked with at the university many headaches.

# Lesson 1: Planning for Migration, Upgrade, and Restructuring

Although it is possible to add a member server running Windows Server 2008 to an existing Microsoft Windows Server 2003 domain, at some point in your organization's migration to Windows Server 2008, you are going to want to upgrade your organization's domain controllers (DCs). In this lesson, you will learn which steps you need to take to move from a network environment that is dependent on a previous version of Microsoft Windows to a Windows Server 2008 Active Directory–based network infrastructure.

---

**After this lesson, you will be able to:**
- Prepare the environment for Windows Server 2008.
- Migrate objects.
- Plan domain consolidation.

**Estimated lesson time: 40 minutes**

---

## Migration Paths

You can take one of three general paths to move from an existing Active Directory environment to an AD DS environment. An AD DS environment is another way of indicating a domain that has Windows Server 2008 DCs. These paths are known as the *domain upgrade*, the *domain restructure*, and the *upgrade-then-restructure*. When planning which method to use, consider factors such as the amount of time the migration should take and the availability of new server hardware.

### Domain Upgrade Migration Path

The domain upgrade migration path involves upgrading the operating system of a Windows Server 2003 DC to Windows Server 2008 or installing Windows Server 2008 DCs into a Windows 2000 Server or Windows Server 2003 domain. Unlike Windows Server 2003, which you can configure to support domains that use both Microsoft Windows NT 4.0 and Windows Server 2003 DCs, Windows Server 2008 DCs cannot coexist in the same domain as Windows NT 4.0 primary and backup DCs. Therefore, if you are planning to add Windows Server 2008 DCs to a domain, you need to ensure that domains in your organization are at the Windows 2000 Native functional level or higher. Domains at the Windows 2000 mixed or Windows Server 2003 interim functional level do not support Windows Server 2008 DCs. There is no direct upgrade path between Windows NT 4.0 and Windows Server 2008. Plan to use the domain upgrade migration path when you will not have access to a significant amount of new server hardware on which to install new deployments of Windows Server 2008.

## Domain Restructure Migration Path

The domain restructure migration path involves copying Active Directory objects from the original domain or forest to the new Windows Server 2008 domain or forest, using tools such as the Active Directory Migration Tool, covered later in this lesson. After all objects are migrated, the DCs in the original domain or forest are decommissioned or redeployed. The domain restructure migration path includes the following advantages:

- The original environment remains the same until the migration is completed. Users are not forced to the new environment until it is tested and ready.
- It enables the selective migration of objects. When you perform a domain upgrade, all objects are upgraded, including those that are redundant, inactive, and no longer necessary. Domain restructure migrations enable organizations to clean up their environments as they transition to the new technology.

The domain restructure migration requires you to have enough new server hardware to support both the original and destination environments concurrently. If the budget does not allow for new server hardware, the domain upgrade migration path is a more feasible alternative. Although it is possible to perform a domain restructure migration using virtualization, you should avoid this approach unless you are planning an AD DS deployment that primarily involves virtualized DCs.

## Upgrade-Then-Restructure Migration Path

The upgrade-then-restructure migration path, also known as a two-phase migration, involves upgrading the original domain or forest and then migrating Active Directory objects to a new Windows Server 2008 domain or forest. This process essentially combines the domain upgrade and domain restructure approaches, enabling an organization to benefit immediately from a Windows Server 2008 upgrade and then to transition to new Windows Server 2008 DC hardware at some point in the future, with the added benefit of removing unnecessary Active Directory objects through the selective migration process.

## Active Directory Migration Tool

You can use the Active Directory Migration Tool v3.1 (ADMT v3) to migrate Active Directory objects within a forest for domain consolidation or to migrate objects to another forest for interforest migration. You can use the ADMT to migrate users, groups, service accounts, computers, and trusts. The ADMT has a simulation mode that enables administrators to evaluate the results of planned migrations prior to performing the actual migration.

---

**MORE INFO**    Obtain the Active Directory Migration Tool

You can obtain the Active Directory Migration Tool from the Microsoft Web site at *http://go.microsoft.com/fwlink/?LinkID=75627.*

---

# Upgrading an Existing Domain to Windows Server 2008

There are two basic strategies for transitioning from an existing domain to a Windows Server 2008 AD DS domain. The first strategy is to introduce new Windows Server 2008 DCs into the forest and then either to retire or upgrade existing Windows 2000 Server or Windows Server 2003 DCs. The second strategy is simply to perform an in-place upgrade of all existing Windows Server 2003 DCs. Both of these strategies are useful when pursuing the domain upgrade migration path.

## Preparing the Environment

You need to perform several steps prior to adding a Windows Server 2008 DC to an existing Active Directory environment, even if you do not intend to change the current domain or forest functional level. These steps include ensuring that existing DCs in the environment have appropriate patches and service packs installed and that the Active Directory schema has been appropriately prepared for the introduction of Windows Server 2008 DCs.

If you are planning to add a Windows Server 2008 DC to a domain that has active Windows 2000 Server DCs, which is possible when using the Windows 2000 Native domain and forest functional level, you must ensure that all Windows 2000 Server DCs have Service Pack 4 and hotfix 265089 installed.

To prepare a forest for the installation of a read-only DC (RODC), run the *adprep /rodcprep* command on the schema master. This command needs to be run only once on the schema master and does not need to be run in each domain in the forest in which you intend to install Windows Server 2008 RODCs. As is the case with *adprep /forestprep*, to execute this command successfully, the user account must be a member of the Enterprise Admins, Schema Admins, and Domain Admins groups. From a planning perspective, consider running *adprep /rodcprep* immediately after running the *adprep /forestprep* command even if you have no immediate plans to deploy RODCs in your environment. If, in the future, it becomes necessary to deploy RODCs in the enterprise, the deployment will be able to proceed without problems that might occur if future administrators do not check whether the forest has been prepared for the deployment of RODCs prior to attempting deployment.

---

**MORE INFO**  **Microsoft Exchange 2000 Server and Windows Services for UNIX 2.0**

Known compatibility problems exist between *adprep.exe* and Exchange 2000 Server and Windows Services for UNIX 2.0 where these products have been deployed in Windows 2000 Server domains. Consult KB article 314649 to resolve the Exchange 2000 Server issue and either install the *Q293783_sfu_2_x86_en.exe* hotfix for Windows Services for UNIX 2.0 or upgrade to Windows Services for UNIX 3.0.

---

After you have completed the forest-level preparation tasks, you must still perform preparation on a per-domain basis before you can install Windows Server 2008 DCs. A user who is a member of that domain's Domain Admins group must run the *adprep /domainprep /gpprep* domain preparation command on the DC that holds the infrastructure master role. After this command has been run, Windows Server 2008 DCs can be introduced to that domain.

---

**MORE INFO**   **More on infrastructure preparation**

To learn more about preparing an existing Active Directory infrastructure for an upgrade to Windows Server 2008 AD DS, consult the following Web page: *http://technet2.microsoft.com /windowsserver2008/en/library/7120ec57-ad86-4369-af22-773ed9b097fc1033.mspx?mfr=true.*

---

### In-Place Domain Controller Upgrade

Upgrading each DC in the domain from Windows Server 2003 to Windows Server 2008 works well within the limitations of the types of upgrades you can perform. For example, you cannot upgrade a computer that has Windows Server 2003 Enterprise to Windows Server 2008 Standard, and you cannot upgrade any Windows Server 2003 DC to a Windows Server 2008 DC that is running the Server Core installation. Before performing an in-place upgrade of a Windows Server 2003 DC, ensure that Service Pack 1 (SP1) or later has been applied. This does not apply to Windows Server 2003 R2 DCs, which are effectively updated to SP1 when initially deployed.

---

**Quick Check**

1. On which DC should you perform the first forest preparation task?
2. Which of the Windows Server 2003 domain functional levels do not support the introduction of Windows Server 2008 DCs?

**Quick Check Answers**

1. You must run *adprep /forestprep* on the DC hosting the schema master role.
2. Windows 2000 Mixed and Windows Server 2003 interim domain functional levels support Windows NT 4.0 DCs. There must be no Windows NT 4.0 DCs in a domain if a Windows Server 2008 DC is to be introduced.

---

## Cross-Forest Authentication

Enterprise-scale organizations often deploy multiple forests. Although these forests are usually designed for separate divisions within the enterprise, a level of integration between these separate network environments is often required. The most common way of allowing users in one forest to access the resources located in another is to configure an interforest trust so that any user in any domain in the trusted forest can access any resource in any domain in the trusting forest. An alternative is an external trust that exists between specific domains in different forests rather than in any domain in each forest. Active Directory Federation Services (AD FS) also provides a method of granting access to forest resources; you will learn about this technology in Lesson 2, "Planning for Interoperability."

When planning a trust, you must consider the following factors:

- Should the trust be bidirectional or one-way?
- Is it necessary to use selective authentication?
- Is it necessary to implement Security Identifier (SID) filtering?

When planning trust direction, ensure that you grant only the minimum required access needed to meet business requirements. This might mean using external trusts rather than forest trusts. Remember that two-way trusts are required only when users in each forest or domain need access to resources located in the other forest or domain. If an organization uses a resource forest scenario, it is necessary to configure only a one-way trust from the forest that hosts accounts to the forest that hosts resources.

You can limit trusts by using selective authentication, which restricts the number of users in the trusted forest who are able to access shared resources in the trusting forest. If you deploy forest-wide authentication rather than selective authentication, any user authenticated over an interforest trust will be assigned the Authenticated Users SID for the trusting forest, essentially granting users from a trusted forest almost all the default rights that users in the trusting forest have. The benefit of selective authentication is that it limits the groups of users who are able to access resources across the trust and enables you to limit which computers in the trusting forest can be accessed across the trust. You can configure selective authentication when you first create the trust or alter the properties of an existing trust as shown in Figure 3-1. If you choose not to implement selective authentication, plan to remove the Authenticated Users group from all sensitive resources in the trusting domain.

SID filtering prevents users from using SIDs stored in the *SIDHistory* attribute when accessing resources in a trusting forest. The *SIDHistory* attribute exists to support the migration of user and group accounts between domains and allows the user accounts to access resources in their original domain during the migration process. A new SID will be assigned to the account when it is moved to the new domain, and that new SID will not be assigned access to the resources that are yet to be migrated from the original domain. SID filtering can block the *SIDHistory* attribute across the forest trust, which ensures that accounts that have been migrated to a trusted forest no longer have access to resources in the original forest unless explicitly specified. When enabled, any SIDs from domains other than the trusted domain are ignored. For example, SID filtering is enabled by default on any trust created using a computer running Windows Server 2008. Disable SID filtering only during the migration of user and group accounts from one forest to another. This allows access to resources during the migration process. After the migration is complete, plan to re-enable SID filtering.

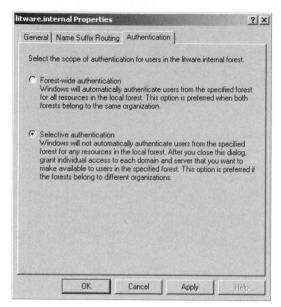

**Figure 3-1**    Configuring selective authentication

## PRACTICE Planning Forest Migration to Windows Server 2008

Tailspin Toys has a fifteen-domain Active Directory forest that contains a mix of domains running at the Windows 2000 Mixed, Windows Server 2003 Interim, and Windows Server 2003 functional levels. All domains running at the Windows 2000 Mixed and Windows Server 2003 Interim functional levels contain Windows NT 4.0 DCs. You are planning the transition of the Tailspin Toys environment so that the forest operates at the Windows Server 2008 functional level.

The *trafalgar.tailspintoys.internal*, *warragul.tailspintoys.internal*, and *bairnsdale.tailspintoys.internal* domains are running at the Windows Server 2003 interim level. Five computers running Windows NT 4.0 are functioning as backup DCs in each of these domains.

The *yarragon.tailspintoys.internal*, *traralgon.tailspintoys.internal*, and *morwell.tailspintoys.internal* domains contain only Windows 2000 Server DCs. The existing DC hardware in each of these domains will support Windows Server 2008 DCs if they are running the Server Core installation. You want to deploy RODCs at several sites within these domains, and budget is available for one new Windows Server 2008 DC, including hardware, for each of these domains.

▶ **Exercise    Plan the Migration of the Tailspin Toys Forest to Windows Server 2008**

In this exercise, you will review the aforementioned business and technical requirements as part of planning a migration to Windows Server 2008 AD DS at Tailspin Toys.

1. Which steps should you include in your plans with respect to the *tailspintoys.internal* root domain?
   - ❏ Join a Windows Server 2008 member server to the domain.
   - ❏ Run *adprep /forestprep* on the schema master.
   - ❏ Run *adprep /rodcprep* on the schema master.

   This is because you must deploy RODCs in several domains in the forest.

2. Which steps should you include in your plans to transition the *yarragon.tailspintoys .internal* domain to the Windows Server 2008 functional level?
   - ❏ Ensure that all Windows 2000 Server DCs have SP4 hotfix 265089 applied.
   - ❏ Ensure that *adprep /rodcprep* has been run on the schema master.
   - ❏ Join the Windows Server 2008 member server to the domain.
   - ❏ Run *adprep /domainprep /gpprep* on the infrastructure master in the domain.
   - ❏ Promote the Windows Server 2008 member server to DC. Seize all domain FSMO roles for this DC.
   - ❏ Demote existing Windows 2000 Server DCs.
   - ❏ Upgrade the domain functional level to Windows Server 2008.
   - ❏ Perform clean installations of Windows Server 2008 Server Core on the hardware originally used by the Windows 2000 DCs.
   - ❏ Promote these computers running Windows Server 2008 Server Core to DCs or RODCs as necessary.

3. What steps must you perform in the *trafalgar.tailspintoys.internal*, *warragul.tailspintoys .internal*, and *bairnsdale.tailspintoys.internal* domains before you can make any modifications to the *tailspintoys.internal* forest?
   - ❏ You must decommission Windows NT 4 DCs.
   - ❏ You must upgrade the domain functional level to Windows Server 2003. (Although Windows 2000 Native would work, these domains were originally at the Windows Server 2003 interim functional level.)

## Lesson Summary

- Run *adprep /forestprep* on the DC hosting the schema master role.
- To upgrade a domain in a forest that has been prepared using *adprep /forestprep*, run the *adprep /domainprep /gpprep* command on the DC that holds the infrastructure master role.
- Selective authentication stops users from trusted domains from being treated automatically as members of the authenticated users group in the trusting domain.
- SID filtering ensures that only SIDs from the trusted domain can be used when users attempt to access resources in the trusting domain. SID filtering is enabled by default on

trusts created between Windows Server 2008 domains. SID filtering is often disabled during cross-forest migration, allowing migrated user accounts access to resources in the source environment until the migration is complete.

■ You can use the Active Directory Migration Tool to migrate objects between domains and forests.

# Lesson Review

You can use the following questions to test your knowledge of the information in Lesson 1, "Planning for Migration, Upgrade, and Restructuring." The questions are also available on the companion CD if you prefer to review them in electronic form.

---

**NOTE   Answers**

Answers to these questions and explanations of why each answer choice is correct or incorrect are located in the "Answers" section at the end of the book.

---

1. Assuming that the FSMO roles are distributed across Windows Server 2003 DCs in the forest root domain so that no one DC hosts more than a single role, on which of the following computers should you run the *adprep /forestprep* command?

    A.  DC hosting the PDC emulator role

    B.  DC hosting the schema master role

    C.  DC hosting the RID master role

    D.  DC hosting the infrastructure master role

    E.  DC hosting the domain naming master role

2. You have upgraded the forest root domain so that it now has Windows Server 2008 DCs. You now plan to upgrade a child domain in the same forest. Assuming that no DC in the forest hosts more than one FSMO role, on which DC in the child domain should you run the *adprep /domainprep /gpprep* command?

    A.  DC hosting the PDC emulator role

    B.  DC hosting the schema master role

    C.  DC hosting the RID master role

    D.  DC hosting the infrastructure master role

    E.  DC hosting the domain naming master role

3. You are planning the migration of several thousand user accounts from the *maffra.contoso .internal* domain to the *traralgon.fabrikam.internal* domain. Each domain is in a separate Active Directory forest. Each Active Directory forest is configured to run at the Windows Server 2008 functional level, and the forests share a two-way forest trust. During the migration, you want to ensure that migrated user accounts are able to access resources in both domains. Which of the following should you plan to do during the migration?

    **A.**  Disable SID filtering.

    **B.**  Enable SID filtering.

    **C.**  Configure Selective Authentication.

    **D.**  Configure name suffix routing.

4. You are planning a two-way forest trust between the Contoso and Fabrikam organizations. You want to ensure that only authorized users from each trusted forest have access to resources in the trusting forest. Many resources are available to authenticated users in each forest. These resources should not be available to users in the trusted forest unless explicitly allowed. Which of the following plans should you make?

    **A.**  Implement selective authentication.

    **B.**  Implement SID filtering.

    **C.**  Implement user principal name (UPN) suffix routing.

    **D.**  Implement forest-wide authentication.

# Lesson 2: Planning for Interoperability

As most people who have been in IT long enough to become enterprise administrators know, few environments use products from a single vendor. Although products from a single vendor generally work well with each other, it can be difficult to integrate information technology products from different companies. Part of an enterprise administrator's job is to make the user experience seamless. You need to ensure that a user who can access a set of shared files on one server, when logged on to a computer running Windows Vista with his or her Active Directory user account, can access exactly the same set of shared files when logged on to a UNIX-based computer with the same user account. In this lesson, you will learn how you can use Windows Server 2008 to enable disparate technologies to interoperate. It is your job as enterprise administrator to plan things so that the workers in your environment need not be aware of the technical complexities of the solution, only that they need to remember one user-name and password to access the resources they need, irrespective of the method they use to access those resources.

---

**After this lesson, you will be able to:**

- Determine the types of scenarios in which it is necessary to deploy AD FS.
- Understand the types of scenarios in which it is necessary to deploy Microsoft Identity Lifecycle Manager 2007 Feature Pack 1.
- Determine which interoperability technology to deploy for UNIX-based computers, based on organizational needs.

**Estimated lesson time: 40 minutes**

---

## Planning AD FS

AD FS enables a user from a partner organization to authenticate to multiple related Web applications from a single sign-on without requiring a forest trust. AD FS accomplishes this by securely sharing digital identity and entitlement rights across a set of preconfigured security boundaries. For example, AD FS enables you to configure a Web application on your network to use a directory service on a trusted partner organization's network for authentication. AD FS enables user accounts from one organization to access the applications of another organization while still enabling full administrative control to each organization's IT departments. Rather than having to create a new account for a person when you need to grant access to a Web application that you manage, you trust the partner organization's directory service. Users from the partner organization can then authenticate to your organization's Web application, using their own organization's credentials. Figure 3-2 displays the AD FS console.

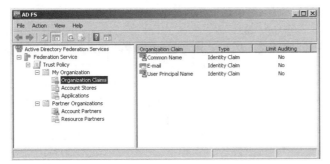

**Figure 3-2**   AD FS console

AD FS requires that one organization have deployed either AD DS or Active Directory Lightweight Directory Services (AD LDS). Although AD FS was available with Windows Server 2003 R2, the version of AD FS that is included with Windows Server 2008 is more tightly integrated with Microsoft Office SharePoint Services 2007 and Active Directory Rights Management Services. Federation trusts are set up between organizations.

An AD FS deployment can include the following roles:

- **Federation Server role**   A server that hosts the Federation Server role routes authentication requests from user accounts in other organizations or from clients on the Internet.
- **Federation Server Proxy role**   Servers with the Federation Server Proxy role are often deployed on screened subnets and forward authentication traffic to servers hosting the Federation Server role from clients on the Internet. You cannot deploy the Federation Server role service and the Federation Service Proxy role service on the same computer.
- **Account Federation server**   The Account Federation server is located on the network of the partner organization and issues security tokens to the user that are then forwarded to your organization's server.
- **AD FS Web Agent**   The AD FS Web Agent is software installed on a Web server that uses security tokens signed by a valid federation server to allow or deny access to a protected application.
- **AD FS–enabled Web servers**   AD FS–enabled Web servers have the AD FS Web Agent installed. These servers must be configured with a relationship to a Federation Server so that authentication can occur.

One of the most important aspects of AD FS is the level of trust that it requires you to give your partner organization for the management of user accounts. After you create a federated trust, you have to trust that your partner organization is managing user accounts properly. If your partner organization is diligent in the way it manages user accounts, this will not pose any problems. If your partner organization is not so diligent, problems could arise. For example, you might work for a manufacturing organization that uses AD FS to allow its partner organizations to log on to a sensitive inventory Web application. Competitor organizations could derive significant commercial benefit by accessing this inventory data. Imagine that a user from the partner organization, who has had access to the inventory Web application, decides to leave his or her job to work for a competitor. If the partner organization is diligent, it will disable the account. If the partner organization is not diligent, that user still might have access to your organization's sensitive data. With AD FS, you have to trust that the partner organization will always manage access to your organization's applications diligently. For many organizations, this can become a political problem. In planning an AD FS strategy, you are likely to spend more time dealing with the political aspects of enabling a partner organization to control access to your organization's Web applications than you are in putting together the technical solution in the first place.

---

**MORE INFO    More on AD FS design**

To learn more about designing an AD FS deployment, consult the following link: *http:// technet2.microsoft.com/windowsserver2008/en/library/efa99362-aa77-46e8-a036 -bfd85cbce7c71033.mspx?mfr=true*.

---

# Microsoft Identity Lifecycle Manager 2007 Feature Pack 1

Identity Lifecycle Manager (ILM) 2007 Feature Pack 1 (FP1) is a tool that enables organizations to manage a single user's identity across a heterogeneous enterprise environment. The identity synchronization and user provisioning component of ILM 2007 FP1 stores aggregate identity information from multiple sources in a central repository called the *metaverse*. Management agents installed on each source work as connectors, translating identity information from connected sources to the metaverse.

ILM 2007 FP1 can synchronize user identity data between Windows Server 2008 AD DS and the following products:

- Active Directory on Windows Server 2003 R2, Windows Server 2003, and Windows 2000 Server
- Active Directory Application Mode on Windows Server 2003 R2
- Microsoft Windows NT 4.0 Domain
- IBM Tivoli Directory Server
- Novell eDirectory 8.6.2, 8.7, and 8.7.x
- Sun Directory Server 4.x and 6.x
- Exchange Server 2007, Exchange Server 2003, Exchange 2000 Server, and Exchange Server 5.5
- Lotus Notes 7.0, 6.x, 5.0, and 4.6
- SAP 5.0 and 4.7
- Microsoft SQL Server 2005, SQL Server 2000, and SQL Server 7

- IBM DB2
- Oracle 10g, 9i, and 8i

ILM 2007 FP1 enables organizations to integrate disparate identity systems. For example, using ILM 2007 FP1, an organization could configure its Exchange Server 2007 deployment to link to the *Human Resources* database. When an employee joins the organization and is added to this database, ILM 2007 FP1 can be configured to set up that employee automatically within Exchange Server 2007 or within any other messaging system for which there is an ILM 2007 FP1 connector.

You can also use ILM 2007 FP1 to manage certificates and smart cards in an enterprise environment. ILM 2007 FP1 integrates with AD DS and Active Directory Certificate Services to provision digital certificates and smart cards directly. You can learn more about Certificate Services in Chapter 9, "Planning and Designing a Public Key Infrastructure."

You can install ILM 2007 FP1 on the Enterprise editions of Windows Server 2003 and Windows Server 2008. ILM 2007 FP1 also needs access to a SQL Server 2008, SQL Server 2005, or SQL Server 2000 database server.

---

**MORE INFO**   **More on the ILM feature pack**

To learn more about the Identity Lifecycle Manager 2007 feature pack, visit *https://www.microsoft.com/windowsserver/ilm2007/overview.mspx*.

---

**Quick Check**

1. What does the deployment of AD FS enable you to accomplish?
2. Where does ILM 2007 FP1 store aggregate identity information?

**Quick Check Answers**

1. The deployment of AD FS enables you to accomplish a single-sign-on solution for a group of related Web applications.
2. In the metaverse, the data for which is stored within an SQL Server database.

# Planning for UNIX Interoperability

As an enterprise administrator, you are aware that many companies do not settle on a single company's operating system solutions for the clients and servers. In some cases, your organization might choose an alternative solution because it meets a particular set of needs at a particular point in time; in other cases, you might inherit a diverse operating system environment when your company acquires a subsidiary. In either situation, it is your job as enterprise administrator to ensure that these diverse systems interoperate in a seamless manner. Windows

Server 2008 includes several features and role services that can assist in integrating UNIX-based operating systems in a Windows Server 2008 network infrastructure.

## Identity Management

Identity Management for UNIX is a role service that enables you to integrate your Windows users in existing environments that host UNIX-based computers. You are most likely to deploy this feature in environments that are predominantly UNIX based and where Windows users and computers running Windows must integrate in an existing UNIX-based infrastructure. Identity Management for UNIX is compatible with Internet Engineering Task Force (IETF) Request for Comments (RFC) 2307, "An Approach for Using LDAP as a Network Information Service." A Lightweight Directory Access Protocol (LDAP) server resolves network password and Network Information Service (NIS) attribute requests. LDAP is a directory services protocol commonly used in UNIX environments in a way very similar to how AD DS is used on Windows networks.

---

**MORE INFO** More on Identity Management for UNIX

To learn more about Identity Management for UNIX, consult the following TechNet link: *http://technet2.microsoft.com/windowsserver2008/en/library/ffad69a4-4a3f-4161-8a0c -dd6c1b9f288f1033.mspx?mfr=true.*

---

## Password Synchronization

The Password Synchronization component of Identity Management for UNIX simplifies the process of maintaining secure passwords in environments in which computers running UNIX and Windows are present and used by staff. Password synchronization is particularly important in environments in which users need to log on regularly to computers running Windows and UNIX. When Password Synchronization is deployed, the user's password on all UNIX computers in the environment will also be changed when a user changes his or her password in AD DS. Similarly, you can configure the Password Synchronization component to change a password automatically in AD DS when a user's UNIX password is changed. You configure the direction of password synchronization by setting the password synchronization properties as shown in Figure 3-3. You access the Password Synchronization Properties dialog box by using the Microsoft Identity Management for UNIX console.

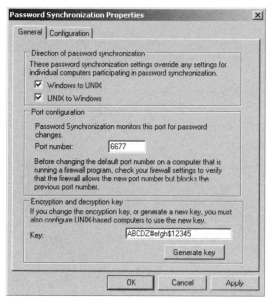

**Figure 3-3**    Configuring password synchronization properties

Password synchronization is supported between Windows Server 2008 and the following UNIX-based operating systems:

- Hewlett Packard HP UX 11i v1
- IBM AIX version 5L 5.2 and 5L 5.3
- Novel SUSE Linux Enterprise Server 10
- Red Hat Enterprise Linux 4 Server
- Sun Microsystems Solaris 10 (SPARC architecture only)

You should deploy Password Synchronization on all DCs in a domain in which it is needed. Any newly deployed DCs in the domain should also have this feature installed. Microsoft also recommends that you demote a DC before removing Password Synchronization. Ensure that the password policies on the UNIX computers and within the Windows domain are similarly restrictive. Inconsistent password policies will result in a synchronization failure if a user is able to change a password on a less restrictive system because the password will not be changed on the more restrictive system due to the password policy. When configuring Password Synchronization, best practice is to ensure that the passwords of sensitive accounts, such as those of administrators from both UNIX and Windows environments, are not replicated. By default, members of the local Windows Administrators and Domain Administrators groups are not replicated.

---

**MORE INFO**    **More on Password Synchronization**

To learn more about Password Synchronization, consult the following TechNet document: *http://technet2.microsoft.com/windowsserver2008/en/library/e755c195-e7e0-4a38-9531 -47a31e6e2aea1033.mspx?mfr=true.*

---

## Subsystem for UNIX-Based Applications

Subsystem for UNIX-based Applications (SUA) is a Windows Server 2008 feature that enables enterprises to run UNIX-based applications on computers running Windows Server 2008. SUA provides a UNIX-like environment, including shells, a set of scripting utilities, and a software development kit (SDK). SUA also provides support for case-sensitive file names, compilation tools, job control, and more than 300 popular UNIX utilities, commands, and shell scripts. You can install Subsystem for UNIX-based Applications as a Windows feature by using the Add Features Wizard.

A computer running Windows Server 2008 that has the SUA feature installed enables two separate command-line environments: a UNIX environment and a Windows environment. Applications execute within a specific environment. A UNIX command executes within the UNIX environment, and a Windows command executes within the Windows environment. Although the environments are different, commands executing in these environments can manipulate files stored on Windows volumes normally. For example, you can use the UNIX-based *grep* command under SUA to search a text file stored on an NTFS volume.

UNIX applications that run on existing computers can be ported to run on Windows Server 2008 under the SUA subsystem. This enables organizations to migrate existing applications that run on UNIX computers to Windows Server 2008. SUA supports 64-bit applications running on a 64-bit version of Windows Server 2008 as well as 32-bit applications running on both the 64-bit and 32-bit versions of Windows Server 2008. SUA supports connectivity to Oracle and SQL Server databases by using the Oracle Call Interface (OCI) and Open Database Connectivity (ODBC) standards. SUA also includes support that enables developers to debug Portable Operating System Interface (POSIX) processes by using Microsoft Visual Studio. POSIX is a collection of standards that define the application programming interface (API) for software that is compatible with UNIX-based operating systems.

Although it is possible to run some UNIX-based operating systems under Hyper-V, many UNIX computers use processor architectures other than x86 or x64. Only operating systems that run on the x86 or x64 architectures are compatible with Hyper-V. When planning the migration of POSIX-compliant applications from UNIX-based computers to Windows Server 2008, first determine whether the application can be migrated to run under the SUA subsystem. If the application cannot be migrated, a virtualization alternative might be necessary. In some cases, it will not be possible to migrate a UNIX-based application to a Windows host or a virtualized UNIX host running under Hyper-V. It is important that you determine what is possible before you make any firm plans to decommission existing UNIX-based computers.

---

**MORE INFO**    **More on Subsystem for UNIX-based Applications**

To learn more about the Windows Server 2008 Subsystem for UNIX-based Applications, consult the following TechNet link: *http://technet2.microsoft.com/windowsserver2008/en/library/f808072e-5b17 -4146-8188-f0b3b7e5c6291033.mspx?mfr=true.*

---

## Server for NIS

Server for NIS enables a Windows Server 2008 DC to act as a master NIS server for one or more NIS domains. Server for NIS provides a single namespace for NIS and Windows domains that an enterprise administrator can manage by using a single set of tools. Server for NIS stores the following NIS map data in AD DS:

- aliases
- bootparams
- ethers
- hosts
- group
- netgroup
- netid
- netmasks
- networks
- passwd
- protocols
- rpc
- services
- pservers
- shadow

It is possible to deploy Server for NIS on other DCs located in the same domain as the master NIS server. This enables these DCs to function as NIS subordinate servers, and NIS data is replicated through AD DS to the servers hosting the Server for NIS role. UNIX-based computers can also function as NIS subordinate servers because Server for NIS uses the same replication protocol to propagate NIS data to UNIX-based subordinates as a UNIX-based NIS master server does. When considering the deployment of Server for NIS in an integrated environment, remember that a computer running Windows Server 2008 must hold the master NIS server role. A computer running Windows Server 2008 cannot function as an NIS subordinate server to a UNIX-based NIS master.

When planning the migration from UNIX-based NIS servers to Windows-based NIS servers, your first task is to move the NIS maps to the new Windows Server 2008 NIS server. After you do this, the computer running Windows Server 2008 can function as an NIS master. It is possible to move multiple NIS domains to a single Windows Server 2008 DC. Although you can configure Server for NIS to support multiple NIS domains concurrently, you can also merge the domains after they have been migrated to the Windows Server 2008 DC running Server for NIS.

You are likely to plan the deployment of Server for NIS when you want to retire an existing NIS server infrastructure although NIS clients are still present on your organizational network. Server for NIS enables you to consolidate your server infrastructure around the Windows Server 2008 operating system while enabling UNIX-based NIS client computers to continue functioning normally on your organizational network.

When planning the deployment of Server for NIS, remember that this component is installed as a role service under the AD DS server role. Server for NIS can be installed only on a Windows Server 2008 DC. You cannot deploy Server for NIS on a standalone computer running Windows Server 2008 or on a member server running Windows Server 2008.

---

**MORE INFO   More on Server for NIS**

To learn more about Server for NIS, consult the following TechNet link: *http:// technet2.microsoft.com/windowsserver2008/en/library/f8ce4afa-e9b4-4e1c-95bd -d8de161c414b1033.mspx?mfr=true.*

---

## Services for Network File System

Services for Network File System (NFS) enables file sharing between Windows-based and UNIX-based computers. Plan to deploy Services for NFS if your environment contains a large number of UNIX-based client computers that need to access the same shared files as the Windows-based client computers on your organization's network. Figure 3-4 shows the NFS Advanced Sharing dialog box on a computer running Windows Server 2008 configured with Services for NFS.

During the deployment of Services for NFS, you must configure AD DS lookup resolution for UNIX group ID and UNIX user ID (GID and UID). You do this by installing the Identity Management for UNIX Active Directory schema extension that is included in Windows Server 2008. Lesson 1 of this chapter covered extending the schema in preparation for the deployment of the first Windows Server 2008 DC in a domain. You can then configure identity mapping by configuring the properties of Services for NFS and specifying the domain in the forest in which Identity Management for UNIX has been installed. Figure 3-5 shows identity mapping configuration for Services for NFS.

**Figure 3-4**   Configuring an NFS share

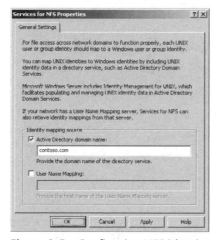

**Figure 3-5**   Configuring NFS identity mapping

---

**MORE INFO**   **More on Services for NFS**

To learn more about Services for NFS, consult the following TechNet document: *http:// technet2.microsoft.com/windowsserver2008/en/library/1f02f8b2-e653-4583-8391 -84d3411badd11033.mspx?mfr=true*.

---

PRACTICE **Planning for Interoperability**

Wingtip Toys is a moderate-sized enterprise that has 15 branch offices located across the southeastern states of Australia. Wingtip Toys wants to move away from its existing network infrastructure that includes both Windows-based and UNIX-based computers to a more homogeneous operating system environment. The company has a mixture of UNIX-based client and server computers at each branch office. UNIX-based client computers authenticate against the NIS service running on a UNIX server at each branch location. All existing UNIX-based client computers currently access shared files from UNIX servers. These shared files should be moved to a Windows-based platform. Previous attempts to achieve this have failed due to problems synchronizing user accounts and passwords between the disparate platforms. Because of budgetary constraints, management has asked that the UNIX servers at Wingtip Toys be decommissioned first, with a gradual transition from UNIX-based client computers to computers running Windows Vista over the next 24 months.

▶ **Exercise    Plan the Interoperability Strategy for Phasing Out UNIX-Based Computers at Wingtip Toys**

In this exercise, you will review the preceding business and technical requirements as part of a planned a migration from UNIX-based computers at Wingtip Toys.

1.  What steps must you perform to ensure that the NIS master server is a computer running Windows Server 2008 rather than a UNIX-based computer?

    ❑ Install Server for NIS on a Windows Server 2008 DC at each site. Configure one Windows Server 2008 DC as the master NIS server.

    ❑ Migrate NIS maps to the new master NIS server.

    ❑ Decommission existing NIS servers.

2.  What steps must you perform to ensure that users who switch between Windows-based and UNIX-based client computers use the same passwords for their user accounts?

    ❑ Install Password Synchronization.

    ❑ Ensure that password policies are compatible.

3.  What steps must you perform prior to decommissioning the UNIX-based file servers that UNIX-based client computers use?

    ❑ Install Services for NFS on the file servers running Windows Server 2008 that will replace the UNIX file servers.

    ❑ Migrate files and permissions from the NFS shares on the UNIX-based computers to the NFS shares on the computers running Windows Server 2008.

    ❑ Decommission the UNIX file servers.

## Lesson Summary

■ Active Directory Federation Services (AD FS) provides a single-sign-on solution for an organization's Web applications. By using AD FS, it is possible to set up federation trusts that allow users from partner organizations to authenticate against local Web applications by using their native environment's credentials.

- Identity Lifecycle Manager 2007 Feature Pack 1 enables user identity information to be shared across a wide range of directories and applications and aggregates user identity data in a metaverse. The metaverse itself is stored in a SQL Server 2000, SQL Server 2005, or SQL Server 2008 database.

- Services for Network File System (NFS) enables UNIX-based computers to access shared files hosted on a computer running Windows Server 2008.

- Subsystem for UNIX-based Applications (SUA) enables POSIX-compliant applications to execute on a computer running Windows Server 2008.

- Services for Network Information Service (NIS) enables a computer running Windows Server 2008 to act as a master NIS server. A computer running Windows Server 2008 cannot function as a subordinate NIS server to a UNIX-based NIS master server.

- Identity Management for UNIX enables Windows-based computers to perform lookups on UNIX-based directories for authentication.

- Password Synchronization enables user account passwords on UNIX-based computers and Windows-based computers to be synchronized. Password policies on both UNIX-based and Windows-based computers must be are similar; otherwise, synchronization errors can occur.

## Lesson Review

You can use the following questions to test your knowledge of the information in Lesson 2, "Planning for Interoperability." The questions are also available on the companion CD if you prefer to review them in electronic form.

---

**NOTE  Answers**

Answers to these questions and explanations of why each answer choice is correct or incorrect are located in the "Answers" section at the end of the book.

---

1. In which of the following situations would you plan to deploy Active Directory Federation Services?

    A. You need to share files on a computer running Windows Server 2008 to clients running UNIX-based operating systems.

    B. You need to synchronize user account passwords between computers running AD DS and UNIX- based computers.

    C. You need to run POSIX-compliant applications on a computer running Windows Server 2008.

    D. You need to provide single-sign-on for a group of related Web applications to users in a partner organization.

2. The organization that you work for wants your assistance in planning the deployment of a solution that will ensure that new-employee data entered in the human resource Oracle 9i database is synchronized with your organization's Windows Server 2008 AD DS and Exchange Server 2007 deployments. Which of the following solutions would you consider deploying to meet this need?

   **A.** AD FS

   **B.** Microsoft Identity Lifecycle Manager 2007 Feature Pack 1

   **C.** Server for NIS

   **D.** Services for NFS

3. Your predominantly Windows-based organization has recently acquired a company that uses UNIX-based computers for all client and server computers. The recently acquired company has a significant amount of spare office space. A nearby branch office has older facilities, so there is a plan to redeploy staff from this older facility to the recently acquired company's site. As part of this redeployment, it will be necessary to introduce computers running Windows Server 2008, functioning as file servers. Which of the following Windows Server 2008 role services or functions should you plan to deploy so that UNIX-based client computers will be able to access files hosted on a Windows Server 2008 file server?

   **A.** Subsystem for UNIX-based Applications

   **B.** Server for NIS

   **C.** Services for NFS

   **D.** Network Policy Server

4. You are putting the finishing touches on a plan to migrate several branch offices to Windows Server 2008. Each branch office currently has an old UNIX-based computer that hosts several POSIX-compliant applications. You want to minimize the amount of hardware present at each branch office. Which of the following items should you include in your Windows Server 2008 branch office migration plan? (Choose two. Each answer forms part of the solution.)

   **A.** Deploy the Terminal Services role.

   **B.** Deploy the Hyper-V role.

   **C.** Deploy the Subsystem for UNIX-based Applications feature.

   **D.** Deploy the Active Directory Federation Services role.

   **E.** Migrate the applications from the UNIX computer to Windows Server 2008.

# Chapter Review

To further practice and reinforce the skills you learned in this chapter, you can perform the following tasks:

- Review the chapter summary.
- Complete the case scenario. This scenario sets up a real-world situation involving the topics of this chapter and asks you to create a solution.
- Complete the suggested practices.
- Take a practice test.

# Chapter Summary

- Run *adprep /forestprep* on the schema master and *adprep /domainprep /gpprep* on each domain's infrastructure master.
- Limit the scope of trusts so that they meet the necessary requirements only. Do not create a two-way trust when a one-way trust is all that is required.
- Selective authentication enables administrators in a trusting forest or domain to allow limited access to specific users from a trusted forest or domain.
- AD FS enable partner organizations to have single sign on for local Web applications without configuring forest-based or domain-based trusts.
- Server for NIS enables a computer running Windows Server 2008 to function as an NIS server for UNIX-based computers.
- Services for NFS enables a computer running Windows Server 2008 to function as a file server for a UNIX-based computer.
- The Password Synchronization component enables account passwords for AD DS–based and UNIX-based computers to be the same.
- SUA enables POSIX-compliant applications to run on computers running Windows Server 2008.

# Case Scenario

In the following case scenario, you will apply what you have learned about patch management and security. You can find answers to these questions in the "Answers" section at the end of this book.

## Case Scenario:  Phasing Out a UNIX-Based Computer at Tailspin Toys

You are assisting Tailspin Toys to integrate the recently purchased Wingtip Toys company in its network infrastructure. The integration will proceed over time, with some tasks of higher priority to the management of Tailspin Toys than others. One high-priority task involves an aging UNIX-based computer at Wingtip Toys that hosts a POSIX-compliant payroll application. This is the only UNIX-based computer in either organization, and management would prefer not to replace the computer with another UNIX-based computer unless absolutely necessary. Wingtip Toys is using Lotus Notes 7.0, and Tailspin Toys uses Exchange Server 2007. The HR department at Tailspin Toys uses an SQL Server 2008–based database to manage employee data. The HR department at Tailspin Toys will now be responsible for managing all new and existing employee data for both organizations. Although the HR database will be managed centrally, each organization's accounting teams will be kept separate, although they will use the existing Tailspin Toys financial Web applications. One problem with this is that the Wingtip Toys accountants find the authentication process quite complicated, and management hopes that you might offer some recommendations to make it simpler. With this information in mind, answer the following questions:

1. What plans could you make to simplify authentication to the Tailspin Toys accounting applications for Wingtip Toys staff?

2. What plans could you make to migrate the Wingtip Toys payroll application to Tailspin Toys?

3. What plans could you make to ensure that the Wingtip Toys mail solution is correctly provisioned when a new employee is hired?

# Suggested Practices

To help you successfully master the exam objectives presented in this chapter, complete the following tasks.

# Plan for Domain or Forest Migration, Upgrade, and Restructuring

Complete the following practice exercise.

- **Practice**   Upgrade a Windows Server 2003 single-domain forest to Windows Server 2008.
  - ❑ Using evaluation software, create a Windows Server 2003 single-domain forest.
  - ❑ Join a Windows Server 2008 member server to this single-domain forest.
  - ❑ Use the *adprep* command to prepare the Windows Server 2003 single-domain forest.
  - ❑ Promote the Windows Server 2008 member server to DC.

❏ Transfer FSMO roles from the Windows Server 2003 DC to the Windows Server 2008 DC.

❏ Demote the Windows Server 2003 DC to member server.

## Plan for Interoperability

Complete the following practice exercise.

■ **Practice** Work with Services for NFS.

❏ Install the Services for Network File System (NFS) role service on a computer running Windows Server 2008.

❏ Configure an NFS share that will be accessible to UNIX-based operating systems.

# Take a Practice Test

The practice tests on this book's companion CD offer many options. For example, you can test yourself on just one exam objective, or you can test yourself on all the 70-647 certification exam content. You can set up the test so that it closely simulates the experience of taking a certification exam, or you can set it up in study mode so that you can look at the correct answers and explanations after you answer each question.

---

**MORE INFO** Practice tests

For details about all the practice test options available, see the "How to Use the Practice Tests" section in this book's introduction.

---

# Chapter 4

# Designing Active Directory Administration and Group Policy Strategy

Designing and planning Active Directory Domain Services (AD DS) and Group Policy is central to the operation of an enterprise network. If your Active Directory structure is wrong or even if it is sound but you are not administering it properly, nothing on your network will work efficiently.

If your Group Policy is not well planned and correctly administered, users will not have the rights they need to do their jobs, or they will find that they can make configuration changes that they should not be able to make. If you do not have a sensible, straightforward, well-documented Group Policy strategy, you might not be able to discover why this is happening. This chapter discusses models for administering AD DS and the principles behind Group Policy design.

### Exam objectives in this chapter:
- Design the Active Directory administrative model.
- Design the enterprise-level group policy strategy.
- Design for data management and data access.

### Lessons in this chapter:
- Lesson 1:  Designing the Active Directory Administrative Model. . . . . . . . . . . . . . . . . 171
- Lesson 2:  Designing Enterprise-Level Group Policy Strategy. . . . . . . . . . . . . . . . . . . . 200

## Before You Begin

To complete the lessons in this chapter, you must have done the following:

- Installed a Windows Server 2008 Enterprise domain controller named Glasgow as described in Chapter 1, "Planning Name Resolution and Internet Protocol Addressing."
- Installed a Windows Server 2008 Enterprise domain controller in the *litware.internal* domain. The computer name is Brisbane. Configure a static IPv4 address of 10.0.0.31 with a subnet mask of 255.255.255.0. The IPv4 address of the Domain Name System (DNS) server is 10.0.0.31. Other than IPv4 configuration and the computer name, accept

all the default installation settings. It's recommended that you use a virtual machine to host this server. To download an evaluation version of Virtual Server 2005 R2, visit *http://www.microsoft.com/technet/virtualserver/evaluation/default.mspx*. You can obtain an evaluation version of Windows Server 2008 Enterprise from the Microsoft Download Center at the following address: *http://www.microsoft.com/downloads/search.aspx*.

- Created the Kim_Akers administrator-level account in the *contoso.internal* domain as described in Chapter 1.

- Created a Tom_Perry administrator-level account with the password P@ssw0rd in the *litware.internal* domain. This account should be a member of Domain Admins, Enterprise Admins, and Schema Admins.

# Lesson 1:  Designing the Active Directory Administrative Model

As an enterprise administrator, you will plan and design the administrative model for AD DS within your enterprise. You are unlikely to create groups, delegate control of organizational units (OUs), or configure and link Group Policy objects yourself, but you will design a delegation structure so that less senior members of staff can carry out the tasks required to implement your plans without being given more rights and permissions than they need to do their job.

Because of the full-trust model in an Active Directory domain tree, domain and server administrators seldom need to configure trusts. Implementing a permission and administration model in a multi-forest enterprise network is, therefore, likely to be a task you do yourself, and you need to work with universal groups and forest trusts.

Your planning should always consider the structures already available to you by default. You should not plan a new domain local security group, for example, when a built-in local security group already exists that facilitates your aims. Therefore, be aware of the security groups that are installed by default or installed automatically when features such as read-only domain controllers (RODCs) are implemented.

You are unlikely to create OUs and Group Policy objects (GPOs) personally, but you need to plan which OUs and GPOs are created and how they are linked. You need to delegate group and OU management. You will not typically audit ordinary users personally, but you do need to audit the high-level activities of your administrative team.

Designing and planning an Active Directory administrative model in the enterprise is a complex task. This lesson discusses the aspects of this task.

> **After this lesson, you will be able to:**
> - Determine a delegation policy that facilitates efficient Active Directory administration but does not allocate unnecessary rights and permissions.
> - Plan an Active Directory group strategy.
> - Plan a compliance auditing strategy to include Group Policy and Active Directory auditing.
> - Plan the administration of Active Directory groups.
> - Plan an organizational structure that includes the design of OU and group structure.
>
> **Estimated lesson time:  55 minutes**

**Real World**

*Ian McLean*

One of the most difficult things a manager needs to learn is how to delegate. As an enterprise administrator, that's what you are—a manager. You're a manager with a high level of technical knowledge, but still a manager, and that's where many excellent server and network administrators fall down. You might be a first-class coder who can produce Microsoft Windows PowerShell and batch files without even thinking about it. You might be a troubleshooting wizard who can identify a network or server fault while others are still rolling up their sleeves; your Group Policy configuration might be immaculate. However, if you are busy changing a password for a forgetful user while the entire enterprise goes wrong for lack of planning, you are not doing your job.

You need to plan. You need to organize. You need to ensure that your staff is given the appropriate training—and that does not mean training people yourself. You need to delegate jobs to people who (in your opinion) know how to do them. You need to ensure that they receive advice and training if they don't.

The main problem for most fledgling enterprise administrators is lack of control. You need to trust your staff, and if one of your junior administrators makes a mistake, you must take the responsibility for a mistake that wasn't yours. You will wear a suit and seldom, if ever, crawl behind wiring racks. You need to accept that your server administrators know more about their particular sections of the network than you do.

Others will configure servers and create OUs. You will plan the structure of your Active Directory forest or forests and the permissions structure in your enterprise. You still need to keep up to date technically—you can't plan a Windows Server 2008 domain unless you know the features Windows Server 2008 offers you—but your job is planning, supervising, and administering.

Enjoy.

# Delegating Active Directory Administration

A well-planned delegation strategy enables you to increase security and manage resources efficiently while meeting administrative requirements. Delegation increases administrative efficiency, decentralizes administration, reduces administrative costs, and improves the manageability of IT infrastructures.

Delegation is the transfer of administrative responsibility for a specific task from a higher authority to a lower authority. From a technical perspective, delegation of administration involves a senior administrator granting a controlled set of permissions to a less experienced administrator to carry out a specific administrative task.

Typically, the administrative model in large organizations with enterprise networks is one in which different divisions and business units share a common IT infrastructure. This IT infrastructure can span multiple organizational and geographic boundaries. Such an environment generally has the following requirements:

- **Organizational structure requirements**  Part of an organization might participate in a shared infrastructure to save costs but require the ability to operate independently from the rest of the organization.
- **Operational requirements**  An organization might place unique constraints on directory service configuration, availability, or security.
- **Legal requirements**  An organization might have legal requirements to operate in a specific manner such as restricting access to confidential information.
- **Administrative requirements**  Different organizations might have different administrative needs, depending on existing and planned IT administration and support models.
- **Organization size**  Organizations can be small, medium, or large. A complex and sophisticated delegation structure for a small organization with a small team of administrators is unlikely to work.

When planning a delegation strategy, you need to have a very good grasp of your organization's requirements. These requirements help you plan the degree of autonomy and isolation within the organization or within sectors of the organization. Autonomy is the ability of the administrators of an organization to manage independently all or part of service management (service autonomy) and all or part of the data stored in or protected by AD DS (data autonomy).

Isolation is the ability of an administrator or an organization to prevent other administrators from controlling or interfering with service management (service isolation) and from controlling or viewing a subset of data in AD DS or on member servers and client computers that have accounts in AD DS (data isolation).

In a large organization, autonomy and isolation need to be carefully managed. You might want to manage some services on an enterprise-wide basis. For example, it is a valid model for even a very large organization to have a single domain tree or even a single domain with many sites. You might want to implement distributed file system replication to replicate AD DS settings throughout the enterprise, but your Australian sites want to control their own password policy. You could use fine-grained security policies in this instance, although this might not be practical for a large number of users, and it requires a domain functional level of Windows Server 2008—not a good idea if you have Microsoft Windows 2000 Server or Microsoft Windows Server 2003 domain controllers (DCs) in a domain. Sometimes strict service or data isolation requires creating a separate forest or a subdomain.

---

**MORE INFO**    Fine-grained password policies

For more information about fine-grained password policies, see *http://technet2.microsoft.com /windowsserver2008/en/library/056a73ef-5c9e-44d7-acc1-4f0bade6cd751033.mspx?mfr=true.*

---

## Classifying Organizations

One of your first steps in planning an organization's delegation structure is to classify the organization. Organizations can be classified based on their size in the following categories:

- **Small organizations**    Typically, these have 25 to 50 workstations and three to five servers.
- **Medium organizations**    Typically, these have 50 to 500 workstations and 4 to 50 servers.
- **Large organizations**    Typically, these have at least 500 workstations and 50 servers.

Small and medium organizations typically have a very small number of administrative groups that are responsible for managing all aspects of AD DS. Small and medium organizations might not need to create an extensive delegation model. Large organizations generally must distribute and delegate administrative authority to various administrative groups, possibly delegating certain aspects of Active Directory management to centralized teams and delegating other aspects to decentralized teams. Although large organizations will find the delegation capabilities of AD DS most useful, small and medium organizations can often achieve enhanced security, increased control, more accountability, and reduced costs by implementing a degree of delegation.

## Delegation Benefits and Principles

By efficiently delegating administrative responsibilities among various administrative groups, you can address the specific requirements of administrative autonomy and successfully manage an AD DS environment. Delegation of administration provides the following benefits:

- Each administrative group has a defined and documented scope of authority and set of responsibilities.
- Administrative authority is decentralized.
- The delegation of administrative responsibility addresses the security concerns of the organization.

When you are planning the delegation of administration, adhere to the following principles:

- **Distribute administrative responsibilities on the basis of least privilege**    This ensures that the individual or group of individuals to whom the task has been delegated can perform only the tasks that are delegated and cannot perform tasks that have not been explicitly delegated or authorized.

- **Increase administrative efficiency**   Many of the responsibilities for managing Active Directory content can be assigned to the directory service itself. This automates management and increases efficiency.
- **Reduce administrative costs**   You can do this by facilitating shared administrative responsibility. For example, you could allocate administrative responsibility for providing account support to all accounts in the organization to a specific group. You need to ensure, however, that the organization's autonomy requirements are met.

## Managing Active Directory Through Delegation

The primary reason for delegating administrative authority is to allow organizations to manage their Active Directory environments and the data stored in AD DS efficiently. Delegation of administration makes Active Directory management easier and enables organizations to address specific administrative needs.

The administrative responsibilities of managing an Active Directory environment fall into two categories:

- **Service management**   Administrative tasks involved in providing secure and reliable delivery of the directory service
- **Data management**   Administrative operations involved in managing the content stored in or protected by the directory service

**Service Management**   Service management includes managing all aspects of the directory service that are essential to ensuring the uninterrupted delivery of the directory service across the enterprise. Service management includes the following administrative tasks:

- Adding and removing DCs
- Managing and monitoring replication
- Ensuring the proper assignment and configuration of operations master roles
- Performing regular backups of the directory database
- Managing domain and DC security policies
- Configuring directory service parameters such as setting the functional level of a forest or putting the directory in the special List-Object security mode

**Data Management**   Data management includes managing the content stored in AD DS as well as content protected by Active Directory. Data management tasks include the following:

- Managing user accounts
- Managing computer accounts
- Managing security groups
- Managing application-specific attributes for AD DS–enabled and AD DS–integrated applications

- Managing workstations
- Managing servers
- Managing resources

You delegate Active Directory administrative functions such as service and data management in response to the geographical, business, and technical infrastructure of an enterprise. A well-implemented delegation model provides coverage for all aspects of Active Directory management, meets autonomy and isolation requirements, efficiently distributes administrative responsibilities (with a limited subset of tasks delegated to nonadministrators), and delegates administrative responsibilities in a security-conscious manner.

## Defining the Administrative Model

To manage an enterprise environment effectively, you need to define how tasks will be assigned and managed. Your plan for delegating responsibility for the network defines the enterprise's administrative model. Microsoft identifies the following three types of administrative models that you can use to allocate the management of the enterprise network logically between individual administrators or departments within the enterprise's IT function:

- Centralized
- Distributed
- Mixed

If no administrative model exists, the environment is managed chaotically, and most administrative tasks are typically handling emergencies. In this case, tasks such as server updates and modifications are frequently performed on the spot without proper testing. When administrative and maintenance tasks are not performed in a consistent manner, securing the environment and auditing administrative events are exceptionally difficult. Environments that do not follow an administrative model are administered reactively rather than proactively.

To identify the correct administrative model, determine which services are needed in each location in the enterprise and where the administrators with the skills to manage these services are located. Placing administrators in branch offices that require very little IT administration is usually a waste of money (which is one of the major reasons that Windows Server 2008 introduced RODCs).

**Centralized Administration Model**    In the centralized administration model, IT-related administration is controlled by one group, typically located at the head office or possibly at the enterprise's research facility. In this model, all critical servers are housed in one location (or a very few locations), which facilitates central backup and an appropriate IT staff member being available when a problem occurs.

For example, if an organization locates mission-critical servers (such as Microsoft Exchange Server 2007 messaging servers) at each site, a qualified staff member might not be available at a remote site if a server needs to be recovered from backup, and remote administration (if possible) would be required. In the centralized administration model, all the servers running Exchange Server 2007 and the appropriate administrator would be located in a central office, enabling recovery and administration to be handled as efficiently and effectively as possible.

The centralized administration model is typically used in organizations that have one large central office with a few branch offices and typically a single Active Directory domain. Delegation is by function rather than by geographical location, and most tasks are allocated to IT staff, although some can be delegated to nonadministrators. For example, the head of the Accounting department could be delegated the task of resetting passwords for all the users in the Accounting OU (but have no rights in the rest of the organization).

**The Distributed Administration Model**    In the distributed administration model, tasks are delegated to IT and non-IT staff members in various locations. The rights to perform administrative tasks can be granted based on geography, department, or job function. Also, administrative control can be granted for a specific network service such as DNS or a Dynamic Host Configuration Protocol (DHCP) server. This enables separation of server and workstation administration without giving nonadministrators the rights to modify network settings or security. A sound, well-planned delegation structure is essential in the distributed administration model.

---

**Exam Tip**    Note that the exam does not include direct references to Dynamic DNS. It will, however, refer to dynamic updates as well as to Active Directory–integrated DNS zones. Any time a DNS server is updated automatically through authorized clients, it is a DDNS server. Keep this in mind when taking the exam.

---

Windows Server 2008 enables granular administrative rights and permissions, giving enterprise administrators more flexibility when assigning tasks to staff members. Distributed administration based only on geographical proximity is commonly found among enterprises that use the distributed administration model. If a server, workstation, or network device needs attention on a site whose size justifies having its own administrator or administrative team, the administrative rights to carry out the required tasks should be delegated to local administrators.

The distributed administration model is commonly used in enterprises that have a number of large, geographically distributed locations—for example, a multinational organization. Such organizations typically have several domains or even several forests. Although rights are delegated to both administrative and nonadministrative staff on a regional basis, a group of enterprise administrators can typically perform high-level administrative tasks across domains and across forests.

**Mixed Administration Model**    The mixed administration model uses both centralized and distributed administration. For example, you could define all security policies and standard server configurations from a central site but delegate the implementation and management of key servers by physical location. Administrators can configure servers in their own location but cannot configure servers in other locations. You can distribute the rights to manage only local user accounts to local administrators and restricted rights over specific OUs to nonadministrative staff. As with the distributed administrative model, an enterprise administrators group would have rights in all locations. This model is used in medium-sized organizations with a few fairly large sites that are geographically separated but in which the main office wants to keep control of certain aspects of the operation.

---

### Quick Check

1. What are the three main aspects of an enterprise's administrative structure that you need to consider when planning an Active Directory administration delegation model?
2. What are the attributes of a well-implemented delegation model?

### Quick Check Answers

1. You need to consider the geographical, business, and technical infrastructure of an enterprise.
2. A well-implemented delegation model could include any or all of the following attributes:
   - ❑ Provides coverage for all aspects of Active Directory management
   - ❑ Meets autonomy and isolation requirements
   - ❑ Distributes administrative responsibilities efficiently
   - ❑ Delegates administrative responsibilities in a security-conscious manner

---

## Using Group Strategy to Delegate Management Tasks

A user to whom you delegate a specific management task or set of tasks is known as a *management stakeholder*. Such users can be enterprise administrators who can perform tasks across multiple domains or multiple forests if the appropriate forest trusts are configured. However, most day-to-day administration in a well-organized enterprise network is carried out by users who do not have administrative rights to an entire domain, forest, or multiple forests. Instead, these users have sufficient rights to carry out specifically defined tasks, typically within a single OU and any child OUs. This follows the principles of autonomy (stakeholders can perform predefined tasks) and isolation (stakeholders can perform only the tasks that are predefined) that were discussed earlier in this lesson.

Stakeholders might be delegated rights to determine who in the organization has permission to read, write, and delete data in a shared folder on a file server. They might be delegated rights to reset passwords in a departmental OU so that they can deal with the situation when a user forgets a password, without needing to call in an administrator. An administrator can be delegated the rights to create and change the membership of a global distribution group and, hence, to determine the membership of a mailing list but have no rights to reconfigure security policies.

A responsible member of staff who is nevertheless not an administrator might be delegated permission to configure a member server as an RODC on a specified site. An administrator at a remote location might be able to configure servers at that location and restore a server from backup but have no rights at other locations. A domain administrator might have rights to a specific domain but not to any of the domains in a separate forest in the enterprise.

Typically, the rights and permissions of stakeholders are conferred through membership of security groups. It is possible to give an individual user rights, but this is bad practice. Familiarize yourself with the built-in domain-wide local security groups that confer limited rights such as Account Operators and Backup Operators. Figure 4-1 shows the built-in local security groups in the Builtin Active Directory container. You cannot change the group type or scope of built-in local security groups.

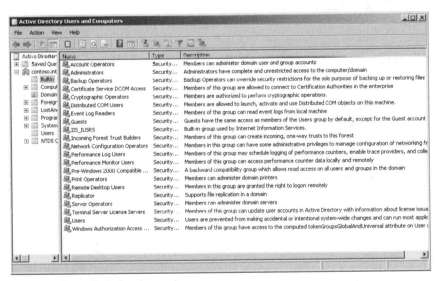

**Figure 4-1**  Built-in local security groups

If you open Group Policy Management Console, look at Default Domain Policy GPO, and access the Back Up Files And Directories user right, you will see on the Explain tab that Backup Operators is one of the security groups that has that right. Figure 4-2 shows this tab.

You allocate rights to security groups in Default Domain Policy GPO, in Default Domain Controllers GPO, or in GPOs linked to specific OUs. For example, Figure 4-3 shows the Back Up Files And Directories user right being allocated to the Sample Group security group (which was created to illustrate this operation and is not a built-in group).

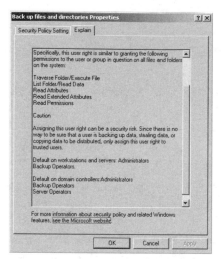

**Figure 4-2**    Default groups with the Back Up Files And Directories user right

**Figure 4-3**    Assigning the Back Up Files And Directories user right to a group

This example is a reminder that to allocate a user right to a security group, you add the group to the user right in a GPO. This is a task you would delegate, but you need to bear the process in mind when you are planning group strategy. You need to keep group strategy as simple as possible. For example, if you created the Sample Group to carry out backup operations in the domain, this would almost certainly be bad design because you already have the built-in Backup Operators group to do this. However, if you want a group that can back up files and directories only in a single OU and give the members of that group no rights other than to that OU, creating a domain local group is a valid strategy.

Allocate user rights to domain local security groups. You can allocate rights to global security groups, universal groups, and even to individual users, but this is bad practice. By the same token, you should not add users directly to local groups. You learned this rule in your very first days of training to be an administrator. Now that you are an experienced administrator looking at high-level planning tasks, the rule is every bit as important.

Add users to global groups. Nest global groups in other global groups. If you use universal groups, add global groups (not users) to universal groups. Add global and universal groups to domain local groups. Assign rights to domain local groups.

Figure 4-4 shows the domain local security groups in the *contoso.internal* domain. These are installed with AD DS or created during configuration operations, for example, when a computer account for an RODC is created in a domain. Chapter 10, "Designing Solutions for Data Sharing, Data Security, and Business Continuity," discusses RODCs in depth. Some domain local security groups can be changed to universal security groups, such as the Allowed RODC Password Replication Group, while others, such as the Cert Publishers group, cannot.

This functionality is determined by whether the operation of a group is confined within the boundaries of a domain (such as publishing certificates) or whether they can cross domains. (Branch-office users in several domains can have their passwords replicated to RODCs for local authentication.) You can create additional domain local security groups and assign them rights in GPOs linked to the domain, to the Domain Controllers OU, or to other OUs in your planned organizational structure.

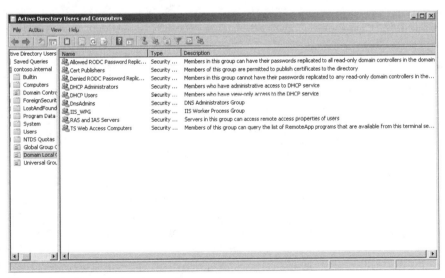

**Figure 4-4** Domain local security groups

Figure 4-5 shows the global security groups created automatically when AD DS was installed to create the *contoso.internal* domain, plus the DnsUpdateProxy group that was created when the default DNS installation for a new domain was specified. The Read-Only Domain Controllers group was created when an RODC computer account was configured, and the RODC_Installers group was created manually. These last two groups will probably not be present on your DC. The DnsUpdateProxy group can be converted to a universal group. The other automatically created groups cannot be.

It is important to remember that even an apparently powerful group such as Domain Admins has no directly allocated user rights but instead gets its rights through membership in the Administrators built-in local group. You *can* allocate rights directly to a global security group, but it is bad practice to do so.

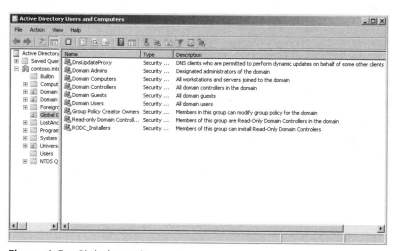

**Figure 4-5**   Global security groups

Figure 4-6 shows the universal security groups created automatically when AD DS was installed to create the *contoso.internal* domain, plus the Enterprise Read-Only Domain Controllers group that was created when an RODC computer account was configured. Universal groups can contain users or (preferably) global security groups from multiple domains and can be allocated rights and permissions across domains. If forest trusts are set up correctly, they can operate across forests.

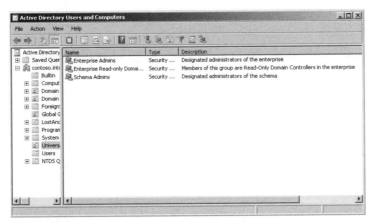

**Figure 4-6**    Universal security groups

---

**MORE INFO**    **Multiple forest considerations**

For more information about operating across forests, see *http://www.microsoft.com/technet /prodtechnol/windowsserver2003/technologies/directory/activedirectory/mtfstwp.mspx#E5D*. Although this article is written for Windows 2000 Server and Windows Server 2003 domains, it is relevant to Windows Server 2008 domains also. Note that the minimum domain functional level in a Windows Server 2008 domain is Windows 2000 Server Native.

---

To an enterprise administrator, universal groups might seem at first to provide an easy answer to cross-domain and cross-forest design, but beware. Universal groups need to be replicated across domains and forests, typically over slow WAN links. They can increase network traffic and thus reduce performance.

Microsoft recommends using as few universal groups as possible. With careful planning, you can do most of what you want to do with global and domain local groups. If you must use a universal group, do not add users. Every time the group membership changes, this triggers more replication traffic. Use only global groups, for example, the Domain Admins group from each of your domains, as members of a universal group. Even if the membership of a Domain Admins group changes, the membership of the universal group—that contains groups and not individual users—remains the same.

## Management Roles

The previous discussion in this lesson has shown that an individual user right in a GPO can be allocated to a user or group. This can be a tedious procedure when extensive rights configuration is required. Roles are collections of rights and permissions, and you should use them in your planning rather than relying on individual rights. For example, Server Manager is a role that consists of a number of rights such as logging on to servers interactively and configuring servers. In general, a role is implemented by a built-in or domain local security group.

Microsoft recommends a number of roles for service management. These role recommendations take into account defined sets of logically related administrative tasks and the security sensitivity and impact of these tasks. The following is the set of recommended roles for delegating service management:

- Forest Configuration Operators
- Domain Configuration Operators
- Security Policy Administrators
- Service Administration Managers
- DC Administrators
- Backup Operators
- Schema Administrators
- Replication Management Administrators
- Replication Monitoring Operators
- DNS Administrators

---

**MORE INFO    Service management**

For more information about service management and the recommended service management roles, see *http://technet2.microsoft.com/windowsserver/en/library/9fa7bfbb-0081-413c-a9f0 -d431bcd20eb81033.mspx?mfr=true*.

---

In addition, Microsoft has engineered a set of recommended roles for delegating data management. These role recommendations take into account the sets of logically related administrative tasks and the security sensitivity and impact of these tasks. The following is the set of recommended roles for delegating data management:

- Business Unit Administrators
- Account Administrators
- Workstation Administrators
- Server Operators
- Resource Administrators
- Security Group Administrators
- Help Desk Operators
- Application-Specific Administrators

---

**MORE INFO    Data management**

For more information about data management and the recommended data management roles, see *http://technet2.microsoft.com/windowsserver/en/library/2aa84f86-de1a-4d2b-b57d -665200e022cd1033.mspx?mfr=true*.

---

## Planning Forest-Level Trusts

In the days before AD DS, domain administrators needed to know about trusts. However, with the full-trust Active Directory model, every domain in a single forest trusts every other domain. Trusts are typically created when your enterprise contains several forests, and cross-forest administration is definitely a task for the enterprise administrator. For this reason, this lesson discusses forest trusts in some depth.

A forest trust (or forest-level trust) allows every domain in one forest to trust every domain in a second forest. Forest trusts can be one-way incoming, one-way outgoing, or two-way. For example, you can configure all the domains in Forest A to trust all the domains in Forest B by creating a one-way trust in either Forest B or Forest A. If, in addition, you want all the domains in Forest B to trust all the domains in Forest A, you need to create a two-way trust.

You can use forest trusts with partner or closely associated organizations. For example, Contoso, Ltd., and Litware, Inc., have merged but do not choose to amalgamate their Active Directory structures in a single forest. Instead, you are asked to plan a forest trust to give employees of one organization rights and permissions in the other.

Forest trusts can form part of an acquisition or takeover strategy. Northwind Traders has acquired Coho Winery. The eventual plan is to reorganize the domain structures of both companies into a single forest, but until this process is complete, you might plan a forest trust between the organizations.

You can also use forest trusts for Active Directory isolation. You might, for example, want to run Exchange Server 2007 as part of a migration strategy to try out the new features and familiarize your technical staff. However, you do not want to install Exchange Server 2007 into your production forest because this could affect your current Exchange Server 2003 deployment. You can create a separate forest in which you can run Exchange Server 2007 but access resources in your production forest while doing so by setting up a forest trust.

## Planning Trust Type and Direction

The most common type of trust that operates across forests is the forest trust, and this is the type of trust discussed in this lesson. You should, however, be aware of the other types of trusts that can be set up with entities outside your forest. These include the following:

- **Shortcut trust**  A forest trust will enable any domain in one forest to trust any domain in another forest. However, if forests are complex, with several layers of child domains, it might take some time for a client in a child domain to locate resources in a child domain in another forest, especially when the operation happens over a WAN link. If users in one child domain frequently need to access resources in another child domain in another forest, you might decide to create a shortcut trust between the two domains.

- **External trust**  You set up an external trust when a domain within your forest requires a trust relationship with a domain that does not belong to a forest. Typically, external trusts are used when migrating resources from Microsoft Windows NT domains, many of which still exist. Windows NT does not use the concept of forests, and a Windows NT domain is a self-contained, autonomous unit. If you plan to migrate resources from a Windows NT domain into an existing Active Directory forest, you can establish an external trust between one of the Active Directory domains and the Windows NT domain.

- **Realm trust**   If a UNIX realm uses Kerberos authentication, you can create a realm trust between a Windows domain and a UNIX realm. This is similar to an external trust except that it is between a Windows domain and a UNIX realm.

When you have selected the type of trust you require—typically a forest trust because shortcut, external, and realm trusts are used in specific situations—you then need to decide whether the trust is one-way or two-way and, if the former, what the trust direction is. One-way trusts can be incoming or outgoing.

If users in Forest A must access resources in Forest B, and users in Forest B must access resources in Forest A, you need to create a two-way trust. Because this is bidirectional, you do not need to specify a direction.

If, however, users in Forest A require access to resources in Forest B, but users in Forest B do not require access to resources in Forest A, Forest A is the trusted forest and Forest B the trusting or resource forest. Forest B trusts the users in Forest A and allows them to access its resources. If you are creating a one-way forest trust in a resource forest, it is an incoming trust. If you are creating a one-way forest trust in a trusted forest, it is an outgoing trust.

Imagine the trust as an arrow. The resources are at the point of the arrow. The users that are trusted to use these resources are at the other end. Figure 4-7 shows this relationship. The arrow is incoming at the trusting (resource) forest and outgoing at the trusted forest.

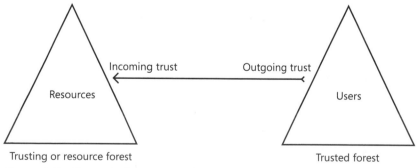

**Figure 4-7**   One-way forest trust relationship

## Creating Forest Trusts

Before you create a forest trust, ensure that the forest functional level of both forests is either Windows Server 2003 or Windows Server 2008. Forest functional levels were discussed in

Chapter 2, "Designing Active Directory Domain Services." Your next step is to ensure that each forest's root domain can access the root domain of the other forest. You need to create the required DNS records and use the *nslookup* tool to ensure that you can resolve domain names in the other forest. You also need to know the username and password for an enterprise administrator account (an administrator account in the root domain) in each forest unless you are setting up only one side of the trust, and an administrator in the other forest is setting up the other end. You create a forest trust in this lesson's practice.

## Planning Data Management

In many enterprise organizations, the Active Directory rights administration structure is not the main concern of the majority of users. They are not concerned about who can configure what. They are concerned about how their data is administered and whether they have the appropriate permissions to read, update, and delete files. A list of data management roles was given earlier in this lesson. It remains only to discuss group management in this context.

Suppose, for example, you have a shared folder on a server called Data Files. In practice, this will probably be a data structure, and you could plan whether to block permission inheritance on subfolders. Your administrators can configure share and NTFS permissions on the folder or folder tree through the Sharing and Security tabs. On the Security tab shown in Figure 4-8, Sample Group has the Modify permission on the folder. Standard users can read the files.

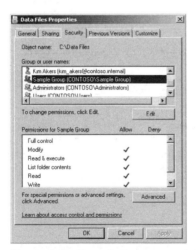

**Figure 4-8**  Sample Group permissions

You can delegate the management of Sample Group to one of its members. For example, Figure 4-9 shows the management of Sample Group delegated to Don Hall. Don can change the group membership.

**Figure 4-9**    Sample Group management

The consequences of this configuration are significant. Don Hall is a standard user with no administrative rights other than the delegated right to manage the Sample Group membership. He cannot set permissions. He cannot manage any other groups. The permissions on the Data Files folder have been set by an administrator. Members of Sample Group have Modify permission. Don cannot change this.

However, he can change the membership of Sample Group. So, safely, and without allocating any administrative rights to anything else, you have delegated to the user Don Hall the facility to determine who can modify files in the Data Files folder. This is a valuable technique. Use it in your planning.

---

**MORE INFO    Delegating data management**

Space considerations prevent a full discussion of data management and how to delegate it—a topic that could easily fill an entire book. For more information, go to *http://technet2.microsoft.com /windowsserver/en/library/83a5fe2d-d74a-42e1-b5a6-d96d181015fc1033.mspx?mfr=true* and follow the links on the left side of the console pane.

---

## Using Starter GPOs

Windows Server 2008 Group Policy introduces starter GPOs; incorporate these in your group strategy planning. Starter GPOs enable you to save baseline templates that you can use when you create new GPOs. You can also export starter GPOs to domains other than those in which they were created.

When you open Group Policy Management Console in Windows Server 2008, you can locate the Starter GPOs container in the left pane below a domain. Until you populate it, this container is empty. You create a starter GPO by right-clicking the Starter GPOs container and selecting New. You can configure GPOs in this container as you would configure any GPO except that only the Administrative Templates settings are available in both Computer Settings and User Settings.

When you create a new starter GPO, you are prompted to name it, and you can add a comment. You can edit your starter GPO and set the Administrative templates you require. When you create a starter GPO, you automatically create a new folder on the DC to which Group Policy Management Console is connected, by default in the C:\Windows\SYSVOL\domain \StarterGPOs path. This is replicated to other DCs as part of SYSVOL replication.

You can create a new (normal) GPO by using a starter GPO as a template by right-clicking the starter GPO and selecting New GPO From Starter GPO. Alternatively you can right-click the Group Policy Objects container, select New, and then specify a starter GPO from the Source Starter GPO drop-down list. You can access the same dialog box and specify a starter GPO if you right-click an OU (or the domain) and select Create A GPO In This Domain, And Link It Here. From a starter GPO, you can easily create multiple GPOs with the same baseline configuration. You need only to configure settings in these GPOs that are not contained in Administrative Templates.

Starter GPOs are not backed up when you choose Back Up All on the Group Policy Management Console Action menu or right-click the Group Policy Objects container and select Back Up All. You must back up starter GPOs separately by right-clicking the Starter GPOs container and selecting Back Up All or by right-clicking individual starter GPOs and selecting Back Up.

---

**MORE INFO**   **GPO comments and administrative template filtering**

The ability to add comments to both starter GPOs and ordinary GPOs is new in Windows Server 2008. You can enter a comment about the entire GPO as well as secondary comments about individual settings. Also new in Windows Server 2008 is the facility to filter a GPO's Administrative Template settings by either setting or comment. For more information, see *http:// technet2.microsoft.com/WindowsServer/en/library/e50f1e64-d7e5-4b6d-87ff-adb3cf8743651033.mspx*.

---

For example, a multinational organization is planning to install five separate Active Directory forests, one for each of its national offices in different countries. You are part of a central planning committee that has decided on 500 Group Policy settings that will be used throughout the enterprise. Each national office will then add its own unique Group Policy settings, to be applied locally.

In this scenario, you would plan to create a starter GPO that has the 500 Group Policy settings applied and distribute it to each national office. You can import and export starter GPOs, which facilitates the distribution of large numbers of policy settings to other environments. You could create a starter GPO in the root domain of each forest and manually apply the 500 settings or create a new GPO in the root domain and do the same. However, this requires significantly more effort than creating a single starter GPO and exporting it to each separate forest. You cannot link to GPOs in other forests.

---

**NOTE**  Exporting a starter GPO

You can use Group Policy Management Console to export and import a starter GPO in cabinet (.cab) file format.

---

Starter GPOs are not the answer to every Group Policy planning scenario. For example, your enterprise has a 20-domain Active Directory forest. You want to apply a consistent set of 300 Group Policy settings to every computer in the forest. When applying these settings in each domain, you do not want to link to GPOs outside that domain.

In this case, you do not need to use starter GPOs. You could instead create a GPO and apply the 300 Group Policy settings and copy the GPO to each of the 20 domains. It is possible to copy GPOs to domains within the same forest. Although you could create a starter GPO, export it, import it into each domain, and then create a new GPO based on the newly imported starter GPO, this is unnecessary and requires more administrative effort.

Another scenario in which you would use starter GPOs is when you are planning the Group Policy strategy for a new organization. Suppose, for example, you want to apply 350 Group Policy settings to each OU but then allow the GPO attached to each departmental OU to be modified and any of those basic settings to be changed if departmental managers request it.

In this case, you would create a starter GPO and apply the 350 basic Group Policy settings. You would create a new GPO for each OU based on the starter GPO and apply each new GPO to the appropriate OU. Changes can then be made to each individual GPO on a per-department basis later. This is not as easily accomplished when you link a single GPO to each OU.

You can view the settings of a starter GPO by selecting it in Group Policy Management Console. You can add comments to each starter GPO, explaining its properties, and use keyword filters to locate appropriate starter GPOs when necessary.

## Using Group Policy Modeling and Results

You or one of your administrators can use the *Group Policy Modeling* node of Group Policy Management Console to verify that planned Group Policy settings have been correctly configured prior to deployment. You can delegate the rights to perform this operation to a member of your team by assigning that user account the Perform Group Policy Modeling Analysis permission.

You can use the *Group Policy Modeling* node to simulate policy settings that will be applied to a computer that is not currently logged on. You can use the *Group Policy Results* node (or Group Policy Results tool) to display policy settings that are applied to computers or users that have actually logged on. If you want to delegate the ability to use planning mode, a user account must be assigned the Perform Group Policy Modeling Analysis right. The Read Group Policy Results permission is required to use the Resultant Set of Policy (RSoP) snap-in tool in logging mode.

### Using Migration Tables

You use migration tables when you import or copy a GPO from one domain or forest to another. These tables deal with domain and forest-specific information that specifies where the GPO was created. Such information does not apply to the domain or forest in which the GPO is being copied or imported. GPOs copied within the same domain, being backed up, or being restored to their original location do not require migration tables.

Your plan would include migration tables if you need to import GPOs that were created in another forest or to copy a GPO to another domain within the same forest. If you want to export a GPO from one forest to another and you need to account for all domain-specific settings that exist for the GPO that you want to export, you would use the Migration Table Editor tool to populate a migration table automatically with domain-specific Group Policy values so that these can be accounted for when the GPO is imported into the target environment.

## Planning to Audit AD DS and Group Policy Compliance

In Windows Server 2008, the global audit policy Audit Directory Service Access is enabled by default. This policy controls whether auditing for directory service events is enabled or disabled. You can configure this policy setting by modifying Default Domain Controllers Policy and then specifying whether to audit successes, audit failures, or not audit at all. You can control which operations to audit by modifying the system access control list (SACL) on an object. You can set a SACL on an AD DS object on the Security tab in that object's Properties dialog box.

Plan how your administrators should configure audit policy. Enabling success or failure auditing is a straightforward procedure. Deciding which objects to audit; whether to audit success, failure, or both; and whether to record new and old values if changes are made is much more difficult. Auditing everything is never an option—too much information is as bad as too little. Your plan needs to be selective.

In Windows 2000 Server and Windows Server 2003, an administrator can specify only whether Active Directory directory service access is audited. Windows Server 2008 gives more granular control. Your auditing policy can include the following:

- Active Directory access
- Active Directory changes (old and new values)
- Active Directory replication

Auditing Active Directory replication is further subdivided so that you can choose two levels of auditing—normal or detailed.

For example, you are an enterprise administrator at Litware, Inc. Previously, on a Windows Server 2003 domain, the auditing options you could plan had limitations. You could determine that the attributes of an object in Active Directory had been changed but not what changes were made. If a change was erroneous, you relied on documentation maintained by your administration team to reverse or correct the alteration. Such documentation was seldom perfect.

Litware has recently upgraded its domain to Windows Server 2008. You can now plan your auditing procedures so that if a change is performed on an object attribute, AD DS logs the previous and current values of the attribute. Only the values that change as a result of the *Modify* operation are logged, so your administrators do not need to search through a long list of attribute values to find the change.

---

### Quick Check

- One of your administrators is setting up Active Directory replication auditing. What are the two auditing levels from which she can choose?

### Quick Check Answer

- Normal or detailed

---

If a new object is created, AD DS logs the values of the attributes that are configured or added at the time of creation. Attributes that take default values are not logged. If an object is moved within a domain, your auditing policy can ensure that the previous and new locations are logged. When an object is moved to a different domain, a *Create* event is generated and logged on the DC in the target domain. If an object is undeleted, your auditing policy can identify the location to which the object is moved. If attributes are added, modified, or deleted during an *Undelete* operation, your administrators can determine the values of those attributes from the Security event log.

If auditing of Directory Service Changes is enabled, AD DS logs events in the Security event log when changes are made to objects that one of your administrators has set up for auditing. Table 4-1 lists these events.

**Table 4-1    Security Events Related to AD DS Objects**

| Event ID | Type of event | Event description |
|----------|---------------|-------------------|
| 5136 | *Modify* | A successful modification has been made to an attribute in the directory. |
| 5137 | *Create* | A new object has been created in the directory. |
| 5138 | *Undelete* | An object has been undeleted in the directory. |
| 5139 | *Move* | An object has been moved within the domain. |

Plan whether to react to such events and how to do so. By default, the events are logged in the Security event log, and members of the Domain Admins, Builtin\Administrators, and Enterprise Admins groups can view them by opening Event Viewer. However, you can design your auditing policy so that an event written to the Security event log initiates a task such as generating an alert or starting an executable program. An administrator can select the event in Event Viewer and choose Attach Task To This Event on the Action menu. Figure 4-10 shows this function.

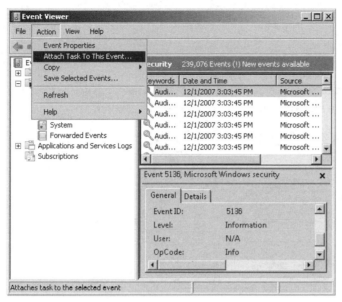

**Figure 4-10** Attaching a task to an AD DS *Modify* event

---

**MORE INFO  AD LDS**

You can also plan to use the new Directory Service Changes audit policy subcategory when planning to audit Active Directory Lightweight Directory Services (AD LDS). For more information about AD LDS, see *http://technet2.microsoft.com/windowsserver2008/en/servermanager /activedirectorylightweightdirectoryservices.mspx* and follow the links.

---

## Planning Organizational Structure

When planning your organizational structure, one of your primary aims is to organize the logical design of your OU hierarchy so that it facilitates the management of Group Policy. This OU hierarchy need not mirror your enterprise's departmental hierarchy. Instead, plan every OU so it has a defined purpose such as delegation of authority or the application of Group Policy. Business needs must drive the OU hierarchy. Plan to delegate administrative authority and designate groups of users to have control over the users and computers or other objects in an OU.

You can add users or groups to user rights policies in a GPO that links to an OU or OU hierarchy, as was discussed earlier in this lesson. You can also plan to delegate control of OUs. You do not need to delegate control of an OU, which is the smallest Active Directory container, to an administrative user. Many of the tasks that can be carried out within an OU are straightforward (for example, resetting passwords when users have forgotten them) and can be easily carried out by nonadministrative users. It is also relatively safe to delegate authority to an OU.

Other than to child OUs, delegated authority over an OU does not give a user rights to any other part of AD DS.

Figure 4-11 shows the Delegation Of Control Wizard, which is currently delegating control of the Sample OU to Sample Group. You can plan a very simple delegation, such as the right to reset passwords and require users to change a password at next logon, to more advanced features such as the ability to link this OU to other GPOs.

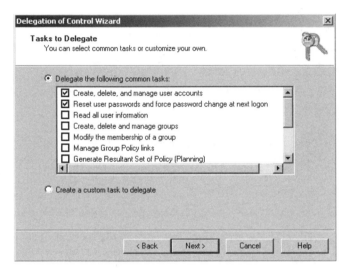

**Figure 4-11**    Delegating control of an OU

Your planned organizational structure should link GPOs to sites, domains, and OUs to implement Group Policy settings as broadly or as narrowly in the organization as necessary. Keep in mind how Group Policy is applied when you plan the scope of application of Group Policy objects. You are probably aware of the following facts, but a spot of review never goes amiss:

- The policy settings in Group Policy objects are inherited and cumulative and apply to all users and computers in an Active Directory container.
- Group Policy objects are processed in the following order: local GPO, site, domain, and OU.
- By default, Group Policy inheritance is evaluated starting with the Active Directory container farthest from the computer or user object. The Active Directory container closest to the computer or user overrides Group Policy set in a higher-level Active Directory container unless you enable the Enforced option for that GPO.
- If you link more than one GPO to an Active Directory container, the GPO processing order (priority) is as follows: the GPO highest in the Group Policy Object Links list, displayed in the Group Policy section of the Active Directory container's Properties page, has precedence by default. If you enable the Enforced option in one or more of the GPOs, the highest GPO that is set to Enforced takes precedence.

**PRACTICE** ## Creating a Forest Trust

In this practice, you create a forest trust between the *contoso.internal* and *litware.internal* forests. You then experiment with adding groups from one forest to groups in another.

### ▶ Exercise   Create a Forest Trust

You need two forests on your network before you can carry out this exercise. Ensure that the forest functional levels of your two forests are at least Windows Server 2003. You might need to raise the domain functional levels of your domains before you can raise forest functional levels. You should also create a conditional forwarder for *litware.internal* on Glasgow and a conditional forwarder for *contoso.internal* on Brisbane, using the servers' respective DNS consoles. If you are unsure how to perform these tasks, refer to the Windows Server 2008 Help files.

1. Log on to the Glasgow DC with the Kim_Akers account.

2. Open Active Directory Domains And Trusts from Administrative Tools. Click Continue to clear the User Account Control (UAC) dialog box and ensure that the tool is connected to the Glasgow DC in the *contoso.internal* domain.

3. Right click the *contoso.internal* domain in the tool's left pane, and choose Properties. On the Trusts tab, click New Trust as shown in Figure 4-12 to launch the New Trust Wizard. Click Next.

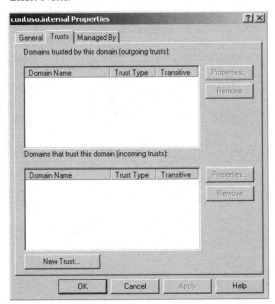

**Figure 4-12**   Accessing the New Trust Wizard

The wizard prompts you to enter the domain, forest, or realm name of the trust.

4. Enter the domain name (**litware.internal**) of the root domain in the forest with which you want to establish the trust, as shown in Figure 4-13.

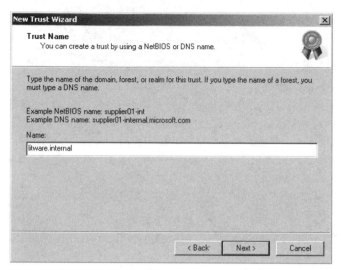

**Figure 4-13**    Specifying the trust endpoint

5. Click Next. The wizard asks whether you are creating a realm trust or a trust with a Windows domain.

6. Select the Trust With A Windows Domain option as shown in Figure 4-14, and click Next.

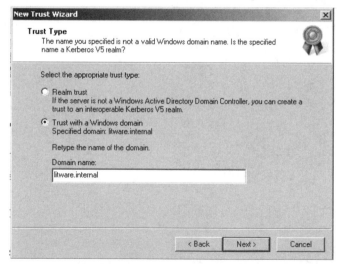

**Figure 4-14**    Specifying a Windows domain trust

You are given the choice between creating a forest trust or an external trust.

7. Choose the Forest Trust option, and click Next. At this point, the wizard asks you whether you want to establish a one-way incoming, one-way outgoing, or two-way trust.

8. Select Two-Way, and click Next to create a two-way trust.

The wizard now asks whether you want to configure only your own side of the trust or both sides of the trust. An administrative password for both forest root domains is required to establish the trust.

9. Choose to configure both sides of the trust. When prompted, enter the username **Tom_Perry** and the password **P@ssw0rd**. You now need to choose between Forest-Wide Authentication and Selective Authentication. Selective Authentication enables you to specify the authentication process in more detail, but it involves much more effort.

10. On the Outgoing Trust Authentication Level–Local Forest page, choose Forest-Wide Authentication. Click Next.

11. On the Outgoing Trust Authentication Level–Specified Forest page, choose Forest-Wide Authentication, and then click Next.

---

**MORE INFO**   **Selective authentication**

For more information about selective authentication, see *http://technet2.microsoft.com /windowsserver/en/library/9266b197-7fc9-4bd8-8864-4c119ceecc001033.mspx?mfr=true*. Although this document and linked documents are part of the Windows Server 2003 library, the information they provide is relevant to Windows Server 2008.

---

The wizard displays a summary of the options you have chosen.

12. Click Next to establish the trust. Click Next.

13. On the Confirm Outgoing Trust page, you can confirm the outgoing link by selecting Yes, Confirm The Outgoing Trust and clicking Next.

14. On the Confirm Incoming Trust page, confirm the incoming trust link by selecting Yes, Confirm The Incoming Trust and clicking Next.

15. On the Completing The New Trust Wizard page, click Finish to close the wizard. Click OK to close the Properties dialog box for the *contoso.internal* domain.

16. Create a universal security group in the *contoso.internal* domain. Add this universal security group to the Administrators builtin security group in the *litware.internal* domain. Experiment to discover the rights and permissions Tom Perry and Kim Akers have in both domains.

## Lesson Summary

- Delegation is the transfer of administrative responsibility for a specific task from a higher to a lower authority. It increases administrative efficiency and reduces administrative costs. Delegation needs to provide both isolation and autonomy.

- When delegating Active Directory administration, you use built-in local, domain local, global, and (sometimes) universal security groups. You can assign rights to security groups and delegate control of OUs to groups.

- Windows Server 2008 introduces new features that enable you to audit changes to Group Policy and Active Directory structure.

- You can delegate the management of groups to a group member without assigning any additional rights over any other part of the enterprise.

- The design of your OU and GPO structure depends on how the organization is structured (geographically or by department) and which administrative model is used.

# Lesson Review

Use the following questions to test your knowledge of the information in Lesson 1, "Designing the Active Directory Administrative Model." The questions are also available on the companion CD if you prefer to review them in electronic form.

---

**NOTE    Answers**

Answers to these questions and explanations of why each answer choice is correct or incorrect are located in the "Answers" section at the end of the book.

---

1. Northwind Traders is a large multinational company with offices located in a number of countries spread over several continents. Each national office has a high degree of autonomy and its own administrative staff. Some Group Policy settings are specified by the head office in Detroit, but the vast majority are configured on a national basis. Active Directory structure is based on geographical structure. Which administrative model does Northwind Traders use?

   A. The centralized model

   B. The hybrid model

   C. The distributed model

   D. The mixed model

2. Which of the following management roles does Microsoft recommend for delegating data management? (Choose all that apply).

   A. Business Unit Administrators

   B. Security Policy Administrators

   C. Service Administration Managers

   D. Resource Administrators

   E. Security Group Administrators

   F. Application-Specific Administrators

   G. Replication Management Administrators

3. Which Windows Server 2008 global audit policy controls whether auditing for directory service events is enabled or disabled, and what is the default setting?

    A. Audit Directory Service Access. This is disabled by default.

    B. Audit Directory Service Access. This is enabled by default.

    C. Directory Service Changes. This is enabled by default.

    D. Directory Service Changes. This is disabled by default.

4. You administer a Windows Server 2008 single-domain Active Directory forest. Your organization recently acquired another company that uses a Windows NT 4.0 domain. You need to set up a trust relationship with the Windows NT 4.0 domain. What sort of trust do you use?

    A. Forest trust

    B. Realm trust

    C. Shortcut trust

    D. External trust

5. You are designing a Group Policy strategy and plan to give members of the software developers' security group permission to link certain GPOs that have already been created to specific OUs within your organization. You do not want to allow members of the software developers' security group to be able to edit these GPOs. Which of the following permissions should you delegate?

    A. Permission to link GPOs

    B. Permissions on a GPO

    C. Permission to generate Group Policy modeling data

    D. Permission to generate Group Policy results

# Lesson 2:  Designing Enterprise-Level Group Policy Strategy

When you design a Group Policy strategy, you can develop some common-sense rules to follow—except they contradict each other. You know what you would like to do, but existing security, permissions, and Active Directory structures make it difficult. And, no, the company will not stop trading for a few weeks while you sort it all out.

This lesson looks at how you plan Group Policy and define a Group Policy hierarchy. It looks at how you control device installation, authentication and authorization, and the new fine-grained password policy that Windows Server 2008 introduces. Mainly, however, it looks at the art of the possible. This is the structure you have—where do you go from here?

---

**After this lesson, you will be able to:**
- Plan a Group Policy hierarchy and implement scope filtering.
- Control device installation through Group Policy.
- Distinguish between multifactor authentication and multifactor authorization.
- Plan a password policy, including the use of fine-grained passwords.
- Plan an authentication policy that uses security certificates and smart cards.

**Estimated lesson time:  40 minutes**

---

## Real World

*Ian McLean*

When I first walked into a senior administrator's post, I confess I was a bit lost.

I knew there was a lot to do and a very short time in which to do it. As in many organizations, the Active Directory and Group Policy structures in the enterprise had been allowed simply to grow with no proper planning. Nobody knew exactly which settings were in force and how to change them.

Fortunately, I knew my job wasn't to Remote Desktop to the nearest DC and start reconfiguring. I needed to get my team together and start planning. I needed to gather what little documentation there was, find out where we were, and decide where we were going.

My team was less than enamored by the thought of meetings, planning, and discussions. They were desperately fighting emergencies. Ten users, nine of them managers and the other the CEO's secretary, had forgotten their passwords and been locked out of their computers. Other users couldn't locate their files on the file server. One more knowledgeable user had discovered she could access files that she shouldn't have been able to.

I'd been there. I'd done all that. The only way that my people wouldn't spend 40 hours a week resolving emergencies was to plan and reorganize the structures. I made my views heard. Loudly.

You probably feel the same when you look at an examination such as 70-647. Where is the comfortable "do this, do that, it will work, and here's the theory behind it"? Instead, you get "you know the theory; you've done this procedure a hundred times. Now plan things properly so you won't need to do it a hundred times more."

It's not a comfort zone. Get used to it.

## Planning a Group Policy Hierarchy

Group Policy is applied through OUs that are linked to GPOs. A domain is itself an OU, and the default domain policies are defined in the Default Domain Policy GPO. Thus, Group Policy hierarchy and structure is closely linked with Active Directory OU structure. You will seldom have the luxury of planning and creating an Active Directory structure, a Group Policy structure, and a Group Policy hierarchy from scratch. You will be faced with current structures and a list of requirements, some of them contradictory.

The effective Group Policy is made up of multiple Group Policy elements that are applied to user objects and to computer objects. You must manage your GPOs so that you keep them well organized and make it as simple as possible to determine which policy elements apply in a given situation.

GPOs that apply at domain and site level can be combined with GPOs that apply to OUs, OU hierarchies, and local computer settings. Several GPOs can link to a single OU, and you need to determine the order in which they are applied. If Group Policy settings in multiple GPOs conflict, the GPO that is applied last defines the settings. This applies unless a GPO earlier in the order has been configured to be enforced. When a GPO is configured to be enforced, its settings override those applied later. You can apply site policy, domain policy, and OU policy. Figure 4-15 shows multiple GPOs linked to a single OU.

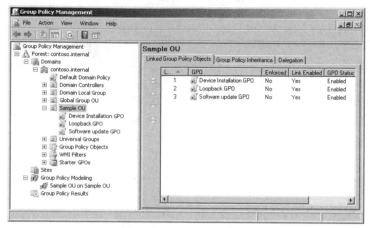

**Figure 4-15**    Linking multiple GPOs to an OU

The link precedence is shown in Figure 4-16. You can change the order of precedence by selecting a GPO link and moving it up or down.

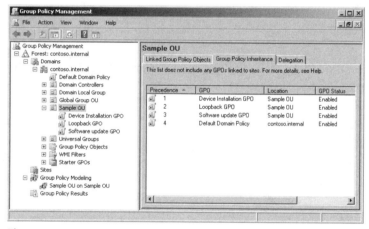

**Figure 4-16**    GPO precedence

## Rules for Planning a GPO Structure

The first rule is to keep things as simple as possible. The ability to block Group Policy inheritance and to enable the Enforced property to prevent inheritance blocking can be useful if used sparingly but can make structures complex and difficult to interpret if overused. The same can be said for Loopback Policy.

You should not have too many non-default settings configured in a single GPO. Design GPOs for a single purpose, for example, a device installation configuration GPO, and name them accordingly. Similarly, give your OUs sensible names. Sales Department OU is descriptive. OU1 is not.

Never link GPOs to OUs across sites and over slow WAN links. If you have two containers in different sites that require the same settings, use two GPOs. In Windows Server 2008, you can use Group Policy Management Console to copy a GPO. The new GPO you create is not linked to any domain or OU; you need to link it to a domain or OU. You can copy a GPO to another site or to another domain in the same forest or export a GPO to a domain in another forest, provided a forest trust is configured.

Always disable unused Group Policy elements. In larger organizations, you might need GPOs at every level of AD DS, but smaller organizations can often design their Group Policy structure so that links take place at a single level within AD DS, and inheritance does the rest. If a GPO contains only user settings and is linked to an OU that contains only users, you can disable the computer settings for that GPO. This simplifies the structure, uses fewer resources, and speeds up user logons.

As an experienced administrator, you will be familiar with the Block Inheritance and Enforced features that you can configure to control Group Policy inheritance. As a planner, you should know when to use these features—they can sometimes be very useful—but mainly when not to use them. Block Inheritance and Enforced are known as exceptions. They add complexity and make your structure difficult to understand. They need careful documentation. Plan to use them as seldom as possible.

## Planning Active Directory Structure

AD DS stores and organizes objects (users, computers, devices, and so on) in a secure hierarchical containment structure that is known as the logical structure. Although the logical structure of AD DS is a hierarchical organization of all users, computers, and other physical resources, the forest and domain form the basis of the logical structure. As previously stated in this lesson, you seldom get to plan and design Active Directory structure from scratch, but you need to consider the principles of good Active Directory design when planning Group Policy structure and strategy.

Forests are the security boundaries of the logical structure. You can plan and design them to provide data and service autonomy and isolation in an organization in ways that can both reflect site and group identities and remove dependencies on the physical topology. Multiple-forest enterprises tend to occur during an acquisition or merger, and you might need to plan whether to retain multiple forests or create a new, single-forest structure.

Domains provide data and service autonomy (but not isolation) and optimize replication within a given region. This separation of logical and physical structures improves manageability and reduces administrative costs because the logical structure is not affected by changes in the physical structure. The logical structure also makes it possible to control access to data. This means that you can use the logical structure to compartmentalize data so that you can control access to it by controlling access to the various compartments.

Information stored in AD DS can come from diverse sources. As a result, it employs a standardized storage mechanism to maintain data integrity. In AD DS, objects are used to store information in the directory, and all objects are defined in the schema. The object definitions contain information—such as data type and syntax—that the directory uses to ensure that the stored data is valid. No data can be stored in the directory unless the objects used to store the data are first defined in the schema. The default schema contains all the object definitions that AD DS needs to function. You can also add object definitions to the schema.

AD DS appears to the administrator and planner as a logical structure that consists of elements such as OUs, domains, and forests. However, the directory itself is implemented through a physical structure that consists of a database stored on all DCs in a forest. The Active Directory data store handles all access to the database and consists of both services and physical files. These services and physical files make the directory available, and they manage the processes of reading and writing the data inside the database that exists on the hard disk of each DC.

## Planning Active Directory Domains and Forests

Domains partition the directory into smaller sections within a single forest. This partitioning results in more control over how data is replicated so that an efficient replication topology can be established, and network bandwidth is not wasted by replicating data where it is not required. OUs make it possible to group resources in a domain for management purposes such as applying Group Policy or delegating control to administrators.

In the days before AD DS, the domain was the security and administrative boundary, and Windows NT 4.0 and Windows NT 3.5 networks typically held a number of domains for this reason. In AD DS, much of what was done in Windows NT domains can now be accomplished by using OUs, and even quite large Active Directory networks can be single domain. The reasons for multiple domains were replication efficiency (still a consideration) and password policies. In a domain at the Windows 2000 Server Native or Windows 2003 domain functional levels, it is not possible to implement different password policies for different users without creating more than one domain. If you raise the domain functional level to Windows Server 2008, however, you can use fine-grained password policies (described later in this lesson), invalidating another reason for multiple domains.

## The Active Directory Schema

The Active Directory schema contains definitions for all the objects used to store information in the directory. There is one schema per forest. However, a copy of the schema exists on every DC in the forest. This way, every DC can quickly access any object definition it might need, and every DC uses the same definition when it creates a given object. The data store relies on the schema to provide object definitions and uses those definitions to enforce data integrity. The result is that all objects are created uniformly. It does not matter which DC creates or modifies an object because all DCs use the same object definition.

## The Active Directory Data Store

The Active Directory data store is made up of several components that together provide directory services to directory clients. These components include the following:

- The directory database in which the data is actually stored
- The Lightweight Directory Access Protocol (LDAP) interface
- The Replication (REPL) and DC management interface
- The Messaging API (MAPI) interface
- The Security Accounts Manager (SAM) interface
- The Directory System Agent (DSA) service component
- The Database Layer service component
- The Extensible Storage Engine (ESE) service component

## Filtering GPOs

When planning your Group Policy structure, bear in mind that you can further refine the application of the policy settings in a GPO by specifying that they should be applied only to specified security groups. These security groups need to be in the container or containers (for example, OU or domain) to which the GPO is linked. They can contain user or computer accounts. If a security group contains user accounts, remove Authenticated Users from the policy scope before you add the security group to the scope.

Figure 4-17 shows the scope of the Device Installation GPO limited to computers in the USA Computers security group. Take note of this facility because it could play a part in your Group Policy design but, like the Enforced option, it is an exception and should be used sparingly.

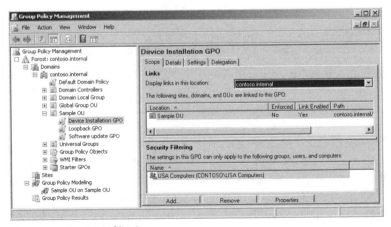

**Figure 4-17**    GPO filtering

# Controlling Device Installation

When you are formulating a plan to control the installation of devices (typically, USB devices) in your enterprise, you can use Group Policy to specify whether devices can be installed and, if so, which criteria should be applied. Depending upon company policy, your plan could have one of the following outcomes:

- Prevent users (except for administrators) from installing any device.
- Allow users to install only devices that are on an approved list. If a device is not on the list, the user cannot install it.
- Prevent users from installing devices that are on a prohibited list. If a device is not on the list, the user can install it.
- Deny read or write access to users for devices that are removable or that use removable media such as CD and DVD burners, external hard drives, and portable devices such as media players, smart phones, or Pocket PC devices.

You need to be familiar with the device installation process and the identification strings that match a device with the device driver packages available on a computer. Obtaining device identities (IDs) and global unique identifiers (GUIDs) is discussed later in this section.

By restricting the devices that users can install, you can reduce the risk of data theft. Users will find it more difficult to make unauthorized copies of company data if they cannot install unapproved devices that support removable media on their computers. You can plan to use Group Policy to deny write access to users for devices that are removable or that use removable media. Restricting device installation can also reduce support costs. You can ensure that users install only those devices that your help desk is trained and equipped to support. This reduces both support costs and user confusion.

In an enterprise environment in which you manage a large number of client computers, you can apply Group Policy settings to manage device installation on computers that are members of a domain or of an OU in a domain. You can choose from one of the following strategies:

- **Prevent installation of all devices**    You plan to prevent standard users from installing any device but to allow administrators to install or update devices. In this scenario, you configure two computer Group Policy settings. The first prevents all users from installing devices, and the second exempts administrators from the restrictions.
- **Allow users to install authorized devices only**    You plan to allow users to install only the devices included on a list of authorized devices. In this scenario, you initially prevent standard users from installing any device. You then create a list of authorized devices and configure Group Policy so that standard users can install only specified devices.
- **Prevent installation of prohibited devices only**    You plan to allow standard users to install most devices but prevent them from installing devices included on a list of prohibited devices. In this scenario, you do not use Group Policy to prohibit installation of

all devices; instead, you create a list of prohibited devices and configure Group Policy so that standard users can install any device except those on the list.

- **Control the use of removable media storage devices** You plan to prevent standard users from writing data to removable storage devices or to devices with removable media such as USB memory drives or a CD or DVD burner. In this scenario, you configure a computer Group Policy to allow read access but deny write access to USB memory devices and to any CD or DVD burner device on users' computers. You can then configure a setting that prevents this policy from affecting users who are members of the Administrators group.

---

**NOTE**  System installation

These plans and policies do not restrict the use of devices by the system, for example, the Windows ReadyBoost feature on Windows Vista clients.

---

## Group Policy Settings That Control Device Installation

Windows Vista and Windows Server 2008 introduce new policy settings that enable you to control device installation. You can configure these policy settings individually on a single computer, but in the enterprise environment, you are more likely to apply them to a large number of computers through Group Policy in an Active Directory domain. These are computer policies and affect any user logged on to a computer, except for the Allow Administrators To Override Device Installation Policies setting, which exempts members of the built-in local Administrators group from any of the device installation restrictions. The following policy settings allow you or members of your administrative team to implement your device installation plan:

- **Prevent Installation Of Devices Not Described By Other Policy Settings**  If this policy setting is enabled, users cannot install or update the drivers for devices unless they are described by either the Allow Installation Of Devices That Match Any Of These Device IDs policy setting or the Allow Installation Of Devices Using Drivers That Match These Device Setup Classes policy setting. If your plan involves disabling or not configuring this policy setting, users can install and update the driver for any device that is not described by the Prevent Installation Of Devices That Match Any Of These Device IDs policy setting, the Prevent Installation Of Devices Using Drivers That Match These Device Setup Classes policy setting, or the Prevent Installation Of Removable Devices policy setting.

- **Allow Administrators To Override Device Installation Restriction Policies**  If this policy setting is enabled, it allows members of the local Administrators group to install and update the drivers for any device, regardless of other policy settings. Administrators can use the Add Hardware Wizard or the Update Driver Wizard to install and update the drivers for any device. If your plan disables or does not configure this policy setting, administrators are subject to all policy settings that restrict device installation.

■ **Prevent Installation Of Devices That Match Any Of These Device IDs**    This policy setting enables you to specify a list of Plug and Play hardware IDs and compatible IDs for devices that users cannot install. Enabling this policy setting prevents users from installing or updating the driver for a device if any of its hardware IDs or compatible IDs is included in the list. If your plan disables or does not configure this policy setting, users can install devices and update their drivers as permitted by other policy settings for device installation. This policy setting takes precedence over any other policy settings that allow users to install a device and prevents users from installing a device even if its ID matches another policy setting that would allow installation.

■ **Prevent Installation Of Devices Using Drivers That Match These Device Setup Classes**    This policy setting enables you to specify a list of Plug and Play device setup class GUIDs that define devices users cannot install. If you enable this policy setting, users cannot install or update drivers for a device that belongs to any of the listed device setup classes. If your plan disables or does not configure this policy setting, users can install and update drivers for devices as permitted by other policy settings for device installation. This policy setting takes precedence over any other policy settings that allow users to install a device and prevents users from installing a device with a GUID on the list even if its ID matches another policy setting that would allow installation.

■ **Allow Installation Of Devices That Match Any Of These Device IDs**    If you enable this policy setting, you can specify a list of Plug and Play hardware IDs and compatible IDs that describe devices users can install. Plan to use this setting only when the Prevent Installation Of Devices Not Described By Other Policy Settings policy setting is enabled and does not take precedence over any policy setting that would prevent users from installing a device. If you enable this policy setting, users can install and update any device with a hardware ID or compatible ID that matches an ID in this list if that installation has not been specifically prevented by the Prevent Installation Of Devices That Match These Device IDs policy setting, the Prevent Installation Of Devices Using Drivers That Match These Device Setup Classes policy setting, or the Prevent Installation Of Removable Devices policy setting. If another policy setting prevents users from installing a device, users cannot install it even if the device is also described by a value in this policy setting. If your plan involves disabling or not configuring this policy setting and no other policy describes the device, the Prevent Installation Of Devices Not Described By Other Policy Settings policy setting determines whether users can install the device.

■ **Allow Installation Of Devices Using Drivers That Match These Device Setup Classes**    If you enable this policy setting, you can specify a list of device setup class GUIDs that describe devices users can install. Plan to use this setting only when the Prevent Installation Of Devices Not Described By Other Policy Settings policy setting is enabled and does not take precedence over any policy setting that would prevent users from installing a device. If you enable this setting, users can install and update any device with a device setup class that matches one of the device setup class GUIDs in this list unless that installation has not been specifically prevented by the Prevent Installation Of Devices That Match Any Of These Device IDs policy setting, the Prevent Installation Of Devices Using Drivers For These Device Setup Classes policy setting, or the Prevent Installation Of Removable Devices policy setting. If another policy setting prevents users from installing a device, users cannot install it even if the device is also described by a value in this policy setting. If your plan involves disabling or not configuring this policy setting and no other policy setting describes the device, the Prevent Installation Of Devices Not Described By Other Policy Settings policy setting determines whether users can install the device.

**NOTE   Planning device installation**

The way the device installation computer policies interact with each other is fairly intuitive and not as complex as it seems when described on paper. If you are formulating plans in this area, practice using these policies until you are familiar with what they do and how they interact. This is a suggested practice later in this chapter and is one of the few instances when an enterprise administrator should carry out configuration rather than delegate it.

Figure 4-18 shows the Device Installation Restriction policies in Group Policy Management Editor. Figure 4-19 shows one of the simplest and most used sets of policy settings that prevents standard users from installing devices but permits administrators to do so.

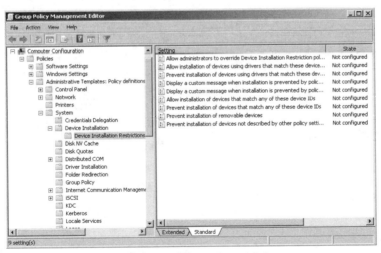

**Figure 4-18**   Device Installation Restriction policies

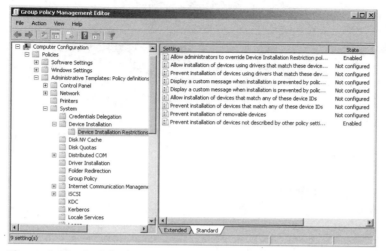

**Figure 4-19**   Standard users cannot install devices, but administrators can

## Obtaining Hardware IDs, Compatible IDs, and GUIDs

You can allow or prevent the installation of specific devices by enabling the appropriate Group Policy setting and adding a list of hardware IDs, compatible IDs, or both. You can also specify device setup class GUIDs that describe devices users can install.

**Hardware IDs**   Hardware IDs provide the most exact match between a device and a driver package. The first string in the list of hardware IDs is referred to as the device ID because it matches the exact make, model, and version of the device. The other hardware IDs in the list match the details of the device less exactly. For example, a hardware ID might identify the make and model of the device but not the specific version. This scheme allows Windows to use a driver for a different version of the device if the driver for the correct revision is not available. Figure 4-20 shows the list of hardware IDs for a USB flash memory device. You can access this from the device's Properties dialog box in Device Manager.

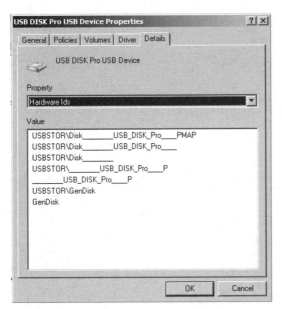

**Figure 4-20**    Hardware IDs

**Compatible IDs**    Windows Server 2008 uses compatible IDs to select a device driver if the operating system cannot find a match with the device ID or any of the other hardware IDs. Compatible IDs are listed in the order of decreasing suitability. These strings are optional and, when provided, they are generic, such as Disk. When a match is made using a compatible ID, you can typically use only the most basic functions of the device. Figure 4-21 shows the list of hardware IDs for a USB flash memory device.

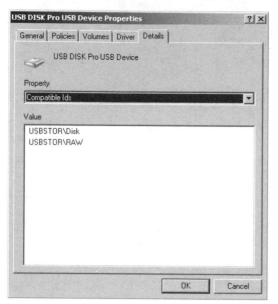

**Figure 4-21**   Compatible IDs

**GUIDs**   A GUID defines a device setup class, which the device manufacturer assigns to a device in the device driver package. The device setup class groups devices that are installed and configured in the same way. For example, all CD drives belong to the CDROM device setup class and use the same co-installer. When Windows Server 2008 starts, it builds a tree structure in memory with the GUIDs for all the detected devices.

In addition to the GUID for the device setup class of the device itself, Windows Server 2008 might need to insert the GUID for the device setup class of the bus to which the device is attached (for example, USB). When you use device setup classes to control users' installation of device drivers, you must specify the GUIDs for all the device's device setup classes, or you might not achieve the results you want. In addition, GUIDs are held in the *HKLM\CurrentControlSet\Control\Class\ClassGUID* registry key and are not as easily obtained as hardware IDs.

For these reasons, hardware IDs rather than GUIDs are typically used to specify the devices than can or cannot be installed. Figure 4-22 shows a hardware ID list specified for the Allow Installation Of Devices That Match Any Of These Device IDs setting.

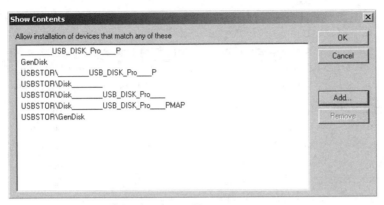

**Figure 4-22**   Specifying hardware IDs

**Exam Tip**   The most likely scenario to appear in the 70-647 examination is one in which users cannot install devices but administrators can. The settings for this scenario are shown in Figure 4-19. The next most likely scenario is that users can install only allowed devices although administrators can install any device. This requires the settings shown in Figure 4-19 plus enabling the Allow Installation Of Devices That Match Any Of These Device IDs setting and adding hardware IDs as shown in Figure 4-22.

# Planning Authentication and Authorization

Authentication involves checking that users are who they say they are. It uses username and password or a security certificate installed on a smart card. Authorization determines whether a user has access to resources through permissions or administrative rights through group membership and delegation. Authorization can happen within a domain, across a domain tree, or between forests. It involves the SAM, access control lists (ACLs), and protocols such as Kerberos v5.

**MORE INFO**   Kerberos authentication

For more information about Kerberos authentication, see *http://technet2.microsoft.com /windowsserver/en/library/4a1daa3e-b45c-44ea-a0b6-fe8910f92f281033.mspx?mfr=true*. Although this is a Windows Server 2003 article, it is valid for Windows Server 2008, as well.

## Multifactor Authentication and Authorization

The network community is always happy to debate when a scenario involves multifactor authentication and when it involves multifactor authorization. Ignore such debates. You have an examination to pass.

Multifactor authentication occurs when you must use two or more distinct methods to authenticate an identity. For example, you are logged on to a domain with an administrative-level account. You need to access a standalone Berkley Internet Daemon (BIND) server through Remote Desktop. You are asked for credentials. They are the same credentials that you used to log on to the domain, but you need to enter them again. This is multifactor authentication.

Multifactor authorization occurs when you need to authenticate two people to accomplish a stated aim. For example, you need to create a two-way forest trust between the *contoso.internal* and *litware.internal* forests. You create one end of the trust logged on to the *contoso.internal* forest as Kim_Akers. To create the other end, you need to provide the credentials for Tom_Perry in the *litware.internal* forest. This is multifactor authorization.

## Using Password Authentication

You can authenticate a user through a username and password. Before you plan a password policy, you need to know what the default settings are. Figure 4-23 shows the default settings for the *contoso.internal* domain.

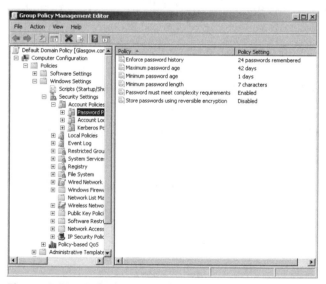

**Figure 4-23**    Default password settings

As an experienced administrator, you should be familiar with password settings. However, you might not be aware of the fine-grained password policies in Windows Server 2008. This topic was discussed in the 70-646 TK. If you studied it for that examination, please treat this section as review.

## Configuring Fine-Grained Password Policies

As a first step in planning fine-grained password and account lockout policies, decide how many password policies you need. Typically, your policy could include at least 3 but seldom more than 10 Password Settings Objects (PSOs). At a minimum, you would probably want to configure the following:

- An administrative-level password policy with strict settings: for example, a minimum password length of 12, a maximum password age of 28 days, and password complexity requirements enabled.

- A user-level password policy with, for example, a minimum password length of 6, a maximum password age of 90 days, and password complexity requirements not enabled.

- A service account password policy with a minimum password length of 32 characters and complexity requirements enabled. (Service account passwords are seldom typed in.) Because of their complexity, service account passwords can typically be set not to expire or to have very long password ages.

You also need to look at your existing group structure. If you have existing Administrators and Users groups, there is no point creating new ones. Ultimately, you need to define a group and Active Directory structure that maps to your fine-grained password and account lockout policies.

You cannot apply PSOs to OUs directly. If your users are organized into OUs, consider creating *shadow groups* for these OUs and then applying the newly defined fine-grained password and account lockout policies to them. A shadow group is a global security group that is logically mapped to an OU to enforce a fine-grained password and account lockout policy. Add OU users as members to the newly created shadow group and then apply the fine-grained password and account lockout policy to this shadow group. If you move a user from one OU to another, you must update user memberships in the corresponding shadow groups.

---

**NOTE  Shadow groups**

You will not find an Add Shadow Group command in Active Directory Users and Computers. A shadow group is simply an ordinary global security group that contains all the user accounts in one or more OUs. When you apply a PSO to a shadow group, you are effectively applying it to users in the corresponding OU.

---

Microsoft applies PSOs to groups rather than to OUs because groups offer better flexibility for managing various sets of users. Windows Server 2008 AD DS creates various groups for administrative accounts, including Domain Admins, Enterprise Admins, Schema Admins, Server Operators, and Backup Operators. You can apply PSOs to these groups or nest them in a single global security group and apply a PSO to that group. Because you use groups rather than OUs, you do not need to modify the OU hierarchy to apply fine-grained passwords. Modifying an OU hierarchy requires detailed planning and increases the risk of errors.

If you intend to use fine-grained passwords, you probably need to raise the functional level of your domain. To work properly, fine-grained password settings require a domain functional level of Windows Server 2008. Planning domain and forest functional levels is discussed in Chapter 2. Changing functional levels involves irreversible changes. You need to be sure, for example, that you will never want to add a Windows Server 2003 DC to your domain.

By default, only members of the Domain Admins group can create PSOs and apply a PSO to a group or user. You do not, however, need to have permissions on the user object or group object to be able to apply a PSO to it. You can delegate Read Property permissions on the default security descriptor of a PSO to any other group (such as help desk personnel). This enables users who are not domain administrators to discover the password and account lock-out settings applied through a PSO to a security group.

You can apply fine-grained password policies only to user objects and global security groups (or *inetOrgPerson* objects if they are used instead of user objects). If your plan identifies a group of computers that requires different password settings, consider techniques such as password filters. Fine-grained password policies cannot be applied to computer objects.

If you use custom password filters in a domain, fine-grained password policies do not interfere with these filters. If you plan to upgrade Windows 2000 Server or Windows Server 2003 domains that currently deploy custom password filters on DCs, you can continue to use those password filters to enforce additional password restrictions.

If you have assigned a PSO to a global security group, but one user in that group requires special settings, you can assign an exceptional PSO directly to that particular user. For example, the CEO of Northwind Traders is a member of the senior managers group, and company policy requires that senior managers use complex passwords. However, the CEO is not willing to do so. In this case, you can create an exceptional PSO and apply it directly to the CEO's user account. The exceptional PSO will override the security group PSO when the password settings (*msDS-ResultantPSO*) for the CEO's user account are determined.

---

### Quick Check

- By default, members of which group can create PSOs?

### Quick Check Answer

- Domain Admins

---

Finally, you can plan to delegate management of fine-grained passwords. When you have created the necessary PSOs and the global security groups associated with these PSOs, you can delegate management of the security groups to responsible users or user groups. For example, a human resources (HR) group could add user accounts to or remove them from the managers group when staff changes occur. If a PSO specifying fine-grained password policy is associated with the managers group, in effect the HR group is determining to whom these policies are applied.

---

**MORE INFO**  **Fine-grained password and account lockout policy configuration**

For more information about fine-grained password and account lockout policies, see *http://technet2.microsoft.com/WindowsServer2008/en/library/2199dcf7-68fd-4315-87cc-ade35f8978ea1033.mspx#BKMK_7*.

---

## Using Smart Card Authentication

If you are using smart cards in your organization to provide additional security and control over user credentials, your users can use those smart cards with authentication credentials to obtain rights account certificates (RACs) and use licenses from an Active Directory Rights Management Services (AD RMS) server (or more commonly in the enterprise environment, an AD RMS cluster), provided a Secure Sockets Layer (SSL) certificate has already been installed.

---

**MORE INFO**  **AD RMS cluster**

For more information about installing an AD RMS cluster, see *http://technet2.microsoft.com /windowsserver2008/en/library/a65941cb-02ef-4194-95ce-7fd213b1e48c1033.mspx?mfr=true*

---

To use smart card authentication, you must also add the Client Certificate Mapping Authentication role service in Server Manager. This is part of the Web Server (IIS) server role. Your next step is to configure the authentication method in IIS. Perform these steps to do so.

1. In Internet Information Services (IIS) Manager, expand the server name in the console tree and, in the results pane of the server Home page, double-click Authentication to open the Authentication page.

2. In the results pane of the Authentication page, right-click Active Directory Client Certificate Authentication, and then choose Enable.

3. Enable client authentication for the Web site that is hosting AD RMS. In IIS Manager, expand the server name in the console tree, expand Sites, and then expand the Web site that is hosting AD RMS. By default, the Web site name is Default Web Site.

4. In the console tree, expand _wmcs, right-click either the certification virtual directory (to support RACs) or the licensing virtual directory (to support user licenses), and then choose Switch To Content View.

5. In the results pane, right-click *certification.asmx* or *license.asmx* as appropriate, and then choose Switch To Features View.

6. In the results pane on the Home page, double-click SSL Settings, and choose the appropriate client certificates setting (Accept or Require).

Accept client certificates if you want clients to have the option to supply authentication credentials by using either a smart card certificate or a username and password. Require client certificates if you want only clients with client-side certificates such as smart cards to be able to connect to the service.

7. Click Apply. If you want to use client authentication for both certification and licensing, repeat this procedure but select the alternate virtual directory the second time.

8. Close IIS Manager. If you are using an AD RMS cluster, repeat the procedure for every other server in the cluster.

Your next task is to force the authentication method to use Client Certificate Mapping Authentication for the AD RMS cluster. Before you do that, back up the applicationhost.config file in the %windir%\system32\inetsrv\config folder.

1. Open an elevated command prompt, and change the directory to **%windir%\system32\inetsrv\config**.

2. Enter **notepad applicationhost.config** and locate the section similar to *Default Web Site/_wmcs/certification/certification.asmx.*

3. If you want to allow smart card authentication in addition to Windows authentication, change:

   ```
   access sslFlags="Ssl, SslNegotiateCert, SslRequireCert, Ssl128"
   ```

   to:

   ```
   access sslFlags="Ssl, SslNegotiateCert, Ssl128"
   ```

4. Add a new line under *windowsAuthentication enabled="true."* In this line, type:

   ```
   clientCertificateMappingAuthentication enabled="true"
   ```

5. If you want to allow only smart card authentication, ensure that SSL client authentication with IIS is required. Add a new line under *windowsAuthentication enabled="true."* In this line, type:

   ```
   clientCertificateMappingAuthentication enabled="true"
   ```

6. Change:

   ```
   windowsAuthentication enabled="true"
   ```

   to:

   ```
   windowsAuthentication enabled="false"
   ```

7. Click File, choose Save, and then close Notepad.

8. In the command prompt window, enter **iisreset**.

   Note that running *iisreset* from a command prompt will restart the services associated with IIS.

Again, if you are using an AD RMS cluster, you repeat the procedure for every other server in the cluster.

After you have configured these settings, a user who attempts to open rights-protected content published by the AD RMS server or cluster is prompted to provide authentication credentials before the server or cluster provides the user with an RAC or user license.

## PRACTICE Implementing Fine-Grained Password Policies

To complete this practice, the domain functional level of the *contoso.internal* domain must be set to Windows Server 2008. If you are unsure how to do this, consult the Windows Server 2008 Help files.

▶ **Exercise    Create a PSO**

In this exercise, you will create a PSO with password policies that are not the same as the default password policies for the *contoso.internal* domain. You associate this with a global security group called special_password that contains the user Don_Hall. Do not attempt this practice until you have raised the domain functional level of the *contoso.internal* domain to Windows Server 2008. If you created a PSO while studying the 70-646 training kit, create another one but change some of the settings.

1. Log on to the Glasgow DC with the Kim_Akers account.
2. If necessary, create a user account for **Don_Hall** with a password of **P@ssw0rd**. Create a global security group called **special_password**. Make Don_Hall a member of special_password. If you are unsure how to do this, consult the Windows Server 2008 Help files.
3. In the Run box, type **adsiedit.msc**.
4. If this is the first time you have used the ADSI Edit console on your test network, right-click ADSI Edit, and then choose Connect To. Type **contoso.internal** in the Name box, and then click OK.
5. Double-click *contoso.internal*.
6. Double-click DC=contoso,DC=internal.
7. Double-click CN=System.
8. Right-click CN=Password Settings Container. Choose New. Choose Object, as shown in Figure 4-24.

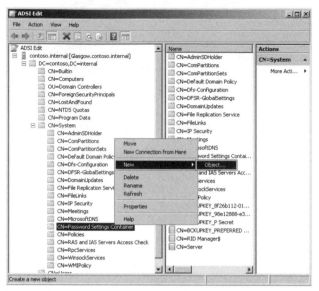

**Figure 4-24**   Creating a password settings object

9.  In the Create Object dialog box, ensure that msDS-PasswordSettings is selected. Click Next.

10. In the Value box for the *CN* attribute, type **PasswdSettings01**. Click Next.

11. In the Value box for the *msDS-PasswordSettingsPrecedence* attribute, type **10**. Click Next.

12. In the Value box for the *msDS-PasswordReversibleEncryptionEnabled* attribute, type **FALSE**. Click Next.

13. In the Value box for the *msDS-PasswordHistoryLength* attribute, type **6**. Click Next.

14. In the Value box for the *msDS-PasswordComplexityEnabled* attribute, type **TRUE**. Click Next.

15. In the Value box for the *msDS-MinimumPasswordLength* attribute, type **6**. Click Next.

16. In the Value box for the *msDS-MinimumPasswordAge* attribute, type **1:00:00:00**. Click Next.

17. In the Value box for the *msDS-MaximumPasswordAge* attribute, type **20:00:00:00**. Click Next.

18. In the Value box for the *msDS-LockoutThreshold* attribute, type **2**. Click Next.

19. In the Value box for the *msDS-LockoutObservationWindow* attribute, type **0:00:15:00**. Click Next.

20. In the Value box for the *msDS-LockoutDuration* attribute, type **0:00:15:00**. Click Next.

21. Click Finish.

22. Open Active Directory Users And Computers, choose View, and then choose Advanced Features.

23. Expand *contoso.internal*, expand System, and then select Password Settings Container.

24. In the details pane, right-click PSO1. Choose Properties.

25. On the Attribute Editor tab, select *msDS-PSOAppliesTo*, as shown in Figure 4-25.

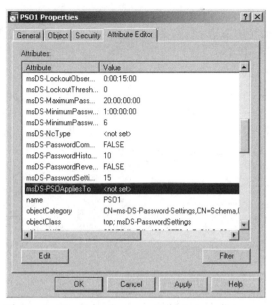

**Figure 4-25**   Selecting an attribute to edit

26.  Click Edit.

27.  Click Add Windows Account.

28.  Type **special_password** in the Enter The Object Names To Select box. Click Check Names.

29.  Click OK. The Multi-Valued Distinguished Name With Security Principal Editor dialog box should look similar to Figure 4-26.

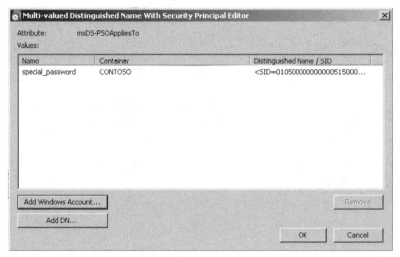

**Figure 4-26**   Adding the special_password global security group to PSO1

30. Click OK, and then click OK again to close the PSO1 Properties dialog box.
31. Test your settings by changing the password for the Don_Hall account to a noncomplex, six-letter password such as **simple**.

## Lesson Summary

- When planning a Group Policy structure, keep it as simple as possible and minimize the use of exceptions. Do not link GPOs to OUs across site links.
- Scope filtering enables you to apply the policy settings in a GPO to selected groups or users in the OU.
- You can use Group Policy to control who can install devices on client workstations and what devices they can install.
- You can authenticate users by username and password or by security certificates held on smart cards. Windows Server 2008 enables you to use fine-grained password policies.

## Lesson Review

Use the following questions to test your knowledge of the information in Lesson 2, "Designing Enterprise-Level Group Policy Strategy." The questions are also available on the companion CD if you prefer to review them in electronic form.

---

**NOTE    Answers**

Answers to these questions and explanations of why each answer choice is correct or incorrect are located in the "Answers" section at the end of the book.

---

1. You are planning your Group Policy structure. Which of the following statements represents good advice?
   A. Keep the number of GPOs to an absolute minimum by having many configuration settings in a single GPO.
   B. If you have two OUs, both at geographically remote sites, that have the same Group Policy settings, link a single GPO to both OUs.
   C. Give your OUs and GPOs meaningful names.
   D. Use features such as the Enforced, Security Filtering, and Loopback Policy settings on GPOs extensively.

2. Which of the following interfaces are components of the Active Directory data store? (Choose all that apply.)

   A. DSA

   B. MAPI

   C. SAM

   D. REPL

   E. LDAP

   F. ESE

3. You want to use Group Policy to control device installation in accordance with company policy. You want administrators to be able to install any device. You do not want standard users to be able to install any but one device that has been approved by the company. You know the Hardware ID for that device. Which of the following configuration steps would you implement? (Choose all that apply.)

   A. Enable Prevent Installation Of Devices Not Described By Other Policy Settings.

   B. Disable or do not configure Prevent Installation Of Devices Not Described By Other Policy Settings.

   C. Enable Allow Administrators To Override Device Installation Restriction Policies.

   D. Disable or do not configure Allow Administrators To Override Device Installation Restriction Policies.

   E. Enable Prevent Installation Of Devices That Match Any Of These Device IDs, and add the Hardware ID of the approved device to the policy setting.

   F. Enable Allow Installation Of Devices That Match Any Of These Device IDs, and add the Hardware ID of the approved device to the policy setting.

# Chapter Review

To further practice and reinforce the skills you learned in this chapter, you can perform the following tasks:

- Review the chapter summary.
- Complete the case scenarios. These scenarios set up real-world situations involving the topics in this chapter and ask you to create a solution.
- Complete the suggested practices.
- Take a practice test.

## Chapter Summary

- Delegation increases administrative efficiency and reduces administrative costs. It provides both isolation and autonomy. You can assign rights to security groups and delegate control of OUs to groups.
- You can delegate the management of groups to a group member and delegate rights to an OU to users or groups without granting rights to any other part of the enterprise.
- Avoid exceptions when planning Group Policy. You can use scope filtering to apply the policy settings in a GPO to selected groups or users in the OU. You can use Group Policy to control device installation.
- New features in Windows Server 2008 enable you to audit changes to Group Policy and Active Directory structure and to use fine-grained password policies.
- The design of your OU and GPO structure depends on how the organization is structured (geographically or by department) and which administrative model is used.

## Case Scenarios

In the following case scenarios, you will apply what you have learned about designing Active Directory administration and Group Policy strategy. You can find answers to these questions in the "Answers" section at the end of this book.

## Case Scenario 1: Designing a Delegation Strategy

You are an enterprise administrator at Northwind Traders. You have just upgraded your domain to Windows Server 2008. You are planning to delegate administrative tasks to members of your team and nonadministrative tasks to security groups that contain standard user accounts. Answer the following questions:

1.  Historically, the administrator team has mostly been involved in emergency resolution, and changes were made to AD DS that were not well documented. The technical director requires you to maintain an audit trail of AD DS changes, including what the original configurations are before changes are made. How do you reassure him?

2.  You have identified an OU that contains several security groups. You ask one of your administrators to create a GPO and to link it to the OU. However, the policy settings in the GPO should apply to only two of the groups and not to the remaining groups. Your team member is unsure how to do this. What do you advise?

3.  A member of your team uses Group Policy to deploy isolation policies to a group of servers in your organization. After deploying the servers, you have determined that the isolation policies are not being applied to several of the servers. Which Group Policy Management Console tool should your team member use to diagnose this problem?

## Case Scenario 2: Planning Authentication and Authorization

You are the enterprise manager at Litware, Inc. Litware has recently upgraded all its DCs to Windows Server 2008, and you are planning authentication and authorization policies that take advantage of the new features Windows Server 2008 provides. Answer the following questions:

1.  Some members of staff (for example, the CEO) want to use simple passwords, although the default policy for the *litware.com* domain enforces complex passwords. Although this is possible in Windows Server 2003, it is difficult to configure and, therefore, was never implemented by Litware. You are asked whether Windows Server 2008 makes this configuration easier. What is your reply?

2.  A member of your administrative team informs you that she cannot get the fine-grained password policy to work, even though all DCs now run Windows Server 2008. What do you advise her to do?

3.  Currently, all staff at Litware can install USB flash memory devices on their client workstations and upload and download files. The technical director sees this as a security risk and wants only administrators to be able to install such devices. However, he does not want to lose the ability to boost Windows Vista client performance through the Windows ReadyBoost feature. What do you tell him?

## Suggested Practices

To help you successfully master the exam objectives presented in this chapter, complete the following tasks.

## Designing the Active Directory Administrative Model

Do both practices in this section.

- **Practice 1**   Investigate management roles. Microsoft-engineered roles for data and system management are listed in this chapter, and a link is given for more information. Follow this link and investigate the Internet. Find out more about these roles.
- **Practice 2**   Investigate compliance auditing. This chapter discusses AD DS and Group Policy auditing, but space prohibits a detailed discussion of every possible setting and option. Search the Internet for more information on this topic.

## Designing Enterprise-Level Group Policy Strategy

Do both practices in this section.

- **Practice 1**   Work with device installation policy settings. The only good way to become familiar with them and how they interact is to configure them and observe the results. Experiment with these settings.
- **Practice 2**   Configure PSOs. A PSO can contain a large number of settings, of which you configured only a small subset in the practice in Lesson 2. Experiment with PSO settings and determine the effects each has on the security policies that affect the users associated with the GPO.

# Take a Practice Test

The practice tests on this book's companion CD offer many options. For example, you can test yourself on just one exam objective, or you can test yourself on all the 70-647 certification exam content. You can set up the test so that it closely simulates the experience of taking a certification exam, or you can set it up in study mode so that you can look at the correct answers and explanations after you answer each question.

---

**MORE INFO**   **Practice tests**

For details about all the practice test options available, see the "How to Use the Practice Tests" section in this book's introduction.

---

# Chapter 5

# Designing a Network Access Strategy

Designing an access strategy for your network in the past strictly involved who should be able to access the network, how they should access the network, and which resources should be made available to these users. Unfortunately, this limited set of criteria falls far short of what else should be included when designing an access strategy. With the advent of more insidious types of attacks through viruses and Trojan horse programs in recent years, it is quite evident that additional requirements are needed prior to allowing a computer access to your secure network.

Protecting the internal network from the ever increasing number of attacks has evolved over the years. From the beginning of the very first stateful firewalls in the mid-1990s to the complex security services offered today, network security experts have steadfastly attempted to keep up with the various threats produced daily. Firewalls; perimeter networks; antivirus, antispam, antispyware programs; and software updates all contribute to the security of networks. All of these are much easier to administer and control when computers attached to the network remain stationary. Newer attacks over the past several years have targeted computers that are not part of the network and have placed dormant pieces of malware on them. When these computers attach to secure networks, some of these newer pieces of malicious software, using various techniques, become active and begin infecting computers and devices on the internal network. Able to penetrate the various layers of defense at the perimeter network by using this newer attack vector with impunity, malware writers can now concentrate on attacking computers that have fewer defense mechanisms.

An initial concern in remote connectivity is the setup of the network perimeter. Perimeter network design has undergone relatively few changes when considering the topology of the perimeter itself. What has changed is the devices and services that are constantly being added and used in the perimeter network. The discussion in this chapter focuses on the devices to deploy in the perimeter to aid in designing a network access protection (NAP) solution. The initial lesson discusses deployment options for a RADIUS (Remote Authentication Dial-In User Service) solution that adequately meets the demands of the environment.

This chapter discusses the components necessary to provide secure remote access connectivity while ensuring the health of the computers and their compliance with stated network policy to help you design a network perimeter when deploying a NAP solution.

### Exam objectives in this chapter:

■ Design for network access.

### Lessons in this chapter:

■ Lesson 1:  Perimeter Networks and Remote Access Strategies ................... 230

■ Lesson 2:  Network Access Policy and Server and Domain Isolation .............. 255

# Before You Begin

To complete the lessons in this chapter, you should have:

■ Experience creating L2TP and PPTP VPN connections.

■ An understanding of authentication protocols used for remote access.

■ Working knowledge of implementing encryption technologies for VPNs.

■ An understanding of firewalls, rules, and security policies for perimeter networks.

■ An understanding of RADIUS and a simple RADIUS configuration.

---

### Real World

*Paul Mancuso*

Prior to undertaking any project involving the design of network security services, I constantly research any new or recently available documentation regarding the features and services of any component involved in the project. Remote access connectivity is quite a fluid subject when it comes to new and innovative devices and services constantly being delivered by the various vendors within the industry. Research becomes even more important due to NAP features and services just arriving to market. There are so many components involved in the process that reading the white papers and studying the example scenarios is imperative because there are so few actual working examples to draw upon at this time. This will rapidly change because Windows Server 2008 brings with it an entire solution that enables third-party vendor solutions to be integrated in the mix.

---

In addition to the research, you should set up a working lab with a bare minimum of half a dozen virtual machines that you can readily assemble into a working design. This enables you to assemble a working solution you can always return to when issues arise in a RADIUS or NAP implementation. The interaction of the various components of a NAP solution requires time studying the interaction and knowing the flow of communication through each of the components involved with the solution. A deep understanding of RADIUS and the attributes involved in each of the NAP enforcement types will aid in designing your NAP solution.

One final note: Ensure that you have checked with any third-party vendor for their compliance with NAP when using their features within your NAP infrastructure. You do not want to be deep into a NAP deployment only to realize that certain attributes you assumed would interact appropriately do not function the way you thought they would. Microsoft also publishes a list at *http://www.microsoft.com/windowsserver2008/en/us /nap-partners.aspx* of all its partners that support NAP.

# Lesson 1:  Perimeter Networks and Remote Access Strategies

Providing secure remote connectivity involves designing access through a perimeter network. Therefore, design a secure perimeter network and decide which services will reside within it first. Services to consider deploying within the perimeter network will most likely include various RADIUS components, VPN servers, publicly accessible application servers, wireless devices, and supporting network infrastructure devices.

Due to the current security-minded environment, your network undoubtedly contains a firewall along with one or more supporting infrastructure devices such as switches and routers as well as application servers such as Web and File Transfer Protocol (FTP) servers that are publicly accessible. In addition, the network might also have a RADIUS service to authenticate virtual private network (VPN) connections or partner access to existing extranets, or possibly to provide secure authentication for a preexisting wireless infrastructure. These network devices and application servers will comprise the current perimeter network that you inherit or are currently administering.

As the enterprise administrator, you are responsible for upgrading the current environment to provide support for:

- An updated RADIUS solution to provide support for an eventual NAP solution.
- A remediation network for the NAP solution.

This lesson provides the background to build a remote access solution and help lay the groundwork for designing a NAP solution.

---

**After this lesson, you will be able to:**
- Understand the technical requirements when designing perimeter networks.
- Understand which services to provide in a perimeter network.
- Determine appropriate firewall services to provide for various types of perimeter networks.
- Design VPN solutions.
- Design a RADIUS solution for a small enterprise.
- Design a RADIUS solution to support branch offices within the same forest.
- Design a RADIUS solution to support a multi-forest environment.

**Estimated lesson time:  45 minutes**

---

# Designing the Perimeter Network

Most perimeter network designs involve one or two firewall devices to protect the edge network. Traffic from the outside passes through one or more inspection points before it is allowed into the perimeter network to access services deployed there or into the secure environment. Typical designs involve a single perimeter device with two or more network interfaces or two inspection points with two security devices, one inspecting traffic into the perimeter network from an untrusted external environment and another inspecting traffic as it enters the secure environment from the perimeter network.

As the enterprise administrator, you must assess the type of traffic you allow into your perimeter network and what traffic is permitted into the secure network. You need to determine how and at what layer you inspect this traffic to fulfill your security requirements successfully. You must assess the services to be deployed in the perimeter network for public accessibility as well as for a secure remote access solution.

## Types of Perimeter Network Architectures

There are many types of perimeter network layouts. The design guides here provide descriptions for the basic security feature sets included in most designs. Network architectures will generally include three distinct regions or zones:

- Border network
- Perimeter network
- Internal network

The border network provides the direct connection to the external environment, which usually is a connection to an ISP, that is often through a router. The border router can offer some protective features such as access lists to manage specific unwanted traffic from certain Internet Control Message Protocol (ICMP) types such as echo requests associated with pinging. A perimeter firewall along with associated security devices and services provides the bulk of protection for the border network. Other than a switch used to provide connectivity to the perimeter security services, there are usually no other network application services of significance within this zone.

The perimeter network is a semi-protected area secured by a perimeter firewall and, possibly, an internal firewall. Services located in this area include Web servers for public access that connect to internal SQL servers along with many other application servers. Most of the discussion in this lesson focuses on other services located within this area.

The internal network is the location of the secure environment. It houses the corporate user and server environment. Some security designs include another firewall service separating the internal user network from the server farms.

Figure 5-1 displays the typical architecture of the three-zone network environment, using two firewall services.

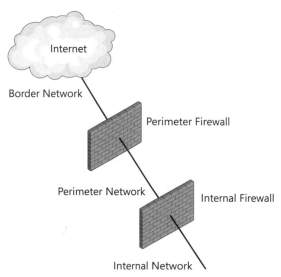

**Figure 5-1**   Perimeter network design employing two firewall devices

If the perimeter firewall is composed of three or more network interfaces, an internal firewall is more of a logical association with the same physical device providing the services for the perimeter firewall than of a physical association with its network interfaces. Figure 5-2 displays an alternative architecture of the network environment employing three or more zones, using a single physical firewall service dividing up separate logical security domains.

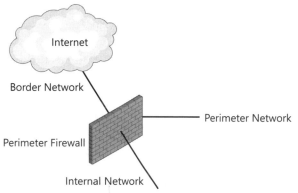

**Figure 5-2**   Perimeter network design employing a single firewall device

These logical designs display a basis for targeting services and security features when designing the perimeter network. As the enterprise administrator, you are responsible for the security of the services that are deployed in the perimeter network. Consider questions such as:

- Which services should be deployed in the perimeter network to provide secure VPN connections?
- Which supporting services are necessary to provide secure VPN connections?
- Do internal users require a secured wireless connection?
- Should the access points for wireless users be deployed as part of the perimeter network design?
- If RADIUS is to be used to centralize management of authentication for remote access and wireless users, which RADIUS components, if any, should be deployed in the perimeter network?

## Securing the Perimeter Network

What is not shown in either design is the type of security services offered by the firewall devices at the perimeter or the internal location in the two firewall device designs. Knowing the types of security devices used to secure access into the perimeter network as well as into the internal environment offers you, the enterprise administrator, a better idea of how services deployed in the perimeter network can be protected. Different types of security devices provide varying levels of security. This lesson focuses only on enterprise-class devices. These devices typically provide one or more of the following:

- Network Address Translation (NAT)
- Stateful inspection
- Circuit-level inspection
- Proxy services
- Application-layer firewalls

NAT uses private IP addresses that have significant meaning when used within your organization. When traffic is sent out to the Internet, these addresses require translation to an acceptable public IP address. NAT was originally devised to overcome the eventual shortage of public IP addresses. One of the benefits of using NAT in your firewall design is that your internal addressing structure is hidden from outside attackers—not a major source of security but a significant fact. A possible detriment when using NAT is that certain services, when run through it, have problems and require services such as NAT editors for Point-to-Point Tunneling Protocol (PPTP) tunnels or NAT Traversal (NAT-T) for IPsec tunnels and Layer 2 Tunneling Protocol (L2TP) tunnels.

Stateful inspection firewalls provide an accounting of all traffic that originated on an interface in a state table. When the connection traffic is returned, the state table determines whether the traffic originated on that interface.

Circuit-level firewalls provide a more in-depth inspection of traffic than does a stateful firewall. Circuit-level firewalls provide session maintenance and enable the use of protocols that require secondary connections such as FTP. Circuit-level firewalls are usually the way stateful inspection services are carried out in today's retail firewalls.

Proxy servers are intermediaries that provide security by requesting a service on behalf of a client; the client is not directly connected to the service. The proxy service can inspect all headers involved in the transaction, providing an extra layer of protection. Frequently requested content can be cached and reused to reduce bandwidth. Proxy servers can also provide authenticated requests, NAT, and authentication request forwarding.

The ultimate in protection is an application-layer firewall. Not only are all the incoming and outgoing packet headers inspected and state tables maintained, but the data streams can be inspected to provide security against attacks hidden in the data payloads of ordinary Web service packets such as HTTP, other Web-related request and data packets, and many other application-specific request and response packets.

---

**MORE INFO**   **Types of firewall services**

The information presented here on types of firewall services is just an overview to provide a basis for discussion on perimeter network design and services deployed within the perimeter network. There is much additional information about firewall types that you can view at *http://www.microsoft.com/technet/security/guidance/networksecurity/firewall.mspx*.

---

**Planning for ISA Server**    Protecting the perimeter network has been a primary focus of Microsoft Internet Security and Acceleration (ISA) Server. ISA Server 2006 is the current version and provides an integrated edge security gateway for remote access, branch office connectivity, and Internet access protection. ISA Server figures prominently in any Microsoft solution because it integrates well with Microsoft remote access services as well as provides secure tunneling for site-to-site VPNs.

---

**NOTE**   **Forefront Edge Security and Access**

ISA Server 2006 is now part of the new Microsoft Forefront Edge Security and Access product line. The Microsoft Forefront line of products provides a comprehensive set of security products from the edge of the network starting with Internet Security and Acceleration (ISA) Server all the way to the desktop, providing firewall services, protection from malware and spyware, network edge security services, and much more.

---

A common use of ISA Server in the perimeter network is in a back-to-back design. The perimeter network is protected by ISA Server operating as a firewall against the outside while providing filtering and reverse proxying of services offered in the perimeter network. A second server running ISA Server stationed between the perimeter network and the internal network acts as an application-layer firewall and proxy server, inspecting and securing all requests as they move inbound to the internal network. The servers running ISA Server at the perimeter firewall or at the internal edge can be deployed in a variety of fashions to provide high availability and load balancing.

Figure 5-3 displays some of the roles that ISA Server can play when deployed in the perimeter network.

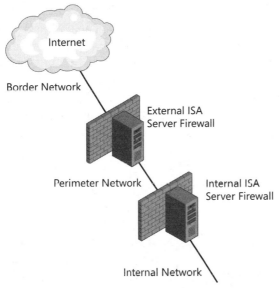

**Figure 5-3**   ISA Server deployed in a back-to-back design

ISA Server 2004 and ISA Server 2006 support Network Access Quarantine Control as a complementary service to Microsoft Windows Server 2003. ISA Server 2004 or ISA Server 2006, when installed on Windows Server 2003 SP1 or later, can use Quarantine Control, which is provided by the Routing and Remote Access service of Windows Server 2003 and is limited to providing access control to VPN and remote access clients only. The service requires custom connection profiles on the clients, along with server-side scripts to check for compliance by remote access clients. The Quarantine Control service does not at this time have any components that allow for integration with the newer NAP service and Network Policy Server (NPS) services in Windows Server 2008 other than NPS providing RADIUS services to VPN clients using ISA Server as the VPN server.

---

**MORE INFO**    ISA Server help

A site often helpful with ideas that involve ISA Server is *http://www.isaserver.org*. This site is well maintained and well organized and offers a wealth of ideas about design, add-ons, and configuration in ISA Server.

---

**NOTE**    ISA Server 2006 and Windows Server 2008

ISA Server 2006, at the time of this writing, is not available for installation on Windows Server 2008 and is available as a 32-bit application server only. Plans for the next version of ISA Server and the Forefront Security products are tailored for Windows Server 2008 and will be available for 64-bit platforms.

---

**Third-Party Firewall Products**    With the security field growing at an increasing pace, third-party firewall products are plentiful. Many of these products fit a paradigm similar to ISA Server. Many of the major firewall product vendors have also included multiple feature sets in their firewall product offerings. This makes it even more attractive to pair a firewall product from one of these top-selling vendors with ISA Server. A common scenario is to use a firewall appliance for the perimeter firewall and an ISA Server cluster for the internal firewall. Many of these third-party products provide an integrated assortment of security services such as:

- Stateful firewall services
- Intrusion prevention services
- Anti-malware services
- Application-layer firewall services

At a minimum, the firewall appliance should provide circuit-level services along with an inline intrusion prevention service module to ensure inspection at the application layer for inbound requests from the border network. ISA Server or an ISA Server cluster installed as the internal firewall can provide proxy, packet filtering, circuit-level firewall services, and application-layer inspection of packets originating from either the border network or the perimeter network for access to internal hosts or responses returned to internal clients.

## Deploying Strategic Services in the Perimeter Network

The perimeter network was originally designed to contain Web services for public use. Over time, the decision to deploy specific applications and services there has undergone much change. The perimeter network might contain not only Web services but also many of the following suggested services:

- Application servers for extranets
- VPN servers for remote access

- Wireless access points to provide public wireless access in your enterprise as well as wireless local area networks (WLANs) for internal corporate use
- Terminal Services (TS) Gateway server role
- Components of RADIUS to provide authentication for wireless access, VPNs, and application servers
- Online Certificate Status Protocol (OCSP) servers to provide timely information regarding the revocation status of a certificate in use

This list is not exhaustive but does describe the more commonly deployed services in the perimeter network. This lesson focuses on the Microsoft best practices for perimeter network design and server placement of these services.

## Planning Web Services Deployment in the Perimeter Network

Web server services commonly deployed in the perimeter network consist of the following:

- Web servers for Internet and extranet access
- FTP servers
- Publicly accessible Domain Name System (DNS) servers

Web servers offer access over HTTP and HTTPS. Even custom applications built for delivery through a Web server use the same ports, minimizing the number of ports to be opened up through the perimeter firewall. This is the strength of using application servers running Internet Information Services (IIS) 7.0 as the application platform for delivery.

Extranet application servers using Secure Socket Layer (SSL) connections might require the services of an OCSP responder, a server responding to requests for certificate revocation similar to what is provided by a lookup on a certificate revocation list, but an OCSP request and response is less resource intensive and more timely concerning the currency of the information. An OCSP responder can be deployed in the perimeter network because there is usually little concern over security. The OCSP responder signs its response, and the one waiting for the response can check the validity of it by using the public key of the OCSP responder.

DNS servers deployed in the perimeter network provide name resolution for publicly accessible Web services and should be restricted to providing responses only to DNS requests for those services. A host-based firewall that includes anti-malware services along with the removal of all unnecessary services is part of the preliminary setup of a secured host in the perimeter zone.

These Web server services should be deployed at the corporate site and can include an alternate site for site redundancy when providing a solution for a disaster recovery plan. Services at the alternate site should be provided the same considerations regarding security.

**Planning IPv6 Access for Web Services**    Windows Server 2008 provides complete support for all related Web services over IPv6 although no special consideration is required because all Internet related services require an IPv4 address for appropriate access for the immediate future. Options for migration to IPv6 are already available in Windows Server 2008 for networks employing IPv6 alongside IPv4 for all Web services.

# Designing a Remote Access Strategy

In designing remote access, an enterprise administrator must consider all required avenues of access. The traditional methods of access have given way to various types of VPN connections and Remote Desktop connections. These two general categories involve many considerations. This portion of the lesson concentrates on deploying VPN servers and providing access for Terminal Server clients.

## Planning for VPN Remote Access Connections

As the enterprise administrator, you must make decisions concerning the following:

- Which VPN protocols for remote access are available?
- Which authentication methods should be supported, considering an eventual NAP deployment?
- How should VPN servers deployed for Internet and extranet access be secured?
- What public key infrastructure (PKI) support is needed for VPN access methods?
- How should NAP be integrated with VPN enforcement?

Each of these items has its own unique set of requirements and dependencies. A decision for one can affect the decisions about others. For instance, choosing to use authentication involving certificates can require a supporting PKI. You must then decide how this choice affects your deployment of a NAP solution. In addition, you might require multiple encryption or authentication protocols and services if you are supporting guest access, extranets with partner firms, and your own remote access clients. Each of these groups of users can have different requirements.

You might want to enforce a stringent security policy, but other factors always come into play. These factors, not listed in any order, include:

- Cost
- Compatibility with existing operating systems
- Compatibility with existing application services
- The inevitable politics involved with enforcing security features on guests and extranets

## Designing a VPN Protocol Solution

Deciding which VPN protocols to use for your remote access policies depends upon several issues such as:

- Which operating systems your VPN clients use.
- Which security requirements exist regarding encrypted communications.
- Which security policies exist to secure communication through your corporate firewall.
- Which authentication mechanisms are acceptable.
- Whether a need exists to deploy a PKI to support the VPN infrastructure.

**VPN Tunneling Protocols**   Windows Server 2008 provides support for three tunneling protocols when configuring remote access connections:

- Point-to-Point Tunneling Protocol (PPTP)
- Layer 2 Tunneling Protocol (L2TP)
- Secure Socket Tunneling Protocol (SSTP)

**Point-to-Point Tunneling Protocol**   PPTP provides a high level of security, still, as a VPN tunneling protocol. Many of the past arguments concerning vulnerabilities were addressed long ago. Its simplicity of deployment as a solution is one of its greatest assets. It is well supported by the operating systems of Microsoft Windows 2000 Professional, Windows 2000 Server, Windows XP, Windows Server 2003, Windows Vista, and Windows Server 2008. PPTP has garnered broad support from the IT industry as well as from many vendors, who support its use within their products.

PPTP, when used in a perimeter network, engenders some concerns when a NAT service is between a PPTP client and a server connection. The NAT service must include a NAT editor such as the one found in the Routing and Remote Access service of Windows Server 2003 and Windows Server 2008. Because ISA Server 2004 and ISA Server 2006 both run on Windows Server 2003 and use the services of the Routing and Remote Access service of Windows Server 2003, a NAT editor is also available for use through ISA Server.

To secure the connections to the VPN server, establish inbound and outbound filters for all communication to ensure that only VPN traffic is allowed. Table 5-1 displays filters you should configure to ensure the security of the VPN server.

**Table 5-1   PPTP Filters on Firewall for VPN Server Deployed in the Perimeter Network**

| Filter Direction | Source Port and IP Address | Destination Port and IP Address | Filter Action |
|---|---|---|---|
| Inbound | Greater than TCP 1023 and source IP address (any) of client | TCP 1723 and IP address of perimeter interface of VPN server | Allows PPTP tunnel maintenance traffic from the PPTP client to the PPTP server |

**Table 5-1    PPTP Filters on Firewall for VPN Server Deployed in the Perimeter Network**

| Filter Direction | Source Port and IP Address | Destination Port and IP Address | Filter Action |
|---|---|---|---|
| Inbound | IP 47 and Source IP address (any) of client | IP 47 and IP address of perimeter interface of VPN server | Defines the PPTP data tunnel from the PPTP client to the PPTP server |
| Outbound | TCP Port 1723 and IP address of perimeter interface | TCP port of client request (any) and IP address of client (any) | Allows PPTP tunnel maintenance traffic from the PPTP server to the PPTP client |
| Outbound | IP 47 and IP address of perimeter interface | IP 47 and IP address of client (any) | Defines the PPTP data tunnel from the PPTP server to the PPTP client |

**Layer 2 Tunneling Protocol**    L2TP provides a more secure connection than PPTP due to several aspects. L2TP provides the same user authentication that PPTP provides as well as computer authentication using IPsec authentication. L2TP with IPsec uses 168-bit triple DES (3DES) encryption for the data and provides per-packet data origin authentication, proving the identity of the user and providing data integrity and replay protection while providing a high level of confidentiality.

L2TP has some constraints, however. Every computer must have a computer certificate. The certificate used by the VPN server and the VPN client computer must come from the same trusted root certification authority (CA). If both the VPN server and the VPN client computer are members of a domain, both computers can use autoenrollment to acquire the necessary computer certificate. If one or both computers are not domain members, an administrator must request certificates on their behalf, using the CA Web enrollment tool. The administrator then needs to install the certificate on the computers by using a flash drive or some other external but secure access method. Computer certificates at the time of this writing cannot be issued to smart cards for use with L2TP certificate authentication of the tunnel.

---

**NOTE    Preshared key vs. a computer certificate**

Although you can use a preshared key instead of a computer certificate for L2TP/IPsec computer authentication, it is considered to be a test lab feature only. This is because using a preshared key is significantly less secure.

---

L2TP has an issue as well with firewall services using NAT. L2TP requires NAT Traversal (NAT-T) to pass through a NAT. This means that an extra UDP port, UDP 4500, must be open on the firewall. The clients connecting to a VPN server behind a firewall using L2TP must also support NAT-T. L2TP requires the filters in Table 5-2 for the perimeter firewall's Internet interface.

**Table 5-2   L2TP Filters on Firewall for VPN Server Deployed in the Perimeter Network**

| Filter Direction | Source Port and IP Address | Destination Port and IP Address | Filter Action |
| --- | --- | --- | --- |
| Inbound | Source IP address (any IP address) of client | UDP port 500 and IP address of perimeter interface of VPN server | Allows Internet Key Exchange (IKE) traffic to the VPN server |
| Inbound | Source IP address (any IP address) of client | IP 47 and IP address of perimeter interface of VPN server | Allows IPsec NAT-T traffic to the VPN server |
| Inbound | Source IP address (any IP address) of client | IP 50 and IP address of perimeter interface of VPN server | Allows IPsec Encapsulating Security Protocol (ESP) traffic to the VPN server |
| Outbound | UDP port 500 and IP address of perimeter interface of VPN server | IP address (any IP address) of client | Allows IKE traffic from the VPN server |
| Outbound | UDP port 4500 and IP address of perimeter interface of VPN server | IP address (any IP address) of client | Allows IPsec NAT-T traffic from the VPN server |
| Outbound | IP 50 and IP address of perimeter interface of VPN server | IP address (any IP address) of client | Allows IPsec ESP traffic from the VPN server |

**Secure Sockets Tunneling Protocol**   SSTP is a new VPN tunnel supported by Windows Vista SP1 and Windows Server 2008. It uses SSL-encrypted HTTP connections for the VPN connection. More specifically, Point-to-Point Protocol (PPP) sessions are encrypted by SSL and transferred over an HTTP connection. This makes using SSTP a great benefit because most companies and organizations such as hotels, Internet cafes, and other Internet hotspots allow TCP port 443 for outbound access. Thus, changes to the firewall are not a great concern when implementing SSTP and deploying the VPN server in the perimeter network.

Another advantage is that SSTP is quite secure. An SSL tunnel is initially formed prior to the transfer of user credentials. SSTP also supports the Extensible Authentication Protocol (EAP) types, Extensible Authentication Protocol-Transport Layer Security (EAP-TLS), and Protected Extensible Authentication Protocol-Transport Layer (PEAP-TLS) for user authentication as well as the Microsoft Challenge Handshake Authentication Protocol (MS-CHAP) v2 authentication methods.

There are some drawbacks to using SSTP. It is supported on Windows Vista SP1 as a VPN client only and on Windows Server 2008 as a VPN client or server. SSTP support will not be added to Windows XP. In addition, users must trust the root certification authority that issued the certificate to the VPN server. VPN clients must have the root CA certificate installed as one of their trusted root CAs to validate this certificate.

Allowing access to a VPN server offering SSTP is fairly simple. More than likely, your firewall is already set to allow access through TCP port 443 for HTTPS. An additional rule is needed only to ensure the passage of TCP port 443 from the border network into the perimeter network to the VPN server perimeter interface.

**Authentication Protocols**    Windows Server 2008 provides support for quite a few authentication protocols. The list now includes:

- PAP
- MS-CHAP
- MS-CHAP v2
- PEAP-MSCHAP v2/EAP-MSCHAP v2
- EAP-TLS
- PEAP-TLS

The list has dwindled a little because support for Shiva Password Authentication Protocol (SPAP) and the Extensible Authentication Protocol-Message Digest have been removed from Windows Server 2008 and Windows Vista VPNs as client choices. It was thought that these two types of authentication provided little value in securing authentication.

---

**NOTE    MS-CHAP and SPAP support in Windows Server 2008**

At the time of writing this book for the release to manufacturing of Windows Server 2008, MS-CHAP (also known as MS-CHAP v1) and SPAP were still included in the NPS and Routing and Remote Access Microsoft Management Consoles (MMCs) although EAP-MD5 is not available. Documentation at *http://technet.microsoft.com/en-us/library/bb726965.aspx#ECAA* states that support was removed for all three. Please note the last section stating the removal of certain technologies. From a VPN client perspective for Windows Vista and Windows Server 2008, EAP-MD5, MS-CHAP, and SPAP are no longer available as choices.

---

From a security perspective, do not choose Password Authentication Protocol (PAP) and MS-CHAP unless necessary to support an incompatible client. MS-CHAP v2 should be used only when strong passwords are enforced.

Among the supported EAP types, EAP-TLS and PEAP-TLS use certificate-based authentication. PEAP supports two EAP types, PEAP-TLS and PEAP-MSCHAP v2. When PEAP is used with the EAP-MSCHAP v2 type, passwords are used to authenticate the user for the connection.

Once again, strong passwords should be enforced to ensure a higher level of security for the connection.

To provide support for certificates when employing certificate-based authentication with either EAP-TLS or PEAP-TLS, users require a user certificate on either a smart card or on their computer. Issuing a certificate through a smart card is not too difficult. Issuing certificates to users who are mostly remote to store on their computers will require one of three solutions:

- Have each user manually request a certificate through either the certificate authority Web enrollment service or the Certificates MMC snap-in.
- Have an administrator request a certificate on the user's behalf and manually install the certificate in the personal store on the user's computer.
- Use Group Policy to distribute a certificate to users.

Having each user perform the request individually solves the dilemma of distributing certificates in most cases. The issue becomes a support problem if too many users need assistance or other technical difficulties arise. The final answer, to use Group Policy, is probably the most efficient but can also have problems. Some users using laptops might not be connected to the network, or the computer itself might not be part of the corporate domain for one reason or another. In most cases, Group Policy works for the majority of users. Traveling users using laptops that are part of the domain need to connect and log on to the domain as part of the process of acquiring a certificate through Group Policy.

Another concern when setting up the environment for remote access connectivity is whether NAP will be instituted in the near future. For VPN connections, NAP includes a VPN enforcement point, which requires a connecting client to use one of the PEAP types for authentication. In choosing which PEAP type to use, PEAP-MSCHAP v2 or PEAP-TLS, PEAP-TLS holds the advantage as a superior authentication protocol for two reasons:

- It does not use a password for authentication but uses a certificate as previously noted.
- PEAP-TLS is superior to EAP-TLS because the exchange of certificates for authentication takes place after the client and the server have created an encrypted tunnel.

The disadvantage in using PEAP-TLS over PEAP-MSCHAP v2 is that all users now require a certificate whereas PEAP-MSCHAP v2 requires only a server certificate. An issue in using PEAP-MSCHAP v2 concerns the certificate issued to the VPN server performing the authentication. If the certificate issued to it is from one of the established trusted public root certification authorities, no other work is required other than purchasing the certificate itself. If the certificate is issued from a standalone root CA by the internal enterprise PKI, then a copy of its certificate needs to be installed on all computers connecting to the VPN using PEAP-MSCHAP v2 for authentication. If the certificate is issued from an enterprise CA, the certificate for the root CA must be distributed through the Web enrollment, the Certificates console, or another manual method.

## Designing Secure VPN Server Deployment

When considering the placement of VPN servers, it has become customary for the VPN servers to be deployed in the perimeter network. Although there are established guidelines for deploying the VPN server outside of the perimeter firewall, it is considered a best practice to deploy the VPN server inside the perimeter zone, behind the perimeter firewall. The previous IP filter tables, Table 5-1 and 5-2, outline the best practices for opening up access to the VPN servers deployed inside the perimeter network.

If the branch offices need VPN connectivity, two choices are available:

- Direct VPN connectivity to VPN servers located at the branch offices
- Centralized management of VPN access to one main office and ensured VPN client access to resources located in their respective branch offices

**VPN Server Deployment at Branch Offices**    If VPN servers are to be deployed at the branch offices, you must give the same consideration when setting up access through the firewall there. The VPN server should be deployed in a perimeter network, often termed a screened subnet, as Figure 5-4 displays. Availability of affordable firewalls such as ISA Server can provide a perimeter network and secure access to resources such as a VPN server, making securing a colocated VPN server an easier chore. Companies can standardize how branch office access is achieved to relieve the complications involved in planning each deployment.

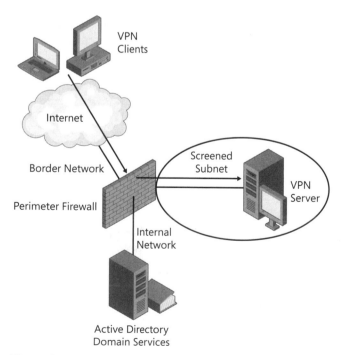

**Figure 5-4**   VPN server deployed in the screened subnet

**MORE INFO**   IP filters

To protect the VPN server further, IP filters can be established with the Windows Server 2008 Firewall feature. Although there is a default program setting for NPS, you can obtain more granular control by running the Security Configuration Wizard. Microsoft refers to this technique for securing ports and services as *role-based security policies*. You can find more information about using this wizard to configure role-based security settings for an NPS server at *http://technet2.microsoft.com /windowsserver2008/en/library/52a98d8a-8823-498c-9be3-3637186e50e61033.mspx?mfr=true*.

**MORE INFO**   Manually configuring Windows Firewall

To learn more about manually configuring Windows Firewall with Advanced Security, use the following link to download an entire document devoted to this topic: *http://www.microsoft.com /downloads/details.aspx?FamilyId=DF192E1B-A92A-4075-9F69-C12B7C54B52B&displaylang=en*.

**Centralized Management of VPN Access**   Clients accessing resources through VPN servers that are centrally located can still access resources anywhere within the enterprise. Because a VPN connection to a VPN client essentially is offering a local area network (LAN) connection remotely, a VPN client will also have access anywhere on that LAN that a normal wired LAN client has access. This is both an advantage and a plausible security issue.

The obvious advantage is the ease in offering resources to the remote client. The VPN client can be anywhere Internet access is available to gain access to data and application servers on your enterprise network in a secure manner. To mediate any possible security issues, the VPN server can enforce strict network routing rules to allow the client access to specific segments of the network. In addition, filter rules can be applied to the VPN connection to disallow a curious VPN client from wandering into areas of the network deemed out of bounds. Because a user with sufficient rights locally can administer his or her own routing tables, the VPN administrator needs to be aware that such users can circumvent simple security applied through routing rules. Inbound IP filters and policies applied to the VPN connection can disable a user's ability to browse networks that are not authorized by the connection.

# Designing a RADIUS Solution for Remote Access

In designing a VPN solution, authentication of VPN clients becomes a paramount concern. In deciding which protocols to use for the tunnel and which authentication protocols are configured for access, the next step is how to manage the authentication of those users.

Managing authentication services for multiple services and for multiple points of access for each of these services rapidly becomes a drain on an administrator's time. As the enterprise administrator, you can see the wisdom in centrally managing authentication and authorization of access to resources.

Microsoft has had an evolving RADIUS strategy ever since the introduction of Routing and Remote Access in Windows 2000 Server. Internet Authentication Service (IAS) was the next iteration and brought along huge improvements. One of the advances was support for a RADIUS proxy. With Windows Server 2008, the VPN and RADIUS solutions are now part of its newly renamed NPS.

NPS encompasses many facets of remote access services. It provides the following services:

- RADIUS client
- RADIUS proxy
- RADIUS server
- RADIUS accounting
- VPN administration for access and polices
- Primary console for administering NAP services

Therefore, when designing your RADIUS solution for VPNs and remote access policies, think about eventually using NAP because NPS plays a central role in this feature.

## Designing a RADIUS Solution for the Main Office

In designing a RADIUS solution, consider all the components of a RADIUS infrastructure that provide authentication, authorization, and accounting. Starting with the access clients and all the way through the RADIUS infrastructure to the back-end user database, an enterprise administrator must carefully plot the location of each of these services. Figure 5-5 displays a real RADIUS design from a high-level overview.

From this overall design, you can see that RADIUS can support authentication for a variety of services and a variety of access client and access servers. Users of Web-based applications from either extranets with partners or publicly accessible application servers can be authenticated using the RADIUS client support built into ISA Server. VPN and dial-up clients can be authenticated through an NPS server configured as a RADIUS client. Finally, wireless clients, either guests or WLAN for the corporate environment, can also use the built-in RADIUS client support in wireless access points to relay RADIUS requests.

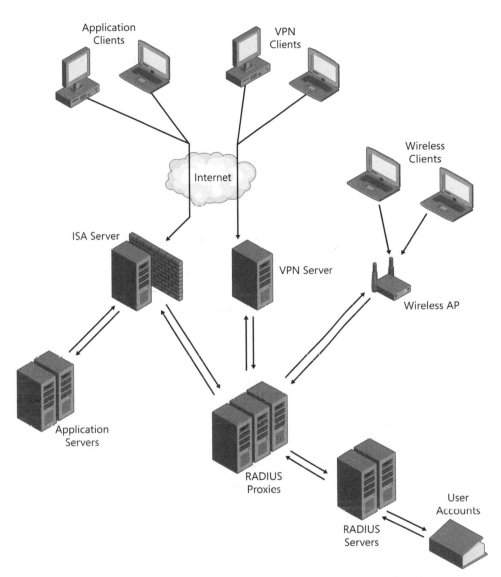

**Figure 5-5**  RADIUS infrastructure, support elements, and example application support

**Deployment Location for RADIUS Services**    Securing your RADIUS solution involves deploying only the essential services in the perimeter network and placing the rest of the services in the secured, internal network. Using Figure 5-5 as a basis for this discussion, you would want to place only the following services in the perimeter network while deploying the rest of the services behind the internal firewall:

- ISA Server
- Application servers (probably in a screened subnet connected to ISA Server, leaving any SQL servers containing the data inside the trusted environment)
- VPN server
- Wireless access point
- RADIUS proxies

**Planning RADIUS Communication**    ISA Server has built-in capabilities to forward authentication requests to a RADIUS server to centralize authentication for users of published Web servers, Web application servers, and Windows SharePoint Services Web sites. The application servers can exist in a screened subnet or in the perimeter network but have access only through an authenticated request from ISA Server. The data that the application servers draw upon can be secured in SQL servers behind the internal firewall.

VPN servers with the NPS role installed can be set up as RADIUS clients and forward all requests to back-end RADIUS proxies. The VPN servers can use a RADIUS server group configuration to ensure high availability and load balancing of requests.

The wireless access points using 802.1x, WPA Enterprise, or WPA2 Enterprise authentication services act as RADIUS clients to forward all RADIUS requests through the RADIUS proxies. The RADIUS proxies then forward those requests to an internal RADIUS server.

**Load Balancing and High Availability of a RADIUS Infrastructure**    Using RADIUS proxies in your RADIUS design is a strong asset in a RADIUS solution for several reasons. There is a fine line between a RADIUS client and a RADIUS proxy. To the RADIUS client, the RADIUS proxy appears to be the RADIUS server where authentication would normally occur. Thus, the communication between the RADIUS clients and the RADIUS proxies is through the RADIUS protocol.

Typically, RADIUS clients do not have a reliable mechanism built into their client architecture for load balancing their requests across multiple RADIUS servers. Load balancing the RADIUS client requests is achieved by configuring some of the RADIUS clients to use specific RADIUS proxy servers as their primary RADIUS servers and configuring other RADIUS clients to use the remaining RADIUS proxy servers as their primary servers. Each of these two RADIUS client groups can then use the other's primary RADIUS server as its secondary RADIUS server.

This type of load balancing is sufficient for the front end of your RADIUS infrastructure. To load balance the back end, the RADIUS proxy servers load balance their requests by round robin with servers of a RADIUS server group.

NPS role service also provides the VPN server role. You can load balance the VPN service, if necessary, by creating an NLB cluster and ensuring that you set the port rule to single or network affinity. The port range for the port rule should encompass the proper TCP port (1723) for PPTP, the UDP ports (500/4500) for L2TP, and TCP port (443) for SSTP.

---

**MORE INFO   IP address and subject name configuration for SSTP NLB cluster**

To ensure proper setup for NLB when using SSTP, the certificate must be the same computer certificate on all VPN servers in the NLB cluster. You can find additional information regarding IP address and subject name configuration for the SSTP NLB cluster at *http://support.microsoft.com /default.aspx/kb/947029*.

---

## Designing a RADIUS Solution for Branch Office Remote Access

If your deployment design calls for distributed VPN remote access, the VPN servers can route their RADIUS requests to the central office's RADIUS server. You can use RADIUS proxies if necessary. To secure the RADIUS communication from the VPN servers through a public network such as the Internet, you can use VPNs linking the branch offices to the main office to carry the RADIUS communication. Because the RADIUS protocol encrypts only select portions of the RADIUS protocol communication, be sure to encrypt the entire RADIUS communication pathway whenever you need RADIUS communication over great distances. This is another advantage that ISA Server delivers when you use it to secure access to the branch offices. ISA Server can also establish the secure VPN that can carry the RADIUS communication between the branch office VPN servers and the main office RADIUS servers.

## Scaling RADIUS Authentication for Multiple Domains and Forests

If your enterprise requires you to authenticate VPN clients from different forests, you have another issue. RADIUS by default provides authentication for users from the same realm of which the RADIUS server is a member. To provide RADIUS authentication for multiple realms, trust relationships must be constructed, or a RADIUS proxy can enable authentication.

For multiple domains of the same forest, no extra trusts are required. For multiple domains with no trusts or one-way trusts, either create the needed trusts or employ a RADIUS proxy.

A RADIUS proxy can resolve the issue if trust relationships are not possible. A RADIUS server in a domain foreign to that of the user receives a RADIUS request for authentication. The RADIUS server without trusts in place with the foreign domain cannot forward the request to an appropriate realm to authenticate the user. By implementing a RADIUS proxy in the communication pathway, the RADIUS requests from the RADIUS clients in specific realms can be proxied to the correct RADIUS servers to provide a successful authentication for the user. Figure 5-6 displays the design details.

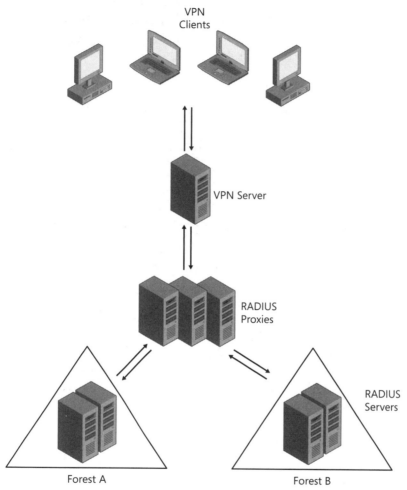

**Figure 5-6**    RADIUS proxies implemented to provide a successful multi-forest solution

PRACTICE **Designing a RADIUS Solution for a Mid-Size Enterprise**

You are the enterprise administrator at Contoso, Ltd. Contoso is a mid-size corporation with offices located in the southeastern United States and the Caribbean. As an enterprise administrator, you are charged with the task of constructing a VPN solution for all branch offices and the main office in Ft. Lauderdale, Florida, for Contoso.

With branch offices in Atlanta, Georgia; New Orleans, Louisiana; Orlando, Florida; St. Thomas in the Virgin Islands; and Grand Cayman in the Cayman Islands, Contoso employs over 2,000 employees. Offices in the United States are connected by the corporate wide area network (WAN). Offices in the Caribbean are connected by a site-to-site VPN connection to the Ft. Lauderdale office.

A single Active Directory Domain Services (AD DS) forest with two domains currently exists for Contoso. The two domains are *contoso.com* and *caribbean.contoso.com*. The Grand Cayman branch office is a recent acquisition from a competing firm, Fabrikam, Inc. Fabrikam has one Active Directory forest with one domain, *fabrikam.com*. You have already moved all Fabrikam domain controllers to the Ft. Lauderdale office in anticipation of centralized management. The branch office at Grand Cayman is being sent a read-only domain controller (RODC) for secure local authentication.

An overall goal is to provide a secure and efficient remote access solution for users in all offices. Certificate authentication of both users and computers is required for the remote access solution instead of the current user password–only authentication provided by MS-CHAP. No dial-up services are offered because all users should connect to their offices through the Internet. Remote access is administered by each office. Administration of remote access policies must be simplified and duplicated on every VPN server. The remote access setup must allow users to authenticate to VPN servers at any of the branch offices or the main office.

Contoso wishes to enforce a level of health for all computers connecting through the VPN. Initially, only a monitored solution is needed to determine the extent of the security problems with VPN clients.

All domains are run internally by a mixture of Windows Server 2003 and Windows Server 2008 domain controllers. All VPN servers are running on Windows Server 2003.

▶ **Exercise 1   Design the VPN Solution**

In this exercise, you will review the current enterprise and, based upon the requirements for the new remote access solution, you will plan a new solution.

1.  What are important factors to consider in the current environment when forming a remote access solution?

    ❑   Multiple forests with no established trusts between them

    ❑   Management's desire to simplify the distributed management of the current authentication scheme used for remote access

    ❑   Use of the Internet for all remote access connections

    ❑   Employment of the highest security by all connections, implying a VPN connection

    ❑   Security requirements to use a certificate-based authentication service

2.  Which authentication protocols can you choose? Why?

    ❑   EAP-TLS and PEAP-TLS are the only authentication protocols that provide certificate-based solutions.

3.  Which VPN protocol should you use?

    ❑ L2TP because it will provide the security required for both the computer and the user. SSTP provides a secure and encrypted tunnel using only a server certificate.

▶ **Exercise 2   Design the RADIUS Solution**

1.  What are the primary considerations in moving the VPN connection toward a RADIUS solution in line with Contoso's overall goals?

    ❑ Windows Server 2003 VPN servers need to be upgraded to Windows Server 2008.

    ❑ In the RADIUS solution, you must consider that a NAP solution will ultimately be deployed.

    ❑ Remote access is currently administered in a distributed fashion. Central administration of remote access policies is a primary goal.

2.  Which components are required of a RADIUS solution for each branch office and the main office?

    ❑ For all U.S.-based branch offices, only a VPN server is necessary because it will act as the RADIUS client, forwarding the authentication requests to the Ft. Lauderdale–based RADIUS proxy servers.

    ❑ For all Caribbean branch offices, only a VPN server is necessary because it, too, will act as a RADIUS client by forwarding the authentication requests to the Ft. Lauderdale–based RADIUS proxy servers.

    ❑ At the Ft. Lauderdale main office, you need a hierarchy of VPN servers acting as RADIUS clients forwarding requests to RADIUS servers, along with RADIUS proxy servers receiving requests from the Cayman Islands, to forward those requests to the appropriate RADIUS servers in the appropriate domain.

## Lesson Summary

■ Perimeter networks serve as the external barrier between the unsecured Internet and the secure internal network.

■ Servers deployed in the perimeter network service direct requests from public computers. Servers in the perimeter network are semi-protected by a perimeter firewall.

■ Servers containing sensitive data such as SQL database servers should be located on the internal network.

■ Network Policy Server (NPS) has replaced Internet Authentication Server (IAS) to provide authentication, authorization, and accounting for RADIUS, management of connection request policies, and network connection policies.

■ Computer certificates can be distributed through Group Policy for managed computers.

■ VPN servers providing the initial point of access for VPN clients should be deployed in the perimeter network. A VPN server can provide the authentication or forward the authentication request to a central location by using RADIUS.

- RADIUS can provide centralized authentication, authorization, and accounting for remote access, 802.1x, and application services.

- A RADIUS configuration involves an access client (which is actually an access server) that forwards the authentication request to a RADIUS server or a RADIUS proxy. If a RADIUS proxy is involved, it too acts much like a RADIUS client and forwards the request to a RADIUS server.

- The RADIUS clients and the RADIUS proxy are usually deployed in the perimeter networks.

## Lesson Review

You can use the following questions to test your knowledge of the information in Lesson 1, "Perimeter Networks and Remote Access Strategies." The questions are also available on the companion CD if you prefer to review them in electronic form.

**NOTE  Answers**

Answers to these questions and explanations of why each answer choice is correct or incorrect are located in the "Answers" section at the end of the book.

1. Which of the following performs RADIUS authentication?
   A. Access client
   B. Access server
   C. RADIUS proxy
   D. RADIUS server

2. Which of the following does not describe an appropriate function of a RADIUS proxy?
   A. Processing requests from access servers and forwarding them to a RADIUS server
   B. Processing incoming connection attempts from access clients
   C. Load balancing RADIUS requests among servers of the RADIUS Server Group
   D. Providing support for multi-forest authentication

3. Which of the following are true statements regarding authentication protocols used for remote access? (Choose all that apply.)

   A. EAP-TLS uses only the server certificate to create secure communication between an authenticating client and the authentication server prior to the computer authenticating.

   B. With PEAP-TLS, the computer and server certificates are exchanged over a secure encrypted tunnel created by only the server certificate.

   C. MS-CHAP v2 uses only a user password to authenticate the user attempting a remote access connection.

   D. MS-CHAP v2 provides for mutual authentication of client and server.

# Lesson 2: Network Access Policy and Server and Domain Isolation

The IT industry long ago saw the issue of network vulnerability due to problematic computers connecting to the network coming and has been furiously investigating solutions to enforce company security policies physically. Network Access Control (NAC) was created to combat this very issue. NAC provides a framework for vendors to produce services and features that can interrogate a computer prior to a connection to the secure, internal network and ensure a computer's compliance with stated health requirements and security settings.

Microsoft has introduced its version of controlling network access with NAP, which provides an enforcement service for health requirement policies prior to network access. NAP offers services, components, and an application programming interface (API) that provide an inherent solution for ensuring the health of servers and networks running Windows Server 2008 as well as of computers running Windows Vista and Windows XP Service Pack 3 as clients.

---

**After this lesson, you will be able to:**

- Describe Network Access Protection (NAP) and the various scenarios for its implementation.
- Describe the architecture and components of NAP.
- Identify purposes for specific NAP enforcement methods.
- Describe the process for implementing NAP policies.

**Estimated lesson time: 45 minutes**

---

## Network Access Protection Overview

Network Access Protection (NAP) provides a platform for validating the health of computer systems prior to allowing access to protected networks. In doing so, a level of assurance can be attained that a computer has at least been "inspected" prior to accessing the private network every time a new connection is made. The validation a computer undergoes can now be logically enforced.

Prior to NAP, a typical connection from an external computer would involve a client connecting across a public network such as the Internet, using a VPN connection. The client connection would initially pass through a firewall or be forwarded by a proxy using the appropriate communication ports required by the chosen security protocol. An authentication service would then examine the credentials of the remote access client. If the credentials were successfully authenticated, the client would be connected to whatever portion of the protected network the connection was previously set up to accomplish.

This scenario has a major flaw. If the remote access client is exactly who it purports to be, provides all the necessary credentials appropriately, and performs only the tasks on the private network that the connection was set up to do, would there still be a problem? Maybe. Suppose the remote access client performs unintended service requests, discovery, research, or—worse—invasive software installations without the knowledge of the user of the computer making the remote access connection. This has become one of the primary reasons for implementing a NAP solution.

---

### Real World

*Paul Mancuso*

After spending a considerable amount of time, effort, and money, you have deployed across an entire network the following security services:

- A top-of-the-line perimeter firewall device
- An antivirus module inside the firewall device whose services you have configured to check for updates once every hour
- An automated update service for workstations and servers to call upon periodically for updates to the operating system and installed applications
- An enterprise anti-malware service that installed anti-malware agents on all client workstations and servers within the environment, with centralized management for setting and configuring changes and updating installed software and agents on deployed computers

Feeling that the enterprise has a reasonable level of security, you go home and think that tomorrow should now be a relatively peaceful day.

In the evening, a salesman visiting a branch office connects his laptop to the protected network. The salesman's laptop is considered safe merely because it is corporate property. A worm that was released into the wild that day had infected the corporate offices of another corporation, where the salesman had plugged the laptop in while delivering a presentation. The worm can now perform functions inside the network from a device considered to be a secure system. Tomorrow comes, and virus reports are coming out of the woodwork.

Several factors could have caused the salesman's laptop to become infected. First, it is presumed that the salesman does not alter the basic security settings of either the security software or the operating system. Also, the laptop is part of the domain; internal group policies were set to ensure the timely scheduling of updates to either the operating system or the security software on all computers, including those the salesman uses. This last presumption leads to missed updates when the salesman is traveling and not connected to the network.

These periodic lapses in acquiring updates provide opportunities for infections when the salesman connects the laptop to unknown environments. The salesman's laptop can acquire all kinds of Trojan horse programs, viruses, and worms. The salesman travels back to the office, plugs the infected laptop into the protected network, and unknowingly unleashes the malicious programming on the laptop into the protected network. The salesman has bypassed all the security precautions the enterprise administrator has painstakingly set up in the network.

With a NAP solution, the possibilities of a traveling employee or guest unleashing an infection into your secured network are lessened. The standard communication flow from a computer being introduced to a network for its initial connection to the network would be altered to pass through a perimeter network as the components of the NAP platform engage. The NAP platform would now involve an entire NAP ecosystem with the connection request of an external client now referred to as a NAP client. The perimeter network would still include the same security services and devices as before, but now the NAP client's request for access takes a detour as the various components of the NAP platform engage to determine the health status of the connecting client. Figure 5-7 shows the difference between a traditional remote access connection and one involving a NAP platform.

Figure 5-7 shows that not only are NAP components now involved in the communication flow, but also that the NAP client might be restricted to an external network referred to as the remediation network, where additional servers using health resources update the client and bring it into compliance.

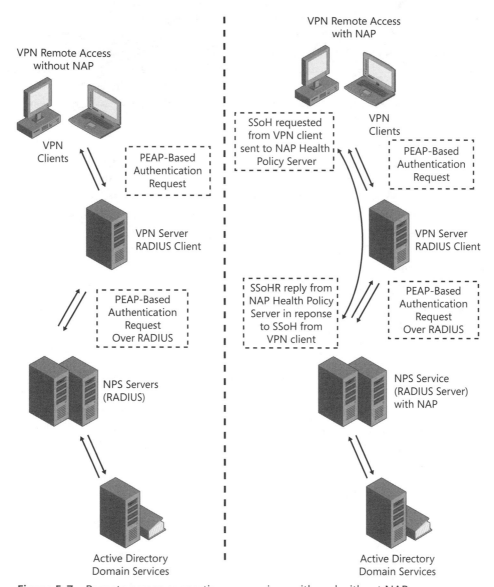

**Figure 5-7** Remote access connection comparison with and without NAP

A complete NAP solution involves three distinct features:

- Health state validation
- Health policy compliance
- Limited access

Health state validation is the process of validating a computer's health and determining its compliance. If the NAP platform is configured for a remediation network, a noncompliant computer is restricted to only the remediation network's subnet until it meets compliance. If the NAP platform has been implemented initially with logging only to quantify compliance issues, the health compliance of a computer is logged, and it is allowed to proceed with the normal connection routine.

To monitor and possibly enforce health policy requirements, administrators create health policies. The health policy component is the heart of a NAP solution. Health policies mandate the level of software updates, operating system build, antivirus revision, and firewall features implemented among many other possible health compliance factors.

When computer systems do not meet the level of health compliance necessary to connect to the private network, an administrator can mandate one of two outcomes, either to allow the connection and log the noncompliant issues or to shunt the connection to a remediation network to configure and update any noncompliant aspect of the computer. This is the limited-access feature of NAP.

---

**NOTE  Network Access Quarantine**

Limited access has some similarities to Network Access Quarantine Control, but only in one principal feature: limiting access for noncompliant computers when making dial-up and VPN connections. Limited access when implemented with a NAP platform provides much capability and a standardized structure. This structure facilitates the addition of third-party enhancements and services. NAP also extends beyond VPN and dial-up communication to include protection when computer systems connect on the LAN. For more information, please visit the Cable Guy article on Network Access Quarantine at *http://technet.microsoft.com/en-us/library/bb877976.aspx.*

---

## Overview of NAP Infrastructure

The NAP infrastructure for all types of enforcement provides a similar architectural overview as displayed in Figure 5-8. Only the devices and regions of interest to a NAP solution are pictured.

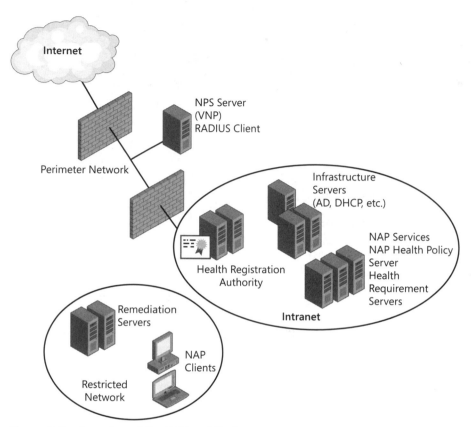

**Figure 5-8**   Overview of the NAP architecture

- The Internet lies outside the perimeter network and is separated by the perimeter firewall. VPN clients access the internal network from this region.

- The perimeter network is segregated by a perimeter and internal firewall.

  VPN servers reside here and provide the initial point of enforcement for a NAP VPN enforcement point. For security purposes, no other NAP service is needed in this location.

- The restricted network is logically separated from the intranet for computers that, although having passed authentication for the NAP enforcement points that require authentication, have not yet acquired the necessary authorization to access the secure intranet. Servers deployed here can include quite a range of NAP support services:

  - ❏ The usual DNS, Windows Internet Name Service (WINS), Active Directory domain controllers, and DHCP servers along with other supporting network infrastructure devices can be deployed.

- ❏ Servers supporting software updates such as Windows Server Update Services (WSUS) can be deployed.
- ❏ For wired switches employing 802.1x enforcement, any switch ports can be associated logically with the restricted network.
- ❏ For wireless access points employing 802.1x enforcement, the entire access point might be logically associated with the restricted network because, at any time, it can be servicing compliant and noncompliant computers.

- ■ The intranet is considered the secured network for most NAP enforcement methods and contains the corporate environment. NAP IPsec enforcement includes an additional logical boundary between two of its zones necessary for IPsec enforcement operation.
  - ❏ The boundary network is where Health Registration Authority servers and, possibly, NAP CAs, NPS servers, and IPsec remediation servers reside.
  - ❏ The secure network is where the remaining portion of all NAP enforcement components resides. These components are the NAP health policy servers, the health requirement servers, the RADIUS proxy servers, and the NPS servers' endpoints.

## Where NAP Works

NAP can be implemented in any scenario in which a computer or network device has left a network and requires a new connection when brought back to the network. Following are specific scenarios of this type of event.

- ■ Desktop computers that have been dormant for periods of time
- ■ Laptops for roaming users
- ■ Personal desktops and laptops of corporate users when connecting to the network to retrieve e-mail and other data
- ■ Laptops of guests
- ■ Laptops and desktops from users of partner firms connected by an extranet

This list comprises the general categories in which a NAP solution would provide a level of assurance of the health of a connected computer. Due to the diversity of these categories, the same level of enforcement of noncompliant computers might not be possible in all situations. Computers that are unmanaged, such as partner computers, home computers, laptops, and those of guests would be sent to the restricted network and, might not be required to undergo remediation, but also would not be allowed into the private network. Managed computers provided by the corporation could institute automatic remediation for any of its computers moved into the restricted network. Options to remediate would vary, depending on the situation.

## Considerations for NAP Enforcement

When deliberating between the types of NAP enforcement methods to institute within your network, you need to know the strengths and weaknesses of each method. How does each method deal with non-NAP capable computers? What is required in each method to administer unmanaged computers (computers not part of the internal AD DS)? In planning a NAP solution, consider that all the NAP enforcement methods have one or more of the following aspects:

- NAP does not stop attackers.
- NAP, to some degree, implies a trust with the NAP client.
- NAP does not remove harmful software from connecting computers.
- NAP should be treated as an assurance feature.

NAP cannot stop an attacker. A malicious user, whether an employee, guest, or outside user, might provide all the necessary compliance for access to your network but still launch an attack when inside your network.

NAP indirectly assumes that the client has not provided false settings, configurations, or modifications to installed software to attain a false positive of compliance. Remember, you are essentially asking the computer owner whether everything on the computer is fine and he or she has not falsified, concealed, or knowingly allowed anyone to configure or install software on this computer. Does this sound similar to the security warnings you might hear a dozen times an hour at any airport?

NAP provides a health statement based on the appearance of sound security configurations, settings, and installed software. It does not scan the computer for malicious software but, rather, assumes that the verified health state of a computer means that another subsystem or configuration on an installed security software application performs that feature.

Finally, NAP is an assurance feature. You are determining that the computers connecting to your network and communicating with the secure internal environment have applied the necessary security precautions to prevent an outbreak. Remember, if someone with malicious intent were to circumvent your NAP solution, the assurance that all other computers have complied with your NAP policies will help deter an attacker from damaging your environment or possibly acquiring sensitive information. As an enterprise administrator, realize your NAP solution was not meant to stop an employee or would-be attacker intent on stealing information; that is not the role a NAP infrastructure is meant to play.

## Planning NAP IPsec Enforcement

When looking for the strongest enforcement method to apply within your network, NAP IPsec enforcement provides the most robust and tamper-resistant solution compared to all other NAP enforcement methods. IPsec enforcement has these advantages:

- Tightly controlled enforcement that not even the local administrator is capable of bypassing
- Upgrades to network infrastructure devices such as hubs, switches, and routers to support NAP are unnecessary
- Granular control to network access
- Easier avenue to end-to-end encryption of sensitive communications

Even by manipulating settings and the configuration of the local computer, administrators cannot bypass health certificates issued by the Health Registration Authority (HRA). Because all other computers are also protected by the same means, there is no way to subvert this requirement. Introducing new switches or other network devices provides no means around the required legitimate health certificate to communicate with hosts expecting the certificate during the IPsec negotiation.

IPsec works at layer 3 and uses a logical connection that is above the physical layers in the network; bypassing it would require modification or extensive reconfiguration of physical hardware.

IPsec allows an administrator to control communication pathways end-to-end. An administrator can create hardened IPsec policies that dictate source and destination IP addresses along with source and destination ports that are allowed for communication and must be encrypted. IPsec enforcement can also control access to the network stringently but use a general approach to managing communication. If you use IPsec enforcement to tightly control access to the secure network, you have already taken a large leap toward encrypting sensitive traffic within your environment.

The disadvantages of an IPsec enforcement solution deserve serious consideration as well:

- It requires creation and maintenance of network zones for the logical separation of network communication.
- It requires the establishment of an internal PKI. If one already exists, it might need a minor overhaul if its creator did not anticipate the additional load that an IPsec enforcement solution will incur.
- It requires another series of servers, which must be managed for configuration, load balancing, and high availability. Loss of the ability to issue health certificates would mean a catastrophic loss of communication within the environment.

When weighing the advantages and disadvantages of a NAP solution using IPsec enforcement, an organization has to consider the increased security that would be provided. IPsec enforcement provides not only the direct benefits offered by a NAP solution but also the increased benefits of data confidentiality when communicating throughout the network environment.

## Designing NAP IPsec Enforcement

When planning NAP IPsec enforcement for any organization, you need to establish the security zones first and determine which services to offer in the boundary network. The three security zones for an IPsec solution are:

- Restricted network
- Boundary network
- Secure network

**Restricted Network**   The restricted network, also referred to as the remediation network, is not the same as the perimeter network. The restricted network is a select network where noncompliant computers have limited access to services to perform remediation. Computers placed into the restricted network consist of either noncompliant NAP clients or non-NAP-capable clients. For IPsec enforcement, the restricted network includes only these devices.

Computers in the restricted network can initiate communication with computers in the restricted and boundary networks. Neither communication is protected by IPsec. Computers in all three networks, however, can initiate communication with computers in the restricted network. This communication is not protected by IPsec either.

Non-NAP-compliant computers have already attempted communication with an HRA and have received a System Statement of Health Response (SSoHR) that contains the Statement of Health Responses (SoHRs) stating which system health agents (SHAs) are noncompliant. The non-NAP-compliant computer in the restricted network will initiate contact with servers in the boundary network to perform remediation. After remediation has been performed, the non-NAP-compliant computer will try again to attain a health certificate. The computer will go through the process of accumulating, across all SHAs, a Statement of Health (SoH) and submit a System Statement of Health (SSoH) to an HRA. The HRA, using System Health Validators (SHVs), will process all SoHs on the SSoH to formulate its SSoHR.

Upon receiving the SSoHR that shows the NAP client as compliant, the HRA also issues a health certificate so that the NAP client is now part of the secure network and initiates IPsec-authenticated communication with computers in either the boundary network or the secure network.

Non-NAP-capable computers are those of guests and other unsupported operating systems such as any version of Windows earlier than Windows XP SP3, Apple Macintosh computers, and UNIX computers. A guest computer can be NAP capable but, because it is unmanaged (not part of AD DS), will more than likely be treated like a non-NAP-capable computer unless network policies dictate otherwise.

**Boundary Network**   The boundary network contains computers responsible for remediation as well as for the HRAs, support services such as DNS, AD DS, and DHCP servers, WSUS and possibly, the NAP CAs. Because the boundary network requires communication from computers residing in the restricted and secure networks, IPsec policies should allow for IPsec-authenticated traffic as well as for unauthenticated traffic. Computers in the boundary network should be managed computers. This enables them to receive their IPsec policies and changes to those policies through Group Policy.

Boundary servers, when communicating with computers in the restricted network, allow unauthenticated communication because computers in the restricted network do not contain the necessary health certificates. When boundary servers communicate with servers in the restricted network, IPsec-authenticated traffic is required.

There is a twist to this last statement. The boundary computers themselves are the ones that offer the update services, have the necessary configuration for compliance, and are part of the NAP components. To ensure that they are capable of initiating IPsec-authenticated communication, they also require a health certificate. To provide these computers with a health certificate, create an IPsec NAP exemption group whose membership includes all the computers of the boundary network. Configure a Group Policy setting that sets the NAP IPsec exemption group for certificate autoenrollment to acquire the necessary health certificate. Because the computers of the exemption group need to hold onto this certificate for the period of time they are performing their services, ensure that the template used to issue the certificate has been set for an extended period of time.

Computers from the restricted network as well as the computers in the boundary network need authentication services. Domain controllers located in the boundary network should be RODCs.

**Secure Network**    The secure network includes all computers that have passed health validation and have acquired a health certificate. The remaining portion of the NAP components related to IPsec enforcement also resides here. These components consist of the following:

- NAP Health Policy servers
- Health Requirement servers
- Root CAs
- RADIUS proxy servers

Computers within this network should be managed computers (part of AD DS). This enables them to acquire their IPsec policies and any configuration changes to your NAP environment through Group Policy.

## Scaling NAP IPsec Enforcement for Small Environments

When deploying components for NAP IPsec enforcement, you have the opportunity to decide which components can be installed together. In smaller environments, it might be appropriate to consolidate several services on one computer. The issue becomes deciding which services to install together.

The HRA must be able to support unprotected communication from NAP clients, and you should, therefore, install the HRA in the boundary network. Because the load on the HRA in a small environment might not be that heavy, you might decide to install it on a computer that has one or more of the following services other computers in the boundary network also need:

- RODCs
- NPS configured for the NAP Health Policy Server role
- NAP CA

If your environment is expected to grow, it would be wise to move some of these components to another server. You can then assume that the server installed with the HRA would be deployed in the boundary network, and another computer with the remaining services would be deployed in the secure network.

---

**IMPORTANT**   **Splitting the HRA and the NAP Health Policy Server role**

If you split the HRA and the NAP Health Policy Server role to two computers, you still need to install the NPS role on the HRA computer. Then configure a RADIUS server group and a connection request policy for the local NPS service to forward requests to the remote RADIUS server group in the secure network.

---

Administrators of extremely small sites of 15 or fewer computers might consider employing ISA Server 2006. ISA Server can create a site-to-site VPN link to the main office boundary network. The connection from the VPN server in the boundary network can be treated like any other local connection requiring IPsec enforcement to obtain a certificate initially. After a computer at the remote office has obtained a health certificate, IPsec rules can be managed granularly to ensure that the branch office computer is able to communicate only with the necessary services at the remote office, through the site-to-site VPN, and in the boundary network for remediation and renewal of certificates. ISA Server would require a certificate as well and should probably be included in the IPsec exemption group. Ensure that a computer certificate is issued to the computer running ISA Server for an extended period of time.

## Scaling NAP IPsec Enforcement for Larger Environments

For larger environments, several components require a thorough design review to ensure high availability and load balancing of specific components. You can begin by deciding which of the following services will be installed individually on at least two or more computers in the boundary network at the corporate office:

- HRA
- RODC
- Subordinate NAP CA
- Remediation server services

By providing fault tolerance for the HRA, the RODCs, and the NAP CA, you are ensuring a healthy environment. Remember that by employing IPsec enforcement, you are required to have these services running constantly. If one or more of these services become unavailable, health certificates will expire, and communication within the network will fail. Ensuring the ability of NAP clients to acquire health certificates is essential because all communication depends upon the necessity of each computer to present a valid health certificate when attempting to communicate with another computer.

In the secure network, deploy at least two NAP health policy servers. Configure the HRA computers as RADIUS clients of the NAP health policy servers. To ensure proper load balancing when configuring the remote RADIUS server group of the NPS service on the HRA computers, use the same priority and weight settings for all members of the RADIUS server group on each of the HRA computers.

For deployments at the branch offices, consider using the deployment models discussed previously for a small company. The services offered at the branch offices would model the same considerations given to a smaller company with a single site.

## PKI Support for IPsec Enforcement

IPsec enforcement use of health certificates requires you, as the enterprise administrator, to reexamine the role PKI currently has within your environment. If a PKI does not exist, you need to deploy one. If one already exists, consider the additional load balancing and management that will be needed.

Smaller environments that already have a PKI probably require only the creation of a subordinate CA for NAP. This CA can be deployed in the boundary networks on the HRA to conserve server resources.

Larger environments require more planning because you now need to consider additional aspects of PKI when employed for use with NAP IPsec enforcement. The load on the CA issuing health certificates will be directly proportional to:

- The number of NAP clients in the environment.
- The lifetime of a health certificate.

The number of NAP clients is not something that you can truly control because deploying a NAP solution would entail using it pervasively throughout the environment.

The lifetime of the health certificate is something you can administer, and it has a direct influence over the load on your NAP CAs. Microsoft recommends for best practices to keep the lifetime at a minimum, preferably four hours. Reducing this time increases the load on the NAP CAs for renewals. Increasing the time, although reducing the load on the NAP CAs, also increases the likelihood that a computer can be out of compliance for a longer period due to changes in the health requirement policy.

**Structure of the PKI**    For most environments, adding an additional subordinate CA to issue health certificates for NAP is sufficient. Microsoft recommends that, in large environments, administrators create an entirely new PKI for NAP. You need to install a new root CA on a server within the secure environment and secure its private key with a hardware security module (HSM). Create subordinate CAs for NAP to issue the health certificates. These can be deployed in the boundary network and given the same security consideration as the RODCs deployed there. This would mean the removal of all unnecessary services and provide a limited attack surface. Securing its private key is not as critical as securing the root CA because certificates issued by it will have a limited lifetime.

You do not need to worry about issuing timely certificate revocation lists (CRLs) for this portion of your PKI because the certificates will expire long before the CRLs are published. In addition, an OCSP responder service is also unnecessary due to the limited lifetime of your health certificates.

**Configuring Additional NAP Components on Clients**    System health agents from third-party members need to be installed on all NAP clients. A variety of software distribution methods is available to an administrator. You can use any one of the following not only for IPsec enforcement but also for VPN enforcement, 802.1x enforcement, and DHCP enforcement, which are discussed later in this chapter:

- Software deployment or logon scripts through Group Policy.
- Desktop management software such as Microsoft System Center Configuration Manager 2007.
- Manual installation for unmanaged computers.
- Shares on remediation servers. Configure the troubleshooting URLs to instruct the user to install the missing SHAs.

---

**NOTE    Troubleshooting URLs**

Troubleshooting URLs are configured as part of the remediation experience in case clients that fail compliance do not have the Configuration Manager client installed. On one of the remediation servers installed in the restricted network, configure a Web URL to help instruct remediation clients on the location of software and options to choose to help acquire a successful health validation.

---

**Configuring NAP Health Policy Servers**    The NPS server running the NAP health policy server can be configured with additional third-party SHVs. Installation instructions for the third-party SHVs are provided by the third-party vendor. The SHVs must be installed on all NAP health policy servers participating in the NAP solution for IPsec as well as for VPN enforcement, 802.1x enforcement, and DHCP enforcement, which are discussed later in this chapter. Windows Server 2008 provides the default Windows Security Health Validator SHV that provides security settings for the Windows Security Center on Windows NAP clients.

# Planning NAP VPN Enforcement

VPN enforcement in NAP is supported for VPN remote access connections by using PPP, specifically working in conjunction with the PPP authentication phase. Windows XP SP3, Windows Vista, and Windows Server 2008 support the remote access quarantine enforcement client for NAP clients.

VPN enforcement design requires you, the enterprise administrator, to consider the following:

- VPN authentication methods
- VPN servers in use
- VPN clients compliant with VPN enforcement
- Configuration of the restricted network for remediation
- Other VPN enforcement considerations such as:
  - ❏ Non-NAP-capable VPN clients
  - ❏ Configuring exemptions
  - ❏ Migration from network access quarantine control to VPN enforcement
  - ❏ Installing support for additional SHAs on NAP clients
  - ❏ Installing support for additional SHVs on NAP health policy servers

When VPN enforcement is employed, VPN clients are evaluated for compliance with health policy immediately after successful PPP authentication. Therefore, VPN clients are left in one of three stages after an attempt to connect through remote access:

- Clients fail authentication and the PPP session ends.
- Clients succeed in authenticating but do not possess a VPN enforcement client.
- Clients succeed in authenticating but do not pass the health inspection and become noncompliant.
- Clients succeed in authenticating, pass the health inspection, and become compliant.

## Planning VPN Authentication Protocol Use for VPN Enforcement

Microsoft supports the use of the two PEAP-based authentication protocols, PEAP-TLS and PEAP-MSCHAP v2, for VPN enforcement. This is due to PEAP-TLS messages used to transmit system health state information between the VPN client and the NAP health policy server.

Your current VPN remote access solution can use PEAP-TLS and PEAP-MSCHAP v2 as you ramp up the environment to support NAP. PEAP-TLS requires support for a computer certificate on each computer within the environment as well as on the NPS server performing RADIUS authentication. PEAP-MSCHAP v2 requires a computer certificate for authentication only on the RADIUS server. The VPN enforcement clients are required to trust the certificate issued to the RADIUS server and need to have the certificate of the root CA in their Trusted

Root Certification Authorities store. You can use Group Policy to issue a required certificate to each computer as well as to update the local computers' Trusted Root Certification authorities.

If a PKI already exists, configuring PEAP-based support for managed computers is a bit easier administratively. Within AD DS, you can use a variety of ways to deliver Group Policy to select accounts. The two easiest methods to accomplish this goal without extensive Group Policy filtering are to:

- Create a computer group and add all the computer accounts to the group membership that participate as VPN enforcement clients.
- Create an organizational unit (OU) and move the computer accounts that participate as VPN enforcement clients into the OU.

Now, apply Group Policy and ensure that the container the Group Policy is applied to is the one that contains just the necessary computer accounts or contains the computer group containing the respective computer account members. If using a computer group to assemble the necessary computer accounts, you can filter Group Policy by ensuring that the specific computer group has the required Read and Apply Group Policy permissions assigned to it.

## Other VPN Enforcement Considerations

Setting up support for VPN enforcement requires you to consider several remaining elements:

- Non-NAP-capable VPN clients
- Migration from network access quarantine control
- Installing or updating SHAs on clients
- Installing additional SHVs on NAP health policy servers

**Non-NAP-Capable VPN Clients**    VPN clients not capable of performing NAP and VPN enforcement need to be treated in one of two ways:

- Allow unlimited access by creating an exemption group.
- Allow only limited access to the restricted network.

To allow unlimited access, create an exemption group whose membership includes the non-NAP-capable computer accounts. Create a network policy by using the Windows Groups condition and selecting the newly created exemption group. On the settings for NAP enforcement on this network policy, ensure that the computer group is allowed full network access for an unlimited time or for a specified time limit. Using a specified time limit allows a period during which a non-NAP-capable client is upgraded to support VPN enforcement.

Using that same policy, you could switch the settings to ensure that the client is allowed only limited access. This would ensure a safer environment but a restriction in access for non-NAP-capable computers. This might severely restrict guests and partner access to a company. Ensure that this is the desired effect prior to implementing this decision.

**Migrating from Network Access Quarantine Control**    Moving to VPN enforcement is a natural progression from Network Access Quarantine Control, which is supported on Windows Server 2003 with the Internet Authentication Service (IAS) RADIUS server.

When upgrading to Windows Server 2008 from Windows Server 2003 running IAS and configured with Network Access Quarantine Control, all the Network Access Quarantine Control settings are brought over. To move toward NAP using VPN enforcement, you must upgrade all the computers running Windows Server 2003 that are running IAS. Although Windows Server 2008 supports Network Access Quarantine Control, Windows Server 2003 with IAS does not support NAP. During the migration from Network Access Quarantine Control to VPN enforcement, you can run them simultaneously. Upgrade your existing clients to support NAP and the clients configured for VPN enforcement.

**Configuring Additional NAP Components on Clients and NAP Health Policy Servers**    The same considerations enumerated in the "Configuring Additional NAP Components on Clients" and "Configuring NAP Health Policy Servers" sections, discussed earlier in this chapter under IPsec enforcement, apply to VPN enforcement as well.

# Planning NAP 802.1x Enforcement

Using 802.1x enforcement means employing NAP at layer 2 over your network and entails both wired and wireless NAP clients configured with an EAPHost NAP enforcement client. Other key components involve an 802.1x-compliant access point and a NAP health policy server. An 802.1x access point can be either a wireless access point or a wired switch, with both being capable of performing 802.1x authentication.

Three Microsoft operating systems provide 802.1x enforcement clients:

- Windows Server 2008 Extensible Authentication Protocol (EAP) Quarantine enforcement client
- Windows Vista Extensible Authentication Protocol (EAP) Quarantine enforcement client
- Windows XP SP2 with two 802.1x enforcement clients
    - A wired client named EAP Quarantine enforcement client
    - A wireless client named Wireless EAPoL Quarantine enforcement client

## Design Considerations for 802.1x Enforcement

The first step toward designing your 802.1x enforcement for NAP is to assess your current access points within your environment. Questions to answer involve the following:

- Are all the switches used at the access layer and back-end server farms 802.1x compatible?
- Which RADIUS attributes do they support for your 802.1x enforcement?
- Which 802.1x authentication methods will you use?

- Which type of 802.1x enforcement, access control list (ACL) or virtual local area network (VLAN), will you use?
- Must you support PXE boot?

Using the inventory list from the documentation of your switches, you can begin assessing the switches involved in the 802.1x enforcement. Contact the vendor's Web site to find out about any known issues with employing NAP and about any necessary updates.

## Access Point Considerations

As 802.1x authentication proliferates, more and more vendors are adding NAP support. There are even blogs devoted to listing security vendors supporting NAP. Finding hardware is not the problem; discerning whether the hardware currently in use is or can be made compliant is the issue. Purchasing new hardware is always an easy way to attain compliance but is also the most expensive.

---

**MORE INFO    802.1x enforcement**

The Microsoft NAP team has provided a specific blog that lists switches tested for 802.1x enforcement. This list is not meant to be exhaustive; in fact, it appears rather to be a list about a single device from the major network infrastructure vendors that was tested for 802.1x enforcement abilities. The assumption is that there is support from each of these vendors in their product line because most of the vendors use a similar operating system across much of the same line of hardware. You can see this blog at *http://blogs.technet.com/nap/archive/2007/07/10/nap-802-1x -enforcement-switches-we-ve-tested-w-nap.aspx.*

---

When examining compliance, look for specific RADIUS support. The Microsoft NAP supports the following vendor-specific attributes (VSA) and RADIUS attributes for defining the restricted network with 802.1x enforcement:

- *Filter-ID for identifying the ACL*
- *Tunnel-Medium-Type*
- *Tunnel-Pvt-Group-ID*
- *Tunnel-Type*
- *Tunnel-Tag*

For setting the periodic re-authentication interval, the standard *Session-Timeout* RADIUS attribute has broad support from most of the hardware vendors.

## ACLs vs. VLANs

802.1x enforcement can implement ACLs or VLANs for restricted access. Which enforcement method you use depends on your access point or switches' support and which type provides the restriction desired within your environment.

Using ACLs, an administrator can define a specific set of packet filters that enable a noncompliant NAP client to communicate only with a specific subset of servers. Because the 802.1x enforcement process occurs over layer 2, the noncompliant NAP client still attempts automatic configuration for its IPv4 configuration or autoconfiguration for IPv6. It attains an address for its usual subnet but now is confined to limited access to specific servers for remediation. The big advantage here is that the ACL also prevents a rogue noncompliant NAP client from attempting to infect other noncompliant NAP clients. Because all the remediation servers should be up to date with their security software and configuration settings, the remediation servers should be fairly impervious to attack as well. This creates an isolated network on a per-port basis because the noncompliant client sees only the remediation network servers until fully compliant.

Using VLANs, an administrator can define a VLAN for remediation. Noncompliant NAT clients and 802.1x NAP clients failing a health check are forced into this VLAN by the wireless access point or a wired switch port on the switch. The VLAN is composed of remediation servers along with other noncompliant NAP clients. This restriction prevents communication outside the VLAN until the NAP client passes its health check. Ensure that this restricted VLAN is used solely for noncompliant NAP clients. Do not configure non NAP capable or unauthenticated NAP clients to use this VLAN. Normally, if an EAPHost NAP enforcement client fails authentication, the computer will not be allowed to communicate through the access point, so these unauthenticated computers will not be placed in the VLAN designated as the restricted network either.

## Planning Authentication Protocols for 802.1x Enforcement

The only two supported authentication protocols for 802.1x enforcement included in Windows XP SP3, Windows Vista, and Windows Server 2008 are the PEAP types, PEAP-TLS and PEAP-MSCHAP v2. If implementing third-party vendor add-ons for 802.1x enforcement, you need to test their solutions because Microsoft NAP supports only PEAP-based solutions.

When implementing an 802.1x enforcement solution, you must consider the PKI when choosing between PEAP-TLS and PEAP-MSCHAP v2. If you're using PEAP-TLS, it will probably be more cost effective to implement an internal Microsoft-based PKI. You need computer certificates for the NPS servers performing RADIUS authentication and the NAP clients using 802.1x enforcement. You can acquire certificates for computer accounts through autoenrollment using Group Policy, by importing a certificate file using either a group certificate (considered less secure) or an individual certificate per computer, or, finally, by using Web enrollment.

The RADIUS servers require a certificate for PEAP-MSCHAP v2. You must install the root CA certificate on all computers employing 802.1x enforcement. For managed computers, it is fairly easy to have clients trust the root CA by using Group Policy. For unmanaged computers, you need to import the root CA certificate into the local computer's Trusted Root Certification Authorities store.

Using 802.1x enforcement also requires you to consider the reauthentication interval. If health policy changes, there is no standard way to enforce client remediation after an 802.1x enforcement client is considered compliant. Setting a time interval that requires clients to reauthenticate provides a reliable means of forcing clients to seek compliance when the health policy is modified. As mentioned earlier, shorter intervals place a greater stress on the NAP infrastructure components such as RADIUS. Microsoft best practices recommends a four-hour interval. You can enforce a reauthentication interval by the following techniques:

- Direct manipulation of the access point's 802.1x configuration
- A VSA configured on the RADIUS server and supported by the 802.1x access point
- The *Session-Timeout* RADIUS attribute

---

### Real World

*Paul Mancuso*

When using PEAP-MSCHAP v2, two PKI considerations come to mind. First, using an internal PKI gives you far greater control over which computer will trust the root CA. Managed computers can easily be configured to trust the root CA through Group Policy. This also establishes a nice baseline so that only managed computers have this trust.

However, this creates a lot of work for an IT department when all that is really necessary to make 802.1x function in relation to a PKI is to purchase a certificate from a PKI vendor whose root CA is already trusted. This eliminates much work on the back end of an 802.1x authentication configuration. The dollar cost is pennies when compared to the time, effort, and additional troubleshooting necessary to set up your own internal PKI and configure Group Policy for managed computers (the easy part), or using one of the manual methods (Web enrollment or importing a certificate file) for unmanaged computers.

---

## Other 802.1x Enforcement Considerations

802.1x enforcement is not without some issues. One of them is the problem of not allowing the use of PXE boot on switch ports where 802.1x enforcement is configured. Also, there might be certain noncapable 802.1x clients within your environment, such as printer servers, fax servers, or computers installed with an operating system that is noncompliant for 802.1x enforcement. You must exempt them from 802.1x enforcement. Configuring exemptions can be as easy as configuring the specific ports used by these network clients to be exempt from

802.1x authentication and 802.1x enforcement or from just 802.1x enforcement if they support 802.1x authentication but not 802.1x enforcement.

Using 802.1x is not the security panacea that will solve all your concerns with keeping out attackers. As stated earlier, NAP is not designed to stop attackers; it is mainly designed to prevent malware outbreaks. In fact, 802.1x authentication has one known flaw regarding man-in-the-middle attacks, but this requires some physical access to your access ports. In addition, 802.1x does not provide the end-to-end security that IPsec enforcement can provide.

802.1x provides the assurance that compliant computers on the network, if attacked by invading malware, are better equipped to ward off the attack. It helps maintain a stable and secure environment.

**Configuring Additional NAP Components on Clients and NAP Health Policy Servers** The same considerations enumerated in the "Configuring Additional NAP Components on Clients" and "Configuring NAP Health Policy Servers" sections, discussed earlier in this chapter under IPsec enforcement, apply to 802.1x enforcement.

# Planning NAP DHCP Enforcement

DHCP enforcement provides for NAP enforcement before an IPv4 client receives its automatic configuration information from a DHCP server. DHCP enforcement uses a limited IPv4 configuration to restrict a DHCP client to a restricted network to perform remediation.

DHCP enforcement combines the use of Windows Server 2008 running the DHCP Server service, the NPS service for RADIUS client capabilities, and the supported Windows clients:

- Windows XP SP3
- Windows Vista
- Windows Server 2008

DHCP enforcement uses the following configurations of IPv4 to restrict a noncompliant client:

- Sets the router option to 0.0.0.0 for noncompliant clients
- Sets the subnet mask for the IPv4 address to 255.255.255.255
- Uses the Classless Static Routes DHCP option to set host routes to specified computers on the restricted network

DHCP enforcement is simple to set up but has some considerable disadvantages when compared to other forms of NAP enforcement:

- It is relatively the weakest form of NAP enforcement.
- A local administrator can override the settings by setting an appropriate manual IPv4 configuration to access the network.
- It does not provide support for IPv6 environments. Currently, DHCP enforcement is an IPv4-only solution.

## Design Considerations for DHCP Enforcement

Several items need to be in place for a successful DHCP enforcement solution:

- All DHCP servers need to be upgraded to Windows Server 2008.
- All DHCP servers need to add the NPS role and configure a Remote Servers group containing the NAP health policy servers.
- Installation of RADIUS infrastructure is necessary if one is not already deployed.
- Consideration is necessary for how to implement exemptions for non-NAP-capable computers.

The network infrastructure, switches, routers, and Active Directory domain controllers require no updates or upgrades. Only the DHCP servers need to be upgraded to Windows Server 2008; install the NPS service and configure the service to function as a RADIUS proxy for the back-end NAP health policy servers.

- The DHCP scopes need to be appropriately configured:
  - ❑ NAP needs to be enabled for the specified scopes where DHCP enforcement is to function.
  - ❑ DHCP scopes need to be configured with the options for noncompliant NAP clients.
- Using either specific Vendor classes or the Default Network Access Protection Class User class, configure the Classless Static Routes option (Option 249) for clients that are noncompliant.

### Configuring Additional NAP Components on Clients and NAP Health Policy Servers

The same considerations enumerated in the "Configuring Additional NAP Components on Clients" and "Configuring NAP Health Policy Servers" sections, discussed earlier in this chapter under IPsec enforcement, apply to DHCP enforcement as well.

## Final Say on DHCP Enforcement

Despite all the disadvantages of DHCP enforcement, it can provide a fine solution for a small company intent on enhancing its malware protection services. For larger environments, DHCP enforcement can provide an inexpensive reporting solution, assuming the necessary Windows Server 2008 components can be installed. For a small environment, as well as for branch offices in larger enterprises, one server can be used to deploy all the necessary components, DHCP, NPS, and NAP health policy server. This is an inexpensive solution to provide at least a fine reporting tool by which to monitor your noncompliant clients' health in your environment and provide a step toward a more secure environment.

# Domain and Server Isolation

Domain isolation and server isolation, introduced initially with Windows Server 2003, are effective means of improving secure communications within an enterprise. By ensuring which computers may communicate with other computers, you provide secure end-to-end authenticated communication. Securing end-to-end communication is not addressed through VPN enforcement, DHCP enforcement, or 802.1x enforcement. NAP IPsec enforcement does provide the same end-to-end authenticated communication service as isolation and, thus, can implement a similar style of security while adding support for health policies.

With domain and server isolation, IPsec authenticated communication defends a computer against network attacks, protection that application-layer user authentication security services do not offer. User authentication does prevent users from attacking specific files and applications, but it is not true security at the lower layers. IPsec authentication would help prevent attacks against services running at the network layer.

## Domain vs. Server Isolation

Domain isolation is a way of ensuring that computers that need to communicate are members of the domain and have received the necessary IPsec policies through Group Policy. This isolates trusted computers from untrusted computers. All incoming requests and subsequently transferred data must be authenticated and protected by IPsec. Using Windows Firewall with Advanced Security policy settings, you can define IPsec and connections security rules that either require or request all inbound traffic to be authenticated with IPsec.

Server isolation is a more selective isolation method than domain isolation. Server isolation enables the enterprise administrator to designate specific hosts within the environment that should require that all client connection requests to it be authenticated by IPsec, much like domain isolation. In addition, you can designate select servers to allow communication with specific clients and servers through:

- Selective certificates used for IPsec authentication.
- Specific IP addresses, using Windows Firewall with Advanced Security policy settings.
- Windows Server 2008, creating firewall rules that permit traffic from computers or users who are members of a select Active Directory security group.
- Windows Server 2003, using the local Group Policy Access This Computer From The Network user right to specify users and computer accounts.

Using either domain or server isolation, exemptions can be made for computers that are not capable of performing IPsec authentication or are not members of AD DS.

## Comparing Server and Domain Isolation to IPsec Enforcement

From a high-level perspective, these technologies are more similar than different. Both technologies use IPsec to provide logical network segmentation. Both server isolation and domain isolation attempt to make the network safer through ensuring that only trusted computers can communicate. IPsec enforcement ensures that computers trusted by health validation are allowed to communicate. Both use IPsec authentication to assure communicating computers mutually of their ability to trust and be trusted. Both technologies can use the default Kerberos authentication or deploy certificates for computer authentication prior to establishing IPsec security associations (SAs).

Server isolation enables an administrator to segment high-value servers further for granular control within the trusted environment. IPsec NAP can define specific zones of security to tighten access even further to high-value servers. Figure 5-9 displays the logical network segmentation that both forms of IPsec isolation can provide.

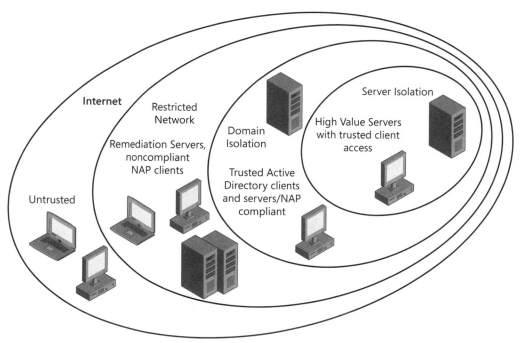

**Figure 5-9**    IPsec providing the logical network segmentation

Adding NAP technology to your IPsec isolation solution now provides the following additional security aspects:

- Formalizes policy validation for healthy computers
- Further restricts computer trust to computers that are managed and healthy

- Uses remediation to enable updating for unhealthy managed computers
- Creates a system of ongoing enforced compliance that offers flexible management for defining trust

### Moving from Server and Domain Isolation to IPsec NAP

If your environment is using Windows 2000 Server or later, you can use IPsec NAP to provide a trusted environment and enforce logical network segmentation for the creation of trusted zones. For networks that have already upgraded to Windows XP SP3 and Windows Vista on the desktop and have begun the upgrade to Windows Server 2008, a steady migration toward NAP can begin.

You can begin introducing health validation in network locations that have already upgraded their operating systems to NAP-capable clients by implementing a pilot program. This pilot program should initially use reporting and quickly move toward the implementation of restriction. After a predominant portion of each network location—branch offices or the main office—have upgraded to NAP-capable clients, you can introduce a NAP solution using reporting. Finally, each office in the network can eventually turn on restriction after a careful review of logs gathered during the implementation of reporting only.

Proper planning is essential to a NAP implementation. It is conceivable that if IPsec NAP is your choice of NAP enforcement, then first instituting server and domain isolation in phases throughout your environment would be a good starting place.

## Lesson Summary

- Gathering the design requirements for a NAP solution involves collecting a list of items necessary to perform each of the desired NAP enforcement types.
- For all NAP enforcement types, ensure that your RADIUS servers are all upgraded to Windows Server 2008. Upgrade only the necessary components of your RADIUS solution, the RADIUS clients and proxies, when called for in your design.
- You can implement NAP enforcement through a VPN, 802.1x, DHCP, or IPsec.
- For all NAP enforcement types, determine non-NAP-capable clients. Segment each type of non-NAP-capable client into respective groups so you can create policies for each type. Determine a NAP solution for the security policies prescribed for each group.
- Maintain adequate supervision for the servers providing remediation in your restricted network.

# Lesson Review

You can use the following questions to test your knowledge of the information in Lesson 2, "Network Access Policy and Server and Domain Isolation." The questions are also available on the companion CD if you prefer to review them in electronic form.

---

**NOTE**  Answers

Answers to these questions and explanations of why each answer choice is correct or incorrect are located in the "Answers" section at the end of the book.

---

1. Choose the appropriate decision points when deciding to implement NAP. (Choose all that apply.)

   A. Provides a safer environment for trusted computers

   B. Enforces a policy on the health level of the computers in the trusted environment

   C. Provides a firewall block against would-be attackers

   D. Ensures that internal computers are more likely to be protected from an attack

2. Choose the correct statement when determining which NAP enforcement method meets a stated policy goal of that NAP enforcement type.

   A. 802.1x enforcement provides end-to-end secure communications of NAP-compliant clients.

   B. DHCP enforcement enables an administrator to mandate the use of a VLAN ID in the restricted network upon failure of a NAP client for compliance.

   C. VPN enforcement provides for confidentiality of each packet's data along its entire path.

   D. IPsec prevents the replay of any portion of a session between two trusted clients.

# Chapter Review

To further practice and reinforce the skills you learned in this chapter, you can perform the following tasks:

- Review the chapter summary.
- Complete the case scenario. This scenario sets up a real-world situation involving the topics of this chapter and asks you to create a solution.
- Complete the suggested practices.
- Take a practice test.

# Chapter Summary

- Design a perimeter network with servers that receive access requests from clients in the border network. Servers on the perimeter network include VPN servers, servers providing Web services, Web application servers, proxy servers servicing Web applications serving as RADIUS clients, and the firewall and network infrastructure devices.
- If you need a PKI to support a remote access solution, determine whether you can scale an existing PKI to support those needs.
- Review the load on your RADIUS servers to determine high availability and load balancing needs, especially if you intend to expand the VPN to support more remote users.
- Determine the security requirements for your choice of VPN protocols. If the highest level of security is required for the VPN due to security policy, and mutual authentication is required for the user and the computer, consider using an EAP-based type of authentication with L2TP to provide the highest level of security for the tunnel, the data, and the VPN client.
- NAP is not designed to lock attackers out of your environment. NAP is designed to ensure that, if attacked, your computers have a well-managed security policy that enhances their ability to fend off an attack.
- You can implement NAP enforcement through IPsec, DHCP, VPN, or 802.1x. IPsec NAP enforcement is the strongest form of NAP enforcement. DHCP enforcement is the weakest form of NAP enforcement.
- Be sure to test a well-documented pilot deployment extensively prior to implementing an enterprise deployment of any NAP solution.

# Case Scenario

In the following case scenario, you will apply what you've learned about designing a network access strategy. You can find answers to these questions in the "Answers" section at the end of this book.

## Case Scenario: Designing a NAP Solution for a Large Enterprise

Contoso, Ltd., is a corporation with 10 branch offices and a main office in Ft. Lauderdale, Florida. The company employs 3,500 people across all its locations. Seven of the branch offices are substantial in size with over 50 employees and computers for all employees at these locations. There is one Active Directory domain in a forest named *contoso.com*.

The company maintains a large data center at the Ft. Lauderdale office. A set of servers at the seven larger branch offices supports authentication, local profiles, data shares, and printing. All servers are for local use only. Remote salespeople and traveling representatives of the company use the three smaller branch offices for meetings. No domain controllers are stationed at any of the branch offices.

The seven larger branch offices are connected to the main office with multiple T1 links to form a link speed between 5 and 10 Mbps. The smaller offices use a business broadband connection through either DSL or cable with asymmetric speeds exceeding 1 Mbps for uploading and 6 Mbps for downloads. At these smaller offices, ISA Server 2004 running on Windows Server 2003 provides local DHCP and firewall services and a site-to-site VPN connection to the main office. Clients at the smaller branch offices consist of a small staff of users for support of the salespeople who travel into the area as well as for a few local salespeople who reside in the area. All the salespeople, including corporate officers, use these smaller offices for meetings.

Remote access is provided through an L2TP VPN that is centrally managed at the Ft. Lauderdale office. A RADIUS solution is already in use because all offices forward their authentication requests to the main office. Each of the branch offices has a single VPN server running Windows Server 2003. The main office has four RADIUS servers running Windows Server 2008.

The company plans to implement NAP using IPsec enforcement at the main office and is currently in the test phase of an IPsec enforcement deployment. Server isolation has been proposed for high-value servers at the main office. All corporate officers along with a smaller, exclusive group of users spread across the enterprise will have access to these servers. IT must complete the NAP IPsec deployment at the main office and evaluate NAP enforcement at the branch offices.

1.  Clients at the larger branch offices access servers at the main office. Several users at two of the branch offices access one of the database clusters that has been deemed a high-value server. How would you apply an IPsec NAP solution at these offices?

2. Support staff at the branch office require access to the servers running Exchange Server as well as access to file servers that all reside at the main office. None of these resource servers have been deemed high-value servers. Will an IPsec NAP enforcement solution be necessary at these branch offices?

# Suggested Practices

To help you successfully master the exam objectives presented in this chapter, complete the following tasks.

## Implement VPNs, RADIUS Solution, and NAP Enforcement

In Practice 1, implement an L2TP VPN by using a VPN access server and a RADIUS server with directory database. In Practice 2, implement NAP by using DHCP, VPN, IPsec, and 802.1x enforcement.

■ **Practice 1**  Using either virtual or physical computers, install the Active Directory Domain Services Server role on one installation of Windows Server 2008. Install an enterprise CA on this same instance with Web enrollment. Install on this same server the Network Policy Server role. Acquire a computer certificate for authentication.

On a second installation of Windows Server 2008, keep it as a workgroup computer and install NPS. Create a connection request policy, using the remote access server as the type of network access server, specifying L2TP as the tunnel type, and enabling the server for 24/7 in day and time restrictions. Ensure that you place the policy at the top of the connection request policies list. Also on this second instance, create a Remote RADIUS Server group, specifying the first Windows Server 2008 as a RADIUS server. (Use only a single subnet and adapter for all computers in this test lab, or you can configure Routing and Remote Access Services [RRAS] and a second adapter on the second instance of Windows Server 2008.)

On the first instance, create a RADIUS client, specifying the second instance of Windows Server 2008 as the RADIUS client. Create a connection request policy stating L2TP as the tunnel type. Create a network policy, using the NAS type of remote access server, VPN as the NAS port type, Authentication Methods set to only Microsoft Protected EAP (PEAP), and edit to ensure that only a certificate is used. Select the option for the client to be assigned a static IPv4 address and type in an appropriate address for connection to this server through the VPN.

Create a Windows Vista installation (SP1 is not required) and maintain the computer as a workgroup member. Configure an L2TP VPN connection, using PEAP-TLS as the only authentication protocol. Ensure that an appropriate IPv4 address is configured for its connection to the RADIUS client VPN server. Acquire an appropriate user certificate (user authentication for the PEAP-TLS) and computer certificate (computer authentication for L2TP), using Web enrollment. Ensure that you also acquire the root CA certificate and make sure that it is stored in the Trusted Root CA store. Test your connection.

- **Practice 2**   Using the Microsoft Step-by-Step guides and either virtual machines or physical computers, practice implementing each of the NAP enforcement types.

  NAP DHCP:

  *http://go.microsoft.com/fwlink/?Linkid=85897*

  Practice NAP VPN enforcement:

  *http://go.microsoft.com/fwlink/?Linkid=85896*

  Practice NAP IPsec enforcement:

  *http://go.microsoft.com/fwlink/?Linkid=85894*

  Practice NAP 802.1x enforcement:

  *http://go.microsoft.com/fwlink/?Linkid=86036*

## Watch a Webcast

For these practices, watch two webcasts about Active Directory Domain Services in Windows Server 2008.

- **Practice 1**   Watch the TechNet webcast, "Protecting Critical Systems and Data with Server and Domain Isolation," at *http://msevents.microsoft.com/CUI/WebCastEventDetails .aspx?culture=en-US&EventID=1032280057&CountryCode=US*.
- **Practice 2**   Watch the Support webcast, "Network Access Protection platform Architecture," at *http://support.microsoft.com/kb/924160*.

## Read a White Paper

In Practice 1, read a white paper about NAP in Windows Server 2008. In Practice 2, read a security guide detailing the steps to creating a security risk management program.

- **Practice 1**   Read the "Network Access Protection Policies in Windows Server 2008" white paper from Microsoft at *http://www.microsoft.com/downloads/details.aspx?FamilyID =8e47649e-962c-42f8-9e6f-21c5ccdcf490&displaylang=en*.
- **Practice 2**   Read the "The Security Risk Management Guide" white paper from Microsoft at *http://www.microsoft.com/downloads/details.aspx?familyid=C782B6D3-28C5-4DDA-A168 -3E4422645459&displaylang=en*.

# Take a Practice Test

The practice tests on this book's companion CD offer many options. For example, you can test yourself on just one exam objective, or you can test yourself on all the 70-647 certification exam content. You can set up the test so that it closely simulates the experience of taking a certification exam, or you can set it up in study mode so that you can look at the correct answers and explanations after you answer each question.

---

**MORE INFO    Practice tests**

For details about all the practice test options available, see the "How to Use the Practice Tests" section in this book's introduction.

---

Chapter 6

# Design a Branch Office Deployment

It seems that every enterprise eventually confronts this issue: whether through the need to have representation in many locations, whether by acquiring another company, or whether by outgrowing the existing office space, at some point you will need to design, deploy, and manage a branch office. The branch office presents a unique collection of challenges. It requires the enterprise administrator to develop a specialized vision and understanding of the many facets of the information system design and the administration demanded by this isolated, and often unsupported and unsecure, facility.

This chapter describes the various real-world pressures and issues that you might be faced with regarding the branch office. It also explains the tools and techniques provided by Windows Server 2008 to help you properly analyze, design, deploy, and maintain a branch office environment. You should develop balanced solutions that address the need for connectivity, performance, and resource access, along with the need for control and security and for legal and regulatory compliance in order to mitigate the pressures and risks associated with the branch office.

**Exam objectives in this chapter:**
- Design the branch office deployment.

**Lessons in this chapter:**
- Lesson 1: Branch Office Deployment. . . . . . . . . . . . . . . . . . . . . . . . . . . . . . . . . . . . . . 290
- Lesson 2: Branch Office Server Security . . . . . . . . . . . . . . . . . . . . . . . . . . . . . . . . . . . 308

# Before You Begin

To complete the lessons in this chapter, you should have:

- An understanding of Windows Server 2008 Active Directory Domain Services (AD DS) and its required infrastructure.
- An understanding of network communications.
- An understanding of the concepts of a security policy.

To complete the lessons in this chapter, you might want to have:

- A lab environment with a Windows Server 2008 Active Directory domain.
- Internet access.
- Access to Microsoft TechNet.

## Real World

*David R. Miller*

In my experience as an enterprise administrator, branch offices are a natural point of vulnerability for an enterprise. They often connect to the organization's most critical information assets, but they are usually not supported, monitored, or secured as thoroughly as the headquarters (HQ) facility. There is an increased likelihood that, because of these vulnerabilities, the branch office will be the point of attack. These attacks can be through electronic means, through improper disposal of information assets, or through the outright theft of computer or network hardware. The successful attack on the branch office can lead to the compromise not only of valuable information assets located at the branch office but also of valuable information assets located at HQ and the entire connected information systems infrastructure.

Many branch office locations are too small to warrant dedicated, full-time, highly skilled, local technical support. Branch offices are typically supported by the more skilled and remote administrative crew at HQ. It is not uncommon for a local junior administrator to provide support services for the branch office. These junior administrators are often of lesser skills and might even not be trusted. Very often, the branch office junior administrators provide support only as a part of their daily responsibilities. This can (and often does) lead to a conflict of interest in their decision-making processes as the local administrator. They will need guidelines and rigid boundaries to manage, control, and monitor their authority and actions in this isolated environment.

These controls might be in the form of written policies, or they might be technical controls implemented at HQ. These technical controls should begin with the delegation of authority to branch office administrators following the principle of least privilege, providing only the barest level of authority and access for junior administrators to perform their limited tasks and meet their limited set of responsibilities. Other controls might include Group Policy object (GPO) restrictions on desktop, applications, software installation, hardware installation, and the like. Still other controls might be implemented on infrastructure systems, like Network Access Protection (NAP) policies and firewall rules on browsing and downloads.

---

**NOTE   Privilege**

Privilege is defined as the collection of rights (the ability to perform system-related functions) and permissions (the ability to access resources and objects) granted to a user or a group of users. A user's level of privilege defines that user's access to an information system.

---

Users in the branch office need a local network infrastructure, like workstations and switches, and at least a firewall and router. They probably also need virtual private network (VPN) capabilities to provide secure connectivity to HQ. They need proper and controlled system configuration. They need application deployment, and they might need access to local and remote resources. They need access to the network infrastructure services, like Dynamic Host Configuration Protocol (DHCP), and the Active Directory Domain Services infrastructure, either locally, remotely, or both. They also need a way to locate these resources and the network infrastructure.

There is a need to implement controls on these users, to maintain the stability and functionality of the information system, to protect the confidentiality and integrity of the valuable information assets, and to conform to legal and regulatory compliance requirements. HQ administrators must balance the need for resource access and performance (availability), with the often conflicting need for control and security (confidentiality and integrity) of the information system.

Together, these branch office issues represent a potential downstream liability for the organization.

# Lesson 1:  Branch Office Deployment

In this lesson, you will be presented with scenario-like branch office issues and the tools and techniques that Windows Server 2008 provides to help resolve those issues.

---

**After this lesson, you will be able to:**

- Describe the server roles and their uses in the branch office implementation.
- Identify the network infrastructure services and know how to deploy them in a branch office environment.
- Describe the components required to provide reliable and secure authentication to branch offices.
- Describe the concept of Administrator Role Separation.
- Describe the advantages and disadvantages of using full, read-only, and Server Core domain controllers in a branch office.
- Describe the benefits and ramifications of performing forest restructuring when implementing branch offices.
- Describe the mechanisms used to improve the availability of information system services and resources in the branch office through device and data redundancy and through replication configuration.

**Estimated lesson time:  50 minutes**

---

# Branch Office Services

## Designing the Active Directory Structure for Branch Office Administration

The first issue to consider in the branch office is the establishment of the proper level of access and authority for the branch office administrator. The branch office administrator is generally less skilled and less trusted than the administrators in the corporate HQ. Branch office administrators are responsible for lower-level administrative functions related to application installation, performing operating system and application updates, and restarting servers and domain controllers (DCs). However, the branch office administrator is generally not authorized to perform Active Directory–related administrative functions. Because branch office administrators are not as skilled or as trusted as the HQ administrators and because they typically are responsible only for their local branch office systems, it is generally not desirable to add the branch office administrators to the Domain Admins group or to other domain-related built-in groups. This is usually too much privilege.

As in Windows Server 2003, you can use the Delegation of Control Wizard in Windows Server 2008 to delegate preconfigured levels of privilege at the Active Directory site, the domain, and the organizational unit (OU). Several additional preconfigured levels of privilege have been added at the domain level to the wizard in Windows Server 2008.

Because the branch office almost always represents an Active Directory site, it might seem that the Delegation of Control Wizard should be used at the site level to delegate privilege to the branch office administrator. However, the preconfigured privileges available at the site level number exactly one—Manage Group Policy Links, just as it was in Windows Server 2003. The Delegation of Control Wizard enables you to create custom tasks to delegate, but when privilege is delegated at the site level, the branch office administrator's level of authority would approximate that of an Enterprise Admin. Enterprise Admin is far too much authority for the branch office administrator and is usually not a good choice for delegation in this case.

If the branch office is configured in Active Directory as its own domain, the branch office administrator can be granted Domain Admin status in his or her home domain. This might or might not be too much authority because members of the Domain Admins group can write GPOs, delegate authority, and define a great deal of policy and control over the domain. Delegation at the domain level would require a skilled and trusted branch office administrator. If the branch office administrator is up to this level of challenge, responsibility, and authority in the enterprise, in which the branch office is its own domain, making the branch office administrator a domain administrator in his or her home domain could be a viable option.

It is generally better to delegate administrative authority at the lowest possible container within the Active Directory structure—the OU. For more granular administrative control, create an OU for each branch office and delegate authority to the branch office administrator at the OU level. Then place all local branch office users and computers into the proper branch office OU. At the OU level, the Delegation of Control Wizard has about a dozen preconfigured levels of privilege. Members of the Enterprise Admins group can still create and link GPOs at the Site level, with the optional "Enforced" setting enabled, for high-level, enterprise administrative control. Members of the Domain Admins group can also create and link GPOs at the domain level, again with the optional "Enforced" setting enabled, for high-level administrative control.

---

**NOTE   Domain restructuring**

Windows Server 2008 provides for domain restructuring in an entirely new way. Branch offices are often isolated from the main office not just geographically but financially (like a different cost center) or administratively (politically), with different network administration, and they might even have different requirements regarding security and compliance concerns.

No matter how the branch office is configured within Active Directory, the branch office might be restructured to better fit the business needs of the enterprise with the control and administration models supported by the different Active Directory containers.

The topic of restructuring domains is covered in Chapter 3, "Planning Migrations, Trusts, and Interoperability."

---

Although you can use delegation of authority at the site, domain, or OU to provide administrative control over member computers and users, what about the domain controller that is physically located in the branch office? Domain controllers should never be moved from the Domain Controllers OU. How can the local branch office administrator manage that operating system and applications? You don't want the local administrator working with Active Directory, but you need his or her help in maintaining the server operating system underlying Active Directory. Windows Server 2008 introduces Administrator Role Separation specifically to address this issue.

## Administrator Role Separation

A new feature of Windows Server 2008 is the ability to delegate local administrative privilege on a domain controller (DC). This grants the delegated user or group local administrator privilege on the server, with the ability to log on to the server, update drivers, and restart the server, but disallows them from being able to manage Active Directory or the Directory Services. This is called Administrator Role Separation.

You must perform Administrator Role Separation delegation on a server-by-server basis. The delegated user or group will not have any administrative privileges on other DCs in the domain. To implement Administrator Role Separation on a single DC, at a command prompt, type:

**DSMGMT.exe**

and press Enter. At the DSMGMT prompt, type:

**local roles**

and press Enter. You can type a question mark (?) to get help at any level in the DSMGMT application. Next, type:

**list roles**

to view the possible delegations on the server. Now, for the delegation, type:

**add <domain>\<username or group name> administrators**

You should receive the following response:

**Successfully Updated Local Role**

Next, to confirm the delegation, type:

**show role administrators**

You should see the user or group that has been delegated the Administrator Role Separation role. Keep in mind that this grants the delegated user or group administrative privilege only on this one DC. To grant administrative privilege to the branch office administrator over users and computers in the branch office, you will also need to delegate privilege at the site, domain, or OU level for the branch office, as appropriate.

## Components and Services in the Branch Office

The branch office typically has relatively few users, relatively few computers, a smaller budget for information services, reduced network infrastructure devices (like servers and firewalls), and, most unfortunately, lesser security and less-skilled administration. The users in the branch office will still need access to enterprise resources, along with a reasonable level of performance, coupled with an appropriate level of security for the information systems. Furthermore, there might be the need to provide additional infrastructure in the branch office to remain in compliance with industry regulations and laws. There needs to be a balance between the needs of the users in the branch office and the cost of providing infrastructure, support, performance, and reliability for the network. It is not prudent business practice to "just throw money" at the issue, hoping that the complaints and other problems go away.

Consequently, a branch office will need an infrastructure to provide information services. This section will explore some of the options and discuss the benefits, along with the price you'll pay to implement the service in the remote and potentially unsupported and nonsecure branch office. As a branch office grows, the need for local services and support also grows. Following is a list of information system components and services that might be desirable in the branch office:

- Client computers
- Servers
    - Member or standalone, to support services like File Services, Print Services, and other infrastructure services
    - Full server or Server Core installation
- Domain controller (DC)
    - Full server: DC or Read-Only DC (RODC)
    - Server Core: DC or RODC
- Global catalog (GC)
- Operations master roles
- Domain Name System (DNS)
- DHCP
- Multisite cluster nodes
- Distributed File System (DFS) or Distributed File System with Replication
- Routing and Remote Access Services
    - For dial-in and VPN, DHCP relay agent, and Network Address Translation (NAT) support

- Windows Server Update Services, to provide Microsoft operating system (OS) and application updates
- Windows Server Virtualization (WSv) services

In addition, the branch office will typically need at least one firewall/router and a wide area network (WAN) link to provide connectivity to the HQ networks, as well as to the Internet. A more detailed discussion of the elements on this list follows.

The branch office network typically connects to the HQ over dedicated WAN links, like a T1 or a T3, or they connect through VPNs over the Internet's public network. In either case, for performance and reliability reasons, it is often desired to place network infrastructure systems in the branch office.

## Windows Deployment Services

What is the value of a branch office without computers? How do you get those standardized operating system and application installations to the branch office? Microsoft has redesigned the earlier Remote Installation Services (RIS) in Windows Server 2008 to enhance the remote deployment and reimaging of computers using preconfigured images complete with applications and settings. Windows Deployment Services (WDS) is a server role that can be added to any Windows Server 2008 server.

WDS is optimized to deploy Windows Vista and Server 2008, but it can deploy earlier versions of Windows operating systems. It relies on preboot execution environment (PXE) technology and requires Transmission Control Protocol/Internet Protocol (TCP/IP) connectivity between the WDS server and the target client. WDS can deploy remote clients using multicast transmission to deploy an image to a large number of client computers simultaneously.

**Windows Server 2008 Server—Member or Standalone**    In the enterprise, the most common deployment of client and server class computers is to make them members of the domain by joining them to the domain. This must be done on the local computer, by script, or by answer file during an unattended installation. Joining these systems to the domain implements the administrative control desired (required) by the administration and by the enterprise security policy. The majority of administrative control is accomplished through the GPO within Active Directory. The benefit to the user of the system is single sign-on to access resources enterprise-wide. The impact of joining the domain for a computer is giving up administrative control of the computer. The administrators in the enterprise now own the control of the system.

For the administrator in the enterprise, almost the only circumstances in which it might be desirable to have a company computer remain a standalone system and not join the domain is when there is little or no need to access enterprise resources and when there is significant risk of the computer being compromised. The compromise could be physical theft or access, or it could be an attack through the network.

**Windows Server 2008 Server Core**   Server Core is the securest installation of Windows Server 2008. Server Core installs a minimal operating system, providing minimal services and applications, with no Windows shell and a limited graphical user interface (GUI). This reduces the maintenance, the management, and the hardware requirements of the server. (Server Core requires only about 1 GB of hard disk drive space for installation and about 2 GB for ongoing server operations.)

Perhaps more significant, Server Core reduces the attack surface of the server, making it the securest installation of Windows Server 2008. It is designed as a bastion host or hardened server, already minimizing the attack vectors of the operating system. Almost always, the way that a hacker is able to compromise a computer is through vulnerabilities in services and applications (program code) running (in memory) on the computer. These vulnerabilities are inherent in all program code. By reducing the number of services and applications that run on a computer, you are reducing the number of attack vectors available to the hacker. This is exactly what Server Core does. It operates with a bare minimum of services and programs running in memory.

Furthermore, if the hacker can break into a running process, the hacker's level of privilege is that of the user account that initially launched the compromised process. After a hacker accesses a computer through one of the vulnerabilities in running program code, the hacker's next objective is to elevate his or her level of privilege in order to acquire greater control over the computer. This is commonly accomplished by triggering the execution of a service (or other process) that runs at a higher level of privilege. Because vulnerabilities are inherent in all program code, the hacker now breaks into the process that runs at the higher level of privilege, acquiring a higher level of privilege on the computer. Again, because Server Core has a reduced set of services and applications installed and available on the computer, the hacker has fewer targets with elevated privilege to execute and exploit. This reduces the likelihood that a hacker can elevate his or her level of privilege on the Server Core server, keeping the hacker at a lower level of privilege. These are the principal mechanisms that make Server Core the securest implementation of Windows Server 2008.

---

**NOTE   The many facets of security**

The reduction of programs in memory and on the hard disk drive does not alone ensure security of the computer. These features, combined with a comprehensive, multilayered, and monitored security structure, are the best defense against hacker compromise of the computer system.

It only takes one vulnerability in a system to enable the hacker to exploit the system. You must attempt to secure them all. Many of these other security measures are addressed later in this chapter.

---

Because Server Core has no Explorer shell and a limited GUI, local administration and administration through a Remote Desktop (Terminal Services) connection must be performed using commands at a command prompt. Figure 6-1 shows the Server Core console.

**Figure 6-1**   The Server 2008 Server Core console

Many Control Panel items are available in Server Core. Type the name of the .cpl item at the command prompt, like **intl.cpl** and **timedate.cpl**. These Control Panel items provide about the only limited GUI for local server administration. Other useful administrative tools are RegEdit.exe, RegEdt32.exe, and bcdedit.exe. You can also use scripts, based on Extensible Markup Language (XML), to configure the Server Core server.

You can also manage the Server Core server remotely, using the Microsoft Management Console (MMC) or through remote command-line tools. The MMC used through a remote connection to the Server Core server is the only way to administer the Server Core server through a GUI interface.

Server Core supports the following server roles:

- Active Directory Domain Services (AD DS)
- Active Directory Lightweight Directory Services (AD LDS)
- DHCP Server
- DNS Server
- File Server
- Print Server
- Streaming Media Services
- Web Server (IIS)

You must select Server Core during the installation of the operating system. Figure 6-2 shows the selection menu from which you need to select the Server Core installation during the installation of Windows Server 2008.

Windows Server 2008 Server Core in the branch office, whether configured as a standalone, member, domain controller, or read-only domain controller server, provides the securest Windows Server 2008 operating system platform because of its server hardening by design. You should use this implementation when the server has a significant risk of being either physically or electronically exposed to compromise or when the server will be supporting the most sensitive data or processes, even in a well-protected LAN or branch office environment. The potential minor cost savings in hardware should typically not be a consideration in making this decision.

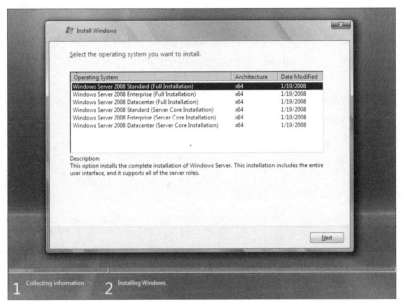

**Figure 6-2** Selecting Windows Server 2008 Full Installation or Server Core Installation

**Windows Server 2008—Full Installation**   The full installation of Windows Server 2008 is what most administrators are used to. It provides all of the desired features through a familiar GUI. Unfortunately, all the "make life easy for the administrator" gadgets, GUIs, tools, utilities, and applications create substantially more opportunities for hackers to break into and take over a server, as previously described.

Windows Server 2008–full installation is generally safe to use on the well-protected LAN or branch office environment where the threat of compromise is reduced and where the server is supporting less than highly sensitive data and processes.

## Adding a Domain Controller

Access to the domain controller server is required for successful authentication of users and computers in the enterprise. Adding a DC to a branch office introduces increased risk, cost, and administrative overhead in human terms, and in terms of directory services, it involves the following:

- The additional hardware (cost) at the branch office.
- Enterprise Admins must create, configure, and maintain a site in Active Directory for the branch office.

- There will be Active Directory replication traffic over the WAN link between HQ and the branch office.

- There will be the need for additional infrastructure devices or services, or both.

- The remote DC must be maintained (at the server level), requiring that Administrator Role Separation be configured.

- There are security concerns about having a copy of the entire Active Directory database, complete with usernames and passwords, along with the additional infrastructure systems and services in this potentially unsecure facility.

On the other hand, having a DC in the branch office provides a notable improvement in performance and reliability for the branch office for the following reasons:

- Branch office users can authenticate faster and can authenticate even if the WAN link is down.

- All other local requests of Active Directory Domain Services respond faster and are successful even if the WAN link is down.

- Not having a DC in the branch office means the branch office relies more heavily on the performance and reliability of the WAN link.

- The DC provides an additional level of fault tolerance to the Active Directory database.

Microsoft recommends the addition of a DC in any site (like a branch office) in the following situations:

- More than 100 users are in the site.

- The site is using an application that relies on a custom Active Directory partition for replication.

- Domain logons must be successful (typically expressed as the requirement to access domain resources) even if the WAN link is down.

---

**NOTE    Active Directory Domain Services binaries**

A new process that runs prior to initializing the Active Directory Installation Wizard is the installation of the DCPromo binaries (executables) onto the server. You can initiate this by adding the AD DS server role to the server. Then you can execute DCPromo. Alternatively, if you don't first install the AD DS server role, you'll see it automatically initiate by simply running DCPromo at a command prompt.

---

In the situations where the DC is required in the branch office, the next decision is "What type of DC shall be deployed in the branch office?" This question has new potential answers in Windows Server 2008. Windows Server 2008 can now provide the following types of DCs, engineered to help satisfy reliability, performance, and security concerns in the branch office.

**Full Domain Controller**   Based on a full installation of controller Windows Server 2008 (as opposed to a Server Core installation), the full domain contains all of the standard components of Active Directory, just as it did in Windows Server 2003. These DCs perform bidirectional replication with other DCs in the domain and forest, just as they did in earlier versions of the operating system.

The full domain controller is the least secure implementation of the DC. It has the full operating system, with many opportunities for the hacker to exploit. It has the full Active Directory database, complete with usernames and passwords. The Active Directory database is writable, providing the opportunity for inappropriate modification, which is a violation of the integrity of the data in the Active Directory database. These potential violations of integrity can be the result of either an authorized user's accidental misconfiguration or willful misuse or of an unauthorized user (hacker) manipulating Active Directory.

**Read-Only Domain Controller**   The RODC is a more secured version of a DC. Based on a full installation of Windows Server 2008 (as opposed to a Server Core installation), the RODC contains all of the standard components of Active Directory, except for account passwords. Clients are not able to write any changes to the RODC, however. Lightweight Directory Access Protocol (LDAP) applications that perform write operations are referred to writable DCs that are located in the nearest site over an available WAN link. RODCs receive only inbound, one-way domain data replication from Windows Server 2008 DCs in the domain.

In addition to the read-only Active Directory database and the one-way replication, RODC features include the following:

- **Credential caching**   Limited contents are stored in the password database in case of compromise. Administrators must configure a Password Replication Policy to allow password replication of only specified accounts to occur to the RODC.
- **Administrator Role Separation**   Described earlier in this lesson.
- **RODC filtered attribute set**   To allow administrators to selectively filter attributes on Active Directory objects, typically for security purposes.
- **Read-only DNS**   All Active Directory–integrated zones get replicated to the read-only DNS server; however, the zones are nondynamic. When clients attempt to update their DNS information, the read-only DNS server returns a referral to the client with the address of a DNS server with a writable copy of the zone.

---

**NOTE**   Increased RODC security comes at a price

Although the RODC provides additional security against unauthorized changes to Active Directory and minimizes the number of passwords that might be compromised if the DC gets stolen from the branch office, the RODC cannot be used to make any changes to Active Directory data. If the WAN link is down, no changes can be made to Active Directory through the RODC.

---

The RODC was largely designed for the branch office implementation. It can be installed on the full installation or the Server Core installation of Windows Server 2008—Server Core, of course, being the more secure of the two. The option to install the DC as a RODC is a new setting in the DCPromo utility, as shown in Figure 6-3.

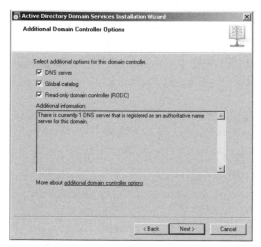

**Figure 6-3**    Selecting the read-only domain controller during DCPromo

The RODC will be covered in more detail in Lesson 2, "Branch Office Server Security."

**Server Core Domain Controller**    As stated previously, Server Core is the securest installation of Windows Server 2008. Server Core installs a minimal operating system, providing minimal services and applications, with no Windows shell and a limited GUI.

Server Core is not a DC by default, but AD DS can be added to the Server Core installation. When the more secure RODC role is added to the Server Core installation, you have the securest DC installation possible, optimized for the risky branch office implementation. You add the AD DS role to the Server Core server using the **DCPromo /unattend <unattend.txt>** command, along with a preconfigured answer file (Unattend.txt) for the DCPromo utility.

Windows Server 2008 Server Core in the branch office, whether configured as a standalone, member, DC, or read-only DC server, provides the securest Windows Server 2008 operating system platform due to its server hardening by design.

**Global Catalog**    The global catalog server is required for successful authentication of users and computers in the enterprise. The global catalog (GC) must reside on a DC. Microsoft recommends that you place a GC in a branch office in the following situations:

- There is a DC in the branch office, and:
- The WAN link is unreliable.
- There are more than 100 users in the branch office.

- Universal group membership caching is not enabled.
- The branch office supports Active Directory–aware or Distributed Component Object Model (DCOM) applications.

Placing a GC in the branch office will improve the performance of LDAP queries, user logons, and Active Directory–aware and DCOM applications for users in the branch office.

Placing a GC in the branch office requires a DC in the branch office, raising the risk of the DC being compromised. Furthermore, it increases the risk of compromise of sensitive GC data, and it increases the amount of AD DS replication traffic to and from the branch office over the WAN links.

**Operations Masters**   Few situations would warrant placing one or more operations masters in a branch office. These are significant components that reside on DCs within the AD DS environment, and placing them in an isolated, and potentially disconnected, branch office could cause problems for the entire forest. About the only cases where it might be appropriate are:

- There is a DC in the branch office, and:
- The branch office is its own domain. A DC in the branch office would hold the relative ID (RID) master, the infrastructure master, and the PDC emulator operations master roles.
- The branch office is its own forest. A DC in the branch office would hold the domain naming master, the schema master, the RID master, the infrastructure master, and the PDC emulator operations master roles.
- The branch office has the bulk of down-level clients in the enterprise. A DC in the branch office would hold the PDC emulator operations master roles.

In almost every other case, the operations master roles should typically remain on the well-secured, stable, and well-connected HQ network.

**Domain Name System**   The Domain Name System (DNS) server is required for successful authentication of users and computers in the enterprise and for Internet access. Clients in the branch office will need to locate AD DS servers and other infrastructure services. It is useful, and can be a requirement, that a DNS server be placed in the branch office. This provides rapid registration and query responses, even if the WAN link to HQ is down or busy.

Providing a DNS server in the branch office is a requirement if the branch office is configured as its own domain in AD DS. Local clients will need local DNS to locate domain-related services. From the perspective of the user or a computer, the act of locating AD DS is accomplished through service location (SRV) records within the DNS zone for the domain. In addition, other AD DS DNS zones throughout the forest must:

- Be configured as Active Directory–integrated DNS zones with proper replication partitions configured.
- Have secondary DNS zones and zone transfers configured.

- Have forwarders or stub zones configured.
- If the branch office domain is a child domain, a delegation record in the parent DNS zone will need to be configured.

**Dynamic Host Configuration Protocol (DHCP) Services**    Another network infrastructure service that is often required is DHCP for the dynamic assignment of IP addresses and other configuration settings to clients. Again, for performance and reliability reasons, placing a DHCP server in the branch office is often desirable. This aids IP connectivity for branch office clients even if the WAN link is down for extended periods.

**Multisite (Branch Office) Clustering with Microsoft Cluster Services**    Failover clusters provide server fault tolerance for highly available applications and services, such as SQL Server, Exchange Server, Windows Server Virtualization (also known as Hyper-V or WSv) servers, DHCP servers, and file and print services. You can place cluster nodes in each branch office site to provide local access with increased availability to applications, services, and data.

**Distributed File System Replication for Data Fault Tolerance**    Another fault tolerant mechanism that can be used in the branch office is distributed file system (DFS) replication. DFS Replication is typically used to replicate data files to multiple and geographically dispersed DFS replica sets, which is ideal for the branch office deployment. DFS Replication has been overhauled in Windows Server 2008, with improvements in performance, data reliability, and replication on demand (called Replicate Now), and it can be used on the new Windows Server 2008 RODC server. DFS Replication is so much better than the earlier (Windows 2000 Server and Windows Server 2003) File Replication Service (FRS) that it replaces FRS for SYSVOL replication for domains configured to use the Windows Server 2008 domain functional level.

**Routing and Remote Access Services**    The Routing and Remote Access Services (RRAS) server hosts several useful but potentially risky services. It is now a component of the Network Policy and Access Services server role, but it can be installed independently of NAP. New in Windows Server 2008 is support for IPv6.

RRAS can be particularly useful in the branch office because it includes the following services:

- VPN server
- Demand-dial routing—for use with establishing on-demand VPNs
- Network address translation (NAT) with:
  - IP routing (small scale, just perfect for satisfying the limited routing needs in the branch office)
  - DHCP relay agent

In addition, RRAS provides support for these typically lesser-used but sometimes helpful services:

- Dial-in connections
- IGMP—Multicast routing
- Routing Information Protocol (RIP) v1 and v2

If you decide to place an RRAS server in the branch office, if it doesn't exist in the branch office already, you'll want to consider the potential placement of a DC in the branch office. If the RRAS server will be authenticating users and VPN connections, you might prefer to provide local authentication services.

The VPN server component of the RRAS server provides tremendous benefits in securing information in transit between the branch office and HQ, between two branch offices, and between the branch office and remote authorized users. It can provide core network infrastructure services with NAT, IP routing, and the DHCP relay agent.

However, remember that a dial-in server, like RRAS, allows remote users, both authorized users and hackers, to gain access to the internal network and its resources. This device is a gap in the security fortress and must be implemented with careful consideration and planning. It requires ongoing monitoring and analysis to maintain and maximize security on this portal into your network infrastructure.

**Windows Server Update Services (WSUS)**   Microsoft Windows Server Update Services (WSUS), currently v3.0 SP1, enables administrators to deploy the latest Microsoft product updates to computers running the Windows operating system. This server downloads, stores, and distributes approved Microsoft operating system and application updates to computers in the enterprise. Placing a WSUS server in a branch office reduces update traffic, either from the HQ or from the Internet. The WSUS server in the branch office can be managed from HQ, so no administrative privilege is required other than local administrator privilege (Administrator Role Separation, which was covered earlier in this chapter) for underlying server support. HQ administration can, of course, grant update approval authority to the branch office administrator, if appropriate.

The down side, again, is the hardware cost, the slightly increased local administration overhead, and the increase of the attack surface of the server and the branch office network.

**Virtualization in the Branch Office**   Another new technology that can be a major benefit in the branch office is Microsoft's Hyper-V technology. Hyper-V provides support for running multiple virtual machines on a single physical computer host. This is referred to as server consolidation. Because most computers operate using only 10 to 25 percent of a computer system's available resources, such as RAM and CPU clock cycles, the hardware is severely underutilized. By running multiple virtual machines on a single physical server host, these server resources are much better utilized, requiring fewer physical servers and providing better return on investment. Having fewer physical devices in the branch office reduces the number and difficulty of physically securing those fewer devices.

Microsoft's virtualization technology provides for rapid and easy deployment of virtual machines and simplifies the migration of virtual machines from one physical host to another. These features can be essential components of the enterprise's business continuity and disaster recovery plans. Hyper-V can be implemented on Windows Server 2008 Server Core servers for increased security and can be clustered to provide server failover fault tolerance.

Hyper-V is included with Windows Server 2008 Standard, Windows Server 2008 Enterprise, and Windows Server 2008 Datacenter. Windows Server 2008 Standard includes one virtual instance per license. Windows Server 2008 Enterprise includes four virtual instances per license. With Windows Server 2008 Datacenter, customers receive unlimited virtual instances per license. You can buy these versions without Hyper-V, but the savings are negligible.

# Branch Office Communications Considerations

Branch office networks need to connect to resources in the HQ network. This connection can be on dedicated lines, like a T1 or T3, or it can communicate over the public wires of the Internet. In either case, these channels of communication should be protected from the sniffer or eavesdropper. Furthermore, it is not uncommon for the WAN link between the branch office and HQ to go down, forcing the network administrator to view WAN links as unreliable. These unsecure and unreliable WAN links are required to carry sensitive corporate, medical, financial, and otherwise private data requiring protection by laws and regulations, as well as data to support AD DS. The types of data an enterprise must consider in its branch office deployment design are the following:

- User data—accessed over the WAN links and for centralized backups at HQ
- DFS replicated data
- AD DS replication data—if the branch office holds a DC
- Global catalog replication data—if the branch office holds a GC
- DNS data—either within AD DS replication Active Directory Integrated zones or in zone transfers
- Multisite clustering heartbeat data

## Site Link Considerations for the Branch Office

Each defined site must connect to AD DS by means of a site link. A site link is the logical connection object between sites for AD DS replication. This logical connection, of course, requires physical connectivity to be in place and to be functioning properly for replication to succeed. Due to the security constraints on different types of data that must be replicated and to provide redundancy for failed replication servers, there are often replication paths for Active Directory replication data that would fail without the addition of site link bridges.

The good news is that from as early as Windows 2000 Server, site link bridging is enabled by default on all site links. If tighter control over replication paths is required, the Bridge All Site Links option can be disabled. The administrator must then manually construct any specific site link bridges required to provide the proper connectivity and redundancy on these logical connections.

Another aspect of AD DS replication, new to Windows Server 2008, is the need to ensure replication to the new RODC. Unfortunately, down-level domain controllers (Windows 2000 Server and Windows Server 2003) do not recognize an RODC because of its one-way replication processes and will not replicate data to it. This requires that any site with only RODCs (one or more) must have a site link directly to a site with at least one Windows Server 2008 DC. The Windows Server 2008 DC does recognize the RODC and will replicate AD DS data to it appropriately.

## Confidentiality for Data in Transit

No matter what type of connection you use, you should employ VPNs to secure data in transit between the branch office and HQ and between remote clients and the branch office. Windows Server 2008 provides VPN support for the following VPN protocols:

- **Point-to-Point Tunneling Protocol (PPTP)** The early and original Microsoft VPN protocol. This VPN is easy to set up and provides reasonable security based on the RC4 cipher for encryption. It uses TCP port 1723.

- **Layer 2 Tunneling Protocol (L2TP)** Operates at layer 2 of the OSI model, so no IP network is required. L2TP provides strong authentication, nonrepudiation, and strong integrity validation by using X.509 digital certificates on the end point servers. It does not provide confidentiality (encryption). It uses TCP port 1701.

- **IP Security (IPsec)** Operates at layer 3 of the OSI model, so an IP network is required. It has become the de facto VPN protocol of choice. With Windows Server 2008, it uses 3DES or AES for encryption and can provide weak authentication and integrity validation based on Kerberos. It can be strengthened to provide strong authentication, nonrepudiation, and integrity validation based on X.509 digital certificates. It uses UDP port 500.

- **Secure Sockets Transport Protocol (SSTP)** This is a new feature in Windows Server 2008. This VPN protocol is based on the very popular Hypertext Transfer Protocol (HTTP) over Secure Sockets Layer (SSL) and Transport Layer Security (TLS), but it has been refined for use on the LAN (versus its original use for Web-based services and applications). It can provide only client-to-server functionality and provides strong authenticity, nonrepudiation, and integrity validation of the server (only), along with weak authentication and integrity validation of the client. SSTP has native support for IPv6. It is based on an X.509 digital certificate on the server, uses the popular RC4 and AES ciphers, and runs over TCP port 443.

## Lesson Summary

- The branch office is typically isolated, with minimal support, infrastructure, and security than the enterprise HQ. Therefore, the branch office is more likely to be compromised than systems at the more developed HQ.
- Delegate privilege to the branch office administrator following the principle of least privilege, using Administrator Role Separation and the Delegation of Control Wizard at the lowest level in the Active Directory hierarchy.
- Consider restructuring the AD DS to optimize administrative control and limit exposure in the branch office.
- Analyze the need for information systems services in the branch office. Balance the needs and benefits of placing these infrastructure services in the remote and less secure branch office with the associated costs and risks.
- Understand the dependencies that services installed in the branch office might require, along with their associated costs and risks.
- Carefully plan and understand the connectivity (WAN links) between the branch office and HQ so that proper security and fault tolerant measures can be implemented.

## Lesson Review

You can use the following questions to test your knowledge of the information in Lesson 1, "Branch Office Deployment." The questions are also available on the companion CD if you prefer to review them in electronic form.

---

**NOTE**  Answers

Answers to these questions and explanations of why each answer choice is correct or incorrect are located in the "Answers" section at the end of the book.

---

1. What new feature of Windows Server 2008 gives a branch office administrator the privilege of logging onto a DC for server administration but does not give the administrator the privilege of administering Active Directory?
    - **A.** Read-only domain controller (RODC)
    - **B.** Server Core domain controller
    - **C.** Administrator Role Separation
    - **D.** BitLocker

2. Which of the following provides user data fault tolerance in a branch office?

   A. Read-only domain controller (RODC)

   B. Clustering

   C. Server Core

   D. DFS Replication

3. Your HQ has a DHCP server. You are designing a new branch office. You need to provide dynamic IP addressing to branch office clients, even if the wide area network (WAN) link fails between headquarters (HQ) and the new branch office. What should you do?

   A. Install a DHCP relay agent in the branch office.

   B. Configure a superscope on the DHCP server in HQ.

   C. Install DHCP on a multisite cluster node in the branch office.

   D. Install demand dial routing in the HQ.

# Lesson 2:  Branch Office Server Security

The branch office should initially be considered inherently unsecure, both physically and electronically. It is a mistake to make assumptions about any level of security until the site has been physically inspected and a comprehensive security policy and program has been defined and implemented specifically for each branch office. Unfortunately, what you'll probably discover is that the information technology component of the branch office is understaffed, under-budgeted, unplanned, and unmonitored.

The pressing need for the security policy and resulting program should be driven by senior management's security posture for the enterprise. The security policy should include disaster recovery planning and business continuity planning and should address every law and regulation with which the company must comply.

Implementation and maintenance of security for the branch office should be the responsibility of an entity other than the IT administration. The security professional and the IT administrator have common concerns, up to a point. The point where they diverge is the one at which you realize that IT's philosophy is "Availability at all cost!" and the security professional's philosophy is "If it isn't secure, pull the plug."

Although the security professional is responsible for the overall security of the branch office, the security professional will usually be located in a distant office, typically HQ. It is the responsibility of local administration and management to become the enforcer of the security policy and program that is handed down from the security professional's team. They are the ones with intimate knowledge and vision of the people, procedures, and structure of the branch office. Although the protection of the confidentiality, integrity, and availability of valuable information assets will be the major content of this lesson, the primary consideration for the security program is human safety. People come first; the issue of protecting the assets of the enterprise immediately follows.

---

**After this lesson, you will be able to:**

- Describe the major components of physical security for the branch office.
- Identify the basic components that establish electronic security on a network.
- Describe the features in Windows Server 2008 that you can use to satisfy specific security targets.
- Describe how to use a read-only domain controller (RODC) to provide increased security in the branch office.
- Describe how to design a Password Replication Policy to maximize security on the RODC.

---

> ■ Describe how to use the Windows Server 2008 Server Core and the Windows Server 2008 Server Core domain controller server installations to provide increased security in the branch office.
> ■ Describe how to secure data in storage on servers in the branch office.
>
> **Estimated lesson time: 50 minutes**

# Overview of Security for the Branch Office

The first component of the security policy and program used to implement security at the branch office is a definition of adequate physical security. Physical security is intended to keep intruders out and to keep the valuable information system assets in. Physical security is implemented in obvious things like solid walls, fences, doors and locks, guards and guard dogs, and internal security zones, like a secure server room with card swipes in and out, designed to provide differing levels of security as users enter the different security zones. Physical security is also implemented in more technical components, like the use of strong passwords, smart cards, and biometrics.

Next, acceptable use policies should be created to include any device or system in the facility and in any device owned by the enterprise that gets issued to the worker. One of the most effective security measures that can be implemented, after the security policy, the security program, and the acceptable use policies, is security awareness training for all users. This should cover facility safety training and an overview of the security policy. Employees should understand that they have specific responsibilities related to the security program and that they must know what the rules of the policy are. They must further understand that violation of any security policy could be grounds for termination. Employees should be constantly reminded and aware of the security concerns of the organization. For example, this can be accomplished through posters or a column in the monthly newsletter citing recent violations and threats, as well as through feedback from IT and through management, when users are identified to be in violation of acceptable use of the computers and information systems.

Security awareness training should be performed at least annually for all employees and should be provided at a higher level and more often as the role of the user rises in the organizational structure in the enterprise. Management personnel must understand their responsibility to know the relevant security policies, as well as their roles as the enforcers of the security policy in their departments. Middle management must provide enforcement at the lower levels of management, and so on.

When employees know what the acceptable use rules are and understand their responsibilities, the security structure should include auditing and monitoring of the facility and as much of the environment as is legal. It should be explained that this monitoring is for the safety and security of the employees, as well as for the assets of the enterprise.

---

**NOTE    A warning about employee monitoring**

The laws in the United States on employee monitoring vary greatly from state to state and even county to county. Typically, the employee must be aware of, and agree to, the monitoring. Furthermore, the monitoring cannot target specific individuals, which would amount to discrimination. The monitoring should be performed routinely and randomly.

Always consult the local legal department for documented guidelines on how, what, and whom can be monitored, and do not exceed these guidelines.

---

You will, of course, enable a comprehensive audit policy on the information systems. You might want to monitor by using CCTV cameras and recording devices, and you might want to record network and Internet usage for any and all employees. You might want to have access to monitor the display on the computer monitor (these can indeed be shadowed by the administration) and be able to search any hard disk drive on the corporate network. You should monitor employees' company e-mail and voicemail. You should monitor the employees any time they are on the company premises, any time they are using company-owned resources (such as cell phones and portable computers), and any time they are acting as a representative of the organization—again, only within the limits of the law. Don't forget that in most cases the organization is legally responsible, and therefore liable, for anything inappropriate that an employee does while on company business or while using any of the organization's devices.

Recording all of this information is beneficial, but it is useless unless someone is specifically responsible for the review of the audit logs, the intrusion detection system (IDS) and intrusion prevention system (IPS) logs, the videotapes, the call logs, the firewall logs, and so on. This is the difficult part. Because the reviewers are looking at the actual map of attacks, exploits, violations, and events that occurred on the system, they must decipher an understanding of what these many logs and events actually say. The responsible person must identify violations, attempted violations, and unexpected vulnerabilities in the environment and develop proposals on the implementation of new and appropriate countermeasures to mitigate the risks and defend against these attacks in the future.

Furthermore, in many cases, these logs must be tightly secured, with their integrity protected and provable, and retained in archives for several years to satisfy legal and regulatory compliance requirements.

# Securing Windows Server 2008 in the Branch Office

Now that the foundation of security is in place, including the security policies, employee safety, physical security, awareness training, and monitoring, the next security objective is the electronic security of the information systems. The threats to information systems that are covered in this section include threats from willful and malicious hacker attack, from malware, from willful or accidental modification of data or system configuration, and from privilege misuse.

# Security Overview for the Information System in the Branch Office

Each branch office implementation must be individually and carefully designed, implemented, and maintained. There are, however, several core security components that virtually every branch office network installation should include.

## Infrastructure Firewalls

The branch office network should be isolated from external networks, including the network at HQ, through one or more firewalls. They can be placed in series (one behind the other) to construct a perimeter network (also known as DMZ, demilitarized zone, and screened subnet) for public resources or resources shared with HQ. They can be placed in parallel and through different Internet service providers (ISPs) to provide redundancy for the WAN link connections to the Internet or to HQ.

## Host-Based Firewalls

In addition to the network-based firewalls, Windows Server 2003, Windows XP, Windows Vista, and Windows Server 2008 all have a built-in, host-based firewall (often called a personal firewall). In general, these host-based firewalls should all be enabled and properly configured to allow only the minimum required traffic into and out of the Windows-based computers. Windows Vista and Windows Server 2008 provide for advanced configuration in the host-based Windows Firewall with Advanced Security.

## The Intrusion Detection System/Intrusion Protection System

Another infrastructure device that you should consider on the branch office network is the Intrusion Detection System/Intrusion Protection System (IDS/IPS). These are third-party devices (or systems). The IDS monitors network traffic, logs data about the traffic, analyzes the traffic based on signatures and anomalies, recognizes potential attacks, and alerts the administrative staff to the perceived attack. The IPS does all that, but it also has the capability to react to the perceived attack. This reaction can be an adjustment to the rule base on one or more firewalls to reject the attacker's frames, or the transmission of TCP NACK to the victim, or the transmission of deauthentication frames to an 802.1x port-based authentication switch to disconnect the victim from the attacker.

## Server Hardening

The next routine security target on all computer systems is server hardening, or creating the bastion host. This reduces the attack surface of the computer by reducing the number of targets available on the system to a hacker. In general, server hardening includes the following:

- Stopping and disabling all unnecessary services and applications
- Renaming the Administrator account

- Creating a new, useless, and disabled user account named Administrator and securing it with an impossible password
- Removing or disabling all unnecessary user accounts
- Delegating remaining user accounts based on the principle of least privilege
- Requiring strong authentication of users
- Performing regular firmware, operating system, and application updates
- Installing, running, and regularly updating antivirus and anti-spyware applications
- Regularly documenting and then reconfirming the system configuration
- Implementing routine auditing on logons, network connections, object access, and system configuration changes

This is the basic hardened server configuration that should be implemented on every computer in the enterprise. However, for critical or exposed servers, you should implement additional lockdowns. They include the following:

- Deleting all nonessential executables (binaries) from the computer
- Deleting all administration tools
- Configuring a GPO to disable and further restrict unused services
- Creating scripts to lock down services and schedule them to run each hour
- Implementing a routine or process to detect changes to the system files or system configuration (you can use the Microsoft System File Checker [SFC.exe] for this purpose. A popular third-party tool named Tripwire is available to validate the integrity of system files, as well.)
- Monitoring system activity and network traffic to and from the hardened server
- Implementing more detailed auditing on logons, network connections, object access, and system configuration changes

The list could go on, but you undoubtedly get the idea. Windows Server 2008 Server Core is a specially designed, hardened server upon installation, as was described in Lesson 1, "Branch Office Deployment."

## Securing Windows Server 2008 in the Branch Office

Windows Server 2008 has introduced several significant enhancements to improve security in installations like the branch office. The most important new additions are the following:

- The Server Core server
- The read-only domain controller (RODC)
- The Password Settings Object (PSO)
- Network Access Protection
- Administrator Role Separation

Server Core and Administrator Role Separation were covered in detail in Lesson 1, "Branch Office Deployment," and NAP is covered in Chapter 5, "Designing a Network Access Strategy." The RODC and the setting of fine-grained password policies with the PSO remain to be discussed.

## The Read-Only Domain Controller

A new security-related feature in Windows Server 2008 is the RODC. It is designed for implementation in environments where:

- There is a need for local access to Active Directory by users, computers, applications, or other entities.
- The physical security of the server cannot be guaranteed.
- The server might be exposed to a hazardous network environment, such as an extranet.
- There are relatively few users.
- WAN link connectivity to the main network might be unreliable.
- Local technical support skills might be limited.

As you review that list, you will undoubtedly realize that it sounds like a  branch office environment. The RODC differs from the full DC in the following ways. The RODC:

- Holds a read-only copy of the Active Directory database.
- Participates in only one-way replication of all replication partitions, including domain data from a Windows Server 2008 DC.
- Participates in only one-way replication of schema, configuration, and application directory partitions, and the global catalog from a Windows Server 2003 DC but not the domain partition.
- Does not receive user or computer credentials (passwords) from Active Directory, by default.
- Can cache only selected user and computer credentials for accounts specified in a Password Replication Policy.
- Supports the removal of specified sensitive attributes from replication through the RODC filtered attribute set.
- Supports Administrator Role Separation.
- Supports a read-only instance of the DNS zones.

**RODC Disadvantages**    Because of the read-only nature of the RODC, it cannot be used as an operations master or a replication bridgehead server. In addition, if Active Directory–aware applications need to write data to Active Directory, the RODC cannot accept those write commands and the application's process will fail. Microsoft Exchange Server is an example of this type of application. An Active Directory write process fails if the request is sent to an RODC. Active Directory–aware applications should be tested with the RODC prior to deployment into production.

The RODC might fail to authenticate smart card logons by default. For any DC to be able to authenticate smart card logons, the DC must receive a domain controller X.509 digital certificate from a trusted certification authority. These digital certificates are typically distributed to the DCs through certificate autoenrollment. The permissions on the certificate template must be modified to allow the RODC to receive this certificate.

The RODC does not advertise properly as a time source, causing the clocks on the branch office client computers to become desynchronized. The simple solution is to configure a Windows Server 2008 full DC server as the PDC emulator operations master for the domain, making it the time master for the domain. Another solution is to manually configure a time master for the domain.

**Installing an RODC**   You need to take a few steps before you can install the first RODC in a domain:

1. Ensure that the forest functional level is Windows Server 2003 or higher. Remember that this means you must purge the forest of any Windows NT Server 4.0 and Windows 2000 Server DCs.
2. Run ADPrep/RODCPrep. This can only be done on the Schema Operations master for the forest and only by a member of the Enterprise Admins group. This step is not required if this is a new Windows Server 2008 forest. Copy the contents of the \sources\adprep folder to the schema master DC, and execute the command from there.
3. Install a Windows Server 2008 DC into the domain. This DC is the replication source for the RODC. The Windows Server 2008 DC must hold the PDC emulator operations master role and be located in the site nearest the site of the RODC, based on site link cost.

Then you can install the RODC on a Windows Server 2008 server. You can install the RODC on a Windows Server 2008 full installation server or on a Windows Server 2008 Server Core installation server. Installing the RODC on the Server Core server provides the greatest level of security because of the hardened server nature of the Server Core server.

**Delegated Installation of the RODC**   The RODC computer object can be created in, or moved to, the DC OU during the installation of the RODC, but this will require membership in the Domain Admins group in the domain for the installer. However, this level of privilege is often not desirable for users in the remote office.

Because the RODC is often located in a remote office with a nondomain administrator user as the installer, it is possible to pre-create the RODC account in the Domain Controllers OU in Active Directory Users and Computers and delegate authority to the remote, nondomain administrator installer who completes the DCPromo installation. Furthermore, you can specify details about the DCPromo installation that get stored on this unoccupied domain controller account object. These details get pushed down to the remote RODC during the DCPromo installation.

In Active Directory Users And Computers, on the Domain Controllers OU, right-click and select the Pre-Create Read-Only Domain Controller Account option, as shown in Figure 6-4. You now see the Active Directory Domain Services Installation Wizard.

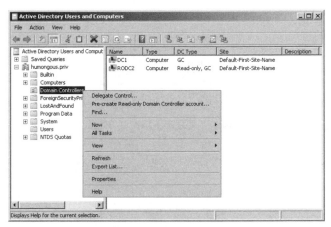

**Figure 6-4**  The delegated RODC installation

To see all configurable options for the RODC, on the Welcome page, select the Use Advanced Mode Installation check box. After a few standard DCPromo pages, such as the Network Credentials page, you are prompted to define information, such as the necessary credentials to pre-create the domain controller account, computer name, site location, and whether you want to configure the RODC to host services such as DNS or the global catalog. You can next specify the Password Replication Policy for the RODC server, as shown in Figure 6-5.

This policy defines the list of passwords that can be replicated to, and cached on, the RODC. This Password Replication Policy will be explained in more detail later in this lesson. The Active Directory Domain Services Installation Wizard next prompts you to specify which user or group of users are delegated the authority to run the DCPromo process on the Windows Server 2008 server in the remote office, as shown in Figure 6-6. The delegated users do not require any additional privileges to complete the installation.

The recommendation for granting privilege, including the privilege to install an RODC, as always, is to follow A-G-DL-P. Place user accounts into global groups, place global groups into domain local groups, and then grant the necessary privileges to the domain local group. The Summary dialog box has an Export button to generate an answer file for use in other similar unattended installations.

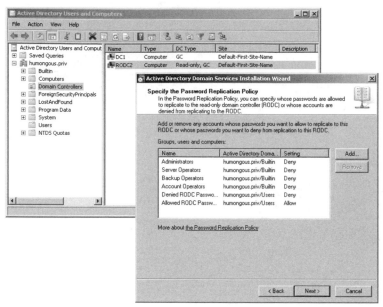

**Figure 6-5** Specifying the Password Replication Policy for the RODC installation

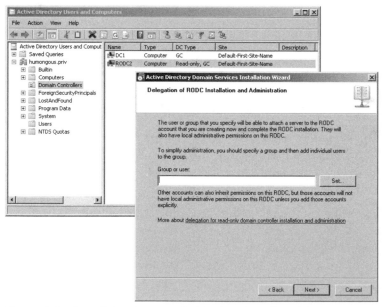

**Figure 6-6** Specifying the nonadministrator installer of the remote RODC

**Installing the RODC from Customized Media**    As you probably recall from Windows Server 2003, the DCPromo utility could be executed using the /ADV switch. This allowed the remote DC to acquire the Active Directory database (NTDS.dit) from a system state data backup copy of a DC in the same domain. This feature has been replaced in Windows Server 2008 with what is called Install From Media (IFM). By using the NTDSUTIL.exe utility with the IFM subcommand, you can create a copy of the NTDS.dit database and remove "cached secrets"—that is, passwords that you do not want to cache on the RODC server.

The RODC installation methods that can use the custom IFM media with passwords removed from the Active Directory database include the following:

- The Active Directory Installation Wizard (DCPromo.exe) where the media can be specified
- From the command line using DCPromo/ReplicationSourcePath
- Within an Answer file

**The RODC Authentication Process**    In Windows Server 2008, the authentication processes have been changed in environments like a branch office where the only DC is an RODC. When a member computer boots up or when a user attempts to log on to a domain account, the request is sent to the local DC—in this case, it is an RODC. The RODC does not cache user or computer credentials by default. The RODC, acting as a relay agent, will then refer the authentication request across the WAN link to a Windows Server 2008 full (writable) DC in the nearest site. This can be slow and will fail the authentication process if the WAN link is down.

To improve performance and reliability, an administrator can create a Password Replication Policy that will replicate the passwords of the users and computers in the remote branch office to the branch office RODC. Now when a member computer boots up or when a user attempts to log on to a domain account, the local RODC can complete the authentication process within the local branch office. A different Password Replication Policy can be created for each RODC.

If a member computer boots up or a user attempts to log on to a domain account and the local RODC does not have its credentials cached, after the authentication process completes through the referral process, the RODC will request that the writable DC replicate the credentials to the RODC for caching. If the account (user or computer) is on the Allowed list of the Password Replication Policy for that RODC, the credentials are replicated from the writable DC to the database of the RODC in the branch office.

If the account is not on the Allowed List of the Password Replication Policy for that RODC, the credentials are not replicated from the writable DC to the RODC, and the authentication process will need to be completed over the WAN link through the referral process every time.

The Password Replication Policy maintains four lists. They are:

- **Allowed List** These passwords (secrets or credentials) can be replicated to the RODC.
- **Denied List** These passwords (secrets or credentials) cannot be replicated to the RODC.
- **Revealed List** A list of accounts whose passwords are cached on RODCs. This list can be used to reset passwords of accounts on RODC servers that become compromised.
- **Authenticated List** A list of accounts that have been successfully authenticated against the RODC.

You can view these lists in Active Directory Users and Computers by displaying the properties of the RODC server's computer object. In the Password Replication Policy tab, you can see the allowed and denied entities by examining the Setting column, as shown in Figure 6-7.

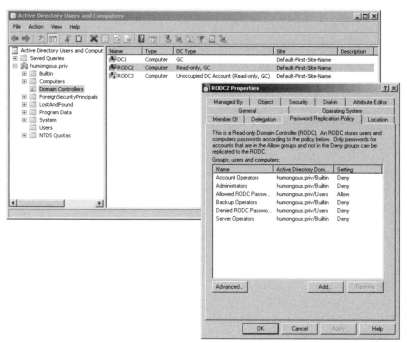

**Figure 6-7** Accessing the Allowed and Denied Lists on the RODC

Click the Advanced button to access the Revealed and Authenticated Lists, as shown in Figure 6-8.

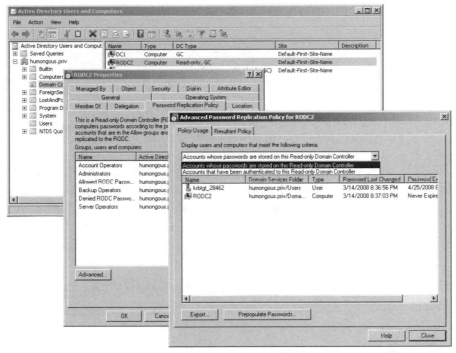

**Figure 6-8**    Accessing the Revealed and Authenticated Lists on the RODC

**Replication Concerns with the RODC**    As stated previously, the RODC can receive domain replication data only from a Windows Server 2008 full (writable) DC. The site with the RODC must be connected to a site with a Windows Server 2008 full (writable) DC in the same domain, by a site link with the lowest cost. If the nearest site (again, based on site link cost) does not contain a Windows Server 2008 full (writable) DC in the same domain, domain data replication to the RODC will fail.

The RODC can receive all other partitions of replication from a Windows Server 2008 DC or a Windows Server 2003 DC.

**Automatic Site Coverage**    Sites are defined in Active Directory by mapping IP subnets to specific sites. Active Directory clients authenticate against and otherwise access DCs in their local site, based on their IP addresses. To ensure that all Active Directory clients are able to identify the appropriate local DC, DNS SRV records are created for DCs and mapped to each site within the DNS zone for the domain.

Because it is possible to create a site without placing a domain controller in the site, Windows 2000 Server, Windows Server 2003, and Windows Server 2008 perform a service called automatic site coverage. If a site is recognized to be without a DC, a DC in the nearest site, based on site link cost, registers a service location (SRV) record for the remote site. This allows the Active Directory clients in the remote site without a local DC to connect to the nearest DC to their site.

However, Windows 2000 Server and Windows Server 2003 do not recognize a Windows Server 2008 RODC and might register a SRV record for a remote site, with only an RODC in it. This is a problem. In DNS for the branch office site there is a SRV record for the RODC that is actually in the branch office site and a SRV record for a Windows 2000 Server DC or a Windows Server 2003 DC in a site remote from the branch office. With DNS round robin (enabled by default), 50 percent of the time Active Directory clients in the branch office site will commute the WAN link to access Active Directory when they have their own RODC locally. This causes increased and unnecessary traffic on the WAN link, degrades performance, and can cause Active Directory–related failures for clients in the branch office site if the WAN link is down.

At the time of this writing, Microsoft recommends using one of five adjustments to resolve this problem:

- Wait for a hotfix from Microsoft.
- Use only Windows Server 2008 DCs in the site nearest to the RODC site.
- Disable automatic site coverage on the Windows 2000 Server DCs and the Windows Server 2003 DCs.
- Adjust the weight of the Windows Server 2003 DC SRV records (this is only a partial solution).
- Use a GPO to adjust the weight of the Windows Server 2003 DC SRV records (this is only a partial solution).

**RODC Compromise**    The main reason to use the RODC is the increased threat of compromise of the DC in an unsecure environment, either by physical theft or access of the system or electronic attack. If the RODC is stolen or becomes otherwise compromised and the hacker cracks into the Active Directory database, the hacker has access to only a few account passwords, so the amount of accounts potentially compromised is reduced. By using the Revealed List for the RODC in Active Directory Users and Computers, you can quickly reset the potentially compromised passwords.

Because the RODC cannot replicate to other DCs, there is no risk of a hacker modifying anything in Active Directory, such as permissions and group membership, and then poisoning the legitimate Active Directory through replication.

If your RODC is stolen, you can easily delete the RODC computer object in Active Directory Users and Computers without a successful DCPromo to remove the DC from Active Directory and without using the NTDSUTIL MetadataCleanup command. (Using the NTDSUTIL MetadataCleanup command to remove Active Directory objects leaves broken links from processes that refer to the now removed object. These broken links will generate numerous errors about the missing object in event logs of DCs for the life of the domain.) To delete the RODC computer object, in Active Directory Users And Computers, right-click the RODC computer object in the Domain Controllers OU, and select Delete. Click OK to close the Warning message dialog box. You can then export a list of all accounts that were cached on the RODC and force the resetting of user and computer passwords for all accounts that were cached on the RODC, as shown in Figure 6-9.

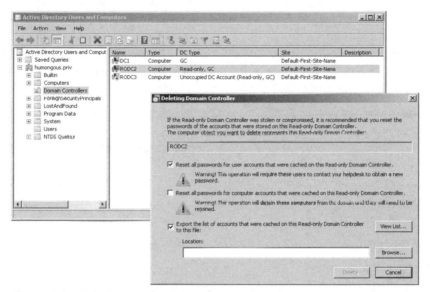

**Figure 6-9**   Deleting a stolen RODC from Active Directory Users and Computers

To summarize, a Windows Server 2008 domain controller in the branch office will maximize performance by having a local copy of all passwords, accepting Active Directory changes, and performing two-way replication. But it also maximizes the amount of sensitive data loss and the risk of poisoning the legitimate Active Directory in the case of compromise.

A Windows Server 2008 RODC in the branch office will support most Active Directory requirements in the branch office while minimizing the amount of sensitive data loss and the risk of poisoning the legitimate Active Directory in the case of compromise. The more accounts you cache, the better the performance but the greater the risk of exposure. The fewer accounts you cache, the poorer the performance but the less the risk of exposure.

Installing the RODC on a Windows Server 2008 Server Core server in the branch office provides the greatest level of security in the branch office by reducing the attack surface of the server and minimizing the amount of sensitive data loss and the risk of poisoning the legitimate Active Directory in the case of compromise.

The RODC supports delegated installation, as well as Administrator Role Separation for increased security.

## The Password Settings Object

New to Microsoft Windows Server 2008 is the ability to define different password and account lockout policies to users in the domain. This support for different policies for different users is called fine-grained password policies. In earlier versions of Windows, only one password and account lockout policy could be effective for all users in the domain. It is a common concern that different users in the domain, like the users in a branch office, require different strengths of passwords and more or less strict account lockout policies. These differing password policies are defined in Password Settings Objects (PSOs) and are applied to users and (preferably) groups of users. PSOs cannot be applied to computer objects or to OUs.

To utilize fine-grained password policies in the branch office, the domain functional level must be set to Windows Server 2008. This requires that all DCs in the domain run Windows Server 2008. Next, create one or more global security groups, one for each different PSO required in the branch office, and populate the group(s) with the appropriate users. Chapter 4, "Planning a Terminal Services Infrastructure," explains in detail how to configure fine-grained password policies.

Using fine-grained password policies, you can configure values, including the following:

- Maximum Password Age
- Minimum Password Age
- Minimum Password Length
- Password History
- Password Complexity
- Reversible Encryption Enabled
- Account Lockout Threshold
- Account Lockout Window
- Account Lockout Duration
- Users or global security groups to which the PSO applies

If you don't like ADSI Edit, you can use LDIFDE. LDIFDE uses a script to configure the new PSO. Save the following script to an ASCII text file and apply an .ldf file extension. Adjust the parameters as desired. For example, you will need to replace the domain name specified in the "dn:" line with your domain name.

```
dn: CN=BoPSO, CN=Password Settings
      Container,CN=System,DC=dc1,DC=litware,DC=internal
changetype: add
objectClass: msDS-PasswordSettings
msDS-MaximumPasswordAge:-1728000000000
msDS-MinimumPasswordAge:-864000000000
msDS-MinimumPasswordLength:8
msDS-PasswordHistoryLength:24
msDS-PasswordComplexityEnabled:TRUE
msDS-PasswordReversibleEncryptionEnabled:FALSE
msDS-LockoutObservationWindow:-18000000000
msDS-LockoutDuration:-18000000000
msDS-LockoutThreshold:0
msDS-PasswordSettingsPrecedence:10
msDS-PSOAppliesTo:CN=BOusers,CN=Users,DC=dc1,DC=litware,DC=internal
```

The time values are calculated using the I8 format. The I8 format breaks the time units into negative 100 nanoseconds (billionths of a second), so all forward-looking time values must be negative. To convert time into I8 values:

- Multiply minutes by -6,000,000,000.
- Multiply hours by -36,000,000,000.
- Multiply days by -864,000,000,000.

After you create the PSO, you can adjust the users and groups to which it is applied by using Active Directory Users and Computers. Complete the following steps:

1. Under the View menu item, select Advanced Features.
2. Expand the Active Directory Users And Computers tree to <Domain Name>, System, and then select the Password Settings Container.
3. In the right pane, right-click the PSO and choose Properties.
4. In the Attribute Editor tab, select the msDS-PsoAppliesTo attribute and click Edit.
5. Add the distinguished name of the user or global security group to which you want to apply the PSO or remove the desired entry.

Fine-grained password policies allow administrators to define unique password and account lockout policies for users and global security groups in a domain. They are well-suited for application to users in the branch office environment, which commonly requires a different level of security.

---

**MORE INFO   Creating the Password Settings Object**

For more detail on the creation of the PSO, see the following Technet article:
*http://technet2.microsoft.com/windowsserver2008/en/library/2199dcf7-68fd-4315*
*-87cc-ade35f8978ea1033.mspx?mfr=true.*

---

## Security for Data in Storage

Another area of security for the nonsecure branch office that you should address is security for data in storage. If a computer is stolen from a branch office, the thief could crack user accounts on the system and access data stored locally on the hard disk drives. If the thief removes the hard disk drives from the original computer and mounts them in another computer where he or she is the administrator, the thief can access all the content. Windows Server 2008 provides two ways to secure this stored data:

- The Encrypting File System (EFS)
- BitLocker

**The Encrypting File System (EFS)**   EFS was introduced in Windows 2000. It provides encryption for data files and folders only. It requires that the underlying volume (partition) be formatted with NT file system (NTFS). It uses self-generated X.509 digital certificates associated with the user account to secure encryption keys for the encrypted content. Ultimately, one accesses the decryption key by knowing the user's password. If the hacker can crack the password, the hacker can decrypt all of the user's EFS protected content.

By default, the local administrator (standalone) or the domain administrator (domain member) is the EFS recovery agent and can decrypt any EFS-secured content. EFS cannot be applied to system or AD DS–related files. All other users who attempt to access another user's EFS content receive an Access Denied error, even if proper permissions are granted.

**BitLocker**   BitLocker was introduced in Windows Vista and is available in Windows Server 2008. A specific partition structure must be configured prior to the installation of the operating system in order for BitLocker to be available for implementation on a system. BitLocker encrypts the entire volume and can be applied to system, boot, and data volumes. BitLocker encryption remains intact even if the hard disk drive is installed in another computer and is mounted by another operating system.

---

**NOTE   BitLocker**

Use BitLocker if you need to secure the NTDS.dit database.

---

BitLocker is based on the Trusted Platform Module (TPM), currently version 1.2. TPM is a microchip that holds the encryption/decryption key and a piece of code in the BIOS used to perform the encryption/decryption process on the specified disk volumes. You can also implement BitLocker on systems without TPM support by storing the encryption/decryption key on a USB thumb drive.

In either case, a recovery key or recovery password, or both, should be exported to external media in case the original encryption/decryption key(s) are lost. By default, no recovery information is backed up. The recovery password is a 48-character numeric value that can be typed into the BitLocker Recovery Console. The recovery key is stored on a USB thumb drive and can be accessed by the BitLocker Recovery Console. In addition, you can generate and store the recovery passwords in AD DS by means of a GPO. The recovery key and recovery password should be securely stored separate from the computer.

---

**NOTE** **BitLocker volume recovery**

For detailed instructions on backing up BitLocker recovery keys in AD DS and on the BitLocker recovery process, see the following Technet article: *http://technet2.microsoft.com/WindowsVista/en /library/3dbad515-5a32-4330-ad6f-d1fb6dfcdd411033.mspx?mfr=true.*

---

## Securing the Branch Office with Network Access Protection

In Windows Server 2008, administrators can use Network Access Protection (NAP) to ensure that remote, local, and branch office clients meet minimum security and configuration compliance requirements for secure connections to branch office and HQ networks. NAP checks the client's health status regarding the state of its firewall, updates, antivirus protection, and anti-spyware protection for the Windows XP SP3, Windows Vista, and Windows Server 2008 operating systems.

---

**NOTE** **Network Access Protocol**

NAP is covered in detail in Chapter 5.

---

# Lesson Summary

- Introduce all the requisite physical security measures in the branch office to establish a reasonably secure physical environment.
- Reduce the number of passwords that might be exposed in the branch office by using an RODC, along with a minimal list of objects in the Password Replication Policy for that RODC.
- Implement the delegated installation of the RODC by pre-creating the RODC account in Active Directory Users and Computers.
- Create custom NTDS.dit content on installation media using the IFM subcommand in NTDSUTIL.exe. IFM stands for installation from media. This replaces the DCPromo/ adv switch used by Windows Server 2003.
- Implement Administrator Role Separation to limit the administrative privileges to the operating system only and not to the AD DS.
- Implement an RODC on a Windows Server 2008 Server Core server to reduce the attack surface of the RODC.

- Understand the need for a Windows Server 2008 full DC in the site nearest to the RODC.
- Consider the impact of automatic site coverage on the registration of SRV records for the site by Windows Server 2003 DCs in nearby sites.
- Implement fine-grained password policies by creating a Password Settings Object and assigning it to users and global security groups.
- Use EFS to encrypt data content while in storage.
- Use BitLocker to encrypt the operating system, the Active Directory database file NTDS.dit, and data content. This protects the operating system's Active Directory database and data even if the drive is mounted in another computer.
- Archive the BitLocker recovery keys in Active Directory to recover data if the TPM module on a system fails.

## Lesson Review

You can use the following questions to test your knowledge of the information in Lesson 2, "Branch Office Server Security." The questions are also available on the companion CD if you prefer to review them in electronic form.

---

**NOTE  Answers**

Answers to these questions and explanations of why each answer choice is correct or incorrect are located in the "Answers" section at the end of the book.

---

1. What type of domain controller should be implemented in the branch office for maximum security?
    - **A.** RODC on a Windows Server full installation
    - **B.** RODC on a Server Core domain controller
    - **C.** Full (writable) domain controller on a Windows Server full installation
    - **D.** Full (writable) domain controller on a Server Core domain controller
2. How can you ensure that replication will successfully occur to a site with only one Windows Server 2008 RODC domain controller?
    - **A.** Place a Windows Server 2008 full (writable) DC in the site nearest to the RODC.
    - **B.** Place a Windows Server 2008 RODC in the site nearest to the RODC.
    - **C.** Make the site link cost to the adjacent site higher than all other costs on site links.
    - **D.** Construct a site link bridge.

3. What is the first action to take if you receive a report that one of the branch offices has had an RODC stolen?

   A. Implement Administrator Role Separation on the replacement RODC.

   B. Use ADSI Edit to construct a new Password Settings Object (PSO).

   C. Construct a new IFM disk.

   D. In Active Directory Users and Computers, delete the RODC.

# Chapter Review

To further practice and reinforce the skills you learned in this chapter, you can perform the following tasks:

- Review the chapter summary.
- Complete the case scenarios. These scenarios set up real-world situations involving the topics of this chapter and ask you to create a solution.
- Complete the suggested practices.
- Take a practice test.

# Chapter Summary

- The branch office has an increased number of physical and network vulnerabilities.
- The resource access needs of the branch office users can vary greatly and must be carefully considered and planned accordingly.
- The branch office will have specific network infrastructure system and service requirements that must be carefully considered and planned.
- The branch office deployment must be designed for the securest implementation and provide only the required services.
- You can restructure the branch office within Active Directory as necessary to maximize security.
- You can provide redundancy of services by installing multisite cluster nodes in the branch office.
- You can provide redundancy of data by configuring DFS Replication in the branch office.
- Placement of a Windows Server Update Services (WSUS) server in the branch office minimizes update-related network traffic to HQ and to the Internet.
- Installing Windows Server 2008 Server Core servers in the branch office reduces the attack surface of the servers.
- You can install RODC domain controllers in the branch office to reduce the risk of exposing passwords.
- Delegate installation of the RODC by pre-creating the RODC account in Active Directory Users and Computers.
- Use Administrator Role Separation to give the branch office administrator the privilege of maintaining the Windows Server 2008 but not to have access to modify Active Directory.
- Use VPNs to secure data in transit between the branch office and HQ.

- The different types of VPNs supported by Windows Server 2008 are PPTP, L2TP, IPsec, and the new SSTP.
- You can use EFS to secure data in storage in the branch office.
- You can use BitLocker to secure data in storage for the operating system, the Active Directory database, and data in the branch office.
- You should archive BitLocker keys in Active Directory to support BitLocker recovery in case the TPM module fails on a computer.

# Case Scenarios

In the following case scenarios, you will apply what you've learned about designing a branch office infrastructure. You can find answers to these questions in the "Answers" section at the end of this book.

## Case Scenario 1:  Contoso Trucking

Contoso Trucking is a trucking company with its HQ in Oshkosh, Wisconsin. Contoso will be adding branch offices in Syracuse and Schenectady, New York. There will be 150 users in Syracuse and 90 users in Schenectady. The tracking program used to schedule trucks and drivers will be required in each office and uses the Active Directory database. All servers in HQ run Windows Server 2008. The intrusion detection system (IDS) on your HQ network shows repeated attacks from your competitor. You have hired a junior administrator for each location.

1. What type of servers should be used in the branch offices?
2. What type of domain controllers should be used in the branch offices?
3. What privileges should the administrators in the branch offices be granted?

## Case Scenario 2:  Contoso Trucking, Part 2

After the two new branch offices are up and running, you grow concerned that the servers in Syracuse could easily be stolen. Furthermore, you decide that the users in Schenectady should have a stronger password policy because of the concentration of financial information they use and process daily.

1. How can you improve security on the operating system and data files that reside on the DCs in Syracuse?
2. How should you satisfy the need for a stronger password policy for users in Schenectady?

## Case Scenario 3:  Contoso Trucking, Part 3

You plan to add another office in Saskatchewan. The junior administrator in Saskatchewan will be buying the server that is to be the local RODC there.

1.  What steps should you take to securely deploy the new RODC in Saskatchewan?
2.  How should you configure delegated authority for the administrator in Saskatchewan?

# Suggested Practices

To help you successfully master the exam objectives presented in this chapter, complete the following tasks.

## Branch Office Deployment

The branch office introduces many challenges regarding functionality, performance, reliability, and security. The following practices will help you understand the many new features of Windows Server 2008 that improve branch office deployment.

- **Practice 1**    On a Windows Server 2008 full installation, implement server hardening techniques, including stopping and disabling services, killing unnecessary applications (especially those that launch at startup), installing all required operating system and application updates, configuring automatic updates, installing antivirus software, installing anti-spyware software, enabling and verifying settings on the firewall, configuring auditing of successful and failed logon attempts and successful and failed object access on a test folder, documenting the system configuration and storing it apart from the server, and minimizing the number of user accounts—deleting and disabling as many as possible.

  Install a Windows Server 2008 RODC and explore the relevant interfaces.

  Configure a Password Replication Policy with two or three user accounts allowed for replication and two or three user accounts denied for replication.

  Install a Windows Server 2008 Server Core and explore the relevant interfaces.

  Install a Windows Server 2008 RODC on a Windows Server 2008 Server Core server.

  Configure Administrator Role Separation on an RODC server.

  Create a PSO and assign it to a sample global security group.

  Perform a fresh installation of Windows Server 2008 full installation and configure it for BitLocker. Remember that a specific partition structure must be created prior to the operating system installation.

# Read a White Paper

- **Practice 2** Read a white paper on the scenarios for installing and configuring the Windows Server 2008 RODC at:

  *http://technet2.microsoft.com/windowsserver2008/en/library/2199dcf7-68fd-4315-87cc -ade35f8978ea1033.mspx?mfr=true*

  Read a white paper on the scenarios for configuring Windows Server 2008 Server Core at:

  *http://technet2.microsoft.com/windowsserver2008/en/library/47a23a74-e13c-46de-8d30 -ad0afb1eaffc1033.mspx?mfr=true*

  Read a white paper on the scenarios for configuring fine-grained password policies at:

  *http://technet2.microsoft.com/windowsserver2008/en/library/2199dcf7-68fd-4315-87cc -ade35f8978ea1033.mspx?mfr=true*

  Read a white paper on the scenarios for configuring Administrator Role Separation at:

  *http://technet2.microsoft.com/windowsserver2008/en/library/c0a45344-f77b-4ea6-8685 -37a51f853b571033.mspx?mfr=true*

  Read a white paper on the scenarios for configuring BitLocker at:

  *http://technet2.microsoft.com/windowsserver2008/en/library/2d130e11-a796-43b7-98ed -d389cad285f51033.mspx?mfr=true*

# Take a Practice Test

The practice tests on this book's companion CD offer many options. For example, you can test yourself on just one exam objective, or you can test yourself on all the 70-647 certification exam content. You can set up the test so that it closely simulates the experience of taking a certification exam, or you can set it up in study mode so that you can look at the correct answers and explanations after you answer each question.

---

**MORE INFO**  **Practice tests**

For details about all the practice test options available, see the "How to Use the Practice Tests" section in this book's introduction.

---

# Chapter 7

# Planning Terminal Services and Application Deployment

Application deployment would be a simple affair if all you needed to do was deploy the same set of applications to all users in your environment. The realities of software licensing mean that large organizations can realize significant cost savings by ensuring that only those workers who need an application have it deployed to their computers. In this chapter, you will learn how to plan the distribution of applications to the workers in your environment by using several tools, each of which is appropriate for a certain set of circumstances. Ways discussed in this chapter of deploying applications to users include Terminal Services, System Center Essentials 2007, System Center Configuration Manager 2007, and traditional deployment through Active Directory Domain Services (AD DS) software publishing functionality.

### Exam objectives in this chapter:
- Plan for Terminal Services.
- Plan for application delivery.

### Lessons in this chapter:

- Lesson 1: Planning a Terminal Services Deployment . . . . . . . . . . . . . . . . . . . . . . . . 334
- Lesson 2: Planning Application Deployment . . . . . . . . . . . . . . . . . . . . . . . . . . . . . 348

## Before You Begin

Ensure that you have installed a Windows Server 2008 Enterprise domain controller named Glasgow as described in Chapter 1, "Planning Name Resolution and Internet Protocol Addressing." No additional configuration is required for this chapter.

# Lesson 1: Planning a Terminal Services Deployment

Planning the deployment of Terminal Services in your enterprise environment means taking into consideration licensing, server resilience, how clients connect, and how applications are deployed to the terminal server. In this lesson, you will learn how each of these factors will influence the plans you develop to deploy Terminal Services in your own organization's enterprise environment.

> **After this lesson, you will be able to:**
> - Plan Terminal Services infrastructure.
> - Plan Terminal Services licensing.
> - Plan Terminal Services session availability.
> - Plan client connections to Terminal Services.
>
> **Estimated lesson time: 40 minutes**

## Planning a Terminal Services Deployment

As an experienced enterprise administrator, you are aware of the role Terminal Services plays on your organizational network. You understand how client computers connect to terminal servers, how to install applications on a terminal server, and the basics of managing and configuring an individual terminal server. In this lesson, you will go beyond the maintenance and configuration of this technology and learn how to plan the deployment of Terminal Services so that it best meets the needs of your organization.

The first step in planning a deployment is understanding how the following Terminal Services components fit together:

- **Terminal server** The server itself is the core component of a Terminal Services deployment. This is the server that clients connect to so they can access their applications.
- **Terminal server farm** A terminal server farm is a collection of terminal servers, used to provide high availability and load balancing to clients on the organizational network. Client connections to terminal server farms are mediated by Terminal Services session directory servers. Terminal server farms are more likely to be deployed at large sites than are individual terminal servers.
- **License servers** License servers provide Terminal Services client access licenses (TS CALs) to terminal servers on the network. Unless a license server is deployed, clients are able to connect to Terminal Services for only a limited amount of time.
- **Terminal Services Gateway servers (TS Gateway)** These servers provide access to terminal servers to clients on untrusted networks. In enterprise networks, you can use a TS Gateway server as a bridge between the standard internal network and a terminal server farm on a network protected by server isolation policies.

When planning the deployment of terminal servers and terminal server farms, ensure that the software the clients use to connect to a terminal server is installed after the Terminal Server role is deployed. Many applications perform a check during installation to determine whether the target of the installation is a terminal server. In some cases, different executable files will be installed when the installation target is a terminal server as opposed to a normal, standalone computer. Alternatively, some applications will generate a pop-up dialog box informing you that installing the application on a terminal server is not recommended and that the vendor does not support this deployment configuration.

Applications that are deployed on a terminal server might conflict with one another in unexpected ways. Your Terminal Services deployment plan should include a testing period so that you can verify that each terminal server's application configuration does not lead to unforeseen conflicts. If conflicts are detected, you will need to plan either to deploy conflicting applications on separate terminal servers or to deploy applications by using Microsoft SoftGrid Application Virtualization, which is covered in more detail in Chapter 8, "Server and Application Virtualization."

## Terminal Services Licensing

Perhaps the most critical aspect of planning the deployment of Terminal Services in enterprise environments is ensuring that licensing is configured appropriately. The loss of one terminal server in an environment in which there are 100 terminal servers is a potential problem. The loss of a license server that has an enterprise scope in an environment in which there are 100 terminal servers is a potential disaster.

All clients that connect to a terminal server require a TS CAL. This license is not included with Windows Vista and is not a part of the standard CALs that you use when licensing a Windows-based server. TS CALs are managed by a Terminal Services license server. When planning a Terminal Services deployment, answer the following questions when considering the deployment of a Terminal Services license server:

- What is the scope of the license server? Will it service clients in the domain or workgroup or manage the licenses for all clients in the forest?
- How will the license server be activated with Microsoft? How will additional licenses be purchased and installed?
- How many license servers are required to service the needs of your organization?
- What type of licenses will be deployed?

### License Server Scope

The license server's discovery scope determines which terminal servers and clients can automatically detect the license server. You configure the license server scope during the installation of the Terminal Services License Server role service, as shown in Figure 7-1. You can change the scope after it is set. The three possible discovery scopes are This Workgroup, This Domain, and The Forest.

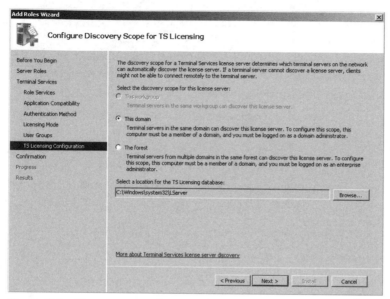

**Figure 7-1**   License server discovery scope

- **This Workgroup**   This scope is not available if the license server is joined to an Active Directory domain. This discovery scope is most often installed on a computer that hosts the Terminal Services role. Terminal servers and clients in the same workgroup can automatically discover this license server.

- **This Domain**   The domain discovery scope enables terminal servers and clients that are members of the same domain to acquire TS CALs automatically. Plan to use this scope if TS CALs in your organization are going to be purchased and managed on a per-domain basis.

- **The Forest**   The forest discovery scope enables terminal servers and clients located anywhere in the same Active Directory forest to acquire TS CALs automatically. You should plan to use this scope when licensing issues are handled on an organizational level rather than at the domain level.

For example, if your organization has a single forest with a separate domain for each state division, but all software purchasing and licensing is handled centrally, you would plan to deploy a license server set to the forest discovery scope. This enables the people responsible for licensing to check a central location to determine your organization's compliance with its Terminal Services licensing responsibilities. It saves them from having to check each state division's Terminal Services license server. If, however, your nationwide organization has software and purchasing managed on a regional basis, it makes sense to deploy Terminal Services licensing servers on the same basis. In that case, you would plan to deploy Terminal Services license servers by using the domain discovery scope.

## License Server Activation

Another important component of a Terminal Services deployment plan is choosing a license server activation method. Before a Terminal Services license server can issue TS CALs, it must be activated with Microsoft in a procedure similar to Windows Product Activation. During the activation process, a Microsoft-issued digital certificate validating both server ownership and identity is installed on the TS license server. This certificate will be used in transactions with Microsoft for the acquisition and installation of further licenses. As shown in Figure 7-2, a license server can be activated through three methods.

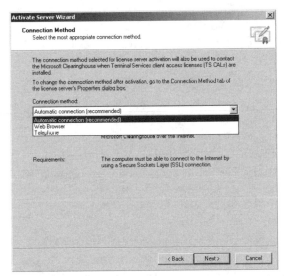

**Figure 7-2**   Three methods of activating a Terminal Services license server

The first method occurs transparently through a wizard, like Windows Product Activation. This method requires the server to be able to connect to the Internet directly, using a Secure Sockets Layer (SSL) connection, which means that it will not work with certain firewall configurations.

The second method involves navigating to a Web page. This method can be used on a computer other than the license server and is appropriate in environments in which the network infrastructure does not support a direct SSL connection from the internal network to an Internet host.

The third method involves placing a telephone call to a Microsoft clearinghouse operator. This is a toll-free call from most locations. The method you use for activation will also validate TS CALs that are purchased at a later date, although you can change this method by editing the Terminal Services license server's properties. If a license server is not activated, it can issue temporary CALs only. These CALs are valid for 90 days.

When planning disaster recovery contingencies for your Terminal Services deployment, consider that if the certificate acquired during the activation process expires or becomes corrupted, you might need to deactivate the license server. A deactivated license server cannot issue permanent Terminal Services Per Device CALs, although it can still issue Terminal Services Per User CALs and temporary Terminal Services Per Device CALs. You can deactivate Terminal Services license servers by using the automatic method or over the telephone, but you cannot deactivate them by using a Web browser on another computer.

## Terminal Services Client Access Licenses

When planning the deployment of Terminal Services, you must determine which sort of TS CAL is most appropriate for your organization. A Windows Server 2008 Terminal Services license server can issue two types of TS CALs: the Per Device CAL and the Per User CAL. The differences between these licenses are as follows:

- **Terminal Services Per Device CAL**   The Terminal Services Per Device CAL gives a specific computer or device the ability to connect to a terminal server. Terminal Services Per Device CALs are automatically reclaimed by the Terminal Services licensing server after a random period between 52 and 89 days. This will not affect clients that regularly use these CALs because any available CAL will simply be reissued the next time the device reconnects. In the event that you run out of available CALs, you can revoke 20 percent of issued Terminal Services Per Device CALs for a specific operating system by using the Terminal Services Licensing Manager console on the license server. For example, 20 percent of issued Windows Vista Terminal Services Per Device CALs can be revoked or 20 percent of issued Microsoft Windows Server 2003 Per Device CALs can be revoked at any one time. Revocation is not a substitute for ensuring that your organization has purchased the requisite number of Terminal Services Per Device CALs for your environment.

- **Terminal Services Per User CAL**   A Terminal Services Per User CAL gives a specific user account the ability to access any terminal server in an organization from any computer or device. Terminal Services Per User CALs are not enforced by Terminal Services licensing, and it is possible to have more client connections occurring in an organization than actual Terminal Services Per User CALs installed on the license server. Failure to have the appropriate number of Terminal Services Per User CALs is a violation of license terms. You can determine the number of Terminal Services Per User CALs in use by using the Terminal Services Licensing Manager console on the license server. You can either examine the *Reports* node or use the console to create a Per User CAL Usage report.

When planning the deployment of Terminal Services license servers, remember that TS CALs can be purchased directly from the server if the terminal server is capable of making a direct SSL connection to the Internet. Alternatively, it is possible to use a separate computer that is connected to the Internet to purchase TS CALs by navigating to a Web site or to use a telephone to call the Microsoft clearinghouse directly.

---

**MORE INFO**   **More on TS CALs**

To learn more about TS CALs, see the following TechNet Web site: *http://technet2.microsoft.com /windowsserver2008/en/library/aa57d355-5b86-4229-9296-a7fcce77dea71033.mspx?mfr=true.*

---

## Backing Up and Restoring a License Server

To back up a Terminal Services license server, you need to back up the system state data and the folder in which the Terminal Services licensing database is installed. You can use Review Configuration, shown in Figure 7-3, to determine the location of the Terminal Services licensing database. To restore the license server, rebuild the server, and reinstall the Terminal Services Licensing Server role, restore the system state data, and then restore the Terminal Services licensing database. When restored to a different computer, unissued licenses will not be restored, and you will need to contact the Microsoft clearinghouse to get the licenses reissued.

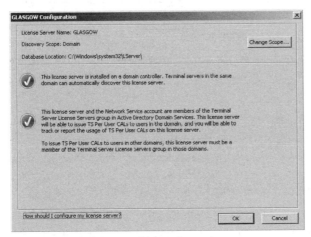

**Figure 7-3**   Reviewing the configuration

## License Server Deployment

When planning the deployment of Windows Server 2008 terminal servers in an environment with Terminal Services running on earlier versions of a Microsoft-based server operating system, consider that Windows Server 2003 Terminal Services license servers and Microsoft Windows 2000 Server Terminal Services license servers cannot issue licenses to Windows Server 2008 terminal servers. Windows Server 2008 license servers, however, support the licensing requirements of earlier versions of Terminal Services. If your organization's Windows Server 2003 terminal servers will coexist with Windows Server 2008 terminal servers for a time, upgrade your organization's license servers to Windows Server 2008 so that they can support both the new and existing terminal servers.

## License Server High Availability

When planning a high availability strategy for license servers, plan the deployment of two separate license servers per scope and install 50 percent of the TS CALs on each license server. Because the location of license servers is published within AD DS, it is not necessary to use a technology such as Domain Name System (DNS) round robin, Network Load Balancing, or Failover Clustering for the deployment of license servers. Your deployment plan for license servers should include regular backups so that if a license server does fail, the purchased licenses can be quickly recovered and redeployed. Remember that licenses that have been installed but not issued will be lost when a server is recovered. It is possible to recover these licenses from the Microsoft clearinghouse, but your license deployment plan should ensure that only the required number of licenses is purchased. You should not purchase a significant number of extra licenses for possible future use. It is easier to purchase those licenses when they will actually be used than worry about recovering unused licenses if the license server fails.

---

**Quick Check**

1. Which type of TS CAL can be revoked?
2. At what point should you install the applications that will be used by Terminal Services clients on the terminal server?

**Quick Check Answers**

1. Per device client access licenses can be revoked.
2. After the Terminal Services server role has been installed on the server.

---

# Deploying Applications Using Terminal Services Web Access

Terminal Services Web Access (TS Web Access) enables clients to connect to a terminal server through a Web page link rather than by entering the terminal server address in the Remote Desktop Connection client software. This enables you to deploy applications through the publication of URLs, which can be distributed through Group Policy.

Unlike the similar functionality that was available in Windows Server 2003, TS Web Access in Windows Server 2008 does not rely on an ActiveX control to provide the Remote Desktop client connection but instead uses the Remote Desktop Client (RDC) software that is installed on client computers. This means that to use TS Web Access, client computers need to be running Windows XP SP2, Windows Vista, Windows Server 2003 SP1, or Windows Server 2008.

A drawback to deploying TS Web Access in an enterprise environment is that TS Web Access must be installed on the terminal server to which it is providing access. It is not possible to connect to a second terminal server by using TS Web Access installed on the first. When considered from the perspective of planning the deployment of applications in an enterprise environment, it means you must distribute a different set of URLs to groups of clients as a method of limiting the number of simultaneous connections to TS Web Access.

In general, you should not plan to use DNS round robin or Network Load Balancing with TS Web Access. Although these technologies will balance incoming connections, they will cause problems with reconnections, with clients occasionally reconnected to servers that are not hosting a currently active session. An exception to this rule is TS Web Access servers located at branch office locations. If your organization has single TS Web Access servers deployed at each branch office location, using DNS round robin and Netmask Ordering will ensure that branch office clients will be connected to their local TS Web Access server.

## Planning the Deployment of Applications by Using RemoteApp

RemoteApp differs from a normal terminal server session in that instead of connecting to a window that displays a remote computer's desktop, an application being executed on the terminal server appears as if it's being executed on the local computer. For example, Figure 7-4 shows WordPad running both locally and as a TS RemoteApp on the same computer running Windows Vista. The visible difference between these two is that one does not have the Windows Vista borders and retains the Windows Server 2008 appearance.

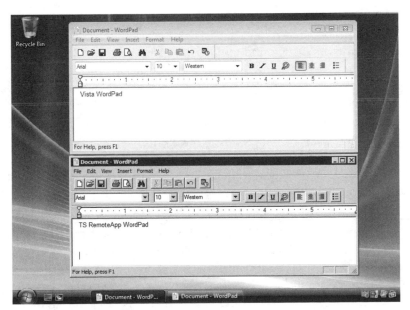

**Figure 7-4** Two different instances of WordPad

When planning the deployment of applications by using RemoteApp, you can use one of three methods:

- Create a Remote Desktop Protocol (RDP) shortcut file and distribute this file to client computers. You can do this by placing the RDP shortcut in a shared folder. This distribution method is inefficient in enterprise environments, although it can work well in smaller, branch office situations.
- Create and distribute a Windows Installer package.
- Have clients connect to the TS Web Access Web site and launch the RemoteApp application from a link on the page. The drawbacks of TS Web Access as an application deployment platform in enterprise environments were covered earlier in this lesson.

---

**MORE INFO   TS RemoteApp**

To learn more about TS RemoteApp, see *http://technet2.microsoft.com/windowsserver2008/en/library /57995ee7-e204-45a4-bcee-5d1f4a51a09f1033.mspx?mfr=true.*

---

## Planning the Deployment of Terminal Server Farms

The Terminal Server Session Broker (TS Session Broker) role service simplifies the process of adding capacity to an existing Terminal Services deployment. TS Session Broker enables load balancing of terminal servers in a group and ensures the reconnection of clients to existing sessions within that group. In TS Session Broker terminology, a group of terminal servers is called a farm.

The TS Session Broker service is a database that keeps track of terminal server sessions. TS Session Broker can work with DNS round robin or with Network Load Balancing to distribute clients to terminal servers. When configured with load balancing, the TS Session Broker service monitors all terminal servers in the group and allocates new clients to the terminal servers that have the largest amount of free resources. When used with DNS round robin, clients are still distributed; the main benefit is that TS Session Broker remembers where a client is connected. Thus, a disconnected session is reconnected appropriately rather than a new session being created on a different terminal server. The limitation of the TS Load Balancing service is that it can be used only with Windows Server 2008 terminal servers. Windows Server 2003 terminal servers cannot participate in a TS Session Broker farm.

When planning the deployment of TS Session Broker load balancing in your organization, you must ensure that clients support RDP 5.2 or later. It is also necessary to ensure that each terminal server in a particular farm has the same application configuration. Configure separate terminal server farms when it is necessary to deploy different groups of applications. For example, application A and application B conflict when deployed together on a single terminal server and must be deployed on separate ones. It would be necessary to plan the deployment of two terminal server farms, one for each application, if you need to extend client capacity by adding additional terminal servers to support each application.

---

**MORE INFO** More on configuring TS Session Broker

To learn more about configuring TS Session Broker, see *http://technet2.microsoft.com /windowsserver2008/en/library/f9fe9c74-77f5-4bba-a6b9-433d823bbfbd1033.mspx?mfr=true.*

---

# Planning the Deployment of Terminal Services Gateway Servers

Plan the deployment of Terminal Services Gateway servers (TS Gateway) when you need to enable Remote Desktop Protocol over HTTPS connections to RDP servers located on protected internal networks to clients on the Internet or untrusted networks. TS Gateway servers are not limited to screened subnets between internal networks and the Internet but can also be deployed to enable access to servers that are the subject of IPsec isolation policies. For example, there might be several terminal servers in your organization that run highly sensitive accounting software. One method of making these servers secure is to apply an IPsec isolation policy to them so that they can respond only to traffic from a very limited set of hosts. You can then deploy a TS Gateway server on your network, applying the same IPsec isolation policy to one of the server's network adapters. This protects the sensitive terminal servers with multiple layers of security. Client access to the servers is not only mediated by authorization policies on the terminal servers running the accounting software themselves but also by the policies applied on the TS Gateway server they must connect through to gain access to these sensitive terminal servers.

## Planning Connection Authorization Policies

Terminal Services connection authorization policies (TS CAPs) specify which users are allowed to connect through the TS Gateway server to resources located on a protected network. This is usually done by specifying a local group on the TS Gateway server or a group within AD DS. Groups can include user or computer accounts. You can also use TS CAPs to specify whether remote clients use password or smart card authentication to access internal network resources through the TS Gateway server. You can use TS CAPs in conjunction with network access protection (NAP) to ensure that clients pass a system health check before being allowed to connect to terminal servers on a protected network.

## Planning Resource Authorization Policies

Terminal Services resource authorization policies (TS RAPs) determine the specific resources on a protected network that an incoming TS Gateway client can connect to. When you create a TS RAP, you specify a group of computers that you want to grant access to and the group of users that you will allow this access to. For example, you could create a group of computers called AccountsComputers that will be accessible to members of the Accountants user group. To be granted access to internal resources, a remote user must meet the conditions of at least one TS CAP and at least one TS RAP.

For example, you might create a TS CAP that specifies that the Accountants group, which has authenticated using smart cards and whose computers have passed a health check and a TS RAP, can access the group of terminal servers that are subject to an IPsec isolation policy. In this situation, the accountants will be unable to make a direct connection to the terminal servers because of the IPsec isolation policy but, assuming they meet the specified conditions, will be able to access the sensitive application published on the terminal servers through the TS Gateway server.

## PRACTICE  Planning Terminal Services

Tailspin Toys is an Australian company headquartered in Sydney. The company uses a single Active Directory forest. Regional branches are located in each Australian state and territory as well as on both of New Zealand's islands. Each regional branch has its own domain in the Tailspin Toys forest. Responsibility for software purchasing and licensing is handled on a branch-by-branch basis by a designated licensing officer. The licensing officer is responsible for ensuring that his or her regional branch complies with its licensing responsibilities.

Tailspin Toys has an existing Terminal Services infrastructure, which you plan to expand as the need for applications installed on terminal servers continues to grow. Although Tailspin Toys has more than 10,000 employees spread across offices in Australia and New Zealand, only a small percentage of employees ever need to access applications hosted on terminal servers; however, they often do so from multiple computers. These employees primarily use two applications. Extensive testing has revealed that installing application Alpha and application Beta on the same terminal server leads to application instability. At present, terminal servers are deployed either with application Alpha or application Beta in each regional office. There are no plans to use Microsoft SoftGrid Application Virtualization at Tailspin Toys.

Another application that runs from Terminal Services, called application Gamma, is used with the company's financial database. This application is used at the Sydney office only. As a method of protecting the company's financial database, you are planning to move all servers that support the database, including a terminal server that hosts application Gamma, to an organizational unit (OU) named Secure Servers. The Secure Servers OU has a Group Policy object (GPO) applied that enforces a certificate-based IPsec server isolation policy. This means that the servers in this OU can communicate only with other hosts that also adhere to an appropriate certificate-based IPsec isolation policy. This provides an added layer of security to these servers, ensuring that the only computers that can communicate with them are authorized to do so.

▶ **Exercise   Plan Tailspin Toys Terminal Services Deployment**

In this exercise, you will review the business and technical requirements to plan a Terminal Services deployment for Tailspin Toys.

1. Twenty members of the accounting team need access to the front-end financial application installed on the terminal server. Which steps can you take to allow this access without giving these users access to any other server that is subject to the IPsec isolation policy?

   ❑ Install a TS Gateway server in the Sydney data center that has two network adapters.

   ❑ Configure an appropriate IPsec isolation policy for one network adapter so that it can communicate with the secured servers.

   ❑ Configure a TS RAP and a TS CAP that allow only the 20 authorized users from the accounting team to use the TS Gateway server to connect to the terminal server that hosts the database front-end application.

2. What plans should you make for the deployment of Terminal Services license servers on the Tailspin Toys network to mirror the company's current software purchasing arrangements and to ensure that a license server is still accessible in the event of a hardware failure?

   ❑ Place two license servers in each domain in the forest. Set the scope on each license server to *Domain*. License purchasing is done on a regional basis, and each domain represents a region.

   ❑ Instruct the licensing officers to purchase Per User TS CALs. These are appropriate because only a small number of users actually access Terminal Services but often do so from multiple computers.

   ❑ Instruct the license administrator in each domain to install 50 percent of the licenses on each TS license server.

3. Clients connecting to TS Alpha and TS Beta at the Sydney head office site are reporting that performance has degraded significantly. It is likely that the number of users at the head office that need to use application Alpha and application Beta will treble in the next financial year. What changes can you implement to improve capacity on TS Alpha and TS Beta to meet this projected growth in demand?

   ❑ Install two terminal server farms, one for TS Alpha and one for TS Beta. Add terminal servers to each farm as required.

   ❑ It is necessary to use separate farms because application Alpha and application Beta conflict when installed on the same terminal server. Each server in a terminal server farm must have an identical application configuration.

## Lesson Summary

- Terminal server license servers must be activated before you can install TS CALs. The discovery scope of a license server determines which clients and TS servers can automatically detect the server.

- TS Session Broker enables you to create a Terminal Services farm. TS Session Broker can be paired with DNS round robin or Network Load Balancing and ensures that disconnected clients are always reconnected to the correct session on the appropriate server.

- TS Web Access allows clients to connect to a terminal server by using a browser shortcut but still requires that the latest Remote Desktop Client software be installed.

- TS Gateway servers can allow clients from unprotected networks to connect to terminal servers on protected networks.

## Lesson Review

You can use the following questions to test your knowledge of the information in Lesson 1, "Planning a Terminal Services Deployment." The questions are also available on the companion CD if you prefer to review them in electronic form.

---

**NOTE    Answers**

Answers to these questions and explanations of why each answer choice is correct or incorrect are located in the "Answers" section at the end of the book.

---

1. You are planning the deployment of Terminal Services licensing for your organization's Australian subsidiary. Your organization has two offices, one located in Brisbane and one located in Adelaide. A data center in Hobart hosts infrastructure servers. Both the Brisbane and Adelaide offices have their own Terminal Services farms. The offices are connected by a high-speed WAN link. Each office has its own AD DS domain, and both are a part of the same forest. The forest root domain is located in the Hobart data center and does not contain standard user or computer accounts. For operational reasons, you want to ensure that CALs purchased and installed at each location are allocated to devices at that location only. Which of the following license server deployment plans should you implement?

    A. Deploy a license server to each location, and set the discovery scope of each license server to *Domain*.

    B. Deploy a license server to each location, and set the discovery scope of each license server to *Forest*.

    C. Deploy a license server to the Hobart data center, and set the discovery scope of the license server to *Forest*.

    D. Deploy a license server to the Hobart data center, and set the discovery scope of the license server to *Domain*.

2. You are planning the deployment of Terminal Services license servers, using the *Domain* scope for each of the domains in your organization's Active Directory forest. Which of the following steps do you need to take prior to installing Per User TS CALs on a TS license server?

    A. Set the forest functional level to Windows Server 2008.

    B. Set the domain functional level of each domain in the forest to Windows Server 2008.

    C. Activate the license server.

    D. Install Internet Information Services (IIS).

3. The organization that you work for is going through a period of growth. Users access business applications from client terminals. You are concerned that the growth in users will outstrip the processing capacity of the host terminal server. Which of the following solutions enables you to increase the client capacity without requiring client reconfiguration?

    A. Use Windows System Resource Manager (WSRM) to ensure that all users are able to access resources equally.

    B. Install Hyper-V on a computer running Windows Server 2008 Enterprise and add virtualized servers as required.

    C. Add terminal servers as required and reconfigure clients to use specific ones.

    D. Create a terminal server farm and add terminal servers as required.

4. You need to ensure that clients connecting to your terminal servers have passed a health check. Which of the following deployments should you implement?

    A. Install OneCare Live on the terminal servers.

    B. Implement TS Session Broker.

    C. Mediate access using a TS Gateway server.

    D. Mediate access using Internet Security and Acceleration (ISA) Server 2006.

# Lesson 2: Planning Application Deployment

A constant challenge for enterprise administrators in large organizations is ensuring that staff members within the organization have access to the specific applications they need to perform their job functions but not to applications they do not need. Just as a missing application costs the organization money in terms of lost productivity, an installed application that is never used costs the organization money in terms of licensing fees. In this lesson, you will learn about three application deployment technologies that can simplify the rollout of important productivity software to users in your enterprise environment. You will learn the benefits and drawbacks of each method and learn which of these solutions is appropriate for a given situation or network environment.

---

**After this lesson, you will be able to:**
- Plan the deployment of applications using Group Policy.
- Plan the deployment of applications using System Center Essentials 2007.
- Plan the deployment of applications using System Center Configuration Manager 2007.

**Estimated lesson time:  40 minutes**

---

## Planning the Deployment of Applications by Using Group Policy

As an enterprise administrator, you are aware that Group Policy enables you to publish software to users, assign software to users, or assign software to computers. You can use a combination of these methods to ensure that applications are available to users on the network, that the software automatically repairs if it becomes corrupted, and that updates and new revisions are installed as appropriate.

Publishing a software installation package to users in a site, domain, or OU enables users to use Add Or Remove Programs in Control Panel to install the software. The Auto-Install publishing option deploys the application when the user attempts to open an associated document. This process is known as document invocation.

You can assign software to users on demand, assign software to users on logon, or assign software to computers. If you assign software to deploy on demand, it is advertised on the desktop. The user installs the software by double-clicking the desktop shortcut, by accessing the software through the Start menu, or by document invocation. If Control Panel is available, the user can also install the software through Add Or Remove Programs. You can also assign software to users so that it installs the next time a user logs off (or reboots the computer) and logs on again. Even if the user removes the software, it becomes available again at logon. Updates and new versions are automatically installed on logon.

If you assign software to users in an OU and users in different OUs use the same computer, then the software might be available to one user and not to another. If you want the software to be available to all users of a computer or group of computers, you can assign software to computers. The software is installed when the computer powers on, and any updates or revisions are installed on reboot. If you assign software to a computer, the computer user cannot remove it. Only a local or domain administrator can remove the software, although a user can repair it.

When planning the deployment of applications, you might have to consider the automatic removal of the application if the computer or user is reassigned. For example, the computer a manager uses in one department is reassigned to an administrative assistant in another department when the manager receives a newer computer. The set of applications the manager uses might be significantly different from the set of applications the administrative assistant uses. If you have configured Group Policy software deployment just to install applications, the set of applications assigned for the administrative assistant are added to those already assigned to the manager. For example, if the manager is assigned applications A, B, C, and D and the administrative assistant applications C, D, E, and F, the computer now has applications A, B, C, D, E, and F installed after reassignment. By configuring software to be removed when the policy falls out of scope, as shown in Figure 7-5, applications A, B, C, and D are removed and applications C, D, E and F are installed when the computer is reassigned to a new user.

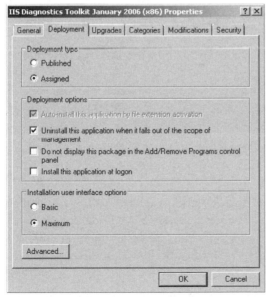

**Figure 7-5**   Ensuring that applications are removed when they fall out of scope

When planning software deployment by using Group Policy, it is important to remember the impact WAN bandwidth limitations will have on deployment. If not configured properly, application files might be pushed to clients across WAN connections, clogging them with traffic and causing the deployment to fail. When planning software deployments, remember technologies, such as distributed file system (DFS), enable you to replicate application packages to branch office locations prior to using Group Policy to publish them. Similarly, use Group Policy filtering to target application deployment precisely when using Group Policy. An excellent tool that assists you with planning application deployment using Group Policy is the *Group Policy Modeling* node of Group Policy Management Console. With this tool, you can simulate an application deployment using Group Policy without having to perform the actual deployment to verify its efficacy.

---

**MORE INFO**   **More on planning application deployment by using Group Policy**

For more information about using Group Policy to deploy software, access the following address: *http://technet2.microsoft.com/windowsserver2008/en/library/3b4568bc-9d3c-4477 -807d-2ea149ff06491033.mspx?mfr=true.*

---

## Planning Application Deployment with System Center Essentials

System Center Essentials (SCE) 2007 is an application deployment solution suitable for organizations that have fewer than 500 clients. Although this number is significantly below what most people would consider an enterprise environment, your particular enterprise might comprise multiple domains or forests that have fewer than 500 clients, in which case, it makes sense to consider SCE 2007 in your application deployment plans.

SCE 2007 provides a single solution for managing an organization's servers, clients, hardware, and software. The tool is built on Windows Server Update Services (WSUS) 3.0 and requires access to a Microsoft SQL Server database to store configuration and reporting data. If your organization does not have a SQL Server 2005 SP2 or SQL Server 2008 instance, the SCE 2007 installation routine installs SQL Server Express.

An administrator can use the SCE 2007 console to assess, configure, and deploy software to targeted groups and computers. SCE 2007 also simplifies the task of deploying operating system upgrades or installing application suites (for example, Office 2007) by providing a wizard that walks you through the process of deploying software by creating a package and targeting installation on clients and servers in your network. You can deploy Microsoft software installation (MSI) and non-MSI applications, drivers, and Microsoft and non-Microsoft hotfix releases. You can target software installations by grouping computers and defining command-line configurations.

Application deployment using SCE 2007 is configured through a wizard that enables you to deploy .msi or .exe packages to clients and servers within your organization. The wizard asks you to specify the destination of the application to be deployed and the application installation deadline. It then enables you to track installation progress and troubleshoot any problems that arise with the deployment.

SCE 2007 automates software and hardware inventory so you can review assets and optimize configuration and ensure that software configurations within your organization meet compliance requirements. You can perform searches, define filters, and generate reports that include up-to-date lists of all installed software applications and installed hardware. This is useful if you want to generate hardware readiness reports for the deployment of major applications or new operating systems.

From the perspective of planning application deployment for large network environments, SCE 2007 sits between using the Active Directory software deployment functionality and the greater functionality of System Center Configuration Manager (SCCM) 2007. SCE 2007 works best for single domain environments with between 300 and 500 client computers. It is possible to deploy only one SCE 2007 server per domain, so when planning application deployment for domains with more than 500 clients, you will need to implement System Center Configuration Manager 2007.

SCE 2007 can be an appropriate application deployment solution for organizations with multiple domains but only when the domains each have fewer than 500 client computers and software application deployment will be managed on the domain rather than at the organizational level. This is because SCE 2007 cannot be used in a hierarchy, and each SCE 2007 server is essentially a standalone solution.

---

**MORE INFO  SCE 2007**

For more information and a link to download trial software, access *http://www.microsoft.com/systemcenter/essentials/default.mspx.*

---

## Planning the Deployment of Applications by Using SCCM 2007

The Microsoft top-tier application deployment solution is SCCM 2007. If planned correctly, you can use an SCCM 2007 installation to manage the application deployment needs of thousands of clients across an enterprise network. This is possible because SCCM 2007 can be deployed in a hierarchy, with multiple software distribution points across different sites. SCCM 2007 also enables you to delegate the deployment of applications to administrators in regional offices.

SCCM 2007 is not limited to application deployment; you can also use it to deploy server and client operating systems and software updates. The software update functionality of SCCM 2007 is covered in more detail in Chapter 11, "Designing Software Update Infrastructure and Managing Compliance." The extensive reporting functionality of SCCM 2007 enables administrators to meter and evaluate software usage, which is very important when you are attempting to assess which computers in an organization have a specific application already deployed.

SCCM 2007 can be configured to work with the Windows Server 2008 Network Policy Server (NPS) to restrict network access to computers that do not meet specified requirements, for example, when installing required security updates. SCCM 2007 can also be configured to perform automatic client remediation, removing unapproved software from clients and installing any applications to meet the organization's software configuration policies.

SCCM 2007 is an agent-based solution, and you must install the agent software on client computers before they can be managed. You can do this automatically for client computers that are members of the same Active Directory forest as the SCCM 2007 server.

SCCM 2007 is deployed on a per-site basis. SCCM 2007 sites can be the same as Active Directory sites or can be independent of the Active Directory structure, so it is important to understand that the same term can be used differently, depending on whether it relates to SCCM 2007 or to AD DS. SCCM 2007 sites have the following properties:

- **Primary site**    A primary site always stores the SCCM 2007 data for itself and for all sites below it in an SCCM hierarchy using a SQL Server database. This database is typically located on the same local area network as the initial SCCM 2007 server and is called the Configuration Manager 2007 site database. The first site in which SCCM 2007 is deployed is always a primary site.

- **Secondary site**    A secondary SCCM site has no local SQL Server database because all configuration data is stored in the database at the primary site. The secondary site is attached to the primary site and administered from there. Secondary sites require no additional SCCM 2007 license and cannot have other sites below them in the hierarchy.

- **Parent sites**    Parent sites have other sites attached to them in a hierarchy.

- **Child sites**    Child sites are attached to sites above them in the hierarchy. A child site can be either a primary site or a secondary site.

- **Central site**    Central sites have no parent sites. These sites are sometimes called standalone sites.

---

**MORE INFO**    **More on sites**

To understand more about SCCM 2007 sites, consult the TechNet article at *http://technet.microsoft.com/en-us/library/bb632547.aspx.*

---

## System Center Configuration Manager 2007 Client Deployment

Before you can use SCCM 2007 to deploy an application to a computer on your network, the client computer must have the SCCM 2007 agent software installed. You can use a number of methods to deploy this software on computer systems in your network. Table 7-1 lists and briefly describes these methods.

**Table 7-1   Methods of Deploying SCCM 2007 Client**

| Installation Method | Description |
| --- | --- |
| Client push installation | Targets the agent to assigned resources |
| Software update point installation | Installs the agent by using the SCCM 2007 software updates feature |
| Group Policy installation | Installs the agent by using Group Policy |
| Logon script installation | Installs the agent by means of a logon script |
| Manual installation | Installs the agent manually |
| Upgrade installation | Installs upgrades to the agent software by using the software distribution feature in SCCM 2007 |
| Client imaging | Pre-stages the agent installation as part of an operating system image |

## Deploying Applications with SCCM 2007

You can use the SCCM 2007 software distribution functionality to push applications and updates to client computers. It uses packages (for example, MSI packages) to deploy software applications. Within those packages, commands known as programs tell the client what executable file to run. A single package can contain multiple programs. Packages can also contain command lines to run files already present on the client. Advertisements specify which clients receive the program and the package. The distribution of applications by using SCCM 2007 involves creating the software distribution package, creating programs to be included in the package, selecting package distribution points, and then creating an advertisement for a program.

A significant difference between using SCCM 2007 and deploying applications through Group Policy is software metering, by which administrators collect software usage data from SCCM 2007 clients. Software metering will inform you of which applications are actively being used as well as of which applications are being installed. This enables organizations to rationalize their software licensing, removing applications that have been deployed but are not used from client computers throughout the organization.

Another advantage of SCCM 2007 over traditional software deployment methods is the ability to use a feature known as Wake On LAN. Wake On LAN can send a wake-up transmission prior to the configured deadline for a software deployment. This enables deployment of applications to computers when their users are not present rather than waiting for installation to proceed when the user first logs on in the morning.

---

**MORE INFO** Wake On LAN

For SCCM 2007 to use Wake On LAN, the System Configuration Manager 2007 client software must be installed on the computer, the client network card must support magic packet format, and the client BIOS must be configured for wake-up packets on the network card. For more information and example scenarios, access *http://technet.microsoft.com/en-gb/library/bb932183.aspx*.

---

## PRACTICE Planning Application Deployment

The Wingtip Toys Active Directory infrastructure consists of three forests, each of which shares a forest trust. As enterprise administrator, you are responsible for planning the software deployment infrastructure for all three forests, although the actual software deployment tasks will be carried out by systems administrators who report directly to you and who have administrative rights only at the forest level.

The *wingtiptoys.internal* forest consists of 20 Active Directory domains, each of which has between 400 and 1,000 computer accounts. These 20 domains are spread across seven Active Directory sites. No domain spans more than a single site. Because of the large number of clients in this forest, the Chief Information Officer (CIO) has asked that application usage be strictly monitored to ensure that only applications that are used are deployed to computers within the organization. All application deployment and configuration data should be stored centrally. Application deployment will also be handled by administrators in the *wingtiptoys.internal* forest root domain and will not be handled by staff at individual sites.

The *wingtiptoys.development* forest consists of five Active Directory domains, one for the development department in each regional head office. Each domain has between 400 and 450 computer accounts and a maximum of 20 servers. Each domain is deployed at a single Active Directory site.

The *wingtiptoys.design* forest consists of a single-site Active Directory domain with 150 computer accounts. It is necessary to deploy several custom applications that are not in Microsoft Installer format to all computers in the *wingtiptoys.design* domain.

Where possible, the technology with the lowest cost should be used. Assume that it costs the least to use software deployment through Group Policy and the most to use SCCM 2007. Although it will be necessary in some instances to deploy third-party applications, your application deployment plans should avoid tools and deployment mechanisms that use third-party products.

▶ **Exercise   Plan the Appropriate Application Deployment Technology**

In this exercise, you will review the business and technical requirements as a precursor to planning an application deployment strategy for the various divisions of Wingtip Toys.

1. Which application deployment method would be most appropriate for use in the *wingtiptoys.design* forest and why?
   - ❑ SCE 2007 is the most appropriate to use in the *wingtiptoys.design* forest. The forest has a single domain, fewer than 500 client computers, and the necessity to install software packages that are not in MSI format. Software packages that are not in MSI format cannot be deployed using standard Group Policy software deployment tools. Some technologies allow conversion of third-party applications to MSI format, but the business and technical requirements specify that these must be avoided. You can learn more about creating MSI packages for third-party products by accessing the following link: *http://support.microsoft.com/default.aspx/kb/257718.*

2. Which application deployment infrastructure plans would you make for the *wingtiptoys.internal* forest? Include information about the infrastructure that will be deployed at each Active Directory site.
   - ❑ Deploy an SCCM 2007 primary site at the *wingtiptoys.internal* forest root site. Application deployment will be managed from here. This site will also host the SCCM configuration database.
   - ❑ Deploy an SCCM 2007 secondary site at the other six Active Directory sites so that application deployment can be managed centrally from the primary site.
   - ❑ Configure SCCM 2007 software metering to monitor application usage.

3. Under what circumstances would it be necessary to use SCCM 2007 rather than SCE 2007 as an application deployment solution for the *wingtiptoys.development* forest?
   - ❑ You would use SCCM 2007 rather than SCE 2007 when administration needs to be performed in a top-down manner. SCE 2007 is limited to 500 clients, which means it would be necessary to deploy an SCE 2007 server in each domain for application deployment, each of which would be managed on an individual basis.
   - ❑ It would be necessary to use SCCM 2007 if the number of clients in each domain grows to more than 500. Each SCE 2007 instance can be used to deploy applications to a maximum of only 500 client computers.
   - ❑ It would be necessary to use SCCM 2007 if centralized reporting for the entire forest was necessary. SCE 2007 can perform reports only for the clients it manages. SCCM 2007 could be generated for every client in the forest.

## Lesson Summary

- ■ Group Policy software deployment enables applications prepared as MSI packages to be distributed to clients by linking GPOs.
- ■ Group Policy software deployment provides no reporting functionality.
- ■ You can target deployments by using GPO filtering.

- System Center Essentials (SCE) 2007 can be used to perform application deployment and reporting, but it is limited to 500 clients.

- SCE 2007 deployment can be targeted to specific computers or users irrespective of OU membership.

- Only one SCE 2007 server can be installed in an Active Directory domain.

- System Center Configuration Manager (SCCM) 2007 can perform sophisticated application deployment and reporting and has no client limitation.

- Like SCE 2007, SCCM 2007 can target specific computers or users for application deployment irrespective of OU membership.

- Software metering enables administrators to rationalize application software licensing.

# Lesson Review

You can use the following questions to test your knowledge of the information in Lesson 2, "Planning Application Deployment." The questions are also available on the companion CD if you prefer to review them in electronic form.

---

**NOTE   Answers**

Answers to these questions and explanations of why each answer choice is correct or incorrect are located in the "Answers" section at the end of the book.

---

1. You are planning an application deployment strategy for a single domain forest that has 600 client computers spread across five Active Directory sites. Which of the following technologies can you use to deploy applications to all client computers in this environment? (Choose two. Each correct answer forms a complete solution.)

    A.   Group Policy software deployment

    B.   System Center Essentials 2007

    C.   System Center Operations Manager 2007

    D.   System Center Configuration Manager 2007

    E.   System Center Virtual Machine Manager 2007

2. You are planning to use Group Policy software deployment to deploy several important applications to client computers on your organization's network. Before performing the actual deployment, you want to verify that the Group Policy configuration will behave in the planned manner. Which of the following tools can you use to verify that the application deployment strategy has been correctly configured prior to application rollout?

    A.   Group Policy Results

    B.   Group Policy Modeling

    **C.** Active Directory Users and Computers

    **D.** Active Directory Sites and Services

3. You are planning the deployment of an important computer-aided design (CAD) application to a select group of users within your organization. You need to ensure that the application will be removed from the users' computers if they are transferred to another department and their user accounts are moved to a new OU within the Active Directory structure. Which of the following plans should you make?

    **A.** Plan to use the Published, rather than Assigned, deployment type.

    **B.** Plan to use the Ignore Language When Deploying This Package advanced deployment option when configuring the software deployment.

    **C.** Plan to use the Install This Application At Logon option when configuring software deployment.

    **D.** Plan to use the Uninstall The Application When It Falls Out Of The Scope Of Management option when configuring software deployment.

4. As part of your application deployment plans, you want to review application deployment every six months to ensure that your organization is using software licenses efficiently. You want to locate those computers in your organization that have unused applications. Which of the following tools enables you to accomplish this?

    **A.** SCCM 2007

    **B.** WSUS 3.0 SP1

    **C.** Group Policy Management Console

    **D.** Active Directory Users and Computers

# Chapter Review

To further practice and reinforce the skills you learned in this chapter, you can perform the following tasks:

- Review the chapter summary.
- Complete the case scenario. This scenario sets up a real-world situation involving the topics of this chapter and asks you to create a solution.
- Complete the suggested practices.
- Take a practice test.

## Chapter Summary

- TS license servers must be activated before they can have TS Per Device and TS Per User CALs installed.
- TS RemoteApp displays just the application, rather than the entire remote desktop, on the Terminal Services client.
- TS Gateway servers enable clients on the Internet to connect to protected terminal servers without requiring the setup of a VPN.
- TS Session Broker enables the creation of terminal server farms and ensures that clients are reconnected to the correct session if they become disconnected.
- Group Policy software deployment enables applications prepared as MSI packages to be distributed to clients by linking Group Policy objects to appropriate Active Directory containers.
- You can use SCE 2007 to perform application deployment and reporting, but it is limited to 500 clients. Only one SCE 2007 server can be installed in an Active Directory domain.
- SCCM 2007 can perform sophisticated application deployment and reporting and has no client limitation. You can use SCCM 2007 reporting to examine how deployed applications are used in an environment so that licensing can be rationalized.

## Case Scenario

In the following case scenario, you will apply what you have learned about Terminal Services and application and server virtualization. You can find answers to these questions in the "Answers" section at the end of this book.

## Case Scenario: Planning a Terminal Services Strategy for Wingtip Toys

You are planning the deployment of Terminal Services for Wingtip Toys. The company has an office in each state of Australia. Because of the decentralized nature of the Wingtip Toys organization, each state office has its own domain in the *wingtiptoys.internal* forest. All clients in the organization are using Windows Vista without any service packs applied. Taking this into consideration, how will you resolve the following design challenges?

1. The purchase and management of TS CALs should be handled separately. What plans should be made for a Terminal Services license server deployment?

2. The terminal server in the Queensland office is reaching capacity and cannot be upgraded further. How can you continue to service clients in the Queensland office and ensure that interrupted sessions are reconnected?

3. What steps must you take to ensure that Windows Vista clients can access RemoteApp applications through TS Web Access?

# Suggested Practices

To help you successfully master the exam objectives presented in this chapter, complete the following tasks.

## Provision Applications

Do all the practices in this section.

- **Practice 1**   Create a Windows Installer package for Notepad by performing these steps:
  - ❑ Install Terminal Services on the Glasgow computer.
  - ❑ Using the TS RemoteApp manager, create the Windows Installer package for the Notepad application.
- **Practice 2**   Install and activate a Terminal Services license server by performing these steps:
  - ❑ Install the Terminal Services License Server role service on the Glasgow computer.
  - ❑ Set the license server scope so that only clients in the *contoso.internal* domain can use the server.
  - ❑ Activate the Terminal Services license server by using the Web page method, using another computer that is connected to the Internet.

# Take a Practice Test

The practice tests on this book's companion CD offer many options. For example, you can test yourself on just one exam objective, or you can test yourself on all the 70-647 certification exam content. You can set up the test so that it closely simulates the experience of taking a certification exam, or you can set it up in study mode so that you can look at the correct answers and explanations after you answer each question.

---

**MORE INFO**  Practice tests

For details about all the practice test options available, see "How to Use the Practice Tests" in this book's introduction.

---

# Chapter 8

# Server and Application Virtualization

Of all the new technologies introduced in Windows Server 2008, few will affect the way you design your network deployment as much as server and application virtualization. Although virtualization products have existed on the Windows Server platform for some time, Hyper-V ties virtualization directly into the operating system. In this chapter, you will learn about Hyper-V functionality and how this technology will influence the decisions you make about deploying Windows Server 2008. The second part of this chapter covers application virtualization. In most deployments, applications are installed and interact directly with the operating system. In application virtualization, a virtualization layer exists between the application and the operating system. This allows the operating system to run applications that might not be compatible if installed in a traditional manner. It also allows applications to be run in a partitioned environment, which means that applications that would normally conflict with each other when run concurrently can be executed side by side without any problems.

### Exam objectives in this chapter:
- Design an operating system virtualization strategy.

### Lessons in this chapter:

- Lesson 1: Planning Operating System Virtualization . . . . . . . . . . . . . . . . . . . . . . . . . 362
- Lesson 2: Planning Application Virtualization . . . . . . . . . . . . . . . . . . . . . . . . . . . . . . 379

## Before You Begin

- To complete the lessons in this chapter, you should have installed a Windows Server 2008 Enterprise domain controller named Glasgow, as described in Chapter 1, "Planning Name Resolution and Internet Protocol Addressing."

No additional configuration is required for this chapter.

# Lesson 1: Planning Operating System Virtualization

In this lesson, you will learn how to design an operating system virtualization strategy. This includes learning how to assess which existing server deployments make good candidates for virtualization, learning how to plan the migration of servers from traditional hardware-based installations to virtual hosts, and learning the most effective locations in an existing network infrastructure to deploy servers that host virtual machines (VMs). This lesson not only explains Hyper-V but also examines Virtual Server 2005 R2 and System Center Virtual Machine Manager 2007. To effectively design an operating system virtualization strategy, you need to understand how these separate components can be integrated to meet your organization's needs.

> **After this lesson, you will be able to:**
> - Understand the differences between operating system virtualization technologies.
> - Understand the benefits of deploying System Center Virtual Machine Manager 2007.
> - Design a server consolidation strategy.
> - Design a virtual host and virtual machine deployment strategy.
>
> **Estimated lesson time: 40 minutes**

Every year the hardware that vendors make available becomes more powerful. Increasingly powerful hardware changes the way that enterprise administrators plan the deployment of server resources. Whereas, in the past, server utilization patterns and performance meant that only a single server role or application could be deployed on computer hardware, today's server hardware can cope with a much higher workload. This means that fewer servers are required to do the same amount of work. Virtualization allows you to fully utilize the increased computing power made available by modern hardware without worrying about the conflicts that might occur if you cohosted important applications and server roles on a single instance of Windows Server 2008. Virtualization provides the following benefits over traditional installations:

- **More efficient use of hardware resources**  Services such as Dynamic Host Configuration Protocol (DHCP) and Domain Name System (DNS), although vital to network infrastructure, are unlikely to push the limits of your server's processor and RAM. Although it is possible to co-locate the DNS and DHCP roles on the one Windows Server 2008 computer, the strategy of separating network roles onto separate partitions allows you to relocate those partitions to other host computers if the circumstances and usage of those roles change.

- **Improved availability**  Consolidating these services onto a single hardware platform can reduce costs and maintenance expenses. Although moving from many platforms to one might look like it would lead to a single point of failure, implementing redundancy technologies (clustering and hot-swappable hardware such as processors, RAM, power supplies, and hard disk drives) provides a greater level of reliability for lower cost. Consider the following situation: four Windows Server 2008 computers are each running a separate application provided to users on your network. If a hardware component fails on one of those servers, the application that the server provides to users of the network is unavailable until the component is replaced. Building one server with redundant components is cheaper than building four servers with redundant components. If a component fails, the built-in redundancy allows all server roles to remain available.

- **Servers need to be only intermittently available**   Some servers need to be available only intermittently. For example, the best practice with a root CA is to use subordinate CAs to issue certificates and to keep the root CA offline. With virtualization, you could keep the entire virtualized root CA server on a removable USB hard disk drive in a safe, only turning it on when necessary and thereby ensuring the security of your certificate infrastructure. Virtualization frees up existing hardware that is rarely used—or makes it unnecessary to buy it.

- **Role sandboxing**   Sandboxing is a term used to describe the partitioning of server resources so that an application or service does not influence other components on the server. Without sandboxing, a failing server application or role has the capacity to bring down an entire server. Just as Web application pools in Internet Information Services (IIS) sandbox Web applications so that the failure of one application will not bring all of them down, running server applications and roles in their own separate virtualized environment ensures that one errant process does not bring down everything else.

- **Greater capacity**   Adding significant hardware capacity to a single server is cheaper than adding incremental hardware upgrades to many servers. You can increase capacity by adding processors and RAM to the host server and then allocating those resources to a virtual server as the need arises.

- **Greater portability**   After a server has been virtualized, moving it to another host if the original host's resources become overwhelmed is relatively simple. For example, suppose that the disks on a Windows Server 2008 Enterprise computer hosting 10 virtualized servers are reaching their input/output (I/O) capacity. Moving some of the virtualized servers to another host is simpler than migrating or upgrading a server. Tools such as System Center Virtual Machine Manager, covered later in the chapter, make the process even simpler.

- **Easier backup and restore**   Tools such as volume shadow copy allow you to back up an entire server's image while the server is still operational. If a host computer fails, the images can be rapidly restored on another host computer. Rather than backing up individual files and folders, you can back up the entire virtualized computer in one operation. System Center Virtual Machine Manager (SCVMM) 2007 allows you to move VMs back and forth to the Storage Area Network (SAN) and even migrate VMs between host computers. SCVMM 2007 is covered in more detail later in the lesson.

# Virtual Server 2005 R2

Virtual Server 2005 R2 SP1 is a product that you can download and install for free from Microsoft's Web site. Virtual Server 2005 R2 SP1 allows you to host and manage VM instances on a 32-bit version of Windows Server 2008. You can also install Virtual Server 2005 R2 SP1 on the 32-bit and 64-bit versions of Windows Server 2003 SP1/R2. It is also possible to install Virtual Server 2005 R2 SP1 on Windows Small Business Server 2003 and Windows XP Professional, though you should never use Windows XP Professional as a virtual host for virtualized servers that are used in a production environment. Virtual Server 2005 R2 SP1 cannot be installed on a Windows Server 2008 computer that has been installed using the Server Core option.

---

**MORE INFO**   Downloading Virtual Server 2005 R2

You can download a free copy of Virtual Server 2005 R2 by accessing the following address on Microsoft's Web site: *http://www.microsoft.com/windowsserversystem/virtualserver/downloads.aspx.*

---

When planning an operating system virtualization strategy, you should consider Virtual Server 2005 R2 SP1 when the computer that you plan to use as a virtual host has a 32-bit, as opposed to a 64-bit, processor. This is because Hyper-V, which is covered later in this lesson, is a Windows Server 2008 feature that is available only on 64-bit versions of Windows Server 2008. For example, say that your organization has a computer with Windows Server 2003 Enterprise installed. The computer has eight processors and 64 GB of RAM, but the processors on the computer are 32-bit rather than 64-bit. Computers with large amounts of RAM make excellent VM hosts, but because the processors on the computer have a 32-bit rather than a 64-bit architecture, it is impossible to install the 64-bit version of Windows Server 2008 on this computer and impossible to use Hyper-V as a VM host. From the planning perspective, you can still install Windows Server 2008 on this computer and use it as a VM host; it is just that the host platform will be Virtual Server 2005 R2 SP1 rather than Hyper-V.

Alternatively, you could have a similarly powerful computer that has the 64-bit version of Windows Server 2003 R2 installed. Your organization might not be ready to upgrade the operating system of this computer to Windows Server 2008, but you might want to use the computer as a VM host. Because Hyper-V can be deployed only on Windows Server 2008 x64, you will need to include Virtual Server 2005 R2 SP1 in your operating system virtualization plans until you can upgrade the computer operating system to Windows Server 2008 x64.

Although you can use Virtual Server 2005 R2 SP1 as a key component in an operating system virtualization strategy, you must remember the following limitations when planning virtual host deployment:

- Virtual Server 2005 R2 SP1 cannot host x64 bit VMs—even if the platform that Virtual Server 2005 R2 SP1 is installed on is a 64-bit operating system.

- Virtual Server 2005 R2 SP1 does not support symmetric multiprocessing (SMP) in the VM environment.
- Virtual Server 2005 R2 SP1 supports a maximum of four virtual network adapters.
- Virtual Server 2005 R2 SP1 supports a maximum of 64 concurrent VMs.

---

**MORE INFO**   **More on Virtual Server 2005**

To learn more about Virtual Server 2005, consult the following page on Microsoft's Web site: *http://www.microsoft.com/windowsserversystem/virtualserver/evaluation/virtualizationfaq.mspx.*

---

# Hyper-V

Hyper-V is a Windows Server 2008 feature that allows you to run virtualized computers under x64 versions of Windows Server 2008. Hyper-V is a hypervisor-based technology. A hypervisor is a software layer between the hardware and the operating system that allows multiple operating systems to run on a host computer at the same time. Hyper-V has many similarities to Virtual Server 2005 R2 in terms of functionality, although, unlike Virtual Server 2005 R2, Hyper-V is built directly into the operating system as a role and does not sit above the operating system as an application. Apart from being a feature included with the operating system, Hyper-V has the following differences from Virtual Server 2005 R2 SP1:

- Hyper-V allows you to run 64-bit VM guests. Hyper-V can concurrently host 32-bit and 64-bit VM guests.
- Hyper-V supports SMP in the VM environment.
- Hyper-V can host as many concurrent VMs as the hardware supports.
- Hyper-V can be configured as a part of a failover cluster, so that a VM fails over across the network to a server running Hyper-V in a recovery site.
- Hyper-V can be used on a Windows Server 2008 computer installed using the Server Core option. You can manage Hyper-V on a Server Core computer using the WMI interface or a remote session using the Hyper-V manager console.
- Hyper-V guests can have a maximum of four virtual SCSI controllers per VM.
- Hyper-V guests can have a maximum of eight virtual network adapters per VM.
- The Enterprise and Datacenter editions of Windows Server 2008 include licenses to run virtualized instances of the operating system using Hyper-V.

## Creating Virtual Machines

Creating a VM on a Hyper-V host is relatively simple and involves running the New Virtual Machine Wizard from the Virtualization Management console. To create the virtual machine, perform the following steps:

1.  Specify a name and location for the VM. Placing a VM on a RAID-5 volume—or, even better, a RAID 0+1 or RAID 1+0 volume—ensures redundancy. You should avoid placing VMs on the same volume as the host operating system. The name of the VM does not need to be simply the computer's name but can include other information about the VM's functionality.

2.  Specify memory allocation. The maximum amount of memory depends on the amount of RAM installed on the host computer. Remember that each active VM must be allocated RAM and that the total amount of allocated RAM for all active VMs and the host operating system cannot exceed the amount installed on the host computer.

3.  Specify networking settings. Specify which of the network cards installed on the host will be used by the VM. Where you expect high network throughput, you might add an extra network card and allocate it solely to a hosted VM.

4.  Specify a virtual hard disk. VMs use flat files to store hard disk data. Hyper-V mounts these files, and they appear to the VM as a normal hard disk drive that can even be formatted and partitioned. When creating a virtual hard disk, you should specify enough space for the operating system to grow, but do not allocate all available space if you intend to add other VMs later.

5.  Specify operating system installation settings. In the final stage of setting up a VM, you specify how you will install the operating system: from an image file, such as an .ISO file; from optical media, such as a DVD-ROM; or from a network-based installation server, such as Windows Deployment Services (WDS).

From this point you can turn on the VM and then begin the installation process using the method that you selected in step 5.

## Managing Virtualized Servers

You manage Hyper-V through the Hyper-V Manager console, shown in Figure 8-1. You can use this console to manage virtual networks, edit and inspect disks, take snapshots, revert to snapshots, and delete snapshots, as well as to edit the settings for individual VMs. You can also mount virtual hard disks as volumes on the host server should the need arise.

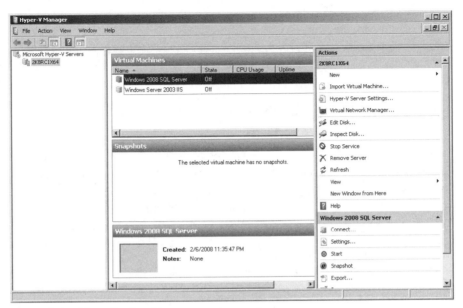

**Figure 8-1**  Virtualization Management console

## Snapshots

Snapshots are similar to a point-in-time backup of a virtualized machine. The great benefit of snapshots is that they allow you to roll back to an earlier instance of an operating system far more quickly than any other technology would. For example, assume that your organization hosts its intranet Web server as a VM under Hyper-V. A snapshot of the intranet Web server is taken every day. Because of an unforeseen problem with the custom content management system, the most recent set of updates to the intranet site have wiped the server completely. In the past, as an administrator, you would have to go to your backup tapes and restore the files. With Hyper-V, you can just roll back to the previous snapshot and everything will be in the state it was when the snapshot was taken.

## Licensing

All operating systems that run in a virtualized environment need to be licensed. Products such as Windows Server 2008 Enterprise and Windows Server 2008 Datacenter allow a certain number of virtual instances to be run without incurring extra license costs because the licenses for these editions include the virtualized component. The applications that run on the virtualized servers also need licenses. As with all licensing queries, in more complicated situations you should check with your Microsoft representative if you are unsure whether you are in compliance.

---

**MORE INFO**   **More on licensing virtual machines**

To learn more about what you need to consider when licensing a VM, see *http://download .microsoft.com/download/6/8/9/68964284-864d-4a6d-aed9-f2c1f8f23e14/virtualization_brief.doc.*

---

## Modifying Hardware Settings

You can edit VM settings. This allows you to add resources like virtual hard disks and more RAM and to configure other settings, such as the Snapshot File Location. Figure 8-2 shows the Integration Services for a specific VM. Integration Services allow information and data to be directly exchanged between host and VM. To function, these services must be installed on the guest operating system. This task is performed after the guest operating system is set up. You can edit some settings, such as the optical drive settings, while the VM is running. Other settings, such as assigning and removing processors from a VM, require you to turn off the VM.

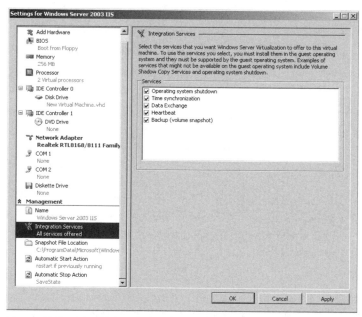

**Figure 8-2**   Modifying the settings of a VM

Not only can you assign processors to VMs, but you can also limit the amount of processor usage by a particular VM. You do this with the Virtual Processor settings shown in Figure 8-3. This way you can stop one VM that has relatively high processing needs from monopolizing the host server's hardware. You can also use the Virtual Processor settings to assign a relative weight to a hosted VM. Rather than specifying a percentage of system resources to which the VM is entitled, you can use ratios to weight VM access to system resources. The benefit of using relative weight is that you do not have to recalculate percentages each time you add or remove VMs from a host. You simply add the new host, assign a relative weight, and let Hyper-V work out the specific percentage of system resources that the VM is entitled to.

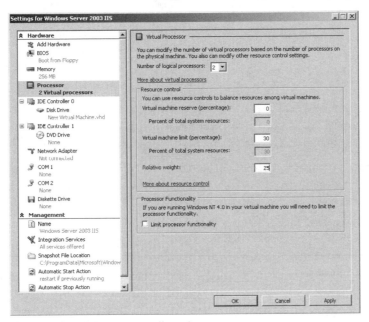

**Figure 8-3**  VM processor allocation

---

## Quick Check

1. On which versions of Windows Server 2008 can you install the Hyper-V role?
2. From the perspective of available host computer hardware, in which cases should you plan the deployment of Virtual Server 2005 R2 SP1 over the deployment of Hyper-V?

### Quick Check Answers

1. You can install the Hyper-V role on the 64-bit editions of the Standard, Enterprise, and Datacenter editions of Windows Server 2008 in both the standard and server-core modes.
2. You should plan the deployment of Virtual Server 2005 R2 SP1 when your host computer hardware has only a 32-bit, rather than a 64-bit, processor.

# Candidates for Virtualization

When you are considering server deployment options, it will be advantageous in some situations to deploy a virtualized server rather than the real thing. One factor is cost: a Windows Server 2008 Enterprise license includes the licenses for four hosted virtual instances. Although you need to consider many other costs when making a comparison, from a licensing perspective, one Windows Server 2008 Enterprise license will cost less than five standard licenses. Also remember that server-grade hardware will always cost significantly more than a Windows Server 2008 Enterprise license, especially if your organization has a licensing agreement with Microsoft.

Although each situation will be different, in certain archetypical situations, you would plan a virtualized server rather than a traditional installation, including the following:

- You want to use WDS at a branch office location for a rollout that will last several days, but you do not have the resources to deploy extra hardware to that location. In this case, you could virtualize a WDS server and turn on the VM only when it was needed. If more operating systems need to be rolled out later, the VM could be turned on.

- You have two applications hosted on the same server that conflict with each other. Because custom applications do not always work together well, sometimes you need to place each application in its own VM. Applications hosted on separate computers are unlikely to conflict with each other! Another solution is to virtualize the application itself. Virtualizing applications is covered later in this lesson.

- You are working with developers who need to test an application. If you have worked as a systems administrator in an environment with developers, you know that some projects are not stable until they are nearly complete, and, until that time, they have a nasty habit of crashing the server. Giving developers their own VM to work with allows them to crash a server as often as they like without your worrying about the impact on anyone outside the development group.

Some server deployments make poor candidates for virtualization. Servers that have high I/O requirements or high CPU requirements make poor candidates. A server that monopolizes CPU, memory, and disk resources on a single computer will require the same level of resources when virtualized, and a traditional server installation will provide better performance than running that same server virtualized on the same hardware. In general, you are reasonably safe in deciding to deploy virtual servers if the server does not have a large performance footprint. When a server is expected to have a significant performance footprint, you will need to develop further metrics to decide whether virtualization offers any advantage.

---

**NOTE    Number of licenses**

Remember that Windows Server 2008 Datacenter (x64) has unlimited licenses for virtual hosts and that Windows Server 2008 Enterprise (x64) has only four.

---

# Planning for Server Consolidation

When you plan the deployment of Windows Server 2008 at a particular site that has an existing Windows server infrastructure, you will be making an assessment about which of the existing servers can be virtualized, which need to be migrated, and which need to be upgraded. If you have deployed System Center Operations Manager in your environment, you can use the product to generate a Virtualization Candidates report, which will give you a list of servers in your environment that make excellent candidates for virtualization given their current usage levels.

When you have determined the need to virtualize a server, the next step is to move that server from its existing hardware to a virtualized partition running under Windows Server 2008. You can use two tools to virtualize a server installed on traditional hardware: the Virtual Server Migration Toolkit (VSMT) and SCVMM. Both tools are compatible not only with Hyper-V but also with Virtual Server 2005 R2.

## Virtual Server Migration Toolkit

VSMT is the best tool to use when you have a small number of servers that need to be virtualized. The tool is command line–based and uses Extensible Markup Language (XML) files to store configuration data that is used during the migration process. You cannot use the VSMT tool to manage virtualized servers—it is purely a tool for migrating existing servers to a virtualized environment.

Unlike the SCVMM 2007 migration tools, it is not possible to use the VSMT to perform migrations without downtime. The VSMT was primarily designed to migrate servers to the Virtual Server 2005 platform. It is because Virtual Server 2005 virtualized operating systems are compatible with Hyper-V that you can use this tool to perform migrations to Windows Server 2008 virtual hosts.

---

**MORE INFO**    **More on the Virtual Server Migration Toolkit**

To find out more about how you can use VSMT to virtualize servers, see the following TechNet article: *http://www.microsoft.com/technet/virtualserver/evaluation/vsmtfaq.mspx.*

---

## System Center Virtual Machine Manager 2007

You should plan to use SCVMM 2007 when you have a large number of VMs to manage in a single location. SCVMM requires a significant infrastructure investment and is primarily designed to manage enterprise-sized virtual server deployments rather than to be something that you would plan to use to migrate a couple of branch office servers into a virtual environment. If you are planning to virtualize a large number of servers, you will find the extra functionality of SCVMM 2007 manager valuable. Unlike VSMT, SCVMM is fully integrated with

Windows PowerShell, giving you more flexibility in migrating servers from physical to virtualized environments.

You should note that deployment of SCVMM requires a connection to a SQL Server database. The Express Edition of SQL Server 2005 SP2 is included with the SCVMM 2007 installation files, or you can use an existing SQL Server 2005 SP2 or SQL Server 2008 instance. SCVMM 2007 uses this database to store VM configuration information.

In addition to virtualizing traditional server installations, you can use SCVMM to do the following:

- Monitor all of the virtualized servers in your environment. A single SCVMM server can be used to manage up to 8,000 VMs.
- Monitor all Hyper-V hosts in your environment. A single SCVMM server can be used to manage up to 400 Hyper-V or Virtual Server 2005 R2 host computers.
- When connected to a Fibre Channel SAN environment, move virtualized servers from one Hyper-V host to another.
- Move virtualized servers to and from libraries.
- Delegate permissions so that users with nonadministrative privileges are able to create and manage their own VMs.
- Migrate servers from physical to virtual without any downtime.

SCVMM 2007 includes capacity planning technology that allows you to assign VMs to the virtual hosts in your environment that have the appropriate available resources to support them based on VM performance data. For example, if you have 10 Windows Server 2008 computers that each host multiple VMs, the capacity planning technology in SCVMM 2007 can make recommendations about where each VM should be deployed based on performance data observations.

SCVMM 2007 increases your operating system virtualization planning options because it includes tools that allow you to make the most efficient use of your VM and virtual host infrastructure. As Figure 8-4 shows, the capacity planning tools available in SCVMM 2007 can be heavily customized, allowing administrators to prioritize the importance of specific resources. For example, you can configure the capacity planning tools to prioritize servers that have available memory over those that have lower CPU utilization.

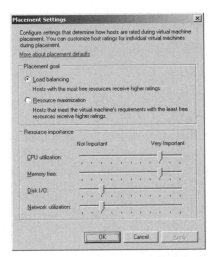

**Figure 8-4** Configuring capacity planning

## Components of a System Center Virtual Machine Manager 2007 Deployment

An SCVMM 2007 deployment consists of several components that can all be installed on the one server or that can be installed on several servers throughout the enterprise. SCVMM 2007 components include the following:

- **SCVMM server** This is the server on which the SCVMM software is installed. You should install this component first. Except under unusual circumstances, there is usually only one SCVMM server in an environment, so you should plan redundancy using failover clustering rather than the deployment of multiple servers. Although it is possible to deploy multiple SCVMM servers in a forest, each SCVMM server requires a separate SCVMM database, although these databases can be hosted on the same SQL Server instance. An SCVMM server cannot be installed in a forest that has a disjointed DNS namespace (multiple separate domain trees within the same forest).

- **SCVMM agent** This component is installed on a VM host running Virtual Server 2005 R2 or Hyper-V and SCVMM library servers. To be automatically managed, all VM hosts must be members of the same forest as the SCVMM server. It is possible to install the SCVMM agent on a computer that is not a member of the same forest and configure a connection manually to the SCVMM server. This is usually done when a virtual host is deployed on a perimeter network. A single SCVMM server can manage a maximum of 400 servers running Hyper-V or Virtual Server 2005 R2 SP1, or both. A Hyper-V or Virtual Server 2005 R2 SP1 host can be managed only by a single SCVMM server.

---

**MORE INFO**    Installing SCVMM agent locally

For more information about installing the SCVMM agent locally, consult the following Tech-Net document: *http://technet.microsoft.com/en-us/library/bb740757.aspx.*

---

■ **SCVMM database**    The SCVMM database can be hosted either on SQL Server 2005 or SQL Server 2008. If no SQL Server instance is specified, the setup routine installs SQL Server Express on the local SCVMM server. The drawback of using SQL Server Express is that the advanced reporting functionality will be unavailable. In addition to using SQL Server 2005 or SQL Server 2008, if you plan to use the advanced reporting functionality of the product, you must also deploy System Center Operations Manager 2007 in the same forest. If the SCVMM database is remote from the SCVMM server, you should secure the connection between the two servers using Secure Sockets Layer (SSL).

---

**MORE INFO**    SCVMM and a remote instance of SQL Server

For more information on the specific steps involved in configuring a remote instance of SQL Server to support SCVMM 2007, consult the following TechNet document: *http://technet .microsoft.com/en-us/library/bb740749.aspx.*

---

■ **SCVMM Administrator console**    Like all management consoles, the SCVMM administrator console can be installed on an administrator workstation to manage SCVMM remotely or used to directly manage the server on which SCVMM components are installed.

■ **SCVMM self-service portal**    This portal allows users who are not SCVMM administrators to manage VMs to which they have been delegated permissions. The portal is Web-based and should be installed on a server that has IIS 6.0 or later and is a member of the same forest as the SCVMM server.

■ **SCVMM library server**    The library is a catalog of resources that are used to create VMs using SCVMM. These resources include ISO images, scripts, hardware profiles, VM templates, virtual hard disks, and stored VMs. A VM template includes a guest operating system profile, a hardware profile, and virtual hard disks. These resources are hosted on a set of shares that are managed through the SCVMM console. The library can be stored across multiple physical servers in an enterprise deployment. If the SCVMM library is not deployed on the VM host server, the network connection between a VM host server and the library it uses should be as fast as possible. A default library share called VMMLibrary is created on the SCVMM server during the installation process unless an administrator determines otherwise. An SCVMM Library server can only be managed by one SCVMM server. You cannot directly share resources between different SCVMM environments.

## SCVMM 2007 in the Branch Office

SCVMM 2007 is usually deployed in a datacenter environment, with all components, including VM hosts, located at the same site. If SCVMM 2007 is going to be used to create, run, and manage VMs at branch and satellite offices, you should deploy a VMM library server and a VM host at the branch office site. This will allow you to deploy new VMs directly from the library to the VM hosts without having to transfer gigabytes of data across the organizational wide area network (WAN) link.

In branch office deployments, the SCVMM library is usually deployed on the same server that functions as the VM host. This allows for rapid deployments because the files used to build new VMs do not need to be copied across the network. The drawback of this type of deployment is that it requires a significant amount of hard disk drive space to store both the library data and the deployed VMs.

---

**MORE INFO**  More on planning SCVMM 2007 deployment

For more information on planning an SCVMM 2007 deployment, consult the following TechNet Web page: *http://technet.microsoft.com/en-us/library/bb963710.aspx*.

---

**MORE INFO**  SCVMM 2007 webcasts

To learn more about using SCVMM 2007, access the following TechNet webcasts: SCVMM 2007 Overview at *http://msevents.microsoft.com/cui/WebCastEventDetails.aspx?culture=en-US&EventID =1032324658&CountryCode=US* and Managing Virtualization at *http://msevents.microsoft.com /cui/WebCastEventDetails.aspx?culture=en-US&EventID=1032349356&CountryCode=US*.

---

## PRACTICE Designing Virtual Server Deployment

Fabrikam, Ltd, is a large Australian company that has three sites spread across the state of Victoria. The headquarters site is in the city of Warrandyte with branch offices in Yarragon and Traralgon. As a part of a shareholder initiative to reduce Fabrikam's fossil fuel usage, the company has been looking for ways to lessen its consumption of electricity. An audit of the company's computer hardware resources has found that it has large numbers of servers deployed throughout all locations, the resources of which are barely being used. Reducing the number of physical servers will reduce the company's use of electricity and also shrink the company's carbon footprint, thus enhancing shareholder value.

Both the Traralgon and Yarragon sites have a large number of Windows Server 2003 computers. All of these computers were originally upgraded from Windows 2000 Server and, hardware that was purchased in early 2001, and are therefore underpowered compared with what is available today. Management believes that the amount of hardware located at the Traralgon and Yarragon sites can be significantly rationalized.

Although operating system virtualization is not being used at the branch office sites, an administrator who has since left the organization realized significant efficiencies by virtualizing 200 existing servers in the Warrandyte datacenter and retiring ageing hardware. These 200 Windows Server 2003 VMs are currently hosted on 10 Windows Server 2003 Enterprise Edition computers. The hosting platform is Virtual Server 2005 R2 SP1. Part of the virtualization plan will involve moving these VMs so that they are hosted under Hyper-V rather than Virtual Server 2005 R2 SP1. The previous administrator determined that all 200 Windows Server 2003 VMs could be hosted on two computers running Windows Server 2008 Datacenter if the computers were provisioned with appropriate hardware. The administrator left before this project moved beyond the early planning stage, and you will need to further develop the plan.

▶ **Exercise    Planning an Operating System Virtualization Strategy for Fabrikam**

In this exercise, you will review the business and technical requirements to plan a virtualized application deployment for Fabrikam, Ltd.

1. What strategy should you use to determine which servers at Fabrikam will make good virtualization candidates and what steps should be taken to migrate these servers?
   - ❑ Plan the deployment of System Center Operations Manager 2007 in the Fabrikam forest. Generate a Virtualization Candidates report.
   - ❑ Deploy SCVMM 2007 and use the product to perform in-place virtualizations of existing servers. For you to do this, each candidate must be a member of the same forest or have the SCVMM 2007 agent installed.

2. What plans should you make to ensure that it is possible to rapidly deploy virtualized servers at the Traralgon and Yarragon branch offices?
   - ❑ It will be necessary to deploy an SCVMM 2007 library at both the Traralgon and Yarragon branch office sites.
   - ❑ It will be necessary to configure distributed file system (DFS) to replicate updated library data to the library site over the WAN links during off-peak period.

3. What plans should you make to migrate the VMs hosted at the Warrandyte datacenter from Virtual Server 2005 R2 to Hyper-V?
   - ❑ Deploy a high-speed SAN at the Warrandyte datacenter.
   - ❑ Deploy a Windows Server 2008 Datacenter host at the Warrandyte datacenter.
   - ❑ Use SCVMM 2007 to migrate the VMs hosted on Virtual Server 2005 R2 to Hyper-V, transferring them across the SAN.

## Lesson Summary

- Hyper-V is an add-on role for 64-bit versions of Windows Server 2008 that you can use to host and manage virtualized operating systems.

- Snapshots allow the state of a server to be taken at a point in time, such as prior to the deployment of an update, so that the server can be rolled back to that state in the future.

- The best candidates for virtualization are servers that do not intensively use processor, RAM, and disk resources.

- The Virtual Server Migration Toolkit (VSMT) provides tools you can use to virtualize existing servers. The toolkit uses XML-based files to assist in the transition from a traditional to a virtualized installation. Use this option if you have a small number of existing servers to virtualize.

- System Center Virtual Machine Manager (SCVMM) allows you to manage many virtual machines (VMs) at once. It includes tools that allow you to move VMs between hosts, allow nonprivileged users to create and manage their own VMs, and perform bulk virtualizations of servers installed on traditional hardware. Use SCVMM only with large VM deployments.

## Lesson Review

You can use the following questions to test your knowledge of the information in Lesson 1, "Planning Operating System Virtualization." The questions are also available on the companion CD if you prefer to review them in electronic form.

---

**NOTE** Answers

Answers to these questions and explanations of why each answer choice is correct or incorrect are located in the "Answers" section at the end of the book.

---

1. Which of the following scenarios provides the most compelling case for the planned deployment of SCVMM 2007?

   A. You need to virtualize four Windows 2000 Server computers.

   B. You want to be able to move virtualized servers between hosts on your Fibre Channel SAN.

   C. You are responsible for managing 10 virtualized Windows Server 2008 servers at your head office location.

   D. You need to automate the deployment of five Windows Server 2008 Enterprise computers with the Hyper-V role installed.

2. On which of the following platforms can you install Hyper-V?

   A. A Server Core installation of the x64 version of Windows Server 2008 Enterprise

   B. A Server Core installation of the x86 version of Windows Server 2008 Datacenter

   C. A standard installation of the x86 version of Windows Server 2008 Enterprise

   D. A standard installation of the x86 version of Windows Server 2008 Datacenter

3. Which of the following are the management limits of a single-server SCVMM 2007 deployment? (Choose two. Each correct answer forms a complete solution.)

   A. 400 virtual machine hosts

   B. 800 virtual machine hosts

   C. 1200 virtual machine hosts

   D. 16000 virtual machines

   E. 8000 virtual machines

4. Which of the following SCVMM 2007 components should you plan to install at branch office locations where you will need to be able to rapidly deploy new VMs to virtual hosts at those sites?

   A. SCVMM database

   B. SCVMM self-service portal

   C. SCVMM server

   D. SCVMM library server

5. You are planning the deployment of SCVMM 2007 to manage several hundred VMs hosted by Windows Server 2008 computers with Hyper-V. Approximately 30 VMs are deployed off two Windows Server 2008 computers on your organization's screened-subnet. Which of the following plans should you make to ensure that all VMs hosted in your environment can be managed using SCVMM 2007 without installing unnecessary instances of the product?

   A. Install the VMM agent manually on the two Windows Server 2008 host computers and configure the internal firewall appropriately.

   B. Install the VMM agent manually on the 30 VMs and configure the internal firewall appropriately.

   C. Install Active Directory Lightweight Directory Services and configure the internal firewall appropriately.

   D. Install SCVMM 2007 on each Windows Server 2008 host computer and configure the internal firewall appropriately.

# Lesson 2: Planning Application Virtualization

This lesson discusses Microsoft SoftGrid Application Virtualization, a technology available from Microsoft that allows applications that would otherwise conflict or not run on a terminal server to be virtualized and served to client computers over the network. This technology differs from the RemoteApp presentation virtualization technology covered in Chapter 7, "Planning Terminal Services and Application Deployment," because the application executes on the client rather than executing on the server with the visual output being displayed on the client.

---

**After this lesson, you will be able to:**
- Understand the benefits of application virtualization.
- Plan the deployment of application virtualization.
- Understand the components necessary for the deployment of Microsoft SoftGrid Application Virtualization.

**Estimated lesson time: 40 minutes**

---

## Microsoft SoftGrid Application Virtualization

Instead of creating a separate partitioned space for the entire operating system, Microsoft SoftGrid Application Virtualization (SoftGrid) creates a separate partitioned space for a specific application when it is run on a SoftGrid client. This allows applications that would otherwise be incompatible with each other to execute concurrently. For example, if it was necessary in your organization to run two versions of an application on the same Windows Vista computer at the same time, you could use SoftGrid to ensure that there were no conflicts between them.

Similarly, if it was necessary in your environment to deploy two versions of the same application using RemoteApp, which was covered in Chapter 7, you would need to use two separate terminal servers and hope that the users in your organization remembered which terminal server to connect to when they needed to run a specific version of the application. This is because, generally speaking, if you install two versions of the same application on the same terminal server, you will run into configuration problems and conflicts. Applications deployed through SoftGrid can share data with locally installed applications, although they cannot perform complex interactions beyond file associations, cut-and-paste, and OLE integration. If your organization uses applications that require more complex integration, it will be necessary to use SoftGrid to deploy applications within a sequenced group called a suite. In a suite configuration, a group of applications runs within the same silo. Silos are discussed later in this lesson.

Applications deployed through SoftGrid can be executed on client computers that have the Microsoft SoftGrid Application Virtualization for Desktop agent installed. The agent functions like VM software, although instead of locally hosting a virtualized operating system, it hosts a virtualized application that is streamed from a computer that has Microsoft System Center Virtual Application Server installed. It is also possible to install Microsoft SoftGrid Application

Virtualization for Terminal Services, which allows you to deploy multiple versions of the same application, or applications, that conflict from a single terminal server or terminal server farm. These applications are streamed to the terminal server from the computer with Microsoft System Center Virtual Application Server installed, as shown in Figure 8-5. A big advantage of SoftGrid is that it allows applications that cannot normally be deployed through Terminal Services to be deployed in this manner.

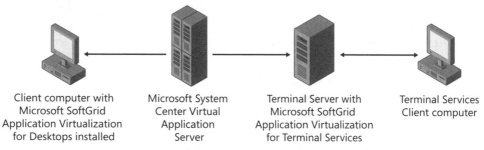

Client computer with Microsoft SoftGrid Application Virtualization for Desktops installed    Microsoft System Center Virtual Application Server    Terminal Server with Microsoft SoftGrid Application Virtualization for Terminal Services    Terminal Services Client computer

**Figure 8-5**    Streaming applications using SoftGrid

---

**MORE INFO**    **Terminal Services and Microsoft SoftGrid Application Virtualization**

To learn more about how Microsoft SoftGrid Application Virtualization works with Terminal Services, see *http://www.microsoft.com/systemcenter/softgrid/evaluation/softgrid-ts.mspx*.

---

You should deploy Microsoft SoftGrid Application Virtualization in your environment when you need to do the following:

- Run multiple versions of the same application on a local client as the silos, ensuring that the differing versions of the applications will not conflict. This is especially useful in application development environments where different versions of the same application need to be tested simultaneously.
- Deploy applications that would normally conflict to the same client.
- Deploy multiple versions of the same application from the same terminal server.
- Deploy applications that are not compatible with Terminal Services from terminal servers. When Microsoft SoftGrid Application Virtualization for Terminal Services is installed on a terminal server, you can deploy applications that are incompatible with Terminal Services.
- Exert greater control over which users can execute specific applications. Each time a user attempts to execute an application, SoftGrid will query Active Directory Domain Services (AD DS) to verify that the user has been authorized to use that application. Audit-based license tracking and strict license enforcement are built into SoftGrid and can be configured to ensure that your organization remains compliant with its application licensing responsibilities.

---

**MORE INFO** SoftGrid Application Virtualization TechCenter

You can learn more about Microsoft SoftGrid Application Virtualization and how you can plan for the deployment of this technology in your environment at *http://technet.microsoft.com/en-us /softgrid/default.aspx*.

---

## Planning the Deployment of Application Virtualization

Planning the deployment of SoftGrid for an organization requires understanding the available components and how they interact with one another. A Microsoft Application Virtualization deployment has the following components:

- **SoftGrid Sequencer** The sequencer is used to package an existing application so it can be deployed through SoftGrid. This component can be installed on the Virtual Application server or deployed separately. Generally it is necessary to have only a single sequencer because this component is used only when preparing applications for their deployment to the Microsoft System Center Virtual Application server.

- **Microsoft System Center Virtual Application Server** This server maintains application packages and streams parts of the application to the client using Real-Time Transport Protocol (RTP) as needed. After parts of the application are transmitted to the client, the components are cached and do not need to be retransmitted when the application is used again. This server also handles authentication and licensing. High availability should be achieved by load balancing identical Microsoft System Center Virtual Application servers. This server must be a member of an AD DS forest.

---

**MORE INFO** Application virtualization white paper

To learn about application virtualization, consult the application virtualization white paper at *http://technet.microsoft.com/en-us/library/bb608285.aspx*.

---

- **SoftGrid Data Store** This component maintains application information in a SQL Server database. It is possible to use SQL Server 2005 Express to support the SoftGrid data store, although enterprise organizations will want to use SQL Server 2005 or 2008 to store this data. This component can be located on the same server as the Virtual Application Server component or located on another computer.

- **SoftGrid Management console** This component manages the SoftGrid infrastructure. Like other consoles, it can be used to remotely manage SoftGrid from an administrator's workstation or used directly when logged on to the System Center Virtual Application server.

- **SoftGrid Client for Desktops** Microsoft SoftGrid Application Virtualization for Desktops client can be installed on Microsoft Windows 2000 Professional, Windows XP Professional, and Windows Vista. This software is necessary if the client computer is going to execute a SoftGrid application directly. This client software can be deployed to client operating systems using traditional application deployment methods. Microsoft SoftGrid Application Virtualization for Terminal Services can be installed on Windows 2000 Server/Advanced Server, Windows Server 2003 with Terminal Services installed, or Windows Server 2008 with the Terminal Services role installed. When client computers access SoftGrid applications using a terminal server, they need only RDP client software. It is not necessary to install the SoftGrid desktop client in this situation.

---

**MORE INFO    SoftGrid server capacity**

To determine the number of Virtual Application servers required for an enterprise environment that uses SoftGrid, consult the following TechNet article: *http://technet.microsoft.com/en-us/library/bb608286.aspx*.

---

## SoftGrid Branch Office Deployments

When planning the deployment of SoftGrid in branch office environments, you should ensure that each branch office has its own Virtual Application server. This is primarily because WAN links are too slow to support the streaming of application data to client computers. In some cases, there will be enough bandwidth from a central location to a branch office to support a Terminal Services session, and using the SoftGrid Terminal Services component on a local terminal server might be the best application deployment solution. Alternatively, if there are only a few clients, you might configure them to access terminal servers across the Internet by connecting to a TS Gateway server located on the screened subnet at your organization's datacenter site.

In most branch office deployment scenarios, SQL Server Express should be deployed on the computer hosting the Virtual Application Server role unless an existing SQL Server 2005 or SQL Server 2008 instance is also present in the branch office environment.

SoftGrid is not currently able to distribute packages intelligently across WAN links. Plans for the rollout of newly sequenced to branch office Virtual Application servers should leverage existing Windows Server 2008 replication tools like DFS. Once they are replicated out to the branch offices, the SoftGrid administrator can configure the local Virtual Application servers with the new SoftGrid packages.

---

**MORE INFO    Branch office configuration guide**

To learn more about the deployment of SoftGrid in branch office environments, consult the following TechNet Web page: *http://technet.microsoft.com/en-au/library/bb608287.aspx*.

---

---

**MORE INFO**  SoftGrid virtual lab

To learn more about Microsoft SoftGrid Application Virtualization, you should take the following TechNet Virtual Lab that is available on Microsoft's Web site: *http://msevents.microsoft.com/CUI /WebCastEventDetails.aspx?EventID=1032346000&EventCategory=3&culture=en-US&CountryCode=US.*

---

## PRACTICE Planning Application Virtualization

You are being retained as a consultant for the development of an application virtualization strategy for Contoso, Ltd. Contoso is a large corporation with offices located throughout Australia. As an enterprise administrator, it is your role to design an operating system virtualization strategy. Contoso's head office is in Melbourne and has 15,000 employees. Contoso has remote offices in Sydney, Adelaide, and Brisbane, each with approximately 5,000 employees. Each remote office is connected to the head office through a leased line WAN.

Approximately 75 percent of the client computers at Contoso have Windows XP Professional SP3 installed. The rest of the client computers at Contoso have Windows Vista Enterprise with SP1 installed. All servers at Contoso have been upgraded to Windows Server 2008.

Contoso is dependent on four line-of-business applications. After these applications were recently patched to deal with several important security issues, it was found that when two or more of these applications run concurrently on a Windows XP or Windows Vista computer, a conflict occurs that causes the computer to experience a STOP error. After further testing of these applications, you have found that two of these applications cannot be installed on a Windows Server 2008 computer with the Terminal Services role deployed. The other two applications can be installed on a terminal server, but the server will encounter a STOP error if any single user executes these applications concurrently.

Almost all users in the Contoso environment will need access to two or more of these applications to perform their daily tasks, and the company's compliance auditors consider rolling back to the unpatched versions of the applications unacceptable. At present, users have been instructed to execute only one application at a time, but there is a growing need to be able to run them concurrently and to cut and paste data between these programs.

Additionally, several groups of users in the organization telecommute. Management wants these users to be able to access these applications while telecommuting, but it will be necessary to ensure that these users' computer updates and antivirus and spyware definitions are up-to-date before they are granted access to the organizational network. Management would prefer any proposed solution to work without deploying a virtual private network (VPN) or dial-up–based remote access solution.

Finally, any solution that you plan to deploy at Contoso should be fault-tolerant and should be able to survive the loss of a single server.

► **Exercise   Planning a Virtualized Application Deployment**

In this exercise, you will review the business and technical requirements to plan a virtualized application deployment for Contoso, Ltd.

1. What aspects of Contoso's operation strongly indicate a necessity to use an application deployment strategy that leverages Microsoft SoftGrid Application Virtualization over other application deployment alternatives?

   ❑ Several line-of-business applications conflict and cause STOP errors when they are run concurrently on a terminal server or on a client computer.

   ❑ Several applications cannot be installed on a terminal server using the standard application deployment method.

   ❑ Using Microsoft SoftGrid Application Virtualization allows these applications to be installed and execute concurrently on a Windows Server 2008 computer with the Terminal Services role installed without conflicts arising due to the virtualized nature of the execution environment.

2. What plans should you make to ensure that Contoso staff at the head and branch offices are able to access important line-of-business applications if a server and WAN links fail completely during a peak business period?

   ❑ At each branch office, plan the installation of the following:

      ● A network load-balanced Microsoft System Center Virtual Application cluster so that SoftGrid applications can be delivered to local terminal servers. These servers need to be local because SoftGrid applications shouldn't be streamed over WAN links. A load-balanced cluster is necessary to meet the availability requirements. SQL Server Express should be deployed on each server.

      ● Configure a two-node network load-balanced terminal server farm. Install Microsoft SoftGrid Application Virtualization for Terminal Services on each terminal server. Load balanced terminal servers are necessary to meet availability requirements.

      ● Client computers at each branch office need to be able to connect only to the terminal server; they do not require the deployment of Microsoft SoftGrid Application Virtualization for Desktops.

3. What plans should you make to allow for the Contoso managers who are telecommuting?

   ❑ Plan the installation of a TS Gateway server on the screened subnet at Contoso HQ. Instruct telecommuting managers to connect to this server over the Internet.

   ❑ Plan the configuration of a TS Gateway server NAP policy to ensure that connecting computers' System Health Validators (SHVs) report on the compliance level of software updates and antivirus and anti-spyware definitions. Configure the TS Gateway server to allow access to only the terminal servers at the HQ site.

## Lesson Summary

- Microsoft SoftGrid Application Virtualization allows applications to be virtualized. This has the advantage of allowing applications that might conflict with each other to be run concurrently.

- Microsoft SoftGrid Application Virtualization differs from Terminal Services in that applications execute on the client rather than on the server.

- You prepare applications for deployment through SoftGrid by using a SoftGrid sequencer.

- A server with Microsoft System Center Virtual Application Server installed is used to stream applications to clients using RTP. High availability should be provided through the use of Network Load Balancing.

- The SoftGrid datastore is a SQL Server database. If no SQL Server 2005 or SQL Server 2008 database is present in the network environment during the installation of Microsoft System Center Virtual Application Server, it is possible to deploy SQL Server Express from the Microsoft System Center Virtual Application Server installation media.

- You can deploy SoftGrid applications to Terminal Services clients by installing Microsoft SoftGrid Application Virtualization for Terminal Services on a terminal server computer. When configured in this way, the application is streamed to the terminal server, which then presents it in a traditional way to the client.

## Lesson Review

You can use the following questions to test your knowledge of the information in Lesson 2, "Planning Application Virtualization." The questions are also available on the companion CD if you prefer to review them in electronic form.

**NOTE  Answers**

Answers to these questions and explanations of why each answer choice is correct or incorrect are located in the "Answers" section at the end of the book.

1. Which of the following high-availability solutions should you plan to deploy to ensure that the Microsoft System Center Virtual Application Server component of your application virtualization is still available if a critical failure occurs in the hardware hosting the component?

    A. Deploy two servers in DNS round robin configuration.

    B. Deploy two servers in failover cluster configuration.

    C. Deploy two servers in Network Load Balancing configuration.

    D. Deploy two servers in a terminal server farm configuration.

2. Which of the following SoftGrid components is used to convert conventional applications so that they can be deployed through Microsoft System Center Virtual Application Server as SoftGrid applications for desktop client computers?

    **A.** SoftGrid data store

    **B.** SoftGrid sequencer

    **C.** SoftGrid Application Virtualization for Terminal Services

    **D.** SoftGrid Application Virtualization for Desktops

3. Your organization is about to open a branch office location in a suburb on the other side of the city from where the HQ site is located. You already use SoftGrid to deploy several mission-critical applications to desktop computers at the HQ site. You plan to do the same for the new branch office location. Which of the following plans should you make to extend the existing Application Virtualization infrastructure to the new branch office? (Choose two. Each correct answer forms a part of the solution.)

    **A.** Plan to deploy the Microsoft SoftGrid Application Virtualization for Clients software to all client computers at the new branch office.

    **B.** Plan to deploy Hyper-V at the new branch office.

    **C.** Plan to deploy SCVMM at the new branch office.

    **D.** Plan to deploy a Microsoft System Center Virtual Application Server at the branch office site.

    **E.** Plan to deploy Microsoft SoftGrid Application Virtualization for Terminal Services at the branch office site.

4. In which of the following situations must you plan to deploy Microsoft SoftGrid Application Virtualization for Terminal Services?

    **A.** You want to deploy Microsoft Office 2007 applications using RemoteApp from a single terminal server.

    **B.** You want to deploy both Microsoft Office 2007 and Microsoft Office XP to Windows Vista client computers.

    **C.** You want to deploy Microsoft Office 2007 applications using RemoteApp from a terminal server farm.

    **D.** You want to deploy Microsoft Office 2007 and Microsoft Office XP from a terminal server farm.

5. You work as a systems administrator for a software development company. During the application development phase, it is necessary to deploy several versions of the same software from the same terminal server. When you attempt to install the applications side by side, a conflict arises. Which of the following solutions should you plan to use?

   A. Deploy the applications using TS RemoteApp.

   B. Deploy a TS Gateway Server.

   C. Deploy Microsoft Application Virtualization.

   D. Deploy the applications using TS Web Access.

# Chapter Review

To further practice and reinforce the skills you learned in this chapter, you can perform the following tasks:

- Review the chapter summary.
- Complete the case scenarios. These scenarios set up real-world situations involving the topics of this chapter and ask you to create a solution.
- Complete the suggested practices.
- Take a practice test.

# Chapter Summary

- Servers that do not have large hardware footprints can be virtualized and hosted on a Windows Server 2008 64-bit computer running the Hyper-V role.
- SCVMM should be deployed when an administrator must manage large numbers of VMs.
- Microsoft Application Virtualization allows applications that could not otherwise be installed on a terminal server, or coexist on a terminal server, to be streamed to clients. This is achieved through application virtualization.

# Case Scenario

In the following case scenario, you will apply what you have learned about Terminal Services and application and server virtualization. You can find answers to these questions in the "Answers" section at the end of this book.

## Case Scenario: Tailspin Toys Server Consolidation

Tailspin Toys has an aging deployment of computers running Windows 2000 Server. Management has decided to transition to a Windows Server 2008 infrastructure. One goal of the transition project is to reduce the number of physical servers and to retire all existing server hardware, which is now more than five years old. You have been brought in as a consultant to assist in the development of plans for server consolidation at a Tailspin Toys branch office. Each site has a unique set of needs and applications. The characteristics of each site are as follows:

1. The Wangaratta site currently hosts a Windows 2000 Server domain controller that also hosts the DHCP and DNS services. A Windows 2000 Server computer hosts a SQL Server 2000 database and two other servers, each of which hosts custom business applications. These applications cannot be co-located with each other or with the SQL Server 2000 database. How could you minimize the number of physical servers using virtualization, and what would the configuration of these servers be?

2. The Yarragon site currently hosts six terminal servers, each of which hosts a separate business application. One of these applications uses a SQL Server 2005 database. These applications cannot be co-located without causing problems on the host terminal servers. Because the Yarragon site has only a small number of users, the hardware resources of the terminal servers are underutilized. How can you minimize the number of terminal servers required to support the staff at the Yarragon site?

# Suggested Practices

To help you successfully master the exam objectives presented in this chapter, complete the following tasks.

## Windows Server Virtualization

Perform the following practice exercise.

■ **Practice**   Obtain a 64-bit evaluation version of Windows Server 2008, and install it on a computer and not within a virtual environment. Join this computer to the *contoso.internal* domain. Install the Hyper-V role. Install a 64-bit evaluation version of Windows Server 2008 as a guest VM.

Download and install the System Center Virtual Machine Manager 2007 VHD file, and join it to the *contoso.internal* domain. Use it to manage the newly installed Windows Server 2008 computer that has the Hyper-V role installed. Use SCVMM 2007 to virtualize server Glasgow.

---

**MORE INFO**   **Obtaining the SCVMM VHD**

You can get the System Center Virtual Machine Manager VHD from the following Web site: *http://technet.microsoft.com/en-au/scvmm/bb962017.aspx.*

---

## Plan Application Virtualization

Perform the following practice exercise.

■ **Practice**   Tailspin Toys has its head office in Sydney, Australia, and branch offices in Brisbane, Adelaide, Hobart, and Melbourne. All client computers at Tailspin Toys have Windows XP Professional installed, and all domain controllers have Windows Server 2008 installed. Tailspin Toys uses five locally produced off-the-shelf software applications, three of which are no longer actively maintained by the respective vendors but which are still mission-critical to Tailspin Toys' operations. Two of these applications have recently been updated to deal with publicly disclosed security vulnerabilities. These updates have caused problems on the client computers when these applications were run concurrently with the three applications that are no longer actively maintained. All applications need to run locally on users' Windows XP Professional computers. Plan a SoftGrid deployment. Include in your plans the necessary server infrastructure and roles, client software deployment required at each site, and planned method of rolling out updates. Your plan should minimize the number of virtualized applications.

# Take a Practice Test

The practice tests on this book's companion CD offer many options. For example, you can test yourself on just one exam objective, or you can test yourself on all the 70-647 certification exam content. You can set up the test so that it closely simulates the experience of taking a certification exam, or you can set it up in study mode so that you can look at the correct answers and explanations after you answer each question.

---

**MORE INFO**   Practice tests

For details about all the practice test options available, see "How to Use the Practice Tests" in this book's introduction.

---

# Chapter 9
# Planning and Designing a Public Key Infrastructure

Planning and designing a public key infrastructure (PKI) for a large organization is a complicated undertaking, but the process can be broken down into three general steps. First, as part of a team of stakeholders, you need to identify and assess the needs of the PKI. Second, you can design the PKI by mapping out the particular certification authorities (CAs) you need to create and the trust relationships among them. Third, you need to design the lifecycle management procedures for each CA: how certificates are issued, renewed, and revoked.

This chapter provides an overview of each of these three steps in the PKI design process.

### Exam objectives in this chapter:
- Design and implement public key infrastructure.

### Lessons in this chapter:

- Lesson 1: Identifying PKI Requirements . . . . . . . . . . . . . . . . . . . . . . . . . . . . . . . . . . . . 393
- Lesson 2: Designing the CA Hierarchy . . . . . . . . . . . . . . . . . . . . . . . . . . . . . . . . . . . . 403
- Lesson 3: Creating a Certificate Management Plan . . . . . . . . . . . . . . . . . . . . . . . . . . . .414

## Before You Begin

To complete the lessons in this chapter, you must have the following:

- A basic understanding of Active Directory Domain Services (AD DS)
- A basic understanding of Active Directory Certificate Services (AD CS)

## Real World

*JC Mackin*

Windows Server 2008 introduces a number of enhancements to Active Directory Certificate Services (AD CS): the inclusion of an Online Certificate Status Protocol (OCSP) responder, support for network device enrollment, support for Cryptography Next Generation (CNG) algorithms, and several other improvements. However, these new features are not available by default if your Active Directory forest predates Windows Server 2008, which is very likely unless your network is brand new.

Before you can take advantage of the new features offered by Windows Server 2008 enterprise CAs, you need to upgrade your pre-existing Active Directory schema. (Note, however, that you *don't* need to upgrade any domain controllers or adjust any forest or domain functional levels.)

Upgrading the Active Directory schema is a straightforward process. To perform this procedure, first locate the schema master in your Active Directory forest. Most sources will give you a complicated way to find this information, but you just need to type the command **netdom query fsmo** on a domain member server at a command prompt. You then perform the following steps on the schema master. First, insert the Windows Server 2008 product DVD into the DVD drive. Then, log on to the domain as a member of the Schema Administrators and Enterprise Administrators groups. Next, open a command prompt and navigate to the X:\sources\adprep directory (where X is the drive assigned to the DVD drive). Finally, type the command **adprep /forestprep**. After the procedure is complete, wait for the changes to replicate to all domain controllers in the forest before you install a Windows Server 2008 enterprise CA.

# Lesson 1:  Identifying PKI Requirements

In Windows Server 2008 networks, a PKI relies on one or more CAs deployed through AD CS. However, deploying a PKI is not as simple as adding the AD CS role in Server Manager. For most medium-sized and large organizations, implementing a PKI requires significant planning. Once the introduction of PKI-enabled applications triggers the need to implement a PKI, you need to review your organization's security policy. Then you need to assess other requirements for the PKI, such as business requirements, external requirements, and Active Directory requirements.

After you assess the needs of your organization in this way, you can design the PKI as a means to enforce your organization's security policies and to ensure that the new PKI remains aligned with the company's business and IT strategy.

---

**After this lesson, you will be able to:**

- Understand the function of a PKI.
- Identify applications that require a PKI.
- Understand many of the factors that you need to consider when performing a needs assessment for a PKI in a Windows Server 2008 network.

**Estimated lesson time:  20 minutes**

---

## Reviewing PKI Concepts

A PKI refers to the set of technologies that enable an organization to use public key cryptography. In public key cryptography, a mathematically related key pair consisting of a public key and a private key is used in the encryption and decryption processes. If the public key is used for encryption, the private key is used for decryption. If the private key is used for encryption, the public key is used for decryption.

More specifically, a PKI is a system of digital certificates, CAs, and other registration authorities (RAs) that provides cryptographic keys for, and authenticates the validity of, each party involved in an electronic transaction.

---

**MORE INFO**  Public key cryptography

For an introduction to public key cryptography, see "Understanding Public Key Cryptography," available at *http://technet.microsoft.com/en-us/library/aa998077(EXCHG.65).aspx*.

---

A PKI consists of the following basic components:

- **Digital certificates**  Electronic credentials that include a public key and that are used to sign and encrypt data. Digital certificates are the foundation of a PKI.

- **One or more CAs**   Trusted entities or services that issue digital certificates. When multiple CAs are used, they are typically arranged in a carefully prescribed order and perform specialized tasks, such as issuing certificates to subordinate CAs or issuing certificates to users.

- **Certificate policy and practice statements**   The two documents that outline how the CA and its certificates are to be used, the degree of trust that can be placed in these certificates, legal liabilities if the trust is broken, and so on.

- **Certificate repositories**   A directory service or other location where certificates are stored and published. In a domain environment, Active Directory is the most likely publication point for certificates issued by Windows-based CAs.

- **Certificate revocation lists (CRLs)**   Lists of certificates that have been revoked before reaching the scheduled expiration date.

---

**MORE INFO   Public key infrastructure**

For an introduction to PKI, see "Cryptography and Microsoft Public Key Infrastructure," available at *http://www.microsoft.com/technet/security/guidance/cryptographyetc/cryptpki.mspx.*

---

## Identifying PKI-Enabled Applications

Typically, an organization decides to deploy a PKI only when that organization introduces one or more applications that depend on a PKI. After the need for a PKI arises, you can begin to define the PKI in a way that best supports these applications.

The following list describes the most common applications and technologies that can lead an organization to consider deploying a PKI:

- **802.1x port-based authentication**   802.1x authentication allows only authenticated users or computers to access either an 802.11 wireless network or a wired Ethernet network. A PKI is required to support 802.1x when the Extensible Authentication Protocol-Transport Layer Security (EAP-TLS), Extensible Authentication Protocol-Tunneled Transport Layer Security (EAP-TTLS), or Protected Extensible Authentication Protocol (PEAP) authentication protocol is used.

- **Digital signatures**   A PKI is used for digital signing. Digital signatures secure Internet transactions by providing a method for verifying who sent the data and that content was not modified in transit. Depending on how a certificate is issued, digital signatures also provide nonrepudiation. In other words, data signers cannot deny that they are the data senders because they are the only users with access to the certificate's private key.

- **Encrypting File System (EFS)**   EFS provides a confidentiality service to NTFS. It employs user key pairs to encrypt and decrypt files and recovery agent key pairs for file recovery purposes. Certificates used for EFS are available from enterprise CAs. In an environment with no Microsoft enterprise CAs, all EFS certificates are self-signed.

- **Internet Protocol security**   Certificates can be used to authenticate the two endpoints in an Internet Protocol Security (IPsec) association. After authentication, IPsec can be used to encrypt and digitally sign all communications between the two endpoints. Certificates do not play a part in the actual encryption and signing of IPsec-protected data—they are used only to authenticate the two endpoints. Note also that in AD DS domains, Kerberos, not certificates, is typically used for authentication.

- **Secure e-mail (S/MIME)**   Secure e-mail, the industry standard for which is Secure/Multipurpose Internet Mail Extensions (S/MIME), provides confidential communication, data integrity, and nonrepudiation for e-mail messages. S/MIME uses certificates to verify a sender's digital identity, the message's point of origin, and message authenticity. It also protects the confidentiality of messages by encrypting their content.

- **Smart card logon**   Smart cards are credit card–sized cards that contain a user certificate. You can use smart cards to provide strong authentication for interactive logons.

- **Code signing**   Code signing protects computers from installation of unauthorized controls, drivers, or applications. Applications that support code signing, such as Microsoft Internet Explorer, can be configured to prevent execution of unsigned controls.

- **Virtual private networks (VPNs)**   VPNs allow remote users to connect to a private network by using tunneling protocols, such as Point-to-Point Tunneling Protocol (PPTP), Layer 2 Tunneling Protocol (L2TP), or Secure Socket Tunneling Protocol (SSTP). Not all VPN types use certificates. However, certificates increase the strength of user authentication and can provide authentication for IPsec if using L2TP with IPsec encryption.

- **Web authentication and encryption**   Distributing Secure Sockets Layer (SSL) certificates to a Web server on either an intranet or the Internet allows a Web client to validate the Web server's identity and encrypt all data sent to and from the Web server. All Web servers offering SSL connections require a server certificate, typically issued by a third-party CA. Optionally, SSL connections can also use client certificates (although this is rarely implemented).

## Identifying Certificate Requirements

After you have determined which PKI-enabled applications your organization plans to deploy, you must determine who must acquire the certificates and the types of certificates that are required. Typically, certificates are deployed to the following subjects:

- **Users**   A digital certificate uniquely identifies a user to a PKI-enabled application. A user can be assigned a single certificate that enables all applications or can receive application-specific certificates, such as an EFS encryption certificate that can be used for one purpose only. The certificates issued to the user are stored in the Current User certificate store.

- **Computers**   A digital certificate uniquely identifies the computer when a user or computer connects to the computer where the certificate is installed. The certificate becomes the computer's identifier and is stored in the Local Machine certificate store. If the Client Authentication object identifier (OID) is included in the certificate in either the Enhanced Key Usage (EKU) extension or the Application Policies extension, an application can use the computer certificate to initiate connections. If the Server Authentication OID is included in the certificate in the EKU or Application Policies extension, the certificate can be used to authenticate the computer's identity when a client application connects.

■ **Network devices**   Several devices on a network allow the installation of certificates for client/server authentication. These devices include, but are not limited to, VPN appliances, firewalls, and routers. The actual process used to install a certificate on a network device is subject to the type of operating system and interfaces of the actual network device.

---

**Exam Tip**    Network device enrollment is a new feature offered by Windows Server 2008, and, therefore, you are likely to see a general question about it on the 70-647 exam. Network device enrollment relies on the Network Device Enrollment Service (NDES). This service is the Microsoft implementation of the Simple Certificate Enrollment Protocol (SCEP), a communication protocol that enables software running on network devices (such as routers and switches, which cannot otherwise be authenticated on the network) to enroll for X.509 certificates from a CA.

---

■ **Services**   Some services require computer certificates for either authentication or encryption. Certificates are not actually issued to a service. Instead, the service certificate is stored either on the Local Machine store or in the user's profile of the associated service account. For example, if a certificate is installed for the World Wide Web (WWW) service of a Web server, the certificate is stored in the Local Machine store. However, the EFS recovery agent certificate for the EFS service is stored in the user profile of the designated EFS recovery agent.

---

**NOTE**   **Where should you install a certificate for a service?**

The easiest way to determine where to install a certificate for a service is to investigate what credentials the service uses to authenticate. If the service uses Local System, then the certificate must be stored in the Local Machine store. If the service uses a user account and password, then the certificate must be stored in that specific user's profile.

---

## Identifying Certificate Security Requirements

Certificate requirements are driven by the PKI-enabled applications your organization plans to use. Identifying these requirements will let you determine the properties of the certificates needed. For each set of certificates, you should identify the following security requirements:

■ **Length of the private key**  In a typical deployment, the length of private keys are nested so that each level in the PKI hierarchy has a key whose length is half that of the level above it. For example, in a PKI, issued user certificates might have 1024-bit keys, issuing CAs might have 2048-bit keys, and root CAs might have 4096-bit keys. Note that, because longer keys are harder to mathematically attack, they support proportionately longer lifetimes.

---

**MORE INFO  CA hierarchies**

CA hierarchies, issuing CAs, and root CAs are discussed in more detail in Lesson 2, "Designing the CA Hierarchy."

---

In choosing a length for each CA in the CA hierarchy, the biggest restriction is the set of applications that will use the CA hierarchy for certificates. Some applications are known not to support keys larger than a certain value.

---

**NOTE  Which technologies limit private key length?**

Technologies known to have issues with CA certificates with key lengths greater than 2048 bits include Cisco VPN 3000 series appliances, Nortel Contivity devices, and some older Java applications.

---

■ **Cryptographic algorithms that are used with certificates**  The standard settings for certificates issued by a Windows Server 2008 CA can meet typical security needs. However, you might want to specify stronger security settings for certificates that are used by certain user groups. For example, you can specify longer private key lengths and shorter certificate lifetimes for certificates used to provide security for very valuable information. You can also specify the use of smart cards for private key storage to provide additional security.

■ **Lifetime of certificates and private keys and the renewal cycle**  A certificate has a predefined validity period that comprises a start date and time and an end date and time. You cannot change an issued certificate's validity period after it has been issued. Certificate lifetimes are determined by the type of certificate, your security requirements, standard practices in your industry, and government regulations.

---

**NOTE  Certificate lifetimes**

When determining certificate lifetimes for a PKI, a good rule of thumb is to make the validity period of the certificate for a parent CA at least twice as long as the certificate for a subordinate CA. In addition, the validity period of the certificate for an issuing CA should be at least twice as long as the maximum validity period of any certificates issued by that same CA. For example, you might give issued user certificates a lifetime of 1 year, the certificate for the issuing CA a lifetime of 5 years, and the certificate for the root CA of the PKI a lifetime of 10 years.

---

■ **Special private key storage and management requirements**    An organization's security policy can require specific security measures for a CA's private key. For example, an organization might have to implement Federal Information Processing Standards (FIPS) 140-2 protection of the CA's private key to meet industry or organizational security requirements.

---

**MORE INFO    Where can you read FIPS 140-2?**

FIPS 140-2, "Security Requirements for Cryptographic Modules," can be found at *http://csrc.nist.gov/publications/fips/fips140-2/fips1402.pdf*.

---

Measures you can take to protect the CA's private key include using a cryptographic software provider (CSP), which stores the CA's private key material on the computer's local hard disk; a smart card CSP, which stores the CA's private key material on a smart card associated with a PIN; and a hardware security module (HSM), which provides the highest security for private keys in dedicated hardware devices.

---

**NOTE    What is a CSP?**

A CSP defines how a certificate's private key is protected and accessed. The CSP will determine where to generate the certificate's key pair when the certificate is requested and will implement mechanisms to protect access to the private key. For example, a CSP might require the input of a PIN to access a smart card's private key. The default CSP in AD CS in Windows Server 2008 is the RSA#Microsoft Software Key Storage Provider. This CSP supports traditional cryptographic algorithms as well as the Suite B algorithms enabled by Cryptographic Next Generation, which is a new feature of Windows Server 2008.

---

**Quick Check**

■ If the lifetime of an issued user certificate is two years, what should normally be the minimum lifetime of the certificate for the issuing CA?

**Quick Check Answer**

■ Four years.

## Reviewing the Company Security Policy

After the need for a PKI is established and the required certificates are identified, you should review the organization's security policy. A security policy is a document, created by members of an organization's legal, human resources, and IT departments, that defines an organization's security standards. The policy usually includes the assets an organization considers valuable, the potential threats to those assets, and, in general terms, the measures that must be taken to protect these assets.

The security policy should be updated to answer high-level PKI questions, such as:

- What applications should be secured with certificates?
- What kind of security services should be offered by using certificates?

In general, when planning and designing a PKI, it is essential to remember that a PKI should enforce your organization's security policy. A PKI, after all, is only as secure as the policies and procedures that the organization implements.

---

**MORE INFO   What does a security policy include?**

One of the most commonly used resources for defining a security policy is ISO 27002 (a renumbering of ISO 17799/BS 7799), "Information Technology: Code of Practice for Information Security Management," which is available for purchase online (for example, at *http://www.standardsdirect.org/iso17799.htm*). Another popular resource is RFC 2196, "The Site Security Handbook," which is available for free at *http://www.ietf.org/rfc/rfc2196.txt*.

---

## Assessing Business Requirements

Business requirements define an organization's goals. Business requirements affect the design of the PKI by allowing the PKI to enhance business goals and processes. For example, the following business requirements can affect a CA hierarchy design.

- **Minimizing PKI-associated costs**   When reviewing CA hierarchy designs, you might have to choose a CA hierarchy that deploys the fewest CAs. For example, some organizations combine the roles of policy CAs and issuing CAs into a single CA in the hierarchy, deploying a two-tier hierarchy rather than a three-tier hierarchy.

- **High availability of certificate issuance**   An organization can require that a CA be consistently available to ensure that no certificate requests fail due to a CA being down for any reason. To ensure that a CA is always available, you should implement clustering on the issuing CA that issues certificates based on the defined certificate template. If your uptime requirements are not as stringent, you might consider publishing the certificate template at more than one CA in the CA hierarchy, protecting against the failure of a single CA.

- **Liability of PKI participants**   A CA hierarchy includes policy CAs that define the liability of the CA. The liability should provide sufficient coverage for transactions that use CA-issued certificates. Your organization's legal department must review this liability definition to ensure that the definitions are legally correct and binding upon all participants in the PKI.

## Assessing External Requirements

In some cases, an organization might have to meet external requirements, such as those defined by other organizations or by the governments of countries in which the organization conducts business.

Examples of external requirements include the following:

- **Enabling external organizations to recognize employee-used certificates**    If you need other organizations to recognize the certificates assigned to entities in your organization, you can choose not to deploy an internal PKI and simply obtain certificates from commercial CAs, such as VeriSign or RSA. Alternatively, you can use cross-certification or qualified subordination to define which external certificates you trust.
- **Using your organization's certificate at partner organizations**    Your employees might use the certificates issued by your CA hierarchy for encryption or signing purposes at another organization. In this case, you might have to create custom certificates to meet the requirements of the other organization.
- **Industry or government legislation**    Several countries have legislation that affects the design of a CA hierarchy. For example, Canada enforces the Personal Information Protection and Electronic Documents Act, which regulates the management of a customer's personal information when held by a private-sector company. The act requires that someone be accountable for compliance and that this person be involved in the deployment and design of the CA hierarchy to ensure that all requirements of the act are enforced in the design.
- **Certificates for nonemployees**    If you issue certificates to nonemployees, you can use a CA hierarchy to deploy a separate certificate policy that includes greater detail for external clients.

## Assessing Active Directory Requirements

You should make several preparations before you install a Windows Server 2008 enterprise CA in a Windows 2000 or 2003 Active Directory environment. These preparations include the following:

- **Determining the number of forests in the environment**    The number of forests will affect the number of enterprise CAs that you require in your AD CS deployment. An enterprise CA can issue certificates only to users and computers with accounts in the same forest. If multiple forests must consume certificates from the PKI, you must deploy at least one enterprise CA per forest.
- **Determining the number of domains in the forest**    If more than one domain is in the forest, one of the major design decisions is which domain will host the CAs. The selection of which domain will host the computer accounts of the CA computers will depend largely on whether your organization uses centralized or decentralized management. In

a centralized model, the CAs will typically be placed in the same domain. In a decentralized environment, you might end up deploying CAs in multiple domains.

- **Determining the membership of the local Administrators groups for a member server** If you use CSPs to protect a CA's private key, all members of the CA's local Administrators group will be able to export the CA's private key. You should start identifying which domain or organizational unit in a domain will best limit the number of local administrators. For example, an organization that has deployed an empty forest root might choose to deploy all enterprise CAs as members of the forest root domain to limit the number of local administrators on the CA.
- **Determining the schema version of the domain** To implement Windows Server 2008 CAs and take advantage of all the new features introduced for AD CS, you must implement the latest version of the Active Directory Domain Services schema. The Windows Servers 2008 schema can be deployed in forests that contain Windows 2000 Server, Windows Server 2003, and Windows Server 2008 domain controllers.

## Assessing Certificate Template Requirements

Certificate templates provide a practical way to implement certificate enrollment in a managed Active Directory environment. Because of the different versions of certificate templates released with each version of Windows Server, compatibility issues must be identified as part of your PKI planning.

Historically, static V1 certificate templates were introduced with Windows 2000. With Windows Server 2003, customization was introduced with V2 certificate templates. With Windows Server 2008, more certificate templates and certificate template properties compared with the Windows Server 2003 templates became available (including properties related to CNG). The new template types in Windows Server 2008 are called V3 templates.

Because of dependencies to the underlying operating system, Windows Server 2008 templates can be assigned only to CAs that are running on a Windows Server 2008. Only Windows Vista client computers and Windows Server 2008 computers can enroll for V3 certificate templates.

If you have installed only V2 certificates in your AD DS forest, you should upgrade the existing templates and add the new V3 certificate templates. If you do not have any certificate templates, all V1, V2, and V3 certificate templates are simply added to the configuration container of your AD DS forest.

## Lesson Summary

- A PKI is a system of digital certificates, CAs, and other registration authorities (RAs) that enables an organization to use public key cryptography.

- The following technologies require a PKI or digital certificates: digital signatures, EFS, SSL, S/MIME, smart cards, and code signing. In addition, the following technologies sometimes require a PKI or digital certificates: 802.1x, IPsec, and VPNs.

- After you have determined which PKI-enabled applications your organization plans to deploy, you must determine who must acquire the certificates, the types of certificates that are required, and the security requirements for those certificates.

- As part of the process of planning a PKI for an organization, you should review the organization's existing security policy, along with its business requirements, Active Directory requirements, certificate template requirements, and any other external requirements.

# Lesson Review

You can use the following questions to test your knowledge of the information in Lesson 1, "Identifying PKI Requirements." The question is also available on the companion CD if you prefer to review it in electronic form.

---

**NOTE** Answers

Answers to these questions and explanations of why each answer choice is correct or incorrect are located in the "Answers" section at the end of the book.

---

1. Which of the following applications does NOT require the use of certificates?
   - A. Encrypting File System (EFS)
   - B. Secure/Multipurpose Internet Mail Extensions (S/MIME)
   - C. Internet Protocol Security (IPsec)
   - D. Secure Sockets Layer (SSL)

# Lesson 2:  Designing the CA Hierarchy

To design the CA hierarchy in a PKI means to determine the actual CAs that your PKI will use and the trust relationships between them. In most medium-sized and large networks, deploying more than one CA is recommended.

This lesson describes the considerations that go into determining how many CAs to deploy, the types of CAs to deploy, and how many tiers of CAs are suitable for your organization's PKI.

> **After this lesson, you will be able to:**
> - Understand the advantages and disadvantages of deploying an internal CA versus relying on an external CA.
> - Understand the advantages and disadvantages of enterprise CAs versus standalone CAs.
> - Understand the difference between a root CA and a subordinate CA.
> - Understand the advantages of using a two-tier or three-tier hierarchy in your PKI.
> - Design a PKI hierarchy for an organization.
>
> **Estimated lesson time:  30 minutes**

## Planning the CA Infrastructure

Before you can implement a PKI that meets the security needs and certificate requirements for your organization, you need to make a number of decisions about how you will deploy CAs. Planning the CA infrastructure for your organization involves making decisions about the following:

- Location of the root CAs
- Internal versus third-party CAs
- CA types and roles
- Number of CAs required

### Designing Root CAs

A CA infrastructure consists of a hierarchy of CAs that trust one another and that authenticate certificates belonging to one another. Within this infrastructure, a final authority, called a root CA, must be in place. The root CA certifies other CAs to publish and manage certificates within the organization.

## Selecting Internal CAs vs. Third-Party CAs

Depending on the functionality that you require, the capabilities of your IT infrastructure and IT administrators, and the costs that your organization can support, you might choose to base your CA infrastructure on internal CAs, third-party CAs, or a combination of internal and third-party CAs.

**Internal CAs**   If your organization conducts most of its business with partner organizations and wants to maintain control of how certificates are issued, internal CAs are the best choice. Internal CAs:

- Allow an organization to maintain direct control over its security policies.
- Allow an organization to align its certificate policy with its overall security policy.
- Can be integrated with the Active Directory Domain Services infrastructure of the organization.
- Can be expanded to include additional functionality and users at relatively little extra cost.

The disadvantages of using internal CAs include the following:

- The organization must manage its own certificates.
- The deployment schedule for internal CAs might be longer than that for CAs available from third-party service providers.
- The organization must accept liability for problems with the PKI.

**External CAs**   If your organization conducts most of its business with external customers and clients and wants to outsource certificate issuing and management processes, you might choose to use third-party CAs. Third-party CAs:

- Allow customers a greater degree of confidence when conducting secure transactions with the organization.
- Allow the organization to take advantage of the expertise of a professional service provider.
- Allow the organization to use certificate-based security technology while developing an internally managed PKI.
- Allow the organization to take advantage of the provider's understanding of the technical, legal, and business issues associated with certificate use.

The disadvantages associated with the use of third-party CAs include the following:

- They typically involve a high per-certificate cost.
- They might require the development of two management standards—one for internally issued certificates and one for commercially issued certificates.
- They allow less flexibility in configuring and managing certificates.
- The organization must have access to the third-party CAs in order to access the CRLs.

- Autoenrollment is not possible.
- Third-party CAs allow only limited integration with the internal directories, applications, and infrastructure of the organization.

## Defining CA Types and Roles

To plan your CA infrastructure, you need to understand the different types of CAs available with Windows Server 2008 and the roles that they can play. Windows Server 2008 Certificate Services supports the following two types of CAs:

- Enterprise
- Standalone

Enterprise and standalone CAs can be configured as either root CAs or subordinate CAs. Subordinate CAs can further be configured as either intermediate CAs (also referred to as policy CAs) or issuing CAs.

Before you create your CA infrastructure, you need to determine the type or types of CAs that you plan to use and define the specialized roles that you plan to have each CA assume.

**Enterprise vs. Standalone CAs**   *Enterprise CAs* are integrated with Active Directory. They publish certificates and CRLs to Active Directory. Enterprise CAs use information stored in Active Directory, including user accounts and security groups, to approve or deny certificate requests. Enterprise CAs use certificate templates. When a certificate is issued, the enterprise CA uses information in the certificate template to generate a certificate with the appropriate attributes for that certificate type.

If you want to enable automated certificate approval and automatic user certificate enrollment, use enterprise CAs to issue certificates. These features are available only when the CA infrastructure is integrated with Active Directory. Additionally, only enterprise CAs can issue certificates that enable smart card logon because this process requires that smart card certificates be mapped automatically to the user accounts in Active Directory.

*Standalone CAs* do not require Active Directory and do not use certificate templates. If you use standalone CAs, all information about the requested certificate type must be included in the certificate request. By default, all certificate requests submitted to standalone CAs are held in a pending queue until a CA administrator approves them. You can configure standalone CAs to issue certificates automatically upon request, but this is less secure and is usually not recommended because the requests are not authenticated.

From a performance perspective, using standalone CAs with automatic issuance enables you to issue certificates faster than you can by using enterprise CAs. However, using standalone CAs to issue large volumes of certificates usually comes at a high administrative cost because an administrator must manually review and then approve or deny each certificate request. For this reason, standalone CAs are best used with public key security applications on extranets and the Internet, when users do not have Windows accounts and when the volume of certificates to be issued and managed is relatively low.

In addition, you must use standalone CAs to issue certificates when you are using a third-party directory service or when Active Directory is not available.

---

**NOTE   Mixing standalone and enterprise CAs**

You can use both enterprise and standalone CAs in your organization.

---

Table 9-1 lists the options that each type of CA supports.

**Table 9-1    Options for Enterprise vs. Standalone CAs**

| Option | Enterprise CA | Standalone CA |
| --- | --- | --- |
| Publish certificates in Active Directory and use Active Directory to validate certificate requests | X | |
| Take the CA offline | | X |
| Configure the CA to issue certificates automatically | X | |
| Allow administrators to approve certificate requests manually | | X |
| Use certificate templates | X | |
| Authenticate requests to Active Directory | X | |

In general, you should deploy a standalone CA if:

- The CA is an offline root or offline intermediate CA.
- Support of templates that you can customize is not required.
- A strong security and approval model is required.
- Fewer certificates are enrolled and the manual work that you must do to issue certificates is acceptable.
- Clients are heterogeneous and cannot benefit from Active Directory.
- It is combined with a third-party RA solution in a multi-forest or heterogeneous environment.
- It issues certificates to routers through NDES SCEP.

You should deploy an enterprise CA if:

- A large number of certificates should be enrolled and approved automatically.
- Availability and redundancy is mandatory.
- Clients need the benefits of Active Directory integration.
- Features such as autoenrollment or modifiable templates are required.
- Key archival and recovery is required to escrow encryption keys.

**Root CAs** A *root CA* is the CA that is at the top of a certification hierarchy, and clients in your organization must trust it unconditionally. All certificate chains terminate at a root CA. Whether you use enterprise or standalone CAs, you need to designate a root CA.

Because there is no higher certifying authority in the certification hierarchy, the subject of the certificate issued by a root CA is also the issuer of the certificate. Likewise, because the certificate chain terminates when it reaches a self-signed CA, all self-signed CAs are root CAs. The decision to designate a CA as a trusted root CA can be made at either the enterprise level or locally by the individual IT administrator.

A root CA serves as the foundation on which you base your CA trust model. It guarantees that the subject public key belongs to the subject identity information that is contained in the certificates it issues. Different CAs might also verify this relationship by using different standards; therefore, it is important to understand the policies and procedures of the root CA before choosing to trust that authority to verify public keys.

The root CA is the most important CA in your hierarchy. If your root CA is compromised, every other CA and certificate in your hierarchy might be compromised. You can maximize the security of the root CA by keeping it disconnected from the network and using subordinate CAs to issue certificates to other subordinate CAs or to end users.

**Subordinate CAs** CAs that are not root CAs are considered subordinate. The first subordinate CA in a hierarchy obtains its CA certificate from the root CA. This first subordinate CA can, in turn, use this key to issue certificates that verify the integrity of another subordinate CA. These higher subordinate CAs are referred to as intermediate CAs. An intermediate CA is subordinate to a root CA, but it also serves as a higher certifying authority to one or more subordinate CAs.

An intermediate CA is often referred to as a policy CA because it is typically used to separate classes of certificates that can be distinguished by policy. For example, policy separation includes the level of assurance that a CA provides or the CA's geographical location to distinguish different types of users. A policy CA can be online or offline.

---

**NOTE** Internal and external policy CAs

Many organizations use one root CA and two policy CAs—one to support internal users and another to support external users.

---

The next level in the CA hierarchy usually contains the issuing CA. The issuing CA issues certificates to users and computers and is almost always online. In many CA hierarchies, the lowest level of subordinate CAs is replaced by RAs, which can act as an intermediary for a CA by authenticating the identity of a user who is applying for a certificate, initiating revocation requests, and assisting in key recovery. Unlike a CA, however, an RA does not issue certificates or CRLs; it merely processes transactions on behalf of the CA.

The hierarchy consisting of a root CA, policy CAs, and issuing CAs is illustrated in Figure 9-1.

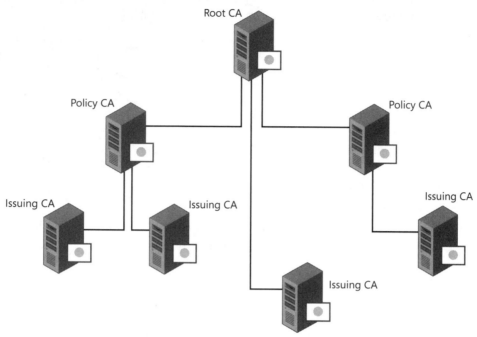

**Figure 9-1**    CA hierarchy roles

## Using Offline CAs

Securing your CA hierarchy is critical. If an intruder can gain access to a CA, either physically or by means of the network, he or she might retrieve the CA's private key and then imperson-ate the CA to gain access to valuable network resources. The compromise of even one CA key invalidates the security protection that it and any CAs below it in the hierarchy provide. For this reason, it is important to avoid connecting root CAs to the network.

To ensure the reliability of your CA infrastructure, you should specify that any nonissuing root and intermediate CAs must be offline. This minimizes the risk of the CA private keys becom-ing compromised. You can take a CA offline in any of the following ways:

- By installing a CA on a standalone computer running Windows 2000, Windows Server 2003, or Windows Server 2008 and configuring it as a standalone CA
- By physically removing the computer from the network
- By shutting down the CA service
- By shutting down the computer

Make sure that you keep CAs in a secure area with limited access.

---

**IMPORTANT**  The root CA should be a standalone, workgroup CA

Installing an offline CA on a server that is a member of a domain can cause problems with a secure channel when you bring the CA back online after a long offline period. This is because the computer account password changes every 30 days. You can get around this by making offline CA computers members of a workgroup. Installing an offline CA as an enterprise CA can cause Active Directory to have problems updating when you disconnect the server from the network. Therefore, do not use an enterprise CA as a root CA.

---

When a CA is supposed to be an offline CA, you can still publish its certificate and CRL in Active Directory. You must be sure to bring an offline CA online at regular intervals, based on your CRL publication schedule, to generate a new CRL for the CA. You must also bring the CA online to process certificate requests for subordinate CA certificates.

Because offline CAs process a small number of certificate requests at infrequent intervals, the administrative costs of maintaining offline CAs are low.

---

## Quick Check
- Why should a root CA remain offline?

## Quick Check Answer
- To protect the entire PKI from becoming compromised in case of a network attack.

---

## Determining the Number of CAs Required

After you have identified your application and user requirements, you can begin to estimate the number of CAs that you need to deploy. If your organization has limited certificate requirements, a small user base, and limited expansion goals, a single CA might be sufficient. By using a single CA, you can still meet a variety of needs by customizing and deploying certificate templates and using role separation. However, if availability or distributed functionality of Certificate Services is a priority, you must deploy multiple CAs. You also need multiple CAs if you want separate CAs to issue certificates for different purposes.

To determine the number of CAs required, answer the following questions in order:

- First, do you require only one CA? If you are supporting only a single application and location, and if 100 percent availability of the CA is not critical, you might be able to use a single CA. Otherwise, you probably require at least one root and multiple subordinate CAs.

- If you need more than one CA, how many root CAs do you require? Generally, it is recommended that you have only one root CA as a single point of trust. This is because significant cost and effort is required to protect a root CA from compromise. With multiple root CAs, root maintenance becomes much more difficult.

However, organizations with a decentralized security administration model, such as corporations with multiple, largely independent business units and no strong central administrative body, might require more than one root CA.

- How many intermediate or policy CAs do you need?
- How many issuing CAs or RAs do you need?

The number of intermediate and issuing CAs that you deploy depends on the following factors:

- **Usage**   Certificates can be issued for a number of purposes (for example, secure e-mail, network authentication, and so on). Each of these uses might involve different issuing policies. Using separate CAs provides a basis for administering each policy separately.
- **Organizational or geographic divisions**   You must have different policies for issuing certificates, depending on the role of an entity or its physical location in the organization. You can create separate subordinate CAs to administer these policies.
- **Distribution of the certificate load**   You can deploy multiple issuing CAs to distribute the certificate load to meet site, network, and server requirements. For example, if network links between sites are slow or discontinuous, you might need to place issuing CAs at each site to meet Certificate Services performance and usability requirements.
- **The need for flexible configuration**   You can tailor the CA environment (key strength, physical protection, protection against network attacks, and so on) to provide a balance between security and usability. For example, you can renew keys and certificates more frequently for the intermediate and issuing CAs that are at high risk for compromise without requiring a change to established root trust relationships. Also, when you use more than one subordinate CA, you can turn off a subsection of the CA hierarchy without affecting established root trust relationships or the rest of the hierarchy.
- **The need for redundant services**   If one enterprise CA fails, redundancy makes it possible for another issuing CA to provide users with uninterrupted service.

Strive to have only as many CAs and RAs as you need to function efficiently. Deploying more CAs than you need creates an unnecessary management burden and introduces additional areas of security vulnerability.

## PRACTICE Planning the CA Infrastructure

You are an enterprise administrator at Humongous Insurance, Inc., a company that specializes in selling automobile insurance at discount prices. The company consists of a headquarters in New York City and three branch offices in Albany, Binghamton, and Buffalo. The company employs about 800 workers among its four office sites. The Humongous Insurance network consists of a single Active Directory domain, *humongousinsurance.com*.

Humongous Insurance is planning to launch a new version of its Web site that allows customers to view confidential data. In advance of the new site launch, the company has recently updated its written security policy. The chief security officer has given you the responsibility of designing a PKI to meet the new security needs of the company. Currently, the company does not have any CA deployed.

The company's updated written security policy includes the following requirements:

- The Web site must require an encrypted Hypertext Transfer Protocol (HTTP) connection when users view account data.
- All e-mail messages sent among employees must be encrypted.
- All remote server administration must be conducted over an encrypted channel.
- At any of the four company branches, access to the company wireless network must require smart card authentication.

▶ **Exercise  Planning for a PKI Deployment**

In this exercise, you review the business and technical requirements and answer specific questions to help you plan for PKI deployment.

1. Name the specific applications implied by the security policy that *require* the use of public key cryptography.

   **Answers:**

   ❑ Web encryption (SSL), for the encrypted HTTP connection when users view account data.

   ❑ Secure e-mail, to encrypt e-mail messages sent among employees.

   ❑ Smart card authentication (with 802.1x), to support the smart card requirement for wireless access.

   (Note that although IPsec is required for the remote server administration over an encrypted channel, IPsec typically uses Kerberos instead of a public key cryptography in an Active Directory environment.)

2. Who must obtain the certificates for each of these applications? In particular, specify whether each application requires certificates for users or computers.

   **Answers:**

   ❑ Web encryption: only the Web server (computer) must obtain a certificate.

   ❑ Secure e-mail: all users in the organization must obtain certificates.

   ❑ Smart card authentication: users needing wireless access must obtain a smart card (which includes a user certificate).

3. For each of the applications, specify whether the certificates required should be assigned by a public CA or an in-house CA.

   **Answers:**

   ❑ Web encryption: the Web server should obtain a certificate from a public CA such as VeriSign or Thawte.

   ❑ Secure e-mail: users should obtain certificates from an in-house CA.

   ❑ Smart card authentication: users should obtain certificates from an in-house CA.

4. For each of the applications that will be supported by an in-house CA, specify whether the CA should be an enterprise CA or a standalone CA.

   **Answers:**

   ❑ Secure e-mail: Enterprise CA

   ❑ Smart card authentication: Enterprise CA

5. Given the size of the company and best practices for PKI deployments, design the CA hierarchy for the certificate infrastructure. Specifically, determine how many tiers for the certificate infrastructure are needed; whether a root CA, intermediate CAs, and issuing CAs are needed; and which of these should be kept online or offline.

   **Answer:**

   ❑ Large companies such as Humongous Insurance should include three tiers in the CA hierarchy. The root CA should be kept offline, the intermediate CAs should also be kept offline, and the issuing CAs should be kept online.

## Lesson Summary

■ To plan a CA infrastructure, you need to determine how many CAs to deploy, the types and roles of CAs to deploy, and the trust relationships among those CAs.

■ Within a PKI, a final authority, called a root CA, must be in place. Beneath this root CA, a PKI can include any number of subordinate CAs. A subordinate CA can act as a parent to verify the integrity of another subordinate CA. When a PKI includes three tiers in this way, the higher subordinate is known as an intermediate CA or policy CA. CAs that actively issue certificates are found at the lowest level of the hierarchy and are known as issuing CAs.

■ As part of the PKI design process, you need to determine whether to use internal CAs, an external CA, or a combination of both.

■ As part of the PKI design process, you need to determine which CAs in your PKI should be enterprise CAs and which should be standalone CAs.

## Lesson Review

You can use the following questions to test your knowledge of the information in Lesson 2, "Designing the CA Hierarchy." The question is also available on the companion CD if you prefer to review it in electronic form.

---

**NOTE**  Answers

Answers to these questions and explanations of why each answer choice is correct or incorrect are located in the "Answers" section at the end of the book.

---

1. You work as an IT administrator in a large company, City Power and Light. The *cpandl.com* network consists of a single Active Directory Domain Services domain.

   You are a member of a team designing a new in-house PKI for use with EFS. Your goals are to minimize the risk that the entire PKI will be compromised and to minimize the administrative overhead of publishing certificates. Which of the following CAs should you deploy for your PKI hierarchy? (Choose two. Each correct answer represents part of the solution.)

   **A.** Offline root CA

   **B.** Online root CA

   **C.** Enterprise subordinate CA

   **D.** Standalone subordinate CA

# Lesson 3: Creating a Certificate Management Plan

Before your CAs issue any certificates, you need to have a plan that describes how certificates will be issued, renewed, and revoked.

This lesson describes the many considerations that go into determining which enrollment, renewal, and revocation methods are most suitable for an organization.

---

**After this lesson, you will be able to:**

- Understand the various certificate enrollment methods and the situations in which each is most suitable.
- Understand the difference between using CRLs and OCSP for certification validity checking and the situations in which each of these methods is most suitable.

**Estimated lesson time:  30 minutes**

---

## Selecting a Certificate Enrollment Method

To enable enrollment, you need to specify the enrollment and renewal processes for your certificates. Enrollment involves either configuring permissions to establish which security principals have Enroll permissions for specific templates (in the case of enterprise CAs) or appointing a certificate administrator who reviews each certificate request and issues or denies the request based on the information provided.

AD CS supports the ability to process certificate requests manually, if administrative approval is required, or automatically, if no approval is necessary. The following enrollment and renewal methods are available:

- **Certificate autoenrollment and renewal**   Allows you to automatically issue certificates that enable PKI applications, such as smart card logon, EFS, SSL, and S/MIME, to users and computers within an AD DS environment. Certificate autoenrollment is based on a combination of Group Policy settings and certificate templates, which allows you to enroll computers when they start up and to enroll users when they log on to their domain.

  To use autoenrollment, you need a Windows Server 2003 or Windows Server 2008 domain controller; a Windows Vista Business, Windows Vista Enterprise, Windows Vista Ultimate, or Windows XP Professional client; and a Windows Server 2003 Advanced Server enterprise CA or a Windows Server 2008 enterprise CA.

- **Certificate Request Wizard and Certificate Renewal Wizard**   Available from the Certificates console, you can use the Certificate Request Wizard to request a certificate from an active enterprise CA on behalf of a user, computer, or service. You can then use the Certificate Renewal Wizard to renew the certificate.

- **Web Enrollment Support pages**   Certificate Web enrollment has been available since its inclusion in the Windows 2000 Server operating system. It is designed to provide an enrollment mechanism for organizations that need to issue and renew certificates for users and computers that are not joined to the domain or that are not connected directly to the network and for users of non-Microsoft operating systems. Instead of relying on the autoenrollment mechanism of a CA or using the Certificate Request Wizard, the Web enrollment support provided by a Windows-based CA allows these users to request and obtain new and renewed certificates through a Web-based user interface over an Internet or intranet connection.

- **Network Device Enrollment Service**   The Network Device Enrollment Service (NDES) is the Microsoft implementation of the SCEP. SCEP is a PKI communication protocol that enables software running on network devices such as routers and switches, which cannot otherwise be authenticated on the network, to enroll for X.509 certificates from a CA.

To select the certificate enrollment and renewal processes that are appropriate for your organization, you need to consider the following:

- **The users, computers, devices, and services for which you intend to provide services**  Determine whether they are internal or external to the organization. Identify the operating systems they are running and determine whether they are connected to Active Directory Domain Services.

- **The policies that you establish to manage certificate distribution**   This includes both the procedural policies that you establish for your PKI and the Group Policy settings that you use to implement those policies.

Selecting certificate enrollment and renewal processes involves making decisions about the following:

- Automatic versus manual requests
- Automatic versus manual approval
- An enrollment and renewal user interface
- CA certificate renewal

## Selecting Automatic vs. Manual Requests

Whether you choose to generate certificate requests automatically or manually depends on the types of certificates that you intend to use and the number and type of clients that you enroll. For example, if you want all users or computers to use a certain type of certificate, it is not practical for you to require that each certificate be requested individually. Although rolling out a new certificate to all users or computers at one time can generate a large amount of network activity, you can control that activity by deploying the certificate requests for each organizational unit one at a time.

On the other hand, you might want to have users or an administrator request certain high-security certificates, such as those used for digital signing or administrative tasks, only when needed. This can improve administrative control over these certificates—particularly if certificate use is not limited by a user or computer OU or security group membership.

You can improve control over your certificates by using one of the following options to limit user certificate requests:

- **Restricted enrollment agent**   In Windows Server 2008 Enterprise and Windows Server 2008 Datacenter, organizations can permit an enrollment agent to enroll only a certain group of users. The restricted enrollment agent features allow an enrollment agent to be used for one or many certificate templates. For each certificate template, you can choose which users or security groups the enrollment agent can enroll on behalf of. The restricted enrollment agent is not available on a Windows Server 2008 Standard–based CA.

- **Restrict access to specific templates**   Configure the discretionary access control list (DACL) for each template so that only the required security principals have Enroll and Read permissions for particular templates.

- **Automate the deployment of computer certificates**   Configure Group Policy to automatically assign the necessary computer certificates by adding the certificate template to the Automatic Certificate Request Settings option in Group Policy.

### Selecting Automatic vs. Manual Approval

Users can request a certificate from a Windows Server 2008 CA either manually or automatically. This request is held until an administrator approves it, if manual approval is required, or until the verification process is completed. When the certificate request has been approved, the autoenrollment process installs the certificate automatically or automatically renews the certificate on behalf of the user, based on the specifications in the certificate template.

Most of the time, you choose the same method for certificate approval that you choose for certificate requests. However, there are exceptions. For example, if you have the appropriate Group Policy and DACL restrictions on your certificate templates, you might decide to approve automatically a certificate request that was generated manually. Conversely, in some cases it is appropriate to manually approve certificate requests that are automatically generated.

However, in general:

- For routine and high-volume certificates, such as e-mail certificates, automatic approval is the best option for certificate approval as long as the certificate requester has already been authenticated with a valid set of domain credentials.

- When a high degree of administrative oversight is required, such as for software code signing certificates, consider processing certificate requests manually. By using the Certificate Request Wizard, you can evaluate every certificate request individually—or you can delegate this responsibility to another administrator.

## Selecting an Enrollment and Renewal User Interface

The user interface that you select for certificate request and approval processing depends on whether you choose automatic or manual certificate request and approval methods. If you decide to use autoenrollment for both certificate requests and certificate approval, you must use a minimal user interface.

However, if all or part of the enrollment process is manual, you must decide between using the Web Enrollment Support pages or the Certificate Request Wizard. The Web Enrollment Support pages are the easier interface for users to use. Users can perform the following tasks from the Web Enrollment Support pages:

- Request and obtain a basic user certificate
- Request and obtain other types of certificates by using advanced options
- Request a certificate by using a certificate request file
- Renew certificates by using a certificate renewal request file
- Save a certificate request to a file
- Save the issued certificate to a file
- Check on pending certificate requests
- Retrieve a CA certificate
- Retrieve the latest certificate revocation list from a CA
- Request smart card certificates on behalf of other users (for use by trusted administrators)

However, administrators might prefer to use the Certificate Request Wizard and the Certificate Renewal Wizard. You can start the wizard from the Certificates snap-in. Because the wizard is linked to the Certificates snap-in, you can also create custom snap-ins that you can distribute to CA administrators to whom you have delegated specific roles.

Unless an organization uses firewalls between one part of the organization and another, you can use the Certificates snap-in or the Web interface interchangeably. If a firewall exists between the CA and the requesting client, you must request certificates by means of the Web Enrollment Support pages or ensure that port 135 and a dynamic port above 1024 are open for Microsoft Management Console (MMC)-based DCOM communication.

Whether you choose to use the Web Enrollment Support Pages or the Certificate Request Wizard and Certificate Renewal Wizard, you might need to prepare documentation that describes how users can request a user certificate, what users can expect after they request the certificate (for example, automatic enrollment or a delay pending administrator approval), and how they can use the certificates after they receive them.

### Using CA Certificate Renewal

When the certificate of a CA expires, the CA can no longer provide certificate services. To provide uninterrupted certificate services, use the Certificates console to renew the CA certificate before its expiration date. The interval that is required for CA renewal depends on the certificate lifetime of the CA.

After you renew a CA, the CA continues to issue certificates by using the new CA certificate, and the cycle starts over. Unexpired certificates that were issued by the prerenewal CA continue to be trusted until they expire or are revoked.

You can use the standard enrollment and renewal methods that are available in Windows Server 2008 to renew your CAs and certificates. You can renew certificates with the same private key and public key set or with new private and public keys. However, if you have special needs, you can develop custom certificate enrollment and renewal applications for CAs.

## Creating a CA Renewal Strategy

Certificate lifetimes can have an impact on the security of your PKI for the following reasons:

- Over time, encryption keys become more vulnerable to attack. In general, the longer that a key pair is in use, the greater the risk that the key can be compromised. To mitigate this risk, you must establish the maximum allowable key lifetimes and renew certificates with new key pairs before these limits are exceeded.

- When a CA certificate expires, all subordinate certificates that are issued by this CA for validation also expire. This is known as time nesting. When a CA certificate is revoked, all certificates that have been issued by the CA must also be reissued.

- End entity certificates expire when the issuing CA certificate reaches the end of its lifetime unless the end entity certificate is renewed with a new key pair that chains to a CA certificate with a longer lifetime.

- You must plan the CA certificate renewal precisely during the PKI deployment phase. If this important planning step is missed, the entire PKI might stop working when the CA certificate expires because all of the certificates that depend on the CA's certificate are then no longer usable for either encryption or signing operations. Remember, however, that a certificate is capable of decrypting data, even if it has expired or been revoked.

# Defining a Revocation Policy

You should draw a revocation policy to define the circumstances under which certificates should be revoked. This revocation policy should describe the circumstances under which certificates are revoked, the individuals who perform revocation, the method by which certificates are revoked, and the manner in which revocation information is distributed to PKI clients.

The most common means of communicating certificate status is by distributing CRLs. In Windows Server 2008 PKIs where the use of conventional CRLs is not an optimal solution, an online responder based on OCSP can be used to manage and distribute revocation status information.

## Certificate Revocation Lists

In some cases a CA must revoke a certificate before the certificate's validity period expires. When a certificate is revoked, the CA includes the serial number of the certificate and the reason for the revocation in the CRL.

Windows Server 2008 supports the issuance of two types of CRLs: base CRLs and delta CRLs.

A *base CRL* contains a list of all the revoked certificates associated with a CA, along with the reason(s) for revocation. All time-valid revoked certificates are signed by a CA's specific private key. If a CA's certificate is renewed with a new key pair, a new base CRL is generated that includes only revoked certificates signed with the CA's new private key.

A *delta CRL* contains only the serial numbers and revocation reasons for certificates revoked since the last base CRL was published. A delta CRL is implemented to provide more timely revocation information from a CA and to decrease the amount of data downloaded when retrieving a CRL. When a new base CRL is published, the revoked certificates in the delta CRL are added to the new base CRL. The next delta CRL will contain only certificates revoked since the new base CRL was published.

The delta CRL is much smaller than a base CRL because only the most recent revocations are included. The base CRL, which contains all revoked certificates, can be downloaded less frequently.

---

**NOTE  Delta CRLs don't work without base CRLs**

If you implement delta CRLs, relying parties must still download the base CRL. It is the combination of the base CRL and the delta CRL that provides the complete information on all revoked certificates.

---

---

**IMPORTANT    Delta CRLs are not always supported**

Not all relying parties support delta CRLs. If a relying party does not support delta CRLs, the relying party will inspect only the base CRL to determine a certificate's revocation status.

---

**Problems with CRLs**    CRLs have historically been the primary method for determining the revocation status of a specific certificate. Although CRLs are widely supported, there are some known issues with using only CRLs to determine a certificate's revocation status.

- **Latency**    The primary issue with CRLs is that there is latency in identifying that a certificate has been revoked. After you have revoked a certificate, relying parties do not recognize the revocation until the next publication of a CRL. The availability is defined by the CRL publication schedule. For example, if you publish an updated base CRL at 7:00 A.M. daily, a certificate revoked at 8:00 A.M. will not be recognized as a revoked certificate until the next day's publication takes place.

- **Caching of CRLs**    When a client computer checks the revocation status of a certificate, it first checks for the desired base CRL or delta CRL in the CryptoAPI cache. If it finds the base CRL or delta CRL, the client computer checks the CRL to determine if the CRL is time-valid. Like certificates, a CRL has a validity period defined by the CRL publication interval. If a time-valid CRL is found in the CryptoAPI cache, that version of the CRL is used for revocation checking, even if an updated version of the CRL has been published manually. The use of the cached version of the CRL is done for performance reasons to prevent excess network traffic. In addition, the use of a cached CRL follows the recommendations in RFC 3280, "Internet X.509 Public Key Infrastructure Certificate and Certificate Revocation List (CRL) Profile," to acquire an updated CRL only when the previous CRL expires.

## Online Certificate Status Protocol (OCSP)

Windows Server 2008 introduces an alternative to CRLs that allows PKI clients to determine in real time whether a certificate has been revoked. Rather than a client downloading a base CRL or delta CRL, the client (OCSP client) sends an HTTP-based certificate status request to a server (referred to as an OCSP responder). The client determines the OCSP responder's URL by inspecting the certificate's Authority Information Access extension. If the extension contains an OCSP responder URL and the client supports OCSP, the client can proceed with sending an OCSP request to the OCSP responder.

---

**NOTE    OCSP is new to Windows Server 2008**

OCSP was not previously available in Windows Server 2003. Prior to Windows Server 2008, you had to implement third-party solutions to use OCSP with a Microsoft CA.

---

Unlike CRLs, which are distributed periodically and contain information about all certificates that have been revoked or suspended, an online responder receives and responds only to requests from clients for information about the status of a single certificate. The responder communicates with the CA that issued the queried certificate to determine the revocation status and returns a digitally signed response indicating the certificate's status. The OCSP responder can communicate directly with the CA or inspect the CRLs issued by the CA to determine the revocation status of the requested certificate.

The advantage of OCSP is that the OCSP responder typically provides more up-to-date revocation information to the OCSP client than a CRL does.

OCSP, however, has disadvantages, as well. One drawback of OCSP is that, for deployments servicing many clients, the OCSP responder can be overwhelmed with requests. For this reason, it is important to deploy your OCSP responder in a Network Load Balancing cluster or other load balancing solution. A second drawback of OCSP is that it is more difficult to implement than CRLs are. A final limitation of OCSP is that it is supported only in Windows Vista and Windows Server 2008.

When planning for certificate validity checking and revocation, OCSP is preferable to CRLs when the timeliness of revocation information is a high priority and minimizing processing workload is a low priority. For large deployments used to support many PKI clients across the Internet, CRLs are a more practical solution.

## Determining Publication Points

The final technical requirement that must be met in your design is determining publication points, either for both CRLs and CA certificates (if you implement CRL checking) or for an OCSP responder (if you implement OCSP).

A PKI client can use the URLs stored in the CRL Distribution Point (CDP) (if CRL checking is being used) and Authority Information Access (AIA) extensions (if OCSP is being used) to determine a certificate's revocation status.

At each CA in the hierarchy, you must define publication points for certificates issued by that CA. These publication points allow access to *that* CA's certificate and CRL. You can use the following protocols when defining publication points:

- **Hypertext Transfer Protocol (HTTP) URLs** HTTP URLs are used for both internal and external publication points. The advantage of HTTP URLs is that there is little lag time between publication and availability. After you publish an updated CRL or CA certificate to an HTTP URL, it is immediately available for download by PKI-enabled applications. In addition, HTTP URLs can typically be downloaded by clients behind firewalls and those who are not full Active Directory clients, including those running an operating system earlier than Microsoft Windows 2000 and non-Microsoft clients.

■ **Lightweight Directory Access Protocol (LDAP) URL**   A CA certificate or CRL that is published to an LDAP URL is, by default, published into the configuration naming context of Active Directory. This means that the CRL or CA certificate is available at all domain controllers in the forest.

---

**NOTE**   **Publishing certificates to LDAP directories**

Although the default LDAP location references Active Directory, you can publish a CA certificate or CRL to any LDAP directory, such as Active Directory Lightweight Directory Services (AD LDS).

---

There are two disadvantages to using the default LDAP URL location:

❑ It can take some time for CRLs or CA certificates to fully replicate to all domain controllers in the forest. The actual time depends on your network's replication latency, especially when the replication must take place between sites and not just between domain controllers in the same site.

❑ Nonsupport of the Active Directory–related LDAP URLs can lead to delays in CRL or CA certificate retrieval. If the default LDAP URL is the first URL in the URL listing, a non–Active Directory enabled client will time out for 10 seconds before it moves on to the next available URL.

---

**MORE INFO**   **Best practices for a PKI**

More information on choosing publication points can be found in the "Best Practices for Implementing a Microsoft Windows Server 2003 Public Key Infrastructure" document at *http://www.microsoft.com/technet/prodtechnol/windowsserver2003/technologies/security/ws3pkibp.mspx*. Even though this is a Windows Server 2003 whitepaper, the concepts still hold true for Windows Server 2008 design.

---

The decision on which protocols to implement for CRL or CA certificate publication points depends on the frequency at which you publish CRLs, the protocols allowed to traverse network firewalls, and your network's operating systems. To ensure maximum availability, the URLs should be ordered so that the most common protocol used for CRL or CA certificate retrieval is listed first in the CDP extension. Other protocols are then listed in their order of use.

After you choose the publication protocols, you must choose *where* to publish the CA certificates and CRLs. The location decision includes the physical servers where you publish the files and the location of the servers on the corporate network: intranet or extranet.

Use the following guidelines when choosing publication points:

■ If most computers are running Windows 2000 or later and are members of the forest, you should include an LDAP URL that references the Active Directory configuration naming context. This location is published to all domain controllers in the forest and ensures availability and fault tolerance.

- If you have several nonforest computers or third-party operating systems, such as UNIX, you should include Web server publication points for HTTP URLs.

- If certificates are to be evaluated from the external network, the CA certificate and CDP must be published to an externally accessible location, such as a Web server or LDAP server in a perimeter subnet of the network.

- File publication points typically are not used for CA certificate and CRL retrieval. File publication points are more common for publishing CA certificates and CRL information to remote servers.

- The URL order is determined by the types of network clients. The order should be set so that the majority of clients can retrieve the CA certificate or CRL from the first URL in the listing. If a client cannot retrieve the CA certificate or CRL from the first URL, the client times out in an attempt to connect and then proceeds through the next URLs in the listing.

- Delta CRLs are published more frequently than base CRLs. You might not want to publish delta CRLs to LDAP locations because of Active Directory replication latency. Instead, publish delta CRLs to HTTP locations. The Active Directory replication interval must allow the delta CRL to be replicated before the prior delta CRL expires if you plan to publish the delta CRL to Active Directory.

---

**NOTE  Publishing to AD LDS**

Delta CRLs can be published to a standalone LDAP server, such as AD LDS, because replication is not an issue with this form of LDAP server.

---

- OCSP URLs must be hosted on highly available resources. If the OCSP responder is unavailable when an OCSP client submits a query, revocation checking will fail.

---

**Quick Check**

- When is it preferable to use Web-based CRL publication points?

**Quick Check Answer**

- When the clients performing certification validity checking are not running Windows or are not members of an Active Directory forest.

---

PRACTICE **Planning a PKI Management Strategy**

You are an enterprise administrator at Fabrikam, Inc., a company based in Buffalo with branch offices in Rochester, Syracuse, Albany, Binghamton, and Elmira. The *fabrikam.com* corporate network consists of a single Active Directory Domain Services domain. The network includes servers that run Windows Server 2003 or Windows Server 2008 and clients that run Windows XP Professional or Windows Vista Enterprise. All computers and employees have accounts in the *fabrikam.com* domain.

Management has recently decided to add support for SSL connections to its external and internal Web servers. Every day, as many as 10,000 independent users from around the world visit the public Web server, which is located in a perimeter network outside of the corporate AD DS domain. The internal Web server is located on a member server in the *fabrikam.com* domain and is used only by employees. You are a member of the team whose job is to define the associated PKI structure along with a certificate enrollment and revocation strategy.

▶ **Exercise   Planning for a PKI Management**

In this exercise, you review the business and technical requirements and answer specific questions to help you plan for PKI deployment.

1. You want the external Web server to support SSL with server authentication and encryption. Should the certificate used to support SSL on this Web server originate from an enterprise CA, a standalone CA, or a public CA?

   **Answer:**
   - ❑ A public CA

2. You want the internal Web server to support SSL with both server and client authentication. Should the certificates used to support SSL on this Web server originate from an enterprise CA, a standalone CA, or a public CA?

   **Answer:**
   - ❑ An enterprise CA

3. If the internal Web server will be used by all employees, what is the best method to distribute certificates to support connections to the server—autoenrollment or Web enrollment?

   **Answer:**
   - ❑ Autoenrollment

4. You want a single technology to support the distribution of revocation information for all clients in your organization. Which revocation technology is best suited to support the CA supporting clients internal to *fabrikam.com*—OCSP or CRLs?

   **Answer:**
   - ❑ CRLs

5. Assume that the headquarters site and all branch offices include a domain controller for the *fabrikam.com* domain. If the currency of revocation data is a low priority and the ease of implementation is a high priority, which type of distribution point should you use to publish certificate validity information—HTTP or LDAP?

   **Answer:**
   - ❑ LDAP

## Lesson Summary

- Part of planning for a PKI involves designing the enrollment, renewal, and revocation processes for certificates.

- AD CS supports the ability to process certificate requests manually, if administrative approval is required, or automatically, if no administrative approval is necessary.

- Autoenrollment allows you to issue certificates automatically to users and computers in an Active Directory domain. Web enrollment provides an enrollment mechanism for organizations that need to issue and renew certificates for users and computers that are not joined to the domain or not connected directly to the network and for users of non-Microsoft operating systems. The Network Device Enrollment Service (NDES) enables software running on network devices to enroll for certificates from a Windows Server 2008 CA.

- A revocation policy should describe the circumstances under which certificates are revoked, the individuals who perform revocation, the method in which certificates are revoked, and the manner in which revocation information is distributed to PKI clients.

- The most common means of communicating certificate status is by distributing CRLs. A base CRL contains a list of all the revoked certificates associated with a CA, along with the reason(s) for revocation. A delta CRL contains only the serial numbers and revocation reasons for certificates revoked since the last base CRL was published. A limitation of CRLs is that there is latency in identifying that a certificate has been revoked.

- OCSP is a new feature of Windows Server 2008 that allows clients to determine in real time the validity of a certificate.

## Lesson Review

You can use the following questions to test your knowledge of the information in Lesson 3, "Creating a Certificate Management Plan." The question is also available on the companion CD if you prefer to review it in electronic form.

---

**NOTE** Answers

Answers to these questions and explanations of why each answer choice is correct or incorrect are located in the "Answers" section at the end of the book.

---

1. You need to design a PKI for your company, Northwind Traders, whose network consists of a single Active Directory domain. You plan to deploy all company CAs on servers running Windows Server 2008. Your goal is to automate the distribution of certificates to users as much as possible.

   Which of the following represents the best method to issue certificates to users who are not members of an AD DS domain?

   A. Online Certificate Status Protocol (OCSP)

   B. Autoenrollment

   C. Simple Certificate Enrollment Protocol (SCEP)

   D. Web enrollment

# Chapter Review

To further practice and reinforce the skills you learned in this chapter, you can

- Review the chapter summary.
- Complete the case scenario. This scenario sets up a real-world situation involving the topics of this chapter and asks you to create solutions.
- Complete the suggested practices.
- Take a practice test.

## Chapter Summary

- Planning a PKI for a large organization can be summarized in three steps. First, you need to identify the needs of the PKI. Second, you need to design the CA hierarchy. Third, you need to determine how certificates are issued, renewed, and revoked.
- A PKI can be triggered by a company's need to support any number of technologies, including EFS, IPsec, VPNs, SSL, S/MIME, smart cards, and digital signatures.
- A PKI should be designed and deployed as a means to support your company's security policies and overall business strategy.
- Designing the CA hierarchy entails determining how many CAs your organization needs, which CAs will be kept online or offline, which CAs should be enterprise CAs or standalone CAs, how many tiers your hierarchy should include, and what the trust relationship should be among deployed CAs.
- Designing a certificate management policy for a PKI entails determining whether certificate issuance should occur manually or automatically, the conditions under which certificates should be revoked, and the method by which clients can check the validity of certificates.

## Case Scenario

In the following case scenario, you will apply what you've learned in this chapter. You can find answers to these questions in the "Answers" section at the end of this book.

### Case Scenario: Planning a PKI

You are an IT administrator in your organization, Litware, Inc. Litware is a publishing company that partners with many independent writers who contribute articles from around the world. The *litware.com* network consists of a single Active Directory domain. In the network, all servers are running Windows Server 2008, and all clients are running Windows Vista Enterprise. All employees have user accounts in the domain, but none of the partners do.

Recently, management has determined that the all e-mail sent between Litware employees and partner writers should be encrypted by using the S/MIME standard. In addition, you want all user certificates to be issued by in-house CAs, not by public CAs.

You are a member of the team whose responsibility is to design a PKI to support the new secure e-mail requirement. Your team has already agreed to use a single root CA for the entire PKI.

1. You want all user certificates issued to partners to have a lifetime of one year by default, but you want all user certificates issued to employees to last three years by default. How many CAs should the PKI include, at a minimum?

2. You want to minimize the administrative difficulty of issuing certificates to users. Which certificate enrollment method should you recommend for Litware employees? For partners?

3. It is a high priority to deliver current information to employees about the validity of certificates issued to partners. Which method should you use to enable employee computers to check for revocation status?

# Suggested Practices

To help you successfully master the exam objectives presented in this chapter, complete the following tasks.

## Watch a Webcast

■ **Practice**  Watch the webcasts "Best Practices for Public Key Infrastructure: Steps to Build an Offline Root Certification Authority (Part 1 of 2)," available at *http://support .microsoft.com/kb/896733*, and "Best Practices for Public Key Infrastructure: Steps to Build an Offline Root Certification Authority (Part 2 of 2)," available at *http://support .microsoft.com/kb/896737*.

## Read a White Paper

■ **Practice**  Read the white paper "Active Directory Certificate Server Enhancements in Windows Server Code Name 'Longhorn.'" You can access this white paper by searching for its title on the *Microsoft.com* Web site or by directly visiting *http://www.microsoft.com /downloads/details.aspx?familyid=9BF17231-D832-4FF9-8FB8-0539BA21AB95 &displaylang=en*.

# Take a Practice Test

The practice tests on this book's companion CD offer many options. For example, you can test yourself on just one exam objective, or you can test yourself on all the 70-647 certification exam content. You can set up the test so that it closely simulates the experience of taking a certification exam, or you can set it up in study mode so that you can look at the correct answers and explanations after you answer each question.

---

**MORE INFO    Practice tests**

For details about all the practice test options available, see the "How to Use the Practice Tests" section in this book's introduction.

---

Chapter 10

# Designing Solutions for Data Sharing, Data Security, and Business Continuity

Before you deploy any new technology in a corporate network, it's important to have a clear idea of the problem that technology is intended to solve. In this way, planning for a new technology always begins with assessing your network needs. When you have defined these needs, you can conduct research to determine which feature or technology can best meet those needs.

This chapter will review features in Windows Server 2008 that address the specific needs for data sharing, data storage security, system recoverabilty, and system availability.

### Exam objectives in this chapter:
- Plan for business continuity.
- Design for data management and access.

### Lessons in this chapter:
- Lesson 1: Planning for Data Sharing and Collaboration . . . . . . . . . . . . . . . . . . . . . . 431
- Lesson 2: Choosing Data Security Solutions . . . . . . . . . . . . . . . . . . . . . . . . . . . . . 448
- Lesson 3: Planning for System Recoverability and Availability . . . . . . . . . . . . . . . . . 459

## Before You Begin

To complete the lessons in this chapter, you must have

- A basic understanding of Windows Server 2008 and of Active Directory Domain Services (AD DS)

**Real World**

JC Mackin

BitLocker is used to protect the data on your disks even if the disks are stolen, and even if (in certain modes) your entire computer is stolen. The computers most likely to benefit from BitLocker are business laptops (because their physical security is easily compromised) and other servers that store critical data.

Unfortunately, however, BitLocker has limited benefit for many computers currently in production. To take advantage of BitLocker encryption, after all, either your computer's motherboard must include a Trusted Platform Module (TPM) version 1.2, or you must insert a prepared USB drive key whenever the computer boots. Because many computers don't currently include a TPM 1.2, the USB key is the only way to take advantage of BitLocker for the many computers that need BitLocker encryption. And, realistically, the USB key does not provide much protection. If you have to insert a USB drive into a computer every time the computer boots, you are likely to keep the USB drive near the computer at all times—in your laptop bag, for example—where it is likely to be stolen right along with your computer.

If you have data that you want to protect with BitLocker and you don't have a TPM 1.2 module on your computer, I would recommend that you choose for your USB drive key a USB drive that is fingerprint-protected. In this case a thief cannot activate the USB drive key even if it is stolen, which ensures that only you can start your computer.

# Lesson 1:  Planning for Data Sharing and Collaboration

Distributed file system (DFS) and SharePoint facilitate data sharing in large organizations, but in very different ways. DFS is a feature whose main benefit is to replicate file shares to remote offices and to provide a consistent Universal Naming Convention (UNC) pathname to file shares regardless of location in a network.

SharePoint, on the other hand, provides access to data through team Web sites. SharePoint sites can store files and documents, but they also provide version control, bulletin boards, calendaring, and many other features.

This lesson reviews the features and design strategies associated with these two data sharing technologies.

> **After this lesson, you will be able to:**
> - Determine whether DFS is a suitable solution for your network.
> - Understand the DFS settings that are integral to an overall DFS design.
> - Determine whether Windows SharePoint Services (WSS) 3.0 is a suitable solution for your network.
> - Determine whether Microsoft Office SharePoint Server (MOSS) 2007 is a suitable solution for your network.
>
> **Estimated lesson time:  60 minutes**

## Planning a DFS Deployment

DFS is a feature in Windows Server 2008 that facilitates access to shared files in a large network. As part of your overall network planning for data sharing and collaboration, you should consider your network needs for file sharing, review the features offered by DFS, and then determine whether this feature can meet those needs.

### Reviewing DFS Concepts and Features

DFS enables an organization to build a single hierarchical view of file shares that remains consistent across sites in a large network. Users access DFS shares by specifying an alias pathname that remains identical regardless of location. With DFS, shared files are replicated among multiple servers so that by specifying the same pathname, users throughout the network access a local copy of the hosted files. When permissions allow changes to a file or folder, changes made to the local copy are also replicated to other DFS servers.

---

**IMPORTANT** DFS fundamentals

If you are not familiar with basic concepts related to DFS, be sure to view the introductory Flash demonstration named Dfs.swf, which you can access by visiting *http://www.microsoft.com /windowsserver2003/evaluation/demos/dfs.html*. Although this demonstration was created for Windows Server 2003, the fundamental concepts about DFS have not changed.

---

DFS is made up of the following network elements:

- **Namespace**   The virtual view of shared folders in an organization. A namespace is made up of the remaining elements on this list.
- **Namespace server**   A namespace server hosts a namespace. A namespace server can be a standalone server, a domain member server, or a domain controller.
- **Namespace root**   The namespace root is the starting point of the namespace. A domain-based namespace can be hosted on multiple namespace servers to increase the availability of the namespace.
- **Folder**   A container in a namespace that redirects clients to a folder target.
- **Folder targets**   A location separate from a folder in which data and content is stored.

The elements that make up a DFS namespace are illustrated in Figure 10-1.

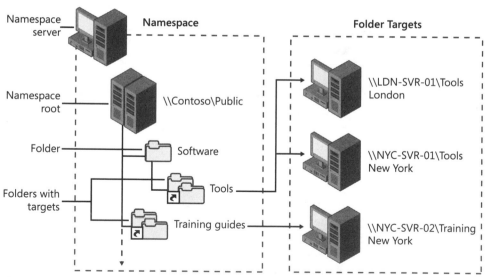

**Figure 10-1**   DFS namespace elements

When you create a new namespace, you can create it as either a domain-based namespace or a standalone namespace. A domain-based namespace is published to Active Directory Domain Services (AD DS) and supports the file replication and built-in fault tolerance features. A standalone namespace stores its configuration information in the Registry of the namespace target that hosts it. Standalone namespaces do not integrate with AD DS and are stored on a single namespace server. Standalone namespaces do not support file replication.

When you create a namespace in Windows Server 2008 mode, two enhancements are added. First, Windows Server 2008 domain-based namespaces support increased scalability (more than 5000 folders). In addition, Windows Server 2008 namespaces support access-based enumeration. (With access-based enumeration, users can see on a file server only the files and folders for which the users have proper permissions.)

To create a domain-based namespace in Windows Server 2008 mode, your servers and domain will need to meet the following requirements:

- The domain functional level must be Windows Server 2008.
- All servers hosting the namespace must run Windows Server 2008.

## DFS Component Technologies

In Windows Server 2008, DFS is based on two underlying technologies: DFS Namespaces and DFS Replication.

- DFS Namespaces allow administrators to group shared folders located on different servers and present them to users as a virtual tree of folders known as a namespace. A namespace provides numerous benefits, including increased availability of data, load sharing, and simplified data migration.
- DFS Replication is a multimaster replication engine that supports replication scheduling and bandwidth throttling. DFS Replication uses a compression protocol called Remote Differential Compression (RDC), which can be used to efficiently update files over a limited-bandwidth network. RDC detects insertions, removals, and rearrangements of data in files, thereby enabling DFS Replication to replicate only the changes when files are updated. Another important feature of DFS Replication is that in choosing replication paths, it leverages the Active Directory site links configured in Active Directory Sites and Services.

Figure 10-2 illustrates how DFS Namespaces and DFS Replication work together. In step 1, client computers contact a namespace server and receive a referral. In step 2, client computers access the first server provided by their referrals. The actual targets on the hosting servers are replicated with each other to allow local referrals.

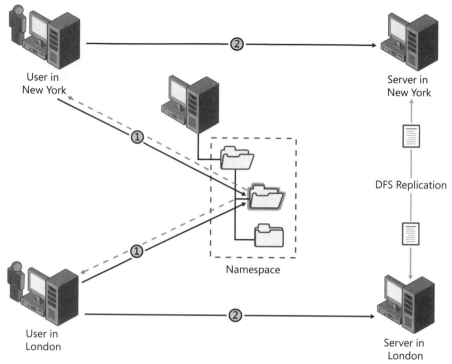

**Figure 10-2**  DFS component technologies

---

**MORE INFO  DFS Replication**

To see a demonstration of a DFS deployment across a branch office and witness some of the features of DFS Replication, it is highly recommended that you watch the 14-minute presentation by Drew McDaniel available at *http://www.microsoft.com/winme/0512/25905 /Branch_Server_demo_mbr.asx*.

---

**MORE INFO  DFS**

For a full introduction to DFS, read "Overview of the Distributed File System Solution in Windows Server 2003 R2," available at *http://go.microsoft.com/fwlink/?LinkId=55315*. Although this paper deals with the version of the distributed file system in Windows Server 2003 R2, the underlying concepts are the same as those in Windows Server 2008.

---

## DFS Namespaces Advanced Settings and Features

You can customize or enable the following settings and features in DFS Namespaces as necessary to design a DFS Namespaces solution for your organization.

## Referral Ordering

A referral is an ordered list of targets, transparent to the user, that a client receives from a domain controller or namespace server when the user accesses the namespace root or a folder with targets in the namespace. The client caches the referral for a configurable period of time.

Targets in the client's Active Directory site are listed first in a referral. (Targets given the target priority "first among all targets" will be listed before targets in the client's site.) The order in which targets outside of the client's site appear in a referral is determined by one of the following referral ordering methods:

- Lowest cost
- Random order
- Exclude targets outside of the client's site

You can set referral ordering on the namespace root, and the ordering method applies to all folders with targets in the namespace. You can also override the namespace root's ordering method for individual folders with targets.

## Failover and Failback

Client failover in DFS Namespaces is the process in which clients attempt to access another target server in a referral after one of the servers fails or is removed from the namespace. Client failback is an optional feature that enables a client to fail back to a preferred, local server after it is restored.

Failback occurs only when a client has failed over to a more expensive server (in terms of site link cost) than the server that is restored. If the restored server has the same cost as the server that the client is currently connected to, failback does not occur to the restored server. For example, if there are two servers (Server 1 and Server 2) in the client's site and Server 1 fails while the client is connected to it, the client will fail over to Server 2. However, the client will not fail back to Server 1 when it is restored because both servers are located in the same site and therefore are associated with the same site link cost.

---

**NOTE  Site link costs**

You can view site link costs by using the Active Directory Sites and Services snap-in.

---

## Target Priority

You can assign a priority to individual targets for a given namespace root or folder. This priority determines how the target is ordered in a referral. The options are:

- First among all targets
- Last among all targets

- First among targets of equal cost
- Last among targets of equal cost

It is important to note that setting target priority on a target will result in that target always being present in a referral, even in cases where you set the Exclude Targets Outside Of The Client's Site option on the folder associated with the target.

## Redundant Domain-Based Namespace Servers

Multiple namespace servers can host a domain-based namespace to increase the availability of the namespace. Putting a namespace server in remote or branch offices also allows clients to contact a namespace server and receive referrals without having to cross expensive wide area network (WAN) connections.

## Namespace Scalability Mode

To maintain a consistent domain-based namespace across namespace servers, it is necessary for namespace servers to periodically poll AD DS to obtain the most current namespace data. If your organization will use more than 16 namespace servers to host a single namespace, it is recommended that you enable namespace scalability mode. When this mode is enabled, namespace servers running Windows Server 2003 and Windows Server 2008 do not send change notification messages to other namespaces servers when the namespace changes nor do they poll the PDC emulator every hour. Instead, they poll their closest domain controller every hour to discover updates to the namespace. (Regardless of whether namespace scalability mode is enabled, changes to the namespace are always made on the PDC emulator.)

---

**NOTE   Root scalability mode**

Namespace scalability mode was known as root scalability mode in Windows Server 2003.

---

**Exam Tip**   On the 70-647 exam, expect to see questions in which you must understand the features and options of DFS Namespaces described in this section.

---

# DFS Replication Advanced Settings and Features

You can customize or enable the following settings and features in DFS Replication as necessary to design a DFS Replication solution for your organization.

## RDC

RDC, which is the basis for DFS replication, is a protocol that can be used to efficiently update files 64 KB or larger over a limited-bandwidth network. RDC detects insertions, removals, rearrangements of data in files regardless of file type, enabling DFS Replication to replicate only the changes when files are updated. To compute the changes to replicate, RDC typically works on an older version of the file with the same name that exists at the appropriate location in the replicated folder tree on the receiving member.

In earlier versions of Windows Server the protocol used to replicate files among folders in a DFS namespace was File Replication Service (FRS). Unlike RDC, FRS copied only entire files, not portions of files. As a result, DFS in earlier versions of Windows is much more bandwidth-intensive than in Windows Server 2008 networks. This change in technology in Windows Server 2008 provides a huge improvement in DFS replication performance, especially across WAN links. Therefore, when planning for DFS, you should plan to upgrade your DFS servers if DFS replication will occur across WAN links.

---

**NOTE  RDC and small files**

RDC is not used on files smaller than 64 KB; in this case the file is compressed before it is replicated. You can also disable RDC on connections that are in a LAN where network bandwidth is not contended.

---

## Cross-File RDC

An additional function of RDC, known as cross-file RDC, can be used to further reduce bandwidth usage. Cross-file RDC is useful when a file exists on the sending member and not the receiving member but similar files exist on the receiving member. Instead of replicating the entire file, DFS Replication can use portions of files that are similar to the replicating file to minimize the amount of data transferred over the WAN. Cross-file RDC can use multiple files as candidate files for RDC seed data.

## Replication Schedule and Bandwidth Throttling

DFS Replication supports replication scheduling and bandwidth throttling in 15-minute increments during a seven-day period. When specifying a replication window, you choose the replication start and stop times as well as the bandwidth to use during that window. The settings for bandwidth usage range from 16 kilobits per second (Kbps) to 256 megabits per second (Mbps) as well as full (unlimited) bandwidth. You can configure a default schedule and bandwidth that applies to all connections between members and optionally create a custom schedule and bandwidth for individual connections.

Because members of a replication group are often located in different time zones, it is important to consider the time zones of the sending and receiving members when you set the schedule. The receiving member initiates replication by interpreting the schedule either in Coordinated Universal Time (UTC) or in the receiving member's local time, depending on which setting you choose. You can choose this setting for the replication group schedule and for custom schedules on individual connections.

## Replication Filters

You can configure file and subfolder filters to prevent files and subfolders from replicating. Both types of filters are set on a per-replicated folder basis. You exclude subfolders by specifying their name or by using the asterisk (*) wildcard character. You exclude files by specifying their name or by using the asterisk (*) wildcard character to specify file names and extensions.

## Staging Folder

DFS Replication uses staging folders to act as caches for new and changed files to be replicated from sending members to receiving members. Each replicated folder uses its own staging folder, and each staging folder has a configurable quota. The quota, which governs when files are purged based on high and low watermarks, must be carefully set based on each replicated folder's replication activity and the disk space available on the server.

## Conflict And Deleted Folder

DFS Replication uses a last writer wins method for determining which version of a file to keep when a file is modified on two or more members and each member has not seen the other's version. The losing file is stored in the Conflict And Deleted folder on the member that resolves the conflict. The Conflict And Deleted folder can also be used to store files that are deleted from replicated folders. Each Conflict And Deleted folder has a quota that governs when files are purged for cleanup purposes.

## Disabled Memberships

A membership defines the relationship between each replicated folder/member pair. Each membership has a status, either enabled or disabled. If you do not want a replicated folder to be replicated to certain members, you can disable the memberships for those members. Doing so allows you to replicate folders to only a subset of replication group members.

---

**Exam Tip**   On the 70-647 exam, expect to see questions in which you must understand the features of DFS Replication described in this section.

---

# Overview of the DFS Design Process

If you decide to implement DFS, you can use the following general outline to plan your DFS design:

1. Identify data to replicate.
2. Make initial namespace decisions.
3. Design the replication topology.

4. Plan for high availability and business continuity.

5. Plan for delegation.

6. Design the namespace hierarchy and functionality.

7. Design replication schedules and bandwidth throttling.

8. Review performance and optimization guidelines.

9. Plan for DFS Replication deployment.

---

**MORE INFO**   Designing DFS

For a detailed description of DFS planning and design, visit *http://technet.microsoft.com* and search for an article entitled "Designing Distributed File Systems."

---

**Quick Check**

- How can you keep a specific file from replicating in a DFS namespace?

**Quick Check Answer**

- Use replication filters.

# Planning a SharePoint Infrastructure

Microsoft provides two related technologies that an organization can use to support collaborative projects among many users. The most recent versions of these technologies, Windows SharePoint Services (WSS) 3.0 and Office SharePoint Server (MOSS) 2007, are suitable in meeting different but related organizational needs. As part of your overall network planning, you should assess the needs of your organization for collaboration and information sharing, review the features offered by these two technologies, and then decide which if either of these technologies is best suited to meet those needs.

## Assessing Needs for Windows SharePoint Services (WSS) 3.0

WSS 3.0 is a free and downloadable add-on to Windows Server 2008. Its purpose is to create a Web-based environment in which users can share information and documents. Organizations can use WSS as the basis for a company intranet or simply as an individual site to facilitate information sharing within teams and departments. Much of the power in WSS is derived from its ability to integrate with Office applications and facilitate collaboration with Office files. Beyond allowing collaboration with Office files out of the box, WSS is also a platform that developers can use to write their own Web-based applications or connect to other established applications.

**Reviewing WSS Features**    WSS features enable Web site–based document storage, collective document editing, document organization, version control, wikis, and blogs. WSS also includes user features like workflows, to-do lists, alerts, bulletin boards, and basic site search.

When determining whether you need to deploy WSS, consider the following points:

- **Document storage**    You should consider deploying WSS if you need a dedicated document storage site for your organization. Whether you require a special site for document storage depends on many factors, such as how many documents need to be stored, how many people are contributing documents, who needs to act on the documents, and so on.

    Document storage sites typically include the following features:

    ❑ The ability to check documents in or out, to track changes to documents, and to keep multiple versions of documents

    ❑ The ability to route documents for approval or through specific processes before publishing them to a larger audience

    ❑ The ability to tag documents with metadata so that documents can be more efficiently sorted and managed

- **Communication**    You should consider deploying WSS if your organization needs a communication site. Communication sites are primarily concerned with distributing information, data, and documents to groups of users. For example, a large organization might have a central site for broadcasting organization-wide information about policies or events (such as a human resources site or a company events site).

    Many communication sites are also used for gathering and sharing information. For example, a community bulletin board is primarily a communication site. People in the community come to the site to read items and to post items for others to read.

    Communication sites are often used for:

    ❑ Describing, publicizing, or announcing an event or other information

    ❑ Viewing calendar or event information

    ❑ Reading documents or editorial articles

    ❑ Posting or uploading information or documents

    ❑ Creating group lists

    ❑ Publishing calendar-based alerts to a group of users

- **Collaboration**    WSS is extremely useful in creating collaboration sites, and your needs for such a site could determine whether deploying WSS is worthwhile for your organization. Collaboration sites are primarily concerned with sharing information and documents, generating ideas, responding to other people's ideas, and tracking progress toward a goal.

Collaboration sites can vary depending on the team type, size, complexity, or objective. For example, a small team that is working on a short-term project (such as organizing an upcoming event or planning a new product launch) has different needs than a larger team (such as a research department in a manufacturing company or the editorial staff in a publishing company) that is working on a series of long-term projects. Members of an organization working together to organize an event (such as a charity event) or to encourage participation in the organization (such as a community or school organization) have their own unique needs.

Collaboration sites often include sections for:

- Sharing information and data
- Sharing documents
- Sharing calendar or event information
- Generating ideas and discussing ideas about a project
- Adding, assigning, and tracking tasks

In general, you can think of WSS 3.0 as a free add-on technology that allows you to quickly build a team Web site in a way that fully integrates with Office 2007.

---

**MORE INFO**  **WSS 3.0 features**

For a fuller description of the features offered by WSS 3.0, read the Microsoft Windows SharePoint Services 3.0 Evaluation Guide, available at *http://technet.microsoft.com/en-us/windowsserver /sharepoint/bb400753.aspx.*

---

---

**MORE INFO**  **Tour a WSS site**

You can view a demo WSS 3.0 site at *http://www.wssdemo.com/default.aspx.*

---

**Understanding WSS Deployment Options**    From a systems administration standpoint, it's important to balance the ease of deployment against other features, such as scalability. To meet different needs, WSS has two main types of deployment options: a standalone configuration and a server farm configuration.

- **Deploying WSS in a standalone configuration**    You can quickly publish a SharePoint site by deploying WSS 3.0 on a single server computer. A standalone configuration is useful if you want to evaluate WSS 3.0 features and capabilities, such as collaboration, document management, and search. A standalone configuration is also useful if you are deploying a small number of Web sites and you want to minimize administrative overhead.

  When you deploy WSS 3.0 on a single server using the default settings, the Setup program automatically installs the Windows Internal Database and uses it to create the configuration database and an initial content database for your SharePoint sites. Windows Internal Database uses SQL Server technology as a relational data store for Windows roles and features only, such as WSS, Active Directory Rights Management Services (AD RMS), UDDI Services, Windows Server Update Services, and Windows System Resources Manager. In addition, Setup installs the SharePoint Central Administration Web site and creates your first SharePoint site collection and site.

In general, the advantage of running WSS on a single computer is that doing so facilitates deployment. The primary drawback of a standalone configuration is that it does not support the scalability needed in larger environments.

- **Deploying WSS in a server farm configuration**  You can deploy WSS 3.0 in a server farm environment if you are hosting a large number of sites, if you want the best possible performance, or if you want to take advantage of the scalability of a multitier topology. A server farm consists of one or more servers dedicated to running the WSS 3.0 application.

In a multitier server farm, multiple WSS front-end servers can connect to a back-end database server that hosts copies of all documents, settings, and related data. This helps organizations increase performance and provide access to data in a variety of scenarios. For example, it allows you to create an extranet that third-party users and organizations (such as business partners) can use for collaboration.

The basic system requirements for a server farm are identical to those of deploying the WSS in a standalone configuration, with one exception. In a server farm, a SharePoint database must be stored on a computer running either Microsoft SQL Server 2000 or SQL Server 2005.

---

**MORE INFO**    Deploying WSS 3.0

For a fuller description of how to deploy WSS 3.0, read "Getting Started with Windows SharePoint Services 3.0," available at *http://go.microsoft.com/fwlink/?LinkId=91963*.

---

## Assessing Needs for Microsoft Office SharePoint Server (MOSS) 2007

Like WSS 3.0, MOSS 2007 allows you to create a Web site that facilitates collaboration, provides content management features, and provides access to information essential to organizational goals and processes. However, MOSS 2007 offers many more features than WSS 3.0 does. Unlike WSS 3.0, in fact, MOSS 2007 is not free but is a separately purchased product.

To determine whether your organization needs MOSS 2007 and not merely WSS 3.0, you should first assess your organization's need for collaboration and then determine whether the features offered by MOSS 2007 can best meet your organization's needs.

**Differences Between WSS 3.0 and MOSS 2007**   MOSS 2007 builds upon the technologies offered by WSS 3.0 to enable community sites that are far more powerful, more customizable, and more tightly integrated with an organization's business processes than those enabled by WSS 3.0.

First, MOSS 2007 facilitates the creation and deployment of powerful Web sites that are more feature-rich and content-rich than those that can be created with WSS 3.0. Sites that are better supported by MOSS 2007 include organizational portal sites and Internet presence sites. MOSS 2007 also comes with many ready-to-use Web site and portal templates, Web Parts, lists, libraries, workflows, and site variations to tailor content to different cultures, markets, and geographic regions.

MOSS 2007 also provides greater support for the authoring, staging, and publishing of custom Web sites than does WSS 3.0. MOSS 2007 enables My Sites, individual mini-sites that can be quickly created to show how users are connected to one another in an organization, the tasks and skills associated with each user, user contact information, and more.

Finally, MOSS 2007 can be much more tightly integrated into an organization's business processes than WSS 3.0 can. Solutions based on MOSS 2007 can provide organization-wide access to business intelligence and other information stored in MOSS 2007 or in line-of-business systems such as SAP. For example, the Business Data Catalog enables you to include data from back-end systems in lists, Web Parts, pages, and search results. In addition, Excel Services provides access to real-time, interactive Office Excel 2007 spreadsheets from a Web browser. MOSS 2007 also provides extended access to information, people, and expertise.

**Examples of Solutions Based on MOSS 2007**    Here are examples of typical solutions that can be built using MOSS 2007 (as opposed to WSS 3.0):

- **Online news magazine**    A publishing organization uses MOSS 2007 to build its branded online magazine site. Article submissions come from inside and outside the organization to be reviewed and accepted by staff editors. This Internet site has a strong community presence because users can log on for personalized information, and it has an extensive search component.

  The Internet site includes subsites for current news and editorials; blogs; and regular columns about politics, business, health, people, personal finance, and science and technology. The site also enables users to sign in to interact with one another and to comment on articles published on the site.

- **Controlled distribution of financial data to clients and business partners**    A bank deploys a solution based on MOSS 2007 to take advantage of Excel Services. The solution enables bank managers to communicate efficiently with clients by providing controlled access to specified workbooks that can be rendered with view-only permissions in a Web browser. The workbooks are accessible in document libraries on a portal; this enables the bank to restrict the availability of financial data to clients who have authenticated access to the portal.

- **Online permit application**    A local government agency uses MOSS 2007 and Office Info-Path 2007 to provide permit application and approval to contractors over the Internet. Contractors use the Web site to apply for permits using an online service. Data entered into the permit application Web form is submitted to a database in the government's Department of Building Inspections network.

  After the application data is submitted, a new permit request (a multipart Office InfoPath 2007 form) is automatically populated to a workspace. When the form is opened, the requesting contractor's company and permit application data is populated into the form's fields. If the request is approved, an electrical permit (also populated with the requestor's contact data and relevant information) is rendered in HTML and posted to the Department of Building Inspections permit site, where the contractor can view and print the permit for posting at the construction site.

- **Corporate Internet presence site**    An international automobile manufacturer has headquarters in Germany; a major subsidiary in Michigan serving the North American market; and regional offices throughout Europe, Asia, and North America. The products are sold internationally, and distinct manufacturing operations serve each regional market. The company's Internet presence Web site is built, administered, and authored using MOSS 2007. It is the focal point for the corporate marketing efforts, and it includes subsites for each product line, along with areas for press releases, investment information, company information, and career opportunities.

Each corporate brand has its own marketing department with individuals responsible for writing that brand's content and updating it on the Web site. The corporate communication department controls the look and feel of the site to make sure the branding and messaging are consistent. The site includes site variations that tailor its content to different languages, cultures, markets, and geographic regions.

Using MOSS 2007 Web sites, the writers for each brand author the site's content and route it for review and approval while managing the creation of multilingual content versions. Using scheduled workflows, the approved and localized content is copied to staging sites where it is tested and ultimately deployed to the public site.

---

**MORE INFO** Deploying MOSS 2007

Like WSS 3.0, MOSS 2007 can be deployed as a standalone server or in a server farm configuration. For more information about deploying MOSS 2007, see "Getting Started with Office SharePoint Server," which you can download at *http://go.microsoft.com/fwlink/?LinkID=91741*.

---

## PRACTICE Designing a Data Sharing Solution

You are an enterprise administrator for A. Datum Corporation, a multinational software company whose headquarters is in New York. To reduce costs, improve efficiency, and encourage creativity, management has recently introduced a plan to increase collaboration between the New York office and the branch offices in Boston, San Jose, London, and Bangaloor. As an enterprise administrator, you and the other members of your team need to choose technologies and configurations that support these new inter-branch projects.

The following points represent the technical requirements for each project:

- A new project with Boston will be used to develop an advertising campaign for the company. Files to be shared between the branches are expected to be very large, and local access to all files is needed.

- Collaboration with the San Jose office should be able to support as many projects as needed among the 100 members of the marketing department. The collaboration solution should enable team members to have ready access to marketing data that is updated in real time. In addition, users should be able to find and contact each other based on skill sets.

- Collaboration with the London office involves copy and tech writing. Employees at the New York and London branches should be able to work together on documents in a way that provides version control.

- Collaboration with the Bangaloor office needs to support many projects related to software development. Team members should be able to have local access to large files that are frequently updated by both New York employees and Bangaloor employees. All development team members should also have access to a central schedule and announcement board.

▶ **Exercise 1    Planning for a Data Sharing Solution**

In this exercise, you make decisions about the data sharing solutions for the various projects in a manner based on the requirements given.

1. At a minimum, which solution or solutions should you implement to meet the stated requirements for the Boston project?

    **Answer: DFS**

    Assuming that the design goals of making files available locally are met, how can you automatically redirect users to files in the opposite branch when the local server is unavailable?

    **Answer: Configure client failover**

2. At a minimum, which solution or solutions should you implement to meet the stated requirements for the San Jose project?

    **Answer: MOSS 2007**

3. At a minimum, which solution or solutions should you implement to meet the stated requirements for the London project?

    **Answer: WSS**

4. At a minimum, which solution or solutions should you implement to meet the stated requirements for the Bangaloor project?

    **Answer: DFS and WSS**

## Lesson Summary

- DFS enables an organization to build a single hierarchical view of file shares that remains consistent across sites in a large network. When you integrate DFS with AD DS, DFS folders can be replicated across sites so that users in various locations can have access to a local copy of the shared files.

- You should deploy DFS if you need to provide local access to the same files across multiple sites. You should customize the deployment by configuring features such as referral ordering, failover, and replications schedules.

- Microsoft provides two related technologies that an organization can use to support collaborative projects among many users. The most recent versions of these technologies, WSS 3.0 and MOSS 2007, are suitable in meeting different but related organizational needs.

- You should consider deploying WSS if you want a free tool that facilitates the creation of team Web sites that enable communication among team members and that provide version control for Office documents.

- You should consider deploying MOSS 2007 if you need to support more powerful community Web sites, such as Internet portals, or if you need to create intranet sites that provide business data that is automatically updated in real time.

## Lesson Review

The following questions are intended to reinforce key information presented in this lesson. The questions are also available on the companion CD if you prefer to review them in electronic form.

---

**NOTE  Answers**

Answers to these questions and explanations of why each answer choice is correct or incorrect are located in the "Answers" section at the end of the book.

---

1. You have implemented a domain-based DFS namespace that spans all five sites of your company network in London, New York, Los Angeles, Toronto, and Sydney. The site link costs among all sites are configured as equal at all five sites.

   A certain folder named Marketing in the DFS namespace includes targets in all five sites. You want users to connect to the local target when available, but when users are unable to connect to the local target, you want their requests to be redirected to the associated target in the New York office.

   How should you enable this functionality?

   A. Configure the New York target priority as first among all targets.

   B. Configure the New York target priority as first among targets of equal cost.

   C. At all four other sites, raise the site link cost to the New York office.

   D. At all four other sites, lower the site link cost to the New York office.

# Lesson 2:  Choosing Data Security Solutions

One of the first steps in designing security for stored data is to choose the security that you will use to protect your data in various locations on your network. A number of data security features are available to protect data, and each available technology is designed to meet specific security needs. For example, BitLocker is designed to protect data on a disk that is stolen or on a computer that has been booted with a stealth operating system. Encrypting File System (EFS) provides a simple method to encrypt chosen files on a disk. Active Directory Rights Management Services (AD RMS) is used to secure files even if they leave your network.

Data protection features vary not only in their application but also in the cost and complexity of their adoption. In general, you need to review the features of each technology and then decide whether your security needs warrant the implementation of the technology in question. In general, the higher your needs to protect specific data, the higher the cost and complexity you should consider to meet your security requirements.

This lesson reviews three data protection technologies: BitLocker, EFS, and AD RMS.

> **After this lesson, you will be able to:**
> - Understand the features and benefits of BitLocker.
> - Understand the benefits of EFS and several considerations for planning an EFS implementation.
> - Understand the features and benefits of AD RMS.
>
> **Estimated lesson time:  35 minutes**

## Protecting Volume Data with BitLocker

BitLocker is a data protection feature available in Windows Server 2008 that provides data encryption for full volumes and integrity checking for early boot components. The purpose of BitLocker is to protect data on a drive that has been stolen or that has been accessed offline in a way that bypasses file permissions (for example, by booting the computer from a stealth operating system).

BitLocker is designed primarily for use with a TPM, which is a hardware module included in many new laptops (as well as some desktops) that are available today. TPM modules must be version 1.2 for use with BitLocker. The TPM module is a permanent part of the motherboard.

If a TPM 1.2 module is not available, a computer can still take advantage of BitLocker's encryption technology as long as the computer's BIOS supports reading from a USB flash device (UFD) before the operating system is loaded. However, you cannot use BitLocker's integrity checking capabilities without a TPM 1.2 module.

---

**MORE INFO**  What is a TPM?

A TPM is essentially a smart card that is attached to a motherboard and that stores keys, pass-words, or digital certificates. For more information about TPMs, visit the Trusted Computing Group TPM FAQ at *https://www.trustedcomputinggroup.org/faq/TPMFAQ/*.

---

## BitLocker Drive Encryption

In Windows Server 2008, BitLocker encrypts system volumes and data volumes. (In Windows Vista, BitLocker can encrypt only system volumes.) To encrypt the full volume, a crypto-graphic key known as the Full Volume Encryption Key (FVEK) is used. This key is stored in the volume metadata and is itself encrypted by another key known as the Volume Master Key (VMK). The VMK is then encrypted again by the TPM, if one is available, or by a startup key located on a user-provided UFD accessed during the startup phase.

## BitLocker Performance Issues

Windows Server 2008 and Windows Vista encrypt and decrypt disk sectors on the fly as data is read from and written to encrypted volumes. As a result, BitLocker does affect performance because these cryptographic operations consume some processor time. However, the actual impact depends on multiple factors, such as caching, hard disk speed, and processor grade.

---

**MORE INFO**  BitLocker fundamentals

For an introduction to BitLocker concepts, read the BitLocker FAQ, which you can find by visiting *http://technet.microsoft.com* and searching for "Windows BitLocker Drive Encryption Frequently Asked Questions." For an introduction to implementing BitLocker, see Windows BitLocker Drive Encryption Step-by-Step Guide (*http://go.microsoft.com/fwlink/?LinkID=53779*).

---

# Choosing a BitLocker Authentication Mode

BitLocker supports four separate authentication modes. The mode you choose depends on the computer's hardware capabilities and the level of security you desire for the computer:

- **BitLocker with a TPM only**  In this authentication mode, BitLocker uses only a TPM to unlock the VMK and enable a volume to be read. Advantages of this mode are that it requires no user intervention, that it protects the data from being read if the drive is stolen, and that it protects the drive against rootkits and other low-level malware. The disadvantage of this authentication mode is that it does not protect data from being read if the entire computer is stolen because the TPM is attached to the internals of the computer.

- **TPM with USB flash device** In this mode, both a TPM and a UFD are required. To start the computer, a user must insert a UFD containing an external key. This effectively authenticates both the user and the integrity of the computer. The advantage of this method is that in principle it protects the data even if the entire computer is stolen (because a thief needs access to the UFD to read the data). The disadvantage is that it requires user intervention every time the computer is started.

- **TPM with PIN** This authentication mode requires both a TPM and a user to provide a PIN every time the computer is started. The advantage of this method is that it protects the volume data if the entire computer is stolen and that it is often easier to provide a PIN than to provide a UFD during startup. The disadvantage of a PIN is that, although this mode is more secure than BitLocker with a TPM only, it is potentially less secure than providing a UFD on a TPM-supplied computer.

- **USB flash device only** This is the only authentication mode that can be used on computers that do not have a TPM. In this mode the user during startup provides a UFD that includes an external key enabling encrypted volumes to be read. The advantage of this method is that it can be used on all computers with a BitLocker-compatible BIOS. The disadvantage of this method is that it does not provide data integrity checking.

## BitLocker Security Design Considerations

Use the following list to help you determine whether to use BitLocker, which authentication mode to implement, and which type of operating system to use.

- Only BitLocker allows you to encrypt all files on a volume, including the page file, hibernation file, registry, and temporary files. If you want to prevent these files from being read if a computer or drive is stolen, use BitLocker and not another encryption technology, such as EFS.

- If you want to protect data stored on all volumes and not just the data on system volumes, you must use BitLocker on Windows Server 2008 and not on Windows Vista.

- If you want BitLocker to detect changes to system data, such as those that might occur from malware or rootkit infection, you must use a system supplied with a TPM. You cannot choose the UFD only authentication method.

- If you want to protect BitLocker with two-factor authentication, you must use a system supplied with a TPM. You can then use a UFD or PIN for authentication in addition to the TPM.

---

**MORE INFO** Planning for BitLocker

For in-depth information about planning the use of BitLocker in Windows, visit the Microsoft Download Center at *http://download.microsoft.com* and search for "Windows BitLocker Drive Encryption Design and Deployment Guides."

---

# Planning for EFS

EFS is the file encryption technology built into Windows that is used optionally to encrypt files stored on NTFS volumes. When a user or program attempts to access a file that is encrypted with EFS, the operating system automatically attempts to acquire a decryption key for the content and, if successful, silently performs encryption and decryption on behalf of the user. When users do not have access to the encryption key, they are not able to open an encrypted file even if they have been assigned Read permissions to that file.

EFS relies on both symmetric and public key cryptography. To support public key cryptography, EFS uses certificates and key pairs. In a workgroup environment these certificates and keys are stored locally on each computer. However, in a domain environment the certificates can be issued by an enterprise certification authority (CA) and managed by Group Policy. With an enterprise CA, a domain user can read his or her encrypted files while logged on to any computer in the domain. In addition, when EFS is deployed with an enterprise CA, a domain user designated as a data recovery agent (DRA) can recover encrypted files stored in the domain.

In general, the advantage of EFS is that it provides a simple method to protect a file from being read on a disk even if that file is accessed offline. The biggest disadvantage of EFS is that it does not protect data sent over the wire or data copied to an alternate location. EFS can protect data only while it stays on an NTFS volume.

---

**MORE INFO　EFS fundamentals**

For a complete introduction to EFS, see Windows Server 2008 Help.

---

When you are planning EFS policy for an organization, it is useful to determine the threats to your system, how EFS handles these threats, and whether to deploy a CA.

To properly plan for and implement EFS, follow these steps:

1. Investigate EFS technology and capabilities.
2. Assess the need for EFS in your environment.
3. Investigate the configuration of EFS using Group Policy.
4. Identify the computer systems and users that require EFS.
5. Identify the level of protection that you require. For example, does your organization require using smart cards with EFS?
6. Configure EFS as appropriate for your environment using Group Policy.

In addition, be sure to follow these EFS best practices:

- Use Group Policy to ensure that the Documents or My Documents folder is encrypted for all users. This practice secures by default the data in which most documents are stored.

- Instruct users to encrypt folders instead of individual files. Encrypting files consistently at the folder level ensures that files are not unexpectedly decrypted.

- The private keys that are associated with recovery certificates are extremely sensitive. These keys must be generated either on a computer that is physically secured, or their certificates must be exported to a .pfx file, protected with a strong password, and saved on a disk that is stored in a physically secure location.

- Recovery agent certificates must be assigned to special recovery agent accounts that are not used for any other purpose.

- Do not destroy recovery certificates or private keys when recovery agents are changed. (Agents are changed periodically.) Keep them all, until all files that might have been encrypted with them are updated.

- Designate two or more recovery agent accounts per organizational unit (OU), depending on the size of the OU. Designate two or more computers for recovery, one for each designated recovery agent account. Grant permissions to appropriate administrators to use the recovery agent accounts. It is a good idea to have two recovery agent accounts to provide redundancy for file recovery. Having two computers that hold these keys provides more redundancy to allow recovery of lost data.

- Implement a recovery agent archive program to make sure that encrypted files can be recovered by using obsolete recovery keys. Recovery certificates and private keys must be exported and stored in a controlled and secure manner. Ideally, as with all secure data, archives must be stored in a controlled access vault and you must have two archives: a master and a backup. The master is kept on-site, while the backup is located in a secure off-site location.

- Avoid using print spool files in your print server architecture, or make sure that print spool files are generated in an encrypted folder.

- EFS does take some CPU overhead every time a user encrypts and decrypts a file. Plan your server usage wisely. Load balance your servers when there are many clients using EFS.

---

### Quick Check

- As a best practice, how many EFS recovery agents should you designate per OU?

**Quick Check Answer**

- Two or more

# Using AD RMS

AD RMS is a technology that allows an organization to control access to, and usage of, confidential data. With an AD RMS–enabled application such as Office, you can create a usage policy to protect a file in the application by controlling rights to that file even when it is moved outside of the company network.

Whenever you choose to protect data by using AD RMS, users who later want to read the data must first be authenticated against the AD RMS server. This authentication can occur anywhere in the world as long as the AD RMS server is accessible over the network and as long as the user's computer is running the AD RMS client, which is built into Windows Vista and Windows Server 2008.

---

**MORE INFO**    **AD RMS in depth**

For in-depth information about AD RMS, see the Active Directory Rights Management Services TechCenter page at *http://go.microsoft.com/fwlink/?LinkId=80907*.

---

AD RMS is installed as a server role and managed through the Active Directory Rights Management Services console, shown in Figure 10-3.

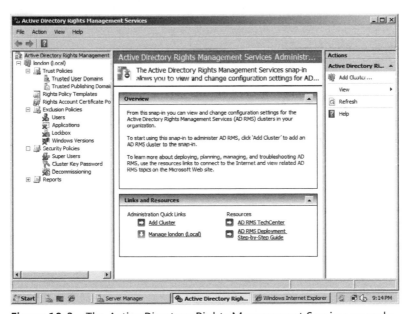

**Figure 10-3**   The Active Directory Rights Management Services console

AD RMS usage policies define three elements for protected files:

- **Trusted entities**    Organizations can specify the entities, including individuals, groups of users, computers, and applications, that are trusted participants in an AD RMS system. By establishing trusted entities, AD RMS can help protect information by enabling access only to properly trusted participants.
- **Usage rights and conditions**    Organizations and individuals can assign usage rights and conditions that define how a specific trusted entity can use rights-protected content. Examples of usage rights are permission to read, copy, print, save, forward, and edit. Usage rights can be accompanied by conditions, such as when those rights expire. Organizations can exclude applications and entities from accessing the rights-protected content.
- **Encryption**    AD RMS encrypts information, making access conditional on the successful validation of the trusted entities. When information is locked, only trusted entities that were granted usage rights under the specified conditions (if any) can unlock or decrypt the information in an AD RMS–enabled application or browser. The application will then enforce the defined usage rights and conditions.

## Creating and Viewing Rights-Protected Information

To protect data with AD RMS, information workers simply follow the same workflow they already use for their information.

Figure 10-4 illustrates how AD RMS works when users publish and consume rights-protected information.

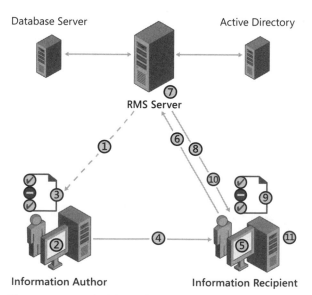

**Figure 10-4**    Workflow of creating and viewing rights-protected information

This process includes the following steps:

1. When a user chooses the option to protect data in an AD RMS–enabled application for the first time, the author receives a client licensor certificate from the AD RMS server. This is a one-time step that enables offline publishing of rights-protected information in the future.

2. Using an AD RMS–enabled application, an author creates a file and defines a set of usage rights and conditions for that file. A publishing license is then generated that contains the usage policies.

3. The application encrypts the file with a symmetric key, which is then encrypted with the public key of the author's AD RMS server. The key is inserted into the publishing license and the publishing license is bound to the file. Only the author's AD RMS server can issue use licenses to decrypt this file.

4. The author distributes the file.

5. A recipient receives a protected file through a regular distribution channel and opens it using an AD RMS–enabled application or browser.

6. If the recipient does not have an account certificate on the current computer, this is the point at which one will be issued.

7. The application sends a request for a use license to the AD RMS server that issued the publishing license for the protected information. The request includes the recipient's account certificate (which contains the recipient's public key) and the publishing license (which contains the symmetric key that encrypted the file).

8. The AD RMS licensing server validates that the recipient is authorized, checks that the recipient is a named user, and creates a use license.

9. During this process, the server decrypts the symmetric key using the private key of the server, reencrypts the symmetric key using the public key of the recipient, and adds the encrypted session key to the use license. This step ensures that only the intended recipient can decrypt the symmetric key and thus decrypt the protected file. The server also adds any relevant conditions to the use license, such as the expiration or an application or operating system exclusion.

10. When the validation is complete, the licensing server returns the use license to the recipient's client computer.

11. After receiving the use license, the application examines both the license and the recipient's account certificate to determine whether any certificate in either chain of trust requires a revocation list. If so, the application checks for a local copy of the revocation list that has not expired. If necessary, it retrieves a current copy of the revocation list. The application then applies any revocation conditions that are relevant in the current context. If no revocation condition blocks access to the file, the application renders the data and the user may exercise the rights he or she has been granted.

This 11-step process is essentially the same whether the recipient is within the publishing organization or outside of it. The recipient is not required to be inside the author's network or domain to request a use license. All that is required is a valid account certificate for the recipient and access to the licensing server that issued the publishing license.

## AD RMS Applications

AD RMS–enabled applications are those that are specifically designed to encrypt and control usage of the information through AD RMS. AD RMS–enabled applications include the following:

- Office System 2003 – Word, Excel, PowerPoint, Outlook
- Office 2007 – Word, Excel, PowerPoint, Outlook, InfoPath
- SharePoint Portal Server 2007
- Exchange Server 2007
- XPS (XML Paper Specification) v1.0
- Internet Explorer 6.0 or later (through use of the RM Add-on for IE)

---

**Exam Tip**    For the 70-647 exam, the most important feature to remember about AD RMS is that it enables users to provide persistent protection for data even as the data leaves the organization. A situation in which AD RMS would be useful would be in protecting confidential e-mail or Word documents even if they are leaked to a third party.

---

## PRACTICE Designing Data Storage Security

You are an enterprise administrator for Consolidated Messenger. The company network consists of a single Active Directory domain. You, along with other members of the data security team, have been given the responsibility of choosing data security solutions for the entire corporate network.

The following points represent the design goals of the data security solutions:

A. No data on critical servers should be accessible even if the hard disks are physically stolen.

B. To start critical servers, you must use a PIN.

C. E-mail marked as confidential must not be readable to unauthorized parties.

D. Users who choose to encrypt personal files must be able to read those files from any computer on the company network.

▶ **Exercise 1   Planning a Data Storage Security Solution**

In this exercise you make decisions about data security in a manner based on the requirements given.

1. Which security feature should you use to meet requirement A?

   **Answer: BitLocker**

   Are there any hardware prerequisites to meet requirement A? If so, what?

   **Answer: No, there are no prerequisites.**

2. Which security feature should you use to meet requirement B?

   **Answer: BitLocker**

   Are there any hardware prerequisites to meet requirement B? If so, what?

   **Answer: Yes, a TPM 1.2 module is needed for the servers in question.**

3. Which security solution should you use to meet requirement C?

   **Answer: AD RMS**

4. What technology should you deploy to meet requirement D?

   **Answer: An enterprise CA**

## Lesson Summary

- BitLocker is a full-volume data encryption feature whose purpose is to protect data on a drive that has been stolen or that has been accessed offline. BitLocker is the only technology available that encrypts complete volumes, including page files and hibernation files. To gain the full benefits of BitLocker, you need to configure the feature on a computer that has a TPM version 1.2.

- BitLocker provides for authentication modes or methods of decrypting disk data: TPM only, TPM with a UFD, TPM with PIN, and UFD only. If you use UFD only mode, BitLocker does not verify the integrity of early boot components.

- EFS is the file encryption technology built into Windows that is used optionally to encrypt files stored on NTFS volumes. EFS is best deployed with an enterprise CA. Although EFS does not enable users to encrypt all files on a drive, EFS is easy to implement and requires no special hardware.

- AD RMS is a technology designed to protect files for AD RMS–compatible applications, such as Office. With AD RMS, protected files and e-mails remain protected even when they leave the company network.

# Lesson Review

The following questions are intended to reinforce key information presented in this lesson. The questions are also available on the companion CD if you prefer to review them in electronic form.

**NOTE**  Answers

Answers to these questions and explanations of why each answer choice is correct or incorrect are located in the "Answers" section at the end of the book.

1.  You want to deploy SQL Server 2005 on a database server to store confidential data that is accessed infrequently. The server itself is rack-mounted and is not likely to be stolen, but the disks are hot-swappable and could feasibly be removed by an intruder. You want to ensure that even if the server's disks are stolen, nobody will be able to read the contents of the disks. You also want the server to be able to restart without administrator assistance.

    What should you do to best meet the requirements of the database server?

    A.  Buy a server with a TPM 1.2 module and use AD RMS to protect the data.

    B.  Use BitLocker to protect the data. You do not need a server with a TPM 1.2.

    C.  Use AD RMS to protect the data. You do not need a server with a TPM 1.2.

    D.  Buy a server with a TPM 1.2 module and use BitLocker to protect the data.

# Lesson 3: Planning for System Recoverability and Availability

When you deploy essential servers, such as domain controllers, Web servers, and database servers, you need to plan how to design the system for recoverability in the event of server failure. In the case of a domain controller, you should plan to use Windows Server Backup (or another backup application) to back up the Active Directory Domain Services (AD DS) database. With Web servers and other application servers that need to support many users, you can use Network Load Balancing (NLB). For database servers, mail servers, and other application servers that use a shared database, you can use failover clustering to support recoverability and service availability.

> **After this lesson, you will be able to:**
> - Design domain controller storage for optimal recoverability.
> - Understand general procedures and considerations for performing maintenance on the AD DS database.
> - Know when you should seize an operations master role.
> - Understand the benefits of Network Load Balancing (NLB) and the scenarios in which it is best used.
> - Understand the benefits of failover clustering and the scenarios in which it is best used.
>
> **Estimated lesson time: 30 minutes**

## Planning AD DS Maintenance and Recovery Procedures

Before you deploy Windows Server 2008 domain controllers, you need to plan AD DS maintenance and recovery procedures, such as backing up and restoring the AD DS database (Ntds.dit), defragmenting the AD DS database, and seizing operations master roles.

### Planning for AD DS Backup

Before you install Windows Server 2008 on a computer you plan to deploy as a domain controller, you should design the storage of that server in a way that best suits its recoverability. Specifically, for each domain controller you should store operating system files, the Active Directory database (Ntds.dit), and the SYSVOL directory all on separate volumes that do not contain other user, operating system, or application data.

The actual backup procedure for AD DS is different in Windows Server 2008 than it is for earlier versions of Windows Server. In Windows Server 2008 you must back up critical volumes on a domain controller rather than backing up only the system state data.

Critical volumes are those that contain the following data:

- The volume that hosts the boot files, which consists of the Bootmgr file and the BCD store
- The volume that hosts the Windows operating system and the Registry
- The volume that hosts the SYSVOL directory
- The volume that hosts the Active Directory database (Ntds.dit)
- The volume that hosts the Active Directory database log files

**Windows Server Backup and *Wbadmin*** Windows Server 2008 includes a new backup application named Windows Server Backup and an associated command-line tool named *wbadmin*. These features are not installed by default. You must install them by using the Add Features option in Server Manager.

---

**NOTE  You cannot back up FAT volumes or partial volumes**

Only NTFS-volumes on locally attached disks can be backed up by using Windows Server Backup. In addition, you cannot use Windows Server Backup to back up selected files or folders; you can back up only entire volumes.

---

You can schedule full server backups and critical-volume backups by using either Windows Server Backup or *wbadmin*. When determining the frequency for AD DS backups, consider the following:

- **The frequency of significant changes to AD DS data**   Significant changes can include changes to the schema, group membership, Active Directory replication or site topology, and policies. They can also include upgrades to operating systems, renaming domain controllers or domains, and migration or creation of new security principals.
- **The effect on business operations if data in AD DS or SYSVOL is lost**   Lost data can include updates to passwords for user accounts, computer accounts, and trusts. It can also include updates to group membership, policies, and the replication topology and its schedules.

In general, it is recommended that you perform backups nightly during times of decreased traffic. For fault tolerance, schedule at least two trusted backups for each domain. You can start by scheduling the backups daily and then adjust the frequency of your backups depending on the previously specified criteria.

Finally, note the following considerations when choosing a storage location for your backups:

- It is recommended that you create a backup volume on a dedicated internal or attached external hard disk drive.
- The destination volume for the backup must be on a separate hard disk from the source volumes.

- In Windows Server Backup, you cannot perform a scheduled backup to a network share. Only manual backups can be performed to a network share.
- Windows Server Backup does not enable you to back up to tape.

---

**NOTE   Can you use Windows Server Backup on a Server Core installation?**

To use the Windows Server Backup graphical user interface (GUI) for managing backup and restore operations on a server that is running a Server Core installation of Windows Server 2008, you must connect remotely from a server that is running a full installation of Windows Server 2008.

---

## Planning for AD DS Recovery

Planning for AD DS recovery entails learning the recovery procedures, learning when to perform each restore type, and deciding whether to install Windows RE on a dedicated partition as part of domain controller deployment.

AD DS recovery includes performing nonauthoritative restores and authoritative restores. A nonauthoritative restore is what you should perform if the Active Directory volume becomes corrupted or is deleted. To perform a nonauthoritative restore of AD DS, you need at least a critical-volume backup. If you cannot start the server, then you must perform a full server recovery instead.

To perform a nonauthoritative restore, you must restart the domain controller in Directory Services Restore Mode (DSRM). Then you can open Windows Server Backup or use the *wbadmin* utility to perform the recovery.

---

**NOTE   Full server recovery and Windows RE**

A full server recovery requires you to start the server with the Windows Server 2008 product DVD and choose the Repair Your Computer option. To avoid having to use the operating system media during recovery, use the Windows Automated Installation Kit to install Windows RE on a separate partition. When you install Windows RE beforehand, you can simply choose it from the boot menu and access Windows Recovery options. For more information about the Windows Automated Installation Kit, visit *http://go.microsoft.com/fwlink/?LinkId=90643*.

---

**MORE INFO   Performing a nonauthoritative restore**

For more information about performing a nonauthoritative restore, search for "Performing a Nonauthoritative Restore of AD DS" on the Microsoft TechNet Web site at *http://technet.microsoft.com*.

---

Unlike a nonauthoritative restore, the purpose of an authoritative restore is to restore an object that has accidentally been deleted. For example, you might need to perform an authoritative restore if an administrator inadvertently deletes an OU containing a large number of users. If you restore the server from backup, the normal, nonauthoritative restore process does not restore the inadvertently deleted OU because the restored domain controller is updated following the restore process to the current status of its replication partners, which have deleted the OU. Recovering the deleted OU instead requires authoritative restore. You can use authoritative restore to mark the OU as authoritative and let the replication process restore it to all the other domain controllers in the domain.

When an object is marked for authoritative restore, its version number is changed so that it is higher than the existing version number of the (deleted) object in the Active Directory replication system. This change ensures that any data that you restore authoritatively is replicated from the restored domain controller to other domain controllers in the forest.

You should not use an authoritative restore to restore an entire domain controller, nor should you use it as part of a change-control infrastructure. Proper delegation of administration and change enforcement will optimize data consistency, integrity, and security.

To perform an authoritative restore, follow this four-step procedure:

1. Start the domain controller in DSRM.
2. Restore the desired backup, which is typically the most recent backup.
3. Use *ntdsutil* to mark desired objects, containers, or partitions as authoritative.
4. Restart in normal mode to propagate the changes.

---

**MORE INFO** Performing an authoritative restore

For more information about performing an authoritative restore, search for "Performing an Authoritative Restore of Deleted AD DS Objects" on the Microsoft TechNet Web site at *http://technet .microsoft.com*.

---

## Stopping AD DS to Perform Maintenance Procedures

Windows Server 2008 introduces a new feature called restartable AD DS that facilitates some Active Directory maintenance procedures. In Windows Server 2008, Active Directory Domain Services appears in the Services console as a service that can be stopped and restarted like any other service. Stopping the AD DS service enables you to perform an offline defragmentation or update of a locally stored AD DS database while you are logged on to a domain controller normally. In earlier versions of Windows you needed to start the computer in DSRM to perform such procedures.

---

**MORE INFO** Offline defragmentation

For specific instructions how to perform an offline defragmentation of the AD DS database by using the *ntdsutil* command-line utility, consult Windows Server 2008 Help.

---

While AD DS is stopped on a particular domain controller, other domain controllers can still service new domain logon requests. Even on the domain controller on which AD DS is stopped, you can continue to log on to the domain if other domain controllers are available to service the logon request. If no other domain controller is available, you can still log on to the server in DSRM by using the local Administrator account and the DSRM password, as in Windows 2000 Server or Windows Server 2003.

---

**NOTE  Can you use *dcpromo* to remove AD DS when AD DS is stopped?**

You can run *dcpromo /forceremoval* to forcefully remove AD DS from a domain controller while AD DS is stopped. However, you should use this procedure only if AD DS cannot be started.

---

Aside from improving the convenience of performing offline maintenance procedures to the AD DS database, stopping the AD DS service provides the additional benefit of preserving the availability of other services while you are performing those maintenance tasks. For example, if a domain controller is also a DHCP server, the domain controller can continue to service DHCP clients when you are performing offline maintenance on AD DS.

---

**NOTE  Stopping AD DS at a command line**

To stop AD DS at a command line, type **net stop ntds**.

---

## Seizing Operations Master Roles

Certain domain and enterprise-wide services that are not suitable for multimaster updates are performed by a single domain controller in AD DS. The domain controllers that are assigned to perform these unique operations are called operations masters or flexible single master operations (FSMO) role holders. If a domain controller that holds an operations master role is lost and cannot be brought back online, you can use the *ntdsutil* utility to seize the lost operations master role.

---

**MORE INFO  Operations master roles**

For an introduction to FSMO roles and for specific instructions about how to use the *ntdsutil* utility to seize FSMO roles, see *http://support.microsoft.com/kb/255504*.

---

A domain controller whose FSMO roles have been seized should not be permitted to communicate with existing domain controllers in the forest. In this scenario, you should either format the hard disk and reinstall the operating system on such domain controllers or forcibly demote such domain controllers on a private network and then remove their metadata on a surviving domain controller in the forest by using the *ntdsutil /metadata cleanup* command.

> ## Quick Check
>
> - If you want to design a domain controller's storage for maximum recoverability, which three elements should all be kept on separate volumes that do not contain user or application data?
>
> ## Quick Check Answer
>
> - The operating system, the Active Directory database (Ntds.dit), and the SYSVOL directory

## Using Network Load Balancing to Support High-Usage Servers

Network Load Balancing (NLB) is used to support a highly used network service or application. An installable feature of Windows Server 2008, NLB transparently distributes client requests among servers in a cluster by using virtual IP addresses and a shared name. From the perspective of the clients, the NLB cluster appears to be a single server.

In a common scenario, for example, NLB is used to create a *Web farm*—a group of computers working to support a Web site or a set of Web sites. In some scenarios it might be possible that a single, powerful server could be used to support the client traffic instead of many smaller Web servers in an NLB farm. However, an NLB farm enables you to gradually increase the power of your solution by adding more servers (called hosts) to the farm as the need arises. NLB also provides the advantage of high availability because in such a cluster there is no single point of failure.

Aside from Web farms, you can also use NLB to create a terminal server farm, a virtual private network (VPN) server farm, or an ISA Server firewall cluster. Figure 10-5 shows a basic configuration of an NLB Web farm located behind an NLB firewall cluster.

As a load balancing mechanism, NLB automatically detects servers that have been disconnected from the cluster and then redistributes client requests to the remaining live hosts. This feature prevents clients from sending requests to the failed servers. NLB also allows you the option to specify a load percentage that each host will handle. Clients are then statistically distributed among hosts so that each server receives its percentage of incoming requests.

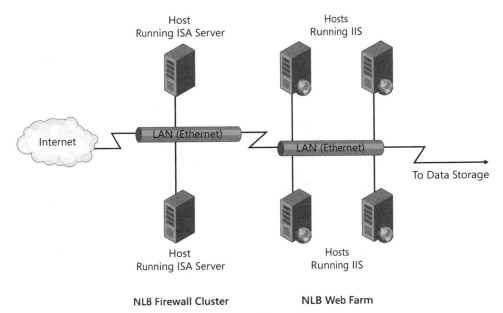

**Figure 10-5** Basic diagram for two connected NLB clusters

## Identifying Applications for NLB

The applications and services that run on NLB include stateful applications (those that maintain session state) and stateless applications. Maintaining session state means that the application or service collects information when first connecting to a cluster host and then retains the information for subsequent requests. During a user session, the same server must handle all the requests from the user in order to access that information. Applications and services that are stateless maintain no user or communication information for subsequent connections.

With a single server, maintaining session state presents no difficulty because the user always connects to the same server. However, when client requests are load balanced within an NLB cluster, without some type of persistence the client might not be directed to the same host for a series of client requests.

In NLB you maintain session state with a *port rule affinity* between the client and a specific cluster host. Port rule affinity directs all client requests from the same IP address to the same NLB host. You can use port rules to specify the port rule affinity between clients and NLB cluster hosts.

Some of the common applications and services well-suited to run on NLB include the following:

- **Web applications**   One of the most common of the solutions that use NLB is a Web farm. A typical challenge in supporting Web applications occurs when an application must maintain a persistent connection to a specific cluster host. For example, if a Web application uses Hypertext Transfer Protocol Secure (HTTPS), the application should, for efficiency, contact the same cluster hosts within the cluster. Connecting to a different cluster host requires establishing a new SSL session, which creates excess network traffic and overhead on the client and server. NLB maintains affinity and reduces the possibility that a new SSL session needs to be established.

- **VPN remote access running on Routing and Remote Access**   Another solution that uses NLB involves using the Routing and Remote Access service in Windows Server 2008 to provide VPN remote connectivity. In the VPN solution, you combine multiple remote access servers running Windows Server 2008 and Routing and Remote Access to create a VPN remote access server farm.

- **Web content caching and firewall running on ISA Server**   You can also use NLB in solutions that include ISA Server to provide network security, network isolation, network address translation, or Web content caching. In ISA Server solutions, the design and deployment are integral parts of the ISA Server design and deployment process.

- **Application hosted on Terminal Services**   When you run applications on Terminal Services, the Terminal Services clients can be load balanced across a number of computers running Terminal Services. NLB works with the Terminal Services Session Broker role service to provide improved scalability and availability for Terminal Services.

- **Custom applications**   NLB might be an appropriate method of improving scalability and availability for applications that your organization or third-party organizations have developed. Custom applications must adhere to the same criteria listed earlier in this section.

**When Not to Use NLB**   In NLB each host in the farm is connected to separate storage, and this data is not replicated among hosts. As a result, NLB is not well-suited to support services in which data is updated by users because data inconsistency among nodes could result. In particular, you should not use NLB to support database servers or file servers. However, many organizations use NLB to support a Web site front end to a single database server.

---

**MORE INFO   NLB best practices**

For a detailed list of NLB best practices, visit *http://technet.microsoft.com* and search for "Network Load Balancing: Configuration Best Practices for Windows 2000 and Windows Server 2003." Although this information was written for earlier versions of Windows Server, the concepts are still valid.

---

## Using Failover Clusters to Maintain High Availability

A failover cluster is a group of two or more computers used to prevent downtime for selected applications and services. The clustered servers (called nodes) are connected by physical cables to each other and to shared storage disks. If one of the cluster nodes fails, another node begins to take over service for the lost node in a process known as failover. As a result of failover, users connecting to the server experience minimal disruption in service.

Servers in a failover cluster can function in a variety of roles, including the roles of file server, print server, mail server, or database server, and they can provide high availability for a variety of other services and applications.

In most cases the failover cluster includes a shared storage unit that is physically connected to all the servers in the cluster, although any given volume in the storage is accessed by only one server at a time.

Figure 10-6 illustrates the process of failover in a basic two-node failover cluster.

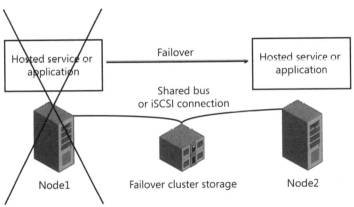

**Figure 10-6**  In a failover cluster, when one server fails, another takes over using the same storage

Server clusters can benefit your organization if:

- Your users depend on regular access to mission-critical data and applications to do their jobs.
- Your organization has established a limit on the amount of planned or unplanned service downtime that you can sustain.
- The cost of the additional hardware that server clusters require is less than the cost of having mission-critical data and applications offline during a failure.

## Comparing NLB and Failover Clusters

NLB clusters and failover clusters are used for different purposes. Whereas NLB is used primarily for increased scalability of Web servers, VPN servers, ISA Server firewalls, and terminal servers, failover clusters are often used most often to increase the availability of database servers. Frequently, in fact, NLB clusters can work as a front end to a failover cluster, as in the case of a Web site that connects to a back-end database, illustrated in Figure 10-7.

Web servers/NLB cluster

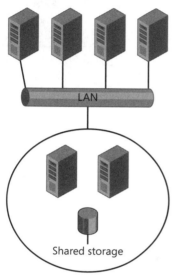

Database server/Failover cluster

**Figure 10-7**    An NLB cluster often acts as the front end to a back-end failover cluster

## Preparing Failover Cluster Hardware

Failover clusters have fairly elaborate hardware requirements. To configure the hardware, review the following list of requirements for the servers, network adapters, cabling, controllers, and storage:

- **Servers**    Use a set of matching computers that contain the same or similar components. (Recommended)
- **Network adapters and cabling**    The network hardware, like other components in the failover cluster solution, must be compatible with Windows Server 2008. If you use iSCSI, your network adapters must be dedicated to either network communication or iSCSI, not both.

In the network infrastructure that connects your cluster nodes, avoid having single points of failure. There are several ways to achieve this. You can connect your cluster nodes by multiple, distinct networks. Alternatively, you can connect your cluster nodes with one network that is constructed with teamed network adapters, redundant switches, redundant routers, or similar hardware that removes single points of failure.

- **Device controllers or appropriate adapters for the storage**   For Serial Attached SCSI or Fibre Channel: If you are using Serial Attached SCSI or Fibre Channel, in all clustered servers the mass-storage device controllers that are dedicated to the cluster storage should be identical. They should also use the same firmware version.

  For iSCSI: If you are using iSCSI, each clustered server must have one or more network adapters or host bus adapters (HBAs) that are dedicated to the cluster storage. The network you use for iSCSI cannot be used for network communication. In all clustered servers, the network adapters you use to connect to the iSCSI storage target should be identical. It is also recommended that you use Gigabit Ethernet or higher. (Note also that for iSCSI you cannot use teamed network adapters.)

- **Storage: You must use shared storage that is compatible with Windows Server 2008**   For a two-node failover cluster, the storage should contain at least two separate volumes configured at the hardware level.

  The first volume will function as the *witness disk*. A witness disk is a volume that holds a copy of the cluster configuration database. Witness disks, known as *quorum disks* in Windows Server 2003, are used in many, but not all, cluster configurations.

  The second volume will contain the files that are being shared to users. Storage requirements include the following:

  - ❑  To use the native disk support included in failover clustering, use basic disks, not dynamic disks.
  - ❑  It is recommended that you format the storage partitions with NTFS (for the witness disk, the partition must be NTFS).

  When deploying a storage area network (SAN) with a failover cluster, be sure to confirm with manufacturers and vendors that the storage, including all drivers, firmware, and software used for the storage, are compatible with failover clusters in Windows Server 2008.

After you have met the hardware requirements and connected the cluster servers to storage, you can then install the Failover Cluster feature.

### What Are Quorum Configurations?

Quorum configurations in a failover cluster determine the number of failures that the cluster can sustain before the cluster stops running. In Windows Server 2008 you can choose from among four quorum configurations. The first option is the node majority quorum configuration, which is recommended for clusters with an odd number of nodes. In node majority, the failover cluster runs as long as a majority of the nodes are running. The second option is the node and disk majority quorum configuration, which is recommended for clusters with an even number of nodes. In node and disk majority, the failover cluster uses a witness disk as a tiebreaker node and the failover cluster then runs as long as a majority of these nodes are online and available. The third option is the node and file share majority quorum configuration. In node and file share majority, which is recommended for clusters that have an even number of nodes and that lack access to a witness disk, a witness file share is used as a tiebreaker node and the failover cluster then runs as long as a majority of these nodes are online and available. The fourth and final option is the No Majority: Disk Only quorum configuration. In this configuration, which is generally not recommended, the failover cluster remains active as long as a single node and its storage remain online.

## Lesson Summary

- You should deploy domain controllers with recovery in mind. Design storage with AD DS elements stored on dedicated volumes, and have in place a plan for recovery procedures.

- In Windows Server 2008 you can stop AD DS as a service, which facilitates certain AD DS maintenance procedures, such as offline defragmentation.

- In NLB many live servers simulate a single server and client requests are distributed to one host in the server farm. NLB is used to support high usage Web servers, terminal servers, ISA Server servers, and VPN servers.

- In a failover cluster, two or more servers (called nodes) share storage and only one node hosts a given service at any given time. Whenever a node fails, another node takes over the services that were hosted by the failed node. Failover clusters are typically used to support high availability for database servers, but they can also be used to support mail servers, print servers, and file servers.

# Lesson Review

The following questions are intended to reinforce key information presented in this lesson. The questions are also available on the companion CD if you prefer to review them in electronic form.

**NOTE**  **Answers**

Answers to these questions and explanations of why each answer choice is correct or incorrect are located in the "Answers" section at the end of the book.

1.  You are planning a failover cluster for a database server. You want the server to include two nodes, and you want to include a witness (quorum) disk in your design. Which quorum configuration should you choose?

    A.  Node majority

    B.  Node and disk majority

    C.  Node and file share majority

    D.  No Majority: Disk Only

# Chapter Review

To further practice and reinforce the skills you learned in this chapter, you can

- Review the chapter summary.
- Complete the case scenario. This scenario sets up a real-world situation involving the topics of this chapter and asks you to create solutions.
- Complete the suggested practices.
- Take a practice test.

## Chapter Summary

- When you need a solution to support data sharing, you should choose DFS if you want to provide users with local access to the same files across multiple sites.
- If you need a solution to support collaboration through team Web sites, you should choose WSS when you want the sites to provide storage and version control for Office documents.
- If you need a solution to support collaboration through team Web sites, you should choose MOSS 2007 when you want the sites to support very advanced features, such as automated integration with business process.
- If you need a solution to encrypt full volumes in case a computer or a drive is stolen, you should choose BitLocker.
- If you need a solution that allows users to encrypt their personal files, you should choose EFS.
- If you need a solution that protects e-mail and Office documents even if they leave your network, you should choose AD RMS.
- You should deploy domain controllers with recovery in mind. Design storage with AD DS elements stored on dedicated volumes, and have a plan in place for recovery procedures.
- NLB is used to provide high availability for Web servers, terminal servers, ISA Server servers, and VPN servers.
- Failover clusters are typically used to provide high availability for database servers, but they can also be used to support mail servers, print servers, and file servers.

# Case Scenario

In the following case scenario you will apply what you've learned in this chapter. You can find answers to these questions in the "Answers" section at the end of this book.

## Case Scenario: Designing Solutions for Sharing, Security, and Availability

You are an IT administrator for Fourth Coffee, Inc., a specialty producer of coffee drinks based in Endicott, New York. The company has been experiencing rapid growth and has recently opened branch offices in Boulder, Austin, and Atlanta.

The *fourthcoffee.com* network consists of a single Active Directory domain. In the network all servers are running Windows Server 2008 and all clients are running Windows Vista Enterprise.

Recently, management has determined that new technical solutions are needed to meet new business needs. These needs have been specified in the following list:

- Project managers in any department of the company should be able to assemble teams made of members from any of the four sites, and every team should be able to create a team Web site quckly and easily. Team Web sites should be used to facilitate communication among team members and to provide announcements, calendars, blogs, and bulletin boards.

- Every department in the company should be associated with a single pathname to its network shares that remains consistent everywhere in the company network. All department shares should be available locally at all four sites, and queries for department shares should not cross WAN links.

- Confidential e-mails should be secured in a way that protects them from being read by unauthorized third parties.

- No single server failure should allow any portion of any database server deployed in the company to go offline.

You are a member of the team whose responsibility is to design solutions to meet these stated needs.

1. At a minimum, what technology should you use to meet the need to assemble team Web sites?
2. Which technology should you use to meet the goals for department file shares? How should you meet the requirement to avoid inter-site communication for department share queries?
3. Which technology should you use to meet the requirement to protect confidential e-mail?
4. Which feature should you use to meet the requirement for database servers?

# Suggested Practices

To help you successfully master the exam objectives presented in this chapter, complete the following tasks.

## Watch a Webcast

■ **Practice**   Watch the webcast, "Deploying Microsoft Windows Rights Management Services," which you can access by visiting *http://msevents.microsoft.com* and searching for event ID #1032286987.

Watch the webcast, "Planning and Deploying the Branch Office Technologies in Windows Server 2003 R2," which you can access by visiting *http://msevents.microsoft.com* and searching for event ID #1032283986. This webcast deals primarily with DFS, which has not changed substantially from Windows Server 2003 R2.

## Read a White Paper

■ **Practice**   Review the white papers, "Planning and Architecture for Office SharePoint Server 2007, Part 1" which you can download at *http://go.microsoft.com/fwlink/?LinkID =79552*, and "Planning and Architecture for Office SharePoint Server 2007, Part 2," which you can download at *http://go.microsoft.com/fwlink/?LinkId=85548*.

Review the white papers, "Planning and Architecture for Windows SharePoint Services 3.0 Technology, Part 1," which you can download at *http://go.microsoft.com/fwlink /?LinkId=79600*, and "Planning and Architecture for Windows SharePoint Services 3.0 Technology, Part 2," which you can download at *http://go.microsoft.com/fwlink/?LinkId =85553*.

# Take a Practice Test

The practice tests on this book's companion CD offer many options. For example, you can test yourself on just one exam objective, or you can test yourself on all the 70-647 certification exam content. You can set up the test so that it closely simulates the experience of taking a certification exam, or you can set it up in study mode so that you can look at the correct answers and explanations after you answer each question.

---

**MORE INFO**   **Practice tests**

For details about all the practice test options available, see the "How to Use the Practice Tests" section in this book's introduction.

---

# Chapter 11

# Designing Software Update Infrastructure and Managing Compliance

When considering the importance of a good software update infrastructure, remember that the most famous worms and viruses have usually used weaknesses for which software updates had already been released. The simple fact is that if you apply newly released software updates to the computers in your organization in a timely manner, your organization will be less vulnerable to worms, viruses, trojans, and bugs than organizations that take a more haphazard approach to update management. In this chapter, you will learn about several software update solutions that you can deploy in your enterprise environment to ensure that all the computers you are responsible for managing have software that is up to date. You will also learn how to generate and apply baseline security policies, a method of ensuring that the configuration of the computers in your organization is as secure as possible while still performing its assigned functions.

### Exam objectives in this chapter:
- Design for software updates and compliance management.

### Lessons in this chapter:

- Lesson 1: Designing a Software Update Infrastructure . . . . . . . . . . . . . . . . . . . . . . . . . 477
- Lesson 2: Managing Software Update Compliance . . . . . . . . . . . . . . . . . . . . . . . . . . . . 496

## Before You Begin

To complete the practices in this chapter, you must have done the following:

- Installed a server running Windows Server 2008 Enterprise configured as a domain controller in the *contoso.internal* domain. Active Directory–integrated Domain Name System (DNS) is installed by default on the first domain controller in a domain.
- Made the following configurations:
  - ❏ Named the computer Glasgow.
  - ❏ Configured a static IPv4 address of 10.0.0.11 with a subnet mask of 255.255.255.0. The IPv4 address of the DNS server is 10.0.0.11.

❑   Other than IPv4 configuration and the computer name, accepted all the default installation settings. You can obtain an evaluation version of the Windows Server 2008 Enterprise software from the Microsoft download center at *http:// www.microsoft.com/Downloads/Search.aspx*.

---

## Real World

*Orin Thomas*

The main reason that many organizations do not apply software updates in a timely manner is the fear of causing some conflict with an existing configuration. Although it is true that software updates do, from time to time, cause problems with existing configurations, such problems are the exception rather than the rule. As an enterprise administrator, you need to take a proactive approach to software update deployment. Rather than taking a wait-and-see approach to the deployment of new updates, you need to develop an update management routine so you can test an update to the point where you are satisfied that it will not cause a problem before rolling it out to all the client computers in your organization. Your routine might involve initially rolling out the update to a set of computers that mirror the configurations deployed in your enterprise, and it might involve deploying the update to a small, select group of test users who can report if the update adversely affects their day-to-day activities. Because Microsoft has a regular schedule for releasing software updates, it is not too difficult for you to make plans to perform update testing regularly after the updates are released. Just remember that a big part of planning software update infrastructure is planning your own time so that you can test and deploy those updates confidently to the computers in your organization.

# Lesson 1:  Designing a Software Update Infrastructure

This lesson examines four software update technologies that are available from Microsoft and informs you about which technology is most appropriate when designing a software update infrastructure for an organization. The lesson begins by examining Microsoft Update and Windows Server Update Services (WSUS) 3.0 SP1, solutions used and appropriate for most small to medium-sized environments. The lesson then covers System Center Essentials (SCE) 2007, a technology that works well as a software update platform in small and medium-sized environments. The lesson finishes by examining System Center Configuration Manager (SCCM) 2007, which is often deployed, among other reasons, as an enterprise software update solution.

> **After this lesson, you will be able to:**
> - Design a patch management solution.
> - Determine which software update product is appropriate for a given set of circumstances.
>
> **Estimated lesson time:  80 minutes**

## Microsoft Update as a Software Update Solution

Two questions are pertinent when planning the deployment of any software update technology. The first is, "How are software updates approved for deployment?" and the second is, "Where are the update files stored and retrieved from after they have been approved for deployment?" How you, as the planner of your organization's software update infrastructure, answer these questions determines the type of solution to incorporate into your designs.

The default configuration of Windows Server 2008 and Windows Vista uses the Microsoft Update servers, hosted by Microsoft and accessible across the Internet, as the source of software update approvals and software update files. When you use this method, the approval of updates is entirely under Microsoft control. Although sole reliance on Microsoft Update reduces an administrator's workload, this method of software update deployment has the following drawbacks in most enterprise environments:

- Each update must be downloaded separately to each client from the Microsoft Update servers. In enterprise environments where there might be thousands of clients, this can have a significant impact on bandwidth usage and cost.
- This method does not allow for testing updates to determine whether they conflict with any existing applications within the environment. Although Microsoft rigorously tests each update prior to deployment, the company cannot test updates against unique custom software deployed in your enterprise environment.

■ There is no provision for centralized reporting. Administrators must use software tools to scan all client computers to determine whether an update has installed correctly. This data cannot be extracted directly from the Microsoft Update servers.

There are certain times when you should plan to use Microsoft Update as a complete software update solution in your enterprise environment. These cases are specific and apply to parts of the organization only, rather than to the organization as a whole. Incorporate Microsoft Update into your patch management design when you must plan for the following scenarios:

■ Your organization has satellite offices or retail outlets where there are a small number of standalone clients. In these circumstances, it is often simpler to enable automatic updates on the clients than to attempt centralized management.

■ Your organization's mobile computers rarely connect to the organizational network, and a central list of approved updates would rarely be accessed. In this situation, you would also use Network Access Protection to ensure that when these mobile computers do connect to the organizational network, their system health is verified before access is granted to the protected network.

In many cases, it is necessary to separate update approvals from update storage. Taking this approach enables you to manage which updates are installed although the update files themselves are downloaded from the Microsoft Update servers on the Internet. You would plan this solution for satellite or branch offices where you must exert control over the distribution of updates but where there is not a strong case to store updates locally. Remember that update approval traffic has only a small bandwidth footprint whereas downloading update files can clog a slow wide area network (WAN) link. For example, imagine that your organization has a small satellite office that has fast Internet connectivity and a virtual private network (VPN) WAN link to a branch office. In this situation, you can configure client computers to poll a software update server for a list of approved updates and then to obtain those updates from the Microsoft Update servers on the Internet. A small amount of data is pulled across the VPN WAN link, but the larger amount of update data is pulled across the Internet link.

# Windows Server Update Services as a Software Update Solution

Rather than having each update downloaded multiple times to clients on the same network, planning the deployment of WSUS enables you to configure the update server settings so that the update server downloads the update once, and clients retrieve the update from the WSUS server. Another feature of WSUS offers administrators the ability to roll back the installation of updates that have already been deployed. WSUS is not limited to updates and can provide a local copy of all content that is published on Microsoft Update. This includes drivers, service packs, feature packs, and security updates.

WSUS 3.0 SP1 is the first version of WSUS compatible with Windows Server 2008. Although not included as a role or feature, the software itself is freely available, and you can install the software on licensed computers running Windows Server 2008. You cannot install WSUS 3.0 SP1 on computers running a Server Core installation of Windows Server 2008, although this functionality might be available in later versions of the update server software. In the first exercise at the end of this lesson, you will install WSUS 3.0 SP1 on a computer running Windows Server 2008.

## Managing WSUS

You can manage a WSUS server locally or remotely by using the Update Services console. WSUS uses administrative roles to assign permissions. Each role can perform a specific set of functions, and you can assign roles to users by adding their user accounts to one of the following local groups:

- **WSUS Administrators**   Users who have accounts that are members of this local group are able to administer the WSUS server. This includes WSUS administration tasks from approving updates and configuring computer groups to configuring automatic approvals and the update source of the server running WSUS. A user who is a member of this group can use the Update Services console to connect remotely to manage WSUS.
- **WSUS Reporters**   Users who have accounts that are members of this local group are able to create reports on the WSUS server. A user who is a member of this group can connect remotely to the server running WSUS, using the Update Services console to run these reports. Lesson 2, "Managing Software Update Compliance," covers reporting in more detail.

## WSUS Deployment Hierarchies

Each WSUS 3.0 SP1 server is capable of providing software updates to 25,000 client computers. This means that, in theory, a single WSUS server can service the requests of all but the largest enterprise environments. In large organizations, WSUS servers are usually deployed in each Active Directory Domain Services (AD DS) site so that update and approval data can be retrieved from a server on the local network rather than over WAN links. You specify the WSUS server's update source during installation. Updates are stored locally on the WSUS server, or client computers use the WSUS server for a list of approved updates and then download those updates from the Microsoft Update servers on the Internet.

WSUS server hierarchies involve an upstream server at the top of the hierarchy and downstream servers that retrieve data from the upstream server. It is possible to have multiple layers in the hierarchy, with each downstream server using the server above it as a source of update approvals and software update files. In many real-world WSUS deployments, the hierarchy structure is used for the approval of updates only, and the downstream servers retrieve the update files from the Microsoft Update servers. This configuration is popular in organizations that have branch offices connected to a head office by slow WAN links but where each branch office has a high-speed link to the Internet. In this configuration, approval data travels to the branch office site across the WAN link, and update files are downloaded from the Internet.

---

**MORE INFO**  WSUS deployment

For detailed information about WSUS deployment, consult the WSUS deployment guide at *http://www.microsoft.com/downloads/details.aspx?FamilyID=208e93d1-e1cd-4f38-ad1e -d993e05657c9&DisplayLang=en.*

---

## WSUS Administration Models

The administration model determines how update approvals flow through the organization. There are two options when configuring the administration model for your organization's downstream WSUS servers. The first option, shown in Figure 11-1, is to configure the downstream WSUS server as a replica of the upstream server. When you configure a WSUS server as a replica, all approvals, settings, computers, and groups from the upstream server are used on the downstream server. The downstream server cannot approve updates when configured in replica mode, although you can change a replica server to the second mode— called autonomous mode—if you urgently need to deploy an update.

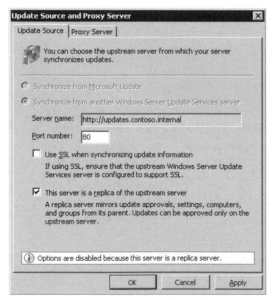

**Figure 11-1**  Downstream replica server

Autonomous mode enables a local WSUS administrator to configure separate update approval settings but still retrieves updates from the upstream WSUS server. Autonomous mode conserves bandwidth for the organization by ensuring that updates are downloaded only once from the Internet but retains the benefit of allowing local administrators discretion over the approval of updates.

When planning the deployment of WSUS in an enterprise environment, it is likely that you will need to use a mixture of autonomous and replica modes. For example, an organization with two Active Directory forests shares a single Internet connection. The organization wants to minimize the number of updates downloaded from the Internet, but the administrators of each forest want control over which updates are deployed in their organization. To resolve this problem, you can place a WSUS server in the first forest and configure it in autonomous mode. You can place a second WSUS server in the second forest and configure it in autonomous mode, but instead of drawing update files from Microsoft Update, these files can be obtained from the WSUS server in the first forest. All future WSUS servers deployed in each environment can then be configured as replicas of their respective forest's autonomous WSUS server.

## WSUS Computer Groups

In the most basic form of WSUS deployment, every computer that is a client of the WSUS server receives approved updates at the same time. Although this method works well for many organizations, other organizations prefer to perform staggered rollouts of updates. Staggered rollouts, usually to a test group of computers, enable organizations to determine whether a software update has an adverse impact on their client computer's configuration. Internally developed custom software can conflict with an update in an unforeseen manner.

By creating a test group, you can deploy newly released updates to a special group of computers in your organization so you can verify that new updates do not conflict with existing deployed configurations. When you are confident that the update causes no problems, you can roll out the update to all clients in the enterprise.

WSUS computer groups have the following properties:

- The two default computer groups are All Computers and Unassigned Computers. Unless a client computer is already assigned to a group, when it contacts the WSUS server for the first time, it will be added to the Unassigned Computers group.
- Groups can be organized in a hierarchy. An update deployed to a group at the top of the hierarchy will also be deployed to computers that are in groups lower in the hierarchy. The Unassigned Computers group is a part of the All Computers hierarchy.
- Computers can be assigned to multiple groups.

As Figure 11-2 shows, administrators can use two methods to assign computer accounts to WSUS groups. The first method is known as server-side targeting. To use this method, choose the Use The Update Services Console option under Computers in the Options section of the Update Services console. A user with WSUS Administrator privileges manually assigns computers in the Unassigned Computers group to specific computer groups, using the WSUS console.

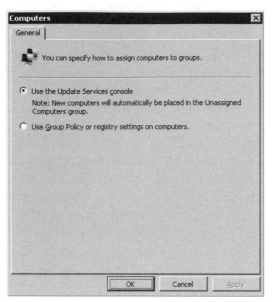

**Figure 11-2** Computer group option

The other method of assigning computers to groups is to use Group Policy or registry settings on clients of the WSUS server. This method, known as client-side targeting, is less time-consuming in enterprise environments and simplifies the group assignment process. Regardless of which method you use to assign computers to groups, you must first create the groups by using the WSUS console.

## Update Installation Behavior

Other than the policies that determine the assignment of computers to WSUS groups and the location of the local WSUS server, the most important WSUS-related group policies relate to how and when WSUS updates are downloaded and installed. As an administrator, you want to avoid the situation of updates never being installed—either because a user intervenes to cancel update installation or because the updates are always scheduled to be installed when the computer is off. You must balance interrupting a user's work with stopping user intervention. No one will be particularly happy to lose several hours of work on an important spreadsheet because you have configured the update settings to install and reboot the computer without alerting the user in advance.

When scheduling update deployments, consider the following policy settings:

- **Enabling Windows Update Power Management To Automatically Wake Up The System To Install Scheduled Updates** This policy works only with instances of Windows Vista that are running on compatible hardware and that have an appropriately configured BIOS. Rather than worrying about whether reboots will interrupt users during the update deployment process, use this policy to awaken computers in the middle of the night, deploy the relevant updates, and then return to sleep. This policy works well in enterprise environments in which hundreds, if not thousands, of computers are deployed, and finding a convenient time during business hours is difficult.

■ **Configure Automatic Updates**    The Configure Automatic Updates policy enables you to specify whether updates are automatically downloaded and scheduled for installation or whether the user is simply notified that updates (either already downloaded or on the WSUS server) are available.

■ **Automatic Updates Detection Frequency**    If this policy is not enabled, the default detection frequency is 22 hours. If you want to configure a more frequent interval, use this policy to do so.

■ **Allow Automatic Updates Immediate Installation**    When enabled, this policy automatically installs all updates that do not require a service interruption or for Microsoft Windows to restart.

■ **No Auto-Restart For Scheduled Automatic Updates Installations**    When this policy is enabled, the computer will not automatically restart but will wait for the user to restart the computer on his or her own time. The user will be notified that the computer needs to be restarted before the installation of updates is completed. If this policy is not enabled, the computer will automatically restart five minutes after the updates are installed to complete update installation.

■ **Delay Restart For Scheduled Installations**    This policy enables you to vary the automatic restart period. As mentioned previously, the default period is five minutes. This policy enables you to set a delay period of up to 30 minutes.

■ **Reschedule Automatic Updates Scheduled Installations**    This policy ensures that a scheduled installation that did not occur—perhaps because the computer was switched off or disconnected from the network—will occur the specified number of minutes after the computer is next started. If this policy is disabled, a missed scheduled installation will occur with the next scheduled installation.

## Planning Automatic Approvals

Part of planning a software update infrastructure for an enterprise environment involves determining the level of administrator intervention required during the approval process. Automatic approval rules enable you to approve specific categories of updates so that they are deployed without requiring administrator intervention. You can configure updates to apply to specific WSUS computer groups, for a specific classification, or for specific products.

You can have multiple automatic approval rules, and you can enable and disable them as necessary. Configure automatic approval rules through the Automatic Approvals dialog box shown in Figure 11-3, which is available under Options in the Update Services console. By default, no updates are automatically approved for distribution by WSUS 3.0 SP1.

**Figure 11-3**   Configuring automatic approvals

Organizational policy influences planning for automatic approval rules more than technical reasons do. In organizations with highly customized software configurations, a rigorous testing process is likely to be in place for all updates, and automatic approval is unlikely to be enabled. In organizations in which administrators do not test updates prior to deployment, using automatic approval rules can minimize staff workload.

## Planning the Deployment of WSUS in Enterprise Environments

The key question that you must deal with in planning the deployment of WSUS in enterprise environments is who is ultimately responsible for approving updates. In some organizations, it can mean that you have to deploy multiple WSUS servers configured in autonomous mode within the same domain; in other organizations, multiple downstream replica servers deployed throughout multiple forests might use a single autonomous WSUS server as an upstream server.

The deployment of WSUS servers themselves in enterprise environments is also dependent on WAN bandwidth configuration. The branch offices of many organizations have a direct connection to the Internet and WAN links, either through a direct link or through a VPN tunnel, to their head office location. In these situations, it makes little sense to pull the software update files over the WAN when they can also be downloaded directly from the Microsoft Update servers on the Internet.

---

## Quick Check

1. In what mode should you deploy a downstream WSUS 3.0 SP1 server if you want it to use the approvals and computer group configuration of the designated upstream server?

2. In what mode should you deploy a downstream WSUS 3.0 SP1 server if the local branch office administrator will be responsible for the approval of software updates?

## Quick Check Answers

1. Put the downstream WSUS server into replica mode if you want it to use the approvals and computer group configuration of the designated upstream server.

2. If a local IT professional is responsible for approving the deployment of updates on a downstream WSUS server, that server needs to be configured to use autonomous, rather than replica, mode.

---

# System Center Essentials 2007

Although limited to managing 500 client computers and 30 servers, SCE 2007 provides more features for the deployment of software updates than WSUS 3.0 SP1 does. The primary difference between the products is that you can also use SCE 2007 to deploy software updates to non-Microsoft products. SCE 2007 provides advanced update distribution control and scheduling flexibility and basic compliance-checking functionality and inventory management. Although SCE 2007 functions as much more than as a platform for deploying software updates, such as providing health reports and software and hardware inventory, this lesson discusses the update functionality in particular. Only SCE 2007 SP1 or later can be installed on a computer running Windows Server 2008.

Unlike WSUS 3.0 SP1, SCE 2007 SP1 is not a free add-on to Windows Server 2008; a nonevaluation version must be purchased from Microsoft when permanently deployed in a production environment. SCE 2008 stores configuration data in a Microsoft SQL Server database. It can either use SQL Server Express, which you can install during the SCE 2007 installation process, or store this data in a separate SQL Server 2005 SP2 or SQL Server 2008 database. The SQL Server 2005 SP2 or SQL Server 2008 database does not need to be hosted on the same server as the other SCE 2007 components, and all SCE 2007, including the database, can be installed on a computer hosting the Active Directory Domain Services (AD DS) role.

SCE offers the following:

- Update management for Microsoft and third-party applications and devices.
- Software deployment of MSI and EXE installed software packages, including third-party applications and Office 2007.

■ Hardware and software inventory with attributes collected for items such as available disk space, RAM usage, and installed applications with version numbers.

SCE 2007 interfaces with client agent software that installs during the SCE 2007 discovery process. SCE discovery involves the SCE 2007 server detecting all computers on the network. When you run the discovery process, you select which of the detected computers the SCE 2007 server will manage. The user account you use to perform the SCE discovery process must have administrative rights on all computers that the SCE 2007 server will manage. After you select a computer for SCE 2007 to manage, the agent software is automatically deployed to that computer.

## SCE 2007 Software Update Configuration

The SCE 2007 software update process is similar to the WSUS 3.0 SP1 software update process, and SCE 2007 SP1 is built on top of WSUS 3.0 SP1. The SCE 2007 SP1 setup process enables you to migrate WSUS 3.0 SP1 settings so that you retain existing computer groups and software update approvals when moving to the new software update platform. As with WSUS 3.0 SP1, you can use computer groups and approval rules with SCE 2007 to stagger and automate the deployment of updates. The biggest difference between the two platforms is that you can use SCE 2007 to deploy updates and service packs to third-party applications. This functionality is not available in WSUS 3.0 SP1.

As also with WSUS 3.0 SP1, the source of Microsoft-related SCE 2007 updates can be either the local SCE 2007 server or Microsoft Update. SCE 2007 can use a local source to deploy updates only for third-party applications. When deploying updates to third-party applications, you run the New Update Wizard to create an update package. When the update package is created, you select the computer groups to which the update package will be deployed.

---

**MORE INFO    Managing updates with SCE 2007**

For more information about incorporating System Center Essentials 2007 into your software update design, consult the following TechNet link: *http://technet.microsoft.com/en-us/library/bb437260.aspx*.

---

## SCE 2007 in the Enterprise

When considering SCE 2007 as a software update solution in an enterprise environment, remember the following facts:

■ SCE 2007 can provide software updates to a maximum of 30 servers and 500 client computers. Most enterprise environments have more computers than this, which might necessitate multiple SCE 2007 servers or mean that you will need to deploy System Center Configuration Manager 2007 if your organization requires advanced software update functionality.

- You can install only one SCE 2007 server in an Active Directory domain. It is possible to have multiple SCE 2007 servers in an Active Directory forest as long as there is only one SCE 2007 server per domain. If the domains in your organization all have fewer than 500 clients and 30 servers, SCE 2007 is a viable software update platform.

- You cannot use SCE 2007 in a workgroup environment. All SCE 2007 clients must be members of the same Active Directory forest.

- SCE 2007 cannot function as part of a WSUS hierarchy. You can deploy WSUS alongside SCE 2007, but the two software update platforms do not directly interoperate.

- You can use SCE 2007 to provide software updates to computers in different domains from the SCE 2007 server as long as these computers are in the same Active Directory forest, and the 500-client, 30-server limit has not been reached.

- You cannot use a single SCE 2007 server as a software update provider for computers in different Active Directory forests.

SCE 2007 works very well as a software update solution in an organization that has a single site and fewer than 500 client computers and 30 server computers. SCE 2007 is not an optimal solution for an organization that has multiple sites connected by WAN links. This is because pushing software updates across WAN links might flood those links with traffic. As mentioned earlier, you cannot deploy SCE 2007 as part of a hierarchy, and you cannot deploy multiple SCE 2007 servers within the same domain.

**MORE INFO** Planning the deployment of SCE 2007

For more information about planning the deployment of SCE 2007 in your enterprise environment, consult the following TechNet link: *http://technet.microsoft.com/en-us/library/bb422980.aspx*.

## System Center Configuration Manager 2007

System Center Configuration Manager (SCCM) 2007 provides a software update solution for enterprise-sized environments that exceed the 500-client, 30-server capacity of SCE 2007. As with SCE 2007, an organization must purchase SCCM 2007 prior to deploying the product permanently as a software update solution. SCCM 2007 does not ship with its own SQL Server database, and you must deploy and configure SQL Server 2005 SP1 or SQL Server 2008 in your environment prior to deploying SCCM 2007. Only SCCM 2007 SP1 or later can be deployed on a computer running Windows Server 2008. Although you can also use SCCM 2007 to deploy operating systems and distribute software, the coverage in this lesson concentrates on the software update deployment and management features of the product.

Like SCE 2007, SCCM 2007 can publish software updates for third-party products. Unlike SCE 2007, SCCM 2007 can also use hierarchies, with primary sites, secondary sites, parent sites, child sites, and central sites. All sites in a hierarchy must be part of the same Active

Directory forest. Each site requires one site server running SCCM 2007. Each site type has the following properties:

- **Primary site**   This is the first SCCM 2007 site. It stores the SCCM 2007 data for itself and for all sites below it in the hierarchy in a SQL Server database.
- **Secondary site**   This site has no local SQL Server database. It is attached to the primary site and administered from the primary site. Secondary sites require no additional SCCM 2007 license. Secondary sites cannot have other sites below them in the hierarchy.
- **Parent sites**   This kind of site has other sites attached to it in a hierarchy.
- **Child sites**   A child site is attached to a site above it in the hierarchy. A child site can be either a primary site or a secondary site.
- **Central site**   Central sites have no parent sites. These sites are sometimes called stand-alone sites.

---

**MORE INFO**   **More on sites**

To understand more about SCCM 2007 sites, consult the following TechNet article: *http://technet.microsoft.com/en-us/library/bb632547.aspx*.

---

SCCM 2007 sites host software update points. Software update points distribute software updates to computers in the organization. WSUS 3.0 SP1 must be installed on a computer running Windows Server 2008 before it can be configured as an SCCM 2007 software update point. When configured as a software update point, you perform all management tasks by using the SCCM 2007 console rather than by the original WSUS administration tools.

---

**MORE INFO**   **Planning software update infrastructure with SCCM 2007**

To learn more about the best practices for planning a software update infrastructure with SCCM 2007, consult the following TechNet article: *http://technet.microsoft.com/en-us/library/bb694244.aspx*.

---

**MORE INFO**   **SCCM 2007 virtual labs**

To learn more about the functionality of SCCM 2007, visit the following TechNet virtual labs: *https://msevents.microsoft.com/cui/webcasteventdetails.aspx?eventid=1032343963&eventcategory =3&culture=en-us&countrycode=us&lc=1033* and *http://msevents.microsoft.com/CUI /WebCastEventDetails.aspx?culture=en-US&EventID=1032343569&CountryCode=US*.

---

**PRACTICE** **Windows Server 2008 Software Update Infrastructure**

In this practice, you will install two software update solutions. In the first exercise, you will deploy Windows Server Update Services 3.0 SP1 on server Glasgow. In the second exercise, you will work with an evaluation virtual hard disk (VHD) of SCE 2007.

Before beginning Exercise 1, "Install WSUS 3.0 SP1 on Windows Server 2008," you must perform the following tasks:

■ Download Windows Server Update Services 3.0 SP1 from *http://go.microsoft.com/fwlink /?LinkId=71266*.

■ Download Report Viewer from *http://www.microsoft.com/Downloads/details.aspx?familyid =8A166CAC-758D-45C8-B637-DD7726E61367&displaylang=en*.

Before beginning Exercise 2, "SCE 2007 VHD," you must perform the following tasks:

■ Download the System Center Essentials 2007 Virtual Hard Disk from *http:// www.microsoft.com/downloads/details.aspx?FamilyID=27342759-e9d6-4073-918c -e9dff77d0206&DisplayLang=en*.

■ Configure Virtual PC, Virtual Server, Hyper-V, or an alternative solution to host this virtual machine. Instructions included with the virtual hard disk explain how to install this computer. Configure the virtual machine so that it has access to the Internet.

▶ **Exercise 1   Install WSUS 3.0 SP1 on Windows Server 2008**

In this practice, you will install WSUS 3.0 SP1 on Windows Server 2008. You will configure this installation so that updates are stored on the Microsoft Update servers. This practice should be considered optional because it requires Internet access. You can configure server Glasgow to access the Internet by adding a second network card or by adding a virtual network card and configuring Virtual Machine network settings appropriately. This practice also assumes that you have not installed IIS on server Glasgow. If IIS has been installed, use the Add Role Services functionality to add the additional required components listed in step 1 instead of performing step 3.

1. Log on to server Glasgow using the Kim_Akers user account.
2. Install Report Viewer on server Glasgow.
3. Use the Server Manager console to add the Web Server (IIS) role. Add any required features. Ensure that the ASP.NET, Windows Authentication, and IIS 6 Metabase Compatibility options are selected.
4. Verify that the features listed in the Confirm Installation Selections dialog box match those shown in Figure 11-4, and then click Install. When the installation process completes, click Close.
5. Double-click the installation file you downloaded to start the WSUS 3.0 SP1 setup process. Install WSUS 3.0 SP1 with the following configurations:
   ❑ Complete a full server installation, including Administration Console.
   ❑ Do not store updates locally.
   ❑ Install the Windows Internal Database locally, as shown in Figure 11-5.
   ❑ Use the existing IIS Default Web Site.

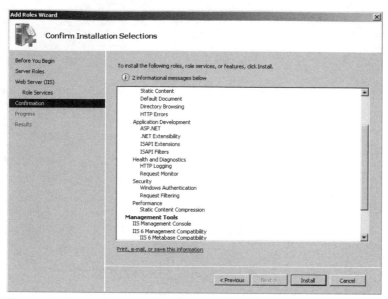

**Figure 11-4**    Preparing IIS for the installation of WSUS

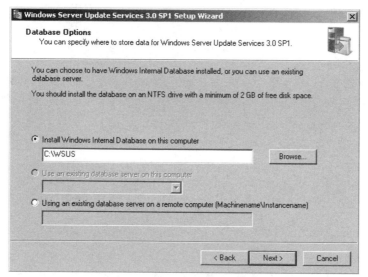

**Figure 11-5**    Configuring WSUS database options

The Windows Server Update Services Configuration Wizard automatically starts when the installation of WSUS 3.0 SP1 is complete.

6. If your Windows Server 2008 computer does not have a connection to the Internet, click Cancel at this point.

7. On the Choose Upstream Server page, shown in Figure 11-6, select Synchronize From Microsoft Update.

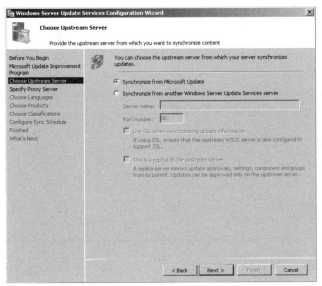

**Figure 11-6**   Configuring synchronization options

8. Unless your organization uses a proxy server that requires authentication, you do not need to specify a proxy server.

9. On the Connect To Upstream Server page, click Start Connecting to contact Microsoft Update to determine the type of updates available, the products that can be updated, and the available languages.

10. On the Choose Products page shown in Figure 11-07, select the All Products check box. On the Choose Classifications page, select the All Classifications check box.

11. On the Set Sync Schedule page, select Synchronize Manually.

12. Ensure that Launch The Windows Server Update Services Administration Console and Begin Initial Synchronization check boxes are cleared, and then finish the installation.

13. When the installation completes, you should open the Update Services console and investigate creating computer groups, creating auto-approval rules and the reporting functionality of WSUS 3.0 SP1. This investigation will help you develop plans to deploy WSUS within your environment.

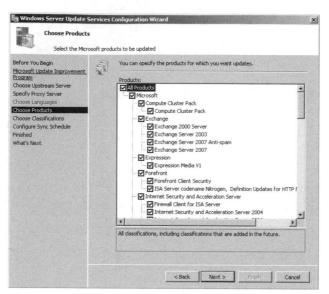

**Figure 11-7**    Choose products that WSUS can update

► **Exercise 2    SCE 2007 VHD**

In this exercise, you will configure the SCE VHD virtual machine and explore the update features available in SCE 2007. To complete the practice, perform the following steps:

1.  Log on to the System Center Essentials 2007 VHD virtual machine, using the username **Administrator** and the password **Evaluation1**.

2.  Use DCPROMO to promote the server to a domain controller (DC) of the new domain, *fabrikam.internal*, in a new forest, using the default settings.

3.  Configure DNS locally on the server, and the Windows Installation Files can be located in the C:\WindowsInstallationFiles\i386 folder. Use **Evaluation1** as the restore mode password.

4.  When you have finished configuring the computer as a DC, double-click the Essentials Setup icon, located on the desktop.

5.  Start the installation by clicking Full Setup on the System Center Essentials 2007 Setup page.

6.  Complete the installation process, accepting the default settings except on the Installation Location page of the setup wizard, on which you should select the Get Update Files From The Microsoft Update Website option, as shown in Figure 11-8. Use the Administrator account as the computer management account. Finish the installation by choosing not to check for updates at this time.

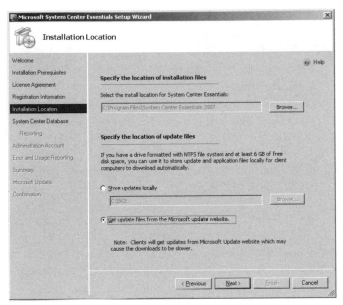

**Figure 11-8**   Location of update files

7. Use the System Center Essentials Console to create computer groups named **Testers**, **Accountants**, and **Research**. Add the computer account for SCEVHDSERVER.fabrikam. internal to each of these groups.

8. From the Updates menu, select Configure Microsoft Update settings. Navigate through the wizard, synchronizing with Microsoft Update and configuring SCE 2007 to provide updates to Exchange Server, Microsoft Office, SQL Server, and Windows. Accept all other default settings.

## Lesson Summary

- WSUS replicas are downstream servers that inherit the configuration of their upstream server.
- Autonomous-mode WSUS servers are downstream servers that retrieve updates from an upstream server, but their approvals and computer groups are configured by a local administrator.
- Server-side targeting assigns computers to WSUS groups, using the WSUS administration console.
- Client-side targeting assigns computers to WSUS groups by using Group Policy or by editing the client computer's registry.
- Deploying updates in a staggered manner or to a test environment enables you to test whether a particular update has an adverse impact on client computers.

- SCE 2007 provides greater functionality than WSUS but also requires access to a SQL Server 2005 SP1 or later database. You can install SQL Server Express during the SCE 2007 setup process.

- SCCM 2007 provides all the extra features of SCE 2007 without the limitation on the number of clients that can be updated.

## Lesson Review

You can use the following questions to test your knowledge of the information in Lesson 1, "Designing a Software Update Infrastructure." The questions are also available on the companion CD if you prefer to review them in electronic form.

---

**NOTE**  Answers

Answers to these questions and explanations of why each answer choice is correct or incorrect are located in the "Answers" section at the end of the book.

---

1. You are planning the deployment of a software update solution to an organization that has 300 computers running Windows Vista and 20 computers running Windows Server 2008, all hosted at a single site. The organization has a single domain forest, and all computers in the organization are members of the Active Directory domain. Which of the following conditions would require you to plan the deployment by using SCE 2007 rather than WSUS 3.0 SP1?

    A. The solution must enable you to roll back updates to third-party products.

    B. The solution must enable you to roll back updates to Microsoft products.

    C. The solution must enable you to deploy service packs for Windows Vista and Windows Server 2008.

    D. The solution must enable you to target the deployment of updates by using computer groups.

2. You are in the process of planning the deployment of WSUS at a university. The university is contains five colleges, each of which has its own separate IT staff and Active Directory forest. The university has a single connection to the Internet through which all traffic passes and wants to minimize the amount of data downloaded from the Microsoft Update servers, but each college's IT staff should have responsibility to approve updates. Which of the following WSUS deployment plans should you use?

    A. Configure one upstream server. Configure a downstream replica server for each college.

    B. Configure a WSUS server in each college. Configure client computers to retrieve approvals from the WSUS server and updates from Microsoft Update.

    C. Configure one upstream server. Configure a WSUS server in each college to use autonomous mode but to retrieve updates from the upstream server.

    D. Configure an autonomous server in each college to retrieve updates from Microsoft Update.

3. You want to stagger the rollout of updates from your organization's WSUS 3.0 SP1 server on a departmental basis. The computer accounts for the computers in each department are located in departmental organizational units (OUs). Which of the following should you do? (Choose two. Each answer forms part of the solution.)

    A. Create WSUS computer groups for each department.

    B. Create Group Policy objects (GPOs) and link them to the domain. In each GPO, specify the name of a departmental WSUS computer group.

    C. Create GPOs and link them to each OU. In each GPO, specify the name of a departmental WSUS computer group.

    D. Create separate security groups for all the computer accounts in each departmental OU.

    E. Create separate security groups for all the user accounts in each departmental OU.

4. Which method can you use to ensure that all security and critical updates deploy to computers in the PatchTest computer group, using WSUS?

    A. Create a scheduled task.

    B. Create an Automatic Approval rule that uses the All Computers group as a target.

    C. Create an Automatic Approval rule that uses the PatchTest WSUS computer group as a target.

    D. Create an Automatic Approval rule that uses the PatchTest security group as a target.

5. You are the enterprise administrator for a large metropolitan university where more than 5,000 computers running Windows Vista and 200 servers running Windows Server 2008 have been deployed. You need to be able to deploy software updates for Microsoft and third-party products while ensuring that software updates will still be available in the event that one of the update servers suffers hardware failure. The university forest has five domains, with client and server computers being spread relatively equally across each domain. Which of the following software update server deployment plans meets the university's needs?

    A. Two WSUS 3.0 SP1 servers

    B. Two SCCM 2007 servers

    C. Two SCE 2007 servers

    D. Five SCE 2007 servers

# Lesson 2:  Managing Software Update Compliance

*Compliance* is a term that encompasses all the configurations necessary for ensuring that the computers in your organization are configured to a specific standard. For example, to meet compliance requirements, all client computers running Windows Vista might need Service Pack 1 and a specific set of updates applied, a certain firewall configured, and a specific set of applications installed. In this lesson, you will learn about several technologies you can use to assess whether software updates that you have approved have actually been deployed to all the computers in your environment. You will also learn how to create a role-based security policy that you can apply to computers in your environment and the tools you can use to verify that the applied policy remains active.

---

**After this lesson, you will be able to:**
- Monitor software update compliance in complex environments.
- Configure and monitor security baselines.

**Estimated lesson time:  40 minutes**

---

## Microsoft Baseline Security Analyzer

The Microsoft Baseline Security Analyzer (MBSA) is a basic tool that enables systems administrators to scan the network to determine which computers are missing updates or are incorrectly configured according to Microsoft best practices recommendations. The best practices scan involves checking Windows Firewall policies, SQL Server – Service Accounts, and other security configuration settings. The MBSA tool can integrate with WSUS, so rather than scanning target systems to see whether any updates are missing from the entire catalog of updates, the MBSA tool will just check whether approved updates are missing from a target computer. You can also use the MBSA tool to detect computers that have not been assigned a software update server. To scan computers with the MBSA tool, your user account must have administrative privileges on the target computer. This enables you to scan computers in your own and trusted forests, assuming your user account has been delegated the appropriate privileges.

As of version 2.1, the MBSA cannot be used to scan computers running Windows Server 2008, although this will be addressed in later versions of the product. Although you can use the MBSA tool to scan most computers in enterprise environments, as Figure 11-9 shows, the MBSA scans are relatively limited in the problems that they can detect on the computers in your environment. Another drawback to the MBSA tool is that the reports it generates are basic. Unlike tools such as SCCM 2007, discussed later in this lesson, you cannot configure the MBSA tool to notify you by e-mail automatically if a server or servers in your environment become noncompliant.

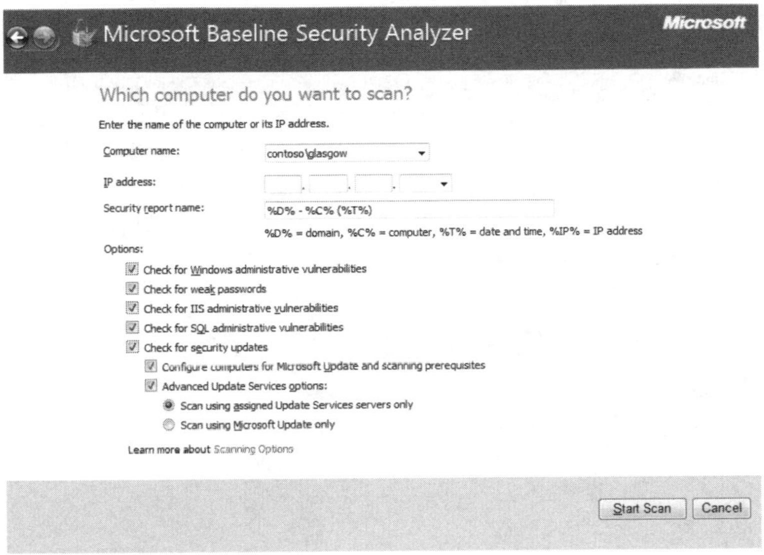

**Figure 11-9**    The MBSA tool

---

**MORE INFO**    **More about the MBSA**

To learn more about the Microsoft Baseline Security Analyzer tool, consult the product Web site at *http://www.microsoft.com/technet/security/tools/mbsahome.mspx*.

---

## WSUS Reporting

You can use WSUS 3.0 SP1 to offer basic software update compliance reporting functionality in enterprise environments. The reports WSUS generates are based on information communicated with WSUS. WSUS does not scan computers to determine whether updates are missing but instead records whether updates have been downloaded to target computers and whether the target computers have reported back to the WSUS server that the update has been successfully installed. Figure 11-10 shows a list of the available WSUS reports.

WSUS reports can be printed or exported to Microsoft Office Excel or PDF format. If WSUS data is written to a SQL Server database, you can perform your own separate analyses by using your own set of database queries. This enables the generation of more sophisticated reports than are offered by the default WSUS configuration.

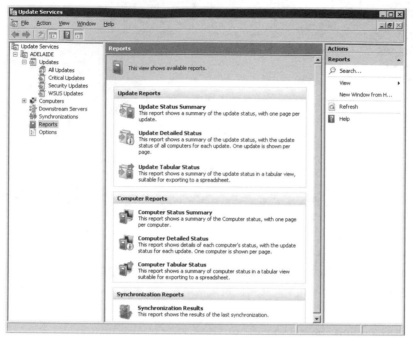

**Figure 11-10**    WSUS reporting options

You can generate the following reports, using WSUS 3.0 SP1 if your user account is a member of the WSUS Reporters or WSUS Administrators groups:

- **Update Status Summary**    This report contains basic information about update deployment, including the number of computers the update is installed on, is needed on, or failed to install on, and for which WSUS has no data. One page is available per update. Figure 11-11 shows an Update Status Summary Report.

- **Update Detailed Status**    This report offers significantly more information about the deployment of updates, providing a list of computers and their update status on an update-per-page basis. When you run a detailed update, you can view the report in summary or tabular format.

- **Update Tabular Status**    This report format provides data in a table on a per-update basis. After this report is generated, you can switch the report to Summary or Update Detailed Status. This form of report is the best to export to Excel because it is already in tabular format, as shown in Figure 11-12.

- **Computer Status Summary**    Similar to the Update Detailed Status report, this report provides update information on a per-computer rather than on a per-update basis. Data is presented in summary form.

- **Computer Detailed Status**    This report format provides detail about the status of specific updates for a particular computer. After this report is generated, you can switch the report to summary or tabular form.

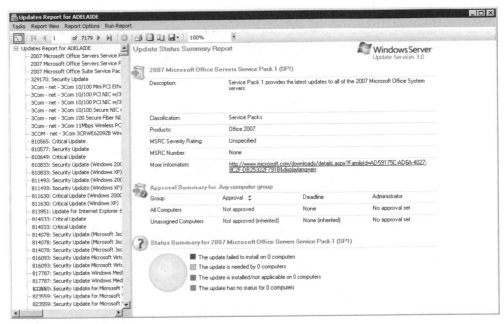

**Figure 11-11** Update Status Summary report

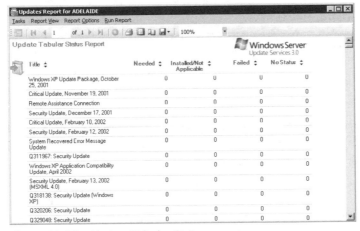

**Figure 11-12** Update Tabular Status report

- **Computer Tabular Status** This report provides a table of update status information, with individual computers as rows. After this report is generated, you can switch the report to summary or tabular form.

- **Synchronization Results** This report shows the result of the last synchronization of the WSUS server.

Enabling the Reporting Rollup For Downstream WSUS servers option enables update, computer, and synchronization data for replica downstream servers to be included in reports generated on the upstream WSUS server. This is an important option in enterprise environments because it displays a complete view of the software update deployment process.

---

**MORE INFO    SCE reporting**

SCE 2007 also offers basic reporting features related to the deployment of updates, although these are similar to what is available with WSUS 3.0 SP1. You can find out more about the reporting options available in System Center Essentials 2007 by completing Exercise 2, "Use the SCE VHD to Perform Compliance Tasks," at the end of this lesson or by consulting the following TechNet article: *http://technet.microsoft.com/en-us/library/bb422813.aspx.*

---

# SCCM 2007 Compliance and Reporting

Configuration management is a feature of SCCM 2007 that enables you to assess whether the configuration of computers within your environment matches what is termed a configuration baseline. A configuration baseline can include a specific operating system version, a set of required applications, a set of optional applications, a set of prohibited applications, a set of software updates, and a set of security settings. When you perform a scan against a configuration baseline, you compare the configuration of the computer you are scanning against the baseline configuration. The results of this scan inform you of whether and how the configuration of the scanned computer deviates from that baseline configuration. If the configuration baseline meets all legal and regulatory requirements, you can use a configuration baseline scan to determine whether a computer is compliant. A host of legal rules and organizational policies generally dictate compliance, so a computer deemed compliant in one organization might not be considered compliant in another.

You can configure SCCM 2007 to scan the computers regularly deployed in your organization against a set of configuration baselines to determine their level of compliance. SCCM 2007 enables you to go even further, automatically subjecting noncompliant computers to a remediation process by which the noncompliant aspects of the configuration are modified. The remediation process might include installing updates, tightening security, and removing prohibited applications so that the computer can be returned to a compliant configuration.

---

**MORE INFO    More on SCCM 2007 configuration management**

For more information about SCCM 2007 configuration management, consult the following TechNet link: *http://technet.microsoft.com/en-us/library/bb680553.aspx.*

---

SCCM 2007 can also be used to generate detailed reports about all aspects of computer configuration in your organization's enterprise environment. SCCM 2007 contains a large number of pre-generated reports. Administrators also can create custom reports on the configuration of client computers so they can tailor the reports for specific circumstances. Administrators who are comfortable with writing SQL queries are able to use the SCCM 2007 query designer rather than a wizard to create custom computer configuration reports. Compared to the MBSA tool, WSUS, and SCE 2007, SCCM 2007 is the most comprehensive reporting and compliance tool available from Microsoft for enterprise administrators.

---

**MORE INFO**  Managing SCCM 2007 reports

For more information about how to manage SCCM reports, consult the following TechNet article: *http://technet.microsoft.com/en-us/library/bb632699.aspx.*

---

# Planning and Deploying Security Baselines

The concept of an attack surface describes the idea that the number of services and applications that a host makes available to the network increases the area that an attacker can target. Hence, a computer hosting a Web server, a DNS server, a Simple Mail Transfer Protocol (SMTP) server, and a Dynamic Host Configuration Protocol (DHCP) server has a larger attack surface than a computer hosting only a DHCP server. Reducing a computer's attack surface is part of the general process known as *server hardening*. Part of the process of hardening a server is enforcing security baseline configurations, a collection of settings, from service startup status through to firewall rules that allow only those parts of the server to operate that are necessary for the server to perform its role. In Windows Server 2008, you harden a computer by applying role-based security policies. You generate, analyze, and apply these policies by using the Security Configuration Wizard and the *scwcmd* command-line utility.

## Security Configuration Wizard

The Security Configuration Wizard is a tool used to reduce the attack surface of a computer running Windows Server 2008. The tool is included in the default installation of Windows Server 2008. You can use this tool to develop security policies that will limit a server to the minimum necessary functionality required for that server to perform its planned role. You can analyze the security policy and then use it to create a GPO that you can apply to all servers that perform the same role across the enterprise.

The first step in deploying role-based security policies in an enterprise environment is to perform *policy prototyping*. Policy prototyping involves creating a security policy on a model server. A model server has a configuration that mirrors the computers in your enterprise environment to which you will be applying the policy. This enables you to test the role-based security policy prior to deploying it in your environment. Role-based security policies include settings for:

- Services
- Network security, which includes Windows Firewall with Advanced Security rules

- Registry values
- Audit policies

As Figure 11-13 shows, the Security Configuration Wizard enables you to create, edit, apply, and roll back role-based security policies. The Security Configuration Wizard writes role-based security policies in XML format.

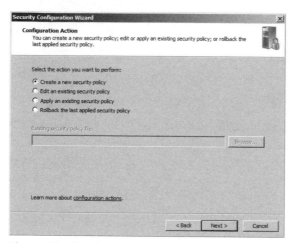

**Figure 11-13**    The Security Configuration Wizard

You can also use the Security Configuration Wizard to apply security templates, which are a set of pre-generated security settings located in the %Systemroot%\security\templates folder of a computer running Windows Server 2008. You can use security templates to apply some security configuration settings to a computer running Windows Server 2008 that you cannot generate just by running the Security Configuration Wizard. For example, you can use security templates to apply software restriction policies, which are Group Policy settings by which you can restrict the applications that a computer running Windows Server 2008 can execute, using security templates. Apply these extra policies by attaching security template .inf files that include the relevant security settings, using the Include Security Templates dialog box. This dialog box also enables you to set the precedence of attached security templates, allowing the settings of one template to override another. These settings remain attached to the XML file and are not directly integrated, although they do become integrated when you use the *scwcmd* command-line utility to translate a role-based security policy into a GPO.

---

**MORE INFO**    **More on security templates**

To learn more about security templates, consult the following TechNet article:
*http://technet2.microsoft.com/windowsserver/en/library/ea9858dc-9bf1-4a42-ada6 -090237ad178a1033.mspx?mfr=true.*

---

## The *scwcmd* Command-Line Tool

The *scwcmd* command-line tool provides greater functionality than the GUI-based Security Configuration Wizard, although you can launch *scwcmd* from an elevated command prompt only. Using the *scwcmd* command-line tool, you can:

- Remotely apply role-based security policy to groups of computers in your organization.
- Analyze the configuration of groups of computers against the role-based security policy.
- Build GPOs that apply the settings in the role-based security policy.

The ability to apply a role-based security policy, using either the *scwcmd* command-line tool or an applied GPO, enables you to enforce a baseline security configuration across the servers in your organization. The ability to analyze the configuration of computers against the role-based security policy enables you to verify that the computers in your organization remain compliant with that role-based security policy. Because the tool is command-line based, you can include it in scheduled tasks. The *scwcmd* command line tool can output reports in HTML format, so enterprise administrators can use it to script regular reports they can use to assess the security health of the computers in their enterprise environment. To create a GPO from a Security Configuration Wizard policy file, issue the following command from an elevated command prompt on a domain controller:

```
scwcmd transform /p:PathAndPolicyFileName /g:NewGPODisplayName
```

After the command executes, the new GPO will be available under the *Group Policy Object* node of the Group Policy Management console.

---

**NOTE** Security Configuration and Analysis tool

The Security Configuration and Analysis tool enables you to check the configuration of a computer against a security template. The *scwcmd* command-line tool enables you to check the configuration of a computer against an XML-formatted security policy file, which includes attached templates. You can find out more about the Security Configuration and Analysis tool by consulting the following link: *http://technet2.microsoft.com/windowsserver/en/library/bf9ae857-c96e-437e-adfb-10166093e4221033.mspx?mfr=true.*

---

Because role-based security policies are stored in XML format, it is a relatively simple process to migrate them to other domains or forests if the need arises. Remotely analyzing the security configuration of a computer by using the *scwcmd* command-line utility requires local administrator privileges on the target computer. It is possible to pass alternate credentials to *scwcmd* so you can use it to analyze the security configuration of computers in separate Active Directory forests if you have the appropriate credentials for that forest.

It is important to understand the rules of precedence in Windows Server 2008 environments where GPOs, Security Configuration Wizard role-based security policies, and security templates are applied. When planning the deployment of multiple security policies through different methods, remember the following:

- Security policies applied using GPOs have the highest precedence and override policies applied through the Security Configuration Wizard or the *scwcmd* command-line utility. Standard GPO precedence rules apply.
- XML-based, role-based security policies have higher precedence than security templates attached to the role-based security policy. The priority of templates is configured when you attach them to the XML role-based security policy generated by the Security Configuration Wizard.

---

**MORE INFO    More on server security policies**

For more information about server security policy management in Windows Server 2008, consult the following TechNet link: *http://technet2.microsoft.com/windowsserver2008/en/library /996d4b3c-0446-461f-b26d-a73fdcefcaf81033.mspx?mfr=true.*

---

## Role-Based Security Policy Best Practices

When planning and creating role-based security policies, keep the following best practices in mind:

- Ensure that your prototype server properly reflects the configuration of the servers to which the policy will apply. Role-based security policies disable all services that are not present on the prototype server when the policy is created.
- Create separate policies for separate software editions. For example, create a separate policy for 64-bit and 32-bit computers running Windows Server 2008 that host the Web Server (IIS) role.
- When possible, group servers that perform the same role into a single OU in the same domain. When this is not possible, use the same OU name for servers with the same role in different domains and forests. This simplifies the application of policy distribution in complex environments.
- Thoroughly test policies before deploying them on production servers.

---

**MORE INFO    More on the Security Configuration Wizard**

To learn more about the Security Configuration Wizard in developing role-based policies for deployment in a Windows Server 2008 environment, consult the following TechNet link: *http://technet2.microsoft.com/windowsserver2008/en/library/52a98d8a-8823-498c-9be3 -3637186e50e61033.mspx?mfr=true.*

---

**PRACTICE** **Role-Based Security and SCE Reporting**

In this practice, you will perform two common enterprise administrator tasks. The first exercise involves the creation and application of a role-based security policy, using the Security Configuration Wizard. The second exercise involves using SCE 2007 evaluation.

▶ **Exercise 1   Create and Apply a Role-Based Security Policy**

In this practice, you will create a role-based security policy based on the current configuration of server Glasgow and save this policy in XML format. You will then transform this XML policy file into a new GPO and apply that GPO to a newly created OU.

1. Log on to server Glasgow, using the Kim_Akers user account.
2. Use the Active Directory Users And Computers snap-in to create an OU named **GlasgowClones** in the *contoso.internal* domain. Create a computer account in the GlasgowClones OU named **London**.
3. Use the Security Configuration Wizard to create a new security policy named **GlasgowPolicy.xml**.
4. Use the *scwcmd* command-line tool to transform the new security policy (located in the \%Systemroot%\Windows\security\msscw\Policies folder) into a GPO named **GlasgowPolicyGPO**.
5. Use the Group Policy Management Console to link GlasgowPolicyGPO to the GlasgowClones OU.
6. Use the Group Policy Modeling Wizard to model the effect that the newly applied GPO has on computer account London.

▶ **Exercise 2   Use the SCE VHD to Perform Compliance Tasks**

In this practice, you will use the SCE 2007 evaluation VHD that you downloaded for Exercise 2 in Lesson 1 to perform several reporting and compliance tasks. To complete this exercise, perform the following steps.

1. Log on to the virtual computer, using the username **Administrator** and the password **Evaluation1**.
2. Open the System Center Essentials 2007 management console. Click Required: Configure Product Features. Navigate through the Feature Configuration Wizard. Review and then accept all default settings except the following.
   a. On the Agentless Exception Monitoring For Computers page, configure SCE 2007 so that it does not collect application errors.
   b. On the Daily Health Report Settings page, select Do Not Configure The Daily Health Report At This Time. Click Configure to complete the configuration process.
3. Click Reporting to open the Reporting View.
4. Select Microsoft Generic Reports Library.

5. Select the Health report and, from the Actions menu, choose Open.

6. Add the *SCEVHDSERVER.fabrikam.internal* object, set the business hours option as shown in Figure 11-14, and then click Run.

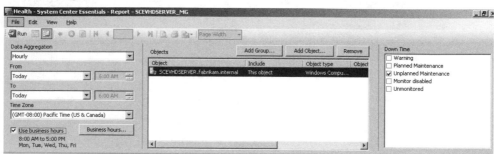

**Figure 11-14**    SCE Health report

7. Select the Updates view. Under Reports, select the Group Update Deployment Status item.

8. In the Choose The Computer Group For This Report drop-down list, select the All Servers group, and then click Run.

---

**MORE INFO    SCE virtual lab**

To learn more about SCE 2007, complete the following virtual lab at *http:// msevents.microsoft.com/CUI/WebCastEventDetails.aspx?EventID=1032335654&EventCategory =3&culture=en-US&CountryCode=US*.

---

## Lesson Summary

■ You can use the MBSA tool to scan computers to determine whether approved updates are installed. The MBSA tool can use a list of updates from an update server or from Microsoft Update. You can use the MBSA tool also to detect a small number of security configuration problems on scanned computers.

■ You can use SCCM 2007 to perform compliance scans, comparing the configuration of scanned computers against a configuration baseline. It is possible to configure SCCM 2007 to resolve configuration differences between the configuration of a scanned computer and the configuration baseline automatically.

■ You can use the Security Configuration Wizard to create a role-based security policy as well as capture the entire configuration of a hardened prototype server. You can then apply this policy to other servers, which automatically changes their security configuration to match that of the prototype server.

# Lesson Review

You can use the following questions to test your knowledge of the information in Lesson 2, "Managing Software Update Compliance." The questions are also available on the companion CD if you prefer to review them in electronic form.

---

**NOTE   Answers**

Answers to these questions and explanations of why each answer choice is correct or incorrect are located in the "Answers" section at the end of the book.

---

1. Tailspin Toys has a single domain forest with 700 client computers running Windows Vista and 24 computers running Windows Server 2008. You are planning the deployment of a product that will be able to perform compliance reporting on all computers in the *tailspintoys.internal* domain to ensure that a specific set of patches are installed and that several security settings have been configured appropriately. Which of the following planned deployments will meet your needs?

   A. A single computer running Windows Server 2008 with SCE 2007 SP1 installed

   B. A single computer running Windows Server 2008 with WSUS 3.0 SP1 installed

   C. Two computers running Windows Server 2008 with SCE 2007 SP1 installed

   D. A single computer running Windows Server 2008 with SCCM 2007 SP1 installed

2. Which of the following tools can you use to apply an XML-formatted, role-based security policy remotely to 400 computers running Windows Server 2008 located throughout an Active Directory forest in which your user account has administrative privileges?

   A. Security Configuration and Analysis tool

   B. Microsoft Baseline Security Analyzer tool

   C. *scwcmd* command-line tool

   D. Windows Server Update Services 3.0 SP1

3. Which of the following security settings, when remotely applied to a group of computers running Windows Server 2008 in an Active Directory forest, will take precedence over all the others?

   A. Security settings applied through Group Policy

   B. Security settings applied using the *scwcmd* command-line tool

   C. Security settings applied using the Security Configuration and Analysis tool

   D. Security settings applied using the Security Configuration Wizard

4. You need a list of computers that a recent update did not install on so that you can send a technician to investigate further. Which of the following WSUS 3.0 SP1 reports should you generate to locate this information quickly?

   A. Update Status Summary

   B. Computer Status Summary

   C. Update Detailed Status

   D. Computer Detailed Status

# Chapter Review

To further practice and reinforce the skills you learned in this chapter, you can perform the following tasks:

- Review the chapter summary.
- Complete the case scenarios. These scenarios set up real-world situations involving the topics of this chapter and ask you to create a solution.
- Complete the suggested practices.
- Take a practice test.

# Chapter Summary

- You can use WSUS Server to centralize the deployment of updates in a Windows Server 2008 environment. It provides basic compliance reporting functionality.
- System Center Essentials 2007 enables you to provide software updates to third-party applications but is limited to only one server per domain and can be used with only 500 client computers and 30 servers.
- System Center Configuration Manager 2007 has advanced reporting functionality that you can use to verify that computers meet compliance requirements.
- You can use the Security Configuration Wizard and *scwcmd* command-line utility to generate, analyze, and apply XML-formatted, role-based security policies.

# Case Scenarios

In the following case scenarios, you will apply what you have learned about patch management and security. You can find answers to these questions in the "Answers" section at the end of this book.

## Case Scenario 1: Deploying WSUS 3.0 SP1 at Fabrikam, Inc.

After using an ad hoc approach to patch management over the last few years, the CIO at Fabrikam, Inc., has decided that during the project to upgrade all existing computers running Windows 2000 Server to Windows Server 2008, WSUS 3.0 SP1 should also be deployed. Fabrikam is located in the state of Victoria, Australia. The head office is located in the Melbourne Central Business District (CBD), and suburban satellite offices are located in Moonee Ponds, Cheltenham, Endeavour Hills, and Glen Waverley.

The current plan is for a WSUS 3.0 SP1 server to be installed on a Windows Server 2008 host at the head office and then for a phased rollout of WSUS servers at the suburban satellite offices. Because all the IT staff work in the Melbourne CBD office, the servers at the satellite offices should use the computer group configuration and the update approvals that are configured on the head office server.

One reason for the ad hoc approach in the past was that Fabrikam uses custom software that sometimes conflicts with updates, causing the installation of those updates to fail. The CIO wants to be able to run reports on updates from her desktop computer to determine when these events occur. The CIO does not require administrative access to the server and never performs hands-on administrative tasks, always delegating this to the systems administrators in her team.

With this information in mind, answer the following questions:

1. To which local group on the computer running Windows Server 2008 hosting WSUS should you add the CIO's user account?

2. How should you configure the update source of downstream WSUS servers at the Fabrikam satellite offices?

3. Which type of report should you instruct the CIO to generate to gain detailed information about the specific computers on which a particular update's installation has failed?

## Case Scenario 2: Security Policies at Coho Vineyard and Coho Winery

Coho Vineyard and Coho Winery are two subsidiary companies owned by the same parent. You work for the parent company, and you are responsible for the planning and deployment of security policies for all subsidiary organizations. Coho Vineyard and Coho Winery each has its own separate single-domain Active Directory forests. These forests do not share a trust relationship. You have separate user accounts with Enterprise Administrator credentials in both forests but most often use a management server located in the *cohovineyard.internal* domain to perform day-to-day tasks. You are planning the deployment of role-based security policies for intranet servers in each organization's forest.

With this information in mind, answer the following questions:

1. The intranet servers use both the 32-bit and 64-bit versions of Windows Server 2008 as their operating system. How many role-based security policies should you develop for these servers?

2. Which tools can you use to create role-based policies for the intranet servers?

3. You want to perform a daily check of the intranet servers in the *cohowinery.internal* forest to verify that their configuration still conforms to the applied security policy. You want to run this check from your management server in the *cohovineyard.internal* forest and have the results output in HTML format. What steps would you take to accomplish this goal?

# Suggested Practices

To help you successfully master the exam objectives presented in this chapter, complete the following tasks.

## Designing for Software Updates and Compliance Management

Complete the following practice exercise.

- **Practice 1**   Install System Center Configuration Manager 2007 in the *contoso.internal* domain by downloading an evaluation version of SQL Server 2008 and System Center Configuration Manager 2007 from the Microsoft Web site. Deploy a new computer running Windows Server 2008. Install SQL Server 2008 and then System Center Configuration Manager 2007.
- **Practice 2**   Prototype and deploy a security policy by installing a new member server in the *contoso.internal* domain and configuring the server with the Web Server (IIS) and DNS Server roles. Use the Security Configuration Wizard to generate a role-based security policy based on the configuration of the newly installed member server. Use the *scwcmd* command-line utility to create a GPO based on these settings.

# Take a Practice Test

The practice tests on this book's companion CD offer many options. For example, you can test yourself on just one exam objective, or you can test yourself on all the 70-647 certification exam content. You can set up the test so that it closely simulates the experience of taking a certification exam, or you can set it up in study mode so that you can look at the correct answers and explanations after you answer each question.

---

**MORE INFO   Practice tests**

For details about all the practice test options available, see the "How to Use the Practice Tests" section in this book's introduction.

---

# Answers

## Chapter 1: Lesson Review Answers

### Lesson 1

1. **Correct Answer: B**

   A. **Incorrect:** Centralized WINS topology uses a single, centralized, high-availability WINS server or WINS server cluster.

   B. **Correct:** Full mesh WINS topology is a distributed WINS design with multiple WINS servers or clusters deployed across the enterprise. Each server or cluster replicates with every other server or cluster.

   C. **Incorrect:** Ring WINS topology is a distributed WINS design created by having each WINS server replicate with a specific neighboring partner, forming a circle.

   D. **Incorrect:** Hub and spoke WINS topology is a distributed WINS design in which a central WINS server is designated as the hub and additional WINS servers only replicate with the hub in the site where they are located.

2. **Correct Answer: A**

   A. **Correct:** You can configure the primary name server, the refresh interval, and the minimum default Time-to-Live (TTL) values for zone resource records in the zone's SOA record.

   B. **Incorrect:** NS records identify the name servers in a DNS zone.

   C. **Incorrect:** SRV records permit AD DS to integrate with DNS and implement DDNS. These records are required for the Locator mechanism to function.

   D. **Incorrect:** Canonical name (CNAME) records map an alias or nickname to the real or canonical name that might lie outside the current zone.

3. **Correct Answer: C**

   A. **Incorrect:** The */createdirectorypartition* switch in the *dnscmd* command is used to create a directory partition and will not enable a DNS server to support Global-Names zones.

   B. **Incorrect:** The */enlistdirectorypartition* switch in the *dnscmd* command is used to add a DNS server to partition replication scope and will not enable a DNS server to support GlobalNames zones.

   C. **Correct:** The */config* switch in the *dnscmd* command is used to enable a DNS server to support GlobalNames zones.

D.  **Incorrect:** The */createbuiltindirectorypartitions* switch in the *dnscmd* command is used to create the default directory partitions and will not enable a DNS server to support GlobalNames zones.

4.  **Correct Answer: A**

A.  **Correct:** You cannot list DNS records by using *nslookup* unless you have allowed zone transfers, even when the records are on the same computer.

B.  **Incorrect:** You run the command console as an administrator when using configuration commands such as *dnscmd*. You do not need to do so when you are displaying but not changing information.

C.  **Incorrect:** You can type **nslookup ls –d adatum.internal** directly from the command prompt. However you can also type **nslookup** and then type **ls –d adatum.internal** from the nslookup> prompt.

D.  **Incorrect:** You can perform most operations on a server, including *nslookup*, by logging on through a Remote Desktop connection. Logging on to servers interactively is bad practice and should be avoided.

5.  **Correct Answer: D**

A.  **Incorrect:** There is no problem with the host record for the Web server. Other users can access the internal Web site.

B.  **Incorrect:** You do not need to flush the DNS cache on the DNS server. The problem is at the user's client computer.

C.  **Incorrect:** The client computer is registered in DNS and can access other Web sites.

D.  **Correct:** A DNS cache entry on the client computer has marked the Web site URL as not resolvable. Flushing the DNS cache on the client computer solves the problem.

# Lesson 2

1.  **Correct Answer: B**

A.  **Incorrect:** A site-local unicast IPv6 address identifies a node in a site or intranet. It is the equivalent of an IPv6 private address, for example, 10.0.0.1.

B.  **Correct:** A global unicast address (or aggregatable global unicast address) is the IPv6 equivalent of an IPv4 public unicast address and is globally routable and reachable on the Internet.

C.  **Incorrect:** A link-local unicast IPv6 address is autoconfigured on a local subnet. It is the equivalent of an IPv4 APIPA address, for example, 169.254.10.123.

D.  **Incorrect:** Two special IPv6 addresses exist. The unspecified address :: indicates the absence of an address and is equivalent to the IPv4 unspecified address 0.0.0.0. The loopback address ::1 identifies a loopback interface and is equivalent to the IPv4 loopback address 127.0.0.1. Neither is the IPv6 equivalent of an IPv4 public unicast addresses.

2. **Correct Answer: A**

   A. **Correct:** The solicited mode address consists of the 104-bit prefix ff02::1:ff (written ff02::1:ff00:0/104) followed by the last 24 bits of the link-local address, in this case, a7:d43a.

   B. **Incorrect:** Although the 104-bit prefix is written ff02::1:ff00:0/104, the /104 indicates that only the first 104 bits (ff02::1:ff) are used. Hence, the solicited mode address is ff02::1:ffa7:d43a.

   C. **Incorrect:** Addresses that start with fec0 are site-local, not solicited node.

   D. **Incorrect:** Addresses that start with fec0 are site-local, not solicited node.

3. **Correct Answer: D**

   A. **Incorrect:** ARP is a broadcast-based protocol used by IPv4 to resolve MAC addresses to IPv4 addresses. ND uses ICMPv6 messages to manage the interaction of neighboring nodes.

   B. **Incorrect:** EUI-64 is not a protocol. It is a standard for 64-bit hardware address.

   C. **Incorrect:** DHCPv6 assigns stateful IPv6 configurations. ND uses ICMPv6 messages to manage the interaction of neighboring nodes.

   D. **Correct:** ND uses ICMPv6 messages to manage the interaction of neighboring nodes.

4. **Correct Answer: A**

   A. **Correct:** In configured tunneling, data passes through a preconfigured tunnel, using encapsulation. The IPv6 packet is carried inside an IPv4 packet. The encapsulating IPv4 header is created at the tunnel entry point and removed at the tunnel exit point. The tunnel endpoint addresses are determined by configuration information.

   B. **Incorrect:** Dual stack requires that hosts and routers provide support for both protocols and can send and receive both IPv4 and IPv6 packets. Tunneling is not required.

   C. **Incorrect:** ISATAP connects IPv6 hosts and routers over an IPv4 network, using a process that views the IPv4 network as a link layer for IPv6 and other nodes on the network as potential IPv6 hosts or routers. This creates a host-to-host, host-to-router, or router-to-host automatic tunnel. A preconfigured tunnel is not required.

   D. **Incorrect:** Teredo is an enhancement to the 6to4 method. It enables nodes that are located behind an IPv4 NAT device to obtain IPv6 connectivity by using UDP to tunnel packets. Teredo requires the use of server and relay elements to assist with path connectivity. It does not require a preconfigured tunnel.

5. **Correct Answer: D**

   A. **Incorrect:** This command displays the IPv6 configuration on all interfaces. It does not configure an IPv6 address.

    B.  **Incorrect:** You can use this command to add the IPv6 address of, for example, a DNS server to an IPv6 configuration. You use *netsh interface ipv6 set address* to configure a static IPv6 address.

    C.  **Incorrect:** This command enables you to change IPv6 interface properties but not an IPv6 address. You use *netsh interface ipv6 set address* to configure a static IPv6 address.

    D.  **Correct:** You use *netsh interface ipv6 set address* to configure a static IPv6 address.

6.  **Correct Answers: A, D, F, and G**

    A.  **Correct:** IPv4 and IPv6 are both supported by Trey's network hardware and service provider. Dual stack is the most straightforward transition strategy.

    B.  **Incorrect:** Trey does not need to encapsulate IPv6 packets inside IPv4 packets. Configured tunneling transition is typically employed if IPv6 is not currently available.

    C.  **Incorrect:** Trey saw no need to configure NAT and use private IPv4 addresses. The organization is unlikely to use site-local addresses, which are the IPv6 equivalent of private addresses.

    D.  **Correct:** Trey uses public IPv4 addresses throughout its network. It is likely to use global unicast addresses in its IPv6 network.

    E.  **Incorrect:** Trey's clients run Windows Vista Ultimate, and its servers run Windows Server 2008. All Trey's clients and servers support IPv6, and the protocol is installed by default.

    F.  **Correct:** There is no guarantee that Trey's network projectors and network printers support IPv6, although they probably do because the company believes in investing in cutting-edge technology.

    G.  **Correct:** Network management systems need to be checked for IPv6 compatibility.

    H.  **Incorrect:** High-level applications are typically independent of the Internet protocol used.

# Chapter 1: Case Scenario Answers

## Case Scenario 1: Configuring DNS

1.  You can configure a zone to support only secure dynamic updates. This ensures that only authenticated users and clients can register information in DNS.

2.  You can configure zone replication to occur only with DNS servers that have NS records and are on the Name Servers list. Alternatively, you can manually specify a list of servers and configure zone replication so that zone information is replicated only to these servers.

3.  When a Windows Server 2008 server is configured as an RODC, it replicates a read-only copy of all Active Directory partitions that DNS uses, including the domain partition,

ForestDNSZones, and DomainDNSZones. Therefore, DNS zone information on RODCs updates automatically (provided the writable DC is configured to allow this).

4. Create an IPv6 reverse lookup zone.

## Case Scenario 2: Implementing IPv6 Connectivity

1. Site-local IPv6 addresses are the direct equivalent of private IPv4 addresses and are routable between VLANs. However, you could also consider configuring every device on your network with an aggregatable global unicast IPv6 address. NAT and CIDR were introduced to address the problem of a lack of IPv4 address space, and this is not a problem in IPv6. You cannot use only link-local IPv6 addresses in this situation because they are not routable.

2. Both IPv4 and IPv6 stacks are available. In this scenario, dual stack is the most straightforward transition strategy.

3. As with DHCP for IPv4, you should configure a dual-scope DHCPv6 server on each subnet. The scope for the local subnet on each server should include 80 percent of the full IPv6 address range for that subnet. The scope for the remote subnet on each server should include the remaining 20 percent of the full IPv6 address range for that subnet.

# Chapter 2: Lesson Review Answers

## Lesson 1

1. **Correct Answer: B**
   A. **Incorrect:** Data autonomy does not require a resource forest. Resource forests provide service isolation to protect areas of the network that need to maintain a state of high availability.
   B. **Correct:** To achieve data autonomy, you can join an existing forest.
   C. **Incorrect:** Data autonomy does not require a new organizational forest. An organizational forest provides service autonomy, service isolation, or data isolation.
   D. **Incorrect:** Data autonomy does not require a new restricted access forest. A restricted access forest is used for data isolation.

2. **Correct Answer: C**
   A. **Incorrect:** A restricted access forest will not provide service autonomy. A restricted access forest is used for data isolation.
   B. **Incorrect:** A resource forest will not provide service autonomy. Resource forests provide service isolation that is used to protect areas of the network that need to maintain a state of high availability.
   C. **Correct:** An organizational forest will provide service autonomy.

D.   **Incorrect:** Joining an existing forest will not provide service autonomy. Joining an existing forest is used to provide data autonomy.

3.   **Correct Answers: A, B, C, and D**

A.   **Correct:** When deciding whether to upgrade existing domains or deploy new domains, determine whether the existing domain model still meets the needs of the organization.

B.   **Correct:** The amount of downtime that can be incurred is an important consideration because the downtime varies between both methods.

C.   **Correct:** Time constraints are an important consideration because the time required varies between both methods.

D.   **Correct:** The budget is an important consideration because the costs vary between both methods.

4.   **Correct Answer: A**

A.   **Correct:** To minimize the impact of a problematic schema change, you must disable outbound replication on the server that holds the schema master operations master role.

B.   **Incorrect:** Disabling inbound replication on the server that holds the schema master operations master role will not minimize the impact because the problematic schema change will be replicated out by the server that holds this role.

C.   **Incorrect:** Deactivating the user class will not minimize the impact of a problematic schema change. Deactivating the user class will cause a forest-wide impact.

D.   **Incorrect:** Restarting the computer that holds the schema master operations master role into Directory Services Restore Mode (DSRM) will not enable you to make the schema change. Schema changes cannot be made in DSRM.

5.   **Correct Answer: B**

A.   **Incorrect:** The forest functional level cannot be raised to Windows Server 2008 because there are domain controllers in the forest that have Windows Server 2003 installed on them. These domain controllers must be upgraded to Windows Server 2008, and the domain functional level must be raised to Windows Server 2008 before the forest functional level can be raised to Windows Server 2008.

B.   **Correct:** To install an RODC, raise the forest functional level to Windows Server 2003, which is the minimal forest functional level required for RODCs.

C.   **Incorrect:** The *adprep /forestprep* command has already been run in this forest because there are Windows Server 2008 domain controllers in the forest.

D.   **Incorrect:** The *adprep /domainprep /gpprep* command has already been run in this forest because there are Windows Server 2008 domain controllers in the forest.

# Lesson 2

1. **Correct Answer: A**

   A. **Correct:** The single site model has all domain controllers in the same site and uses intrasite replication.

   B. **Incorrect:** The multiple sites model uses intersite replication, not intrasite replication, because domain controllers are distributed across one or more sites.

   C. **Incorrect:** The hub and spoke replication topology has multiple sites and uses intersite replication, not intrasite replication.

   D. **Incorrect:** The full mesh replication topology has multiple sites and uses intersite replication, not intrasite replication.

2. **Correct Answer: C**

   A. **Incorrect:** The single site model has all domain controllers in the same site and, therefore, does not provide efficient replication when the network consists of faster network connections between major computing hubs and slower links connecting branch offices.

   B. **Incorrect:** There is no replication topology referred to as the ring replication topology in terms of AD DS replication.

   C. **Correct:** The hub and spoke replication topology provides the most efficient replication when the network consists of faster network connections between major computing hubs and slower links connecting branch offices.

   D. **Incorrect:** The full mesh replication topology is used when each site connects to every other site. The propagation of change orders for replicating AD DS can impose a heavy burden on the network and is not efficient when the network consists of faster network connections between major computing hubs and slower links connecting branch offices.

3. **Correct Answer: A**

   A. **Correct:** The server that holds the PDC emulator operations master role should be placed in the location represented by the hub site because this site would have the largest number of users in a hub and spoke replication topology.

   B. **Incorrect:** The server that holds the PDC emulator operations master role should not be placed in a spoke site because those locations have fewer users than the hub site. The PDC emulator should always be placed in a location where it services the highest number of users.

   C. **Incorrect:** The server that holds the PDC emulator operations master role cannot be placed in every location represented by a spoke site because there can be only one PDC emulator per domain.

   D. **Incorrect:** The server that holds the PDC emulator operations master role should not be placed on the server that holds the global catalog server role in a spoke site because a spoke sites have fewer users than the hub site. The PDC emulator should always be placed in a location where it services the highest number of users.

4. **Correct Answer: A**

   A. **Correct:** When the forest model consists of multiple domains, and not all domain controllers are global catalog servers, the infrastructure master role must be placed on a server that is not a global catalog server.

   B. **Incorrect:** When the forest model consists of multiple domains, and not all domain controllers are global catalog servers, the infrastructure master role cannot be on a server that is a global catalog server because in this scenario, a global catalog server will not receive any updates for the objects the infrastructure master role holder needs to know about.

   C. **Incorrect:** There can be only one infrastructure master role holder per domain. Therefore, the infrastructure master role holder cannot be placed on every global catalog server in the forest.

   D. **Incorrect:** Placing the infrastructure master role holder on a single server in the forest root domain will suffice for the forest root domain. However, because there is one infrastructure master role holder per domain, this is not a complete solution.

# Chapter 2: Case Scenario Answers

## Case Scenario 1: Designing the AD DS Forest

1. No. Joining the Wingtip Toys computers to the Tailspin Toys forest will not provide service isolation and will allow the Tailspin Toys administrators to manage the entire forest.

2. Yes. Creating a new organizational forest for Wingtip Toys will meet the service isolation requirements and separate the administration capabilities between Tailspin Toys and Wingtip Toys administrators.

## Case Scenario 2: Designing AD DS Sites

1. No. Not all locations are connected to a central location. Therefore, the hub and spoke topology will not work.

2. Yes. Using a hybrid topology will work. The U.S., Canada, Mexico, and Italy locations will be using a hub and spoke in this hybrid, with the U.S. location as the hub. The Argentina location will connect directly to the Mexico location, which necessitates a hybrid topology.

## Case Scenario 3: Designing the Placement of Domain Controllers

1. No. A global catalog server will also act as a writable domain controller. Therefore, if this server is compromised through lack of physical security, it can be used to further compromise AD DS and AD DS data.

2. Yes. An RODC in the Argentina location will be the best solution because physical security cannot be guaranteed in this location, and RODCs are read-only.

# Chapter 3: Lesson Review Answers

## Lesson 1

1. **Correct Answer: B**
   A. **Incorrect:** You must run *adprep /forestprep* on the DC hosting the schema master role.
   B. **Correct:** You must run *adprep /forestprep* on the DC hosting the schema master role.
   C. **Incorrect:** You must run *adprep /forestprep* on the DC hosting the schema master role.
   D. **Incorrect:** You must run *adprep /forestprep* on the DC hosting the schema master role.
   E. **Incorrect:** You must run *adprep /forestprep* on the DC hosting the schema master role.

2. **Correct Answer: D**
   A. **Incorrect:** You should run *adprep /domainprep /gpprep* on the computer hosting the infrastructure master role, not on the computer hosting the PDC emulator role.
   B. **Incorrect:** You should run *adprep /domainprep /gpprep* on the computer hosting the infrastructure master role.
   C. **Incorrect:** You should run *adprep /domainprep /gpprep* on the computer hosting the infrastructure master role, not on the computer hosting the RID master role.
   D. **Correct:** You should run the *adprep /domainprep /gpprep* command on the infrastructure master when preparing a domain for the introduction of a Windows Server 2008 DC when the forest has already been prepared.
   E. **Incorrect:** You should run *adprep /domainprep /gpprep* on the infrastructure master, not on the domain naming master. There is only one domain naming master per forest.

3.  **Correct Answer: A**

    A.  **Correct:** Disabling SID filtering enables the *SIDHistory* attribute, allowing SIDs tied to accounts that have been migrated to new domains or forests to access resources in the original domain or forest.

    B.  **Incorrect:** SID filtering is enabled by default.

    C.  **Incorrect:** Selective Authentication limits which users can access resources across a forest trust.

    D.  **Incorrect:** Name suffix routing routes authentication requests to a specific forest.

4.  **Correct Answer: A**

    A.  **Correct:** When selective authentication is configured for a trust relationship, users from the trusted forest will not automatically be authenticated for resources in the trusting forest. Users from the trusted forest must be explicitly granted access to resources.

    B.  **Incorrect:** SID filtering is automatically enabled on Windows Server 2008 trusts as a security measure; it will not ensure that users from a trusted forest are automatically treated as authenticated users by the trusting forest.

    C.  **Incorrect:** UPN suffix routing is used to specify where user authentication occurs, not to ensure that users from a trusted forest are automatically treated as authenticated users by the trusting forest.

    D.  **Incorrect:** Forest-wide authentication means that users from a trusted forest are automatically treated as authenticated users by the trusting forest.

# Lesson 2

1.  **Correct Answer: D**

    A.  **Incorrect:** Services for NFS enables you to serve files from a computer running Windows Server 2008 to UNIX-based client computers.

    B.  **Incorrect:** The Password Synchronization component of Identity Management for UNIX enables you to synchronize passwords between AD DS and UNIX-based computers.

    C.  **Incorrect:** Subsystem for UNIX-based Applications enables you to run POSIX-compliant applications on a computer running Windows Server 2008.

    D.  **Correct:** Active Directory Federation Services enables you to implement a single-sign-on solution for a group of related Web applications.

2.  **Correct Answer: B**

    A.  **Incorrect:** AD FS provides a single-sign-on solution for Web applications. It does not synchronize identity data across different products.

    B. **Correct:** Microsoft Identity Lifecycle Manager Feature Pack 1 can be used as a tool to synchronize user identity data across a heterogeneous environment. This includes synchronizing user identity data stored in a human resources database running on Oracle 9i with a Windows Server 2008 AD DS infrastructure and an Exchange Server 2007 deployment.

    C. **Incorrect:** Services for NIS does synchronize identity data between NIS and AD DS, but the solution required in this question involves different products. The necessary outcome cannot be achieved by using Services for NIS.

    D. **Incorrect:** Services for NFS is a file-sharing solution that enables UNIX-based operating systems to access shared files on computers running Windows Server 2008. It cannot be used to synchronize identity data.

3. **Correct Answer: C**

    A. **Incorrect:** Subsystem for UNIX-based Applications enables POSIX applications to execute on a computer running Windows Server 2008.

    B. **Incorrect:** Server for NIS enables a computer running Windows Server 2008 to function as an NIS server for UNIX computers. It is not used to share files between a computer running Windows Server 2008 and UNIX-based client computers.

    C. **Correct:** Services for NFS enables UNIX-based client computers to access shared files on computers running Windows Server 2008.

    D. **Incorrect:** Network Policy Server is not related to shared files.

4. **Correct Answers: C and E**

    A. **Incorrect:** You would not plan to use the Terminal Services role as a method of migrating UNIX-based applications to Windows Server 2008.

    B. **Incorrect:** Although it might be possible to virtualize some UNIX-based operating systems under Hyper-V, they cannot all be virtualized because many such operating systems run on architectures other than x64 or x86.

    C. **Correct:** The Subsystem for UNIX-based Applications feature enables POSIX compliant applications to run on a computer running Windows Server 2008.

    D. **Incorrect:** Active Directory Federation Services does not allow POSIX-compliant applications to run on a computer running Windows Server 2008.

    E. **Correct:** After SUA has been installed, the POSIX applications still need to be migrated to the new platform.

# Chapter 3: Case Scenario Answers

## Case Scenario: Phasing Out a UNIX-Based Computer at Tailspin Toys

1. Authentication can be simplified by using Active Directory Federation Services and setting up a federation partnership between Wingtip Toys and Tailspin Toys.

2. Because the application is POSIX-compliant, it probably can be migrated to run under the Windows Server 2008 Subsystem for UNIX-based Applications environment.

3. You can use Identity Lifecycle Manager 2007 Feature Pack 1 to synchronize identity data between the Tailspin Toys HR database running on SQL Server 2008 and the Wingtip Toys mail infrastructure running on Lotus Notes 7.0.

# Chapter 4: Lesson Review Answers

## Lesson 1

1. **Correct Answer: C**
   - A. **Incorrect:** In the centralized model, Group Policy is set at a single central location that is locally administered by a single administration team. This model is best suited to organizations with a single main office and small branch offices.
   - B. **Incorrect:** The hybrid model is more commonly known as the mixed model. This model is best suited to medium-sized organizations with a main office and a number of subsidiaries, each of which has a few local administrators. Most Group Policy settings are defined at the central office, but the subsidiaries can configure and administer local configurations.
   - C. **Correct:** Northwind Traders is a large multinational organization. Each national office has considerable autonomy and its own administration team. This is the distributed administrative model.
   - D. **Incorrect:** The mixed model is best suited to medium-sized organizations with a main office and a number of subsidiaries, each of which has a few local administrators. Most Group Policy settings are defined at the central office, but the subsidiaries can configure and administer local configurations.

2. **Correct Answers: A, D, E, and F**
   - A. **Correct:** Microsoft recommends the Business Unit Administrators management role for delegating data management.
   - B. **Incorrect:** Microsoft recommends the Security Policy Administrators management role for delegating service management, not data management.
   - C. **Incorrect:** Microsoft recommends the Service Administration Managers management role for delegating service management, not data management.

D. **Correct:** Microsoft recommends the Resource Administrators management role for delegating data management.

E. **Correct:** Microsoft recommends the Security Group Administrators management role for delegating data management.

F. **Correct:** Microsoft recommends the Application-Specific Administrators role for delegating data management.

G. **Incorrect:** Microsoft recommends the Replication Management Administrators management role for delegating service management, not data management.

3. **Correct Answer: B**

A. **Incorrect:** Audit Directory Service Access controls whether auditing for directory service events is enabled or disabled. However, the policy is enabled by default.

B. **Correct:** Audit Directory Service Access controls whether auditing for directory service events is enabled or disabled. This policy is enabled by default.

C. **Incorrect:** If Directory Service Changes is enabled, AD DS logs events in the Security event log. This setting does not control whether auditing for directory service events is enabled or disabled.

D. **Incorrect:** If Directory Service Changes is disabled, AD DS does not log events in the Security event log. This setting does not control whether auditing for directory service events is enabled or disabled.

4. **Correct Answer: D**

A. **Incorrect:** A forest trust sets up a trust relationship between the domains in two forests. Windows NT 4.0 domains do not use forests.

B. **Incorrect:** If a UNIX realm uses Kerberos authentication, you can create a realm trust between a Windows domain and the UNIX realm. You cannot create a realm trust between two Windows domains.

C. **Incorrect:** If users in one child domain in a forest frequently need to access resources in another child domain in another forest, you might decide to create a shortcut trust between the two domains. You cannot create a shortcut trust to a Windows NT 4.0 domain.

D. **Correct:** You set up an external trust when a domain within your forest requires a trust relationship with a domain that does not belong to a forest. Typically, external trusts are used when migrating resources from Windows NT domains.

5. **Correct Answer: A**

A. **Correct:** You should delegate permission to link GPOs. This enables existing GPOs to be linked without allowing those GPOs to be modified.

B. **Incorrect:** You should delegate permissions to existing OUs in this scenario, not to GPOs.

C. **Incorrect:** The software developers' security group does not need to generate Group Policy modeling data to link GPOs.

D. **Incorrect:** The software developers' security group does not need to generate Group Policy results to link GPOs.

# Lesson 2

1. **Correct Answer: C**

   A. **Incorrect:** Although having too many GPOs (often with the same settings) is a common mistake, it is also a bad idea to have too few. However, if a GPO has many policy settings configured in different areas, it can be difficult to understand everything it does or to give it a descriptive name.

   B. **Incorrect:** Linking GPOs to OUs across sites can slow replication and increase traffic over slow WAN links.

   C. **Correct:** Both GPOs and OUs should have descriptive names. You might know what GPO06 does right now, but will you remember in three months' time? If you had called it (for example) Kiosk Policy, its function would be much clearer. Similarly, an OU named Human Resources is more helpful than OU23.

   D. **Incorrect:** Features such as Block Inheritance, Enforced, Security Filtering, and Loopback Policy can be useful in the situations for which they were designed. However, they add complexity and make your Group Policy design more difficult to understand. Use these exceptions only when you can identify a real advantage in doing so.

2. **Correct Answers: B, C, D, and E**

   A. **Incorrect:** DSA is a service component in the Active Directory data store, not an interface.

   B. **Correct:** MAPI is an interface in the Active Directory data store.

   C. **Correct:** SAM is an interface in the Active Directory data store.

   D. **Correct:** REPL is an interface in the Active Directory data store.

   E. **Correct:** LDAP is an interface in the Active Directory data store.

   F. **Incorrect:** ESE is a service component in the Active Directory data store, not an interface.

3. **Correct Answers: A, C, and F**

   A. **Correct:** Enabling Prevent Installation Of Devices Not Described By Other Policy Settings prevents standard users from installing devices except for those devices permitted by other settings.

   B. **Incorrect:** Disabling or not configuring Prevent Installation Of Devices Not Described By Other Policy Settings permits standard users to install any device except those specifically prohibited by other settings.

C. **Correct:** Enabling Allow Administrators To Override Device Installation Restriction Policies permits administrators to install any device.

D. **Incorrect:** Disabling or not configuring Allow Administrators To Override Device Installation Restriction Policies results in administrators having the same device installation rights as standard users, which is not what is required.

E. **Incorrect:** Enabling Prevent Installation Of Devices That Match Any Of These Device IDs and adding the Hardware ID of the approved device to the policy setting would explicitly prohibit the installation of that device.

F. **Correct:** Enabling Allow Installation Of Devices That Match Any Of These Device IDs and adding the Hardware ID of the approved device to the policy setting would explicitly permit installation of that device and would override the Prevent Installation Of Devices Not Described By Other Policy Settings setting for that device only.

# Chapter 4: Case Scenario Answers

## Case Scenario 1: Designing a Delegation Strategy

1. Windows Server 2008 provides granular AD DS auditing that enables you to audit the changes made to AD DS configuration and to record what the settings are before they are changed.

2. Advise your team member to use scope filtering. This enables security groups to be defined when the GPO is linked to the OU so that the GPO settings apply only to these groups.

3. The Group Policy Results tool.

## Case Scenario 2: Planning Authentication and Authorization

1. Windows Server 2008 introduces fine-grained password policies that enable settings other than the default to be set for specified users or for security groups. You can apply a PSO to a group or an exceptional PSO directly to a user account. In Windows 2003 domains, variations in password policy typically require additional domains.

2. Your team member needs to check domain functional levels and raise them to Windows Server 2008, if necessary.

3. You can use Group Policy to prevent all users except administrators from installing devices on their workstations. This does not affect the Windows ReadyBoost feature, which is a System installation.

# Chapter 5: Lesson Review Answers

## Lesson 1

1. **Correct Answer: D**

   A. **Incorrect:** The access client would be the VPN client that initiates the connection attempt.

   B. **Incorrect:** The access server is also known as the RADIUS client. In this scenario, it receives the inbound connection attempt from the access client and forwards the authentication request to a remote server through RADIUS.

   C. **Incorrect:** The RADIUS proxy is an intermediary between RADIUS clients and RADIUS servers to facilitate load balancing and forwarding of requests to the appropriate RADIUS server for authentication.

   D. **Correct:** The RADIUS server is the final RADIUS component in the chain of forwarded requests starting from a RADIUS client. It is the endpoint at which a directory server is presented with an authentication request from the RADIUS server.

2. **Correct Answer: B**

   A. **Incorrect:** One of the primary uses of a RADIUS proxy is accepting inbound RADIUS requests from access servers.

   B. **Correct:** The RADIUS client or an access server performs this service.

   C. **Incorrect:** The RADIUS proxy is essential in a RADIUS solution that requires load balancing of requests to back-end RADIUS servers. Normally, access clients can provide load balanced RADIUS requests by offsetting configurations on the access clients. One access client has a specified primary RADIUS server and a secondary RADIUS server whereas a second access client has them listed opposite of the first access client.

   D. **Incorrect:** Multi-forest environments using RADIUS for authentication of a provided service require a RADIUS proxy to ensure the delivery of a RADIUS request to an appropriate RADIUS server in the same realm as the user account requesting authentication.

3. **Correct Answer: A, C, and D**

   A. **Correct:** The server certificate is first presented to the client and is used to create the encrypted channel between the client and the server.

   B. **Incorrect:** PEAP-TLS uses the server's certificate along with the computer's certificate to create an encrypted tunnel prior to the exchange of certificates for mutual authentication.

   C. **Correct:** MS-CHAP v2 uses only the user password for the user's authentication. No other authentication medium is provided for the user.

   D.   **Correct:** MS-CHAP v2 does provide for mutual authentication of both the client
        and the server.

## Lesson 2

   1.   **Correct Answer: A, B, and D**

   A.   **Correct:** NAP provides a safer internal environment where trusted computers have
        successfully passed a health validation.

   B.   **Correct:** Enforcing a policy that mandates the health level of a computer and
        requires validation of it prior to entrance into the trusted environment ensures
        protection.

   C.   **Incorrect:** NAP does not provide a firewall block against attackers. NAP does
        ensure that all computers have an appropriately configured firewall but provides
        no assurance that computers cannot be attacked.

   D.   **Correct:** Enforcing validation of a health policy prior to a computer's entrance into
        the trusted network enhances the network's ability to fend off an attack.

   2.   **Correct Answer: D**

   A.   **Incorrect:** 802.1x ensures only that a client accessing the trusted environment
        through an access point has passed a health validation check.

   B.   **Incorrect:** DHCP enforcement uses the Classless Static Routes option (option
        249) of DHCP to define the servers in the restricted network for a noncompliant
        NAP client requiring remediation.

   C.   **Incorrect:** VPN enforcement does provide for the confidentiality of the data up to
        the point at which the access server accepts the inbound connection request;
        encryption beyond this point depends on the VPN connection protocols and any
        other protocol for data confidentiality.

   D.   **Correct:** IPsec prevents not only the replay of a communication session but also
        enables data confidentiality, data integrity, IPsec authentication of the communi-
        cation channel, and data origin authentication.

# Chapter 5: Case Scenario Answers

## Case Scenario: Designing a NAP Solution for a Large Enterprise

   1.   Using the NAP IPsec enforcement requires that all managed computers be trusted.
        Regardless of the fact that these are branch offices, the users here will be accessing ser-
        vices at the main office. Thus, services accessed by users will require user authentication
        at the very least. Access to any resource, including domain controllers, will require IPsec-
        authenticated access.

2. Again, regardless of the location; how few users; and whether any user requires access to domain services such as domain controllers, file servers, or e-mail, the user will be required to access those resources from a computer that can provide IPsec-authenticated communication.

# Chapter 6: Lesson Review Answers

## Lesson 1

1. **Correct Answer: C**

   A. **Incorrect:** The RODC will refer modifications to a writable D

   B. **Incorrect:** Server Core installs a limited set of services and applications and has a constrained interface, but it does not prohibit an administrator from modifying Active Directory.

   C. **Correct:** Administrator Role Separation allows the branch office administrator the privilege of managing the underlying server operating system but not Active Directory.

   D. **Incorrect:** BitLocker provides encryption of entire volumes on a drive in a system but does not stop a logged-on branch office administrator from administering Active Directory.

2. **Correct Answer: D**

   A. **Incorrect:** The RODC provides increased security for Active Directory but does not provide user data fault tolerance.

   B. **Incorrect:** Clustering can be used to provide server and application fault tolerance, but it has no built-in mechanism to provide user data fault tolerance.

   C. **Incorrect:** Server Core provides increased security thorough a reduced attack surface, but it does not provide user data fault tolerance.

   D. **Correct:** DFS Replication is used to replicate user data to multiple locations, such as branch offices, making the data fault tolerant.

3. **Correct Answer: C**

   A. **Incorrect:** The relay agent would still need to traverse the WAN link.

   B. **Incorrect:** With the WAN link down, clients in the branch office could not access any scope in the HQ.

   C. **Correct:** The DHCP cluster would provide fault tolerance for IP addressing, even with the failed WAN link.

   D. **Incorrect:** Demand dial routing, although it might provide redundancy in the WAN link, does not address the DHCP needs of the branch office.

# Lesson 2

1. **Correct Answer: B**
   - A. **Incorrect:** The full installation of Windows Server 2008 has more features, services, and applications installed by default, making it more vulnerable to attack.
   - B. **Correct:** Server Core installs a limited set of services and applications and has a constrained interface, making this the securest installation in the branch office.
   - C. **Incorrect:** The full (writable) version of the DC can be used to steal more passwords and to violate the integrity of the data in Active Directory.
   - D. **Incorrect:** The full (writable) version of the DC can be used to steal more passwords and to violate the integrity of the data in Active Directory.

2. **Correct Answer: A**
   - A. **Correct:** The RODC requires a writable Windows Server 2008 DC in the nearest site, based on site link cost, to the RODC site.
   - B. **Incorrect:** RODCs cannot perform outbound replication and, therefore, could not be a replication source.
   - C. **Incorrect:** Site link costs should be the lowest to ensure replication.
   - D. **Incorrect:** Site link bridging is not a factor of replication to an ROD

3. **Correct Answer: D**
   - A. **Incorrect:** Administrator Role Separation allows the local administrator to maintain the replacement RODC server, but not Active Directory. This will not protect passwords on the stolen ROD
   - B. **Incorrect:** The PSO is used to specify and assign fine-grained password policies to users and groups, not to protect exposed passwords.
   - C. **Incorrect:** The IFM disk might be used to perform a remote installation of the replacement RODC, but this should not be the first action taken.
   - D. **Correct:** You can use the Delete RODC Wizard to reset user and computer passwords, as well as to export a list of users with passwords on the stolen ROD

# Chapter 6: Case Scenario Answers

## Case Scenario 1: Contoso Trucking

1. Because these offices will probably be under constant hacker attack by your competitor, these servers should all be Windows Server 2008 Server Core servers.
2. All DCs should be RODCs due to the unskilled administrators and the risk of exposure from the hacker attacks.

3. The junior administrators should be granted local administrator privileges using Administrator Role Separation.

## Case Scenario 2: Contoso Trucking, Part 2

1. Initialize BitLocker on the drives in Syracuse. This might require a reinstallation of the operating system to create the proper partition structure to support BitLocker.

2. Raise the domain functional level to Windows Server 2008. Create a global security group named Schenectady Users and add all Schenectady users to the group. Use ADSI Edit or LDIFDE to create a PSO with the following settings (for example):

   ❑ Maximum Password Age = 30 days
   ❑ Minimum Password Age = 25 days
   ❑ Minimum Password Length = 12 characters
   ❑ Password History = 24
   ❑ Password Complexity = Enabled
   ❑ Reversible Encryption Enabled = False
   ❑ Account Lockout Threshold = 3
   ❑ Account Lockout Window = 30 minutes
   ❑ Account Lockout Duration = 0 (Only an administrator can unlock the account.)
   ❑ Users or global security groups that the PSO applies to = Schenectady Users

## Case Scenario 3: Contoso Trucking, Part 3

1. Pre-create the RODC account in Active Directory Users and Computers. Grant the new junior administrator in Saskatchewan the authority to install the RODC. Create IFM media using *ntdsutil* and remove the password attribute from all users. Supply the IFM media to the administrator in Saskatchewan.

2. Configure Administrator Role Separation for the administrator in Saskatchewan. Create an OU named Saskatchewan. Place all Saskatchewan users and computers into the Saskatchewan OU. Delegate the appropriate level of privilege to the junior administrator in Saskatchewan.

# Chapter 7: Lesson Review Answers

## Lesson 1

1. **Correct Answer: A**

   A. **Correct:** If a license server's discovery scope is set to *Domain*, only computers within the local domain will be able to request CALs from that server.

B. **Incorrect:** If a license server's discovery scope is set to *Forest*, it is possible that clients from other domains in the forest will acquire licenses from it even if there is a server closer to them—for example, when their local server runs out of CALs.

C. **Incorrect:** A license server located in the root domain with a scope set to *Forest* will provide CALs to clients in the forest but will not do so in a way that meets with the location requirements of the scenario.

D. **Incorrect:** A license server located in the root domain with a scope set to *Domain* will provide CALs to clients in the root domain only, not in the specific branch office locations mentioned in the question.

2. **Correct Answer: C**

A. **Incorrect:** It is not necessary to set the forest functional level to Windows Server 2008 prior to deploying a Terminal Services license server.

B. **Incorrect:** It is not necessary to set the domain functional level to Windows Server 2008 to install licenses on a Terminal Services license server.

C. **Correct:** It is necessary to activate the TS license server prior to the installation of CALs.

D. **Incorrect:** It is not necessary to install IIS on a TS license server.

3. **Correct Answer: D**

A. **Incorrect:** Using WSRM policies will not enable adding capacity as needed.

B. **Incorrect:** Hyper-V would not work as a solution because there is an upper limit to processor capacity on the virtual host. This solution requires the ability to add processor capacity as required.

C. **Incorrect:** Although adding terminal servers would meet emerging capacity needs, it would not meet the requirement that clients do not need to be reconfigured.

D. **Correct:** Planning the deployment of a terminal server farm enables you to add and remove servers from the farm as necessary without altering client configuration.

4. **Correct Answer: C**

A. **Incorrect:** OneCare Live and other antivirus solutions can check for viruses and malware after a client connection has been made but cannot block unhealthy clients from connecting.

B. **Incorrect:** TS Session Broker is used to manage sessions that connect to terminal server farms—you cannot use it to ensure that connecting clients pass health checks.

C. **Correct:** A TS Gateway server can be used in conjunction with NAP to disallow computers that have not passed a health check to connect to the terminal server.

D. **Incorrect:** ISA Server 2006 cannot be used to block clients from connecting to a terminal server if they do not pass a health check. It is possible to use NAP in conjunction with ISA Server 2006 but not specifically to block access to Terminal Services clients.

# Lesson 2

1. **Correct Answers: A and D**

   A. **Correct:** You can use Group Policy software deployment in this situation to deploy applications to all clients on the network.

   B. **Incorrect:** System Center Essentials 2007 is limited to managing 500 clients.

   C. **Incorrect:** System Center Operations Manager 2007 is not an application deployment tool.

   D. **Correct:** You can use System Center Configuration Manager 2007 in this situation to deploy applications to all clients on the network.

   E. **Incorrect:** System Center Virtual Machine Manager 2007 is not an application deployment tool.

2. **Correct Answer: B**

   A. **Incorrect:** Group Policy Results works only with computers or users who have logged on and is not a suitable tool for simulating an application deployment strategy.

   B. **Correct:** Group Policy Modeling enables you to simulate an application deployment strategy when using Group Policy software deployment.

   C. **Incorrect:** You cannot use Active Directory Computers and Users to simulate Group Policy software deployment.

   D. **Incorrect:** You cannot use Active Directory Sites and Services to simulate a Group Policy software deployment.

3. **Correct Answer: D**

   A. **Incorrect:** An application can be configured to be uninstalled when it falls out of the scope of management whether it is published or assigned.

   B. **Incorrect:** The language options will not remove an application if the user account is moved to another OU.

   C. **Incorrect:** The Install This Application At Logon option will not remove an application if the user account is moved to another OU.

   D. **Correct:** Plan to use the Uninstall The Application When It Falls Out Of The Scope Of Management option when an application needs to be removed because a user or computer account is moved from the location in Active Directory that prompted the initial application deployment.

4. **Correct Answer: A**

   A. **Correct:** The SCCM 2007 software metering functionality enables you to determine the frequency with which applications installed on a computer are actually used. You can determine whether the application is necessary by tracking usage patterns.

B. **Incorrect:** You cannot use WSUS 3.0 SP1 to perform software metering.

C. **Incorrect:** You cannot use Group Policy Management Console to perform software metering.

D. **Incorrect:** You cannot use Active Directory Users and Computers to perform software metering.

# Chapter 7: Case Scenario Answers

## Case Scenario: Planning a Terminal Services Strategy for Wingtip Toys

1. Deploy a Terminal Services license server centrally and use the *Forest* discovery scope.
2. Create a Terminal Services farm by using TS Session Broker.
3. To access RemoteApp applications through TS Web Access, you must upgrade Windows Vista clients to SP1 and Windows XP clients to SP3.

# Chapter 8: Lesson Review Answers

## Lesson 1

1. **Correct Answer: B**

   A. **Incorrect:** VSMT is a more appropriate tool to virtualize a small number of existing servers.

   B. **Correct:** You can use SCVMM 2007 to move virtualized servers between virtual hosts over a Fibre Channel SAN. Because you cannot use other types of tools to accomplish this type of migration, this scenario presents the most compelling case for the deployment of SCVMM 2007.

   C. **Incorrect:** You can use SCVMM 2007 to manage and monitor thousands of VMs. Although it is possible to manage 10 VMs using this product, the built-in Hyper-V tools are more than adequate to such a task. Because one answer in this set requires SCVMM 2007, this answer is not the most compelling.

   D. **Incorrect:** Automating server deployment is accomplished through Windows Deployment Services (WDS) rather than SCVMM.

2. **Correct Answer: A**

   A. **Correct:** It is possible to install the Hyper-V role only on an x64 version of Windows Server 2008. It is possible to install Hyper-V on a Server Core computer.

   B. **Incorrect:** It is possible to install the Hyper-V role only on an x64 version of Windows Server 2008.

C.  **Incorrect:** It is possible to install the Hyper-V role only on an x64 version of Windows Server 2008.

D.  **Incorrect:** It is possible to install the Hyper-V role only on an x64 version of Windows Server 2008.

3.  **Correct Answers: A and E**

A.  **Correct:** A single SCVMM 2007 deployment can be used to manage 8000 VMs and 400 VM hosts.

B.  **Incorrect:** A single SCVMM 2007 deployment can manage only 400 VM hosts.

C.  **Incorrect:** A single SCVMM 2007 deployment can manage only 400 VM hosts.

D.  **Incorrect:** A single SCVMM 2007 deployment can manage only 8000 VMs.

E.  **Correct:** A single SCVMM 2007 deployment can be used to manage 8000 VMs and 400 VM hosts.

4.  **Correct Answer: D**

A.  **Incorrect:** The SCVMM database needs to have good connectivity only to the SCVMM server. An SCVMM library server needs to have good connectivity to a virtual host for the rapid deployment of new VMs.

B.  **Incorrect:** The question mentions nothing about SCVMM self-service portals, and these are not required to ensure that rapid VM deployment can occur to branch office VM hosts.

C.  **Incorrect:** Only one SCVMM server needs to be deployed in an organization, and this server can be used to manage rapid deployments at a branch office location if a library server is there.

D.  **Correct:** You should deploy an SCVMM 2007 library server at a branch office location when you need to use SCVMM 2007 to rapidly deploy new VMs to a branch office virtual host.

5.  **Correct Answer: A**

A.  **Correct:** The SCVMM 2007 agent must be installed manually on VM hosts that are configured as standalone servers.

B.  **Incorrect:** VMM agents are installed on host computers and not on VMs.

C.  **Incorrect:** Active Directory Lightweight Directory Services does not need to be installed to allow SCVMM 2007 to manage standalone virtual hosts.

D.  **Incorrect:** It is not necessary to install extra instances of SCVMM 2007 because it is possible to manage standalone servers if the agent software is manually installed.

# Lesson 2

1. **Correct Answer: C**

   A. **Incorrect:** Although DNS round robin splits load on the basis of request, it is not fault tolerant and will still direct clients to a failed host until manually configured otherwise.

   B. **Incorrect:** Microsoft System Center Virtual Application Server is not a cluster-aware application.

   C. **Correct:** Microsoft recommends that you use Network Load Balancing as a high-availability solution for the Microsoft System Center Virtual Application Server component of an application virtualization solution.

   D. **Incorrect:** A terminal server farm does not function as a high-availability solution for the Microsoft System Center Virtual Application Server component of an application virtualization deployment.

2. **Correct Answer: B**

   A. **Incorrect:** The data store is a SQL Server database that holds configuration data.

   B. **Correct:** The SoftGrid sequencer is used to convert traditional applications so that they can be deployed through Microsoft System Center Virtual Application Server to SoftGrid clients.

   C. **Incorrect:** Neither the Terminal Services nor desktop client software is used to perform the SoftGrid sequencing process.

   D. **Incorrect:** Neither the Terminal Services nor desktop client software is used to perform the SoftGrid sequencing process.

3. **Correct Answers: A and D**

   A. **Correct:** This client software is required to ensure that SoftGrid applications can be run on the local computer.

   B. **Incorrect:** Hyper-V is not a component of a SoftGrid Application Virtualization Deployment.

   C. **Incorrect:** SCVMM is not a component of a SoftGrid Application Virtualization Deployment.

   D. **Correct:** A Microsoft System Center Virtual Application Server needs to be deployed at the local site to ensure that SoftGrid applications can be delivered to local clients.

   E. **Incorrect:** There is no need to deploy Microsoft SoftGrid Application Virtualization for Terminal Services at the branch office site because Terminal Services is not in use.

4. **Correct Answer: D**

   A. **Incorrect:** It is not necessary to deploy SoftGrid in this situation.

B.  **Incorrect:** Although in this situation you should plan to deploy SoftGrid, it is not necessary to use a terminal server.

C.  **Incorrect:** In this situation it is not necessary to deploy SoftGrid.

D.  **Correct:** Microsoft SoftGrid Application Virtualization for Terminal Services is necessary only when you need to virtualize applications on the terminal server before serving them to clients.

5.  **Correct Answer: C**

A.  **Incorrect:** You should use Microsoft Application Virtualization—TS RemoteApp will not resolve the problem of applications conflicting when installed on the same terminal server.

B.  **Incorrect:** You should use Microsoft Application Virtualization—a TS Gateway Server will not resolve the problem of applications conflicting when installed on the same terminal server.

C.  **Correct:** Microsoft Application Virtualization allows applications that would normally conflict—including different versions of the same application—to be deployed from the same terminal server.

D.  **Incorrect:** You should use Microsoft Application Virtualization—TS Web Access will not resolve the problem of applications conflicting when installed on the same terminal server.

# Chapter 8: Case Scenario Answers

## Case Scenario 1: Tailspin Toys Server Consolidation

1.  Install the 64-bit version of Windows Server 2008 Enterprise and deploy Hyper-V. Virtualize the server that hosts the domain controller, DNS, and DHCP services on one virtual server. Virtualize the server that hosts the SQL Server 2000 database and individually virtualize each of the servers hosting the business application. This would require one physical server. It would also be possible to upgrade the existing servers to Windows Server 2008 without requiring extra licenses because the Enterprise edition includes four licenses for virtualized instances of Windows Server 2008.

2.  Although it would be possible to virtualize each terminal server, this would not meet the goal of reducing the number of terminal servers (though it would meet the goal of minimizing the amount of server hardware). In this situation, you can reduce the amount of hardware and terminal servers by deploying Microsoft Application Virtualization, which allows applications to run in virtualized silos so that they do not conflict with each other. Rather than virtualizing the server, this solution virtualizes the applications.

# Chapter 9: Lesson Review Answers

## Lesson 1

1. **Correct Answer: C**

   A. **Incorrect:** EFS encrypts data by using a combination of symmetric and asymmetric methods. EFS requires the use of certificates.

   B. **Incorrect:** S/MIME uses certificates and public key cryptography to encrypt e-mail.

   C. **Correct:** IPsec can rely on a certificate infrastructure for authentication, but this is not a requirement. In Windows domains, IPsec usually relies on Kerberos instead.

   D. **Incorrect:** SSL requires the use of a server certificate.

## Lesson 2

1. **Correct Answers: A and C**

   A. **Correct:** By taking the root CA offline, you can minimize the risk that the entire PKI will be compromised.

   B. **Incorrect:** Leaving the root CA online leaves that CA open to being compromised. When the root CA is compromised, the entire PKI is compromised.

   C. **Correct:** In this case, the subordinate CA is an issuing CA. By deploying the CA as an enterprise CA, you can automate the distribution of certificates to domain members.

   D. **Incorrect:** Using a standalone CA does not minimize the administrative overhead of publishing certificates.

## Lesson 3

1. **Correct Answer: D**

   A. **Incorrect:** OCSP is a protocol that enables real-time certificate validity checking. It doesn't enable certificate enrollment.

   B. **Incorrect:** Autoenrollment is available as a certificate enrollment method only for enterprise CAs and only to members of the local Active Directory forest.

   C. **Incorrect:** SCEP is a protocol used to issue certificates to network devices, not to users.

   D. **Correct:** Web enrollment provides the most automated method to issue certificates to users who are not members of an Active Directory domain.

# Chapter 9: Case Scenario Answers

## Case Scenario: Planning a PKI

1. The PKI should include three CAs, including the root CA. You should have one policy CA for the partners and another policy CA for employees.
2. Employees should use autoenrollment. Partners should use Web enrollment.
3. OCSP.

# Chapter 10: Lesson Review Answers

## Lesson 1

1. **Correct Answer: B**
    A. **Incorrect:** If you configure the target priority as first among all targets, users in the other four sites will be directed to the New York target even if the local target is available.
    B. **Correct:** This option achieves the desired effect. By default, users will be directed to the target in their own site, but if the local target is unavailable, they will be directed to the New York site.
    C. **Incorrect:** You do not want to change the site link cost because this would unintentionally affect other features, such as AD DS replication.
    D. **Incorrect:** You do not want to change the site link cost because this would unintentionally affect other features, such as AD DS replication.

## Lesson 2

1. **Correct Answer: D**
    A. **Incorrect:** You cannot use AD RMS to protect data in a SQL Server database.
    B. **Incorrect:** You need a TPM 1.2 if you want the server to be able to restart without administrator assistance.
    C. **Incorrect:** You cannot use AD RMS to protect data in a SQL Server database.
    D. **Correct:** If your server includes a TPM 1.2 module, you can use BitLocker encryption to protect the data and prevent the disks from being read on another server. In addition, if you choose the TPM-only authentication mode, you can allow the server to restart without requiring an administrator to enter a PIN or provide a USB drive key.

## Lesson 3

1. **Correct Answer: B**
    A. **Incorrect:** Node majority is best used for an odd number of nodes.
    B. **Correct:** This is the quorum configuration used with an even number of nodes and a witness disk.
    C. **Incorrect:** This is the best quorum configuration to use when you have an even number of nodes and no witness disk. (A file share replaces the witness disk.)
    D. **Incorrect:** This option is not recommended. It is used when any single node and its storage remains online. It does not use a witness disk.

# Chapter 10: Case Scenario Answers

## Case Scenario: Designing Solutions for Sharing, Security, and Availability

1. WSS
2. DFS and a domain-based namespace. To avoid inter-site queries, you should deploy a namespace server at all four sites.
3. AD RMS
4. Failover clustering

# Chapter 11: Lesson Review Answers

## Lesson 1

1. **Correct Answer: A**
    A. **Correct:** You can use SCE 2007 to deploy updates to third-party products, and you can roll back the deployment of these updates if necessary.
    B. **Incorrect:** Both WSUS 3.0 SP1 and SCE 2007 can be used to roll back software updates for Microsoft products.
    C. **Incorrect:** Both WSUS 3.0 SP1 and SCE 2007 can be used to deploy service packs for Windows Vista and Windows Server 2008.
    D. **Incorrect:** Both WSUS 3.0 and SCE 2007 enable the targeted deployment of updates by using computer groups.

2. **Correct Answer: C**
    A. **Incorrect:** Because each college's IT department needs the ability to approve updates, you should not configure downstream servers as replicas.

  **B.**  **Incorrect:** Replica servers do not enable local administrators to approve updates.

  **C.**  **Correct:** Configuring one upstream server to retrieve updates from the Internet and five downstream autonomous servers—one for each college—meets the question's objectives of minimizing bandwidth use and enabling each college's IT department to approve or reject updates.

  **D.**  **Incorrect:** Although five autonomous servers would enable college IT departments to approve updates, it would not minimize the amount of traffic between the university and Microsoft Update.

3.  **Correct Answers: A and C**

  **A.**  **Correct:** You need to create computer groups on the WSUS server and then assign clients to these computer groups, using GPOs applied to departmental OUs.

  **B.**  **Incorrect:** You need to assign the GPOs to OUs rather than to the domain.

  **C.**  **Correct:** You need to create computer groups on the WSUS server and then assign clients to these computer groups, using GPOs applied to departmental OUs.

  **D.**  **Incorrect:** You do not need to create a security group, but you must create a WSUS computer group.

  **E.**  **Incorrect:** You do not need to create a security group, but you must create a WSUS computer group.

4.  **Correct Answer: C**

  **A.**  **Incorrect:** Although it might be possible with a significant amount of effort, creating a scheduled task is not the best way to deploy updates by using WSUS. You should create an Automatic Approval rule that uses the PatchTest WSUS computer group as a target.

  **B.**  **Incorrect:** An Automatic Approval rule that deploys updates to the All Computers group will deploy updates to all computers, not to the PatchTest WSUS group as specified in the question text.

  **C.**  **Correct:** Automatic Approval rules use WSUS computer groups as targets for update deployment.

  **D.**  **Incorrect:** Automatic Approval rules do not use security groups as targets for update deployment.

5.  **Correct Answer: B**

  **A.**  **Incorrect:** You cannot use WSUS 3.0 SP1 to deploy updates for third-party applications.

  **B.**  **Correct:** You can use SCCM 2007 to deploy updates for third-party applications, and a single SCCM 2007 server can service more than 5,000 computers running Windows Vista and 200 computers running Windows Server 2008 if the other SCCM 2007 server fails.

C. **Incorrect:** An SCE 2007 server is limited to providing updates to 500 clients and 30 servers. In the event that one SCE 2007 server fails, it will not be able to provide coverage to all the hosts at the university.

D. **Incorrect:** Five SCE 2007 servers will not provide adequate coverage for the university environment. At most, five SCE 2007 servers can cover 2,500 computers running Windows Vista and 150 computers running Windows Server 2008.

# Lesson 2

1. **Correct Answer: D**

   A. **Incorrect:** You cannot use SCE 2007 SP1 to manage more than 500 client computers or 30 server computers.

   B. **Incorrect:** You cannot use WSUS 3.0 SP1 to generate compliance reports, although it can generate simple patch deployment reports.

   C. **Incorrect:** You can deploy only one SCE 2007 SP1 instance in a domain.

   D. **Correct:** You can use only SCCM 2007 SP1 in a single domain environment to provide update and configuration compliance reporting when there are more than 500 client computers or 30 servers.

2. **Correct Answer: C**

   A. **Incorrect:** You use the Security Configuration and Analysis tool to apply template files rather than XML-formatted, role-based security policies.

   B. **Incorrect:** You cannot use the Microsoft Baseline Security Analyzer tool to apply security policies.

   C. **Correct:** You can use the *scwcmd* command-line tool to apply an XML-formatted, role-based security policy remotely.

   D. **Incorrect:** You cannot use Windows Server Update Services 3.0 SP1 to apply role-based security policies.

3. **Correct Answer: A**

   A. **Correct:** Security settings applied through Group Policy objects override security settings applied using the *scwcmd* command-line tool, the Security Configuration Wizard, and the Security Configuration and Analysis tool.

   B. **Incorrect:** Security settings applied through the *scwcmd* command-line tool can be overridden by security settings applied through GPOs.

   C. **Incorrect:** Security settings applied through the Security Configuration and Analysis tool can be overridden by security settings applied through GPOs.

   D. **Incorrect:** Security settings applied through the Security Configuration Wizard tool can be overridden by security settings applied through GPOs.

4.  **Correct Answer: C**

    A.  **Incorrect:** Update Status Summary will provide information about the number of computers the update did not install on but will not provide detailed information about specific computers.

    B.  **Incorrect:** Computer Status Summary will provide summary information about computers and updates but will not provide detailed information about specific computers.

    C.  **Correct:** The Update Detailed Status report provides a per-update report with a list of computers and their update status. Navigating to the page that holds information about the problematic update will enable you to locate the necessary computers quickly.

    D.  **Incorrect:** A Computer Detailed Status report will give you one-computer-per-page information about the status of particular updates. Although it would be possible to check every page of such a report to determine which computers did not have the update, this requires significantly more effort than having a single page that lists each computer's status for a particular update.

# Chapter 11: Case Scenario Answers

## Case Scenario 1: Deploying WSUS 3.0 SP1 at Fabrikam, Inc.

1.  Add the CIO's account to the WSUS Reporters local group. This will enable the CIO to run reports without being assigned unnecessary administrative privileges.

2.  Configure the downstream WSUS servers at the Fabrikam satellite offices as WSUS replicas. This way, the downstream servers will inherit the update approvals and the computer group configuration at the head office WSUS server automatically.

3.  Instruct the CIO to generate an Update Detailed Status report. This will enable her to bring up an update report page that will list the specific computers on which the update failed to install.

## Case Scenario 2: Security Policies at Coho Vineyard and Coho Winery

1.  Create a role-based security policy for each proce-ssor architecture.

2.  You can use the Security Configuration Wizard or the *scwcmd* command-line utility to create role-based security policies for the intranet servers.

3.  Create a script that uses *scwcmd* and your administrative credentials in the *cohowinery .internal* forest to check the configuration of the intranet servers and to output the report in HTML format. Run the script as a scheduled task on your management server in the *cohovineyard.internal* forest.

# Glossary

**The .NET framework**  A software component that is included in Windows operating systems. It provides precoded solutions to common program requirements, and controls the execution of programs written for the framework. Most new applications created for the Windows platforms use the .NET framework.

**ACID properties**  A set of properties that guarantee that single logical operations (in particular database transactions) are processed reliably. Atomicity guarantees that either all of the tasks of a transaction are performed or none of them is. Consistency requires that the data is in a legal state when the transaction begins and when it ends. Isolation guarantees that the application makes operations in a transaction appear isolated from all other operations. Durability guarantees that after the user has been notified of success, the transaction will persist, and not be undone.

**Access control**  A combination of share and NTFS permissions and user rights that should ensure that users can access the resources they require but prevent inappropriate access to resources that users are not entitled to access.

**Access control entry (ACE)**  An assignment of permissions to a security principal.

**Access control list (ACL)**  A list of ACEs. ACLs are sometimes known as permission sets.

**Address space**  The total number of addresses (theoretically) available with an Internet protocol.

**Anycast address**  An IPv6 address that can identify a number of hosts. Packets addressed to an anycast address are delivered to the closest interface (in terms of routing distance) that is identified by the address.

**Application accessibility**  Refers to the features that permit a wide range of users to run an application. Direct accessibilty requires that an application be designed so that the greatest number of people possible can use it without needing special adaptive software or hardware. Further accessibility is provided by interfaces specifically designed to improve accessibility for (for example) physically impaired users or users with sight or hearing impairment.

**Application availability**  The readiness of an application (and the service it runs under) to handle customer requests and to return timely and accurate responses.

**Application resilience**  Ensures that if an installed application is corrupted or if its executable file is deleted, the application automatically reinstalls. It also ensures that applications are kept up to date and new updates, service packs, and application revisions install as required.

**ASP.NET**  A Microsoft Web application framework that programmers use to build dynamic Web sites, Web applications, and extensible markup language (XML) Web services.

**Authoritative restore**  A technique by which objects deleted from Active Directory can be recovered.

**Autoenrollment**  A process by which a digital certificate is automatically assigned without administrator or user intervention.

**Autonomous mode**  A downstream WSUS server administration mode that uses different approvals to the upstream server.

**Bare metal restore**  When a restore is performed without loading an operating system.

**Boot partition**  The boot partition hosts the operating system files. The easiest way to remember this when considering the system partition is that the labels are counterintuitive.

**BootP-enabled**  A BootP-enabled router or layer-3 switch can pass DHCP or DHCPv6 traffic to remote subnets so that a DHCP server can allocate addresses from different scopes to different subnets.

**Collector computer**  A computer that is sent Event Log data or a computer that polls a set of computers for Event Log data. The Event Log data of multiple computers can be viewed on a collector computer.

**Component object model (COM)**  A Microsoft platform for component-based software engineering (CBSE). COM is used to enable dynamic object creation and interprocess communication in any programming language that supports the technology.

**CA**  Certificate Authority. A special server that issues digital certificates to users, computers, and services.

**CRL**  Certificate Revocation List. A list of certificate serial numbers for certificates that are no longer considered valid by the issuing authority.

**DFS namespace**  A hierarchy of DFS folders.

**DFS replication (DFSR)**  Fast, efficient multi-master replication that ensures that data within a DFS namespace is consistent and up to date. In Windows Server 2008, DFSR also replicates Active Directory information.

**DHCP**  Dynamic Host Configuration Protocol. This protocol is used to provide IPv4 and IPv6 addressing information dynamically to clients on the network.

**DFS root**  In standalone DFS, the root is the namespace server. In domain-based DNS, the root is the domain.

**DNS round robin**  This technique, not limited to Windows Server 2008, creates multiple answers for an individual host in the DNS to create a primitive form of load balancing.

**Data collector set**  Can include performance monitor data, event trace data, and computer configuration information.

**Delegation**  The assigning of administrative privileges to nonadministrative users.

**Directory services restore mode**  A special operating mode of a Windows Server 2008 domain controller that allows for the restoration of Active Directory objects.

**Distributed file system (DFS)**  An arrangement in which resources can be distributed in folder targets on one or more servers and users can access resources via virtual DFS folders without needing to know where they are stored physically.

**Domain isolation policy**  A policy that restricts computers to only accepting incoming communication from other computers that are members of the same domain.

**Downstream server**  A server that receives approvals and/or updates from another WSUS server in the organization.

**EFS**  Encrypting File System. A technology that allows individual files and folders to be encrypted.

**EAP-TLS**  Extensible Authentication Protocol-Transport Layer Security is an authentication protocol that supports advanced authentication mechanisms such as digital certificates and smart cards.

**Failover clustering**  Formerly known as server clustering, Failover Clustering creates a logical grouping of servers, also known as nodes, that can service requests for applications with shared data stores.

**Forward lookup zone**  A DNS zone that enables a host name to be resolved to an IP address.

**Functional levels**  The levels at which a domain and forest operate. Higher functional levels provide more functionality but support fewer operating system versions.

**Group policy object (GPO)**  An AD DS object that contains Group Policy settings. GPOs are typically linked to one or more OUs.

**Group policy setting**   A configurable setting that determines the security and resource access applied to a user or computer account that is held in an OU.

**Hyper-V**   The name of the Windows Server Virtualization feature.

**Indexing**   Creating an index of the most common file and non-file data types on a server. You can index on file content in addition to data type.

**L2TP/IPsec**   A VPN protocol that uses IPsec to encrypt data and verify its integrity.

**LUN**   Logical Unit Number. A LUN is a logical reference to a portion of a storage subsystem. A LUN can be a partition on a single disk, an entire disk, or even a group of disks.

**Line-of-business (LOB) application**   A custom application that addresses operational requirements for a specific organization (or group of organizations).

**Multicast**   A transmission type where multiple hosts are sent data from one host across the network, but the data is transmitted only once to the hosts in the multicast groups rather than being transmitted in full to each host individually.

**Multicast address**   An address (IPv4 or IPv6) that identifies several hosts. Packets addressed to a multicast address are delivered to all interfaces that are identified by the address.

**Network access protection (NAP)**   A management feature that determines whether a client computer joining a network meets predefined configuration conditions, such as whether security updates have been applied and the operating system is up to date. If the client is not compliant, network access is restricted until remediation takes place.

**Network load balancing**   A high-availability feature of Windows Server 2008 that creates a virtual network adapter between two or more servers and sends requests to the servers based on administrator-defined criteria.

**Offline file**   A file that is automatically downloaded from a server so that a user can work on it offline and automatically uploaded to the server when the user's client computer is again online. The process of uploading and downloading offline files is known as synchronization.

**Organizational unit (OU)**   An AD DS container that can hold user accounts, computer accounts, or both.

**PPP**   Point-to-Point Protocol is a data-link protocol that is used for transmitting data.

**PPTP**   Point-to-Point Tunneling Protocol is a VPN protocol based on PPP.

**PXE**   Preboot Execution Environment. Allows compatible network clients to start an operating system from a network source rather than from local media such as a hard disk or CD-ROM.

**Password settings container (PSC)**   An object class in AD DS that contains PSOs.

**Password settings object (PSO)**   An AD DS object that contains security settings that can be different from the security settings for the domain.

**Privilege**   The ability to perform an administrative action, such as change a user password or create an Active Directory object.

**Quorum model**   The technique by which a Windows Server 2008 Failover Cluster determines the minimum number of cluster members to continue operating. Windows Server 2008 has four such models.

**Quota**   A setting that determines the amount of storage space in a shared folder or volume that an individual user is entitled to use. Soft quotas can be exceeded. Hard quotas cannot.

**RADIUS**   An authenticating, authorizing, and accounting protocol used with remote access traffic.

**Read-only domain controllers (RODC)**   A domain controller that holds AD DS information and can authenticate users and resolve DNS inquiries, but which does not permit connected user to make any changes to AD DS structure. RODCs contain only a small subset of the domain's user name and password information (if any).

**Reliability**     A measurement of how stable a computer's operating system, applications, services, and hardware are.

**Remediation**     The process of updating a client computer so that it becomes compliant and can be granted full network access. Automatic remediation through System Center Configuration Manager 2007 requires that the tool's software updates feature is installed and enabled.

**Replica mode**     A downstream WSUS server administration mode where all configuration information is inherited from the upstream server.

**Reverse lookup zone**     A DNS zone that enables an IP address to be resolved to a host name.

**Route aggregation**     A property of Internet protocol addresses that permits a number of contiguous address blocks to be combined and summarized as a larger address block.

**SSTP**     A VPN protocol that uses SSL to encrypt PPP traffic.

**Scope**     A range of contiguous addresses that can be allocated by a stateful address allocation protocol such as DHCP or DHCPv6.

**Shadow group**     A security group that contains all the user accounts in an associated OU. You cannot apply a PSO to an OU, so you apply it to the shadow group instead.

**Silo**     In Microsoft Application Virtualization, a silo is a virtualized partition in which an application executes.

**Softgrid**     Previous name of Microsoft Application Virtualization.

**System partition**     The system partition is the disk partition that the computer starts from. The easiest way to remember this when considering the boot partition is that the labels are counterintuitive.

**System state backup**     Backs up all Windows Server 2008 configuration data, such as the registry, Active Directory, and server role data.

**Two-stage installation**     A procedure where an administrator creates a computer account and a nonadministrative user installs the operating system on the computer. Two-stage installation is typically used to install RODCs.

**Unicast address**     An address (IPv4 or IPv6) that uniquely identifies a host on a network.

**VPN**     Virtual Private Network allows hosts to the Internet to use encrypted tunnels to communicate with each other in such a way that it appears that the hosts are all on the same local network.

**Virtualized**     A virtualized server or application runs in its own separate environment under the management of a host or parent computer.

**Volume shadow copy service (VSS)**     A set of application program interfaces (APIs) that enable the capture of shadow copies of disk volumes while applications on a system continue to write to the volumes.

**Wake on LAN**     A feature that wakes a client computer from sleep mode so that (for example) updates can be applied. The computer's network adapter needs to be capable of receiving and processing wake-up packages.

**Windows PE**     The Windows Preinstallation Environment is a stripped-down, bootable environment that allows maintenance tasks to occur. It is most often used in network installations where a computer does not have a PXE-compliant network adapter.

# Index

## Symbols
* (wildcard character), 438

## A
A (host) records
  DHCP support, 36
  DNS standard type, 10
  registering, 22
  split DNS, 24–25
AAAA (host) records, 10, 32
acceptance use policies, 309
access control lists (ACLs), 213, 272–273
Account Administrators, 184
Account Federation servers, 153
account lockout policies
  additional information, 217
  password policies and, 215, 322
ACLs (access control lists), 213, 272–273
Active Directory Certificate Services. See AD CS (Active
    Directory Certificate Services)
Active Directory data store, 205
Active Directory database, 459
Active Directory Domain Services. See AD DS (Active
    Directory Domain Services)
Active Directory Domain Services Installation Wizard,
    315
Active Directory Federation Services. See AD FS (Active
    Directory Federation Services)
Active Directory Lightweight Directory Service. See AD LDS
    (Active Directory Lightweight Directory Service)
Active Directory Migration Tool (ADMT), 144
Active Directory Rights Management Service. See AD RMS
    (Active Directory Rights Management Service)
Active Directory schema, 204
Active Directory Sites and Services snap-in, 435
Active Directory Users and Computers, 323
Active Directory–integrated DNS
  dynamic updates, 27
  name resolution, 23, 26
  planning DNS infrastructure, 28
  planning GlobalNames zone, 29
  read-only, 299
AD CS (Active Directory Certificate Services)
  assessing CA requirements, 400–401

certificate request processing, 414
ILM support, 155
AD DS (Active Directory Domain Services)
  AD FS support, 153
  additional information, 82
  audit planning, 191–193
  branch office considerations, 301
  conditional forwarding, 8
  container configuration, 182
  dcpromo binaries, 298
  delegating administration, 172–178
  delegating management tasks, 178–191
  designing domain controller placement, 122–126,
    133–134
  designing domain structure, 90–97, 107–108
  designing forest structure, 81–90, 106–107
  designing functional levels, 97–101, 108–109
  designing physical topology, 112
  designing printer location policies, 127–129
  designing replication, 117–122, 132–133
  designing schema, 101–103
  designing site structure, 114–117, 131–132
  designing trusts, 103–105, 109
  DFS Namespaces, 433
  disaster recovery, 459
  DNS support, 4–5, 28
  functionality, 79
  GlobalNames DNS zones, 17
  identifying role, 82–83
  ILM support, 154–155
  integrating with DNS infrastructure, 28
  IPsec support, 264–265
  license servers, 340
  managing through delegation, 175–176
  migration paths, 143
  planning backups, 459–461
  planning recovery, 461–462
  planning structure, 193–194, 203–204
  preparing, 145–146
  real world example, 80, 84–85, 113, 172
  recovery passwords, 324
  SCE support, 485
  schemas, 401
  Server Core support, 296
  Server for NIS, 159

stopping, 462–463
virtualization support, 381
VPN authentication, 270
WSUS support, 479
AD FS (Active Directory Federation Services)
additional information, 154
cross-forest authentication, 146
planning, 152–154
Web servers, 153
AD FS Web Agent, 153
AD LDS (Active Directory Lightweight Directory Service)
AD FS support, 153
additional information, 193
forest structure, 82
publishing certificates, 422–423
Server Core support, 296
AD RMS (Active Directory Rights Management Service)
AD FS support, 153
additional information, 217, 453
applications supported, 456
overview, 448, 453
persistent protection, 456
rights-protected information, 454–456
smart card authentication, 217–218
usage policies, 454
WSS support, 441
Add Features Wizard, 158
Address Resolution Protocol (ARP), 47
administration models
audit planning, 191–193
branch offices, 290–292
centralized, 176–177
classifying organizations, 174
delegation, 172–173, 177–191
delegation benefits/principles, 174–175
distributed, 176–177
domain structures, 90
managing Active Directory, 175–176
mixed, 176–177
planning structure, 193–194
types supported, 176–177
WSUS support, 479–481
Administrative Templates settings, 189
Administrator Role Separation, 292, 299, 312
ADMT (Active Directory Migration Tool), 144
adprep /domainprep /gpprep command, 103, 145
adprep /forestprep command, 103, 145–146, 392
adprep /rodcprep command, 103, 145, 314
ADSI Edit tool, 322
AES (Advanced Encryption Services), 99, 305

AFSDB (Andrew File System Database) records, 10
aggregatable addresses, 47
AIA (Authority Information Access), 421
All Computers group, 481
Allowed RODC Password Replication Group, 181
Andrew File System Database (AFSDB) records, 10
anycast addresses, 39, 45
API (application programming interface), 255
APIPA (automatic IP addressing), 36, 46
application programming interface (API), 255
applications
analyzing network requirements, 63–65
Application-Specific Administrators, 184
deploying on terminal servers, 335
deploying with Group Policy, 348–350
deploying with SCCM, 351–354
deploying with SCE, 350–351
deploying with TS RemoteApp, 341–342
deploying with TS Web Access, 340–341
PKI-enabled, 394–395
planning deployment, 354–355
site-aware, 117
Subsystem for UNIX-based Applications, 158–159
terminal servers, 335
virtualization support, 379–384
Application-Specific Administrators, 184
Apply Group Policy permission, 270
ARP (Address Resolution Protocol), 47
asterisk (*), 438
ATM (Asynchronous Transfer Mode) records, 10, 43
Audit Directory Service Access policy, 191
auditing considerations, 191–193, 310
Authenticated Users SID, 147
authentication. *See also* BitLocker
802.1x enforcement, 273–274
cross-forest, 146–147
gathering site requirements, 114
intra-forest, 103–105
L2TP support, 240
multifactor, 214
password, 214
PKI support, 238
PKI-enabled applications, 394–395
planning, 213–219
RADIUS support, 237, 248–250, 269
RODC process, 317–319
selective, 147–148
smart card, 217–219, 243
VPN support, 269–270
authoritative restores, 461–462

Authority Information Access (AIA), 421
authorization
    multifactor, 214
    planning, 213–219, 343–344
autodiscovery feature (WINS), 18
autoenrollment, certificates, 414–416
automatic IP addressing (APIPA), 36, 46
automatic site coverage, 116, 319–320
automatic tunneling, 52–53
automatic updates, 483–484
autonomy
    additional information, 86
    data, 85, 173
    defined, 85, 173
    forest design models, 86, 89–90
    gathering requirements, 85–86
    management stakeholders, 178
    service, 85, 173
availability. *See* service availability

**B**

background zone loading, 15–16
backing up
    AD DS planning, 459–461
    license servers, 339
    virtualization considerations, 363
Backup Operators, 184, 215
bandwidth
    cross-file RDC, 437
    deployment considerations, 349
    DFS Replication, 437
    gathering site requirements, 115
base CRLs, 419, 423
bastion hosts, 311–312
bcdedit.exe tool, 296
BIND (Berkeley Internet Daemon), 28, 214
BitLocker
    additional information, 449–450
    choosing authentication mode, 449–450
    data storage security, 324–325
    overview, 448
    performance issues, 449
    protecting volume data, 448–449
    real world example, 430
    security design considerations, 450
border networks, 231
boundary networks
    IPsec support, 264–266
    ISA Server, 266

branch offices
    Active Directory structure, 290–292
    adding domain controllers, 297–304
    additional information, 382
    Administrator role separation, 292
    communications considerations, 304–305
    components and services, 293–294
    designing RADIUS solution, 249
    host-based firewalls, 311
    IDS/IPS, 311
    infrastructure firewalls, 311
    PSOs in, 322–323
    real world example, 288–289
    RODC considerations, 313–322
    SCVMM support, 375
    security considerations, 308–312, 324–325
    server hardening, 311–312
    SoftGrid deployments, 382–383
    virtualization support, 303–304
    VPN server deployment, 244–245
    Windows Deployment Services, 294–297
Bridge All Site Links option, 121, 305
Business Unit Administrators, 184

**C**

CA hierarchies
    assessing Active Directory requirements, 400–401
    assessing business requirements, 399
    assessing external requirements, 400
    designing, 403–410
    legal requirements, 400
    security requirements, 397
caching
    credential, 299
    CRLs, 420
    negative, 12
    NLB support, 466
    proxy servers, 234
    universal group, 124–125
capacity planning, 372
CAs (certification authorities)
    assessing Active Directory requirements, 400–401
    assessing business requirements, 399
    assessing external requirements, 400
    certificate renewal, 418
    defined, 394
    defining types/roles, 405–408
    determining number required, 409–410
    EFS support, 451

enterprise, 405–406
intermediate, 407
internal vs. third-party, 404–405
issuing, 407
NAP support, 264, 267
offline, 408–409
PKI support, 267, 393
planning infrastructure, 403–412
policy, 407
root, 403, 407, 409
standalone, 405–406
VPN support, 240, 242
CDP (CRL Distribution Point), 421–423
central sites, 488
centralized administration model, 176–177
centralized management, 245
Cert Publishers group, 181
certificate policy statements, 394
certificate practice statements, 394
Certificate Renewal Wizard, 414, 417
certificate repositories, 394
Certificate Request Wizard, 414, 417
certificate revocation lists. *See* CRLs (certificate
    revocation lists)
certificate templates, 401
certificates. *See* digital certificates
Certificates snap-in (MMC), 243, 417
certification authorities. *See* CAs (certification
    authorities)
child sites, 488
CIDR (classless interdomain routing), 36, 38
Client Authentication OID, 395
Client Certificate Mapping Authentication role, 217
client-side targeting, 482
CNAME (canonical name) records
    DNS standard type, 10
    GlobalNames DNS zones, 17
    split DNS, 24–25
CNG (Cryptographic Next Generation), 392, 398, 401
collaborative projects. *See* WSS (Windows SharePoint
    Services)
colon-hexadecimal representation, 38
comments, adding to starter GPOs, 189
compatible IDs, 211–212
compliance
    auditing, 191–193
    defined, 496
    health policy, 259
    SCCM support, 500–501
    SCE support, 505–506

software update, 496–504
computer certificates, 240
conditional forwarders, 8, 25
cone NATs, 48, 50
configuration management, 500
configured tunneling transition, 52
Conflict and Deleted folder, 438
connectivity
    forest structures, 84
    troubleshooting, 58–59
    verifying, 54–58
Coordinated Universal Time (UTC), 437
corporate namespaces
    defined, 22
    name resolution, 23
    usage suggestions, 23
cost considerations
    delegating administration, 175
    domain structures, 95
    PKI-associated, 399
    site links, 120, 435
CPL file extension, 296
Create event, 192
credential caching, 299
CRL Distribution Point (CDP), 421–423
CRLs (certificate revocation lists)
    base, 419, 423
    creating, 419–420
    defined, 394
    delta, 419, 423
    PKI support, 268
    problems with, 420
    publishing certificates, 421–423
cross-file RDC, 437
CryptoAPI cache, 420
Cryptographic Next Generation (CNG), 392, 398, 401
CSP (cryptographic software provider), 398

**D**

DACL (discretionary access control list), 416
data autonomy
    defined, 173
    forest structures, 85–86, 89–90
data confidentiality, 305
data isolation
    defined, 173
    forest structures, 85–86, 89–90
data management
    additional information, 184
    defined, 175

delegating, 188
   planning, 187–188
   recommended roles, 184
   tasks included, 175–176
data recovery agent (DRA), 451–452
data security. *See* security
data sharing
   designing solutions, 445–446
   DFS design process, 438–439
   DFS Namespaces settings, 434–436
   DFS Replication settings, 436–438
   planning DFS deployment, 431–434
   shared folders, 187
   SharePoint infrastructure, 439–445
data storage
   backup considerations, 460–461
   branch office considerations, 324–325
data stores, 205, 381
DC Administrators, 184
DCOM (Distributed Component Object Model)
   certificate enrollment, 417
   global catalog servers, 124, 301
dcpromo command
   AD DS support, 298, 300, 463
   DNS support, 4
   RODC support, 315, 317, 321
DDNS servers, 177
Default Domain Controllers GPO, 179, 191
Default Domain Policy GPO, 179, 201
defragmentation, 462
delegation
   Active Directory administration, 172–178
   administration models, 177
   Administrator Role Separation, 292
   data management, 188
   defined, 172
   deploying applications, 351
   glue records, 7
   management tasks, 178–191
   managing Active Directory, 175–176
   real world example, 172
   RODC installation, 314–315
   SCVMM support, 372
Delegation of Control Wizard, 194, 290–291
delta CRLs, 419, 423
demilitarized zone (DMZ), 311
Device Installation Restriction policies, 207–209
DFS (distributed file system)
   additional information, 432, 434, 439
   component technologies, 433–434

data sharing, 431
design process overview, 438–439
folder targets, 432
folders, 432
namespace root, 432
namespace servers, 432
namespaces, 432–433
planning deployments, 431–434
DFS Namespaces
   AD DS support, 433
   advanced settings, 434–436
   failover and failback, 435
   namespace scalability mode, 436
   overview, 433
   redundant domain-based namespace servers, 436
   referral ordering, 435
   target priority, 435–436
DFS Replication
   additional information, 434
   advanced settings, 436–438
   bandwidth throttling, 437
   Conflict and Deleted folder, 438
   cross-file RDC, 437
   disabled memberships, 438
   overview, 433
   RDC protocol, 436–437
   replication filters, 438
   replication schedule, 437
   staging folder, 438
DFSR (distributed file system replication), 23, 302
DHCP (Dynamic Host Configuration Protocol)
   branch office considerations, 302
   distributed administration model, 177
   DNS support, 5, 22
   infrastructure models, 36
   integrating with NAP, 64–65
   IP addressing, 21, 36, 46
   IPsec support, 264
   planning NAP enforcement, 260, 275–276
   RRAS support, 302
   site-local addresses, 41
   software distribution methods, 268
DHCP Server role, 69–71, 296
DHCPv6 protocol
   configuring clients, 60–62
   dual-stack transition, 52
   integrating with NAP, 64–65
   setting up scope, 71–72
   site-local addresses, 41
   stateful configuration, 46

DHCPv6 Recursive Name Service option, 60
digital certificates
    creating renewal strategy, 418
    defined, 393
    defining revocation policy, 419–423
    determining lifetimes, 397
    EFS support, 451
    enrollment methods, 414–418
    identifying requirements, 395–398
    PKI support, 393
    selecting enrollment methods, 414–418
digital signatures, 394
Directory Services Restore Mode (DSRM), 462–463
Directory System Agent (DSA), 205
disaster recovery
    AD DS planning, 461–462
    domain controllers, 459
    license server activation, 338
    placement of operations masters, 125
discretionary access control list (DACL), 416
distributed administration model, 176–177
Distributed Component Object Model (DCOM)
    certificate enrollment, 417
    global catalog servers, 124, 301
distributed file system. *See* DFS (distributed file system)
distributed file system replication (DFSR), 23, 302
DMZ (demilitarized zone), 311
DNS (Domain Name System)
    administering, 10–15
    branch office considerations, 301–302
    configuring, 5–6, 30–34
    forwarders, 8
    IPsec support, 264
    name resolution, 4–10
    new features/enhancements, 15–22
    planning infrastructure, 22–30
    stub zones, 6–7
    zone replication, 9
DNS Administrators, 184
DNS forwarding
    integrating infrastructures, 28
    overview, 8
    planning, 25
DNS Manager snap-in (MMC), 10
DNS namespaces, 23, 97
DNS round robin, 341–342
DNS servers
    branch office considerations, 301–302
    conditional forwarders, 8
    delegation, 7

dynamic updates, 177
file-backed, 5
forwarders, 8
GlobalNames DNS zones, 17
glue records, 7
IP addressing, 36, 60
negative caching, 12
perimeter networks, 237
planning GlobalNames zone, 30
recursive queries, 25
root hints, 27–28
RPC support, 16
scavenging resource records, 27
Server Core support, 296
virtual, 61
zone replication, 9
DNS zones
    AD DS support, 28
    automatic site coverage, 319
    background loading, 15–16
    branch office considerations, 301
    DHCP support, 36
    dynamic updates, 27
    GlobalNames, 15
    planning zone types, 26–27
    root hints, 27
dnscmd command
    functionality, 11
    GlobalNames DNS zones, 17
    IPv4 addresses, 21
    IPv6 addresses, 21
    troubleshooting connectivity, 59
documentation, network requirements, 65–66
Domain Admins group
    applying PSOs, 215–216
    branch office considerations, 291
    installing RODCs, 314
    preparing environments, 145
    Security event log, 192
    suggested practices, 183
    user rights, 182
Domain Configuration Operators, 184
domain controllers. *See also* RODCs (read-only domain
        controllers)
    adding in branch offices, 297–304
    boundary networks, 265–266
    branch office considerations, 292
    delegating administration, 173
    designing placement, 122–126, 133–134
    determining operating system, 98

disaster recovery, 459, 462
DNS support, 4
domain functional level support, 98
FSMO considerations, 463
in-place upgrades, 146
logging on, 66
password synchronization, 157
planning AD DS backups, 459–460
preparing environment, 145–146
primary, 125, 301
real world example, 122
Server for NIS, 159–160
shadow copies, 15
domain functional levels
designing, 98–99
domain-wide features, 99
password considerations, 216
raising, 99
supported domain controllers, 98
domain isolation, 277–279
domain models
additional information, 93
global catalog server placement, 124
regional, 92, 95, 123
single, 91–92, 126
Domain Name System. *See* DNS (Domain Name System)
domain naming master, 125
domain trees, 97
domain upgrade migration path, 143
domains
AD DS structure, 203–204
assessing CA requirements, 400
deployment considerations, 94–95
designing models, 91–93
determining number required, 93–94
forest root, 95–97
forest trusts, 185
gathering design requirements, 90–91
gathering site requirements, 115
migration paths, 143–144
planning GlobalNames zone, 29–30
RADIUS authentication, 249–250
restructuring, 144, 291
role-based security policies, 503
SCE support, 487
trust types, 185–186
upgrade considerations, 94–95, 143
dotted decimal notation, 38
DRA (data recovery agent), 451–452
DSA (Directory System Agent), 205

DSMGMT.exe tool, 292
DSRM (Directory Services Restore Mode), 462–463
dual IP layer, 51–52
dual stack transition, 51–52
Dynamic Host Configuration Protocol. *See* DHCP (Dynamic Host Configuration Protocol)
dynamic updates
additional information, 6
DDNS servers, 177
DNS zones, 27
dynamicObject class, 100

**E**

EAP (Extensible Authentication Protocol), 241, 271
EAPHost NAP enforcement client, 271, 273
EAP-MD, 242
EAP-MSCHAPv2, 242
EAP-TLS (Extensible Authentication Protocol-Transport Layer Security)
PKI-enabled applications, 394
remote access support, 242
SSTP support, 241
EAP-TTLS, 394
EFS (Encrypting File System)
additional information, 451
certificate enrollment, 414
data security solutions, 451–452
data storage security, 324
identifying PKI requirements, 394, 396
overview, 448
802.1x standard
additional information, 272
PKI-enabled applications, 394
planning NAP enforcement, 261, 271–275
real world example, 274
software distribution methods, 268
EKU (Enhanced Key Usage), 395
e-mail
AD RMS support, 456
MBSA limitations, 496
monitoring, 310
PKI-enabled applications, 395
employee monitoring, 310
Encapsulating Security Protocol (ESP), 241
Encrypting File System. *See* EFS (Encrypting File System)
encryption
AD RMS. *See* AD RMS (Active Directory Rights Management Service)

BitLocker. *See* BitLocker
digital certificates, 396
EFS. *See* EFS (Encrypting File System)
PKI-enabled applications, 395
public key cryptography, 393
Enhanced Key Usage (EKU), 395
Enroll permission, 416
Enterprise Admins group
    adding domain controllers, 317
    applying PSOs, 215
    branch office considerations, 291
    preparing environments, 145
    Security event log, 192
enterprise CAs, 405–406, 451
ESE (Extensible Storage Engine), 205
ESP (Encapsulating Security Protocol), 241
EUI-64 (Extended Unique Identifier 64-bit), 40
Event Viewer, 192
Exchange Server
    AD RMS support, 456
    additional information, 145
    centralized administration model, 176
    forest trusts, 185
    global catalog servers, 124
    site structures, 117
explicit tunnels, 52
exporting starter GPOs, 190
Extended Unique Identifier 64-bit (EUI-64), 40
Extensible Authentication Protocol (EAP), 241
Extensible Markup Language (XML)
    role-based security policies, 502–503
    Server Core support, 296
    VSMT support, 371
Extensible Storage Engine (ESE), 205
external CAs, 404–405
external trusts, 185

**F**

failback, 435
failover, 435
failover clustering
    disaster recovery, 459
    high availability, 467–470
    NLB comparison, 468
    preparing hardware, 468–470
    quorum configurations, 470
FAT system, 460
fault tolerance, 267, 302
Federal Information Processing Standards (FIPS), 398

Federation Server Proxy role, 153
Federation Server role, 153
File Replication Service (FRS), 302, 437
File Transfer Protocol (FTP), 230, 237
filtering
    Administrative Templates settings, 189
    DFS Replication, 438
    GPOs (Group Policy Objects), 205
    IP filters, 245
    L2TP support, 241
    password policies and, 216
    PPTP support, 239–240
    RODC support, 299
    SID support, 147
FIPS (Federal Information Processing Standards), 398
FIPS 140-2 standard, 398
firewalls
    additional information, 234
    application-layer, 234
    branch office considerations, 311
    circuit-level, 234, 236
    internal networks, 231
    L2TP support, 241
    perimeter networks, 231–234, 311
    personal, 311
    PPTP filters, 239–240
    security considerations, 230
    stateful inspection, 234
    third-party products, 236
    types of services, 234
flexible single master operations (FSMO), 463
folder targets, 432
folders
    Conflict and Deleted folder, 438
    defined, 432
    disabled memberships, 438
    referral ordering, 435
    staging, 438
    target priority, 435
Forest Configuration Operators, 184
forest functional levels, 99–101
forest models
    additional information, 89
    mapping design requirements, 89–90
    organizational, 87
    resource, 88
    restricted access, 88
forest root domains
    deploying, 97
    designing, 95–97

designing controller placement, 123
selecting, 95
forest trusts
  creating, 186, 195–197
  planning, 185
forests
  AD DS structure, 203–204
  additional information, 86
  assessing CA requirements, 400
  branch office considerations, 301
  cross-forest authentication, 146–147
  designing models, 87–90
  determining number needed, 86
  gathering requirements, 83–86
  identifying AD DS role, 82–83
  intra-forest authentication, 103–105
  planning GlobalNames zone, 29
  RADIUS authentication, 249–250
  real world example, 84–85
  role-based security policies, 503
  SCE support, 487
  trust paths for authentication, 103–105
Format Prefix (FP), 39
forwarders. *See also* DNS forwarding
  branch office considerations, 302
  conditional, 8, 25
  defined, 8
FP (Format Prefix), 39
FQDNs (fully qualified domain names), 4, 23
FRS (File Replication Service), 302, 437
FSMO (flexible single master operations), 463
FTP (File Transfer Protocol), 230, 237
full mesh replication, 118
full server recovery, 461
fully qualified domain names (FQDNs), 4, 23
functional levels
  additional information, 97
  designing, 97–101, 108–109
  domain, 99
  forest, 99–101
  functionality, 97
  password considerations, 216

## G

GC (global catalog), 300–301
global catalog servers
  adding domain controllers, 300–301
  designing placement, 124
  infrastructure master role, 126

global groups
  allocating rights, 182
  applying PSOs, 216
  nesting, 181
  suggested practices, 183
global unicast addresses
  additional information, 40
  defined, 38
  Format Prefix, 39
  overview, 39–40
global unique identifiers (GUIDs), 206, 212
GlobalNames DNS zone
  functionality, 15
  legacy support, 17
  planning, 29–30
glue records, 7, 26
GPOs (Group Policy Objects)
  adding comments, 189
  filtering, 205
  migration tables, 191
  planning hierarchy, 201–205
  planning organizational structure, 194
  planning rules, 202–203
  recovery passwords, 324
  scwcmd tool, 503
  Security Configuration Wizard, 501
  security groups, 181
  starter, 188–190
grep command, 158
group ID, 44, 160
Group Policy
  auditing compliance, 191–193
  authentication protocols, 243
  certificate enrollment, 415–416
  controlling device installation, 206–213
  deploying applications, 348–350
  domain isolation, 277
  EFS support, 451
  IPsec support, 265
  planning authentication, 213–219
  planning authorization, 213–219
  planning hierarchy, 201–205
  planning organizational structure, 193–194
  real world example, 200–201
  VPN authentication, 269–270
  WSUS support, 482
Group Policy Management Console
  delegating management tasks, 179
  Group Policy Modeling node, 190, 349
  Group Policy Object node, 503

Group Policy Results node, 190
starter GPOs, 188
Group Policy Objects. *See* GPOs (Group Policy Objects)
GUIDs (global unique identifiers), 206, 212

## H

hardware considerations
analyzing network requirements, 62–63
controlling device installation, 206–213
failover clustering, 468–470
virtualization, 362, 368
hardware IDs, 210–211, 213
hardware security module (HSM), 268, 398
Help Desk Operators, 184
high availability. *See* service availability
HRA (Health Registration Authority)
fault tolerance, 267
IPsec support, 263–264, 266
NAP Health Policy Server role, 266
NAP support, 261
HSM (hardware security module), 268, 398
HTTP (Hypertext Transfer Protocol), 305, 421
HTTPS (Hypertext Transfer Protocol Secure), 466
hub and spoke replication, 117
hybrid replication, 119
Hypertext Transfer Protocol (HTTP), 305, 421
Hypertext Transfer Protocol Secure (HTTPS), 466
Hyper-V
branch office considerations, 302–304
creating virtual machines, 365–366
functionality, 365
limitations, 364
managing virtualized servers, 366–368
operating systems and, 361
SCVMM support, 372–373
UNIX support, 158

## I

IANA (Internet Assigned Numbers Authority), 39, 43
IAS (Internet Authentication Service), 246, 271
ICMP (Internet Control Message Protocol), 231
ICMPv4 Redirect messages, 47
ICMPv4 router discovery, 47
ICMPv6 (Internet Control Message Protocol for IPv6), 47
ID (interface identity), 40
Identity Lifecycle Manager (ILM), 154–155
Identity Management for UNIX role service, 156–158
IDS/IPS (Intrusion Detection System/Intrusion
Protection System), 310–311

IEEE (Institute of Electrical and Electronics Engineers), 40
IEEE 802 standard, 40
IETF (Internet Engineering Task Force), 156
IIS (Internet Information Services), 217–218, 237
IKE (Internet Key Exchange), 241
ILM (Identity Lifecycle Manager), 154–155
incremental zone transfer, 9
inetOrgPerson objects
domain functional levels, 99
forest functional levels, 100
password policies, 216
information services
audit policy, 310
branch office considerations, 293–294
infrastructure master role, 125–126
Institute of Electrical and Electronics Engineers (IEEE), 40
Integration Services, 368
interface ID
anycast addresses, 39
defined, 42, 54
link-local addresses, 42
multicast addresses, 39
ping command, 54, 57
privacy issues, 40
site-local addresses, 41, 45
unicast addresses, 38
Interface ID field, 41, 45
interface identity (ID), 40
intermediate CAs, 407
internal CAs, 404–405
internal networks, 231
Internet Assigned Numbers Authority (IANA), 39, 43
Internet Authentication Service (IAS), 246, 271
Internet Control Message Protocol (ICMP), 231
Internet Control Message Protocol for IPv6 (ICMPv6), 47
Internet Engineering Task Force (IETF), 156
Internet Explorer, 456
Internet Information Services (IIS), 217–218, 237
Internet Key Exchange (IKE), 241
Internet Protocol Security. *See* IPsec (Internet Protocol
Security)
Internet Security and Acceleration (ISA), 25
Internet service providers (ISPs), 311
Internetwork Packet Exchange addresses. *See* IPX
addresses
interoperability planning
ILM tool, 154–155
planning AD FS, 152–154
UNIX considerations, 155–161
Intersite Topology Generator (ISTG), 113

Inter-Site Transport contain, 120
intranets, 261
Intra-site Automatic Tunnel Addressing Protocol
    (ISATAP), 53
Intrusion Detection System/Intrusion Protection System
    (IDS/IPS), 310–311
intrusion prevention services, 236
IP addressing. *See also* IPv4 addresses; IPv6 addresses
    aggregatable addresses, 47
    APIPA support, 36, 46
    L2TP filters, 241
    name resolution, 4
    PPTP filters, 239–240
    real world example, 37
    scope, 39
    SSTP support, 249
IP filters, 245
IP Security Policies Management snap-in (MMC), 58–59
ipconfig command
    functionality, 12, 57
    IPv6 support, 54
    troubleshooting connectivity, 59
IPsec (Internet Protocol Security)
    data confidentiality, 305
    domain isolation, 278–279
    IP addressing, 46
    IP Security Policies Management MMC snap-in, 58–59
    NAT-T support, 233
    PKI support, 263, 267–268
    PKI-enabled applications, 395
    planning NAP enforcement, 261–268
    scaling NAP enforcement, 265–267
    security zones, 262–265
    server isolation, 277–279
    TS Gateway servers, 343
IPSec6 tool, 58
IPv4 addresses
    aggregatable addresses, 47
    analyzing structure, 37
    APIPA support, 36
    DHCP support, 275
    DNS support, 4
    dnscmd tool, 21
    dotted decimal notation, 38
    IPv4 headers, 47
    IPv4-compatible addresses, 48, 52
    IPv4-mapped addresses, 48
    IPv6 advantages, 45–48
    public unicast addresses, 38, 41
    slash notation, 38

ToS field, 46
IPv4-to-IPv6 transition
    6to4 tunneling, 53
    additional information, 51
    automatic tunneling, 52–53
    cone NATs, 48, 50
    configured tunneling transition, 52
    dual stack transition, 51–52
    IPv4-compatible addresses, 48, 52
    IPv4-mapped addresses, 48
    IPv6 tools, 54–62
    ISATAP addresses, 50–51
    ISATAP protocol, 53
    planning, 51–53
    Teredo addresses, 48–49
    Teredo protocol, 53
IPv6 addresses
    additional information, 21, 39
    advantages, 45–48
    aggregatable addresses, 47
    analyzing structure, 37
    anycast addresses, 39, 45
    autoconfiguration, 41
    DHCP limitations, 275
    displaying, 54–55
    DNS support, 4, 10, 15
    dnscmd tool, 21
    interface support, 39
    IPv6 headers, 46–47
    multicast addresses, 39, 43–45
    prefixes, 38
    syntax, 38
    types supported, 38–39
    unicast addresses, 38–43
IPv6 protocol
    analyzing hardware requirements, 62–63
    analyzing software/application requirements, 63–65
    configuring interfaces, 55–56, 66–68
    documenting requirements, 65–66
    planning networks, 62–66
    tools supported, 54–62
    troubleshooting connectivity, 58–59
    verifying configuration, 54–55
    verifying connectivity, 54–58
    verifying TCP connections, 59–60
    Web services, 238
IPX (Internetwork Packet Exchange) addresses, 39, 43
ISA (Internet Security and Acceleration), 25
ISA Server
    additional information, 236

boundary networks, 266
firewalls, 236
NLB support, 464
planning, 234–236
RADIUS support, 248–249
ISATAP (Intra-site Automatic Tunnel Addressing
Protocol), 53
ISATAP addresses, 50–51
ISO 10646, 22
ISO 27002, 399
ISO file extension, 366
isolation
additional information, 86
data, 85, 173
defined, 85, 173
domain, 277–279
forest design models, 86, 89–90
forest trusts, 185
gathering requirements, 85–86
management stakeholders, 178
server, 277–279
service, 85–86, 89–90, 173
ISPs (Internet service providers), 311
issuing CAs, 407
ISTG (Intersite Topology Generator), 113

**K**
KCC (Knowledge Consistency Checker), 100, 121
Kerberos authentication protocol
additional information, 213
data confidentiality, 305
domain functional levels, 99
functionality, 213
realm trusts, 186
RPC over IP replication, 120
keys
key pairs, 451
preshared, 240
private, 393, 397–398, 452
public, 393, 451
recovery, 324
symmetric, 451, 455
Knowledge Consistency Checker (KCC), 100, 121

**L**
L2TP (Layer 2 Tunneling Protocol)
data confidentiality, 305
NAT support, 233
UDP ports, 249

VPN support, 239–241
LAN (local area network), 245
latency, 420
LDAP (Lightweight Directory Access Protocol)
Active Directory data store, 205
forest functional levels, 100
publishing certificates, 422
RODC limitations, 299
UNIX environments, 156
LDF file extension, 322
LDIFDE tool, 322
least privilege, 174, 291
legal requirements
CA hierarchy design, 400
delegating, 173
employee monitoring, 310
forest structures, 84
licensing
activating servers, 337–338
AD RMS, 455
backing up/restoring servers, 339
defined, 334
deploying, 335, 339
high availability, 340
scope considerations, 335–336
TS CALs, 334–335, 338–339
virtual machines, 367–368, 370
Lightweight Directory Access Protocol. *See* LDAP
(Lightweight Directory Access Protocol)
link-local addresses
configuration example, 42
ND messages, 44
overview, 39, 41–42
load balancing. *See* NLB (Network Load Balancing)
local Administrators group, 401, 463
local area network (LAN), 245
Local Machine certificate store, 395–396
location considerations
designing printer location policies, 127–129
gathering site requirements, 114
license servers, 340
RADIUS solutions, 248
location schema, 127–129

**M**
MAC (Media Access Control) addresses, 40, 44
Mackin, JC, 392, 430
Manage Group Policy Links privilege, 291
management roles, 183–184

management stakeholders, 178–179
Mancuso, Paul, 228, 256, 274
MAPI interface, 205
MBSA (Microsoft Baseline Security Analyzer)
    additional information, 497
    functionality, 496–497
    WSUS reporting, 496–500
McDaniel, Drew, 434
McLean, Ian, 37, 172, 200
Media Access Control (MAC) addresses, 40, 44
memberships, 438
Message Queuing, 124
metaverse repository, 154
Microsoft Baseline Security Analyzer. *See* MBSA
    (Microsoft Baseline Security Analyzer)
Microsoft Challenge Handshake Authentication Protocol
    (MS-CHAP), 241–242
Microsoft Exchange Server. *See* Exchange Server
Microsoft Forefront Edge Security and Access product
    line, 234
Microsoft Identity Lifecycle Manager (ILM), 154–155
Microsoft Identity Management for UNIX console, 156
Microsoft Management Console. *See* MMC (Microsoft
    Management Console)
Microsoft Office, 456
Microsoft Office SharePoint Server. *See* MOSS (Microsoft
    Office SharePoint Server)
Microsoft Security Bulletin MS06-064, 48
Microsoft SoftGrid Application Virtualization
    additional information, 381, 383
    branch office considerations, 382–383
    components supported, 381–382
    functionality, 379–380
    terminal servers, 335
Microsoft software installation (MSI), 350
Microsoft SQL Server
    SCE requirements, 485
    SCVMM requirements, 372, 374
Microsoft System Center Configuration Manager, 268
Microsoft System Center Virtual Application Server, 379,
    381
Microsoft Update, 477–478
migration considerations
    cross-forest authentication, 146–147
    GPO migration tables, 191
    migration paths, 143–145
    NAP enforcement, 270
    Network Access Quarantine Control, 271
    preparing environment, 145–146
    real world example, 142

    SCVMM support, 371–372
    VSMT limitations, 371
Migration Table Editor tool, 191
Miller, David R., 288
mixed administration model, 176–177
MMC (Microsoft Management Console)
    Certificates snap-in, 243, 417
    DNS Manager snap-in, 10
    IP Security Policies Management snap-in, 58–59
    managing Server Core, 296
    Windows Firewall With Advanced Security snap-in,
       58–59, 245, 277
Modify event, 192–193
MOSS (Microsoft Office SharePoint Server)
    additional information, 443–445
    examples of solutions, 444–445
    overview, 442
    WSS comparison, 443
Move event, 192
MS-CHAP (Microsoft Challenge Handshake
    Authentication Protocol), 241–242
MSI (Microsoft software installation), 350
multicast addresses
    defined, 39
    flags field, 43
    group ID, 44
    scope field, 44
    solicited-node, 44–45
    structure, 43
    Transient (T) flag, 43
multifactor authentication, 214
multifactor authorization, 214
multinetting technique, 38
multiple domain model, 126
multiple sites model, 116–117
MX (Mail Exchanger) records, 10, 24

**N**
NAC (Network Access Control), 255
name resolution
    configuring DNS, 5–6, 30–34
    corporate namespaces, 23
    GlobalNames DNS zones, 17
    new DNS features, 15–22
    planning DNS, 4–15
    planning DNS infrastructure, 22–30
    real world example, 4
namespace root
    defined, 432

referral ordering, 435
target priority, 435–436
namespace scalability mode, 436
namespace servers
defined, 432
namespace scalability mode, 436
redundant domain-based, 436
namespaces. *See also* DFS Namespaces
delegated, 23
planning, 22–24, 97
NAP (Network Access Protection)
branch office security, 312, 325
connection authorization policies, 343
enforcement considerations, 262
functionality, 255–259
health policy compliance, 259
health state validation, 259
infrastructure overview, 259–261
integrating with DHCP, 64–65
limited access feature, 259
Network Access Quarantine Control, 235
planning 802.1x enforcement, 271–275
planning DHCP enforcement, 275–276
planning IPsec enforcement, 262–268
planning VPN enforcement, 269–271
RADIUS support, 246
real world example, 256–257
remote access strategy, 243
support services, 260–261
typical scenarios, 261
NAP Health Policy Server role, 266, 268, 276
NAT (Network Address Translation)
cone NATs, 48, 50
IP addressing, 36
L2TP constraints, 240
NLB support, 466
perimeter networks, 233
PPTP support, 233, 239
RRAS support, 302
NAT-T (NAT Traversal), 233, 240
ND (Neighbor Discovery), 41, 44, 47
NDES (Network Device Enrollment Service), 396, 415
negative caching, 12
Neighbor Discovery (ND), 41, 44, 47
nesting global groups, 181
net stop ntds command, 463
NetBIOS (Network Basic Input Output System), 18
NetBT (NetBIOS over TCP/IP), 17
Netdom.exe tool, 99
Netmask Ordering, 341

netsh interface ipv6 6to4 command, 50
netsh interface ipv6 add dnsserver command, 56, 59
netsh interface ipv6 add route command, 59
netsh interface ipv6 add v6v4 tunnel command, 50
netsh interface ipv6 delete destinationcache command, 57
netsh interface ipv6 delete neighbors command, 56
netsh interface ipv6 delete route command, 59
netsh interface ipv6 isatap command, 50
netsh interface ipv6 set address command, 50, 55
netsh interface ipv6 set interface command, 56
netsh interface ipv6 set route command, 59
netsh interface ipv6 show address command, 54–56
netsh interface ipv6 show destinationcache command, 57
netsh interface ipv6 show dnsservers command, 15, 59
netsh interface ipv6 show neighbors command, 54
netsh interface ipv6 show route command, 58–59
netstat command, 54, 59
Network Access Control (NAC), 255
Network Access Protection. *See* NAP (Network Access Protection)
Network Access Quarantine Control, 235, 259, 271
network access strategy. *See* remote access strategy
Network Address Translation. *See* NAT (Network Address Translation)
Network Device Enrollment Service (NDES), 396, 415
Network File System (NFS), 160–161
Network Information Services (NIS), 156, 159–160
network interface cards (NICs), 47
Network Load Balancing. *See* NLB (Network Load Balancing)
network operating system (NOS), 82
network planning
additional information, 66
analyzing hardware requirements, 62–63
analyzing software/application requirements, 63–65
documenting requirements, 65–66
gathering requirements, 83–84, 114–115
printer location policies, 127–129
Network Policy Server. *See* NPS (Network Policy Server)
Network Service Access Point addresses. *See* NSAP addresses
New Virtual Machine Wizard, 365
next-level aggregator (NLA), 40
NFS (Network File System), 160–161
NICs (network interface cards), 47
NIS (Network Information Services), 156, 159–160
NLA (next-level aggregator), 40
NLB (Network Load Balancing)
best practices, 466
disaster recovery, 459

failover cluster comparison, 468
high-usage servers, 464–466
limitations, 466
RADIUS support, 248–249
SSTP support, 249
TS Session Broker, 342
TS Web Access, 341
nodes, 39
nonauthoritative restores, 461
NOS (network operating system), 82
NPS (Network Policy Server)
    authentication protocols, 242
    bound networks, 266
    IP filters, 245
    NAP support, 261
    Network Access Quarantine Control, 235
    RADIUS support, 246, 248
    SCCM support, 352
NS (name server) records, 7, 10
NSAP (Network Service Access Point) addresses, 39, 43
nslookup command
    forest trusts, 186
    functionality, 12–14
    troubleshooting connectivity, 59
Ntds.dit database, 324, 459
ntdsutil utility
    MetadataCleanup command, 321, 463
    offline defragmentation, 462
    seizing FSMO roles, 463
NTFS (NT file system)
    backup considerations, 460
    EFS support, 324, 451

**O**

object identifier (OID), 395
OCI (Oracle Call Interface), 158
OCSP (Online Certificate Status Protocol)
    certificate revocation, 420–421
    perimeter networks, 237
Office System 2003, 456
offline CAs, 408–409
offline defragmentation, 462
OID (object identifier), 395
Online Certificate Status Protocol (OCSP)
    certificate revocation, 420–421
    perimeter networks, 237
Open Systems Interconnection (OSI), 43, 305
operating systems
    determining for domain controllers, 98

domain functional levels, 98–99
forest functional levels, 100–101
Hyper-V support, 361
password synchronization, 157
planning virtualization, 362–375
operational requirements, 83–84, 173
operations masters roles
    additional information, 463
    branch office considerations, 301
    designing placement, 125–126
    seizing, 463–464
Oracle Call Interface (OCI), 158
organizational forest model, 87
organizational units. *See* OUs (organizational units)
organizations
    classifying, 174
    planning structure, 193–194
OSI (Open Systems Interconnection), 43, 305
OUs (organizational units)
    applying Group Policy, 201
    DNS namespaces, 24
    EFS support, 452
    planning structure, 193–194
    shadow groups, 215

**P**

PAP (Password Authentication Protocol), 242
parent sites, 488
partitions
    BitLocker considerations, 324
    defined, 5
    DNS namespaces, 24
    domains, 204
password authentication, 214
Password Authentication Protocol (PAP), 242
password policies
    additional information, 174, 217
    administrative-level, 215
    branch office considerations, 322–323
    configuring, 215–217
    delegating management, 216
    domain functional levels, 99
    domain structures, 90
    forest structures, 84–85
    implementing, 219–222
    Password Replication Policy, 313, 315–319
    recovery keys, 324
    service account, 215
    user-level, 215

Password Settings Objects. *See* PSOs (Password Settings Objects)

password synchronization, 156–158

pathping command, 54, 57

PDCs (primary domain controllers), 125, 301, 436

PEAP (Protected Extensible Authentication Protocol), 394

PEAP-MSCHAPv2
    802.1x enforcement, 273
    remote access support, 242–243
    VPN authentication, 269

PEAP-TLS (Protected Extensible Authentication Protocol-Transport Layer Security)
    802.1x enforcement, 273
    remote access support, 242–243
    SSTP support, 241

perimeter networks. *See also* remote access strategy
    defined, 231
    deploying strategic services, 236–238
    designing, 231
    firewalls, 231–234, 311
    ISA Server, 234–236
    NAP architecture, 260
    security considerations, 230, 233–236
    types of architectures, 231–233

persistent protection, 456

personal firewalls, 311

personal identification number (PIN), 450

physical security, 309

physical topology
    additional information, 114
    automatic site coverage, 116
    designing domain controller placement, 122–126, 133–134
    designing printer location policies, 127–129
    designing replication, 117–122, 132–133
    designing site structure, 114–117, 131–132
    real world example, 113

PIN (personal identification number), 450

ping command, 12, 54, 57

ping6 command, 54

PKI (public key infrastructure)
    802.1x enforcement, 273
    additional information, 394
    assessing Active Directory requirements, 400–401
    assessing business requirements, 399
    assessing certificate template requirements, 401
    assessing external requirements, 400
    authentication support, 238
    best practices, 422
    components supported, 393–394

creating certificate management plans, 414–423
    defined, 393
    designing CA hierarchy, 403–410
    identifying certificate requirements, 395–398
    identifying enabled applications, 394–395
    IPsec support, 263, 267–268
    participant liability, 399
    planning deployment, 411–412
    planning management strategy, 423–424
    real world example, 392
    reviewing security policies, 398–399
    structure, 268
    VPN support, 238

Point-to-Point Protocol (PPP), 241

Point-to-Point Tunneling Protocol. *See* PPTP (Point-to-Point Tunneling Protocol)

Policelli, John, 4, 80, 84, 113, 122

policy CAs, 407

policy prototyping, 501

Portable Operating System Interface (POSIX), 158

POSIX (Portable Operating System Interface), 158

PPP (Point-to-Point Protocol), 241

PPTP (Point-to-Point Tunneling Protocol)
    data confidentiality, 305
    NAT support, 233, 239
    TCP ports, 249
    VPN support, 239–240

preboot execution environment (PXE), 294

preshared keys, 240

primary domain controllers (PDCs), 125, 301, 436

primary sites, 488

print services, 296, 302

printer location policies, 127–129

private keys
    EFS support, 452
    functionality, 393
    length restrictions, 397
    storage requirements, 398

privileges, 288, 315

Properties dialog box, 191

Protected Extensible Authentication Protocol (PEAP), 394

proxy servers, 234

PSOs (Password Settings Objects)
    branch office considerations, 312, 322–323
    configuring policies, 215–216
    creating, 222, 323

PTR (pointer) records, 10, 36

public key cryptography, 393, 451

public key infrastructure. *See* PKI (public key infrastructure)

publication points, 421–423
pull partners, 18
push partners, 18
PXE (preboot execution environment), 294

## Q

QoS (Quality of Service), 46
quorum configurations, 470

## R

RACs (rights account certificates), 217
RADIUS (Remote Authentication Dial-In User Service)
    authentication, 237, 249–250, 269
    design considerations, 245–246
    design mid-size enterprise solution, 250–252
    designing branch office access, 249
    designing main office solution, 246–249
    DHCP support, 276
    NAP support, 261
    restricted network attributes, 272
RAs (registration authorities), 393
RDC (Remote Desktop Client), 340, 436–437
RDP (Remote Desktop Protocol), 312–313
Read permission, 270, 416
Read Property permission, 216
read-only domain controllers. See RODCs (read-only
    domain controllers)
realm trusts, 186
Real-Time Transport Protocol (RTP), 381
recovery. See disaster recovery
recovery keys, 324
recursion, 25
referral ordering, 435
RegEdit.exe tool, 296
RegEdit32.exe tool, 296
regional domain model
    designing controller placement, 123
    forest root domain, 95
    overview, 92
registration authorities (RAs), 393
relative identifier (RID) master, 125, 301
remediation process
    IPsec support, 264
    remediation servers, 261, 266, 268
    SCCM support, 500
remote access strategy
    designing RADIUS solution, 245–250
    designing VPN protocol solution, 239–243
    designing VPN server deployment, 244–245

ISA Server, 234
    planning VPN connections, 238
    real world example, 228–229
    security considerations, 230
Remote Authentication Dial-In User Service. See RADIUS
    (Remote Authentication Dial-In User Service)
Remote Desktop Client. See RDC (Remote Desktop
    Client)
Remote Desktop Protocol (RDP), 342–343
Remote Installation Services (RIS), 294
remote procedure calls (RPCs), 16, 120, 125
replication. See also DFS Replication
    branch office considerations, 302, 305
    designing, 132–133
    designing domain structures, 91
    designing site link bridging, 121–122
    designing site link properties, 120–121
    designing site links, 119–120
    designing site models, 115–117
    designing topology, 117–119
    full mesh, 118
    gathering site requirements, 114
    hub and spoke, 117
    hybrid, 119
    RODC considerations, 319
Replication Management Administrators, 184
Replication Monitoring Operators, 184
reporting
    SCCM options, 500–501
    SCE options, 500
    WSUS options, 497–500
Resource Administrators, 184
resource forest model, 88
restoring
    license servers, 339
    virtualization considerations, 363
restricted access forest model, 88
restricted networks
    802.1x enforcement, 272
    IPsec support, 264
reverse lookup zones
    additional information, 21
    configuring, 32–34
    dnscmd support, 10
revocation policies, 419–423
RFCs (Request for Comments)
    RFC 1123, 22
    RFC 2044, 22
    RFC 2136, 5
    RFC 2181, 22

RFC 2196, 399
RFC 2307, 156
RFC 2373, 38–39, 44
RFC 2374, 40
RFC 2893, 52
RFC 3041, 40
RFC 3053, 52
RFC 4057, 66
RFC 4213, 51
RFC 4214, 53
RFC 4380, 53
RFC 4941, 40
RID (relative identifier) master, 125, 301
rights account certificates (RACs), 217
RIP (Routing Information Protocol), 303
RIS (Remote Installation Services), 294
RODCs (read-only domain controllers)
    additional information, 15
    authentication process, 317–319
    automatic site coverage, 319–320
    boundary networks, 265–266
    branch office considerations, 299–300, 313–322
    compromise considerations, 320–322
    delegated installation, 314–315
    designing placement, 124
    disadvantages, 313–314
    DNS support, 15, 23
    forest functional levels, 100
    installing, 103, 314
    installing from customized media, 317
    planning zone types, 26
    preparing environment, 145
    replication concerns, 319
    security considerations, 299, 312
role-based security policies, 245, 501–502, 504–505
roles
    certification authority, 405–408
    data management, 184
    defined, 183
    sandboxing, 363
    service management, 184
root CAs, 403, 407, 409
root hints, 27–28
root scalability mode, 436
route aggregation, 47
route command, 54
route print command, 57, 59
Routing and Remote Access Services (RRAS) role service
    branch office considerations, 302
    DHCP support, 60

NLB support, 466
Routing Information Protocol (RIP), 303
routing tables, 47
RPC over IP replication, 120
RPCs (remote procedure calls), 16, 120, 125
RRAS role service. *See* Routing and Remote Access
    Services (RRAS) role service
RSA CA, 400
RTP (Real-Time Transport Protocol), 381

**S**
SACL (system access control list), 191
SAM (Security Accounts Manager), 205, 213
SAN (Storage Area Network), 363, 469
sandboxing, 363
SAs (security associations), 278
SCCM (System Center Configuration Manager)
    additional information, 488
    compliance, 500–501
    deploying applications, 351–354
    functionality, 487
    reporting, 500–501
    server consolidation, 371
    site type properties, 487–488
    WakeOn LAN feature, 353–354
SCE (System Center Essentials)
    additional information, 486–487
    compliance, 505–506
    configuring, 486, 492–493
    deploying applications, 350–351
    functionality, 485–487
    software update reports, 500
Schema Admins group, 145, 184, 215
schema master, 125
schemas
    Active Directory, 204
    AD DS, 401
    additional information, 103
    deployment process, 102
    designing modification process, 101
    location, 127–129
    upgrading, 102–103
scope
    DHCPv6, 71–73
    IP addresses, 39
    license servers, 335–336
scope field, 44
screened subnet, 311
SCVMM (System Center Virtual Machine Manager)

additional information, 375
branch office considerations, 375
deployment components, 373–374
functionality, 363, 371–373
planning deployment, 375
SCVMM Administrator console, 374
SCVMM agent, 373–374
SCVMM database, 374
SCVMM library server, 374
SCVMM server, 373
scwcmd tool, 503–504
secondary sites, 488
secure dynamic updates, 6
secure networks, 264–265
Secure Socket Tunneling Protocol. *See* SSTP (Secure
    Socket Tunneling Protocol)
Secure Sockets Layer. *See* SSL (Secure Sockets Layer)
Secure/Multipurpose Internet Mail Extensions
    (S/MIME), 395, 414
security
    AD RMS. *See* AD RMS (Active Directory Rights
        Management Service)
    auditing events, 192
    BitLocker. *See* BitLocker
    branch office considerations, 308–312, 324–325
    certificate requirements, 396–398
    data confidentiality, 305
    delegating administration and, 173
    designing, 456–457
    designing RODC placement, 124
    domain structures, 90
    EFS. *See* EFS (Encrypting File System)
    facets to consider, 295
    firewalls. *See* firewalls
    forest structures, 83–84
    IPv6 addressing, 46
    namespace considerations, 22
    new features, 312
    perimeter networks, 230, 233–236
    persistent protection, 456
    physical, 309
    planning/deploying baselines, 501–504
    real world example, 430
    remote access strategy. *See* remote access strategy
    RODC support, 299
    TS Gateway servers, 343
    WINS considerations, 18
Security Accounts Manager (SAM), 205, 213
security associations (SAs), 278
Security Configuration and Analysis tool, 503

Security Configuration Wizard, 245, 501–502, 504
Security event log, 192
Security Group Administrators, 184
security groups, 179–183, 216
security identifier (SID), 99
security policies
    acceptance use policies, 309
    branch office considerations, 308–310, 324–325
    new features, 312
    reviewing, 398–399
    role-based, 245, 501–502, 504–505
    scwcmd tool, 503–504
    security awareness training, 309
    Security Configuration Wizard, 245, 501–502
Security Policy Administrators, 184
security templates, 502–504
security tokens, 153
security zones, 262–265
selective authentication, 147–148
Server Authentication OID, 395
Server Core, 295–296, 300, 312, 461
server farms
    defined, 334, 464
    NLB support, 464, 466
    planning deployment, 335, 342–343
    WSS support, 442
Server for NIS, 159–160
server hardening
    branch office considerations, 311–312
    defined, 501
    enforcing security baselines, 501–504
server isolation, 277–279
Server Manager role, 183, 217, 460
Server Operators, 184, 215
server-side targeting, 481
service accounts, 215
Service Administration Managers, 184
service autonomy
    defined, 173
    forest structures, 85–86, 89–90
service availability
    certificate issuance, 399
    failover clusters, 467–470
    license servers, 340
    NLB support, 464–466
    RADIUS support, 248–249
    virtualization, 362
service isolation
    defined, 173
    forest structures, 85–86, 89–90

Service Level Agreements (SLAs), 94
service location, 114. *See also* SRV records
service management
  additional information, 184
  defined, 175
  recommended roles, 184
  tasks included, 175
Services for NFS, 160–161
shadow copies, 15
shadow groups, 215
SharePoint. *See* WSS (Windows SharePoint Services)
SHAs (system health agents), 264, 270
Shiva Password Authentication Protocol (SPAP), 242
shortcut trusts
  defined, 185
  designing, 105, 109
SHVs (System Health Validators), 264, 268, 270
SID (security identifier), 99
SID filtering, 147
SIDHistory attribute, 147
Simple Mail Transfer Protocol (SMTP), 116, 120
single domain model, 91–92, 126
single site model, 115
site IDs, 55
site link bridges, 121–122
site links
  branch office considerations, 304–305
  designing, 119–120
  determining costs, 120, 435
  determining intervals, 121
  determining schedules, 121
site models
  automatic site coverage, 116, 319–320
  deploying applications with SCCM, 352
  designing, 115–117
  multiple sites, 116–117
  SCCM considerations, 487–488
  single site, 115
site structure. *See* physical topology
site-local addresses
  configuration example, 42
  Interface ID field, 41, 45
  overview, 39, 41–42
6to4 tunneling, 53
6to4cfg tool, 51
SLAs (Service Level Agreements), 94
slash notation, 38
smart cards
  authentication, 217–219, 243
  certificate enrollment, 414

  PKI-enabled applications, 395
  TPM support, 449
S/MIME (Secure/Multipurpose Internet Mail
    Extensions), 395, 414
SMTP (Simple Mail Transfer Protocol), 116, 120
snapshots, 367
SOA (Start of Authority) records, 10, 27
SoftGrid Client for Desktops, 381
SoftGrid data store, 381
SoftGrid Management console, 381
SoftGrid Sequencer, 381
software metering, 353
software requirements, 63–65, 350
software restriction policies, 502
software update points, 488
software updates
  managing compliance, 496–504
  MBSA support, 496–500
  Microsoft Update, 477–478
  planning security baselines, 501–504
  real world example, 476
  SCCM support, 487–488, 500–501
  SCE support, 485–487, 492–493
  WSUS support, 478–484, 489–491
SoH (Statement of Health), 264
SoHR (Statement of Health Response), 264
solicited-node multicast addresses, 44–45
SPAP (Shiva Password Authentication Protocol), 242
special addresses, 39, 43
split DNS, 24–25
  additional information, 25
SQL Server (Microsoft)
  SCE requirements, 485
  SCVMM requirements, 372, 374
SRV records
  automatic site coverage, 116, 319–320
  DNS standard type, 10
  GlobalNames DNS zones, 17
SSL (Secure Sockets Layer)
  certificate enrollment, 414
  data confidentiality, 305
  license servers, 337
  NLB support, 466
  perimeter networks, 237
  PKI-enabled applications, 395
  smart card authentication, 217
SSoH (System Statement of Health), 264
SSoHR (System Statement of Health Response), 264
SSTP (Secure Socket Tunneling Protocol)
  data confidentiality, 305

TCP ports, 249
VPN support, 239, 241–242
staging folders, 438
stakeholders delegating tasks, 178–179
standalone CAs, 405–406
starter GPOs, 188–190
stateful address configuration, 41, 46
stateful inspection firewalls, 234
stateless address configuration, 40–41, 46
Statement of Health (SoH), 264
Statement of Health Response (SoHR), 264
storage. *See* data storage
Storage Area Network (SAN), 363, 469
stub zones
    branch office considerations, 302
    creating, 7
    defined, 6
    DNS support, 6–7
    glue records, 26
SUA (Subsystem for UNIX-based Applications), 158–159
subnet ID, 38
subnet masks, 38
subnet-router anycast addresses, 45
subordinate CAs, 407–408
Subsystem for UNIX-based Applications (SUA), 158–159
symmetric keys, 451, 455
synchronization, password, 156–158
system access control list (SACL), 191
System Center Configuration Manager. *See* SCCM (System Center Configuration Manager)
System Center Essentials. *See* SCE (System Center Essentials)
System Center Virtual Machine Manager. *See* SCVMM (System Center Virtual Machine Manager)
system health agents (SHAs), 264, 270
System Health Validators (SHVs), 264, 268, 270
system recoverability. *See* disaster recovery
System Statement of Health (SSoH), 264
System Statement of Health Response (SSoHR), 264
Systeminfo command, 98
SYSVOL directory, 459–460


**T**

TCP (Transmission Control Protocol), 46
TCP/IP (Transmission Control Protocol/Internet Protocol), 294
TCP/IPv6 GUI, 50, 55, 59
telnet command, 59–60
Teredo addresses, 48–49

Teredo protocol, 53
terminal server farms, 334–335, 342–343
terminal servers, 334–335, 341
Terminal Services. *See* TS (Terminal Services)
third-party CAs, 404–405
Thomas, Orin, 142, 476
3DES encryption, 240, 305
Time-to-Live (TTL), 27
TLA (top-level aggregator), 39
TLS (Transport Layer Security), 305. *See also* EAP-TLS; PEAP-TLS
top-level aggregator (TLA), 39
ToS (Type of Service) field, 46
TPM (Trusted Platform Module)
    BitLocker support, 324, 430, 448–449
    defined, 449
tracert command, 54, 57
training, security awareness, 309
Transient (T), 43
Transmission Control Protocol (TCP), 46
Transmission Control Protocol/Internet Protocol (TCP/IP), 294
Transport Layer Security (TLS), 305. *See also* EAP-TLS; PEAP-TLS
troubleshooting
    IPv6 connectivity, 58–59
    URLs, 268
Trusted Platform Module (TPM)
    BitLocker support, 324, 430, 448
    defined, 449
Trusted Root Certification Authorities store, 269, 273
trusts
    AD FS support, 153
    designing, 109, 147
    external, 185
    forest, 185–186, 195–197
    intra-forest authentication, 103–105
    planning direction, 186
    realm, 186
    shortcut, 105, 109, 185
    types listed, 185–186
TS (Terminal Services)
    components supported, 334–335
    deploying applications, 340–342
    licensing, 334–340
    NLB support, 466
    planning deployment, 334–335, 344–345
    virtualization support, 379–382
TS CALs, 334–335, 338–339
TS CAPs, 343

TS Gateway servers
  gateways, 334
  perimeter networks, 237
  planning deployment, 334–335, 343–344
TS Per Device CAL, 338
TS Per User CAL, 338
TS RAPs, 343–344
TS RemoteApp, 341–342
TS Session Broker, 342–343, 466
TS Web Access, 340–341
TTL (Time-to-Live), 27
tunnel brokers, 52
Type of Service (ToS) field, 46

## U

UDDI Services, 441
UDP (User Datagram Protocol)
  IPv4 addressing, 46
  L2TP support, 249
  NAT support, 240
  Teredo prefix, 48
UFD (USB flash drive), 448, 450
Unassigned Computers group, 481
UNC (Universal Naming Convention), 431
Undelete event, 192
unicast addresses
  defined, 38
  global, 38–40
  IPX, 39
  link-local, 39, 41–42
  node support, 39
  NSAP, 39
  site-local, 39, 41–42
  special, 39, 43
  structure, 38
  types supported, 39
universal groups
  caching, 124–125
  global groups and, 181–182
  suggested practices, 183
Universal Naming Convention (UNC), 431
UNIX environments
  identity management, 156
  password synchronization, 156–158
  Server for NIS, 159–160
  Services for NFS, 160–161
  Subsystem for UNIX-based Applications, 158–159
URLs
  publishing certificates, 421–423
  troubleshooting, 268

USB flash drive (UFD), 448, 450
User Datagram Protocol. *See* UDP (User Datagram Protocol)
user ID, 160
user rights
  allocating, 179–181
  GPOs, 193, 277
  server isolation, 277
userPassword attribute, 99
UTC (Coordinated Universal Time), 437

## V

VeriSign CA, 400
virtual DNS servers, 61
virtual local area networks (VLANs)
  802.1x enforcement, 272
  ACLs vs., 272–273
  IPv6 addresses, 61
virtual machines. *See* VMs (virtual machines)
virtual private networks. *See* VPNs (virtual private networks)
Virtual Server 2005 R2
  additional information, 365
  downloading, 364
  functionality, 364
  limitations, 364–365
  SCVMM support, 373
Virtual Server Migration Toolkit (VSMT), 371
Virtualization Management console, 365, 367
virtualization technology. *See also* Hyper-V
  additional information, 381
  application considerations, 379–384
  benefits, 362–363
  branch office considerations, 302–304
  candidates for, 370
  designing deployment, 375–376
  Microsoft SoftGrid Application Virtualization, 335
  operating system considerations, 362–375
  virtual DNS servers, 61
  Virtual Server 2005 R2, 364–365
  Windows Server Virtualization, 302
VLANs (virtual local area networks)
  802.1x enforcement, 272
  ACLs vs., 272–273
  IPv6 addresses, 61
VMK (Volume Master Key), 449
VMMLibrary share, 374
VMs (virtual machines)
  creating, 365–366
  licensing, 367–368, 370

managing, 366–368, 371
memory considerations, 364
modifying hardware settings, 368
SCVMM support, 373–375
voicemail, monitoring, 310
Volume Master Key (VMK), 449
VPN servers, 244–245
VPNs (virtual private networks)
authentication support, 269–270
designing protocol solution, 239–243, 251–252
designing server deployment, 244–245
ISA Server, 234–235
L2TP support, 240–241
load balancing, 249
NLB support, 464
PKI-enabled applications, 395
planning connections, 238
planning NAP enforcement, 269–271
PPTP support, 239–240
RADIUS support, 230, 248–249
software distribution methods, 268
software update considerations, 478
SSTP support, 241–242
VSMT (Virtual Server Migration Toolkit), 371

## W

WakeOn LAN feature, 353–354
WAN (wide area network)
branch office considerations, 294
DFS Replication, 437
hub and spoke replication, 117
regional domain model, 92
SCE limitations, 487
SoftGrid limitations, 382
software update considerations, 478
wbadmin tool, 460–461
WDS (Windows Deployment Services)
branch office considerations, 294–297
creating virtual machines, 366, 370
Web Enrollment Support pages, 415, 417
Web farms
defined, 464
NLB support, 464, 466
WSS support, 442
Web servers
AD FS–enabled, 153
disaster recovery, 459
IPv6 access, 238
perimeter networks, 236–238

Web Server server role, 217, 296
wide area network. *See* WAN (wide area network)
wildcard character, 438
Windows Automated Installation Kit, 461
Windows Deployment Services. *See* WDS (Windows Deployment Services)
Windows Firewall With Advanced Security snap-in (MMC), 58–59, 245, 277
Windows Internal Database, 441
Windows Internet Name Service. *See* WINS (Windows Internet Name Service)
Windows PowerShell, 371
Windows RE, 461
Windows ReadyBoost feature, 207
Windows Security Health Validator SHV, 268
Windows Server 2008 Server, 294
Windows Server 2008 Server Core, 295–296, 300, 312
Windows Server Backup, 460–461
Windows Server Update Services. *See* WSUS (Windows Server Update Services)
Windows Server Virtualization, 302
Windows Services for UNIX, 145
Windows SharePoint Services. *See* WSS (Windows SharePoint Services)
Windows System Resources Manager, 441
WINS (Windows Internet Name Service)
autodiscovery feature, 18
centralized topology, 18
DNS support, 5
full mesh topology, 18
hub and spoke topology, 20–21
IP addressing, 36
NAP support, 260
NetBT support, 17
planning replication, 17–20
ring topology, 19
wireless access points, 248, 261
WLANs (wireless local area networks), 237
Workstation Administrators, 184
WPA Enterprise, 248
WSS (Windows SharePoint Services)
AD RMS support, 456
additional information, 441–442
assessing needs for MOSS, 442–445
collaboration sites, 440–441
communication sites, 440
deployment options, 441–442
document storage sites, 440
MOSS comparison, 443
overview, 431

WSUS (Windows Server Update Services)
  additional information, 480
  administration models, 479–481
  branch office considerations, 303
  computer groups, 481–482
  deployment hierarchies, 479–480
  functionality, 478–501
  installing, 482–483, 489–491
  IPsec support, 264
  managing, 479
  MBSA support, 496–500
  NAP support, 261
  planning automatic approvals, 483–484
  planning deployment, 484
  SCE support, 350, 486–487
  scheduling updates, 482–483
  WSS support, 441
WSUS Administrators group, 479, 481
WSUS Reporters group, 479

**X**
XML (Extensible Markup Language)
  role-based security policies, 502–503
  Server Core support, 296
  VSMT support, 371
XPS (XML Paper Specification), 456

**Z**
zone ID, 57
zone transfers
  branch office considerations, 301
  configuring, 9
  defined, 9
  DNS namespaces, 22
  incremental, 9
  planning DNS zones, 27

# Windows Server 2008 Resource Kit—
# Your Definitive Resource!

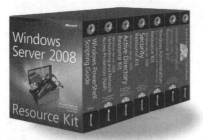

**Windows Server® 2008
Resource Kit**

Microsoft® MVPs with
Microsoft Windows Server Team

ISBN 9780735623613

Your definitive reference for deployment and operations—from the experts who
know the technology best. Get in-depth technical information on Active Directory®,
Windows PowerShell™ scripting, advanced administration, networking and network
access protection, security administration, IIS, and other critical topics—plus an
essential toolkit of resources on CD.

## *Also available as single volumes*

**Windows Server 2008
Security Resource Kit**

Jesper M. Johansson et al. with
Microsoft Security Team

ISBN 9780735625044

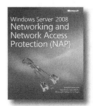

**Windows Server 2008
Networking and Network
Access Protection (NAP)**

Joseph Davies, Tony Northrup,
Microsoft Networking Team

ISBN 9780735624221

**Windows Server 2008
Active Directory Resource Kit**

Stan Reimer et al. with
Microsoft Active Directory Team

ISBN 9780735625150

**Windows® Administration
Resource Kit: Productivity
Solutions for IT Professionals**

Dan Holme

ISBN 9780735624313

**Windows Powershell
Scripting Guide**

Ed Wilson

ISBN 9780735622791

**Internet Information
Services (IIS) 7.0
Resource Kit**

Mike Volodarsky et al. with
Microsoft IIS Team

ISBN 9780735624412

*See our complete line of books at:* **microsoft.com/mspress**

# 2007 Microsoft® Office System Resources for Developers and Administrators

## Microsoft Office SharePoint® Server 2007 Administrator's Companion

Bill English with the Microsoft SharePoint Community Experts
ISBN 9780735622821

Get your mission-critical collaboration and information management systems up and running. This comprehensive, single-volume reference details features and capabilities of SharePoint Server 2007. It delivers easy-to-follow procedures, practical workarounds, and key troubleshooting tactics—for on-the-job results.

## Microsoft Windows SharePoint Services Version 3.0 Inside Out

Jim Buyens
ISBN 9780735623231

Conquer Microsoft Windows SharePoint Services— from the inside out! This ultimate, in-depth reference packs hundreds of time-saving solutions, troubleshooting tips, and workarounds. You're beyond the basics, so now learn how the experts tackle information sharing and team collaboration— and challenge yourself to new levels of mastery!

## Microsoft SharePoint Products and Technologies Administrator's Pocket Consultant

Ben Curry
ISBN 9780735623828

Portable and precise, this pocket-sized guide delivers immediate answers for the day-to-day administration of Sharepoint Products and Technologies. Featuring easy-to-scan tables, step-by-step instructions, and handy lists, this book offers the straightforward information you need to get the job done—whether you're at your desk or in the field!

## Inside Microsoft Windows® SharePoint Services Version 3

Ted Pattison and Daniel Larson
ISBN 9780735623200

Get in-depth insights on Microsoft Windows SharePoint Services with this hands-on guide. You get a bottom-up view of the platform architecture, code samples, and task-oriented guidance for developing custom applications with Microsoft Visual Studio® 2005 and Collaborative Application Markup Language (CAML).

## Inside Microsoft Office SharePoint Server 2007

Patrick Tisseghem
ISBN 9780735623682

Dig deep—and master the intricacies of Office SharePoint Server 2007. A bottom-up view of the platform architecture shows you how to manage and customize key components and how to integrate with Office programs—helping you create custom enterprise content management solutions.

## Microsoft Office Communications Server 2007 Resource Kit

Microsoft Office Communications Server Team
ISBN 9780735624061

Your definitive reference to Office Communications Server 2007—direct from the experts who know the technology best. This comprehensive guide offers in-depth technical information and best practices for planning, designing, deploying, managing, and optimizing your systems. Includes a toolkit of valuable resources on CD.

**Programming Applications for Microsoft Office Outlook® 2007**

Randy Byrne and Ryan Gregg
ISBN 9780735622494

**Microsoft Office Visio® 2007 Programming Step by Step**

David A. Edson
ISBN 9780735623798

*See more resources at* **microsoft.com/mspress** *and* **microsoft.com/learning**

# Prepare for Certification with Self-Paced Training Kits

## Official Exam Prep Guides—
### Plus Practice Tests

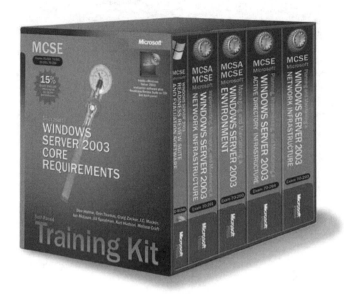

Ace your preparation for the skills measured by the MCP exams—and on the job. With official *Self-Paced Training Kits* from Microsoft, you'll work at your own pace through a system of lessons, hands-on exercises, troubleshooting labs, and review questions. Then test yourself with the Readiness Review Suite on CD, which provides hundreds of challenging questions for in-depth self-assessment and practice.

- **MCSE Self-Paced Training Kit (Exams 70-290, 70-291, 70-293, 70-294): Microsoft® Windows Server™ 2003 Core Requirements.** 4-Volume Boxed Set. ISBN: 0-7356-1953-0. (Individual volumes are available separately.)

- **MCSA/MCSE Self-Paced Training Kit (Exam 70-270): Installing, Configuring, and Administering Microsoft Windows® XP Professional, Second Edition.** ISBN: 0-7356-2152-7.

- **MCSE Self-Paced Training Kit (Exam 70-298): Designing Security for a Microsoft Windows Server 2003 Network.** ISBN: 0-7356-1969-7.

- **MCSA/MCSE Self-Paced Training Kit (Exam 70-350): Implementing Microsoft Internet Security and Acceleration Server 2004.** ISBN: 0-7356-2169-1.

- **MCSA/MCSE Self-Paced Training Kit (Exam 70-284): Implementing and Managing Microsoft Exchange Server 2003.** ISBN: 0-7356-1899-2.

*For more information about Microsoft Press® books, visit:* **www.microsoft.com/mspress**

*For more information about learning tools such as online assessments, e-learning, and certification, visit:* **www.microsoft.com/mspress** *and* **www.microsoft.com/learning**

# System Requirements

We recommend that you use a test workstation, test server, or staging server to complete the exercises in each lab. The following are the minimum system requirements your computer needs to meet to complete the practice exercises in this book. For more information, see the Introduction.

## Hardware Requirements

You can complete almost all practice exercises in this book using virtual machines rather than real server hardware. The minimum and recommended hardware requirements for Windows Server 2008 are as follows:

- A minimum of two computers or virtual machines with a minimum 1GHz (x86) or 1.4GHz (x64) processor (2GHz or faster recommended)
- 512 MB of RAM or more (2 GB recommended; 4 GB enables you to host all the virtual machines specified for all the practice exercises in the book)
- 15 GB free hard disk space (40 GB recommended; 60 GB enables you to host all the virtual machines specified for all the practice exercises in the book)
- CD-ROM drive or DVD-ROM drive
- Super VGA (1,024 x 768) or higher resolution video adapter and monitor
- Keyboard and Microsoft mouse or compatible pointing device

## Software Requirements

- Windows Server 2008 Enterprise server configured as a domain controller
- Windows Vista (Enterprise, Business, or Ultimate)

# What do you think of this book?

# We want to hear from you!

Do you have a few minutes to participate in a brief online survey?

Microsoft is interested in hearing your feedback so we can continually improve our books and learning resources for you.

To participate in our survey, please visit:

**www.microsoft.com/learning/booksurvey/**

...and enter this book's ISBN-10 or ISBN-13 number (located above barcode on back cover*). As a thank-you to survey participants in the United States and Canada, each month we'll randomly select five respondents to win one of five $100 gift certificates from a leading online merchant. At the conclusion of the survey, you can enter the drawing by providing your e-mail address, which will be used for prize notification only.

Thanks in advance for your input. Your opinion counts!

\* Where to find the ISBN on back cover

ISBN-13: 000-0-0000-0000-0
ISBN-10: 0-0000-0000-0

Example only. Each book has unique ISBN.

**Microsoft**®
*Press*

No purchase necessary. Void where prohibited. Open only to residents of the 50 United States (includes District of Columbia) and Canada (void in Quebec). For official rules and entry dates see:

**www.microsoft.com/learning/booksurvey/**